Professional Java SOAP Programming

Henry Bequet

Wrox Press Ltd. ®

Professional Java SOAP Programming

First published December 2001

Published by Wrox Press Ltd,
Arden House, 1102 Warwick Road, Acocks Green,
Birmingham, B27 6BH, UK
Printed in the United States

ISBN 1-861006-10-1

Trademark Acknowledgements

Credits

Author
Henry Bequet

Technical Architect
Chanoch Wiggers

Technical Editors
Helen Callaghan
Ian Nutt

Managing Editor
Louay Fatoohi

Author Agent
Lorraine Clarke

Project Administrator
Laura Hall

Indexer
Fiona Murray

Proof Readers
Fiona Berryman

Technical Reviewers
Chris Crane
Dave Writz
David Whitney
Jeremy Crosbie
John Davies
Kapil Apshankar
Phil Powers De George
Romin Irani
Steve Baker
Justin Foley
Tee Parham
Jay Bourland
Phil Hanna

Production Project Coordinator
Abbie Forletta

Cover
Chris Morris

About the Author

Henry Bequet

Henry Bequet is Vice President of Internet Development with Sagent Technology, a business intelligence firm. Henry is a SUN-certified Java 2 programmer who specializes in developing scalable distributed Web applications using XML, SOAP, Java, and C++.

Henry was born in rainy Belgium but he now lives in sunny Boulder, Colorado with his wife and two children where he enjoys software development, skiing, and roller-skating.

Acknowledgements

A book like this one would not be possible without the work and support of many people. I would like to apologize in advance for any omissions in this list of the wonderful people who helped me along the way.

Special thanks Ken Gardner, the Chairman and Founder of Sagent Technology, Inc., not only for supporting the idea of this book, but also for believing early on that XML and SOAP are viable technologies for performance-minded applications. I am also grateful to Ken for being willing to write the foreword of this book.

I would like to thank the people who help me on a daily basis in the Boulder office of Sagent, especially Chuck Bardeen, Derek Brouwer, Rich Dobbs, Tee Parham, Wentao Liu, Jay Bourland, and Tom Hayward.

I also want to acknowledge the team at Wrox Press that supported me in this endeavor: Chanoch Wiggers, Helen Callaghan, and Laura Hall. Many thanks to the reviewers of the book: Chris Crane, Dave Writz, David Whitney, Jeremy Crosbie, John Davies, Kapil Apshankar, Phil Powers De George, Romin Irani, Steve Baker, Justin Foley, Tee Parham, Jay Bourland, and Phil Hanna

I do not want to forget Beach Clow and John Biard who listened to my ideas and approved the project that started my work in XML-based distributed applications: Centrus Real-Time.

Finally, special thanks go to my family, Anne-Françoise, Julie and Christophe, who make the journey worthwhile.

To all, my warmest thanks and deepest appreciation.

Pour Anne-Françoise
Sans toi, la vie n'a pas de sens

JAVA

Table of Contents

JAVA

Introduction

My involvement with distributed XML applications started in early 1999 with the development of a document-based web application for the marketing industry. If you forget about the domain-specific issues, the requirements of the application boiled down to the following bullet items:

- The application or service must be open: clients running on virtually any platform, written in virtually any programming language must be able to access the service.
- The application must be available over the Internet and clients must be able to access the service through firewalls.
- The application must be available 24 hours a day, 7 days a week, and 365 days a year.
- The application must securely encrypt the data transmitted over the Internet.
- The application must be scalable to the point of being able to handle billions of transactions per year.

Based on my previous experience with web applications and XML, those requirements suggest XML over HTTP:

- XML and HTTP are standard protocols that are implemented on virtually all platforms in use today.
- Standard HTTP traffic is usually permitted to go through firewalls, or at least system administrators are very familiar with HTTP and can configure it to meet their security requirements.
- The stateless nature of HTTP makes it easy to replicate machines for maximum availability.
- HTTPS specifies an easy to implement, widely available, and secure encryption mechanism.
- The stateless nature of HTTP provides for straightforward scalability: new machines can be added as the load on the servers increases.

At the time, there were already plenty of books on XML as a web-publishing tool, but few people were using XML and HTTP as a distributed application protocol. Most of the information that was available on the subject had to be hunted down in cutting-edge magazine articles and Internet newsgroups. My work would have been greatly simplified if I could have picked up a book on distributed architecture using XML as an encoding mechanism and HTTP as a transport. Alas, I could not find such a book.

After the aforementioned application was released and deployed, I started working on a Business Intelligence (BI) application that involved the development of a web-based Application Programming Interface (API) with requirements very similar to the marketing application that our team had just finished. Essentially, we were to use a similar architecture, but instead of being document-based, the application would be procedure-based.

This is where I discovered SOAP, the Simple Object Access Protocol. SOAP is a system for accessing remote objects and data in distributed environments in a language and system independent way. I also encountered XML-RPC, a somewhat overlapping specification for making remote procedure calls using XML over the Internet.

I immediately started to look for books on XML-RPC and SOAP but was disappointed by what I found. I could not find a book that would present the caveats and pitfalls of SOAP development in a production environment that demanded performance. There were a couple of books that introduced XML-RPC or SOAP, but they left my team and me in the dark as far as the challenges of a real-life, scalable, and secure application would face. After the first alpha release of the SOAP-based application, I thought that other people would benefit from our experience so I contacted Wrox Press about a practical book on SOAP and a few weeks later, I was busy translating the vision to reality.

We will introduce many new technologies in the course of this book, to name a few: XML, XSL, XSLT, XML Schemas, SOAP, WSDL, UDDI. Since this book is a practical book, based on the author's experience with those technologies, you will find many examples to help you along the way. In addition to simple introductory examples, we will organize the book around a sample application: LeSavon.com. The drawback of a sample application that tries to emulate real-life experience is the added complexity and the unnecessary details that one must take into account when developing a mission-critical system. We have tried as much as possible to avoid those pitfalls, but we do not claim to have completely succeeded. We hope that the reader will forgive us and keep in mind that the ultimate goal is to help replicate our success.

Because this book is about sharing our experience in deploying SOAP-based, performance-minded distributed applications, you will not find any Alpha or Beta products used in the development of the sample application. However, because the field of web services is not mature and evolving quickly, you will find discussions about tools and utilities that are not production-worthy. We were careful not to depend on those tools for the mission-critical aspects of our sample application. A good example of experimental tools is our use of IBM's Web Service ToolKit (WSTK) that we will use in Chapter 11 to expedite the development of WSDL documents, but that could be bypassed by manually writing the WSDL files.

In the development and deployment of our web services, we will limit ourselves to freely and readily available tools. This restriction will not inhibit our creativity and productivity in any ways, as you will discover for yourself in the pages to come.

Ken Gardner, Chairman and Founder of Sagent Technology, Inc.

Prerequisites of this Book

Some prerequisite knowledge is assumed in the text of this book:

- Knowledge of object-oriented concepts such as objects, classes, overriding and overloading method, and interfaces.
- A working knowledge of Java in general and Java server-side development (servlets and JSP).
- An understanding of the Internet and its use will be helpful to put things in perspective, but is not required.

This book will briefly introduce HTTP and XML in Chapter 2.

Organization of this Book

The book is organized in three parts: Distributed Application Protocols, Sample Application, and Web Services.

In Chapter 1, Distributed Application Protocols, we look at the major distributed application protocols and compare their pros and cons. We then review the SOAP specification in detail and we take a closer look at the SOAP implementation that we will use in this book, Apache SOAP, in Chapter 2.

In Chapter 3, Setting Up your SOAP Server, we get down to the details of downloading and configuring the necessary software to get your SOAP server up and running.

From this point onward, we move into the second part of the book. We begin with a discussion of the requirements for the sample application (Chapter 4) and go on to design the SOAP Server, where we design and implement SOAP services (Chapter 5). In Chapter 6, we write a client framework that will come handy when we wrap up the development of the sample application with its user interface.

No discussion of application development is complete without coverage of Security and Personalization. In chapter 7, we show a possible integration strategy to an LDAP-based enterprise security system to integrate security and personalization. Chapter 8, Caching, discusses how the addition of a rule-based cache system can tremendously improve the performance of our application.

We also look at the performance of our application (Chapter 9), analyzing the sample application to validate the design and implementation choices that we made in the previous chapters. Finally, Chapter 10, Web Application, concludes the second part of the book with the addition of a web-based Graphical User Interface (GUI) to our sample application.

In the third part of the book, we formally define web services and discover that the sample application is indeed a web service. Chapter 11, WSDL, introduces the reader to the Web Service Description Language (WSDL), a key technology that promotes the interoperability of software components over the Web. In Chapter 12, Universal Description, Discovery, and Integration (UDDI), we publish the sample application as a web service and discuss how potential users can query the UDDI registry to discover our services.

Conventions

To help you get the most from the text and keep track of what's happening, we've used a number of conventions throughout the book.

For instance:

> **These boxes hold important, not-to-be forgotten information which is directly relevant to the surrounding text.**

While the background style is used for asides to the current discussion.

As for styles in the text:

- When we introduce them, we **highlight** important words.
- We show keyboard strokes like this: *Ctrl-A*.
- We show filenames and code within the text like so: `doGet()`.
- Text on user interfaces and URLs are shown as: Menu.

We present code in three different ways. Definitions of methods and properties are shown as follows:

```
protected void doGet(HttpServletRequest req, HttpServletResponse resp)
                     throws ServletException, IOException
```

Example code is shown:

```
In our code examples, the code foreground style shows new, important,
    pertinent code
while code background shows code that's less important in the present context,
    or has been seen before.
```

Customer Support

We always value hearing from our readers, and we want to know what you think about this book: what you liked, what you didn't like, and what you think we can do better next time. You can send us your comments, either by returning the reply card in the back of the book, or by e-mail to feedback@wrox.com. Please be sure to mention the book title in your message.

How to Download the Sample Code for the Book

When you visit the Wrox site, http://www.wrox.com/, simply locate the title through our Search facility or by using one of the title lists. Click on Download in the Code column, or on Download Code on the book's detail page.

The files that are available for download from our site have been archived using WinZip. When you have saved the attachments to a folder on your hard-drive, you need to extract the files using a de-compression program such as WinZip or PKUnzip. When you extract the files, the code is usually extracted into chapter folders. When you start the extraction process, ensure your software (WinZip, PKUnzip, etc.) is set to use folder names.

Errata

We've made every effort to make sure that there are no errors in the text or in the code. However, no one is perfect and mistakes do occur. If you find an error in one of our books, like a spelling mistake or a faulty piece of code, we would be very grateful for feedback. By sending in errata you may save another reader hours of frustration, and of course, you will be helping us provide even higher quality information. Simply e-mail the information to support@wrox.com, your information will be checked and if correct, posted to the errata page for that title, or used in subsequent editions of the book.

To find errata on the web site, go to http://www.wrox.com/, and simply locate the title through our Advanced Search or title list. Click on the Book Errata link, which is below the cover graphic on the book's detail page.

E-mail Support

If you wish to directly query a problem in the book with an expert who knows the book in detail then e-mail support@wrox.com, with the title of the book and the last four numbers of the ISBN in the subject field of the e-mail. A typical e-mail should include the following things:

- The **title of the book, last four digits of the ISBN**, and **page number** of the problem in the Subject field.
- Your **name, contact information**, and the **problem** in the body of the message.

We *won't* send you junk mail. We need the details to save your time and ours. When you send an e-mail message, it will go through the following chain of support:

- Customer Support – Your message is delivered to our customer support staff, who are the first people to read it. They have files on most frequently asked questions and will answer anything general about the book or the web site immediately.
- Editorial – Deeper queries are forwarded to the technical editor responsible for that book. They have experience with the programming language or particular product, and are able to answer detailed technical questions on the subject.
- The Authors – Finally, in the unlikely event that the editor cannot answer your problem, he or she will forward the request to the author. We do try to protect the author from any distractions to their writing; however, we are quite happy to forward specific requests to them. All Wrox authors help with the support on their books. They will e-mail the customer and the editor with their response, and again all readers should benefit.

The Wrox Support process can only offer support to issues that are directly pertinent to the content of our published title. Support for questions that fall outside the scope of normal book support, is provided via the community lists of our http://p2p.wrox.com/ forum.

p2p.wrox.com

For author and peer discussion join the P2P mailing lists. Our unique system provides **programmer to programmer™** contact on mailing lists, forums, and newsgroups, all in addition to our one-to-one e-mail support system. If you post a query to P2P, you can be confident that it is being examined by the many Wrox authors and other industry experts who are present on our mailing lists. At p2p.wrox.com you will find a number of different lists that will help you, not only while you read this book, but also as you develop your own applications. Particularly appropriate to this book are the **j2ee**, and **pro_java_server** lists.

To subscribe to a mailing list just follow these steps:

1. Go to http://p2p.wrox.com/.
2. Choose the appropriate category from the left menu bar.
3. Click on the mailing list you wish to join.
4. Follow the instructions to subscribe and fill in your e-mail address and password.
5. Reply to the confirmation e-mail you receive.
6. Use the subscription manager to join more lists and set your e-mail preferences.

Why this System Offers the Best Support

You can choose to join the mailing lists or you can receive them as a weekly digest. If you don't have the time, or facility, to receive the mailing list, then you can search our online archives. Junk and spam mails are deleted, and your own e-mail address is protected by the unique Lyris system. Queries about joining or leaving lists, and any other general queries about lists, should be sent to listsupport@p2p.wrox.com.

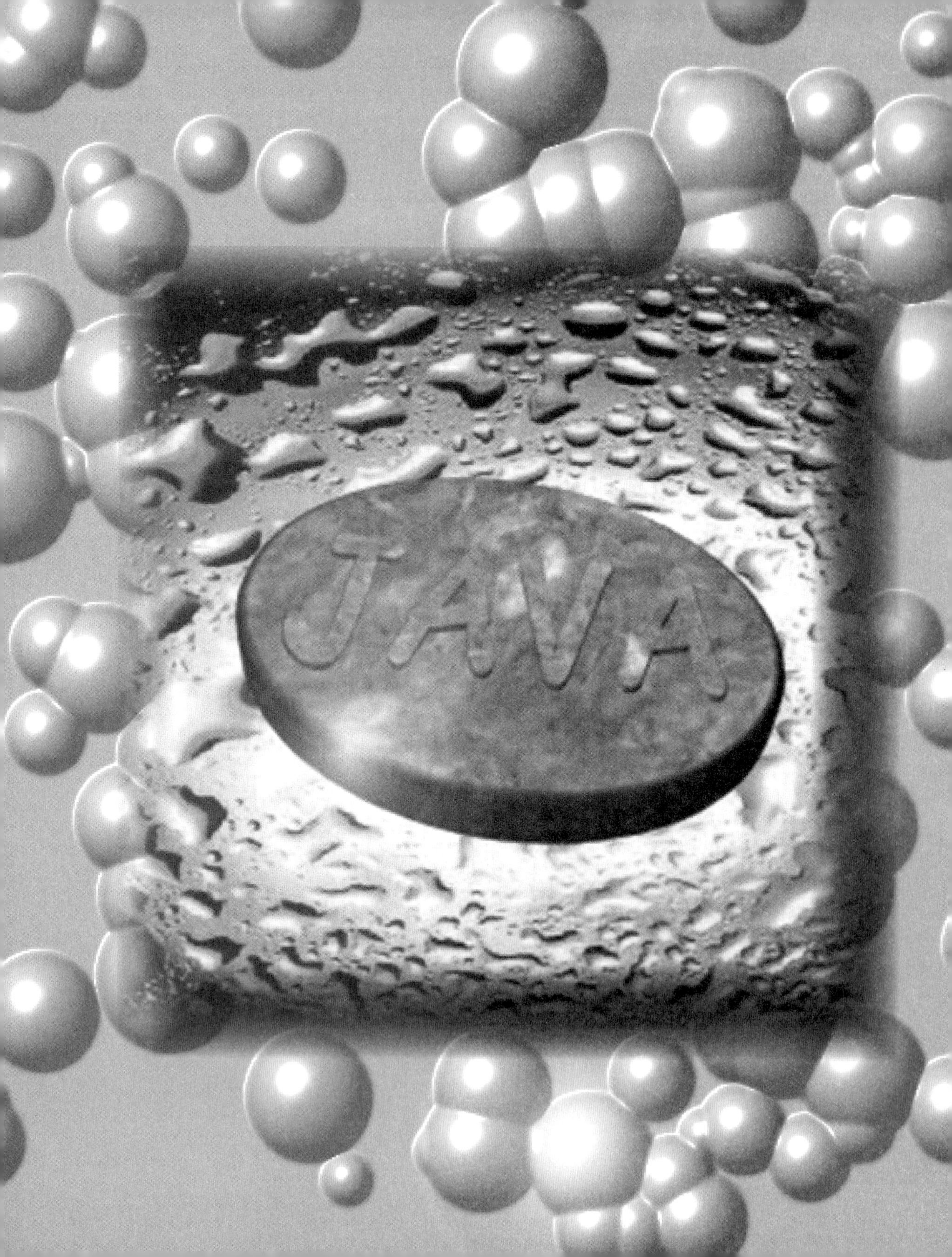
JAVA

1

DISTRIBUTED Application Protocols

This chapter aims to give a short history and introduction to distributed application protocols, such as CORBA and DCOM. If you are already familiar with those protocols and want to jump into SOAP directly, feel free to skip this chapter and go directly to Chapter 2 where we review the SOAP specification.

We will not write any code in this chapter and will keep the discussion general. Links to resources on the Internet are provided in the coming pages, should you be interested in learning more about the protocols discussed in this chapter.

Rather than giving an exhaustive description of CORBA or DCOM, we will look at these protocols from a high-level standpoint. Our goal here is to have an idea of the state of the technology and an understanding of the pros and cons of defining the architecture of your application in the context of distributed applications.

Like most design decisions, choosing a communication protocol for a distributed application is a balancing act between your requirements and how much you're willing to sacrifice in development time, performance, and openness, amongst other things. For instance, if you are designing a real time application over a dedicated network, SOAP might not be your best choice. On the other hand, if you are designing a business-to-business integration tool that provides data cleansing services (verification of addresses, spelling, etc.) over the Internet, SOAP is likely to be a good fit. Other examples can be given. We will elaborate further on these trade-offs in the coming pages.

The remainder of this chapter is dedicated to the review of the following protocols:

- CORBA
- COM/DCOM/COM+
- RMI
- XML-RPC
- SOAP
- EbXML

Documents and Procedures

Before starting our review of the main distributed application protocols, we need to say a few words about the semantics of the payload contained in the messages that travel between remote machines.

There are many ways to classify distributed protocols. A taxonomy that is often used is based on the content type of the data packets. Procedure-oriented payloads, also known as **Remote Procedure Calls (RPC)**, contain a representation or encoding of a procedure, function or method call. Document-oriented payloads contain a document that represents a data structure rather than a procedure call. An example of such a document is a purchase order that is sent from the buyer of products and services to the supplier.

We could argue that the difference is largely academic, because these two payload contents overlap each other. On one hand, a document-oriented payload is similar to a procedure-oriented payload since you can represent a serialized method call as a data structure. Actually, we will see in Chapter 2 that SOAP encodes method calls as a structure. On the other hand, procedure-oriented payloads can contain document-based payloads since the content of a document can be passed as an argument. We will concentrate on RPC payloads in this book.

Let's begin our review of distributed protocols with one of the most popular distributed object protocols: CORBA.

CORBA

The **Common Object Request Broker Architecture (CORBA)** was introduced in 1990 by the Object Management Group (OMG). It was a specification for distributing objects over a network. The OMG is a consortium of some 800 companies representing virtually every large company in the computing industry, and hundreds of other small and medium size companies. In addition to CORBA specifications, the OMG is responsible for a variety of other technologies like the **Unified Modelling Language (UML)** or the **Common Warehouse Metamodel (CWM)**.

CORBA is a specification for client/server architecture. As shown in the following diagram, clients invoke remote objects on servers via a runtime component called the **Object Request Broker (ORB)**:

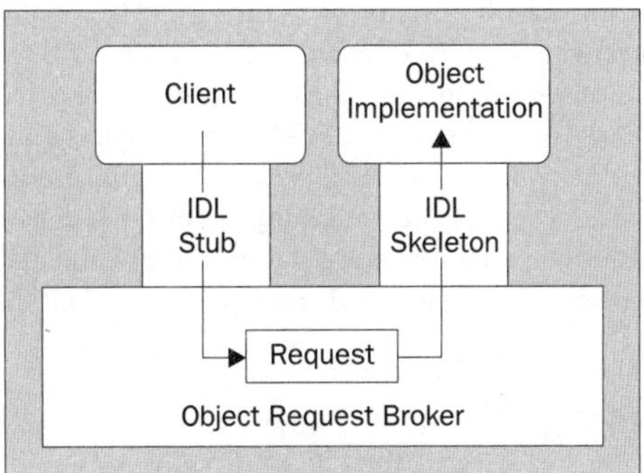

The following figure shows that the remote invocation of objects involves ORB-to-ORB communication using the **Internet Inter-ORB Protocol (IIOP)**. IIOP is the TCP/IP serialization of the General Inter-ORB (GIOP) protocol, an abstract protocol that does not have a transport mapping defined. Other protocols can be used as well, but the use of a GIOP-based protocol is required for OMG compliance.

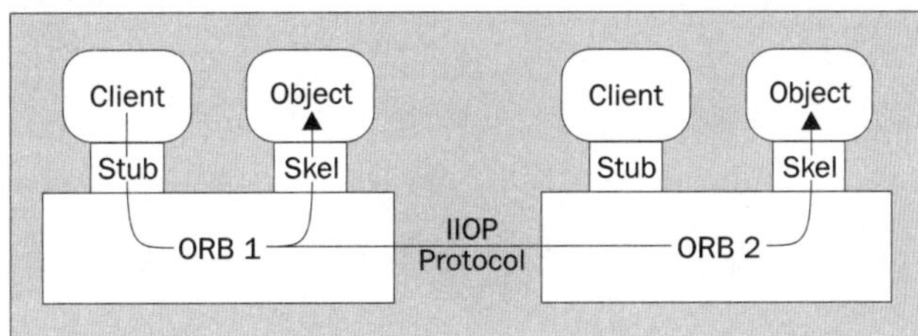

The object interfaces are described using the **Interface Description Language (IDL)**, a language modelled on C++. Language bindings that facilitate the process of supplying and invoking remote objects are available. The compilation of IDL produces an implementation of the proxy design pattern, also known as client **stubs** and object **skeletons**, which are used by clients and providers of CORBA services.

CORBA offers many advantages from completeness to multi-language support. However, CORBA is a complex specification that requires a heavy infrastructure to work adequately.

A language binding for CORBA that is especially relevant for a book on Java development is Java IDL. Java IDL gives the Java developer access to CORBA in a platform-independent way. With Java IDL, distributed applications written in Java can invoke objects on remote servers using CORBA-compliant services. Like any CORBA implementation, Java IDL includes runtime components such as a Java Object Request Broker.

> *You can find more information about CORBA at the Object Management Group web site:* http://www.omg.org. *You can also visit the CORBA site itself at* http://www.corba.org .

The acceptance of CORBA on non-UNIX platforms has been limited, partly because the existence of COM/DCOM which we will introduce in the next section.

COM/DCOM

During the development of the 32-bit version of Windows, Microsoft was looking for a technology that would allow developers to reuse software components written by different groups using different programming languages. CORBA could not be the technology, partly for political and marketing reasons, but also for a good technical reason: developers at Microsoft wanted a technology that would not incur any overhead over a straight C++ call when all components were inside the same process (in-process). The Microsoft engineers selected the **Component Object Model (COM)** that borrows key concepts from CORBA, including a runtime environment and the IDL language, but without any overhead for in-process calls. In 1997, the networked version of COM was introduced: **Distributed COM (DCOM)**.

COM+ is a refinement of COM and DCOM. The main contribution of COM+ is the introduction of runtime services that simplify the work of the COM developer.

In COM and its derived technologies, an object is a software component that supports at least one interface called `IUnknown`. The object can be created by a DLL or by an executable. The `IUnknown` interface contains two methods that govern the lifetime of an object (`AddRef()` and `Release()`) and one method to discover the capability of the object during runtime (`QueryInterface()`). As shown in the next figure, COM does not require any runtime environment when the client and the server are in the same process:

However, in the case of communication across processes or computers, the architecture is similar to CORBA. For process-to-process communication on the same machine client, calls go through the COM runtime components, and the serialization is handled by the **Local Procedure Call (LPC)** protocol.

The **Distributed Computing Environment** (**DCE**) provides services for distributed computing, including a distributed time system to keep clocks closely synchronized.

The remote calls are similar, with the LPC component being replaced by the DCOM network protocol:

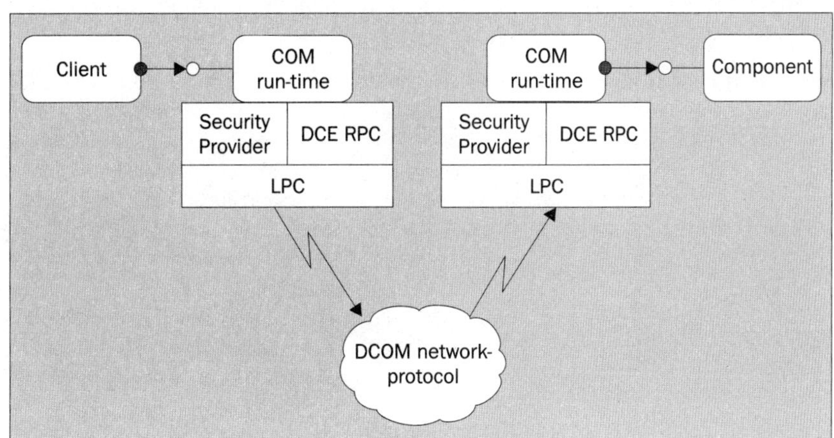

Because COM and DCOM inherited their foundation from CORBA, they have similar pros and cons: they are complete and complex protocols and as such require significant computing and networking power. Since it is a binary standard, DCOM is language-independent (there is a Java 1.X implementation), but in practice it is only used with C++ and Visual Basic objects on the Windows platform. Like CORBA, DCOM suffers from a steep learning curve.

> *More information on COM can be found at* http://www.microsoft.com/com/tech/com.asp.

RMI

Java's **Remote Method Invocation (RMI)** provides remote invocation of Java objects. The definition and implementation of objects is entirely within the realm of Java. This specificity allows for a quite elegant solution that can rapidly be implemented by a Java developer. Its main weakness is its lack of openness to other distributed protocols. This limited interoperability is often an impediment to the success of RMI in the enterprise.

In RMI, the client and the server use two different implementations of the same Java interface, as shown in the following diagram:

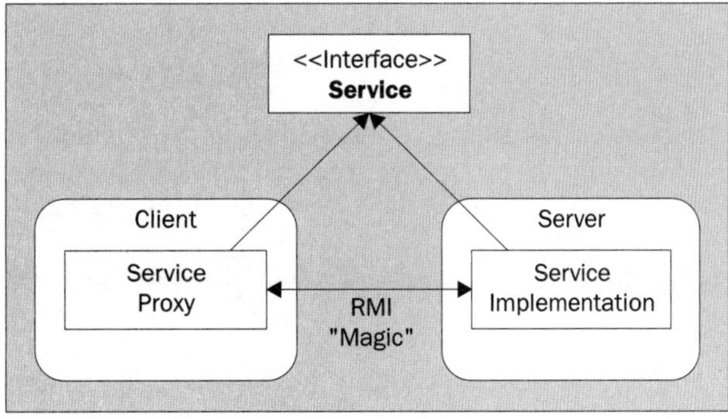

The client implementation or proxy serializes method calls and sends them to the server, where the "real" implementation of the service lives. We will use a similar methodology to implement a SOAP proxy in Chapter 6.

The architecture of RMI is layered as shown on the next figure. This should look somewhat familiar:

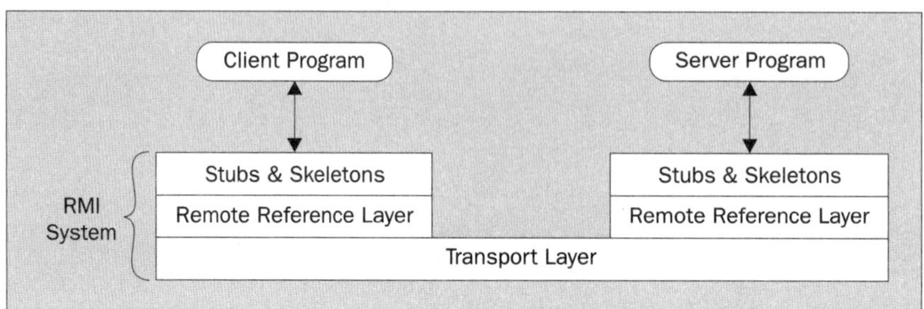

The stubs and skeletons layer is an implementation of the proxy design pattern, similar to the one we saw for DCOM and CORBA. The stubs know how to forward object calls over the RMI communication link using the remote reference layer. On the server-side, the skeleton knows how to communicate with the stub across the wire. If the server is passed a call-back method, such as an event notification for instance, the roles are reversed – the server has a stub for that method and the client has a skeleton for its method.

The remote and reference layer is responsible for handling remote object creation and remote method invocation using the transport layer.

The transport layer is responsible for handling the communication between **Java Virtual Machines (JVMs)**. The JVMs may be local or on different machines.

The main advantage of this layered architecture is that one layer can be replaced without affecting the other layers. For instance, the default RMI transport that uses the **Java Remote Method Protocol (JRMP)** over TCP/IP can be replaced by IIOP. When using IIOP as its transport, RMI can be used to remotely invoke CORBA services. RMI-IIOP also allows the Java programmer to work completely in the Java programming language like in the default JRMP.

> *More information on Java RMI can be found at* http://java.sun.com/products/jdk/rmi/.

XML – RPC

XML Remote Procedure Call (XML-RPC) is the precursor to the **Simple Object Access Protocol (SOAP)**. XML-RPC was introduced in 1998 by UserLand Frontier, partly as a reaction to the complexity and limitations of the traditional distributed object systems that we discussed earlier.

XML-RPC is a simple remote procedure call specification that uses XML as the encoding and HTTP as the transport. One important point to stress is that XML-RPC is a remote procedure call specification; in other words, it does not know anything about objects. The same argument has been made about SOAP, but we will defer that discussion to Chapter 2. XML-RPC also lacks support for protocols other than HTTP(S).

One major feature of XML-RPC is its simplicity. If you look at the following request, you will see that an XML-RPC request is almost self-explanatory:

```
POST /RPC2 HTTP/1.0
User-Agent: XML-RPC Client
Host: 127.0.0.1
Content-Type: text/xml
Content-length: 173

<?xml version="1.0"?>
  <methodCall>
    <methodName>getOrderCustomer</methodName>
      <params>
        <param>
          <value><i4>1012345</i4></value>
        </param>
      </params>
  </methodCall>
```

If you are familiar with HTTP and XML, you can find as much information in the XML-RPC call as you would in the equivalent Java call:

```
int orderID  = 1012345;
String customer = getOrderCustomer(orderID);
```

All requests in XML-RPC are HTTP `POST` requests. The URI on the first line of the HTTP request is optional in cases where the server only handles XML-RPC. The `User-Agent` and the `Host` must be specified. The content of the HTTP request must be of type `text/xml`.

The top-level element is `<methodCall/>` to signify that the content of the XML document is a serialized method call. The `<methodName/>` element as its name suggests contains the name of the method to be invoked. The `<params/>` element is a container for the parameters of the call. The default type is `string`, but you can specify other types similarly to the sample above, where the order identifier is a 4-byte integer.

When the XML-RPC server receives the request, it parses the XML document and makes the actual call. The response to the call is the return value of the method:

```
HTTP/1.1 200 OK
Connection: close
Content-Length: 136
Content-Type: text/xml
Date: Thu, 11 Oct 2001 01:12:17 GMT
Server: XML-RPC1 LINUX RED HAT 7.1

<?xml version="1.0"?>
  <methodResponse>
    <params>
      <param>
        <value>aterieur</value>
      </param>
    </params>
  </methodResponse>
```

The response is as straightforward as the request: the HTTP response contains an XML document that encodes the return value of the method inside the `<methodResponse/>` tag. The return value is encoded, as are the input arguments, using the `<params/>` and `<param/>` elements.

XML-RPC also supports complex types not shown in the previous examples: structures (`<struct/>`) and arrays (`<array/>`).

We will see in the next chapter that SOAP builds on these simple ideas and XML standards to define a language and platform-independent communication protocol.

> *More information on XML-RPC can be found at* http://www.xmlrpc.com.

SOAP

Since Chapter 2 is dedicated to the presentation of the SOAP specification, we will not go into much detail about the protocol, but we will give a short history of SOAP, a high-level description, and a brief discussion of its pros and cons.

> *The SOAP specification can be found at* http://www.w3.org/TR/SOAP. *For your convenience, you can find the SOAP specification in its entirety in Appendix A.*

The SOAP 1.0 specification was released in 1999, and was largely sponsored by Microsoft. The SOAP 1.1 specification was not radically different from 1.0, but the framework differed because 1.1 was submitted in May 2000 to the **Worldwide Web Consortium (W3C)** as a collaborative effort between several companies: IBM, Microsoft, DevelopMentor, Lotus, and UserLand.

According to Don Box of DevelopMentor (http://www.develop.com/dbox/postsoap.html), the SOAP specification could have been released back in 1998, but because of disagreements between teams working on an early version of XML Schemas and on SOAP, things did not happen that way. Instead, Dave Winer of UserLand released the specification of XML-RPC that we discussed in the previous section.

The fact that there were disagreements between a team working on a metadata specification like XML Schemas and a team working on a distributed application protocol might seem surprising at first. However, as we will discover in Chapter 2, the majority of the SOAP specification deals with metadata. In Chapter 11, we will also introduce the **Web Services Description Language (WSDL)**, which is the recommended metadata exchange mechanism adopted by the W3C. WSDL makes extensive use of XML Schemas.

SOAP borrows many concepts from XML-RPC. Concisely, SOAP is XML-RPC with better metadata exchange, better packet structure definition, and a more open architecture for the use of other transport protocols than HTTP. We will justify these generalizations in Chapter 2.

We will have a detailed discussion about the pros and cons of SOAP in Chapter 4 when we review the requirements and the high-level design of the sample application. However, it is appropriate to review the main advantages and disadvantages of SOAP here.

The major selling points of SOAP come from the essence of the protocol: a set of open standards and simple rules governing the use of those standards. From HTTP and XML, SOAP inherits openness, secure Internet support, robustness, and scalability. XML and XML Schemas bring a well-defined metadata exchange infrastructure. The disadvantages of SOAP also find their roots in HTTP, XML, XML Schemas and the simplicity of the specification.

The chattiness or verbosity of SOAP comes mainly from the use of XML and XML Schemas. The higher latency of SOAP requests when compared to other protocols like DCOM or GIOP come from the statelessness of HTTP. We will work hard in the remainder of this book to overcome those disadvantages, but there are cases when SOAP is not the right technology. Once again, those issues will be discussed at length in Chapter 4.

Despite its current pluralistic support, SOAP 1.1 has had a hard time being accepted after its release. As you might expect, IBM and Microsoft embraced it with the release of WSTK and .NET, but other major players like Sun kept their distance for about a year. However, in mid 2001 Sun started showing timid signs of getting on the SOAP and Web service bandwagon with prototypes like JAXM and JAX-RPC.

The submission of the SOAP specification to the W3C and the W3C willingness to work on the next release of SOAP as part of the XML Protocols working group indicate that it is only a matter of a time before most vendors wholeheartedly support SOAP. The web service paradigm, which we will briefly introduce in the next section, should fuel the SOAP engine.

Web Services

Web pages are a universal means of communication: they can be typed and published on practically all platforms. The same freedom of choice is available to the consumers of the web pages: there is a wide variety of browsers and Operating Systems (OS) for them to use. The platform used to publish the page has no relationship to the platform used to view the page, except when it comes to standard protocols like HTTP and HTML. As we all know, this model has been widely successful, probably well beyond the intentions of the original designers at the **Centre Européen de Recherche Nucléaire (CERN)**.

The universality of the HTML/HTTP paradigm was initially geared for humans: a human publishes a page and another human consumes the page. The concept has been stretched on both the publishing side and the consuming side. Pages are generated by CGI scripts, JSP, servlets, and other similar technologies. Web crawlers and spiders consume and digest pages on behalf of humans to produce summaries or indexes. Nevertheless, these extensions to the initial model remain focused on human interactions: web pages are published by humans for humans.

Web service technology is an attempt at replicating the success of the ubiquity of the web publishing paradigm for software. In other words, a web service is a software component that can be called from any language running on any platform. We will refine this crude definition in Chapter 11.

The platform used to create and publish the provider of a service is completely unrelated to the platform used to consume the service. The technologies that will make this model succeed are a mix of existing web publishing technologies like HTTP and XML, combined with new technologies like SOAP, WSDL, and UDDI, which are aimed at software.

In the chapters to come, we will explore these technologies and see for ourselves how they can enable open communication between software components, regardless of the development language and the deployment platform.

ebXML

There is renewed interest in technologies related to **Electronic Data Interchange (EDI)** in general and **ebXML (electronic business XML)** in particular. One motivating factor for this activity is that technologies like XML, SOAP, and Web Services are perceived as having the potential to overcome some of the shortcomings of EDI. Let's spend a few minutes discussing the problems, the potential solutions, and the connection between EDI and SOAP.

ebXML is a specification sponsored by the **United Nations Centre for Trade Facilitation and Electronic Business (UN/CEFACT)** and by the **Organization for the Advancement of Structured Information Standards (OASIS)**. ebXML finds its roots in EDI, which is a technology that has been in existence for over 25 years. EDI allows companies to reduce the paper overhead of doing business by standardizing the exchange of information over private networks or **Value-Added Networks (VANs)**. The significant EDI drawbacks that have prevented its wide acceptance are its complexity and its cost of deployment. The ubiquity of the Internet and its open protocols (HTTP, XML, etc.) offer the opportunity to address those issues and give EDI a new lease of life. ebXML is an attempt to maximize this opportunity.

> *You can find more information about ebXML at* http://ebxml.org.

The protocols that we have discussed in this chapter so far define the interactions between two or more software programs. ebXML goes beyond that level of communication since it standardizes the way companies publish their business processes in a **Business Process Specification Schema (BPS Schema)**. In other words, there is a lot more to ebXML than inter-process communication. However, ebXML specifies how software components must interact once trading partners have agreed on the schemas defining their processes. In fact, SOAP has recently been added as a recommended envelope for the ebXML business message payload.

Summary

In this first chapter, we have reviewed some of the major distributed protocols in use today. The protocols that we discussed vary in complexity, scope, and reach.

Protocols like CORBA and DCOM tend to be very complex since they specify a development and deployment infrastructure in addition to the definition of a wire protocol. Other protocols like Java RMI limit complexity by confining their reach to one programming language.

We spent some time reviewing the anatomy of an XML-RPC request and its response. We saw that the model is simple and straightforward. The simplicity of the model will contribute to wide acceptance, if not of the specific technology, at least of the concepts used by the technology.

We briefly described ebXML as an emerging B2B standard that attempts to leverage the legacy of EDI rather than approaching the whole problem from scratch. ebXML standardizes more than interactions between software programs since it defines business processes and their usage across companies.

The HTML and HTTP standards have allowed for ubiquitous publication and consumption of web pages. The web service technology promises to replicate this unprecedented success story for software components. We will describe in detail the technologies necessary for the implementation and deployment of web services throughout the remainder of the book.

The first building block to ensure that our web services may talk to one another is a communication protocol, which we will discuss in the next chapter – one entirely dedicated to the SOAP specification.

JAVA

2

SOAP

In the first chapter, we discussed several distributed object protocols and compared them to SOAP. Although it is not possible to cover all protocols, we now have a good idea of where SOAP stands: it is a simple XML-based protocol that supports RPC and messaging, primarily over HTTP. In this chapter, we will look at SOAP in more detail.

To broaden our understanding of SOAP and how the Apache framework implements this protocol, we will follow the organization of the SOAP specification. However, this chapter is meant to be an introduction to SOAP, not a reference. For an authoritative guide, you should always refer back to the SOAP 1.1 specification.

> *The SOAP 1.1 specification can be found at* http://www.w3c.org/TR/SOAP/*, and the salient points are contained in Appendix A.*

While we are looking through the SOAP specification, we will point out features that are either partially supported or not implemented in the Apache SOAP framework. The comprehensive list of what is and is not supported can be found at http://xml.apache.org/soap/features.html. The list of known interoperability issues with the Apache SOAP framework can be found at http://xml.apache.org/soap/docs/guide/interop.html.

Before getting into the specifics of SOAP, we will first have a look at the technologies that constitute its foundation.

We will then describe the anatomy of a SOAP packet:

- The SOAP envelope
- The SOAP header
- The SOAP body
- The SOAP fault

We will primarily focus on HTTP as the transport for SOAP packets.

We will then talk more specifically about the SOAP header and the SOAP envelope – this carries a request, a response, or a fault – and then we will discuss each of these in detail. In the course of this discussion, we will introduce the important topic of encoding and XML metadata.

Core Technologies

One of the design goals of SOAP is to be an open technology, from both a platform and a programming language point of view. The SOAP architects decided to meet this requirement by leveraging as many existing technologies as possible rather than inventing new ones.

For you, the SOAP developer, this means that you must be familiar with a variety of web technologies before being able to understand the SOAP specification. In no particular order, those technologies are:

- HTTP
- XML
- XML Namespaces
- XML Schemas

In addition, you must also be familiar with the prerequisites that we mentioned in the introduction to this book: basic object-oriented concepts and Java. We will introduce these core web technologies in the following sections. If you are already familiar with some or all of them, feel free to skip those sections and go directly to the SOAP section.

We will first talk about the protocol closest to the bits that travel over the wire: HTTP.

HTTP

The **Hypertext Transfer Protocol (HTTP)** is used to transport virtually all traffic on the World-Wide Web (WWW). HTTP is a client-server model: a client submits a request to the server, which in turn sends a response.

SOAP makes extensive use of the following HTTP features: HTTP headers (including `Content-Type`), `POST`, and HTTP return codes (`2`*nn* for success, `3`*nn* for redirection, `4`*nn* for client errors, and `5`*nn* for server errors). See http://www.w3.org/Protocols/Specs.html for further details.

The HTTP protocol specifies the format of the request and the response:

- The first line
- Zero or more header lines
- A **Carriage Return-Linefeed (CRLF)** by itself
- An optional body

The following code snippet shows an example of an HTTP request.

```
GET /Authors/soap.html HTTP/1.1
Host: www.wrox.com
Content-Type: text/html; charset=utf-8
Content-Length: 0
```

The first line of the HTTP header carries the verb (more on that later), the path (URL portion after the host name), and the version of HTTP that the client understands (if it is a request). The `Content-Type` defines the **Multipurpose Internet Mail Extensions (MIME)** type of the request. The type of the previous request is `text/html`, which is used for most web pages. It simply specifies that the data being transmitted is text and that the text is an HTML document.

As a SOAP developer, you will mostly deal with `text/xml`: the data is text and contains an XML document. As its name suggests, the `Content-Length` defines the number of bytes in the request. In this particular case the content length is 0, which is typical for a web page request that does not need to submit any data to the server.

> **The Multipurpose Internet Mail Extensions (MIME) extend the format of Internet mail to allow non-ASCII information to be transmitted in e-mail headers and messages. As usual with Internet standards, MIME is used for many more applications than its intended target – for instance, you can use MIME to add non-textual information (such as JPEG pictures) to SOAP packets.**
>
> **See RFC 1521 at http://www.cis.ohio-state.edu/cgi-bin/rfc/rfc1521.html for more details.**

If all goes well, the server response will start with `HTTP/1.0 200 OK`, where `1.0` is replaced by the version of HTTP that is supported by the server. This is followed by the content of the requested resource.

The following HTTP response contains a simple HTML document.

```
HTTP/1.1. 200 OK
Content-Type: text/html; charset=utf-8
Content-Length: 25

<html>Hello World!</html>
```

Note that the example in the previous HTTP response contains the encoding of the document. The value of `Content-Length` is in bytes (after the empty CRLF). There are other header fields such as `Date` and `Expiration`.

The **Unicode Transformation Format (UTF)** is an algorithmic mapping from a UNICODE character to a unique sequence of bytes (one to four bytes). There are actually seven different forms of encoding for UNICODE characters (UTF-16, UTF-32, etc.). The major advantage of UTF-8 is that it is compact and therefore conserves precious network bandwidth. See http://www.unicode.org for more information.

However, things do not always go smoothly. To handle the more difficult cases, HTTP defines ranges of return codes:

- `1`*`nn`*
  This status is informational. It is typically sent by the server to indicate some kind of status. For instance, `100` means that the server is willing to accept the request and the client may proceed with the rest of the request.
- `2`*`nn`*
  The request succeeded – `200` means the request was `OK`.
- `3`*`nn`*
  The request has been moved. This response is accompanied with the new URL, telling the user where to get the data. This is not really an error, but an indication that the document should be retrieved from an alternate location.
- `4`*`nn`*
  The request submitted by the client is in error. For instance, `401` means that the client does not have access to the resource and `404` means that the resource does not exist (presumably, the client requested the wrong URL).
- `5nn`
  The server is in error. This is usually a sign that something went wrong on the server side. For instance, as a SOAP developer, you will typically encounter a `500` error when an uncaught exception is thrown by a service.

In the code snippet below, the response indicates that the requested URL cannot be found.

```
HTTP/1.1 404 Object Not Found
Server: Microsoft-IIS/5.0
Date: Wed, 12 Sep 2001 23:57:41 GMT
Connection: close
Content-Length: 3252
Content-Type: text/html
```

We can also see more header entries in that figure. Their meaning is obvious, except for the `Connection: close` that signifies that the server explicitly requests that the client close the HTTP connection (a browser, most of the time). HTTP is a stateless protocol; unless otherwise instructed by the server, the connection is closed once the request has been satisfied. Web browsers will keep a connection open as long as they are displaying a page for efficiency reasons, since a page is usually made of multiple resources (frames, bitmaps, etc.).

Most of the time, the HTTP protocol uses TCP/IP sockets to handle the connection between the client and the server. In TCP/IP sockets, the client and the server agree on a port number to use to start the connection. Different protocols based on TCP/IP use different port numbers. The standard port for HTTP is port `80`, although any port can be used, if the client and the server agree on an alternate port number.

As we discussed earlier, HTTP is used to retrieve any data (resource) from a server. The resource can be a text file as we saw earlier, but it can also be a binary file, or a remote executable. Resources are identified by **Universal Resource Locators (URLs),** which define not only where to get the resource, but also how to get it. A URL starts with the protocol that is used to retrieve the data. For instance, `ftp://` indicates that the data can be retrieved using the File Transfer Protocol (FTP).

With HTTP, a URL typically looks like the following:

```
http://server-name:port-number/file-path
```

The port number is assumed to be `80`, when it is not present. Arguments can be added to the URL if needed. For instance, the following URLs are valid for HTTP:

- `http://www.wrox.com`
- `http://myserver:1234/mystuff`
- `http://myserver:1234/mysservlet?value=private`

To allow the client to have a meaningful dialog with the server, HTTP defines a set of methods for requesting information from a server. The principal methods are:

- `GET`
  This method is typically used to retrieve a file, or trigger the execution of some code on the server. The arguments, if any, are part of the URL requested. `GET` is not safe when used with HTTPS (secure HTTP) since only the header and the body are encrypted, and not the URL. In other words, even if you are using HTTPS, everyone will be able to see the entire URL. If you look at the example above, this means that `value=private` would be in the open and therefore not very private.

- `POST`
  This method is similar to `GET` but the arguments for the requests are included as part of the body of the request. `POST` is safe when used with HTTPS.

- `PUT`
  This allows a client to upload a file to the server.

- `DELETE`
  This allows a client to delete a file from the server. Most installations do not support `PUT` and `DELETE` because of the inherent risk in these verbs. `PUT` and `DELETE` do not play a role in SOAP.

XML

HTML documents are portable and easy to use. This ease of use was a key ingredient to the success of HTML: with a simple editor like Notepad or Vi, anybody can publish his or her own pages on the Web. The primary drawback of HTML documents is that they do not offer much in terms of content management and document structure: HTML documents do not contain semantic information, they only contain presentation information.

For instance, if one is looking for published work on Winston Churchill as opposed to published work by Winston Churchill, one is left with thousands of possible hits to sort through. You might think that a better search engine would solve the issue, but a better search engine would only try to cope with the lack of semantics in the target documents.

HTML also suffers from a lack of reusability, mostly because it does not separate data from presentation. For example, imagine that you need to show the monthly sales figures to two radically different audiences: sales representatives and company executives. Sales representatives will want the minute details of each account to see where they should make a difference. Company executives are only interested in the aggregated data to see the trend. To show different levels of details in the sales figures, you must write two completely different HTML pages. The following document is an HTML page that might be returned as a hit in a search of work published by Winston Churchill. You will notice that the result set contains only books, but the concept could be extended to other results like articles, recordings, and so on.

```
<HTML>
  <HEAD>
    <TITLE>Books on Winston Churchill</TITLE>
  </HEAD>
  <BODY>
    <H1>Pre 1950</H1>
    <P>The Blitz
    <P>Breaking Enigma
    <H1>Post 1950</H1>
    <P>The Making of the Iron Lady
    <P>The Churchill Doctrine
  </BODY>
</HTML>
```

There is no structure (the apparent structure merely improves readability not analysis) and no semantics in the HTML document: the name `Churchill` is devoid of any meaning.

Another limitation of HTML is the fact that it is a rigid standard – developers cannot define custom tags for specific applications, such as server-side code execution or metadata definition.

A possible solution to those issues is the **eXtensible Markup Language (XML)**. Like HTML documents, XML documents are portable and easy to use. In addition, XML pages can share a common data structure, which leads to more reusability. An XML document containing sales figures can be used to drive the content of HTML pages for sales associates, a printed annual report, and an executive summary.

The following XML document would be returned as a result for a search about Winston Churchill.

```
<?xml version="1.0" encoding="UTF-8"?>
<subjects>
  <subject name="Winston Churchill">
    <category name="Pre 1950">
      <books>
        <book title="The Blitz"/>
        <book title="Breaking Enigma"/>
      </books>
    </category>
    <category name="Post 1950">
      <books>
        <book title="The Making of the IronLady"/>
        <book title="The Churchill Doctrine"/>
      </books>
    </category>
  </subject>
</subjects>
```

Once again, we have limited the scope to `<books/>`, but the returned document could include elements like `<dvds/>`, `<articles/>` and so on.

In the case of our search result in XML:

- The structure of the document is exposed through the hierarchy of nested tags. For instance, it is clear that the books inside `<category name="Post 1950"/>` are distinct from the books inside `<category name="Pre 1950"/>`.
- It is clear that the subject matter is Winston Churchill because of the `<subject name="Winston Churchill"/>` element.

Like HTML, XML defines the concepts of elements and attributes.

Elements represent a unit in the data hierarchy, and can be nested within other elements and have elements nested within them. They are part of the process of imposing order upon data values. Elements are delimited by a beginning tag and an end tag, as in `<category>some value<category/>`. The beginning tag is `<category>`, the end tag is `<category/>`, and the value is `some value`. An element may be empty, and have no value as in `<category/>`. Elements nested in other elements are called **child elements** of their parent elements. For instance, in the previous example, `<books>` is the parent element of `<book>`.

Attributes are merely name-value pairs contained inside the first tag of the element. For instance, in `<category name="Pre 1950"/>` an attribute name within `<category>` is `name` and the attribute value is `Pre 1950`.

The first line of the document requires further explanation:

```
<?xml version="1.0" encoding="UTF-8"?>
```

All XML documents start with the <?xml version="1.0"?> element, possibly followed an encoding attribute. This element is a particular form of what the XML specification calls a **processing instruction**: it indicates that the document is an XML document. In the previous example, the processing instruction indicates that the document is an XML document encoded using UTF-8. All XML documents are encoded in UNICODE.

We need to make one last point before we move on to a more complicated example: contrary to HTML, XML is case-sensitive. So the following documents are **not** equivalent:

```
<?xml version="1.0" encoding="UTF-8"?>
<subjects>
  <subject name="Winston Churchill"/>
</subjects>
```

```
<?xml version="1.0" encoding="UTF-8"?>
<Subjects>
  <Subject name="Winston Churchill"/>
</Subjects>
```

By the same token, the following document is not valid XML (the </subjects> tag does not match the <Subjects> tag):

```
<?xml version="1.0" encoding="UTF-8"?>
<Subjects>
  <Subject name="Winston Churchill"/>
</subjects>
```

The XML example that we have just analyzed demonstrated that it is possible to add structure and semantics to a document by defining a hierarchy of tags. We can take this example a little further by defining a more complex hierarchy. Let's assume that we want to add more tags to the document above to further classify books based on their physical aspect. To implement this classification, we have defined a <category> tag to mean hardcover or paperback, as opposed to chronological taxonomy. Clearly, we need a way to distinguish between the two classifications, or we would wind up with something like the following (ambiguous) XML document:

```
<?xml version="1.0" encoding="UTF-8"?>
<subjects>
  <subject name="Winston Churchill">
    <category name="Pre 1950">
      <books>
        <book title="The Blitz" size="medium">
          <category>hardcover</category>
          <price currency="lira" value="10345.00"/>
          <price currency="us dollars" value="19.99"/>
        </book>
        <book title="Breaking Enigma" size="medium">
          <category>hardcover</category>
          <price currency="us dollars" value="49.99"/>
        </book>
```

```
      </books>
    </category>
    <category name="Post 1950">
      <books>
        <book title="The Making of the IronLady" size="large">
          <category>hardcover</category>
        </book>
        <book title="The Churchill Doctrine" size="medium">
          <category>paperback</category>
          <price currency="us dollars" value="9.99"/>
        </book>
      </books>
    </category>
  </subject>
</subjects>
```

Lifting that ambiguity by qualifying XML tags is the purpose of **XML namespaces**. Note that this kind of ambiguity is more likely to happen when more than one person defines the XML document or when XML documents are merged together.

The latest XML specification can be found at http://www.w3c.org/XML/.

XML Namespaces

Before we talk specifically about XML namespaces, we need to revisit the URL that we introduced with the HTTP protocol. URLs are in fact part of a larger taxonomy: **Uniform Resource Identifiers** or **URIs**. A URI is a string (sequence of characters) that uniquely identifies a resource. As you can see in the diagram below, URIs are divided into two sub-categories: the URL that we discussed earlier and the **Uniform Resource Name** or **URN**.

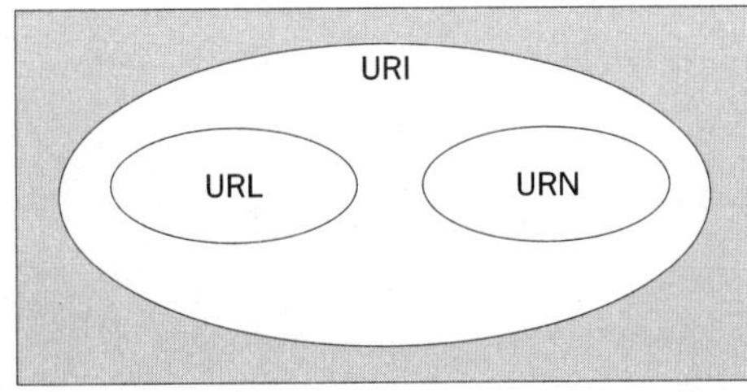

If you have done any IDL or COM development, think of URNs as human-understandable UUIDs and GUIDs.

A URN is a location-independent string representing the resource: there is no claim made as to where the resource is or how to get to it because a URN is simply a unique string. The syntax allows for global uniqueness:

```
"urn:" <namespace-identifier> ":" <namespace-specific-string>
```

The namespace identifier can be anything that is unique to your organization, for example: `http://www.wrox.com`. The namespace-specific string can be anything you want; so long as it is made of letters, numbers, parentheses, hyphens, etc. The exact syntax of URNs is defined in RFC 2141 and this can be downloaded from http://www.cis.ohio-state.edu/cgi-bin/rfc/rfc2141.html.

In summary, use a URL to locate a resource and use a URN to identify a resource in a location-independent fashion.

What does this have to do with XML namespaces? The short answer is that to uniquely identify XML elements, you need globally unique identifiers: URIs. More specifically, namespaces are used in XML documents so that elements with identical names can coexist in the same document. This concept is not a novelty: as Java programmers, we use package names all the time to segregate the space of class and interface names. XML namespaces are not any different – they allow different people to define identical tags with different semantics.

To declare a namespace explicitly, use the following syntax:

```
"xmlns:" <prefix> "=" <URI>.
```

For instance `xmlns:cvrs="http://www.wrox.com/covers"` declares the namespace `cvrs` that is referenced in the XML document using the prefix `cvrs` as in `<cvrs:category>` or `<Envelope cvrs:color="red">`. Once again, these URLs do not necessarily represent a "live" document; they are simply a unique identifier. The namespace declaration is made on the first element that uses the namespace, *after* the element tag, which is somewhat counter-intuitive, as you can see in the following code snippet:

```
<?xml version="1.0" encoding="UTF-8"?>
<cvrs:category xmlns:cvrs="http://www.wrox.com/lesavon/covers">
  paperback
</cvrs:category>
```

Note that namespaces explicitly declared are inherited; the following XML fragments are equivalent:

```
<SOAP-ENV:Envelope
xmlns:SOAP-ENV="http://schemas.xmlsoap.org/soap/envelope/"
xmlns:cvrs="htttp://www.wrox.com">
  <Body>
    <cvrs:MyStruct>
      <value>123</value>
    </cvrs:MyStruct>
  </Body>
</SOAP-ENV:Envelope>
```

```
<SOAP-ENV:Envelope
xmlns:SOAP-ENV="http://schemas.xmlsoap.org/soap/envelope/"
xmlns:cvrs="htttp://www.wrox.com">
  <SOAP-ENV:Body>
    <cvrs:MyStruct>
      <cvrs:value>123</cvrs:value>
    </cvrs:MyStruct>
  </SOAP-ENV:Body>
</SOAP-ENV:Envelope>
```

In both documents, the top-level element is <SOAP-ENV:Envelope/> where SOAP-ENV refers to the http://schemas.xmlsoap.org/soap/envelope/ namespace. In the first document, the namespace of the <Body> element is inherited from the top-level element and is therefore equivalent to <SOAP-ENV:Body>. By the same reasoning, <value> is equivalent to <cvrs:value>.

Interestingly (and potentially confusingly) enough, the following document is equivalent to the previous two examples:

```
<cvrs:Envelope
xmlns:cvrs="http://schemas.xmlsoap.org/soap/envelope/"
xmlns:SOAP-ENV="htttp://www.wrox.com">
  <cvrs:Body>
    <SOAP-ENV:MyStruct>
      <SOAP-ENV:value>123</SOAP-ENV:value>
    </SOAP-ENV:MyStruct>
  </cvrs:Body>
</cvrs:Envelope>
```

This is due to the fact that the actual value of the prefix is irrelevant, only the actual URI of the namespace defines the identity of the namespace.

We can also declare a default namespace with the syntax xmlns="some-uri" (no prefix in this case). All elements that are not explicitly prefixed are assumed to be part of the default namespace.

The next XML document shows our book description using namespaces. The default namespace of the document is http://www.wrox.com. Tags like <subjects> and <titles> now belong to that namespace. The <cvrs:category> tag belongs to its own namespace, as do the <cover> element and the size attribute because of the namespace scoping rules that we discussed earlier.

```
<?xml version="1.0" encoding="utf-8"?>
<subjects xmlns="http://www.wrox.com"
    xmlns:cvrs="http://www.wrox.com/covers">
  <subject name="Winston Churchill">
    <category name="Pre 1950">
      <books>
        <book title="The Blitz">
          <cvrs:category>
            <cover size="medium">hardcover</cover>
          </cvrs:category>
        </book>
        <book title="Breaking Enigma">
          <cvrs:category>
            <cover size="medium">hardcover</cover>
          </cvrs:category>
        </book>
      </books>
    </category>
    <category name="Post 1950">
      <books>
        <book title="The Making of the Iron Lady">
          <cvrs:category>
            <cover size="large">hardcover</cover>
```

```
            </cvrs:category>
          </book>
          <book title="The Churchill Doctrine">
            <cvrs:category>
              <cover size="medium">paperback</cover>
              <price>1999</price>
            </cvrs:category>
          </book>
        </books>
      </category>
    </subject>
  </subjects>
```

If you would like more information on namespaces, the latest XML namespace specification is available at http://www.w3.org/TR/REC-xml-names/.

Now that we have seen how namespaces can be used in XML to render tag and attribute names less ambiguous by associating them with a globally unique identifier, we can turn our attention to XML schemas.

XML Schema

There are two major problems with the previous namespace-aware XML document. The first problem is within its structure. If you look carefully, you will see that the last book has a price tag while the others do not. Is that the intention of the designer or is it an omission? If the price is not listed, does it have a default value? This ambiguity is a source of confusion and potential bugs.

Another problem with the price is the unit. Since everything is text in an XML document, you do not know if that `1999` is a key for a lookup table, the price in Belgian francs (you need a few of those for a $), or the price in pennies. Solving these kinds of problems leads us on to XML schemas.

When XML was introduced it came with Document Type Definitions (DTD) that are becoming out of favor for several reasons, not least of which is that DTDs have a distinct non-XML grammar. Another problem they have is a lack of flexibility when it comes to defining complex data types.

To give you an idea of how schemas are put together, let's build an XML schema for our sample document. Actually, we will write two XML schemas.

The XML Schemas discussed in this section can be found in the `ProJavaSoap/Chapter02/` *directory. The schema for* `http://www.wrox.com/lesavon` *can be found in* `winston.xsd` *and the schema for* `http://www.wrox.com/lesavon/covers` *can be found in* `covers.xsd`.

The first schema (`winston.xsd`) is for the namespace: `http://www.wrox.com/lesavon`:

```
<?xml version="1.0" encoding="UTF-8"?>
<!-- winston.xsd: schema for winston.xml - Henry Bequet 08/15/01 -->
<xs:schema xmlns:xs="http://www.w3.org/2001/XMLSchema"
  xmlns="http://www.wrox.com/lesavon"
  xmlns:cvrs="http://www.wrox.com/lesavon/covers"
  targetNamespace="http://www.wrox.com/lesavon">
```

An XML schema is an XML document with `<xs:schema/>` as the root element. The default namespace for the document is `http://www.wrox.com/lesavon`, and this is also the target namespace for the XML schema. The `xs:` or `xsd:` prefix is usually reserved for schema definitions. The `xsi:` prefix is used for schema instances. The target namespace is the namespace for which the schema is defined.

We will reference elements and attributes for another namespace (`http://www.wrox.com/lesavon/covers`) in another schema (`covers.xsd`) – we use the prefix `cvrs` for that namespace. The `covers.xsd` is brought into the main schema (`winston.xsd`) using the `import` statement:

```
<xs:import namespace="http://www.wrox.com/lesavon/covers"
  schemaLocation="covers.xsd"/>
```

Our top-level element is `<subjects>` and contains elements tagged `subject`.

```
<!-- the tag subjects is a collection of subject tags;
     the order is not important -->
<xs:element name="subjects">
```

An element can be of complex type or of simple type. A simple element may not contain other elements or attributes. Complex elements may contain elements and attributes. To declare a complex element, you use the `complexType` declaration as we did for `<subjects>`.

```
  <xs:complexType>
```

The `<xsd:all>` tag indicates that the subject tags can appear in any order. The use of the attribute `ref` in XML schemas allows the reuse of definitions. It also helps readability by preventing schemas from becoming too deeply nested.

```
    <xs:all>
      <xs:element ref="subject"/>
    </xs:all>
  </xs:complexType>
</xs:element>
```

The `<subject>` element is declared as a reference to the following element:

```
<!-- the tag subject is a list of category tags;
     the order is important -->
<xs:element name="subject">
  <xs:complexType>
```

The `<xsd:sequence>` indicates that the subelements must appear in a specific order.

```
    <xs:sequence>
```

The declaration expresses that the type <subject> contains as many <category> elements as necessary: its cardinality starts at zero and is unbounded.

```
      <xs:element ref="category" maxOccurs="unbounded"/>
    </xs:sequence>
```

The xs:attribute defines the attribute of the <subject> tag (name). The name attribute is mandatory in the target document because of the use="required" declaration. The definition of the attribute also defines its type: xs:string, which stands for "a string as defined in the XML schema referenced by the http://www.w3c.org/1999/XMLSchema namespace", or a UNICODE string.

Other types like integer, float, and double are also supported. (For instance, if you look in the covers.xsd file, you will see that a price is a decimal.)

```
    <xs:attribute name="name" type="xs:string" use="required"/>
  </xs:complexType>
</xs:element>

<!-- a category has a name and contain one books tag -->
<xs:element name="category">
  <xs:complexType>
    <!-- a category contains one and only one books tag -->
    <xs:sequence>
      <xs:element ref="books" minOccurs="1" maxOccurs="1"/>
    </xs:sequence>
    <!-- the name of a category is a string and is required -->
    <xs:attribute name="name" type="xs:string" use="required"/>
  </xs:complexType>
</xs:element>

<!-- the tag books is a list of book tags;
     the order is important -->
<xs:element name="books">
  <xs:complexType>
    <xs:sequence>
      <xs:element ref="book" maxOccurs="unbounded"/>
    </xs:sequence>
  </xs:complexType>
</xs:element>

<!-- the tag book has a title; the title is a string and is required -->
<xs:element name="book">
  <xs:complexType>
    <xs:sequence>
```

The external references to the file are easily handled using namespaces:

```
      <xs:element ref="cvrs:category" minOccurs="1" maxOccurs="1"/>
```

We can qualify elements with a namespace as well. The remainder of the XML schema should contain no surprises at this point.

```
          <xs:element ref="cvrs:price" minOccurs="0" maxOccurs="unbounded"/>
        </xs:sequence>
        <xs:attribute name="title" type="xs:string" use="required"/>
        <xs:attribute ref="cvrs:size" use="required"/>
      </xs:complexType>
    </xs:element>
</xs:schema>
```

The second schema (`covers.xsd`) is for the namespace `http://www.wrox.com/lesavon/covers`.

```
<?xml version="1.0" encoding="UTF-8"?>
<!-- covers.xds: schema for winston.xml (covers ns) - Henry Bequet 08/15/01 -->
<xs:schema xmlns:xs="http://www.w3.org/2001/XMLSchema"
  xmlns="http://www.wrox.com/lesavon/covers"
  xmlns:cvrs="http://www.wrox.com/lesavon/covers"
  targetNamespace="http://www.wrox.com/lesavon/covers">
  <xs:attribute name="size" type="xs:string"/>
  <xs:element name="category" type="xs:string"/>
  <xs:element name="price">
    <xs:complexType>
      <xs:attribute name="currency" type="xs:string"/>
      <xs:attribute name="value" type="xs:decimal"/>
    </xs:complexType>
  </xs:element>
</xs:schema>
```

The modified version of the Winston Churchill document that uses these XML schemas (`winston.xml`) is shown below:

```
<?xml version="1.0" encoding="UTF-8"?>
<!-- winston.xml: sample xml with schema - Henry Bequet 08/15/01 -->
<subjects
  xmlns="http://www.wrox.com/lesavon"
  xmlns:xsi="http://www.w3.org/2001/XMLSchema-instance"
  xmlns:cvrs="http://www.wrox.com/lesavon/covers"
  xsi:schemaLocation="http://www.wrox.com/lesavon winston.xsd
                      http://www.wrox.com/lesavon/covers covers.xsd">
  <subject name="Winston Churchill">
    <category name="Pre 1950">
      <books>
        <book title="The Blitz" cvrs:size="medium">
          <cvrs:category>Hardcover</cvrs:category>
          <cvrs:price currency="lira" value="10345.00"/>
          <cvrs:price currency="us dollars" value="19.99"/>
        </book>
        <book title="Breaking Enigma" cvrs:size="medium">
          <cvrs:category>Hardcover</cvrs:category>
          <cvrs:price currency="us dollars" value="49.99"/>
        </book>
      </books>
```

```
      </category>
      <category name="Post 1950">
        <books>
          <book title="The Making of the IronLady" cvrs:size="large">
            <cvrs:category>Hardcover</cvrs:category>
          </book>
          <book title="The Churchill Doctrine" cvrs:size="medium">
            <cvrs:category>Paperback</cvrs:category>
            <cvrs:price currency="us dollars" value="9.99"/>
          </book>
        </books>
      </category>
    </subject>
  </subjects>
```

In order to test that our XML document is valid, we need an XML schema-aware parser. For instance, we can use Xerces 1.4.3, which we download from Apache (see below). The code samples that we use in this chapter are included as XML files (`.xml`) and XML schema definition files (`.xsd`) to give you a practical example to try. You can find these files in the code download, in the folder `ProJavaSoap/Chapter02/`.

SOAP 2.2 requires a JAXP-compatible and namespace-aware XML parser like Xerces 1.1.2 or later, however the samples for this chapter require Xerces 1.4.3. Before parsing the samples, make sure that `xerces.jar` and `xercesSamples.jar` are at the beginning of your classpath. You can download the 1.4.3 version of Xerces from http://xml.apache.org/dist/xerces-j/:

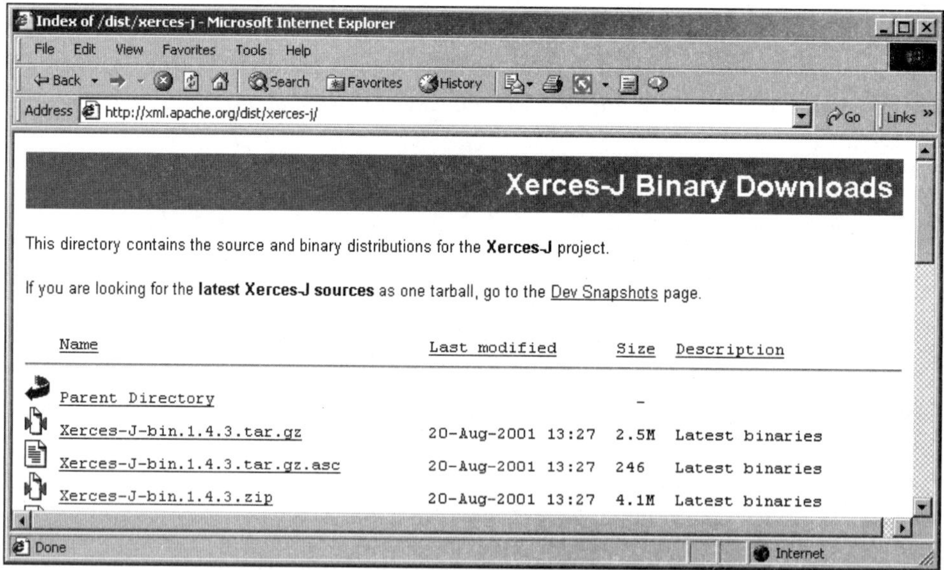

The file we are interested in for the Windows platform is Xerces-J-bin-1.4.3.zip. Download and expand it into a directory structure using a ZIP file utility like WinZip (http://www.winzip.com/). Your installation directory should look like the following screenshot:

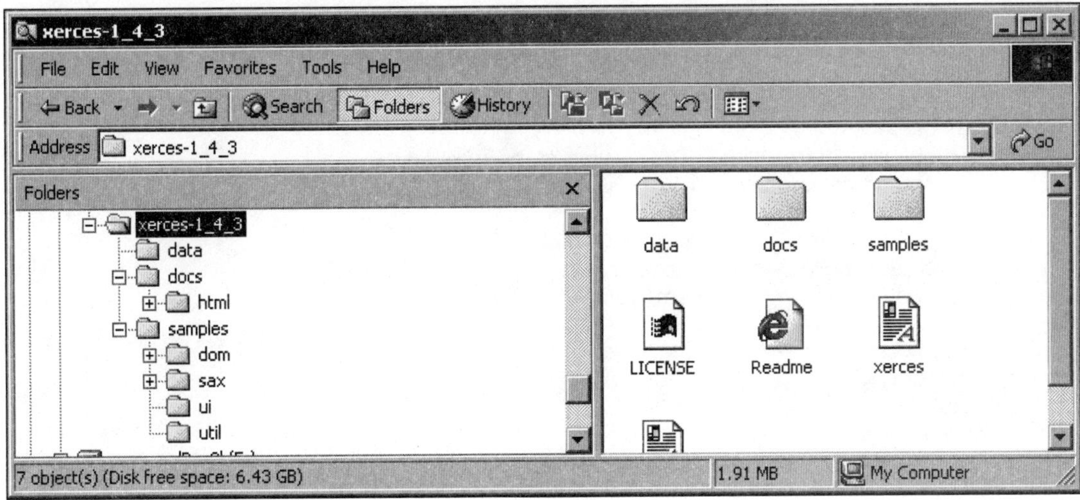

The download and install procedure is similar for LINUX, but you should download the Xerces-J-bin-1.4.3.tar.gz file instead of Xerces-J-bin-1.4.3.zip. To uncompress and explode the tar file, simply use the following commands:

```
$ gzip -d Xerces-J-bin-1.4.3.tar.gz
$ tar -xf Xerces-J-bin-1.4.3.tar
```

The result will be a directory tree named `xerces-1_4_3`. We will show how to run the samples on Windows for the remainder of this chapter, but these instructions are easily translatable to LINUX.

To validate the samples, we can use the `DOMWriter` class that comes with the Xerces samples. The `DOMWriter` class reads, parses, and prints the input document. Copy the code download for this chapter on to your own hard drive, and run the following:

```
C:\ProJavaSoap\Chapter02>set CLASSPATH=.;C:\xerces-1_4_3\xerces.jar;
C:\xerces-1_4_3\xercesSamples.jar

C:\ProJavaSoap\Chapter02>java dom.DOMWriter -f winstonNoSchema.xml
winstonNoSchema.xml:
<?xml version="1.0" encoding="UTF-8"?>
<subjects>
  <subject name="Winston Churchill">
    <category name="Pre 1950">
      <books>
        <book size="medium" title="The Blitz">
          <category>Hardcover</category>
          <price currency="lira" value="10345.00"></price>
          <price currency="us dollars" value="19.99"></price>
        </book>
        <book size="medium" title="Breaking Enigma">
          <category>Hardcover</category>
          <price currency="us dollars" value="49.99"></price>
```

```
      </book>
    </books>
  </category>
  <category name="Post 1950">
    <books>
      <book size="large" title="The Making of the IronLady">
        <category>Hardcover</category>
      </book>
      <book size="medium" title="The Churchill Doctrine">
        <category>Paperback</category>
        <price currency="us dollars" value="9.99"></price>
      </book>
    </books>
  </category>
 </subject>
</subjects>

C:\ProJavaSoap\Chapter02>
```

And the following command can be used to parse and validate the `winston.xml` file:

```
C:\ProJavaSoap\Chapter02>java dom.DOMWriter -n -v -s -f winston.xml
winston.xml:
<?xml version="1.0" encoding="UTF-8"?>
<subjects xmlns="http://www.wrox.com/lesavon"xmlns:cvrs=
   "http://www.wrox.com/lesavon/covers" xmlns:xsi=
   "http://www.w3.org/2001/XMLSchema-instance" xsi:schemaLocation=
   "http://www.wrox.com/lesavon winston.xsd
   http://www.wrox.com/lesavon/covers covers.xsd">
 <subject name="Winston Churchill">
  <category name="Pre 1950">
    <books>
      <book cvrs:size="medium" title="The Blitz">
        <cvrs:category>Hardcover</cvrs:category>
        <cvrs:price currency="lira" value="10345.00"></cvrs:price>
        <cvrs:price currency="us dollars" value="19.99"></cvrs:price>
      </book>
      <book cvrs:size="medium" title="Breaking Enigma">
        <cvrs:category>Hardcover</cvrs:category>
        <cvrs:price currency="us dollars" value="49.99"></cvrs:price>
      </book>
    </books>
  </category>
  <category name="Post 1950">
    <books>
      <book cvrs:size="large" title="The Making of the IronLady">
        <cvrs:category>Hardcover</cvrs:category>
      </book>
      <book cvrs:size="medium" title="The Churchill Doctrine">
        <cvrs:category>Paperback</cvrs:category>
        <cvrs:price currency="us dollars" value="9.99"></cvrs:price>
```

```
      </book>
    </books>
  </category>
 </subject>
</subjects>

C:\ProJavaSoap\Chapter02>
```

Note that if you try to validate the `winstonNoSchema.xml` file, you will get errors. We would expect this, since it does not include a schema:

```
C:\ProJavaSoap\Chapter02>java dom.DOMWriter -n -v -s -f winstonNoSchema.xml
winstonNoSchema.xml:
[Error] winstonNoSchema.xml:3:11: Element type "subjects" must be declared.
[Error] winstonNoSchema.xml:4:37: Element type "subject" must be declared.
[Error] winstonNoSchema.xml:5:31: Element type "category" must be declared.
[Error] winstonNoSchema.xml:6:14: Element type "books" must be declared.
[Error] winstonNoSchema.xml:7:47: Element type "book" must be declared.
[Error] winstonNoSchema.xml:8:21: Element type "category" must be declared.
[Error] winstonNoSchema.xml:9:52: Element type "price" must be declared.
...
```

This short introduction to XML schemas does not intend to be an exhaustive coverage of the topic, since the XML schema specification amounts to hundreds of pages. The point of this short discussion is to give you enough information to be able to understand the encoding of a SOAP packet.

> *If you would like more information about XML Schemas, the latest XML Schema specification can be downloaded from* http://www.w3.org/XML/Schema.

We will see in the next section that the main use of XML schemas in SOAP is for serialization: without XML schemas (or their equivalent), we would have no means of exchanging metadata between the client and the server. Without this common understanding of metadata, interoperability will never be a reality.

Now that we have a better understanding of the technologies used by SOAP, we can have a closer look at the SOAP specification itself. We will start with a high-level view of the SOAP packet.

SOAP

As we saw in Chapter 1, *SOAP is a lightweight protocol for exchange of information in a decentralized, distributed environment.* To achieve the goal of exchanging information, SOAP uses XML to encode its payload.

Let's look at an example that we will refine as we dig deeper into the specification:

```
POST /realtimequotes/ncrouter HTTP/1.1
Host: mysoapserver
Content-Type: text/xml; charset=utf-8
...
                                                    HTTP Header

<?xml version='1.0' encoding='UTF-8'?>

<SOAP-ENV:Envelope
 xmlns:SOAP-ENV="http://..."
 ...

  <SOAP-ENV:Header>
     <t:transaction
     xmlns:t="some-URI"...
  </SOAP-ENV:Header>
                                          (Optional) SOAP Header

  <SOAP-ENV:Body>
       <m:getLastTradePrice xmlns:m="trading-uri">
            <ticker>SUNW</ticker>
       </m:getLastTradePrice>                        SOAP Body
  </SOAP-ENV:Body>                       (May contain a SOAP Fault)
</SOAP-ENV:Envelope>                                 SOAP Envelope

                                                       SOAP Packet
```

Aside from the HTTP-specific data, the XML document above contains three parts specified by XML elements (the meaning of each part will be explained further in subsequent sections):

- **Envelope:** `<SOAP-ENV:Envelope>`
  The SOAP envelope is analogous to a snail mail envelope, but without the address which is the responsibility of the transport and included in the HTTP header. The envelope specifies global settings such as the encoding.

- **Header:** `<SOAP-ENV:Header>`
  The header is optional. If it is present, it contains header entries that define SOAP settings, such as the ultimate destination of a message (more on that later) and application-specific settings (the transaction identifier, for instance).

- **Body:** `<SOAP-ENV:Body>`
  The body must be present and must follow the header, if any. The body contains a message, an RPC call, or a fault.

Unfortunately, software components sometimes fail, hence the necessity of having a standard placeholder for exceptional situations like a version mismatch, or a badly formed request. The SOAP fault (`<SOAP-ENV:Fault>`) is the placeholder for bad news.

Before we dig deeper into the specifications of the SOAP protocol, there are two points that are usually misunderstood about SOAP and that are worth clarifying:

1. **SOAP is a one-way protocol.**
   SOAP does not require a response message to be sent as a response to the "request" message. Despite the fact that the SOAP specification does not explicitly define how to use SOAP with a messaging protocol, such as the **Simple Mail Transport Protocol (SMTP)**, the architects of SOAP have that feature in mind. The Apache SOAP implementation supports SMTP as a transport.

2. **SOAP is not (exclusively) an RPC protocol.**
   SOAP is usually used to trigger a remote method call, but nothing in the protocol specification forces a SOAP server to invoke a method as a result of a SOAP message being received. We will see an example of this functionality in the *Messaging* section, where we will describe a document-based protocol as opposed to a procedure-based protocol.

Looking at the SOAP 1.1 specification, we can see that *Section 7 (Using SOAP for RPC)* describes how to use SOAP for RPC. Roughly, SOAP serializes a function call as an XML structure containing:

- A method name
- An optional method signature
- A list of arguments
- An optional header

The URI of the target object is not part of the serialized data: it is the responsibility of the transport protocol to carry the URI.

HTTP Bindings

Although it is possible to carry a SOAP payload using several HTTP methods, and even other protocols than HTTP, the SOAP 1.1 specification only defines HTTP bindings for HTTP `POST` requests. The definition of the SOAP bindings affects three areas of HTTP: the HTTP header, the HTTP response, and the HTTP extension framework.

> *In an HTTP `POST`, the request (SOAP or other) is part of the body of the document, as opposed to an HTTP `GET` where the request is part of the URL.*

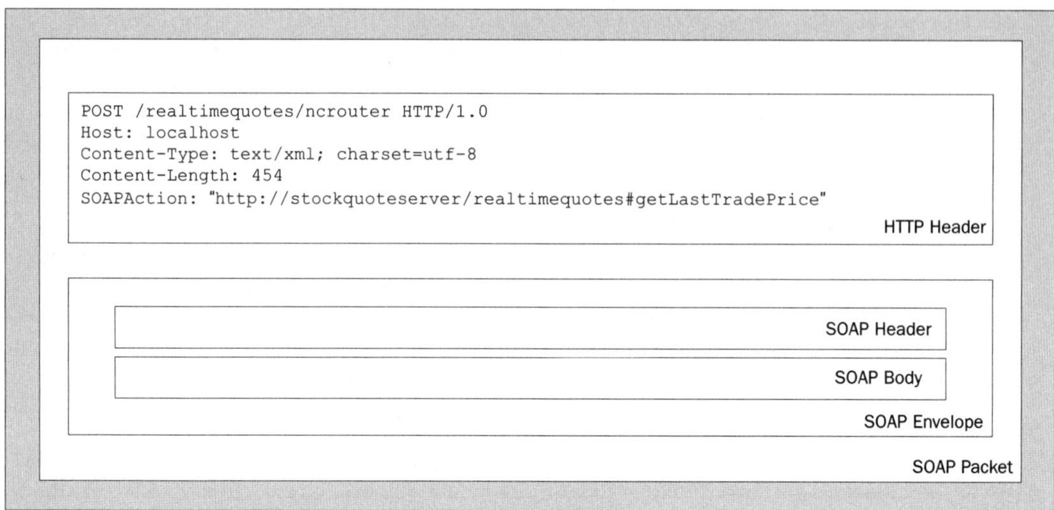
POST /realtimequotes/ncrouter HTTP/1.0
Host: localhost
Content-Type: text/xml; charset=utf-8
Content-Length: 454
SOAPAction: "http://stockquoteserver/realtimequotes#getLastTradePrice"
HTTP Header
SOAP Header
SOAP Body
SOAP Envelope
SOAP Packet

SOAPAction HTTP Header

The main goal of the `SOAPAction` HTTP header field is to provide a way for servers to quickly filter SOAP requests. An example of this situation is a firewall that needs to quickly filter out requests for unauthorized services. The value of the `SOAPAction` header must be specified by the client; however, its format is very loose as it is defined to be a URI in RFC 2396.

It is not a good idea to "stuff" the `SOAPAction` with complicated URIs that would promptly be rejected or simply not understood by a firewall designed to deal with vanilla HTTP requests. In particular, it is important to ensure that we do not have `CRLF` in the `SOAPAction`. This would terminate the HTTP header prematurely and give you strange errors concerning the trailing part of your `SOAPAction`, which would not be a valid XML document.

The following values for a `SOAPAction` are legal:

- `SOAPAction: "http://www.wrox.com/leavon/ncrouter/Orders#getOrderList"`
- `SOAPAction: "OrderService.java"`
- `SOAPAction: "http://wwww.wroxpress.com"`
- `SOAPAction: ""`
- `SOAPAction:`

An empty string value (`""`) means that the intent of the request is provided by the HTTP request URI, and no value means that there is no indication of the intent of the SOAP request.

The intent of a SOAP request can also be indicated by the first child of the <Body> element as shown in the following example, which comes from a call to the `getOrderObject()` method:

```
<?xml version='1.0' encoding='UTF-8'?>
<SOAP-ENV:Envelope
 xmlns:SOAP-ENV="http://schemas.xmlsoap.org/soap/envelope/"
 xmlns:xsi="http://www.w3.org/1999/XMLSchema-instance"
 xmlns:xsd="http://www.w3.org/1999/XMLSchema">
 <SOAP-ENV:Body>
   <ns1:getOrderObject xmlns:ns1="urn:order"
    SOAP-ENV:encodingStyle="http://xml.apache.org/xml-soap/literalxml">
     <!-- Arguments have been omitted -->
   </ns1:getOrder>
  </SOAP-ENV:Body>
</SOAP-ENV:Envelope>
```

Since there is nothing in the SOAP specification requiring the `SOAPAction` to be in sync with the reality of the request, it might be risky to rely on it for security purposes, unless your server-side implementation forces the `SOAPAction` and the first child of the <SOAP-ENV:Body> tag to match. The Apache SOAP implementation does not perform any validation of the `SOAPAction` header entry.

SOAP 1.0 supports the mandatory `SOAPMethodName` that must match the first element of the <SOAP-ENV:Body>. Since SOAP 1.0 implementations must reject a SOAP request that does not have a matching value for `SOAPMethodName` and the first child of the <Body> element, this can be used to reliably filter calls at the firewall level. This feature was dropped in favor of **HTTP Extensions**, which can be used to achieve the same purpose, as we will see in the section on *HTTP Extension Framework* later.

Another potential use of `SOAPAction` is to route the SOAP request to the appropriate web service. The Apache SOAP framework does not use the `SOAPAction` for routing; it uses the namespace of the first child of the body element to route the SOAP request (the `"trading-uri"` in our example).

Specifically, the Apache SOAP framework will set the `SOAPAction` based on the second argument you pass to `Call.invoke()`. The statement `call.invoke(url, "this is the SOAPAction")` will generate the following SOAP request:

```
POST /realtimequotes/ncrouter HTTP/1.0
Host: localhost
Content-Type: text/xml; charset=utf-8
Content-Length: 454
SOAPAction: "this is the SOAPAction"
...
```

We will have a closer look at the API of the Apache SOAP framework in Chapter 3, when we write the `HelloWorld` sample.

If the target server is running Apache SOAP, then the request will be processed normally: the Apache SOAP router ignores the `SOAPAction`.

> **Note: this could lead to interoperability issues with a SOAP client that submits a SOAP request with the `SOAPAction` set to the target URL and no namespace on the first child of the `<SOAP-ENV:Body>` element.**

HTTP Response

The HTTP binding for SOAP follows the semantics of the HTTP standard when it comes to status codes. In particular, a `2nn` status code means that the request has been processed successfully. For instance, an HTTP return code of `200` means `OK`. In case of an error occurring while processing the request, the server must return a `500` status code (Internal Server Error) and include a SOAP fault as part of the response. Ideally, a SOAP server should always return a `text/xml` content type, no matter what the error. In practice, this is not true, since most SOAP implementations (including Apache SOAP) are deployed as part of a web site. This means that when the SOAP request does not make it to the SOAP server implementation, we will more than likely get an HTTP error with a `text/html` content type, as opposed to `text/xml`.

For instance, if we submit a SOAP request to the wrong URL, on a servlet engine such as Tomcat, it will respond with the following error:

```
HTTP/1.0 404 Not Found
Content-Type: text/html
Content-Length: 201
Servlet-Engine: Tomcat Web Server/3.2.3 (JSP 1.1; Servlet 2.2; Java 1.3.0; Windows
2000 5.0 x86; java.vendor=Sun Microsystems Inc.)

<head><title>Not Found (404)</title></head>
<body><h1>Not Found (404)</h1>
<b>Original request:</b> /lesavon/the-missing-router<br><br>
<b>Not found request:</b> /lesavon/the-missing-router</body>
```

Unless the application server that hosts the SOAP server is customized to return SOAP errors, it will return error messages intended for a browser. In other words, your client application must be prepared to deal with an error encoded in `text/html` rather than `text/xml`.

The HTTP Extension Framework

We have seen earlier that the `SOAPAction` HTTP header could be used to give a description of the intent of the SOAP call to a firewall. One drawback of the `SOAPAction` HTTP header is that it is not an HTTP header (as defined by the HTTP protocol) and there is a possibility of conflict with some other extension. Whenever you are working with XML and you encounter an ambiguity, namespaces are normally never far away.

The **HTTP Extension Framework** defines a mechanism to dynamically extend the functionality of HTTP clients and servers using namespaces. The extensions are dynamic because they do not need to be registered with some standard organization, but in practice, client and server components know about the extensions prior to runtime. The HTTP Extension Framework goes far beyond the reach of SOAP, since it can be used to extend the HTTP protocol for transmitting any type of data, not only SOAP payloads.

> *The HTTP Extension Framework can be downloaded from http://www.w3.org/Protocols/HTTP/ietf-http-ext.*

This is how it works:

1. Software designers agree on an extension and assign the extension a globally unique URI. For SOAP, we will use `http://schemas.xmlsoap.org/soap/envelope`.

2. A client or a server that implements that extension declares its use via the URI in the HTTP header. The declaration of the URI and its associated namespace is done according to the HTTP Extension Framework (see below).

3. The HTTP application can implement the desired behavior without any risk of conflict.

Let's look at an (extended) HTTP request, to see how HTTP extensions work in practice:

```
M-POST /realtimequotes/ncrouter/ HTTP/1.0
Man: "http://schemas.xmlsoap.org/soap/envelope"; ns=144
Host: localhost
Content-Type: text/xml; charset="utf-8"
Content-Length: 454
144-SOAPAction: http://stockquoteserver/realtimequotes#getLastTradePrice

<SOAP-ENV:Envelope xmlns...
  ...
</SOAP-ENV:Envelope>
```

The first difference between the previous HTTP request and what we have seen earlier is the HTTP verb: `M-POST` rather than `POST`. The `M-POST` defines a mandatory HTTP request. An HTTP request is called a mandatory request if it includes at least one mandatory extension declaration. All HTTP verbs are supported (`M-POST, M-GET`, etc.). The example above contains the mandatory extension declaration:

```
Man: "http://schemas.xmlsoap.org/soap/envelope"; ns=144
```

In other words, once the `Man:` header is present, the remainder of the HTTP header must contain at least one extension declaration for the specified URI. In our case, the mandatory extension declaration is the following header element:

```
144-SOAPAction: http://stockquoteserver/realtimequotes#getLastTradePrice
```

As you have probably noticed, `SOAPAction` is prefixed by `144`; the prefix for the URI specified in the `Man:` header element.

The HTTP Extension Framework also defines optional headers with the `Opt:` header element, but they are not used as part of SOAP.

All this discussion would be pointless, if it were not for the fact that the server has the right to force clients to follow an extended protocol. Let's assume that the client submits a SOAP request with a plain HTTP `POST`. The server can then return a `501` HTTP error code (Not Extended) to notify the requester that it must submit a mandatory HTTP request, in other words, a request with `M-POST` and a `Man:` header element. If the server still doesn't like the request, for instance because the `Man:` header element is not for the `http://schemas.xmlsoap.org/soap/envelope` URI, then the server can reject the request again.

SOAP Envelope

The SOAP envelope is the top-level element of the XML document representing the message. The example shown in the following XML document uses UTF-8 encoding, but we can also use another encoding, such as UTF-16.

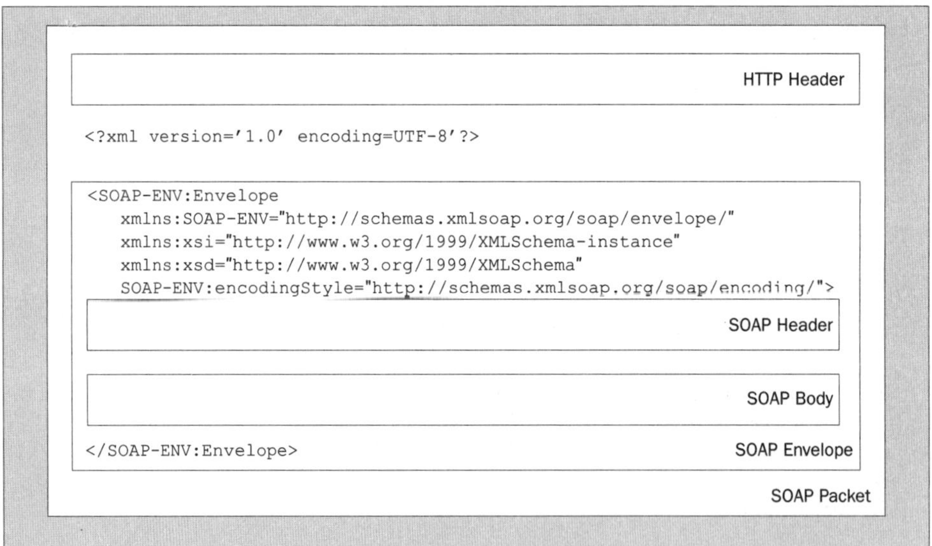
HTTP Header
<?xml version='1.0' encoding=UTF-8'?>
<SOAP-ENV:Envelope
xmlns:SOAP-ENV="http://schemas.xmlsoap.org/soap/envelope/"
xmlns:xsi="http://www.w3.org/1999/XMLSchema-instance"
xmlns:xsd="http://www.w3.org/1999/XMLSchema"
SOAP-ENV:encodingStyle="http://schemas.xmlsoap.org/soap/encoding/">
SOAP Header
SOAP Body
</SOAP-ENV:Envelope>
SOAP Envelope
SOAP Packet

The SOAP envelope must be present and it must be called `Envelope` (not `envelope`). The previous example contains three namespace declarations:

- `xmlns:SOAP-ENV="http://schemas.xmlsoap.org/soap/envelope/"`
  This namespace is used for SOAP itself: all elements and attributes defined in the SOAP specification (`Envelope, Body, mustUnderstand`) are part of this namespace.

- `xmlns:xsd="http://www.w3.org/1999/XMLSchema"`
  This namespace is used to reference elements and attributes from the master schema at the w3 website. For instance, to reference a float type, we will use `<xsd:float>`.

- `xmlns:xsi="http://www.w3.org/1999/XMLSchema-instance"`
  This namespace exists to reference elements and attributes from an instance of the `xsd:` schema.

The namespace declarations are optional, so the following `<Envelope>` is a valid SOAP request:

```
<Envelope>
  <Body/> <!-- an empty body is valid, but the body must be present -->
</Envelope>
```

The `encodingStyle` attribute indicates the serialization rules used in the SOAP message. It is a global attribute scoped to all the children of the envelope. Note that children of the SOAP envelope can explicitly override this setting. We will see a practical use of this scoped encoding when we talk about the serialization of XML documents. The serialization rules as defined in Section 5 of the SOAP specification are identified by the URI `http://schemas.xmlsoap.org/soap/encoding/`. The absence of the `encodingStyle` attribute indicates that there are no restrictions on the default encoding used in the SOAP message. Once again, this global setting can be overridden by child elements.

Envelope Versioning Model

SOAP does not define a traditional versioning model like 1.0, 1.1, etc. SOAP relies on namespaces to define versions. The envelope of a SOAP message must reference the `"http://schemas.xmlsoap.org/soap/envelope/"` namespace. If a SOAP server receives a request that references another namespace, it must reject the request with a `<VersionMismatch>` element in a `<Fault>` element (see below).

SOAP Header

Despite the fact that the Apache SOAP implementation does not use the SOAP header, it is worth mentioning. The main motivation behind the SOAP header is to provide a mechanism to extend the protocol. For instance, you could add state management or transactional support to SOAP headers. As you can see below, the header is the first child element of the envelope element:

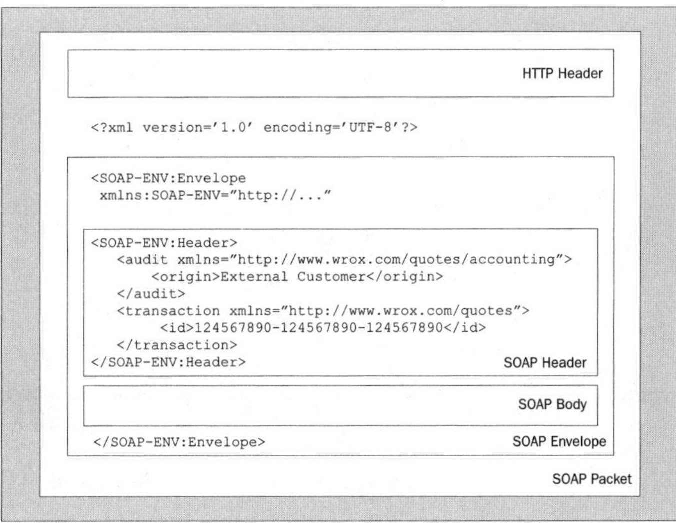
HTTP Header
<?xml version='1.0' encoding='UTF-8'?>
<SOAP-ENV:Envelope
xmlns:SOAP-ENV="http://..."
<SOAP-ENV:Header>
<audit xmlns="http://www.wrox.com/quotes/accounting">
<origin>External Customer</origin>
</audit>
<transaction xmlns="http://www.wrox.com/quotes">
<id>124567890-124567890-124567890</id>
</transaction>
</SOAP-ENV:Header>
SOAP Header
SOAP Body
</SOAP-ENV:Envelope>
SOAP Envelope
SOAP Packet

The header is optional. Elements for the SOAP headers must be qualified by a namespace. The `mustUnderstand` attribute requires a little explanation. The purpose of the `mustUnderstand` attribute is to support robust evolution of APIs. Imagine that (as the example above suggests) we decide to use SOAP headers to implement a transaction management mechanism. If a SOAP server received the message and decided to ignore the `<transaction>` element, consequences could be disastrous. To prevent this kind of unwanted behavior, header entries flagged with the `mustUnderstand="1"` attribute cannot be ignored (`mustUnderstand` can be 0 (false) or 1 (true)):

```
...
<SOAP-ENV:Header>
  <transaction xmlns="http://www.wrox.com/lesavon" SOAP-
      ENV:mustUnderstand="1">
    <id>124567890-124567890-124567890</id>
  </transaction>
</SOAP-ENV:Header>
...
```

When the `mustUnderstand` attribute is set on unknown header entries, servers must reject the request with a SOAP fault code set to `"Must Understand"`, as we will see in the later section dealing with SOAP faults.

The Apache SOAP implementation does not support the `mustUnderstand` attribute.

SOAP Body

The body of a SOAP message is where most of the information is usually located. The SOAP body is meant to contain mandatory information for the ultimate recipient of the message. In this book, we are mostly interested in the RPC calls being serialized in the SOAP body, but we will also see some error messages in the *SOAP Fault* section.

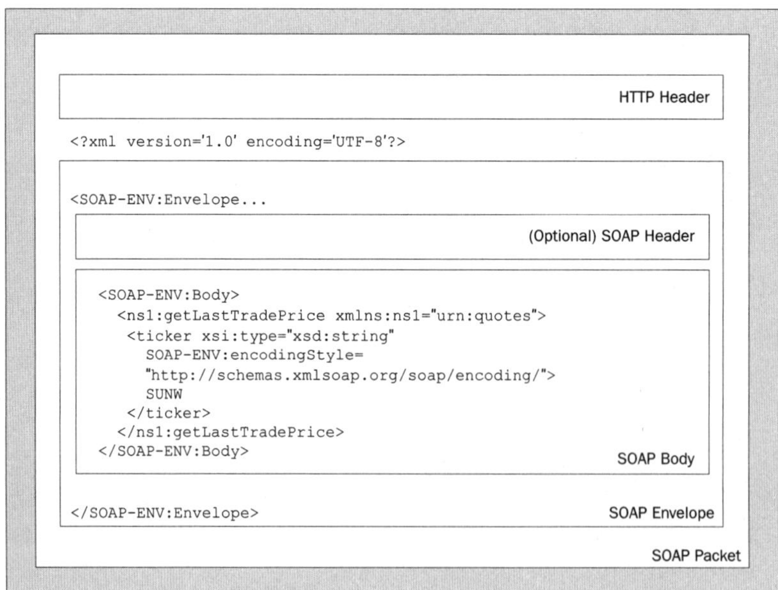
HTTP Header
<?xml version='1.0' encoding='UTF-8'?>
<SOAP-ENV:Envelope...
(Optional) SOAP Header
<SOAP-ENV:Body>
<ns1:getLastTradePrice xmlns:ns1="urn:quotes">
<ticker xsi:type="xsd:string"
SOAP-ENV:encodingStyle=
"http://schemas.xmlsoap.org/soap/encoding/">
SUNW
</ticker>
</ns1:getLastTradePrice>
</SOAP-ENV:Body>
SOAP Body
</SOAP-ENV:Envelope>
SOAP Envelope
SOAP Packet

The diagram above shows a simple example of a SOAP body. As you can see, the <Body> element is namespace-qualified, although this is optional. The SOAP body in the example above contains one entry called a **<Body> entry**. RPC calls usually contain one <Body> entry: the serialized method call. This statement will become clearer in the next section when we talk about encoding, but an RPC call is serialized similarly to a structure, where the field names are in fact argument names.

The content of the SOAP body is left up to the application with the exception of the SOAP fault that we discussed earlier, the only <Body> entry defined by SOAP. However, the body must obey certain rules:

- The <Body> element must be encoded as an immediate child of the <Envelope> element. If a header is present, then the <Body> element must immediately follow the header. If no header is present, then the <Body> element must be the first direct child of the SOAP envelope.
- The SOAP body must be encoded using XML. The SOAP encoding rules (see the section about *Encoding*) may be followed and the encodingStyle attribute may optionally be used to indicate which encoding rules are being used. The SOAP encoding rules are identified by the namespace http://schema.xmlsoap.org/soap/encoding.

  Other possible forms of encoding supported by the Apache SOAP framework include literal XML and XMI-based serialization. Literal XML is plain XML, XML that does not correspond to the encoding of an RPC call. We would typically use literal XML if the argument to a method were an XML document. XMI is the **XML Metadata Interchange** standard supported by the OMG. More information can be found at http://www.omg.org. In short, XMI is roughly equivalent to XML schemas. We will not use XMI in this book due to its limited acceptance, but it is worth being aware of it.
- The <Body> entries are serialized as independent elements, however for RPC we should only have one <Body> entry: the serialized method call.

SOAP Fault

The following diagram shows that the SOAP <Fault> element appears as a <Body> entry.

```
HTTP Header

<?xml version='1.0' encoding='UTF-8'?>

<SOAP-ENV:Evelope
  xmlns:SOAP-ENV="http://..."
  ...

SOAP Header

<SOAP-ENV:Body>
 <Fault>
  <faultcode>Server</faultcode>
  <faultstring>service: 'urn:quotes' unknown</faultstring>
  <faultactor>/realtimequotes/ncrouter</faultstring>
  </Fault>
</SOAP-ENV:Body>
SOAP Body

</SOAP-ENV:Envelope>
SOAP Envelope

SOAP Packet
```

The SOAP Fault is optional, but there can only be one `<Fault>` element per `<Body>` element. The SOAP `<Fault>` element contains up to four elements:

- `<faultcode/>`
  The `<faultcode>` element allows the client to algorithmically identify the source of the fault. As you can see from the following table, this mechanism is similar to what we saw for HTTP when it comes to differentiating the source of the error. However, rather than using numerical values, SOAP uses XML qualified names. The version mismatch and `mustUnderstand` fault codes are particular to SOAP.

Name	Meaning
`Version Mismatch`	The namespace for the SOAP envelope is not `"http://schemas.xmlsoap.org/soap/envelope/"`.
`mustUnderstand`	One of the header entries was not understood by the receiving party and the `mustUnderstand` flag was set to `"1"` (true).
`Client`	The message received was incorrectly formed. A typical example of this would be a lack of serialization information.
`Server`	The receiving web service could not process the message. This situation would arise if the application were to throw an exception. The detail section of the fault might contain the stack of exception.

- `<faultstring/>`
  Once again, the strong affinity of SOAP to HTTP shows up in the `<faultstring>` element, since it is similar to the reason phrase that we saw earlier. Note that the `<faultstring>` must be present. The `<faultstring/>` is mostly intended for human readers as opposed to the `<faultcode/>`, which is intended for algorithmic use.

- `<faultactor/>`
  The `<faultactor>` element names the service that generated the fault. The `NullPointerException` in the example below was thrown inside the `ncrouter` of the `lesavon` context. The `<faultactor>` is more meaningful in a situation where there is more than one recipient for the SOAP message. We will look at an example of this when we talk about the `SOAPActor` in the *Messaging* section.

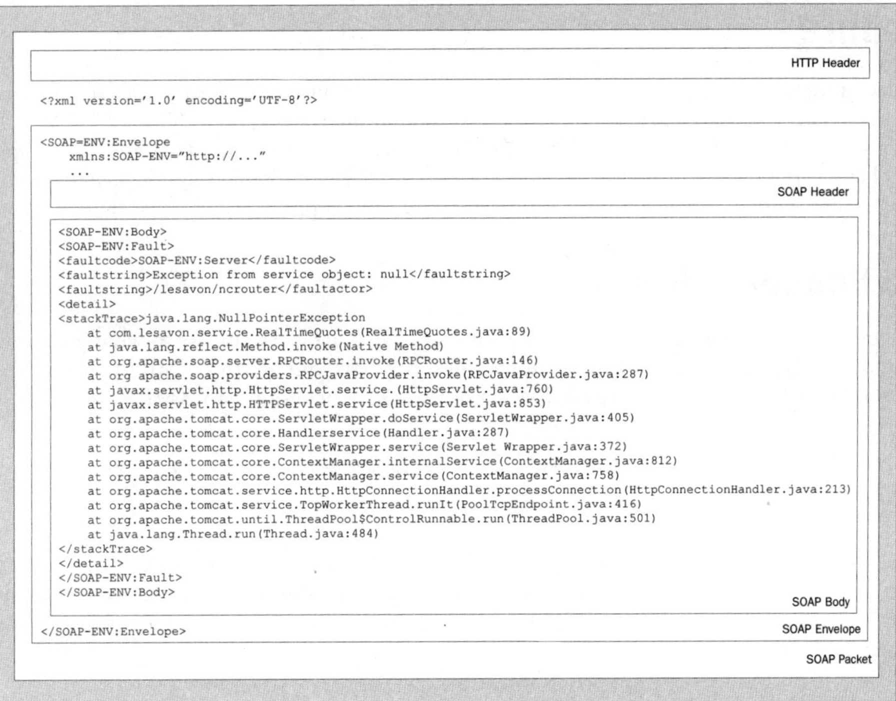

HTTP Header
<?xml version='1.0' encoding='UTF-8'?>
<SOAP=ENV:Envelope
xmlns:SOAP-ENV="http://..."
...
SOAP Header
<SOAP-ENV:Body>
<SOAP-ENV:Fault>
<faultcode>SOAP-ENV:Server</faultcode>
<faultstring>Exception from service object: null</faultstring>
<faultstring>/lesavon/ncrouter</faultactor>
<detail>
<stackTrace>java.lang.NullPointerException
at com.lesavon.service.RealTimeQuotes(RealTimeQuotes.java:89)
at java.lang.reflect.Method.invoke(Native Method)
at org.apache.soap.server.RPCRouter.invoke(RPCRouter.java:146)
at org apache.soap.providers.RPCJavaProvider.invoke(RPCJavaProvider.java:287)
at javax.servlet.http.HttpServlet.service.(HttpServlet.java:760)
at javax.servlet.http.HTTPServlet.service(HttpServlet.java:853)
at org.apache.tomcat.core.ServletWrapper.doService(ServletWrapper.java:405)
at org.apache.tomcat.core.Handlerservice(Handler.java:287)
at org.apache.tomcat.core.ServletWrapper.service(Servlet Wrapper.java:372)
at org.apache.tomcat.core.ContextManager.internalService(ContextManager.java:812)
at org.apache.tomcat.core.ContextManager.service(ContextManager.java:758)
at org.apache.tomcat.service.http.HttpConnectionHandler.processConnection(HttpConnectionHandler.java:213)
at org.apache.tomcat.service.TopWorkerThread.runIt(PoolTcpEndpoint.java:416)
at org.apache.tomcat.until.ThreadPool$ControlRunnable.run(ThreadPool.java:501)
at java.lang.Thread.run(Thread.java:484)
</stackTrace>
</detail>
</SOAP-ENV:Fault>
</SOAP-ENV:Body>
SOAP Body
</SOAP-ENV:Envelope>
SOAP Envelope
SOAP Packet

- `<detail/>`
  The `<detail>` element is meant to carry application-specific information. It must be present if the application could not process the `<Body>` element. In other words, its presence or absence can be used to test if the error was related to processing the body. For instance, the fault example with an unknown service does not contain a `<detail>` element, as the request never made it to the service (in this case because the service was not registered).

Note that the Apache SOAP implementation will not generate a `<detail>` element if you do not include a fault listener in your deployment descriptor. We will look more closely at deployment descriptors in the next chapter, when we write the `HelloWorld` sample. Instead of the fault shown in the previous example, you would get the following:

```
<SOAP-ENV:Fault>
  <faultcode>SOAP-ENV:Server</faultcode>
  <faultstring>Exception from service object: null</faultstring>
  <faultactor>/realtimequotes/ncrouter</faultactor>
</SOAP-ENV:Fault>
```

In addition to these four elements, a SOAP fault may contain additional namespace-qualified elements.

Next, we will discuss the rules that SOAP defines to encode its payloads.

Encoding

The encoding section of the SOAP 1.1 specification represents more than half of the volume of the document. This is mostly attributable to the fact that, at the time of the release of SOAP 1.1, XML schemas were still in a state of flux. Had XML schemas been a true standard, the SOAP specification would have shrunk to of a fraction of its size. Unfortunately, the XML schema specification is still not complete, and arguably needs a few more features to fully support SOAP encoding.

Basic Encoding Rules

As we mentioned previously, the encoding rules of SOAP are very similar to what you would expect to find in other programming languages and database systems. SOAP uses XML to encode its payload: however, SOAP defines a more restrictive set of rules for encoding than XML.

> *The specification for the data types supported by XML Schemas can be found at* http://www.w3.org/TR/xmlschema-2/.

The schema used for SOAP encoding can be found at http://schemas.xmlsoap.org/soap/encoding/. To define the specific rules of encoding for your data, you can either reference an external schema or use the `xsi:type` mechanism. Apache SOAP use the latter, as you can see in this example that encodes a string and an integer:

```
<?xml version='1.0' encoding='UTF-8'?>
<SOAP-ENV:Envelope
 xmlns:SOAP-ENV="http://schemas.xmlsoap.org/soap/envelope/"
 xmlns:xsi="http://www.w3.org/1999/XMLSchema-instance"
 xmlns:xsd="http://www.w3.org/1999/XMLSchema">
 <SOAP-ENV:Body>
   <ns1:getOrder xmlns:ns1="urn:order"
    SOAP-ENV:encodingStyle="http://xml.apache.org/xml-soap/literalxml">
     <arg0 xsi:type="xsd:string"
      SOAP-ENV:encodingStyle="http://schemas.xmlsoap.org/soap/encoding/">
       atase
     </arg0>
     <arg1 xsi:type="xsd:int"
      SOAP-ENV:encodingStyle="http://schemas.xmlsoap.org/soap/encoding/">
       123456010
     </arg1>
   </ns1:getOrder>
  </SOAP-ENV:Body>
</SOAP-ENV:Envelope>
```

The advantage of using the `xsi:type` mechanism is that the SOAP document is self-describing, in both its structure and in the values of its data types. The disadvantage is that there is no schema describing the SOAP messages.

The rules governing serializations are strict. The complete rules are available in the specification, but here are the essential ones:

- **All values are represented as element content.**
  In other words, attributes may not be used to represent values or pass arguments to remote methods. For instance, the ticker value that we saw earlier may not be represented as `<ticker value="sunw"/>`.
- **A simple value is represented as character data.**
  In particular, a simple value may not contain elements, since this would make it a complex value. In addition, strings may be represented as character data.
- **A compound value is encoded as a sequence of elements.**
  A compound value is a structure simply encoded as an unordered list of elements. For instance, the complex number `(1, 2i)` could be encoded with its real and imaginary numbers:

```
<arg0 xsi:type="complex">
  <real xsi:type="xsd:double">1</real>
  <img xsi:type="xsd:double">2</img>
</arg0>
```

- **Each field of a compound element is distinguished using a role name "accessor", which is the name of the field.**
  The accessor is the XML element used to access the data. For instance, the accessor of the first argument in the previous example is `<arg0/>`.
- **Arrays are compound values of type `SOAP:Array`.**
  SOAP arrays have one or more dimensions. The elements of an array are accessed using an ordinal position or accessor. SOAP arrays may be heterogeneous arrays. The serialization rules for SOAP arrays support sparse arrays as well as partially transmitted arrays, but Apache SOAP does not support that specific serialization.

The SOAP specification allows for a role name accessor and an ordinal accessor to be used at the same time. However, in this book, we will only work with ordinal accessors to arrays (natural integers like `1, 2, 3`), which is typically what you will encounter in RPC development as in `array[0]` or `array[144]`.

The following table contains a few examples so you can see the implications of those rules. For each example, we have included the Java definition of the data along with the serialized version as produced by the Apache SOAP framework. As we mentioned earlier, this serialization is not the only valid serialization for SOAP.

Java Declaration	SOAP Serialization
`int index = 144;`	`<index xsi:type="xsd:int">144</index>`
`String str = "1234";`	`<str xsi:type="xsd:string">1234</str>`

Table continued on following page

```
Class Cl1 { int index;
  float fl1;
  ...
};
```

```
<item
  xmlns:ns3="urn:your-service-urn"
  xsi:type="ns3:Cl1">
  <index xsi:type="xsd:int">
   1
  </index>
  <fl1 xsi:type="xsd:float">1.0</fl1>
</item>
```

```
int ints[] = new { 1, 2,
3 };
```

```
<ns2:Array
  xmlns:ns2=
"http://schemas.xmlsoap.org/soap/encoding/"
  xsi:type="ns2:Array"
  ns2:arrayType="xsd:int[3]">
  <item xsi:type="xsd:int">1</item>
  <item xsi:type="xsd:int">2</item>
  <item xsi:type="xsd:int">3</item>
</ns2:Array>
```

```
String strArray = {
  "first", "second",
"third"};
```

```
<ns2:Array
  xmlns:ns2=
"http://schemas.xmlsoap.org/soap/encoding/"
  xsi:type="ns2:Array"
  ns2:arrayType="xsd:string[3]">
  <item xsi:type="xsd:string">first</item>
  <item xsi:type="xsd:string">second</item>
  <item xsi:type="xsd:string">third</item>
</ns2:Array>
```

With the serialization rules mentioned so far, we should have enough information to understand the SOAP messages that we will work with in this book. For completeness, we will briefly mention another important feature of SOAP encoding: multiple references.

Multi-References

SOAP was designed as a wire-level protocol, and as such it needs to pay special attention to the amount of data that is transmitted in its messages. For instance, if you are sending an array of strings to the server and several of those strings are identical, you would be duplicating the strings with the serialization rules that we have mentioned so far:

```
<ns2:Array
  xmlns:xsi="http://www.w3.org/1999/XMLSchema-instance"
  xmlns:ns2="http://schemas.xmlsoap.org/soap/encoding/"
  xsi:type="ns2:Array"
  ns2:arrayType="xsd:string[3]">
  <item xsi:type="xsd:string">This is a long string to transmit on the
     wire</item>
  <item xsi:type="xsd:string">This is a long string to transmit on the
     wire</item>
  <item xsi:type="xsd:string">This is a long string to transmit on the
     wire</item>
  <item xsi:type="xsd:string">This is a long string to transmit on the
     wire</item>
</ns2:Array>
```

This particular example does not use a particularly long string, but our application could. This is where the use of **multi-reference accessors** allows for a more compact representation:

```
<ns2:Array
  xmlns:xsi="http://www.w3.org/1999/XMLSchema-instance"
  xmlns:ns2="http://schemas.xmlsoap.org/soap/encoding/"
  xsi:type="ns2:Array"
  ns2:arrayType="xsd:string[3]">
  <item soap:href="#id1"/>
  <item soap:href="#id1"/>
  <item soap:href="#id1"/>
  <item soap:href="#id1"/>
  <item xsi:type="xsd:string" soap:id="id1">
    This is a long string to transmit on the wire
  </item>
</ns2:Array>
```

More importantly, multi-reference accessors allow you to preserve the semantics of a method call (or of any data type) from the client to the server. Consider the following case:

```
String s1 = "My first string";
myMethod(s1, s1);
```

Without multi-reference, the call would be serialized as follows:

```
<ns1:myMethod
  xmlns:ns1="urn:my-service"
  SOAP-ENV:encodingStyle="http://schemas.xmlsoap.org/soap/encoding/">
  <firstString xsi:type="xsd:string">My First String</firstString>
  <secondString xsi:type="xsd:string">My First String</secondString>
</ns1:myMethod>
```

With that information, it is impossible for the server-side doing the un-marshaling to reconstitute the intent of the call. However, if the call is serialized using multi-references, the semantics of the call can be preserved, because the SOAP payload carries the information that the first and second argument of the call are in fact identical:

```
<ns1:myMethod
  xmlns:ns1="urn:my-service"
  SOAP-ENV:encodingStyle="http://schemas.xmlsoap.org/soap/encoding/">
  <firstString xsi:type="xsd:string" soap:href="#id1"/>
  <secondString xsi:type="xsd:string" soap:id="id1">
    My First String
  </secondString>
</ns1:myMethod>
```

When working with the Apache SOAP framework, you must remember that it does not support multi-referencing. Therefore, you need to be careful when defining your method signatures.

Enumerations

The Java language does not support an enumerated type. However, many other programming languages do, including XML schema. SOAP defines its enumerated type in the same way as XML schemas do: an enumerated type or enumeration is a list of distinct values compatible with the base type of the enumeration. For instance, if you wanted to represent a `Color` enumerated type, you could base your representation on the type `string` as shown in the following example:

```
<?xml version='1.0' encoding='UTF-8'?>
<SOAP-ENV:Envelope
 xmlns:SOAP-ENV="http://schemas.xmlsoap.org/soap/envelope/"
 xmlns:xsi="http://www.w3.org/1999/XMLSchema-instance"
 xmlns:xsd="http://www.w3.org/1999/XMLSchema">
 <SOAP-ENV:Body>
  <ns1:getRGB xmlns:ns1="urn:rgb-converter"
   SOAP-ENV:encodingStyle="http://schemas.xmlsoap.org/soap/encoding/">
   <arg0 xsi:type="xsd:string">red</arg0>
  </ns1:getOrderList>
 </SOAP-ENV:Body>
</SOAP-ENV:Envelope>
```

You could also base your representation on the type `int`, as demonstrated in the following SOAP request:

```
<?xml version='1.0' encoding='UTF-8'?>
<SOAP-ENV:Envelope
 xmlns:SOAP-ENV="http://schemas.xmlsoap.org/soap/envelope/"
 xmlns:xsi="http://www.w3.org/1999/XMLSchema-instance"
 xmlns:xsd="http://www.w3.org/1999/XMLSchema">
 <SOAP-ENV:Body>
  <ns1:getRGB xmlns:ns1="urn:rgb-converter"
   SOAP-ENV:encodingStyle="http://schemas.xmlsoap.org/soap/encoding/">
   <arg0 xsi:type="xsd:int">0</arg0>
  </ns1:getOrderList>
 </SOAP-ENV:Body>
</SOAP-ENV:Envelope>
```

As you can see in the previous examples, an enumerated type is simply serialized according to its base type.

Default Values

SOAP does not define a clear semantic for elements that do not have an accessor. For instance, if the argument of a method is omitted and no overloaded implementation is available, what should the receiving end do? The specifics are left to the implementation, since the SOAP specification merely suggests resolution through the use of Booleans and numeric values. In practice, you will maximize your chances of interoperability by not relying on default values.

Since we are on the subject of overloading methods, it is worth mentioning that SOAP will allow you to overload a method simply by changing its return value. However, this kind of overloading (since it is not legal in Java) might also hamper your ability to work with other services.

Messaging

When we discussed distributed application protocols in Chapter 1, we introduced the concept of **document-based** (also known as **message-based**) services, as opposed to the **procedure-based** services that we have been talking about in the previous sections.

As we said in Chapter 1, the fundamental difference between the two systems is not architectural, since it is based on the payload exchanged between computers: message-based systems do not encode a procedure call, they simply carry a document or a data structure. SOAP is designed to support message-based services as well as procedure-based services. Similarly to procedure-based services, message-based services can either be one way, or be based on a request-response protocol. We will review a one-way message-based service shortly.

So, when should we use a message service as opposed to an RPC service? A key advantage of a message service is its flexibility. Consider the following scenario. You have a customer database, and you want to periodically check and possibly update the quality of your data. If your database already has an XML import/export capability, you can export your customer addresses into a large XML document and send it to an address standardization provider.

> **Standardizing an address is the process of putting a mailing address in a canonical form that your local post office will deliver. For instance in the US, `123 Pearl Street Colorado Boulder` would transformed into `123 Pearl St, Boulder Co 80301`. Standardization of addresses is used in data quality applications.**

As a response, you get back a modified document with the standardized addresses, which you can now import back into your database for updates. In an RPC system, you have to convert the customer addresses into one or more method calls, submit the request, and then do the reverse operation when you receive the response. You can see that with messaging you can leverage existing import/export infrastructure that you already have in place.

Another example of the usefulness of message systems is in setting up SOAP services to audit SOAP messages as they pass through. The following diagram shows just such an arrangement – the first recipient of the SOAP request is the audit system, which passes the request to its final destination as specified by the `actor` attribute.

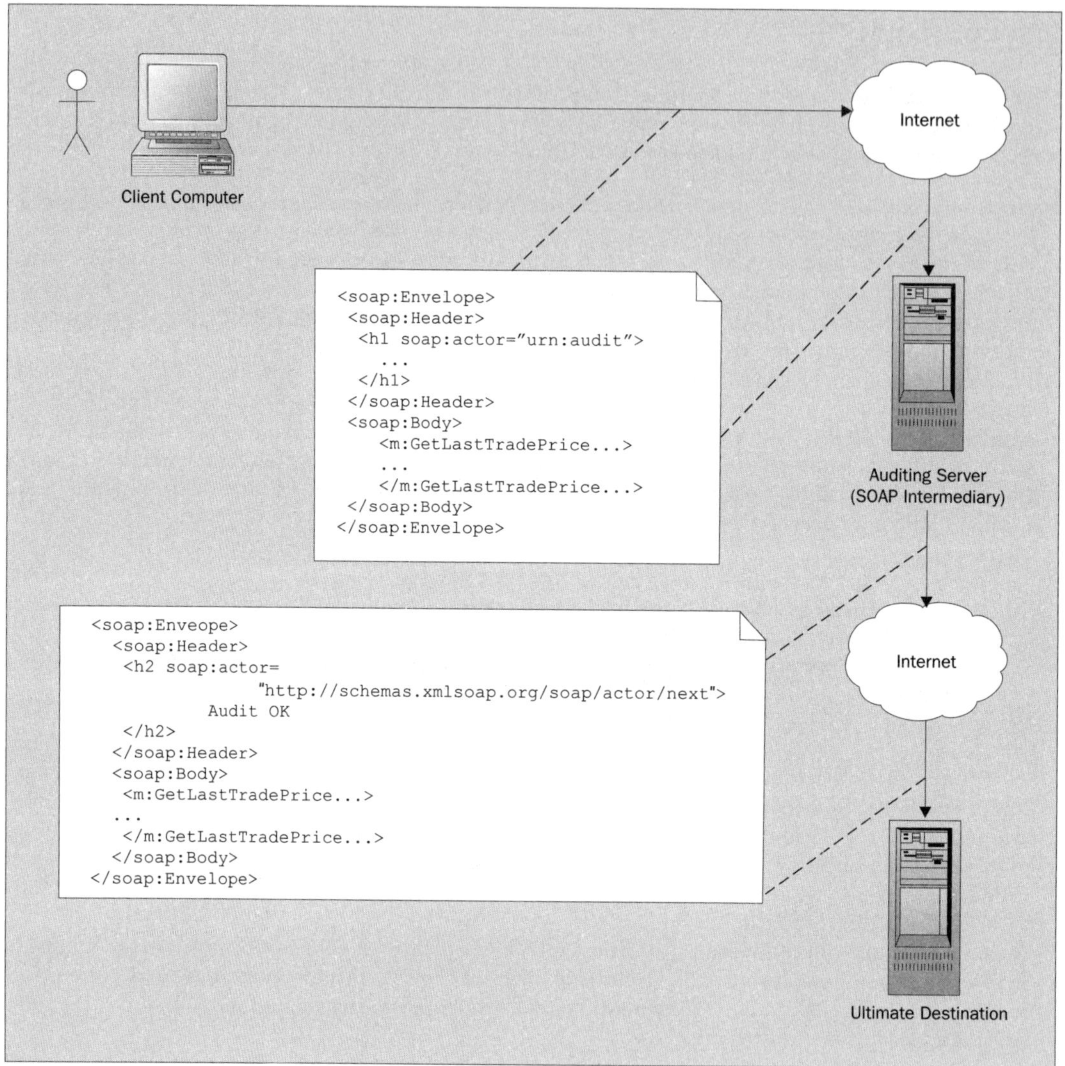

Most messaging protocols are asynchronous, so you might be tempted to list that characteristic as an advantage of messaging over RPC. However, as we have seen, SOAP is fundamentally a one-way protocol that supports asynchronous connections for RPC packets and document-based messages.

The audit system is called a **SOAP intermediary**, an application that is capable of both receiving and forwarding SOAP messages. There might be cases where you need to give specific directives to a SOAP intermediary. For instance, imagine that you have been given a promotional key and you want to tell the billing system that you are entitled to preferential treatment. Such a requirement could be handled with a **SOAP actor**.

A SOAP actor is a global attribute that can be used to indicate the intended recipient of a header element. Like any global identifier in XML, a SOAP actor is a URI. When a SOAP intermediary receives a header element intended for its use, it must not forward it to the next recipient of the message. (You do not want to dispense a double discount, do you?) In the previous diagram, the `<h1/>` header entry is morphed into the `<h2/>` header entry to notify the ultimate recipient of the message that the audit has been performed successfully.

The header elements that we saw previously while introducing SOAP actors did not have a SOAP actor attribute, and as such were intended for the ultimate destination of the SOAP message. This use of header elements shows you another example of how the header is used to extend the protocol. Note that the Apache SOAP framework does not support SOAP actors.

Because SOAP serializes method calls similarly to structures, the distinction between an RPC service and a message service is largely academic until you actually get to the implementation of your service. When it comes to RPC services, the Apache SOAP implementation relies on the service providing a remote method to call. All you need to do to implement a procedure-based service is to provide a Java method that implements the functionality. For instance, let's imagine that you want to expose a method through SOAP using the Apache SOAP framework. Specifically, to expose a method that returns `"Hello World!"`, we would only need to write the following code:

```
package com.lesavon.service;
public class HelloWorldService {
    public String getMessage() {
        return "Hello World!";
    }
}
```

We will discuss this idea in more detail in Chapter 3, but the important point here is that you can develop your RPC service using only Java without knowing anything about SOAP or the Apache SOAP framework. When it comes to the development of a message service, you have to provide a callback method containing low-level (in other words, implementation-dependent) objects. The signature for the callback method in Apache SOAP is:

```
void name(SOAPEnvelope request-envelope,
     SOAPContext request-context,
     SOAPContext response-context);
```

where `SOAPEnvelope` and `SOAPContext` are classes of the Apache SOAP implementation. In the case of RPC services, the Apache SOAP implementation is able to hide the details of SOAP development.

Where Are the Objects?

So where are the objects in the Simple **Object** Access Protocol? Surely, you cannot say that you have a distributed object-oriented protocol if you cannot hold a reference to a remote object! In particular, how can a protocol be called object-oriented if it does not support the fundamental characteristics of an object, characteristics that are apparent in most object-oriented languages from SmallTalk, to C++/C#, to Java?

The main features of objects are:

- **Instance Methods**: the ability to automatically associate data to a set of functions, also known as methods in that concept
- **Polymorphism**: the ability to define the behavior of an object at runtime
- **Data Encapsulation**: the ability to hide the inner data of an object from the users of the object

The polymorphic accessors of SOAP are closer to method overloading than they are to method overriding. They are not polymorphic in the object-oriented sense.

In short, an object has instance data and polymorphic behavior.

The Apache SOAP implementation allows us to map SOAP calls to (static) class methods. We will discuss the lifetime of remote services when we introduce deployment descriptors.

The only "object" calls that we can make using SOAP are calls to static methods, since we cannot specifically call a remote object without a remote reference to that object. We could argue that the serialization of objects is specified in SOAP, but the data that travels inside a SOAP packet could just as easily represent a structure. There is no guarantee that an object is on the other side of the wire.

In other words, we can use SOAP to implement distributed object-oriented systems, but a purely function-based implementation is perfectly compatible with the specifications of SOAP.

Summary

In this chapter, we looked at the SOAP specification in more detail. We saw that the specification addresses three major pieces of functionality:

- The SOAP envelope, which along with the header and the body defines a framework for exchanging messages in a distributed architecture
- The encoding rules, which define an XML-based serialization mechanism that can be used for interoperability
- The SOAP RPC mechanism, that uses structure-like serialization rules for method call encoding

In addition, SOAP defines HTTP as its preferred transport without precluding the use of other transports, such as SMTP. The use of HTTP is a key ingredient to the acceptance of SOAP by security-minded network administrators.

For the most part, SOAP is true to its goal of simplicity. Arguably the 'S' in SOAP gets lost in Section 5 where the SOAP specification tackles encoding, since it takes more than half of the overall document. However, this complexity should disappear as the XML Schema specification is accepted as standard.

What the SOAP specification does not specify is even more remarkable:

- SOAP defines no proprietary protocol to carry its payload.
- SOAP defines no lifetime and no garbage collection rules.
- SOAP defines no remote activation.
- SOAP defines no object-by-reference mechanism.
- SOAP defines no batching process.
- SOAP defines no programming language bindings.
- SOAP defines no compatibility to the legacy systems that we discussed in Chapter 1 (CORBA, DCOM, amongst others).

Historically, these features are the toughest to implement and the hardest to get accepted across platforms.

In this chapter, we looked at the features of the Apache SOAP framework that we will be using in the remainder of the book. We also discussed some potential interoperability issues, such as the use of the `SOAPAction` header element.

Hopefully, this chapter gave you the urge to start developing web services using SOAP. In the next chapter, we will set up our SOAP development environment. We will also write the unavoidable `HelloWorld!` program, only this time with a SOAP flavor.

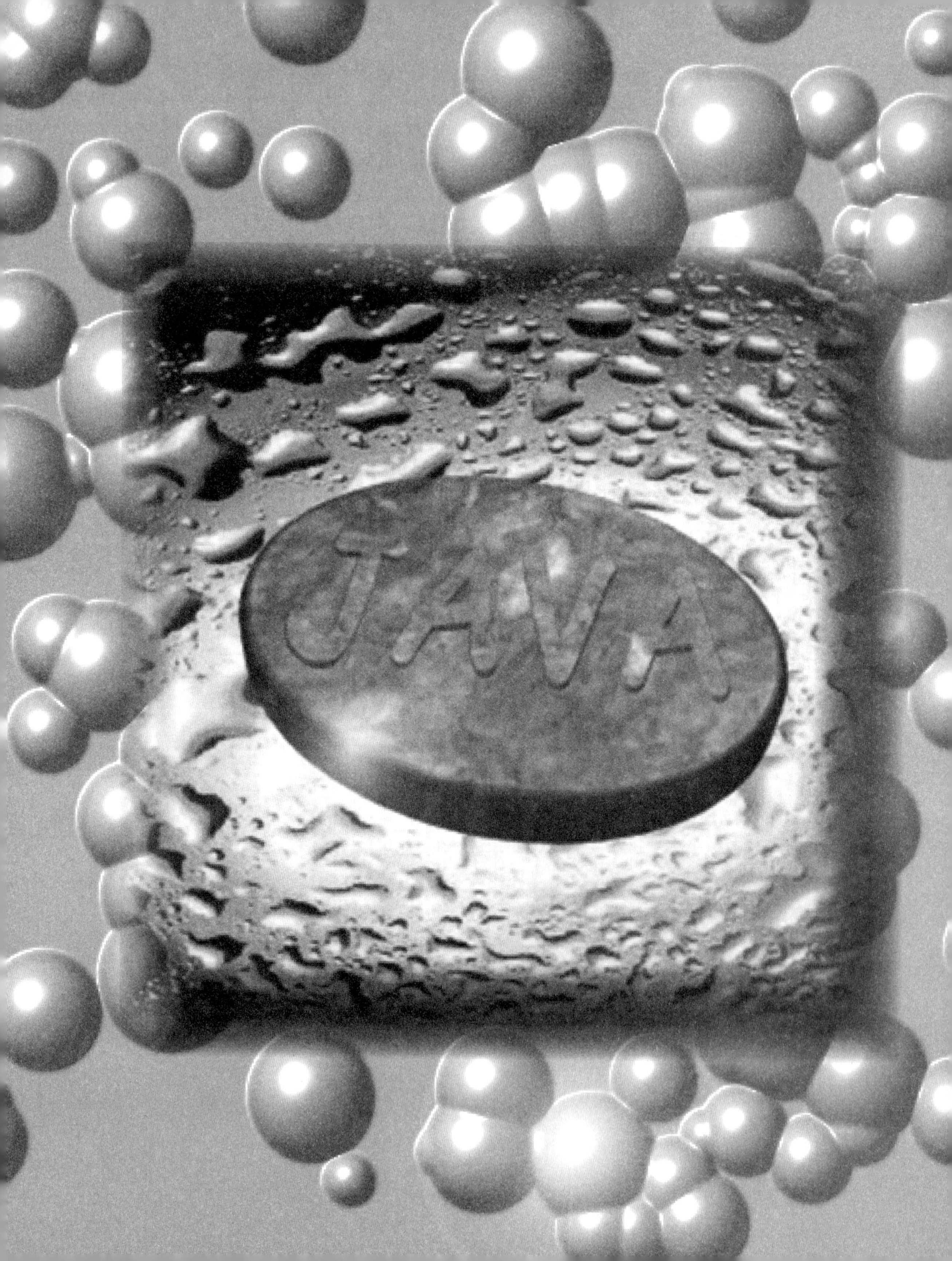
JAVA

3

Setting Up Your SOAP Server

In this chapter we will cover how to set up the development environment for our SOAP projects, using freely available tools such as Apache, Tomcat, and the Apache SOAP framework. As we will discover in the pages to come, a SOAP server relies on many software components. Setting up a SOAP server involves integrating many different types of components from web servers to servlet engines, and including the SOAP engine itself. Setting up a SOAP development environment is not a trivial task: we will have to download and install specific versions of software components, and we have to make sure that the right component is loaded in memory at the right time. Configuration issues occupy a large place in the problems that frustrate newcomers to SOAP development.

We will cover setting up the environment in detail in order to make this process as smooth as possible. There is also a troubleshooting section at the end of this chapter.

We will go through the steps of downloading and configuring the software on the two major classes of Operating Systems (OS): Windows and UNIX. To show you an example of how it is done on Windows, we will use Windows 2000, and we will use Linux Red Hat to represent the UNIX family. The screenshots for the most part show a Windows development, but in areas where this differs from Linux both will be shown. Directory paths will, on the whole, be shown relative to C:\ (In other words, Windows is the default environment). Adapt this to your own system as necessary.

We will conclude the chapter with a short discussion on two popular web servers: Apache and IIS. Since you do not need a web server for development, we will not go through the steps required to install them. However, when we go on to talk about security in Chapter 7 we will detail how to set up authentication with a web server, as it is part of the architecture of the sample application.

Without any more delay, let's describe the software needed for the application. We will first describe the various contributory components, followed by a look at the setup instructions for Linux and Windows.

Pieces of the Puzzle

The following figure shows some of the software components that we will be using during the course of this book, and how they relate to one other:

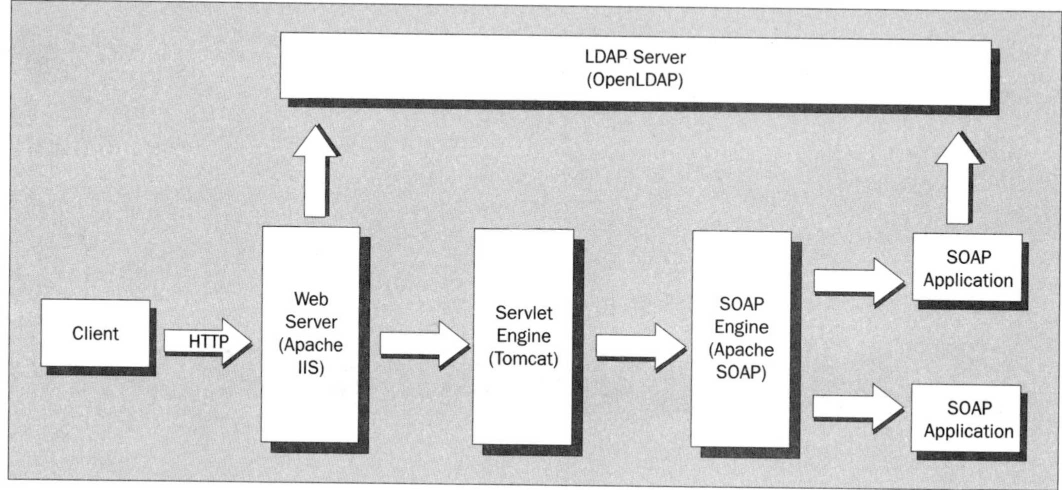

1. **J2EE**
   First things first: without the enterprise version of the Java SDK, no java SOAP development is possible. We will not go into details about setting up the SDK – if you are reading this book, chances are that you already know how to develop Java applications. Sun's web site contains detailed information on how to set up a Java development environment. The Java 2 Enterprise Edition (J2EE) can be downloaded from http://java.sun.com/j2ee/. If you need further help downloading and installing the J2EE than that offered by Sun, please refer to *Professional Java Server Programming J2EE Edition* by Wrox Press.

2. **A Servlet Engine**
   A servlet engine, such as Tomcat, is responsible for creating and starting the Java Virtual Machine (JVM). It will also invoke your servlet according to the protocol defined in the J2EE architecture.

3. **A SOAP Engine**
   A SOAP engine generates and parses requests and responses according to the SOAP specification that we reviewed in Chapter 2. We rely largely on the Java Apache SOAP engine in this book. The SOAP engine will be called a SOAP framework (in other words, a set of classes for development) when the focus is SOAP development rather than SOAP deployment. Note that you will use the same `soap.jar` file for development and for deployment.

The setup of the SOAP engine is liable to be the most challenging.

With the three software packages that we have just mentioned, you have enough plumbing to develop SOAP applications. However, you might want to consider downloading the following components for deployment:

4. **A Web Server**
   The web server listens to HTTP requests and forwards them to the SOAP engine when appropriate. Note that most servlet engines, including Tomcat, come with a web server. This means that during early development we can leave the external web server out of the picture. However, during testing and in production we should rely on a tested web server like Apache or IIS for performance and security considerations. We will discuss the specifics of this at the end of this chapter.

5. **An LDAP Server**
   As we will see in Chapter 7, security and personalization can be added to our application using the **Lightweight Directory Access Protocol (LDAP)**. We will rely primarily on a freely available LDAP implementation (OpenLDAP) for our samples. Creating an LDAP database is a rather complex operation, so we will defer discussion on this topic until Chapter 7.

Let's start with the list of components that we will have to download, and a short description of their purpose and their location on the Web.

Downloads

The following table contains the list of downloads that we will require, as well as a short description of the software that they contain. The downloads are available in the site addresses listed below. Follow the links on each site to obtain the relevant files. Alternatively, a document is available in the code download section of http://www.wrox.com that details the absolute addresses for these downloads. This document will be maintained to ensure up to date links.

Software	Description	URL
Tomcat (3.2.3)	**Servlet Engine** A servlet engine instantiates the Java virtual machine to execute servlets and Java Server Pages. The servlet engine also takes care of compiling JSP pages into servlets.	http://jakarta.apache.org
SOAP (2.2)	**SOAP Engine** The SOAP Engine (or framework when used for development) is the set of classes that provide SOAP functionality.	http://xml.apache.org

Table continued on following page

Software	Description	URL
Xerces (1.4.3)	**XML Parser** JAXP-compatible namespace-aware XML parser.	http://xml.apache.org
JavaMail (1.2)	**SMTP** Simple Mail Transport Protocol support used by Apache SOAP.	http://java.sun.com/
JAF (1.0.1)	**Java Bean Activation Framework (JAF)** MIME attachment support used by Apache SOAP.	http://java.sun.com/

We will be downloading and initializing these software components in the order listed in the table. The downloadable files for Linux and Windows can be found from the same URLs. However, the file names might be different due to the differing file formats on these platforms. We will describe the exact file names as we go through the steps required to download and install these components.

As we mentioned in the introduction, you should have installed the J2SDKEE version 1.3.1 or greater. We will review the setups for Windows 2000 and for Linux. Modifying these instructions for your specific platform should be a minor variation on those two themes. Essentially, the OS commands to explode the ZIP files and manipulate their contents differ slightly, but the methodology is the same.

Tomcat

The servlet engine that we will use in this book is the reference implementation by Apache: Tomcat. We will use version 3.2.3, since that is the version recommended by the developers of Apache SOAP.

The installation and configuration instructions for Tomcat are straightforward. Let's begin with the download.

Download

Your point of entry on the Internet to download or learn about any software that comes out of the Apache organization is http://www.apache.org. As you can see below, the Apache organization has a lot to offer:

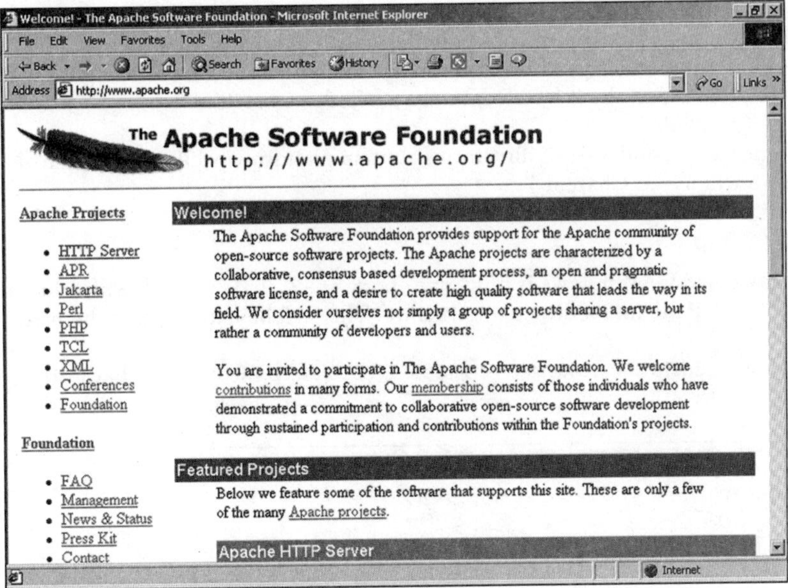

Go to the download page for Tomcat v3.2.3 from http://jakarta.apache.org, which contains various incarnations of the same files:

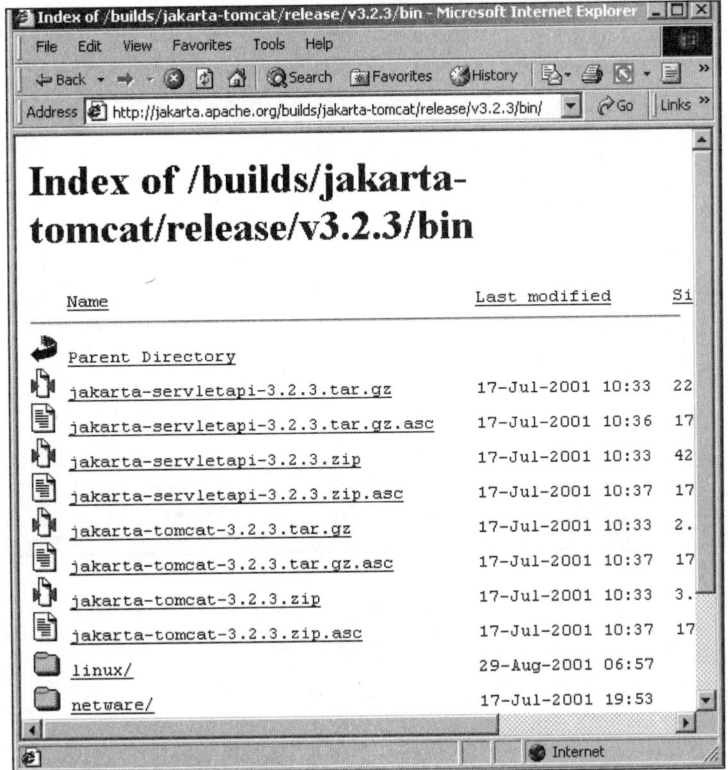

Some files are for the Windows platform and some are for the UNIX platform. Signed versions are also available that guarantee that the distribution files have not been tampered with. This is probably useless if you get and install the files from the Apache site, but has some value if we put the file on a server for later redistribution, especially if we elect to use a Windows machine.

The `Linux`, `netware`, and `win32` directories contain platform-specific code, such as the Jakarta DLL for IIS that we will use in Chapter 7.

Windows 2000 Setup

The file to download for Windows is `jakarta-tomcat-3.2.3.zip`. Download it now. The next step is to expand the ZIP file into a directory structure. This will be explained in the next section.

The first step is to unzip the `jakarta-tomcat-3.2.3.zip` file onto the hard drive, which in our case is `C:\`.

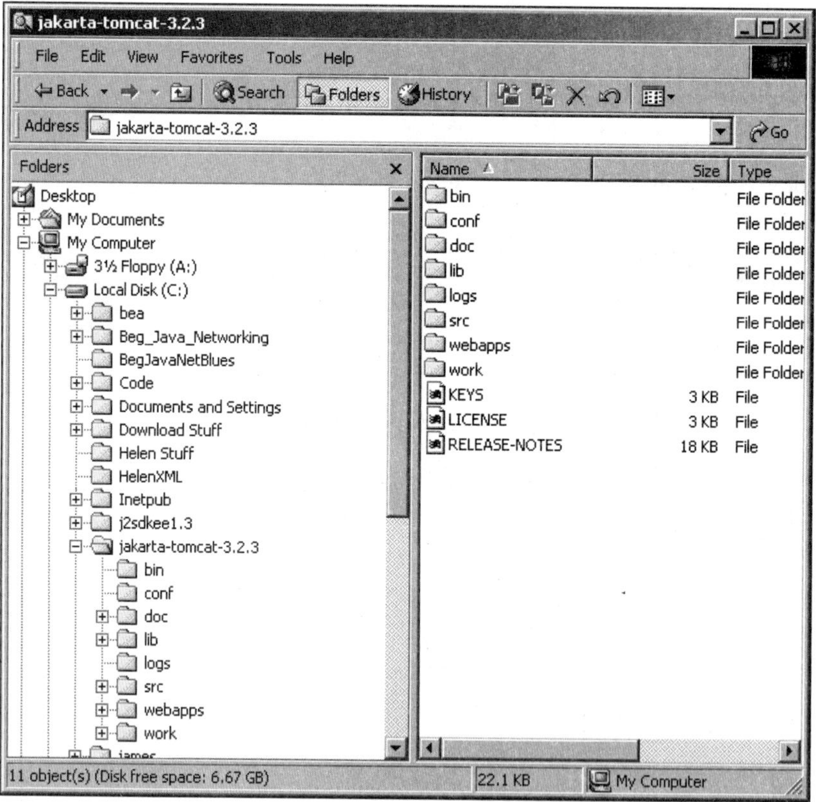

Go into the `bin` folder and double-click on `startup.bat`. This should start Tomcat in a separate window as shown in the next figure:

```
Tomcat 3.2
2001-10-09 13:18:55 - ContextManager: Adding context Ctx( /examples )
2001-10-09 13:18:55 - ContextManager: Adding context Ctx( /admin )
Starting tomcat. Check logs/tomcat.log for error messages
2001-10-09 13:18:55 - ContextManager: Adding context Ctx(  )
2001-10-09 13:18:55 - ContextManager: Adding context Ctx( /test )
2001-10-09 13:18:56 - PoolTcpConnector: Starting HttpConnectionHandler on 8080
2001-10-09 13:18:56 - PoolTcpConnector: Starting Ajp12ConnectionHandler on 8007
```

Linux Setup

We will be using Red Hat Linux 7.1 to demonstrate the configuration steps for Tomcat and SOAP. We will also use EMACS to show you the minor edits that you have to perform in configuration files.

The file to download for Linux is `Jakarta-tomcat-3.2.3.tar.gz`. If you click on the hyperlink, you should get a dialog box:

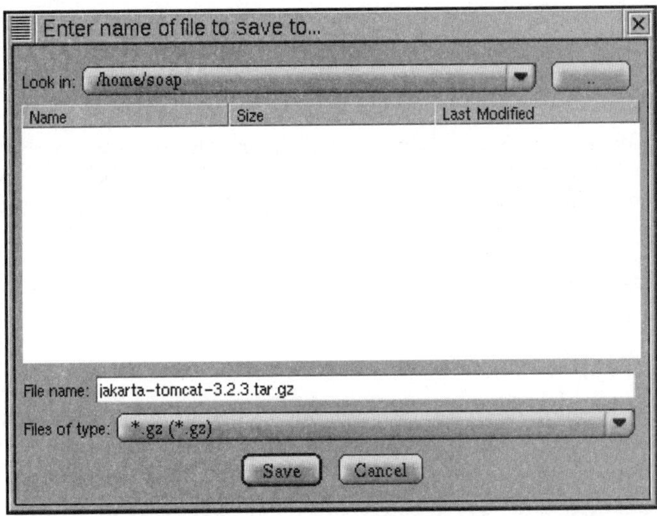

Be sure to set the path to what you want (you do not want to download the file to the home directory – you might want to set up a user called `soap` in the `usr` directory, and operate all of the code from their `home` directory.). The first step is to decompress the file using `gzip`:

```
gzip -d Jakarta-tomcat-3.2.3.tar.gz
```

As the output of the `ls` command shows in the figure above, the result of that command will be `Jakarta-tomcat-3.2.3.tar`, an archive file that we need to expand into a directory.

Do this using the following tar command:

```
tar -xf Jakarta-tomcat-3.2.3.tar
```

The result of the tar command is a directory called Jakarta-tomcat-3.2.3.

The next step is to define two shell variables:

- JAVA_HOME
  $JAVA_HOME points to the directory where we installed the JDK 1.3.1 or later. The Tomcat shell scripts use this variable.
- TOMCAT_HOME
  $TOMCAT_HOME points to the directory where we installed Tomcat. The Tomcat shell scripts use this variable.

We also need to make sure that the shell scripts inside the Tomcat/bin directory can be executed. Starting Tomcat is achieved with the tomcat.sh command:

```
$TOMCAT_HOME/bin/tomcat.sh run
```

Testing Tomcat

At this point, we have the web server bundled with Tomcat listening to port 8080 for HTTP requests. Port 8080 is the default port, but you can change it by modifying the conf/server.xml file. For development, we are happy with port 8080, but for security reasons you will want to change the settings for deployment, as we will discuss further in Chapter 7.

To test that everything is working, simply bring up the browser and key in the URL to our server:

```
http://<machine-name>:8080
```

Make sure to replace <machine-name> with the name of your own server (or with 127.0.0.1 or localhost if you are bringing up the browser on the machine where you installed Tomcat). The following figure shows Tomcat's home page for localhost. Note that Tomcat automatically redirects the browser to the index.html page.

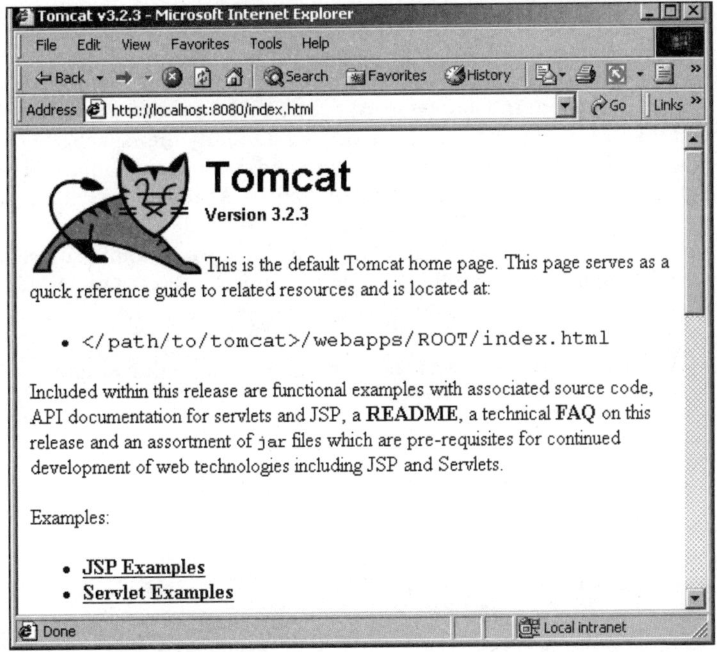

Since we didn't go to all of this trouble to see an HTML page, we will click on the Servlet Examples link, find the `Hello World` servlet example, and then click on Execute:

At this point, we have downloaded and configured Tomcat to process servlets and Java Server Pages (JSP). We will need to do some minor adjustments to Tomcat's configuration for SOAP, but for the most part Tomcat is ready to support our SOAP development.

We can now move on to the more delicate part of setting up our environment: downloading and configuring Apache SOAP.

Apache SOAP

Apache SOAP is a Java implementation of the SOAP submission to the World Wide Web Consortium (W3C). We reviewed it in detail in Chapter 2. Apache SOAP implements a client component and a server component that we use in this book. We will even modify the Apache SOAP implementation to customize its security and automatic XML generation and parsing capabilities. These enhancements will be discussed later – for now, we will concentrate on getting Apache SOAP 2.2 up and running.

Apache SOAP is a little trickier to configure than Tomcat because it builds on several software components: a servlet engine (Tomcat), a messaging framework (JavaMail), a MIME extension framework to handle non-textual data, and, of course, an XML parser.

We will first download all the components we need and then we will configure them to work correctly.

Download

The first component that we will download is Apache SOAP itself.

Begin by navigating to http://xml.apache.org/dist/soap/version-2.2/:

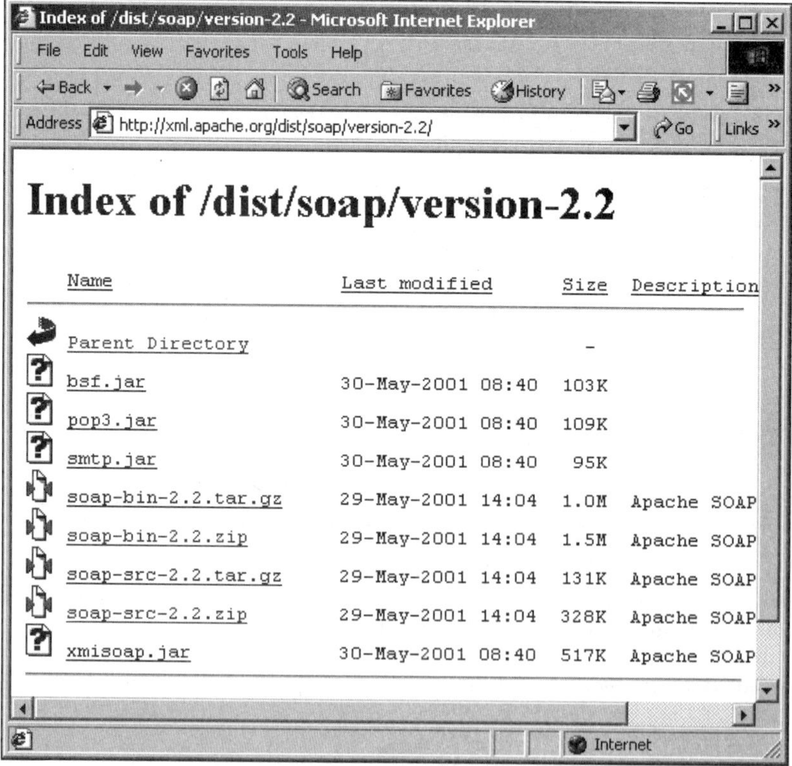

Windows Installation for SOAP

The file we are interested in for SOAP on the Windows platform is `soap-bin-2.2.zip`. The download procedure is similar to the one we performed a few moments ago for Tomcat. The `soap-src-2.2.zip` file contains the source without the binaries, as you may have guessed from the name and the size.

Using WinZip or a similar tool, you need to extract the files and directories from the ZIP file. At the end of the extraction process, you should have the following directory structure:

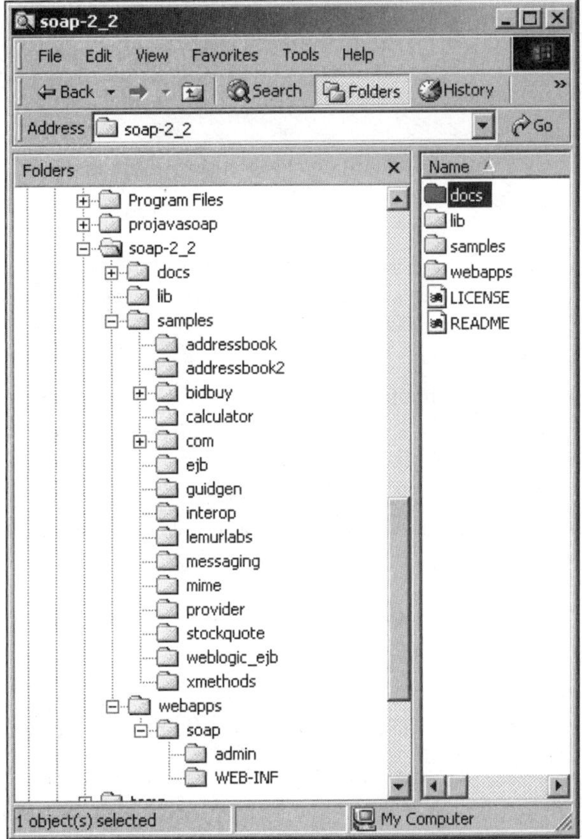

Linux Installation for SOAP

The SOAP download file for the Linux platform is `soap-bin-2.2.tar.gz`. The download procedure is similar to that for Tomcat. The `soap-src-2.2.tar.gz` file contains the source without the binaries, as you may have guessed from the name and the size.

Since the file is a compressed file, the first thing we need to do is to decompress it with `gzip`:

```
gzip -d soap-bin-2.2.tar.gz
```

As the output of the `ls` command shows in the figure above, the result of this command will be `soap-bin-2.2.tar`, an archive file that we need to expand into a directory, just as we did for Tomcat. Note that the other files are the files left from the previous steps. Once again, you create the directory structure using `tar`:

```
tar -xf soap-bin-2.2.tar
```

The top-level files and directories in the `SOAP2_2` directory are:

- `docs`
  This directory contains two types of documentation – documentation to set up a running environment for SOAP, and API documentation for people like us who want to develop using the Apache SOAP framework.

- `lib`
  The `lib` directory should only contain the `soap.jar` file and a DLL for the development of COM-based SOAP services.

- `samples`
  The `samples` directory contains various samples that may or may not apply to your platform. You might want to revisit the samples after you are done with this chapter to begin experimenting with Apache SOAP.

- `webapps`
  The `webapps` directory contains one directory and one file. The `soap.war` file is a Web Archive file that contains the SOAP admin web application that we will use in a few moments to check that our installation is kosher.

- `LICENSE` and `README`
  Those two files contain the usual Apache legal notice and the `README` file that refers you to the documentation directory.

Note that if you want to build the Apache SOAP framework you will have additional directories and files:

- `src`
  The `src` directory contains the source and will only be present is you explicitly download the `soap-bin-2.2.tar.gz` file.

- `build` and `build.xml`
  The `build` directory is the target of the build. The `build` directory will not be created unless you start a build. You might be looking for a `make` file, but you will not see one. Builds are handled by a platform-independent Java-based utility called ANT. We will review ANT in Chapter 5, but for now simply think of it as `make` on steroids.

As part of the Apache SOAP installation for Windows, you get the `TcpTunnelGui` utility. It is a TCP tracing utility. We will use it later in this chapter to show the XML payload that travels over HTTP. If you do any serious SOAP development, chances are that you will use it quite frequently. It is also an excellent tool to learn about SOAP messages.

By now, you are probably ready to see SOAP in action. Alas, you must download and configure a few more components before actually seeing a live demonstration of SOAP.

Xerces

The first component that we need to download is an XML parser. You are probably aware that Tomcat ships with an XML parser since it uses XML documents such as `server.xml` and `web.xml`. However, if you have read Chapter 2, you know that SOAP relies heavily on namespaces and XML schemas, so we need a parser that handles namespaces correctly. By the way, this may seem obvious to you, but a quick search through the SOAP development mailing list reveals that over 500 messages have to do with people selecting the wrong parser. We will discuss the symptoms of this problem in the troubleshooting section at the end of this chapter.

An XML parser that can do the job for us is the Xerces parser from Apache (http://xml.apache.org/dist/xerces-j):

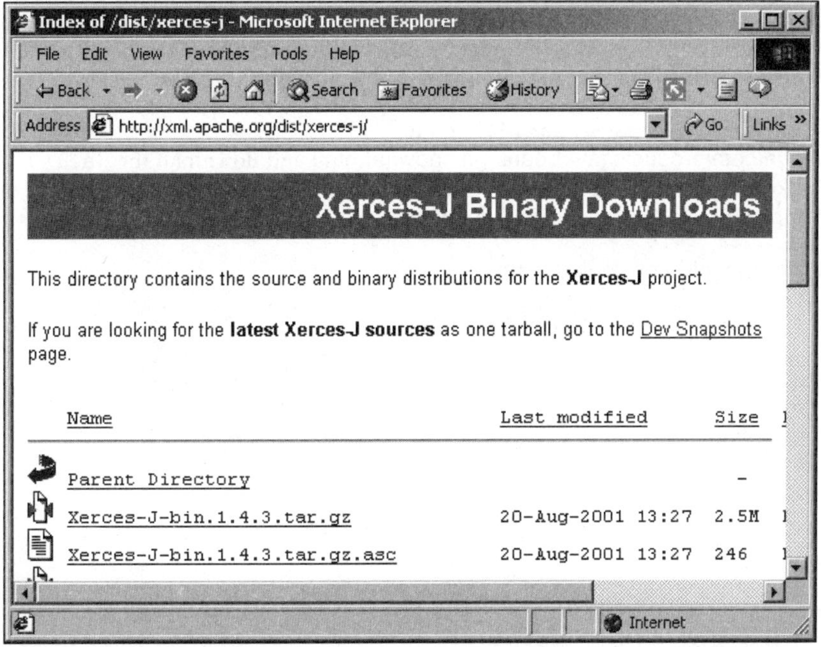

The file we are interested in for Windows is `Xerces-J-bin-1.4.3.zip`. Download and expand it into a directory structure as we did before. In order to keep all of the JAR files that we use in one place, you can copy `xerces-1_4_3\xerces.jar` to the `soap-2_2\lib` directory, but that step is optional.

Note that there is a C++ version of Xerces, hence the –J. Linux users should be interested in the file called `Xerces-J-bin-1.4.3.tar.gz`. Download this file and expand it into a directory structure as we did earlier for Tomcat and Apache SOAP.

JavaMail

The next component to download is JavaMail. Apache SOAP uses it in the messaging component of its implementation. You can get to `mail.jar` by entering the URL http://java.sun.com/products/javamail:

Download the `javamail-1_2.zip` file to your machine – the process should be familiar by now, as should extracting the ZIP file to your installation directory. Copy `javamail-1_2\mail.jar` to the `soap-2_2\lib` directory to keep the JAR files together.

Linux users will need to uncompress the ZIP file and generate the directory structure in one step using the `unzip` command:

```
C:\ProJavaSoap>unzip -q javamail-1_2.zip
```

The `-q` flag stands for "quiet" because `unzip` is verbose by default, and gives you a list of the directories and files that it extracts from an archive.

JavaBean Activation Framework

The last component that we need also comes from SUN. The **JavaBean Activation Framework (JAF)** is used by the Apache SOAP package to invoke software extensions that can handle non-textual data like bitmaps. The installation is essentially the same as it was for the JavaMail package.

To get the file we need, `activation.jar`, go to http://java.sun.com/products/javabeans/glasgow/jaf.html and download the `jaf1_0_1.zip` file, which we handle like the previous ZIP files. The JAR file we need is `jaf-1_0_1\activation.jar`, which should be copied to the `soap-2_2\lib` directory.

The installation should now look like this:

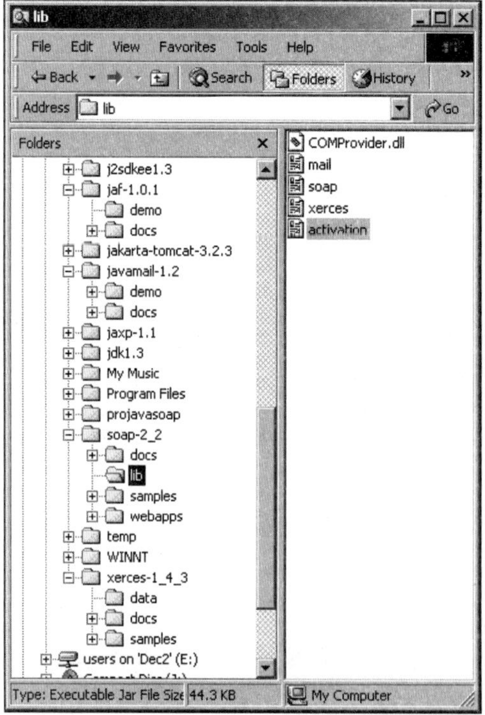

The end is near. At this point, we have downloaded all the software that we need; however, we still have to modify a couple of setup files before actually running our programs.

Setup

The classpath must be configured to include the components we depend on, and we must tell Tomcat where to find the applications that we will build.

Setting up your classpath to include the JAR files we need is essential. There are many necessary JAR files and the order is important.

Classpath for Tomcat – Windows 2000

If you are running on Windows, you now need to alter `tomcat.bat`, which can be found in the `jakarta-tomcat-3.2.3\bin` folder. To compile and run the samples in this book, the classpath must be set to the following value by adding these lines of code to the file:

```
:installClasspath
set SOAP_HOME=c:\soap-2_2
set SOAP_LIB=%SOAP_HOME%\lib
set CP=%SOAP_LIB%\xerces.jar;%CP%
set CP=%SOAP_LIB%\mail.jar;%CP%
set CP=%SOAP_LIB%\activation.jar;%CP%
set CP=%SOAP_LIB%\soap.jar;%CP%
set CP=C:\ProJavaSoap\Chapter03\HelloWorld\WEB-INF\classes;%CP%
echo Using CLASSPATH: %CP%
echo.
set CLASSPATH=%CP%
```

Classpath for Tomcat – Linux

On Linux, your `tomcat.sh` should look something like the following screenshot. However, you will have to replace the path with the directory where we will install `HelloWorld`.

```
if [ "$oldCP" != "" ]; then
    CLASSPATH=${CLASSPATH}:${oldCP}
fi
export SOAP_HOME=/usr/soap/home/soap-2_2
export SOAP_LIB=$SOAP_HOME/lib
CLASSPATH=$SOAP_LIB/xerces.jar:$CLASSPATH
CLASSPATH=$SOAP_LIB/mail.jar:$CLASSPATH
CLASSPATH=$SOAP_LIB/activation.jar:$CLASSPATH
CLASSPATH=$SOAP_LIB/soap.jar:$CLASSPATH
CLASSPATH=$CLASSPATH:/usr/soap/home/ProJavaSoap/WEB-INF/classes

export CLASSPATH
```

In General

We mentioned that the XML parser that we downloaded must be loaded before the XML parser that comes standard with Tomcat, so you need to make sure that `xerces.jar` – or its equivalent if you have decided to use an alternate parser – is at the beginning of your classpath.

Tomcat must be running to take requests from the `HelloWorldClient`. However, because of what appears to be a bug in Tomcat 3.2 (both on Windows and Linux), you must explicitly set the classpath to include the `HelloWorldService` class. According to the J2EE specifications, the `WEB-INF/classes` directory should automatically be included in the classpath.

By now, you are ready to install and run SOAP applications. But before going through an execution, we will first configure the Apache SOAP administration application that allows us to see what SOAP services are installed, or **registered**, on the server.

SOAP Configuration

There are several ways to install a web application in Tomcat. An easy way to install a web application is to modify the `server.xml` file that is located in the `conf` directory of your Tomcat installation. Scroll down to the bottom of this file and simply add a context as shown below:

```
            <Context path="/examples"
                     docBase="webapps/ROOT" />
        </Host>
        -->
            <Context path="/soap"
                     docBase="C:/soap-2_2/webapps/soap"
                     reloadable="true" >
            </Context>
    </ContextManager>
</Server>
```

Make sure that you modify the `docBase` attribute to reflect your actual installation. The `reloadable` attribute is used for debugging: it means that Tomcat will check for modified files and reload them. For a production installation, we will want to turn that feature off.

You will need to start or restart Tomcat after saving the `tomcat.bat/tomcat.sh` and `server.xml` files, in order for the changes to take effect.

Testing Apache SOAP

In this step, we will test that the SOAP server is configured properly but we will not use a SOAP service (we need to write one before we can use it). The development of our first SOAP service is described later in this chapter in the section called *Our First SOAP Service.*

To start Tomcat and see what classpath is used, open a DOS window and follow the instructions shown on this screenshot:

```
C:\WINNT\System32\cmd.exe - tomcat run
C:\jakarta-tomcat-3.2.3\bin>tomcat run
Including all jars in C:\jakarta-tomcat-3.2.3\lib in your CLASSPATH.

Using CLASSPATH: c:\soap-2_2\lib\soap.jar;c:\soap-2_2\lib\activation.jar;c:\soap
-2_2\lib\mail.jar;c:\soap-2_2\lib\xerces.jar;C:\jakarta-tomcat-3.2.3\classes;C:\
jakarta-tomcat-3.2.3\lib\ant.jar;C:\jakarta-tomcat-3.2.3\lib\jasper.jar;C:\jakar
ta-tomcat-3.2.3\lib\jaxp.jar;C:\jakarta-tomcat-3.2.3\lib\parser.jar;C:\jakarta-t
omcat-3.2.3\lib\servlet.jar;C:\jakarta-tomcat-3.2.3\lib\webserver.jar;.;;C:\jdk1
.3\lib\tools.jar

2001-10-10 14:45:55 - ContextManager: Adding context Ctx( /examples )
2001-10-10 14:45:55 - ContextManager: Adding context Ctx( /admin )
2001-10-10 14:45:55 - ContextManager: Adding context Ctx( /soap )
Starting tomcat. Check logs/tomcat.log for error messages
2001-10-10 14:45:55 - ContextManager: Adding context Ctx(  )
2001-10-10 14:45:55 - ContextManager: Adding context Ctx( /test )
2001-10-10 14:45:57 - PoolTcpConnector: Starting HttpConnectionHandler on 8080
2001-10-10 14:45:57 - PoolTcpConnector: Starting Ajp12ConnectionHandler on 8007
```

This command is almost identical to the one we entered earlier to test Tomcat itself. The only changes were to the configuration files used by Tomcat. If you look carefully at the picture above, you will notice two changes from the previous run of Tomcat:

1. The classpath has changed. It now includes the JAR files that we have downloaded. Pay special attention to `xerces.jar`, for, as we said earlier, it must be at the beginning of your classpath (or at least before any other XML parser). Note that at this point the XML parser delivered with Tomcat has been replaced by Xerces.

2. A new application or context has been added: /soap.

To test that you can actually go to the /soap application, go to your favorite web browser and enter the following URL: http://<machine-name>:8080/soap, where `<machine-name>` is the name of your server, or the loopback address (`localhost` or 127.0.0.1).

The following figure shows SOAP's home page for localhost:

If you click on Visit, you should see the following screen:

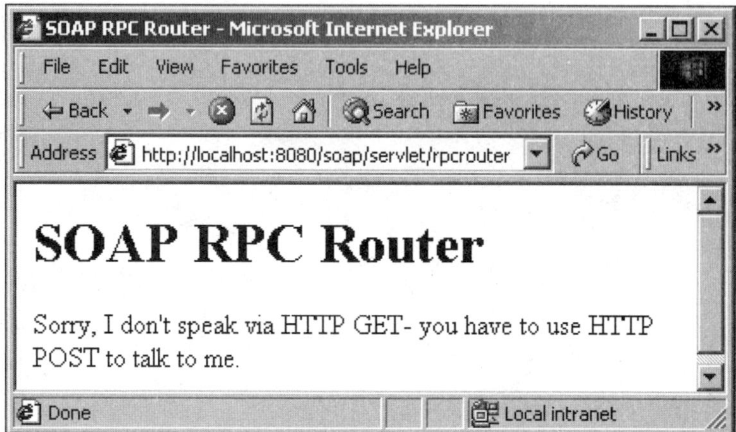

Surely, this is the sign of something going wrong! However, this message only means that everything is working as it should.

Another test that we can go through at this point is to run the SOAP Apache administration page or simply `admin`. To get to the administration page, go back to the SOAP home page and click on `Run` to bring up the following screen:

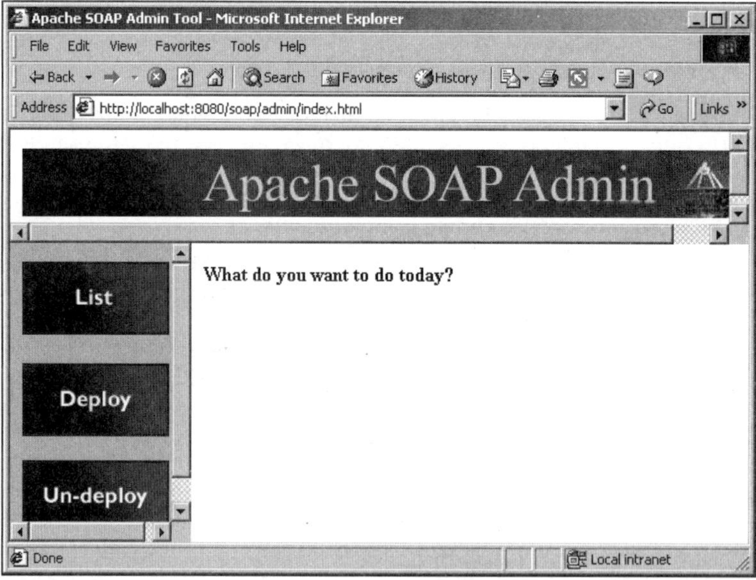

Try clicking on the List button and you will see we have no SOAP services deployed yet. We will deploy a service later when we write our own in the *Our First SOAP Service* section. We now have a SOAP server configured on our machine.

Our First SOAP Service

Our first SOAP service will be quite trivial, but its development will introduce the Apache SOAP framework. As we mentioned earlier, detailed documentation on the coding, registration, and testing of a SOAP service can be found with the Apache SOAP installation under the `docs/index.html` directory. Note that the `HelloWorld` service is part of the code download for this book and is not included as part of the Apache SOAP engine.

The `HelloWorld` SOAP service contains one method that returns a string. The Java signature of the method is:

```
public String getMessage(String callerName);
```

This simple example will allow us to achieve several objectives:

- Write a SOAP service
- Register the SOAP service
- Write a SOAP client
- Build the service and the client
- Run the client and the service
- Examine the SOAP payloads from the client to the server and vice-versa

We will start with the class of the SOAP service.

The Service Class

Creating the service is probably the simplest operation of this process. Have a look at the code in `HelloWorldService.java`:

> *The sample code for this chapter can be found in* `ProJavaSoap\Chapter03`*.* `HelloWorldService.java` *is in* `ProJavaSoap\Chapter03\HelloWorld\src\com\lesavon\service`.

```
// HelloWorldService.java

package com.lesavon.service;

public class HelloWorldService {

  // Returns the string "Hello <callerName>!" to the caller.
  public String getMessage(String callerName) {
    return "Hello " + callerName + "!";
  }
}
```

Most of the actual code is a one-line method. However, this level of simplicity can only be achieved because the Apache SOAP framework and the packages that it uses provide a lot of functionality.

Deployment Descriptor

In the SOAP Apache framework, when a SOAP request comes from the client, it does not directly go to the SOAP service. Look at the figure below: the SOAP request is sent to `org.apache.soap.server.http.RPCRouterServlet`. The `RPCRouterServlet` uses deployment descriptors to decide where to route the request.

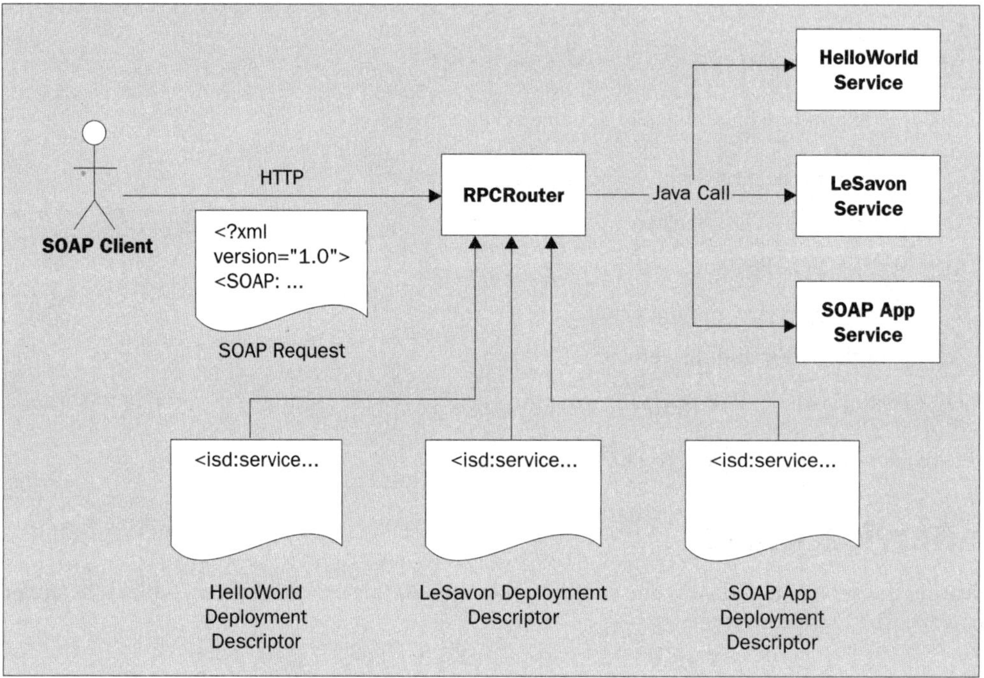

A deployment descriptor is an XML document that contains information about SOAP services. It contains information such as the name of the service and the Java class that implements the service. The action of sending a deployment descriptor to the Apache SOAP engine is called **registration** or **deployment** of the SOAP service. Once a SOAP service is registered, clients can make calls to the `RPCRouter` servlet and have it re-direct the call to the appropriate SOAP service.

We will have a closer look at this mechanism in the *Programmatic Registration* section, but before that we will register our service using the Apache SOAP administration page, introduced during the setup phase of our SOAP server.

Interactive Registration

For this registration demonstration we will use a Windows client, but since it is browser-based, the steps will be identical no matter what your platform of choice is. The look and feel, however, will be specific to the platform.

To deploy a SOAP service using the administration GUI, you need to go to the following URL: http://localhost:8080/soap/admin/index.html.

You will need to replace localhost with the actual machine name or address if you are not running this upon your local machine. This URL brings up the administration page that we have seen earlier. Click on the Deploy button to bring up the deployment screen:

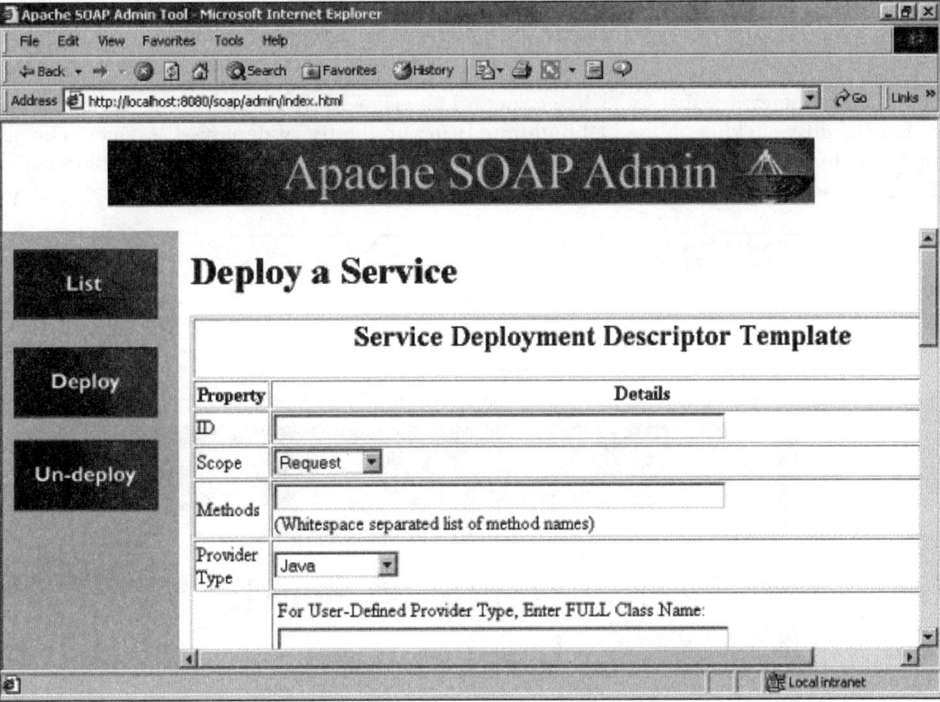

The deployment screen is a Java Server Page (JSP) that contains more details than we need since we will only be using a Java-based SOAP service:

- The identifier, or ID of the service is `helloworld`, but it could be any SOAP service name that is unique to the server hosting your service.
- We will describe the scope of the service in Chapter 7, so don't worry about its meaning at this point: simply take the default which is Request.
- The list of methods must be separated by a space, but in our case we have only one method: `getMessage`.
- The next thing that you need to specify is the class that implements the service: `com.lesavon.service.HelloWorldService`.
- The Static? box allows you to tell the SOAP engine that it should not create an instance of the class to invoke methods but work with class methods. The default is no, which we must use since we have not defined the `getMessage()` method as static.

There is some more information on the bottom of the page that has to do with serialization, or in other words: converting objects in and out of XML documents. We do not need to specify any class to handle the serialization of our arguments and return values, since we only have strings and the Apache SOAP engine handles the serialization of strings automatically. Note the Apache SOAP engine also handles all the basic Java types (integer, long, float, etc.) and their corresponding classes.

We have entered enough information for the JSP to generate a deployment descriptor, so click on the Deploy button at the bottom of the page (not shown) to bring up a page with the message that the service helloworld has been deployed.

Finally, a success message that looks like a success message! We can double-check that everything went as we expected by clicking on the List button to bring up the list of deployed services. This list should contain only one service at this point, helloworld. Click on the hyperlink (helloworld) to bring up the details of the `HelloWorld` service:

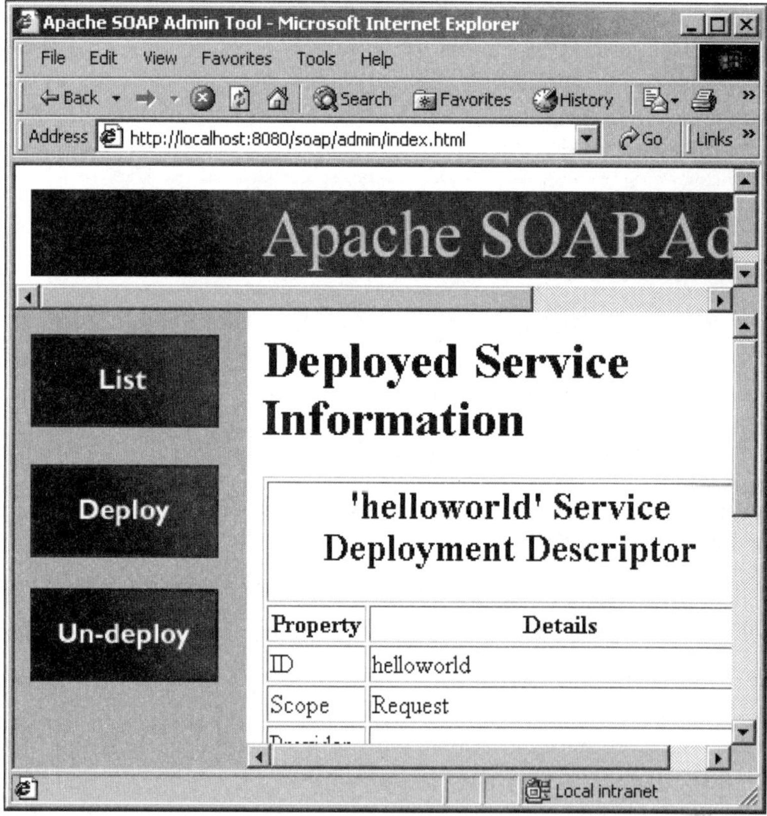

Before we move to a more automated way of specifying a deployment descriptor, we need to make a couple of points:

1. We haven't specified that the java class should be compiled, and yet we successfully registered the service. This shows that the deployment page and the SOAP engine do not check for the existence of the class when saving the deployment descriptor. This is a potential source of trouble: a simple misspelling will be rewarded with cryptic class not found messages at runtime.

2. We have registered our class with the Tomcat `soap/` context. Somehow, we need to make our class known to that context or the `RPCRouter` servlet will not be able to instantiate our class. We will look at a couple of ways to make the class available to this context when we create a web application for `HelloWorld`.

3. We can use the **Un-deploy** button to remove a service from the list of registered services.

Let's now perform the same task using a Java client.

Programmatic Registration

As we have seen at the beginning of this section, the deployment descriptor is an XML document that contains information about the service: the name of the service, the class providing the service, and the methods of the service. The deployment descriptor for `HelloWorld` contains a simple description of the service:

```
<isd:service xmlns:isd="http://xml.apache.org/xml-soap/deployment"
    id="urn:helloworld">
  <isd:provider type="java" scope="Request" methods="getMessage">
    <isd:java class="com.lesavon.service.HelloWorldService" static="false"/>
  </isd:provider>
</isd:service>
```

You can find the deployment descriptor for the `HelloWorld` service in the `ProJavaSoap/Chapter03/HelloWorld/HelloWorld.xml` file. The identifier for the service is `urn:helloworld`. The identifier must be unique to the `RPCRouter` servlet, or router for short. The `<isd:provider/>` element contains the description of our service, including the fully qualified name of the class that implements the service. The `static="false"` attribute indicates that the exposed methods (see below) are not static methods on the class as mentioned previously.

Let's have a closer look at the attributes of the `<isd:provider/>` element:

- `type="java"`
  The types of providers are Java, Enterprise Java Beans (EJB) and script. We will only work with Java-based services in this book. Each provider type has its own set of attributes and nodes.

- `scope="Request"`
  The possible scopes are request, session, and application. The request scope indicates that the java object will be destroyed once the request is completed. Services with the session scope will reuse objects for the duration of the session. The application scope indicates that the object will remain in memory as long as the servlet that routed the request is not destroyed or the servlet engine is not shutdown, which should qualify as the ultimate destruction for a servlet.

- `methods="getMessage"`
  The list of exposed methods separated by a comma. The `HelloWorld` service has only one method, but the sample application that we will build in the following chapters supports several methods per service, so we can see how this would work.

When using SOAP Apache out of the box, you must register your service by submitting its deployment descriptor to the `RPCRouter` servlet. In the previous section, we asked the SOAP administration page to do the work for us, but in this section, we will explicitly submit the deployment descriptor to the router.

To submit the deployment descriptor to the server, you must call the `deploy()` method of the service manager. Since we need to perform this operation remotely, we can use SOAP. To bootstrap the process, when the `RPCRouter` servlet is loaded in memory, it automatically registers the service manager with the following URN:

```
urn:xml-soap-service-management-service
```

The service manager (`org.apache.soap.server.ServiceManager`) class has four methods that are relevant to this discussion:

- `public void deploy(DeploymentDescriptor dd)`
  This method deploys a service by adding its descriptor to the list of deployed services. Deployed services are stored in a hash table that is serialized to `DeployedServices.ds`, in order for deployed services to persist between executions of the servlet engine.
- `public String[] list()`
  This method returns the list of services that are currently registered on the server. The list is returned as an array of strings containing the service identifiers. To get a description of the service, you need to call the `query()` method shown below.
- `public DeploymentDescriptor query(String serviceName)`
  The `query()` method returns the deployment descriptor of the service, identified by the name passed as input.
- `public DeploymentDescriptor undeploy(String id)`
  The `undeploy()` method removes the service, passed as input, from the list of deployed services. It returns the deployment descriptor of the service that was removed.

Once the service is deployed, the `RPCRouter` servlet can look it up in the hash table to route the traffic to the proper service. Routing in this case means creating an instance of the service class listed in the deployment descriptor and invoking the correct method through reflection. If the method is provided by a static implementation then there is no need for creating an instance of the class. The lifetime of the service depends on the scope declared in the deployment descriptor.

Let's have a closer look at how the deployment descriptor is passed to the server. A utility class (`org.apache.soap.server.ServiceManagerClient`) that comes with Apache-SOAP bundles a deployment descriptor into a SOAP request and submits it to the server. For example, to deploy the `HelloWorld` service, you would type the following command:

```
C:\ProJavaSoap\Chapter03\HelloWorld>java
org.apache.soap.server.ServiceManagerClient
http://localhost:8080/soap/servlet/rpcrouter deploy HelloWorld.xml
```

Remember that all of the JAR files we placed in the `soap-2_2/lib` directory (`xerces.jar`, `soap.jar`, `mail.jar`, and `activation.jar`) have to be in the classpath on the command line in order for the above to run.

The URL of the server to deploy the service is `http://localhost:8080/soap/servlet/rpcrouter`. The command to execute is `deploy` and this command takes one argument: `HelloWorld.xml`, the deployment descriptor. The actual payload sent to the server is broken down below:

```
<?xml version='1.0' encoding='UTF-8'?>
  <SOAP-ENV:Envelope
  xmlns:SOAP-ENV="http://schemas.xmlsoap.org/soap/envelope/"
  xmlns:xsi="http://www.w3.org/1999/XMLSchema-instance"
  xmlns:xsd="http://www.w3.org/1999/XMLSchema">
  <SOAP-ENV:Body>
    <ns1:deploy
    xmlns:ns1="urn:xml-soap-service-management-service"
```

The SOAP request will be sent to the `ServiceManager` class.

```
    SOAP-ENV:encodingStyle="http://schemas.xmlsoap.org/soap/encoding/">
```

The parameters are encoded using SOAP encoding as opposed to literal XML encoding, which we discussed in Chapter 2.

You will notice that the only argument for the `deploy()` method is passed in as a deployment descriptor object, not as a deployment descriptor file. The `ServiceManagerClient` class has parsed the `HelloWorld.xml` file, constructed a `DeploymentDescriptor` object, and serialized the object into XML. We will revisit the subject of serialization further when we talk about custom serialization in Chapter 5. For the moment, take a look at the XML contained between the `<descriptor>` and `<descriptor/>` tags. The information contained in the deployment descriptor file was forwarded to the SOAP server along with some default values. These default values are highlighted.

```
<descriptor xmlns:ns2="http://xml.apache.org/xml-soap"
    xsi:type="ns2:DeploymentDescriptor">
  <faultListener
    xmlns:ns3="http://schemas.xmlsoap.org/soap/encoding/"
    xsi:type="ns3:Array" ns3:arrayType="xsd:string[0]">
  </faultListener>
  <providerClass
    xsi:type="xsd:string">
    com.lesavon.service.HelloWorldService
  </providerClass>
  <serviceType xsi:type="xsd:int">0</serviceType>
  <serviceClass xsi:type="xsd:string" xsi:null="true"/>
  <methods
    xmlns:ns4="http://schemas.xmlsoap.org/soap/encoding/"
    xsi:type="ns4:Array" ns4:arrayType="xsd:string[1]">
    <item xsi:type="xsd:string">getMessage</item>
  </methods>
  <providerType xsi:type="xsd:byte">0</providerType>
```

```
        <scriptLanguage xsi:type="xsd:string" xsi:null="true"/>
        <mappings
          xmlns:ns5="http://schemas.xmlsoap.org/soap/encoding/"
          xsi:type="ns5:Array" ns5:arrayType="ns2:TypeMapping[]"
          xsi:null="true"/>
        <checkMustUnderstands
             xsi:type="xsd:boolean">false</checkMustUnderstands>
        <defaultSMRClass xsi:type="xsd:string" xsi:null="true"/>
        <ID xsi:type="xsd:string">urn:helloworld</ID>
        <props xsi:type="ns2:Map" xsi:null="true"/>
        <isStatic xsi:type="xsd:boolean">false</isStatic>
        <scriptFilenameOrString xsi:type="xsd:string" xsi:null="true"/>
        <scope xsi:type="xsd:int">0</scope>
      </descriptor>
      </ns1:deploy>
    </SOAP-ENV:Body>
  </SOAP-ENV:Envelope>
```

The server will respond with a simple OK:

```
  <?xml version='1.0' encoding='UTF-8'?>
    <SOAP-ENV:Envelope xmlns:SOAP-
      ENV="http://schemas.xmlsoap.org/soap/envelope/"
      xmlns:xsi="http://www.w3.org/1999/XMLSchema-instance"
      xmlns:xsd="http://www.w3.org/1999/XMLSchema">
    <SOAP-ENV:Body>
      <ns1:deployResponse
        xmlns:ns1="urn:xml-soap-service-management-service"
        SOAP-ENV:encodingStyle="http://schemas.xmlsoap.org/soap/encoding/">
```

A void() method (see the signature of deploy() earlier) returns an empty response in Apache SOAP.

```
      </ns1:deployResponse>
    </SOAP-ENV:Body>
  </SOAP-ENV:Envelope>
```

The server will attempt to deploy any service as long as the deployment descriptor passed in is correct. In particular, the server will deploy a service that is served by a class that does not exist, or a class that is unreachable because of classpath issues, for instance. You will only get error messages when you actually try to call the service. This is one fact to keep in mind while debugging your services.

At this point, our service is registered and we have a class to handle our requests.

Before we can actually run this service, we need to write some client code. As you will see in the next section, writing a client is slightly more complex since it involves generating a SOAP request and posting it to the server. However, you will be pleased to find out that the details are taken care of by Apache SOAP.

The HelloWorld Web Application

We have seen in the previous section that the RPCRouter servlet invokes a method of our class: HelloWorldService.getMessage(). There are several ways to make our class known to the router, and they all have their advantages and shortcomings.

The easy way is to copy the HelloWorldService class to the soap-2_2/WEB-INF/classes directory. It is easy enough and does the job for a quick test. However, when it comes to writing an application intended for deployment, you will probably need other resources than just the class. For instance, you are likely to define HTML, JSP pages and even other servlets for your application. In addition, copying your class into another application's hierarchy does not represent the clean separation of web applications that the J2EE architects had in mind.

Even though defining a separate web application for a class as simple as HelloWorldService seems like overkill, we will benefit from this experience when we write the main sample application of this book: LeSavon.com.

The main instrument in the definition of a web application is the web.xml file. The following web.xml file is in ProJavaSoap\Chapter03\HelloWorld\etc directory.

```
<!DOCTYPE web-app
  PUBLIC "-//Sun Microsystems, Inc.//DTD Web Application 2.2//EN"
  "http://java.sun.com/j2ee/dtds/web-app_2_2.dtd">
<web-app>
  <display-name>Hello World Sample</display-name>
  <description>
    This is Hello World Service.
  </description>

  <servlet>
    <servlet-name>Apache-SOAP RPC Router</servlet-name>
    <display-name>Apache-SOAP RPC Router</display-name>
    <description>The Apache-SOAP RPC Router.</description>
    <servlet-class>
      org.apache.soap.server.http.RPCRouterServlet
    </servlet-class>
    <init-param>
      <param-name>faultListener</param-name>
      <param-value>org.apache.soap.server.DOMFaultListener</param-value>
    </init-param>
  </servlet>
  <servlet-mapping>
    <servlet-name>Apache-SOAP RPC Router</servlet-name>
    <url-pattern>/rpcrouter</url-pattern>
  </servlet-mapping>
</web-app>
```

A detailed description of web application description files, as defined in the J2EE recommendations, is outside the scope of this book. For the purposes of our sample, it is important to know that the web.xml file contains the description of the servlets that are part of our application. As we have discussed before, there is only one servlet: the RPCRouterServlet servlet. The DOMFaultListener class is invoked by SOAP Apache to complement the fault generated by the framework. We can register our own fault listener to add to the information returned back to the client.

We also need to modify the `conf\server.xml` file again to let Tomcat know where to find our servlets and JSP. This is done by adding a context to `server.xml` similar to the one we added earlier for the SOAP web application:

```
<Context path="/helloworld"
    docBase="C:/ProJavaSoap/Chapter03/HelloWorld"
    debug="9"
    reloadable="true" >
</Context>
```

We will need to replace the value of the `docBase` attribute with the actual root tree of our application.

The HelloWorld Client

`HelloWorldClient` is a standalone Java application with no GUI. Let's have a look at the code to see how the client side of Apache SOAP is used:

> *The* `HelloWorldClient.java` *file is in the* `ProJavaSoap\Chapter03\HelloWorld\src\com\lesavon\test` *directory.*

```
// HelloWorldClient.java

package com.lesavon.test;

import java.net.URL;
import java.util.Vector;
import java.util.Arrays;
```

The `URL` class allows us to specify the URL of the SOAP service. We will use arrays and vectors to build the argument list for the call to `getMessage()`.

```
import org.apache.soap.Constants;
import org.apache.soap.SOAPException;
import org.apache.soap.Envelope;
import org.apache.soap.Fault;
import org.apache.soap.rpc.Call;
import org.apache.soap.rpc.Response;
import org.apache.soap.rpc.Parameter;
```

The `Constants` class defines useful values like the type of encoding to be used in the call. A `SOAPException` is thrown by the framework when something goes wrong and the `Fault` class encapsulates a `SOAP:FAULT` section from the SOAP payload. The `rpc.*` classes allow us to build the call to the service.

```
public class HelloWorldClient {
  public static void main(String args[]) {
    String methodName = "com.lesavon.test.HelloWorldClient.main";
    String url = "http://localhost:8080/helloworld/rpcrouter";
    String uri = "urn:helloworld";   // must match HelloWorld.xml
    String remoteMethod = "getMessage";
    String caller = "reader";
```

The `rpcrouter` is the servlet that we will define in the next section (*Building the `HelloWorld` Sample*) when we write the `web.xml` for the `HelloWorld` application. The value of the `uri` variable must match the name that we gave during the registration process: either manually entered in the deployment page or in the `HelloWorld.xml` file.

```
    if (args.length != 0) {
      System.err.println("HelloWorldClient: invokes a SOAP service.");

      System.err.println("Usage: HelloWorldClient");
      System.exit(1);
    }

    System.out.println(methodName + ": Starting test...");

    try {
      Call call = new Call();
      Parameter param = new Parameter("caller", caller.getClass(), caller,
                                      Constants.NS_URI_SOAP_ENC);
```

A `Parameter` represents an argument to an RPC call. The only argument of a call to `getMessage()` is a string. The name that will be passed as argument name is `caller`. The type of the argument is `String(caller.getClass())`, and the encoding is SOAP encoding. The other possibility for encoding is literal XML encoding, for returning an XML document, as opposed to the serialization of Java object as XML.

```
      call.setTargetObjectURI(uri);
      call.setMethodName(remoteMethod);
      call.setParams(new Vector(Arrays.asList(new Parameter[] {
        param
      })));

      Response resp = call.invoke(new URL(url), "");
```

Once we have set the URI for our service, the name of the method, and the parameters of the call, we are ready to invoke the remote service. The parameters are set with a vector since you typically have more than one parameter. As we saw in Chapter 2, the second argument of `invoke()` is the value of the `SOAPAction` header field. It is ignored by the Apache SOAP server, but is likely to be used by other SOAP engines. Since this test routine is for Apache SOAP only, we could leave the value blank.

```
      // Check the response.
      if (resp.generatedFault()) {
        Fault fault = resp.getFault();

        System.out.println(methodName + ": Call to " + remoteMethod
                           + " returned a fault!");
        System.out.println("  Fault code: " + fault.getFaultCode());
        System.out.println("  Fault string: " + fault.getFaultString());
      } else {
        if (resp.getReturnValue() != null) {
          Object result = resp.getReturnValue().getValue();
```

```
            System.out.println("Call to " + remoteMethod
                             + " returned an object of "
                             + result.getClass() + ": " + result);
          }
        }
      } catch (Exception exception) {
        System.err.println(methodName + ": Error, caught exception: "
                         + exception);
      }

      System.out.println(methodName + ": All done!");
    }
  }
```

If the call fails, a fault will be generated as part of the response. The fault typically returns a string describing what went wrong along with a fault code. As we saw in Chapter 2, the fault codes can take the following values:

- `VersionMismatch` – This is for future use since we have only one supported version of SOAP at this point.
- `MustUnderstand` – This is also for future use since Apache SOAP does not implement the "must understand" concept of SOAP that we discussed in Chapter 2. This could lead to interoperability issues since Apache SOAP will typically ignore whether a class is valid or not. For a discussion on the subject, please refer to Chapter 2. A workaround is to use the `MustUnderstand` flag, which can be set in the deployment descriptor.
- `Client` – The request sent by the client is in error.
- `Server` – The server is in error, for instance a service threw an exception.
- `Protocol` – The SOAP protocol was violated in some way. For instance, the content of a request is `text/html` rather than `text/xml`.

Most of the time, client-side problems will throw an exception and server-side problems will give you a fault. The reasoning is that if the server fails to handle the request, it is not necessarily a problem. In Chapter 5, we will introduce a proxy that always throws an exception. To see how it works in practice, we will go through a few problem scenarios after a successful run of the `HelloWorld` client.

Building the HelloWorld Sample

We have now written enough code for a web service and the client that invokes it. Before we can see our code in action, we must first build it. In Chapter 5, we will use the ANT utility that is used to build Tomcat, amongst other things. To keep things simple in this chapter, we will build the directory tree by hand on a Windows platform. A similar set of instructions needs to be followed on UNIX, but using the appropriate OS-specific commands, for instance `mkdir usr/soap/home/ProJavaSoap/Chapter03/HelloWorld` instead of `mkdir C:\ProJavaSoap/Chapter03\HelloWorld`.

The build steps are shown below – merely enter the correct commands at the prompts:

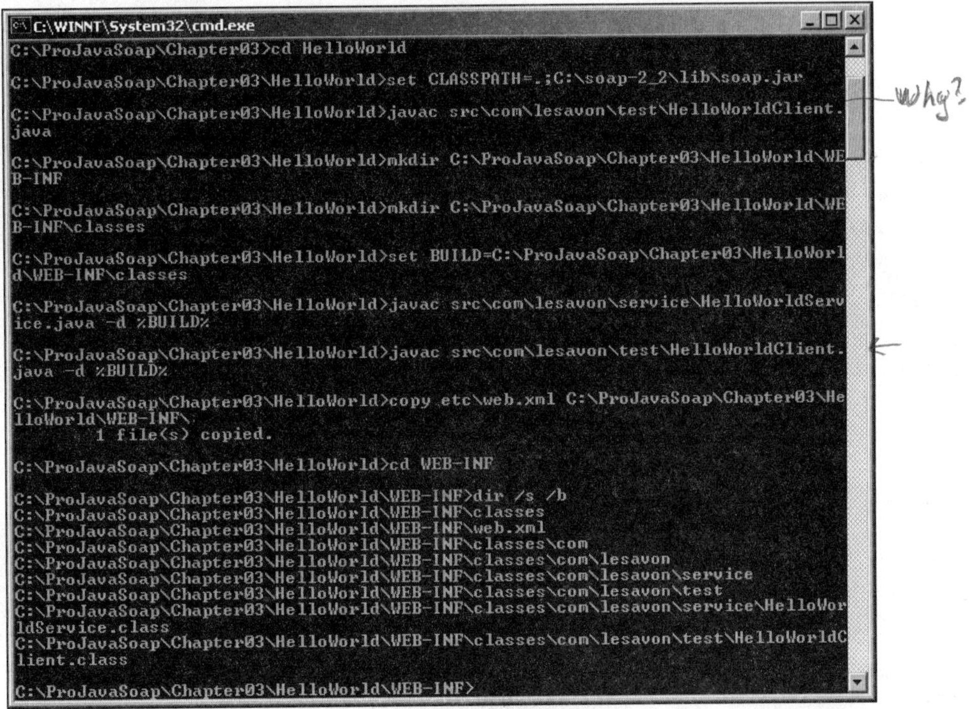

Note that if you want to use the GUI-based deployment that we reviewed in the previous section, you will need to copy the administration tree from the SOAP application (`soap-2_2\webapps\soap\admin`) to the `HelloWorld` application. For instance, on Windows, the `HelloWorld` application tree would look like this:

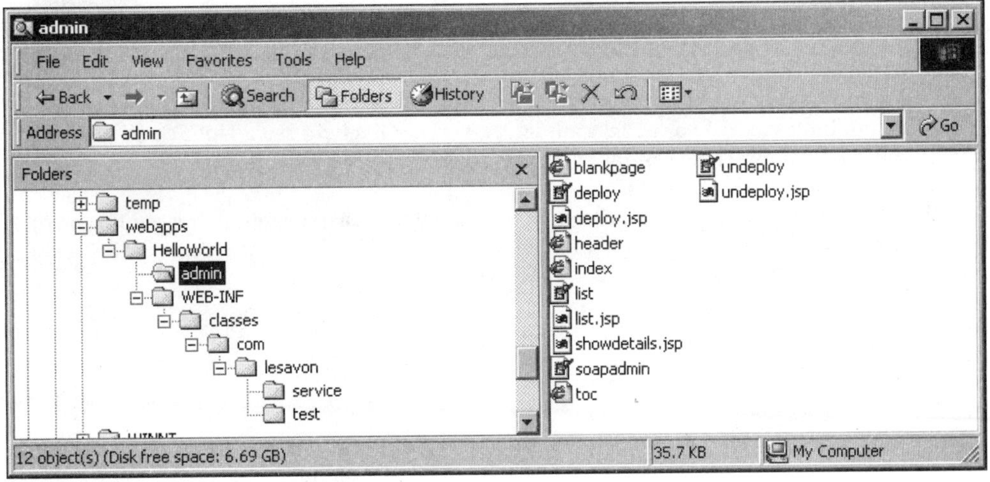

The value of the `docBase` attribute that we specified earlier in the `jakarta-tomcat-3.2.3\conf\server.xml` file must match our build directory: `C:ProJavaSoap\Chapter03\HelloWorld`.

As we have seen before, registering the service can be accomplished with the help of the `ServiceManagerClient`. Before running the sample, let's make sure that everything is fine with the router itself. If the router is not set up properly then your service will not work. This check involves two steps:

1. Check that the router takes requests.

2. Check that the router handles the registration of our service properly.

When we set up Tomcat earlier, we registered the Apache router servlet: `rpcrouter` using the `web.xml` file. The following URL – http://localhost:8080/helloworld/rpcrouter – entered on a browser, should show the output below. Be sure to restart Tomcat before trying this out.

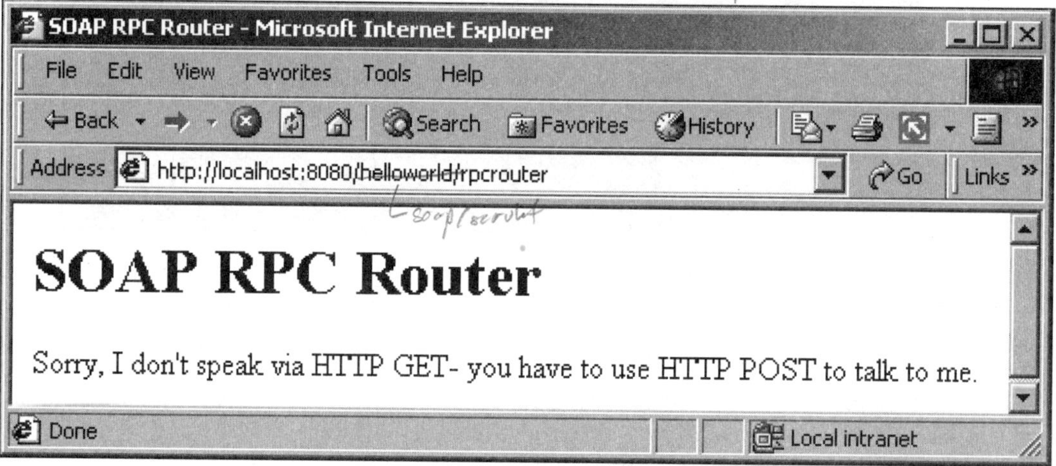

As we have said before, this is the sign that everything is well as far as the router is concerned. Note that if you have not built the `HelloWorld` sample yet, you are likely to see a Not Found (404) error: the content of the virtual directory cannot be found.

We will look at some other potential errors at the end of this chapter, but if you get this error, check that the classes for the example were compiled correctly and written to the correct directory – `C:\ProJavaSoap\Chapter03\HelloWorld\WEB-INF\classes`.

Once the router is taking requests, we can send the deployment descriptor as described earlier in the *Programmatic Registration* section. The result of the registration is shown on the following figure:

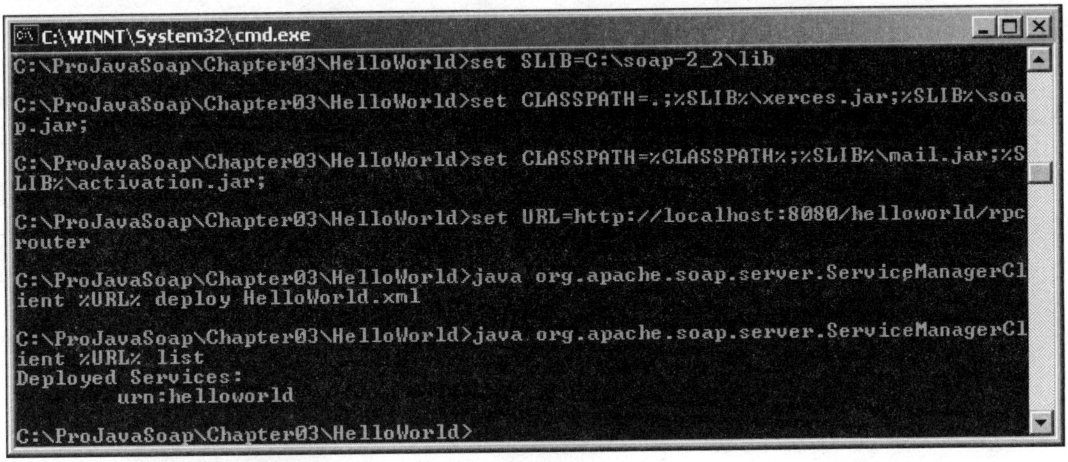

```
C:\WINNT\System32\cmd.exe
C:\ProJavaSoap\Chapter03\HelloWorld>set SLIB=C:\soap-2_2\lib

C:\ProJavaSoap\Chapter03\HelloWorld>set CLASSPATH=.;%SLIB%\xerces.jar;%SLIB%\soa
p.jar;

C:\ProJavaSoap\Chapter03\HelloWorld>set CLASSPATH=%CLASSPATH%;%SLIB%\mail.jar;%S
LIB%\activation.jar;

C:\ProJavaSoap\Chapter03\HelloWorld>set URL=http://localhost:8080/helloworld/rpc
router

C:\ProJavaSoap\Chapter03\HelloWorld>java org.apache.soap.server.ServiceManagerCl
ient %URL% deploy HelloWorld.xml

C:\ProJavaSoap\Chapter03\HelloWorld>java org.apache.soap.server.ServiceManagerCl
ient %URL% list
Deployed Services:
        urn:helloworld

C:\ProJavaSoap\Chapter03\HelloWorld>
```

Now that the `HelloWorld` sample has been built, that the router is set up and that our service is registered, we are ready to run our first SOAP service.

Running the HelloWorld Sample

After modifying the classpath, be sure to start or restart Tomcat for the changes to take effect. To run our sample, we start the client application (on Windows 2000):

```
C:\WINNT\System32\cmd.exe
C:\ProJavaSoap\Chapter03\HelloWorld\WEB-INF\classes>java com.lesavon.test.HelloW
orldClient
com.lesavon.test.HelloWorldClient.main: Starting test...
Call to getMessage returned an object of class java.lang.String: Hello reader!
com.lesavon.test.HelloWorldClient.main: All done!

C:\ProJavaSoap\Chapter03\HelloWorld\WEB-INF\classes>_
```

For this example to run, a SOAP request has been sent to the server and a SOAP response was returned. The request sent to the server looks like this (including the HTTP header):

```
POST /helloworld/rpcrouter HTTP/1.0
Host: localhost
Content-Type: text/xml; charset=utf-8
Content-Length: 454
SOAPAction: ""
```

This is the HTTP portion of the request, the header. It tells the server that we are posting a request that is 454 bytes long and that the content is `text/xml`.

```
<?xml version='1.0' encoding='UTF-8'?>
<SOAP-ENV:Envelope
     xmlns:SOAP-ENV="http://schemas.xmlsoap.org/soap/envelope/"
     xmlns:xsi="http://www.w3.org/1999/XMLSchema-instance"
     xmlns:xsd="http://www.w3.org/1999/XMLSchema">
```

The document is an XML document and the top-level element is a SOAP envelope.

```
<SOAP-ENV:Body>
  <ns1:getMessage xmlns:ns1="urn:helloworld">
```

The request is for the `urn:helloworld` so we will use that identifier for the name space. The request is a call to `getMessage()`.

```
<caller xsi:type="xsd:string"
        SOAP-ENV:encodingStyle="http://schemas.xmlsoap.org/soap/encoding/">
  reader
</caller>
```

The argument of the call is a `String` with value `reader`. The name of tag `<caller>` was the name specified as the first argument to the constructor of the `Parameter` object.

```
    </ns1:getMessage>
  </SOAP-ENV:Body>
</SOAP-ENV:Envelope>
```

After receiving and processing our request, the server will return the following response (including the HTTP header):

```
HTTP/1.0 200 OK
Content-Type: text/xml; charset=utf-8
Content-Length: 479
Set-Cookie2: JSESSIONID=hj2ogyv4n1;Version=1;Discard;Path="/helloworld"
Set-Cookie: JSESSIONID=hj2ogyv4n1;Path=/helloworld
Servlet-Engine: Tomcat Web Server/3.2.1 (JSP 1.1; Servlet 2.2; Java 1.3.0; Windows
2000 5.0 x86; java.vendor=Sun Microsystems Inc.)
```

The 479-byte response is `text/xml`.

```
<?xml version='1.0' encoding='UTF-8'?>
<SOAP-ENV:Envelope
     xmlns:SOAP-ENV="http://schemas.xmlsoap.org/soap/envelope/"
     xmlns:xsi="http://www.w3.org/1999/XMLSchema-instance"
     xmlns:xsd="http://www.w3.org/1999/XMLSchema">
```

The response document is an XML document and the top-level element is a SOAP envelope.

```
<SOAP-ENV:Body>
  <ns1:getMessageResponse
         xmlns:ns1="urn:helloworld"
         SOAP-ENV:encodingStyle="http://schemas.xmlsoap.org/soap/encoding/">
```

The body contains the response of a call to `getMessage()` of the `urn:helloworld` service.

```
<return xsi:type="xsd:string">Hello reader!</return>
```

The actual return value is a string; its value is `Hello reader!`.

```
      </ns1:getMessageResponse>
    </SOAP-ENV:Body>
  </SOAP-ENV:Envelope>
```

Et voilà: you have designed, written, built, and executed your first SOAP service. Alas, things do not always go that smoothly or you would not have to buy a book to accomplish this task. In other words, it is probably a good idea to discuss what happens when reality kicks in.

Testing and Debugging

A significant challenge in debugging distributed applications is to monitor what travels on the wire. SOAP applications are not different, but you will be glad to know that there are a couple of tools available to help your debugging.

The tcpTrace Utility

The `tcpTrace` utility is a freeware tool that can be downloaded from http://www.pocketsoap.com/tcpTrace. It comes as a ZIP file that contains the `tcpTrace.exe` utility. To extract the executable, you can use the same methodology as we used in setting up the JAR files for Apache SOAP.

`tcpTrace` finds its roots in the Apache `TcpTunnelGui`. The `tcpTrace` utility creates a TCP tunnel between one port on your machine and a remote host. You can also create a tunnel between two different ports on your local machine. As the figure below shows, the `tcpTrace` utility first prompts you for:

- **Local port**
  The port number that you will connect to on your local machine to establish the TCP tunnel
- **Destination server**
  The server name or IP address that is the other end of the tunnel
- **Destination port number**
  The port number for the server at the other end of the tunnel

To run the program, merely click on the `tcpTrace.exe` icon.

In the figure below, a tunnel is being created from port 8081 (on localhost) to port 8080 on localhost. The net effect of creating the tunnel is that you can visualize the SOAP traffic directed to port 8081. Since the `tcpTrace` utility listens to TCP traffic, you can use it to monitor any text TCP-based traffic. In particular, the tool excels in debugging JSP or servlets.

The tool also provides a few extra features, such as a logging capability. However, we will only use the interactive display in this book.

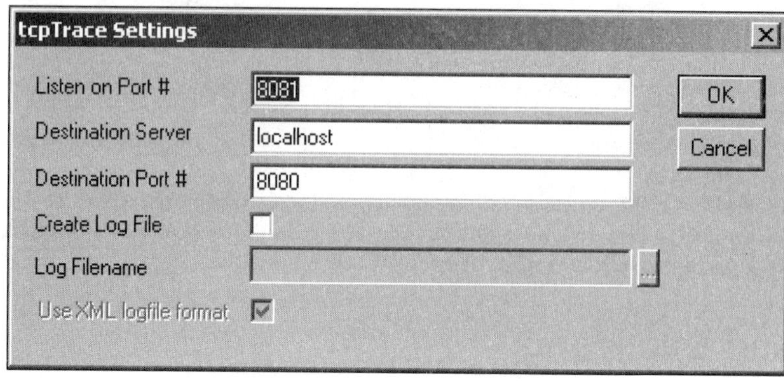

Let's run the `HelloWorldClient` that we just built, after making sure that the destination URL specifies port 8081 rather than port 8080:

```
...
public class HelloWorldClient {
  public static void main(String args[]) {
    String methodName = "com.lesavon.test.HelloWorldClient.main";

    String url = "http://localhost:8081/helloworld/rpcrouter";

    String uri = "urn:helloworld";    // must match HelloWorld.xml
    String remoteMethod = "getMessage";
    String caller = "reader";
...
```

When this file is altered, make sure that the tcpTrace is running and the files recompiled before you start Tomcat again, otherwise Tomcat will throw a "`connection refused`" error.

The next figure shows the request and its response. The HTTP header is displayed as well:

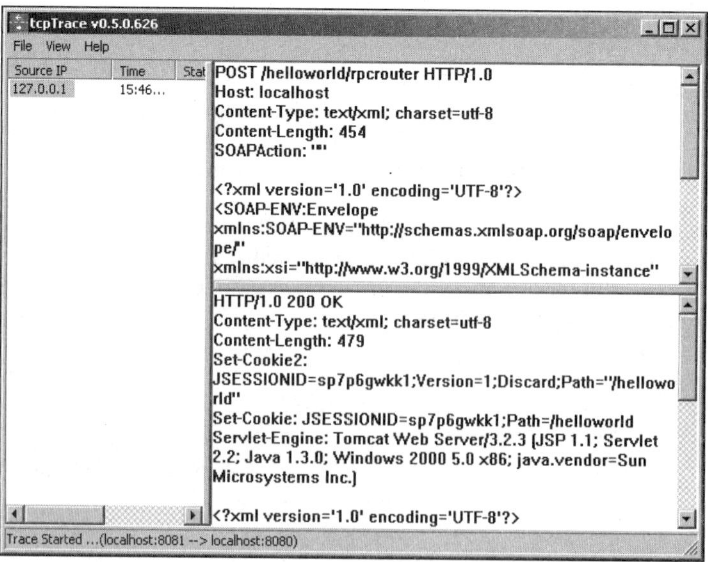

There are also command line options. For more details, you can visit http://www.pocketsoap.com/tcpTrace. If you wanted to use a platform-independent tool, the `TcpTunnelGui` utility comes with the Apache SOAP distribution.

We invoke `TcpTunnelGui` by specifying the local port, the target server and the target port on the command line. Open a new window, making sure that `soap.jar` is in the classpath, and enter the following (remember to shut off `tcpTrace` beforehand, or a `BindException` will be thrown:

```
C:\ProJavaSoap\Chapter03\HelloWorld>java
org.apache.soap.util.net.TcpTunnelGui 8081 localhost 8080
```

Now run `HelloWorldClient` again. The figure below shows the traffic generated by the `HelloWorld` sample using `TcpTunnelGui`.

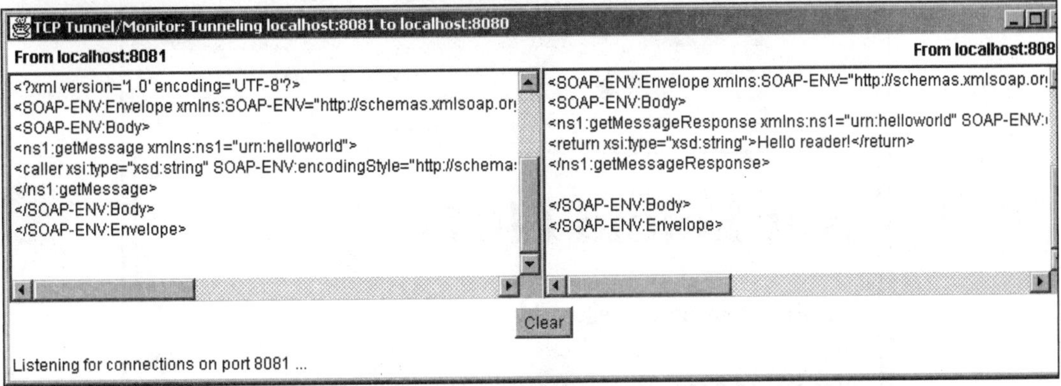

`TcpTunnelGui` and `tcpTrace` provide you with essentially the same information, and if you are using a Windows platform your choice will be mostly a matter of taste.

Troubleshooting

Let's have a look at a few common problems and how they show themselves in the `tcpTrace` utility.

Server Down

If Tomcat is not running, or if it is refusing connections for whatever reason, you will not see any connections in `tcpTrace` until a socket exception is thrown. One thing to watch for is the debugger: if you are debugging the server side, the server might not respond to a request because it is stopped at a breakpoint.

Bad URL

If you specify a bad URL to Apache SOAP, the result will typically be a SOAP client exception thrown within a few seconds:

```
[SOAPException: faultCode=SOAP-ENV:Client; msg=Error opening socket: nothere;
targetException=java.lang.IllegalArgumentException: Error opening socket: nothere]
```

The default time out for TCP/IP connections is 3,000 milliseconds on most computers. Keep in mind that servlet URLs are case sensitive: the figure below shows that `hellworld/rpcrouter` instead of `helloworld/rpcrouter` will fail with an HTTP 404 return code.

Classpath Issues

Client-side classpath issues are usually the easiest to deal with: you will get a `ClassNotFoundException` thrown on the client side; the payload will not make it to the server.

Classpath issues on the server side are a little trickier. You will get a `SOAPException` thrown on the server as shown in the screenshot below. For this particular case, the `HelloWorldService.class` file was removed from the server. The output on the client side is:

```
com.lesavon.test.HelloWorldClient.main: Starting test...
com.lesavon.test.HelloWorldClient.main: Call to getMessage returned a fault!
  Fault code: SOAP-ENV:Server.BadTargetObjectURI
  Fault string: Unable to resolve target object:
com.lesavon.service.HelloWorldService
com.lesavon.test.HelloWorldClient.main: All done!
```

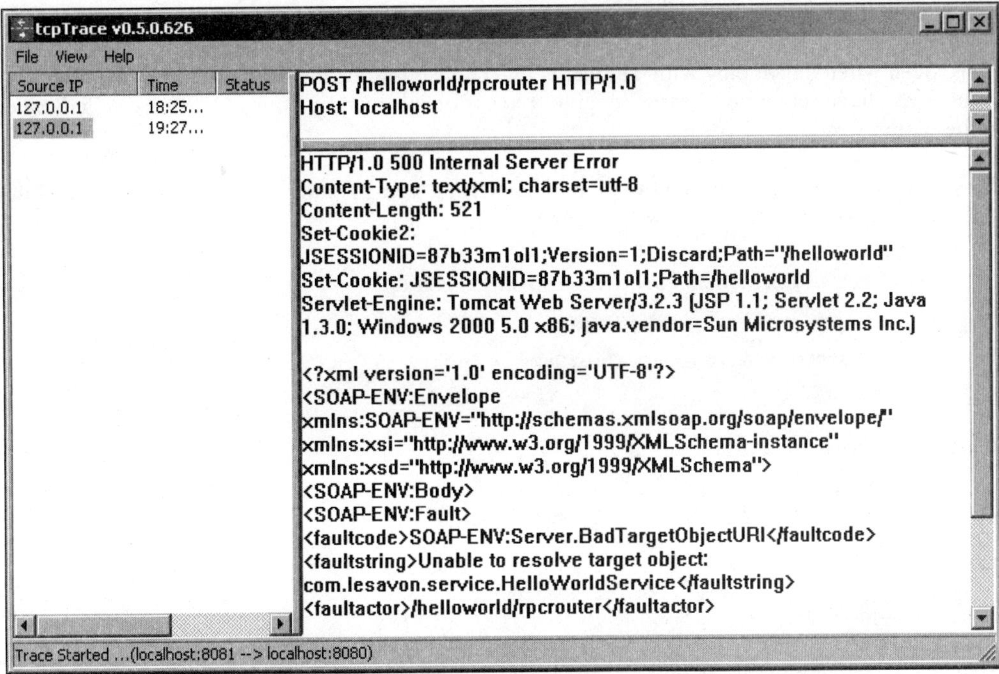

xerces.jar

`xerces.jar` must be the first reference in the classpath for things to work smoothly. Essentially, the class loader will not be able to resolve the DOM level 2 methods, and will throw a "`No Such Method`" exception.

Serialization Issues

Serialization issues will typically arise when the default serializer cannot handle the class that needs to be serialized. On the client side, the problem will manifest itself with a `SOAPException`:

```
com.lesavon.test.HelloWorldClient.main: Starting test...
com.lesavon.test.HelloWorldClient.main: Error, caught exception: [SOAPException:
faultCode=SOAP-ENV:Client; msg=No Serializer found to serialize a
'some.missing.Class' using encoding style
'http://schemas.xmlsoap.org/soap/encoding/'.;
targetException=java.lang.IllegalArgumentException: No Serializer found to
serialize a 'some.missing.Class' using encoding style
'http://schemas.xmlsoap.org/soap/encoding/'.]
com.lesavon.test.HelloWorldClient.main: All done!
```

If you do not register a serializer, you will get the same exception wrapped in a SOAP payload (see below). We will discuss serialization in detail in Chapter 5, when we develop a custom serializer.

You will probably encounter other problems when debugging SOAP applications, but the cases that we just reviewed should cover the majority of your problems. One diagnostic tool that should not be overlooked when developing with Tomcat is the Tomcat logs or the Tomcat output window, depending on how you have set up your servlet engine. Exceptions thrown by your SOAP service will be displayed in the output window.

They will also be wrapped in the SOAP payload. Here, a `null` pointer exception was forced in the `HelloWorldService.getMessage()` method:

```
public String getMessage(String callerName) {
    ((Object)null).toString();
    return "Hello " + callerName + "!";
}
```

to artificially create this problem:

```
<?xml version='1.0' encoding='UTF-8'?>
<SOAP-ENV:Envelope xmlns:SOAP-ENV="http://schemas.xmlsoap.org/soap/envelope/"
xmlns:xsi="http://www.w3.org/1999/XMLSchema-instance"
xmlns:xsd="http://www.w3.org/1999/XMLSchema">
<SOAP-ENV:Body>
<SOAP-ENV:Fault>
<faultcode>SOAP-ENV:Server</faultcode>
<faultstring>Exception from service object: null</faultstring>
<faultactor>/helloworld/rpcrouter</faultactor>
</SOAP-ENV:Fault>
</SOAP-ENV:Body>
</SOAP-ENV:Envelope>
```

Before concluding this chapter, let's say a few words about web servers.

Web Servers

Depending on your platform, the definition of the best web server will vary. Apache runs on many flavors of UNIX and on most flavors of Windows. But, according to Apache, it is not as robust on Windows as it is on UNIX. On Windows, many people elect to work with IIS because of its openness to Windows tools and close integration to the OS. However, the frequency of the security patches for IIS is testimony to the risks of that openness and close integration. You will have to make the choice that is best for your application and deployment scenario. In this section, we will briefly introduce both web servers.

As we said earlier, you could skip the installation of a web server for your development since most servlet engines come bundled with a web server. However, you should be aware that for production and testing, you will certainly need a production-ready web server for two reasons:

1. **Security**
   Web servers are regularly updated with patches to plug security holes that have been discovered by the hackers of the moment. Servlet engine releases are usually not maintained with the same level of scrutiny.

2. **Performance**
   Web servers are designed to return static pages in the most optimal way through various features such as caching. Servlet engines are designed to perform with servlets and JSP pages, not static pages. Since most applications in production have some amount of static pages, your overall solution will perform better if a web server is set up to return static pages.

Let's now get into the specifics of Apache and IIS.

Apache

You can download the Apache web server from http://httpd.apache.org/. The Apache web server is not written in Java; it is largely a C development. Its primary platform is UNIX, but it can be used for development and production on other platforms, including Windows. The installation comes with instructions for most popular OS. Like all Apache projects, you can download just the binaries or the binaries and the sources.

Setting up the Apache server for production is a complicated endeavor that is outside the scope of SOAP development. However, the instructions contained in the `docs/manuals/` directory that comes with the Apache distribution will get you going quickly in a development environment. Alternatively, refer to *Professional Apache* by Wrox Press Ltd, ISBN 1861003021.

We will discuss how to setup LDAP-based authentication with Apache in Chapter 7.

IIS

The **Internet Information Server (IIS)** comes with your installation of Windows 2000 Professional or Server. However, if you are using Windows 2000 Professional, IIS is not installed by default, and must be selected when you install the OS. It can also be added later using the Add/Remove Windows Components window in Control Panel. To see if you have IIS installed, go to Control Panel, into Internet Services Manager, and if it is present it should open up a console. If not, then it can be loaded from your Windows installation.

If you are using Windows NT or even Windows 9X, you will have to install the Windows Option Pack; (this pack is ostensibly for NT, but can be used by 95 and 98 also). The option pack can be downloaded from Microsoft's web site http://www.microsoft.com/ntserver/nts/downloads/recommended/NT4OptPk/default.asp. Note that on the non-server versions of NT and Windows 9X, the web server is called the **Personal Web Server (PWS)**, but it is equivalent to IIS for development purposes. Nothing special needs to be done if you are using IIS for SOAP development.

Summary

In this chapter, we have introduced the platform setup and software tools that we will be using in the remainder of this book. As we have pointed out, SOAP development can be done with freely available tools.

We detailed the necessary steps for downloading and configuring those tools on the Windows and UNIX platform, by reviewing the installation and configuration specifics for Windows 2000 and Linux Red Hat 7.1.

Using the aforementioned tools, we put together our first web service: `HelloWorldService`, and we went through the necessary requirements for Apache SOAP to route client calls to our service. We also looked at the SOAP/XML messages that travel over the network during registration and execution of our sample service: helloworld.

We concluded the chapter with some troubleshooting techniques that will hopefully come in handy for the SOAP developer.

Now that we have a Java environment for SOAP development, we can define the requirements of our sample application. This is the main topic of Chapter 4.

JAVA

4

LeSavon.com

In this chapter, we will state and describe the requirements for the main sample application of this book, **LeSavon.com**. The sample application aims at showing the SOAP components of a distributed application. It will greatly simplify, sometimes to an extreme, these external components. By focusing on the topic of this book – SOAP and Web services – we hope to avoid distracting the reader with issues that are not directly related to SOAP. One notable exception is the security system that we will describe in detail.

> *A distributed application is a system with programs or components running on multiple machines. The different* ***components*** *or* ***tiers*** *of the distributed application can have a* ***master-slave*** *or a* ***peer relationship****.*

A production-grade application usually involves a lot more components than web services; a database, a data mart, and a data warehouse are typical examples of the pieces that make up a mission-critical application. A data mart is a database, or a collection of databases, designed to help managers make strategic decisions about their business. A collection of data marts is usually called a data warehouse.

The main advantage of data marts over traditional databases is that the data model of a data mart is optimized to give the best response time for business-oriented queries.

Although, this book will not go into details about how to set up and deploy a security infrastructure, it will dedicate an entire chapter to the subject of security itself, because an enterprise SOAP application cannot be successful without being tightly integrated to the security system of an enterprise.

By limiting the dependencies of our sample application to other backend systems, we also simplify the task of downloading and setting up the sample application. This simplicity is a feature that the reader will surely appreciate!

Before we proceed, we need to define more clearly what we want to achieve in this chapter. The requirements we will present here are not complete by any means. However, bringing them to a more complete and more solid state would involve discussions on topics such as cost, ergonomics, and so on.

Although these issues must be addressed when gathering requirements for a production system, they have very little to do with distributed applications and SOAP. So do not expect these requirements to be complete, but expect them to give you a good idea of the requirements that can be addressed by SOAP.

High Level Requirements

The LeSavon Company sells perfumes and cosmetics through catalog orders. Traditionally, LeSavon customers have been calling Customer Service Representatives (CSRs) to inquire about the status of their order. To save money, resources, and to respond to a growing demand from its customer base, the company wants to provide an Internet service where customers can review their orders. The new service will be called LeSavon.com.

The LeSavon Company does not intend to replace the existing human interactions between the company and its customers. The goal is to provide a system to supplement the existing process. It is believed that the new system will reduce cost because some customers will prefer to use the Internet and therefore will not require support from the call center.

For the purposes of this book, the characteristics of an order are simple:

1. There is only one item per order.
2. There is no order status as such; the mere presence of an order in the database indicates that it is being processed. In this simplified world, there are no canceled orders, no back orders, and so on.

In the first phase of the development, the application will be read-only – there is no capability to modify orders.

LeSavon has been developing its applications as two-tier applications without a middle tier to enforce business rules. Business applications can be classified depending on the number of **tiers** that are used to develop them. A tier is a logical component of an application that can be deployed on a computer by itself. Very often, there is a one-to-one correspondence between the tiers of an application and the machines used for its deployment, but that is not always the case. The simplest application is the single tier standalone program model, which has the advantage of being simple but with the disadvantage that no shared resources can be accessed.

The two-tier model brings a client-server relationship to the picture. It has the advantage of allowing fast and secure access to shared resources. Typically in this arrangement, the server is used to access some kind of database. However, the two-tier model does not scale (does not handle a large community of users) very well and has the disadvantage of duplicating business logic in all the client applications.

The management of LeSavon recognizes the shortcomings of two-tier architecture, but does not want to allocate the necessary resources to undergo that development because it feels that providing an Internet service is more important than consolidating the current applications.

The three-tier model adds a **middle tier**, often called a **business layer**, to the two-tier architecture. Although, it increases the complexity of the overall application, the three-tier model does not duplicate business logic and it scales well.

The **n-tier architecture** comes into play when you explode the tiers of the three-tier model into several other tiers. An example would be to explode the clients into a SOAP layer and web application layer. The n-tier model raises the bar in complexity and cost, but offers a of lot flexibility in terms of extensibility (in other words, the ease with which new client applications can be added), scalability, security, and robustness.

For the time being, the designers of LeSavon.com must live with the current two-tier architecture – at least outside of the new code. To better balance the needs of a better architecture and the limited resources, the architecture of LeSavon.com will create a business layer and expose its classes as SOAP services. The fact that the SOAP services will provide customers with direct access to the database and limited business rules is not viewed as a major liability at this point, as LeSavon.com will be limited to read-only operations in the first phase of the project.

The development language and the deployment platform of the potential business layer have not been decided yet.

There is a need for two user communities:

- Regular users
- Administrators

Administrator accounts must be more secure since they contain more privileges than regular user accounts. As part of taking orders, the company automatically creates a user account for their customers, so customer accounts will automatically be part of the regular user community.

LeSavon will initially provide the service free to its customers, so there is no need to keep track of system usage.

Since LeSavon already uses a directory service accessible via the **Lightweight Directory Access Protocol** or **LDAP** (see side note), the application should use the existing infrastructure to implement its security requirements. LDAP, its applications, and security will be presented in Chapter 7. The sample application provides a default security implementation that does not use LDAP, if you want to focus solely on the SOAP aspects of the application.

The Lightweight Directory Access Protocol (LDAP) is a protocol that has been gaining a significant amount of attention lately. A directory service provides access to named objects with attributes. This is similar to an electronic phone book, but with a lot more attributes than a name and an address. Entries in a directory can be as diverse as a computer, a printer, or a user. LDAP is a protocol to access the data stored in a directory service.

The figure below shows a high-level diagram of the anticipated use of the application:

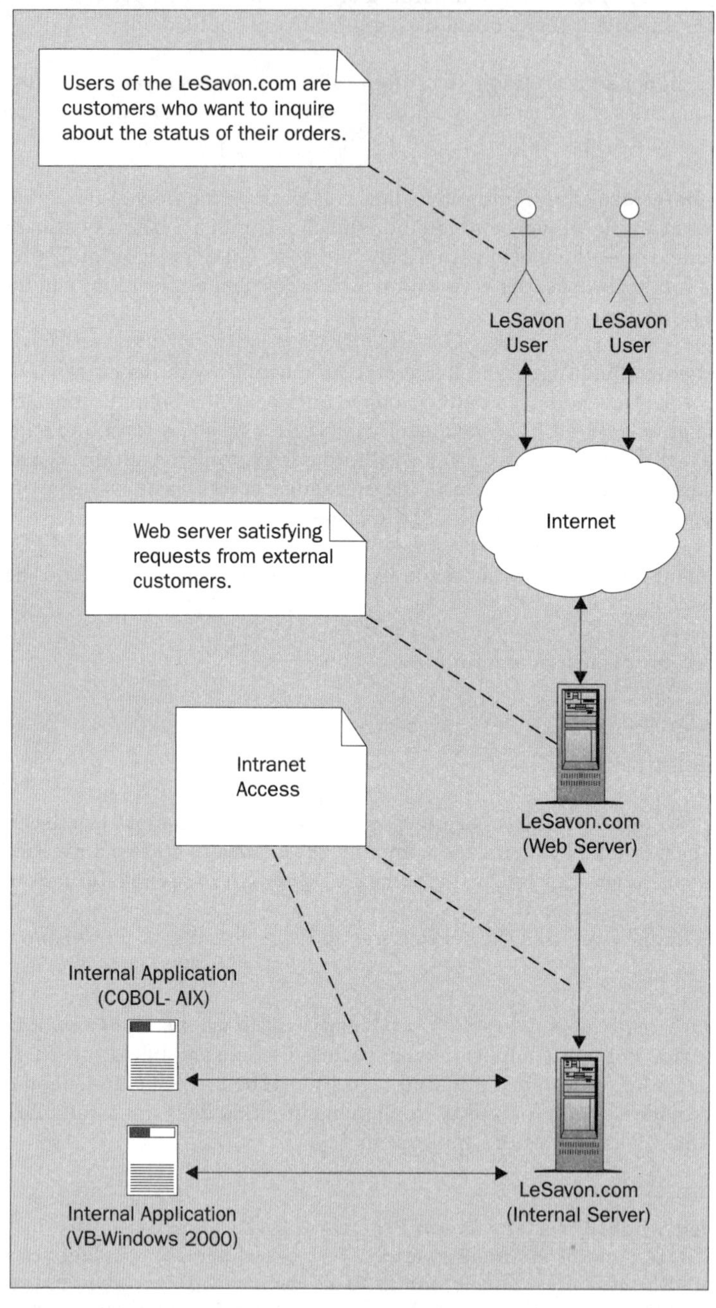

Browser-Based GUI

The application must be available over the Internet to allow customers to check their order from the comfort of their home. The user interface must be accessible to a wide variety of browsers including Microsoft Internet Explorer and Netscape Communicator. The user interface must also be running on a wide variety of platforms from all the releases of Windows to the Macintosh to Linux. The designers of LeSavon.com feel that they can meet this requirement by limiting the user interface to HTML 3.2. In particular, there will be no client-side scripting.

At the time of writing, the latest version of HTML is 4.01. However, HTML 3.2 should give us all the features we need to build a simple user interface.

The application must provide end-users with a personalized user interface. Parameters like fonts, colors, and default home page should be customizable on a user basis. The customization implementation must be open to accommodate future requirements.

Platform-Independent Implementation

LeSavon wishes to develop an application for the long term. Since hardware and software technologies change rapidly, the company wants to have a platform-independent application. Ideally, the company would like to run the application on its existing hardware and buy more hardware as the load increases.

The company currently runs hardware with the following operating systems: Windows (NT and 2000), LINUX, SOLARIS, and AIX. The company would like to keep its options open on the OS front for this new application.

Platform-Independent API

Early in the requirement cycle, the general accounting department expressed a desire to use LeSavon.com as an interface to the OLTP database. An **On-Line Transaction Processing** (**OLTP**) database is the mission-critical database that a company uses to run its business. That requirement was reflected in the anticipated use of the application, as we saw earlier. To satisfy this requirement, and keep the design of the applications at LeSavon facing in the direction of multi-tier architecture, the designers of LeSavon.com have proposed an Application Programming Interface (API). The API must be platform-independent because the accounting department runs a variety of OS from AIX, to Linux to Windows 2000.

The existence of the accounting department as a customer brings up the issue of batch access; the accounting department is mostly interested in reports that are inherently batch operations. The architecture and implementation of LeSavon.com will have to keep that potential usage in mind.

We touched earlier upon the fact that the Customer Service Representatives (CSRs) handle most of the interactions with customers. Once the CSRs heard that a Web application was being developed for customers to review their orders on line, they decided to bring their own requirements to the table.

After several meetings with CSRs, designers, and management, it was decided that at least for the first release, a third community of users, namely CSRs, would not be added. Instead, CSRs will use the system by pretending to be a customer. The management of LeSavon was pleased to find out that the planned API would allow additional development on top of LeSavon.com without any redesign. Once again, the API must be open in its platform support because the CSR department runs all of its applications on Windows 2000.

These additional requirements have brought to light the fact that individual customers are not the only potential users of the system. A company that buys products in large quantities from LeSavon could be interested in finding out the status of its orders, potentially as a batch operation for their reporting system. For cost reasons, the decision was made to limit the user interface to individual customers and focus on interactive access to the system while keeping in mind the batch requirements that might come later in the context of business-to-business transactions.

These new requirements and the new community slightly alters the anticipated use of the application as you can see in the following diagram:

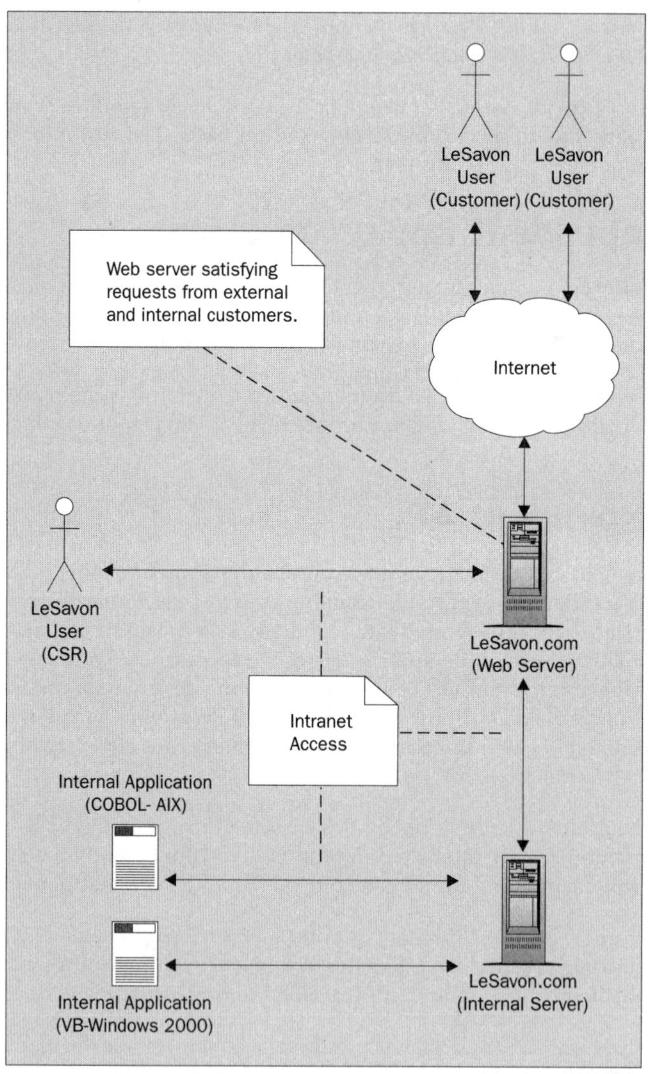

Scalability

Since LeSavon expects to be widely successful and grow quite significantly over the next few years, the application must be able to grow with the business. In other words, the application must be able to scale without requiring any re-engineering.

For the purpose of this application, a small load is 20 simultaneous users or less; a medium load is 100 simultaneous users or less; a large load is 1,000 simultaneous users or less.

24 by 7

The application must be available twenty-four hours a day, seven days a week, because customers are likely to access the service at any time, especially after hours. LeSavon believes that a lack of availability of the application would discourage users from using it in the first place and therefore, not meet its goals of increased customer satisfaction and cost reduction. Internet industry experience seems to support the management of LeSavon in that assumption.

The availability requirement seems obvious – who would design a system for failure? The important requirement here is to plan for failure. By stating that the application must provide continuous service, we are stating that even in the case of the failure of one of the components of the application (software or hardware) the service will still be provided.

The initial deployment will involve single redundancy (double the number of machines) of the architecture; however, the architecture must support a higher level of redundancy.

Since the initial load is expected to be small, the first deployed solution will be on two machines to provide high availability. An inexpensive solution like DNS round robin will be used initially, but an HTTP load balancing hardware solution should be possible to accommodate heavier application loads.

The high availability techniques mentioned here will be discussed at length in Chapter 9, in the discussion on performance.

Now that we have a grasp of the requirements, we can move into a discussion on the high-level architecture.

High Level Architecture

The application is divided into three tiers:

- The presentation tier
- The business tier accessed using SOAP
- The backend or database tier

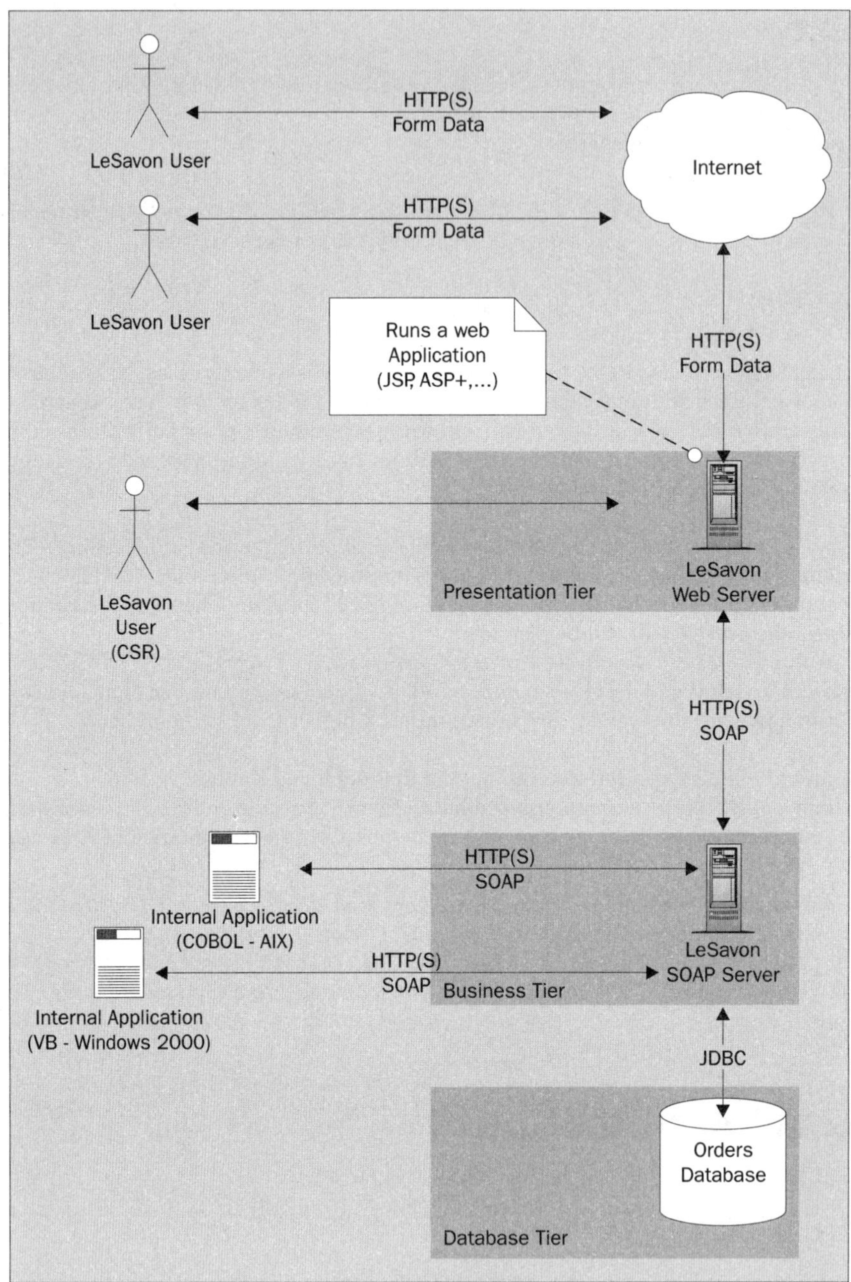

The external web server (LeSavon Web Server in the figure above) runs the presentation layer. There are a variety of valid platforms and frameworks for the presentation: JSP, ASP, CGI, and Perl, amongst others. The presentation layer makes calls to the business layer using SOAP. As we stated earlier, the main advantage of the middle tier is that it can be used to unify the business logic across the enterprise.

We will see in Chapter 6 that calls made using SOAP can easily be transformed into `in-proc` *calls using the proxy pattern.*

As you can see in the figure above, other applications besides the sample application can make calls to the SOAP layer.

The third tier in the case of the sample application is a simplistic JDBC-accessible database, but it could be any backend system of your enterprise: an Online Transaction Processing Database (OLTP), a data mart, or an Enterprise Resource Planning (ERP) system. In fact, the third tier could be broken down to as many as tiers necessary. For example, a data mart solution communicates with OLTP databases as well as a repository database, and this drives the execution of an **Extract Transform and Load (ETL)** tool that ultimately populates the data mart.

An OLTP database is optimised for queries and modifications to the database needed to run the day-to-day operations. The OLTP database is usually not suitable for Business Intelligence (BI) processing, which is the realm of data marts and data warehouses. The data is moved on a regular basis, sometimes in quasi real-time, from the OLTP database to the data marts using a process called Extract Load and Transform (ETL). We will not use a data mart in the sample application, but it is important to keep all the usages of the system in mind when designing an application to avoid interfering with any existing processes.

This sequence diagram shows the interactions for the *display list of orders* use case:

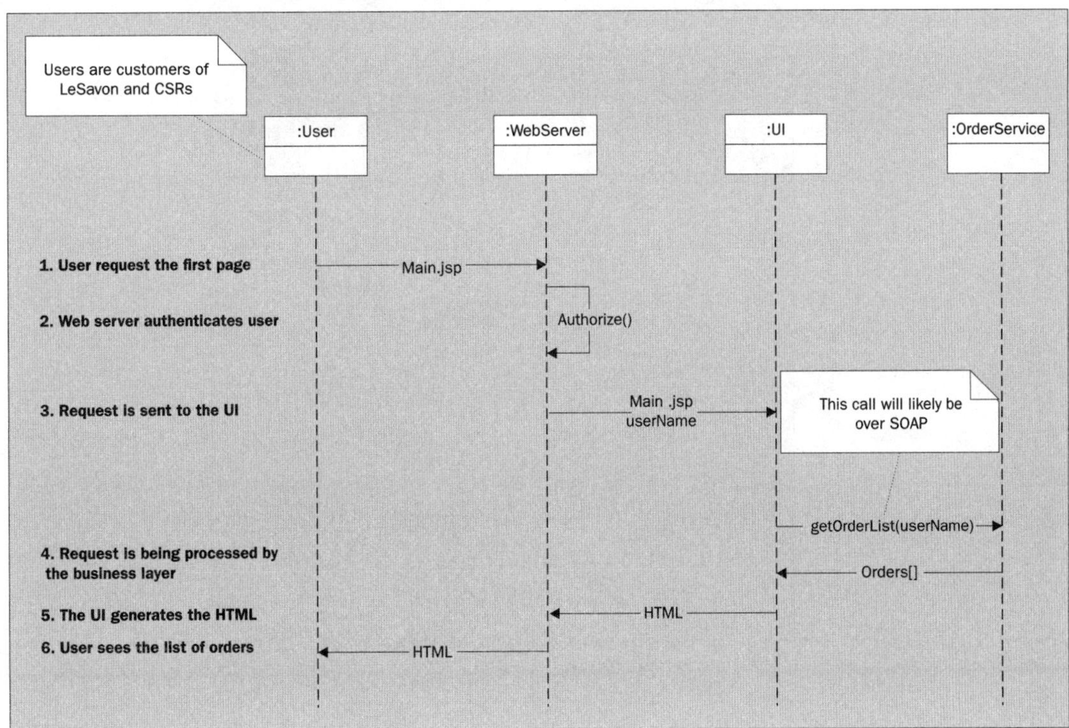

The other use cases follow a similar pattern. You will notice that the Web server adds the authorized user name prior to forwarding the request to the JSP/servlet engine.

The following two figures show two potential scenarios for deployment. In the first, the load balancer provides high availability for the external Web server:

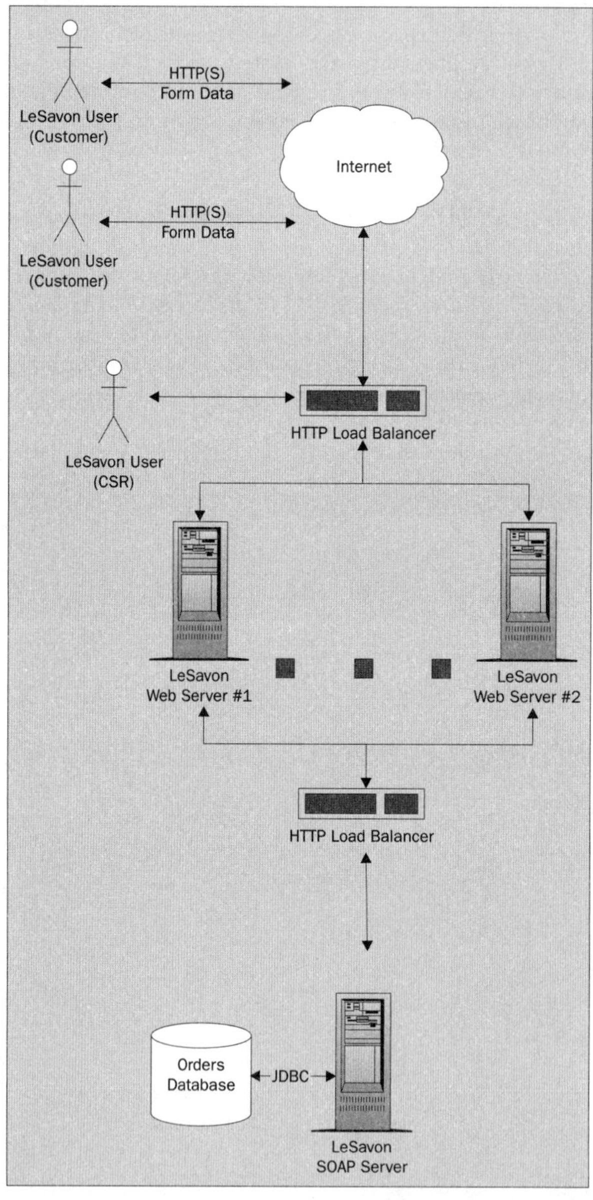

In the second scenario, the load balancer provides high availability for the backend as well. The same load balancer could be used for the external web servers and the SOAP server:

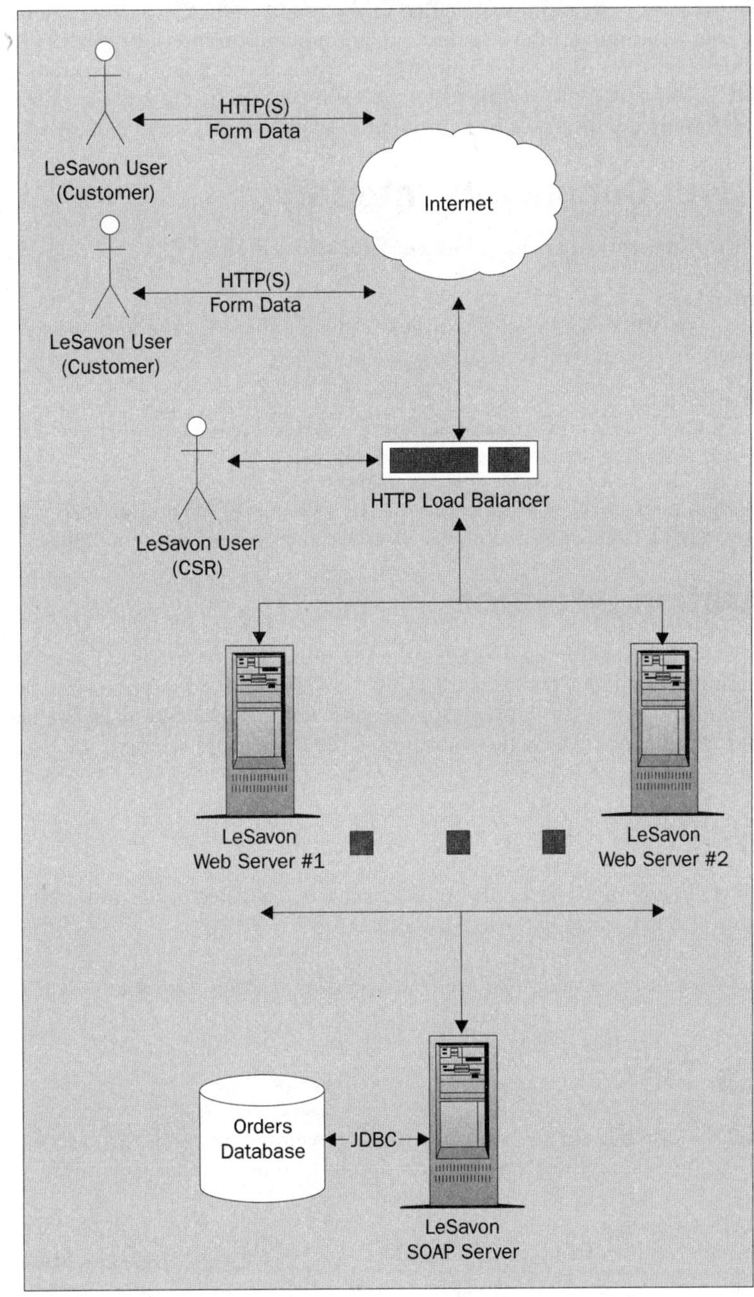

Presentation Tier

To serve the two user communities specified in the requirements, we will implement two user interfaces; one general user community interface and one administration interface. Since this system is largely an excuse to show examples of SOAP clients using various technologies, the actual Graphical User Interface (GUI) will be kept as simple as possible. In particular, there are no help screens – a feature that would definitely be necessary in a production application.

General User Community Interface

The GUI for the general user community contains two screens:

- **Order List**
  This page contains a list of the orders in the database for the authenticated user. Each order is a hyperlink to the order details page.

- **Order Details**
  This page contains the information on the order that was not displayed in the Order List screen, including article, quantity, and unit price.

There is no login page because we will rely on the web server for authentication. By the time a request has been processed by our application, it will already have been authenticated.

Administration Interface

In addition, an administration page is presented to users with administration privileges. The administration page contains two areas: a SOAP service area and a cache area. In the SOAP service area, the administrator can list the registered services of the application. In the cache area, the administrator can manage the cache according to the concepts discussed in Chapter 8.

Security

Since LDAP is already in use at LeSavon and because it satisfies our requirements for customization, the sample application will make extensive use of LDAP.

The security and the personalization strategies (and LDAP) will be described in detail in Chapter 7.

Business Tier

We have said that the middle tier was going to be developed using SOAP as the protocol. The choice of SOAP is a fundamental architecture decision that has some key characteristics:

1. **SOAP is stateless**
   We have seen in Chapter 2 that SOAP is a stateless protocol. In practical terms, this means that the client can never be sure of the server that processes its request: when techniques like load balancing are used, multiple servers are used and from the client's perspective, each server is as likely to service requests as the next. We will discuss the implications of statelessness in a moment.

2. **SOAP is platform-independent**
   Since it is a wire-level specification, SOAP allows applications running on different OS to call each other.

Is SOAP a 'wire-level' protocol?

The SOAP 1.1 specification states that 'SOAP is an XML-based protocol for exchange of information in a decentralized, distributed environment.' As such, SOAP defines the rules of encoding for your objects and data structures for serialization inside the `<Body>` *element that travels over a transport protocol like HTTP. In that sense, the SOAP specification defines the format of the data that travels over the wire.*

The main difference between SOAP and other distributed protocols like DCOM or RMI is that SOAP focuses exclusively on the format of the data that travels over the wire. By contrast, RMI will specify what exceptions you should throw in your methods and DCOM will specify what interfaces you must support in your objects.

SOAP does not specify any application, language, or process-level constraints.

3. **SOAP is language-independent**
   Most programming languages can be used to code SOAP services and SOAP clients. In this book, we will focus mostly on Java.

We have touched on the issue of state in our server-side application. This is a fundamental choice that needs careful scrutiny. For most applications, there is always some state that needs to be maintained. In the sample application, we maintain the state of a customer's orders in the database. We also maintain personalization information in a distributed directory service.

The issue is not so much if the overall application is stateless or state-full, but if one particular tier of the application is stateless or state full. The following table evaluates the benefits of stateless tiers in a distributed environment:

Criteria		
Simplicity	**Plus** The application designer can count multiple requests to be serviced in the same context.	**Minus** The developer must be prepared to restore some state between requests.
Scalability	**Plus** Machines can be duplicated at will since they do not maintain any state.	**Minus** State must be shared by multiple machines by either relying on complex infrastructure like EJB or forcing all requests to go all the way to the database.
Latency	**Plus** The responsiveness of the application can be maximized by keeping a cache of data structures that are expensive to compute (database connections, list of items, and so on.)	**Minus** A minimal state must be recomputed for each request. However, there are techniques to minimize the impact of the statelessness on latency (see side note).

Criteria		
Robustness	**Plus** Since machines can be duplicated at will, maximum robustness can be easily achieved through redundancy.	**Minus** The complexity of the infrastructure or the fact that all machines are not equivalent make it hard to increase robustness through redundancy.

Based on this table, deciding on a solution may be difficult, unless you have your priorities well defined. If scalability and robustness are your most important requirements, and you need to keep costs down, then a stateless application is probably the way to go. On the other hand, if you want developers to have the easiest possible environment and your application will never need to scale beyond a few users, then state full will be the best choice.

If you decide to design a stateless application like LeSavon.com, there are steps that you can take to minimize the penalties to your end users. For instance, you could maintain a state to improve the latency of your application, but be ready to re-build that state if it is not present on the machine when the request arrives. We will discuss how caching can be used to dramatically improve your performance in Chapter 8.

On the issue of simplicity, the use of a framework like Apache-SOAP helps a great deal. We will also investigate techniques to simplify the development task even further.

Now that we have a grasp of the issues surrounding state in our application, we can turn our attention to SOAP itself. As we saw in the above table, the stateless nature of SOAP means that the service can easily be scaled out: you can add as many machines as you need into production without having to recode your application. Since scaling in (putting more power into one machine) has its limits, it is important to know that scaling out is an option.

The other major advantage of statelessness is that it allows us to satisfy the availability requirement: when one server goes down, another server can take over without the client noticing any loss of connectivity.

We will discuss statelessness, scalability, and high availability further in Chapter 9.

SOAP is a good idea if the three characteristics that we mentioned earlier – statelessness, language independence, and platform-independence – are important to you. If you need to scale your application to thousands of simultaneous users, and if your backend servers and middle tier applications run on multiple platforms, then SOAP is a good choice because it is a platform-independent and language-neutral protocol. However, if your application is coded purely in Java from beginning to end, then the J2EE model is probably a better choice.

At this point, you might wonder if it is possible to mix solutions: even if your application is J2EE compliant in the backend, there is still some value in SOAP. For instance, your backend services might be running on Enterprise Java Beans (EJBs), and in this case, the SOAP tier provides a platform-independent interface to a Java-centric system.

A subject that inevitably comes up in a discussion about SOAP is performance. Is a web service-based application inherently slower than an application written with other distributed technologies like CORBA, DCOM, or RMI in mind? This depends on your definition of faster. We can measure performance in terms of latency (the time it takes for a user to get her answer back) and scalability (the time it takes for a lot of users to get their answer back).

There is little argument that the latency of a SOAP call is higher than the latency of a DCOM, CORBA, or RMI call. The SOAP protocol tends to generate verbose requests and responses. In addition, an open, document-based, stateless protocol has to do more work to handle a client request: the request must be parsed, serialized from a text representation to a binary representation, and some state might have to be restored. All of this takes time.

In choosing between SOAP and other technologies, you will have to ask yourself how much latency is acceptable to your application. If a GUI-based application increases the latency from 100ms to 200ms, nobody will complain, especially if the latency remains at about 200ms no matter how many clients hit your server.

Before we talk about our simplistic backend tier, we need to say one more word about state. Would it be a good idea to implement a mechanism on top of SOAP to preserve state on the server? Cookies allow us to define a state on top of a stateless protocol, HTTP. We could implement the same feature on top of SOAP.

Well in practice this is not advisable. In order for cookies to work in a distributed environment, such as the one described earlier, the load balancing software or hardware contains intelligence to scan the cookies in the HTTP header and make a client use the same server whenever possible. If we were to add an argument to our SOAP calls to maintain state, then load balancers would not monitor that argument and our calls would not "stick" to a preferred server. If we want to define an affinity to a server in a distributed environment, then we must rely on HTTP. Application servers also support sharing cookies between servers to distribute the state, but that increases the cost and complexity of the system.

We will discuss the issues of load sharing, load balancing, and fail-over in Chapter 9.

So what if we really want to develop a state-full application on top of SOAP? The protocol specification does not support it, but it does not prevent it either. It is possible, but it's not pretty.

Let's assume that we have solved the issue of stickiness in a distributed environment by either ignoring it (for example, we will always deploy the application on one server) or by writing our own transport that keeps track of HTTP cookies. In order to stay within the realm of SOAP, we will have to exchange the state as part of the `<header>` or the `<body>` element. If we decide to use the `<header>` we are extending the SOAP protocol and will get out of the realm of objects.

If we decide to stay within the realm of objects then we must use the `<body>` element and serialize a state token (in other words, a cookie) as part of our argument list and return it as part of the return value. In other words, the API will not look natural to Java developers, it will start looking like an add-on that is hard to maintain from a developer standpoint. It is unnatural because remote calls will be different than in-process calls or in-process calls will carry a superfluous argument. It is hard to maintain because the client developer must keep track of state tokens and then deal with expiring states and similar issues.

In Chapter 5, we will modify the Apache SOAP HTTP support to add HTTP header fields to SOAP messages.

Overall, this added level of complexity moves out of the realm of a simple and open protocol like the Simple Object Access Protocol. If the application cannot be designed with a stateless API, SOAP is probably not the right choice for the application.

In summary, adding state into an application as an afterthought is a bad decision. As we said earlier, deciding the statelessness of your tier is a fundamental decision: once you have made it you need to stick to it or go back to the drawing board and redesign your application.

Backend Tier

The backend tier of the sample application does not use SOAP as an interface. Therefore, we will make assumptions to keep things as simple as possible to focus on the topic of this book: SOAP development in Java. In particular, we will not rely on the availability of a Relational Database Management System (RDBMS) like Oracle, SQL Server, or MySQL to run the sample application.

Simplifications

You could be forgiven for thinking that LeSavon is a company that does not have its act together from an IT standpoint: no standardization on platforms, no uniformity of development environments or programming languages, and no business layer for its mission-critical applications. Alas, this is not unusual for a company that has grown from a startup to a mid-size company. In a typical situation, consultants bring in their favorite tools and technologies to do the initial development.

As the company grows through mergers and acquisitions, the picture gets muddier and muddier with the acquired companies relying on their own software and hardware systems. This set of requirements is not as far fetched as it might look at first sight!

As we mentioned earlier, we will make some major simplifications to the LeSavon.com application. Most of these simplifications would prevent a real-life application from being usable. To develop and deploy your application using LeSavon.com as a model, you will have to replace those simplifications and assumptions by the variables of your particular situation. However, the SOAP aspects of the LeSavon.com have not been simplified and you will be able to use most of the SOAP code presented in this book as-is in production applications.

Let's now discuss the major simplifications of the sample application. For each item, we will discuss a possible production solution.

Database

For LeSavon, data on customers and orders is essential to the daily operations of the business. That data is not to be handled lightly and as such, must be stored and accessed with a state-of-the-art RDBMS. The production database must include a careful data design to guarantee the integrity of the data at all times. In addition, processes must be put in place to handle disaster and recovery scenarios. Although these are very interesting subjects, these matters have little to do with SOAP development. To keep our discussion focused on Web services, the sample code uses a text file. To bring the sample code closer to reality, you can use JDBC. However, setting up a JDBC driver requires you to own an RDBMS and demands some setting up. As an example of such configuration, we will set up Sun's JDBC-ODBC bridge on Windows 2000. For performance reasons, this is usually not a valid choice for a production system, but it uses the same tools as a real application.

The text file used by the sample application as a database is a **tab-delimited** file that contains only a few customer records:

```
OrderID     Client    Article                 UnitPrice Quantity  TotalPrice
123456001   atase     Senteur de Provence     20        5         100
123456002   aterieur  Senteur de Provence     20        3         60
123456003   pdefer    Parfum de Lilas         35        3         105
123456004   piglote   Senteur de Provence     20        1         20
123456005   atase     Eau de Mouille          50        2         100
123456006   piglote   Parfum de Lilas         35        1         35
123456007   aterieur  Crystal de Roches       25        1         25
123456008   pdefer    Senteur de Provence     20        1         20
123456009   aterieur  Quartz de Petits Noeuds 45        2         90
123456010   atase     Parfum de Lilas         35        1         35
123456011   atase     Crystal de Roches       25        1         25
123456012   atase     Quartz de Petits Noeuds 45        1         45
123456013   pdefer    Eau de Mouille          50        2         100
```

The file is the `C:\projavasoap\Ch4\Database\Order.txt` file. We will use it in our application as the data source.

> *The `C:\` root directory is used throughout the book to indicate the root directory where the sample application is installed.*

The read-only nature of our modifications to the backend database will not impair our ability to put together a valid SOAP-based architecture. However, in order to preserve the statelessness of the SOAP server, SOAP calls that modify the database must be bundled into one atomic operation. If that is not possible, then you should consider creating one more tier that handles the modifications to the database (possibly using EJBs) and leave stateless operations in the SOAP layer.

Order

We can define an in memory representation of an order using the `Order.java` class as follows. The implementation is almost trivial since our definition of an order is the simplest possible. There are two points, however, that are worth making:

- The `Order` class is modeled after the JavaBean design pattern: public empty constructor and accessor/mutator methods.
- The class provides a `toXML()` method in addition to overriding `toString()`.

The main reason for following that pattern is that we can then use the `org.apache.soap.encoding.soapenc.BeanSerializer` class provided by the Apache SOAP framework to handle serialization. Serialization in this context means getting Java objects in and out of XML. The `BeanSerializer` automatically handles serialization of JavaBeans, so to take advantage of that capability, we need to define the `Order` class as a Java Bean.

The `toXML()` method will come handy in the implementation of the `OrderService` class:

```
/*
 * Order.java    1.0 03/06/2001
 */
package com.lesavon;

public class Order {
    int    id;
    String client;
    String article;
    int    unitPrice;
    int    quantity;
    int    totalPrice;
```

Each of the class properties corresponds to a column in the **Order.txt** data file in order. We provide an empty constructor, but we will use the constructor that accepts values for all the above properties:

```
public Order() {}

public Order(int id, String client, String article, int unitPrice,
  int quantity, int totalPrice) {
  this.article    = article;
  this.unitPrice  = unitPrice;
  this.quantity   = quantity;
  this.totalPrice = totalPrice;
  this.client     = client;
  this.id         = id;
}
```

We also offer standard accessor/mutator pairs (omitted here for brevity's sake) for each of the class properties defined above. Review the source code provided in the code download if you are in doubt. Other methods defined here are the `equals()` method, which we override to check for matching properties with the passed `Order` object:

```
public boolean equals(Order order) {
  return (id == order.id)
         && (article.compareTo(order.client) == 0)
         && (client.compareToIgnoreCase(order.client) == 0)
         && (quantity == order.quantity)
         && (totalPrice == order.totalPrice)
         && (unitPrice == order.unitPrice);
}
```

We also provide a `toString()` method; this method will give a string of the form:

com.lesavon.Order: id = id, client: client, article: article, unit price: unitPrice, quantity: quantity, total price: totalPrice

```
public String toString() {
  return "com.lesavon.Order: id = " + id
         + ", client: " + client
```

```
            + ", article: " + article
            + ", unit price: " + unitPrice
            + ", quantity: " + quantity
            + ", total price: " + totalPrice;
  }
```

Finally, we also provide a `toXML()` method that creates an `<order>` with each of the properties as attributes with their corresponding values:

```
    public String toXML() {
      return "<order id=\"" + id
              + "\" client=\"" + client
              + "\" article=\"" + article
              + "\" unitPrice=\"" + unitPrice
              + "\" quantity=\"" + quantity
              + "\" totalPrice=\"" + totalPrice
              + "\"/>";
    }
  }
```

Orders loaded from the database will be created as `Order` objects in the application.

Simple Data Access Layer

A good strategy to isolate your application from the details of accessing a database is to use the adapter design pattern to implement a data access layer in which its primary function is to read and write data. This is different from JDBC since, at least in theory, it allows you to access non-relational data.

The adapter design pattern is a structural pattern that converts the interface of a class into another interface understood by the clients of the interface. The main advantage of the adapter pattern is that it allows classes to work together easily. In the case of the data access layer of the sample application, we use the adapter pattern to unify JDBC and file I/O under one umbrella: `com.lesavon.service.DataAccess`.

Since we only need to access one database table, or equivalent, for the purposes of our application, the interface that defines the data access layer is rather trivial. Before we go on, we should defined our own exception class that can wrap application specific information. The class itself is simple. You should create it, saving it to the c:\ProJavaSoap\Chapter04\src folder:

SavonException.java

```
  /*
   * SavonException.java     1.0 02/06/2001
   *
   */
  package com.lesavon;

  import org.apache.soap.Constants;
  import org.apache.soap.Fault;
  import org.apache.soap.SOAPException;
```

```
public class SavonException extends SOAPException {
  Exception exception;
  Fault     fault;

  public SavonException(String description) {
    super(Constants.FAULT_CODE_SERVER, description);
  }

  public SavonException(Fault fault) {
    super(Constants.FAULT_CODE_SERVER,
          "Code = " + fault.getFaultCode() +
          ", String = " + fault.getFaultString());
    this.fault = fault;
  }

  public SavonException(String description, Exception exception) {
    super(Constants.FAULT_CODE_SERVER, description);
    this.exception = exception;
  }

  public String toString() {
    String string = super.toString();
    if (exception != null) {
      string += " - nested: " + exception.toString();
    }

    return string;
  }

  public Fault getFault() {
    return fault;
  }
}
```

The code for the `OrderService` class will be discussed in detail in the following chapter. This class provides the implementation for the SOAP service that we will deploy. Before we are able to deploy the service, we will need to develop this class.

The `OrderService` class will use the following class, `DataAccess`, as the adapter class to provide data access abstraction. The class will provide a single method `getOrderList()` that returns an array of `Order` objects representing current orders:

```
// DataAccess.java

package com.lesavon.service;

import com.lesavon.Order;
import com.lesavon.SavonException;

interface DataAccess {

  Order[] getOrderList(String userName) throws SavonException;
}
```

The only method is `getOrderList()`, which returns a list of orders for a given user. We will use the same interface for text and database access through JDBC.

The `TextAccess` class implements the database access to a test file:

```
// TextAccess.java

package com.lesavon.service;

import java.io.File;
import java.io.StringReader;
import java.io.IOException;
import java.io.FileReader;
import java.io.LineNumberReader;
```

We use the `java.io.LineNumberReader` to read the tab-separated file.

```
import java.util.Vector;
import java.util.StringTokenizer;

import com.lesavon.Order;
import com.lesavon.SavonException;
```

The `java.util.StringTokenizer` will allow us to parse the lines of the files into `com.lesavon.Order` objects that we will temporarily store in a vector.

```
public class TextAccess implements DataAccess {
  final String FILE_PATH = "C:\ProJavaSoap\Chapter04\Database\      orders.txt";
  final int MIN_SIZE = 13;    // Vector of result initial size

  public TextAccess() throws IOException {

    // We make sure that the file exists and that we can read it
    File file = new File(FILE_PATH);
    if (!file.exists() ||!file.canRead()) {
      throw new java.io.FileNotFoundException("Cannot open " + FILE_PATH
                                              + " for reading.");
    }
  }
```

The constructor makes sure that the file exists and that we can actually read the data.

```
  public Order[] getOrderList(String userName) throws SavonException {
    Vector ordersVector = new Vector(MIN_SIZE);

    try {
      LineNumberReader reader =
                new LineNumberReader(new FileReader(FILE_PATH));
      String line = reader.readLine();    // first line = field names

      while ((line = reader.readLine()) != null) {
        StringTokenizer tokenizer = new StringTokenizer(line, "\t");
```

This last line tokenizes each line by tabs.

```
            ordersVector.add(new Order(
                                Integer.parseInt(tokenizer.nextToken()),
                                tokenizer.nextToken(),
                                tokenizer.nextToken(),
                                Integer.parseInt(tokenizer.nextToken()),
                                Integer.parseInt(tokenizer.nextToken()),
                                Integer.parseInt(tokenizer.nextToken())));
          }

          Order order = null;
          for(int index=0; index<ordersVector.size(); index++) {
            order = (Order)ordersVector.elementAt(index);
            if(!order.getClient().equals(userName)) {
               ordersVector.remove(order);
               index--;
            }
```

Note the last line of this section of code. Removing an element from a vector will shift all of the elements left (or up) one element. The next element to check is therefore in the same position as the current index value. The next iteration of the for loop will increment the index so we must decrement it by one.

```
          }
          reader.close();
        } catch (Exception exception) {
          System.err.println("Unable to read text file: " + FILE_PATH + ": "
                                   + exception);
        }

        return (Order[]) ordersVector.toArray(new Order[ordersVector.size()]);
      }
    }
```

The `getOrderList()` function does not contain any surprises: it opens the file, reads the lines, and parses them into `Order` objects. You will notice that we store the list of orders in a vector that we convert to an array, since they are easy to deal with and the list should be final.

The next section explores a slight variation on the same theme: reading the `orders.txt` file using JDBC rather than file I/O.

JDBC-ODBC Bridge

The `JDBCAccess` class implements the `DataAccess` interface. Most of the implementation is similar to what we saw in `TextAccess`:

```
// JDBCAccess.java

package com.lesavon.service;
```

```
import java.sql.ResultSet;
import java.sql.Connection;
import java.sql.Statement;
import java.sql.DriverManager;
```

The `java.sql` classes provide JDBC support.

```
import java.util.Vector;

import com.lesavon.Order;
import com.lesavon.SavonException;

public class JDBCAccess implements DataAccess {
  final String CONNECTION_STRING = "jdbc:odbc:LeSavon";    // JDBC connection
```

JDBC requires the definition of a connection string that specifies what driver to use in addition to arguments for the driver. In this case, we use the JDBC to ODBC bridge. If you want to use another driver, you will need to replace this connection string along with the class name of the driver (see below). The alternate values for these variables are specific to your RDBMS vendor. The remainder of the class will remain identical.

```
  final int MIN_SIZE            = 13;    // Vector of result initial size
  final String ORDER_ID         = "OrderID";
  final String CLIENT           = "Client";
  final String ARTICLE          = "Article";
  final String UNIT_PRICE       = "UnitPrice";
  final String QUANTITY         = "Quantity";
  final String TOTAL_PRICE      = "TotalPrice";
  final String BASE_QUERY       = "select OrderID, Client, Article, "
    + "UnitPrice, Quantity, TotalPrice from orders.txt where client=";
```

The string constants will be used to retrieve data from the record set. The base query string is the SQL statement that returns the records for the orders of the specified user. We will complete the SQL statement when we know the client name.

```
  public JDBCAccess() throws SavonException {
    try {
      Class.forName("sun.jdbc.odbc.JdbcOdbcDriver");    // Load the driver
    } catch (ClassNotFoundException classNotFoundException) {
      throw new SavonException(
        "Cannot load jdbc/odbc bridge for JDBCAccess",
         classNotFoundException);
    }
  }
```

In the constructor, we make sure that we can load the driver. As mentioned before, you will need to change the class name of the driver if you want to use another driver than the JDBC-ODBC bridge.

```
  public Order[] getOrderList(String userName) throws SavonException {
    Vector ordersVector = new Vector(MIN_SIZE);

try {

      ResultSet rs =
        DriverManager.getConnection(CONNECTION_STRING, userName, null)
          .createStatement()
            .executeQuery(BASE_QUERY + "'" + userName + "'");
```

```
        // Turn the results of the query into an array of plain objects.
        while (rs.next()) {
          ordersVector.add(new Order(rs.getInt(ORDER_ID),
                                     rs.getString(CLIENT),
                                     rs.getString(ARTICLE),
                                     rs.getInt(UNIT_PRICE),
                                     rs.getInt(QUANTITY),
                                     rs.getInt(TOTAL_PRICE)));
        }
      } catch (Exception exception) {
        System.err.println("Unable to connect to the database: " + exception);
      }

      return (Order[]) ordersVector.toArray(new Order[ordersVector.size()]);
    }
}
```

Once again, the implementation of the `getOrderList()` is straightforward; get a recordset for the SQL query results, navigate the record set until the end of the file, and parse each record into an `Order` object. The remainder of the code is identical to what we saw in `TextAccess`.

The connection string that we encountered earlier specified an ODBC data source `jdbc:odbc:LeSavon`. Setting up an ODBC data source requires a little bit of work, so let's review the necessary steps for the Windows 2000 platform. Other Windows platforms like NT use similar steps. As you will see in the coming pages, the process is typical of Windows: it is heavy on the number of dialog boxes and clicks you have to go through, but each step is easy to perform.

Several ODBC drivers can be used, but an easy way to access a tab-separated file like `orders.txt` is through the Microsoft ODBC text file driver. The first step is to bring up the ODBC Data Source Administrator that you can find in the Control Panel (Start->Settings->Control Panel->Administrative Tools->Data Source (ODBC)):

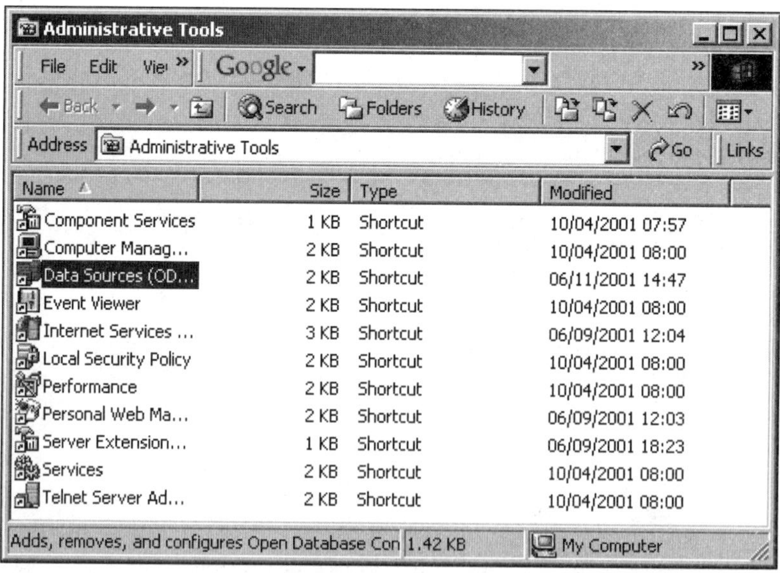

Now bring up the System DSN tab:

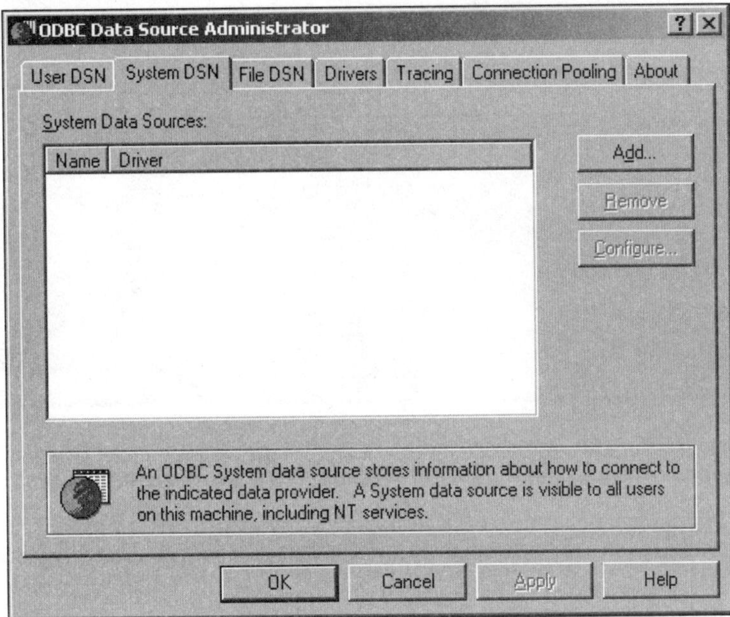

Depending on the data sources that you have already set up on your machine, your display might look slightly different. The next step is to add the data source by clicking on the Add button, which brings up the following dialog box:

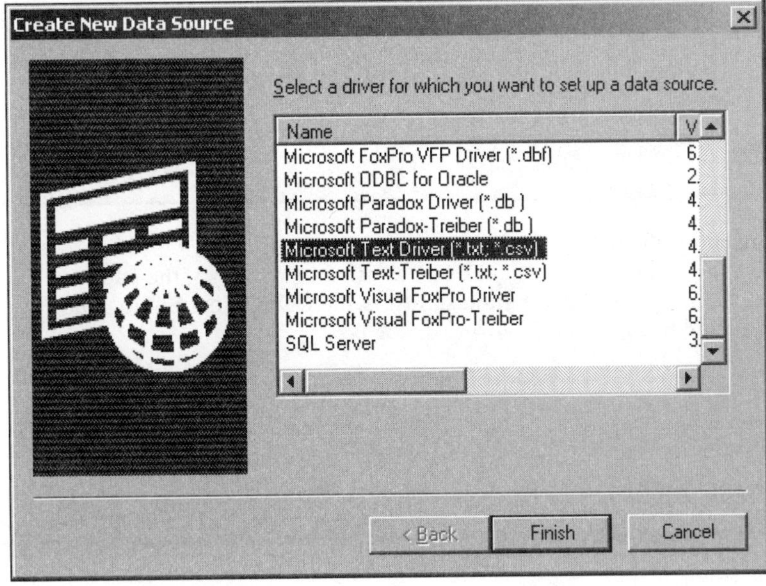

Select the driver highlighted in the figure above, and then click on Finish to bring up the next step:

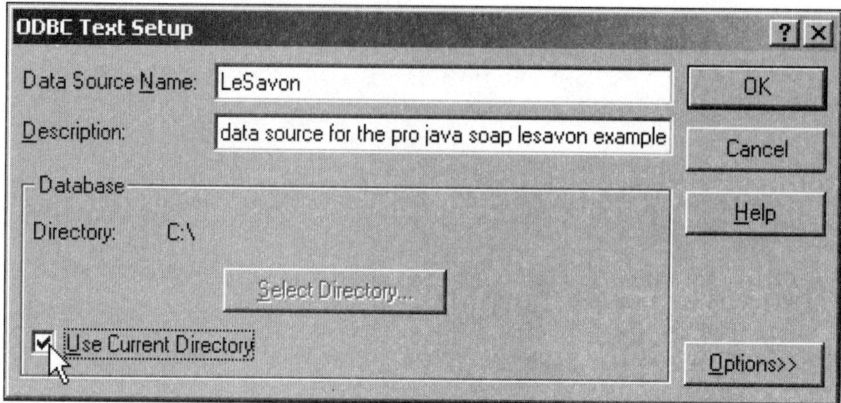

You need to set the directory to where the `orders.txt` file is located, so un-select the Use Current Directory checkbox and click on the Select Directory button to bring up this dialog box:

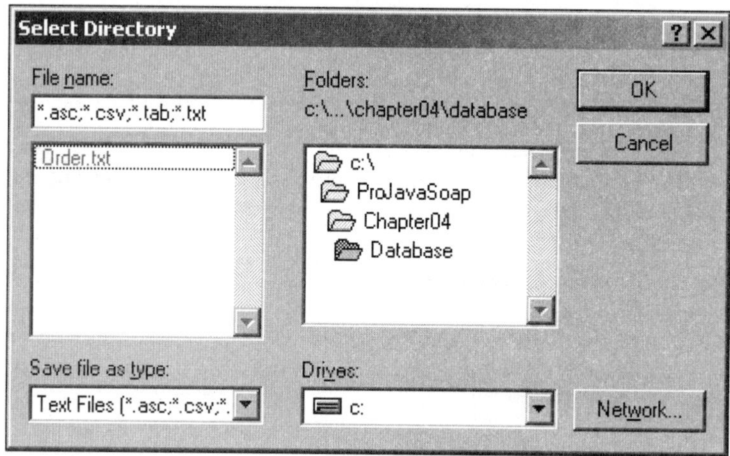

On the test machine, the root directory is `c:\` and the file is in `c:\ProJavaSoap\Chapter04\Database` (as usual in Windows, the paths are case-insensitive). Click OK and then click on the Options button shown in the ODBC Text Setup dialog box that we saw earlier. That should bring up the following dialog box:

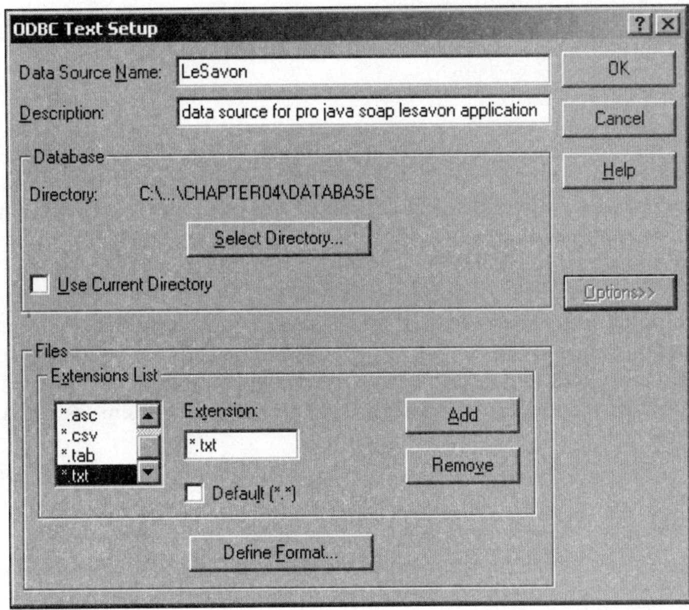

Click on the Define Format button to bring up the Define Text Format dialog box. Select order.txt and select the Column Name Header bullet point. Next, choose the Tab Delimited format from the drop down menu. Next, enter 13 for the number of Rows to Scan. This is the number of data rows that the file contains – it does not include the first row which represents column names. Selecting Guess now should bring up the following appropriate headings, which should be checked against their suggested data types for accuracy. In the figure below, we can see that `OrderID` has been assigned an integer data type that is sufficient for this example. `Client` and `Article` are appropriately assigned `Char` types of 255 lengths while the rest are assigned integer data types:

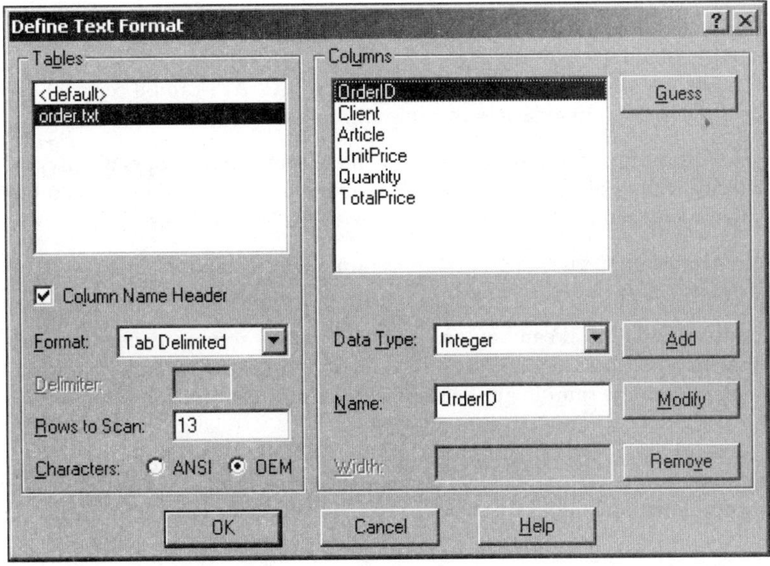

Click on OK for all the dialog boxes to apply your changes. Before dismissing the ODBC Data Source Administrator, make sure that it includes the LeSavon data source.

Security

As we discussed earlier, the user interface is protected by the authorization infrastructure of the web server. However, the security of the API is somewhat naïve, since it only requires a user name and not a password for user-related functionality such as getting a list of orders for a specific user. This is not unusual with a limited set of features.

Well known shipping companies let you track your packages with a tracking number and some additional information such the zip code or the postal code of the sender. Note that the administration API requires a user name and a password. If your application needs to protect the functionality available to the regular user community then you can use the same methodology as the administration API.

> *Security implementations that protect the user interface as well as the backend API will be presented in Chapter 7.*

Whilst we are on the topic of security, the LDAP database (discussed in detail in Chapter 7) is not ready for production since it uses clear-text passwords and authentication. This makes your life easier in development, but you must test with a secure LDAP implementation.

Reality Check

So, what is real in the sample application? In the following areas, the sample application is equivalent to mission-critical applications in that:

- The overall architecture of the sample application is secure, scalable, and robust. It provides scalable (in and out) services that can be deployed in a 24 by 7 environment.
- The overall architecture of the sample application is open, both from a platform and language standpoint. Since it is written in Java, LeSavon.com can be deployed on all the platforms and OS that we mentioned so far. In addition, the SOAP API can be remotely accessed by applications written in a variety of programming languages on virtually any platform.
- The SOAP administration functionality is secure and robust. Specifically, the transport layer, the administration of the cache, and the personalization and security can be used in a production environment.
- Care is also taken to guarantee that the sample application performs well, even under stress. Performance is discussed at length in Chapters 8 and 9.
- The sample application can be deployed on as many servers as needed and administered from any machine that has the application installed. However, the administration features implemented in the sample application are not sufficient for a production system.

Nevertheless, it would be naïve to take code from the entire sample application as-is and put it into production without evaluation and testing, because there are probably assumptions and shortcuts that the author forgot to mention.

Summary

In this chapter, we have presented the requirements of our sample application: LeSavon.com. The LeSavon Company uses a very heterogeneous computing environment from a hardware and software standpoint. The company wants to use LeSavon.com as a bridge to the future: it will unify the existing applications in their current form and it will provide a scalable multi-tier architecture.

Our goal in the coming chapters will be to demonstrate that web services and SOAP can be the unifying technology for the applications of our fictitious company. We have discussed why the sample application is a sample and not a production-ready system. However, we have shown in what areas it must be modified to accommodate the needs of your mission-critical application.

We also reviewed some cases where SOAP should be avoided. Although SOAP provides openness, scalability, and availability, in certain circumstances these are not sufficient to offlay the cost in added complexity and performance degradation.

We also described the data access layer and the two implementations that allow us to work with Java file IO or with a more realistic JDBC-based implementation.

In our development of the sample application, we will start with the implementation of the SOAP API using web services and then move on to the clients. We will then connect to our services using a Javaclient. Prior to coding the web services that make up the SOAP API, we must decide what services we want to implement and how they will interface to each other.

The business layer that we will deploy as a SOAP server for the sample application is the subject of Chapter 5.

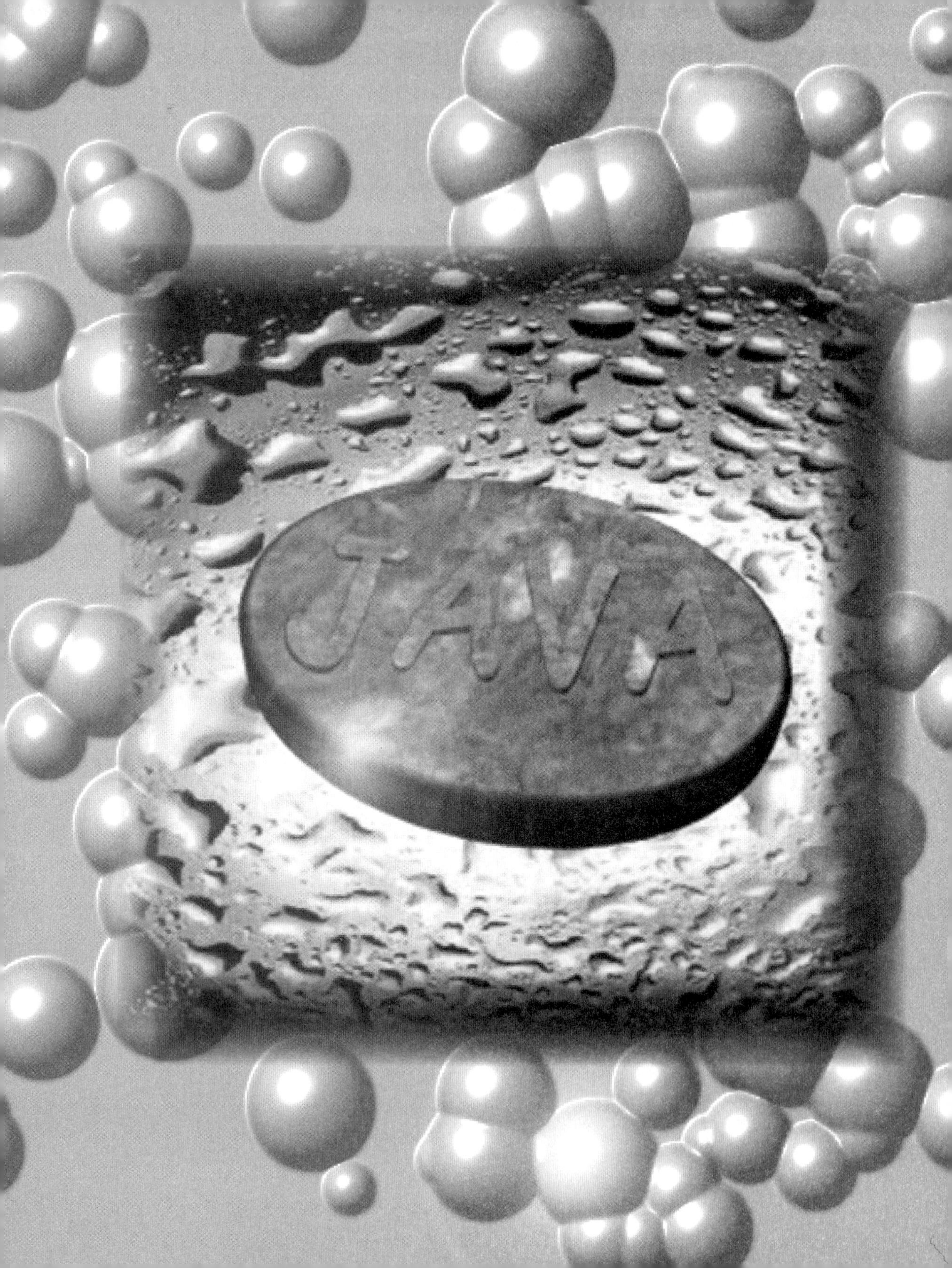
JAVA

5

SOAP Server

In this chapter, we will concentrate on the server for the sample application. We will start by discussing the architecture of the sample application in a little more detail. Then we will write the four components of the SOAP server:

- A cached router
- A un-cached router
- The `RemoteOrder` interface and its implementation, the `OrderService` class
- The `RemoteAdmin` interface and its implementation, the `AdminService` class

The cached router, referred to as the *router* from now on, improves the responsiveness of the application by caching responses for a given period of time, expiring them as required, and storing new request responses in the cache. It does this by calling the un-cached router, or *ncrouter*, which forwards the call to the implementing service, the `OrderService` class.

We will also take a closer look at deploying and un-deploying SOAP services (registration) in a secure environment. Finally, we will conclude the chapter with a look at custom serialization and good practices for SOAP service design. We will test the service with a minimal command line client.

You might be wondering where the **Graphical User Interface (GUI)** clients are in this picture. The GUI clients are not part of the SOAP server (they are not Web services) and will be discussed as part of the clients. Per our requirements, which we discussed in the previous chapter, the GUI is browser-based and as such contains two tiers: a server tier that generates the pages and a client tier that displays the pages. In practice, the server tier of the GUI can run on the same server as the SOAP server.The design of the sample application will make switching back and forth between the two solutions a trivial task.

We begin our description of the SOAP server with the architecture of LeSavon.com.

LeSavon.com Architecture

We took some liberties with the Unified Modeling Language (UML) since we need to represent calls over HTTP in addition to straight method calls. The entry points to the sample application are two servlets: *router* and *ncrouter.* The servlets implementing these functions route SOAP traffic.

The `com.lesavon.service.Serveur` class implements the function of the *router.* It will check if a response to a request is stored in the cache, and will return it if so. Otherwise, it calls the ncrouter, which will forward the call to the relevant service.

The `org.apache.soap.server.http.RPCRouterServlet` class provides the function of the *ncrouter.* We used this class in Chapter 3 with the HelloWorld example. We don't need to amend the implementation provided by apache for this part of the application; it will suffice for our purposes.

The *ncrouter* will also field administration calls; a client can administer the cache by flushing or refreshing it.

In reality, the entry point to LeSavon.com is the Web server that handles authentication. The figure below shows the collaboration diagram between the classes on the server-side for a call to `com.lesavon.RemoteOrder.getOrderList()`.

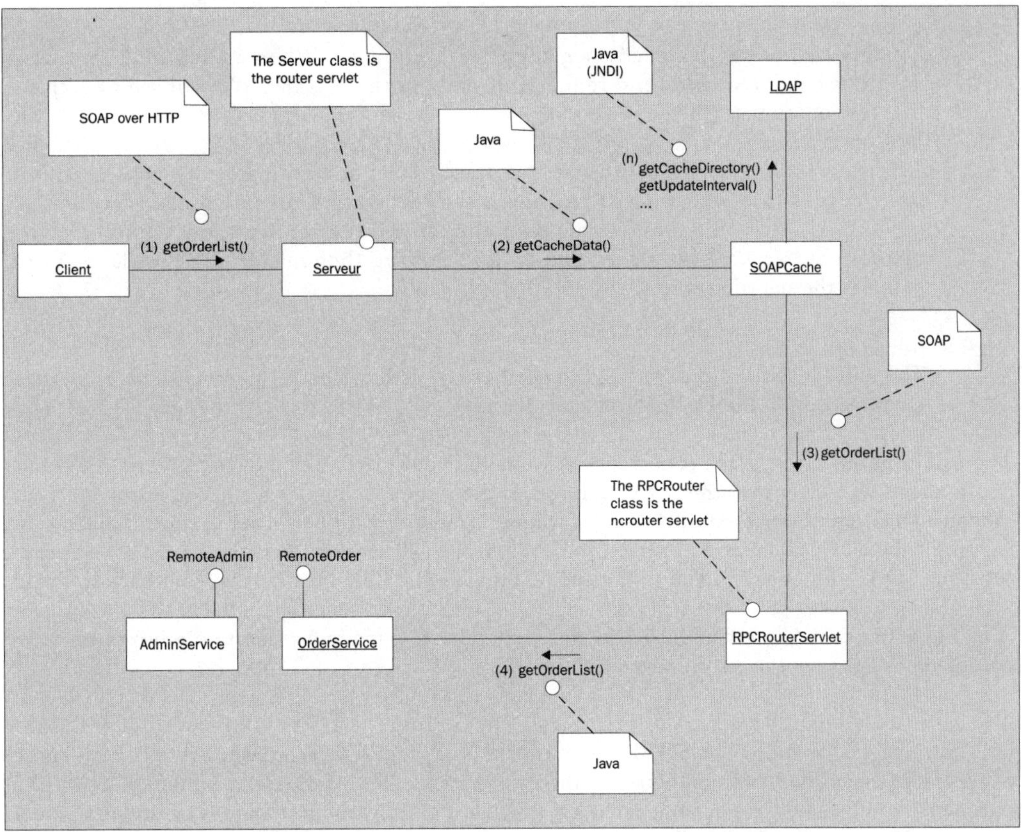

The signature of the `RemoteOrder.getOrderList()` method that returns the list of orders for a given user:

```
public Order[] getOrderList(String userName) throws SavonException;
```

There are two different flows suggested by the diagram above. Let's review the steps for the first flow described by the previous figure:

1. `getOrderList()`
   The client calls `getOrderList()` using SOAP over HTTP. The target URL for the client in this diagram is the `Serveur` class.

2. `getCacheData()`
   On receiving the request, the *router* forwards the request to the `SOAPCache` class that, as its name suggests, implements a cache for SOAP requests. If the cache has the response, then that response can be returned and the client has the list of orders from `getOrderList()`. If it does not, then it calls the *ncrouter* class, `RPCRouterServlet`.

3. `getOrderList()`
   For this call, the SOAP cache is a client of the *ncrouter*. When a client does not want to use the cache, it should send requests directly to the *ncrouter*. We will see how this works in a few moments.

   To process the request, `RPCRouterServlet` parses and validates the SOAP request. The *ncrouter* goes through its list of registered services to find the target class for the `getOrderList()` method. In this case, the target is `OrderService`, which implements the `RemoteService` interface. The `OrderService` then makes JDBC calls to access the data for the list of services.

4. `getOrderList()`
   The call to `OrderService.getOrderList()` is handled as in-process Java, as we saw in Chapter 3 with the HelloWorld service.

The call from the cache to the router servlet is made over SOAP. Using SOAP gives us flexibility during deployment: we can deploy the SOAP service on the same machine as the cache or on another machine. However, with flexibility usually comes a trade-off with performance: a call made over SOAP is going to be slower than an in-process call. When the call makes it back to the `SOAPCache`, the resulting SOAP response is saved to the cache. Finally, the SOAP response is sent back to the client.

A call to a non-cached method is slightly different since it is made directly to the `ncrouter` servlet, completely bypassing the `router` servlet.

The calls labeled `getCacheDirectory()` and `getUpdateInterval()` are not part of this flow and require some explanation. The SOAP cache runs a background thread designed to refresh and clean up SOAP responses. The thread will query a directory service (in this diagram, LDAP) to get the value of parameters such as the path for the cache on disk, how often responses should be updated, etc. In other words, calls from the SOAP cache to the directory service will happen asynchronously.

We will ignore the issues internal to the development of the SOAP cache in this chapter, and instead focus on the implications of `SOAPCache` to the design and development of the SOAP server.

Flushing the Cache

The application administration system allows administrators to manage the service. It requires login, and allows the administrator to flush and refresh the cache. The figure below shows a call to the `flush()` method. `RPCRouterServlet` routes the call to the `AdminService` object.

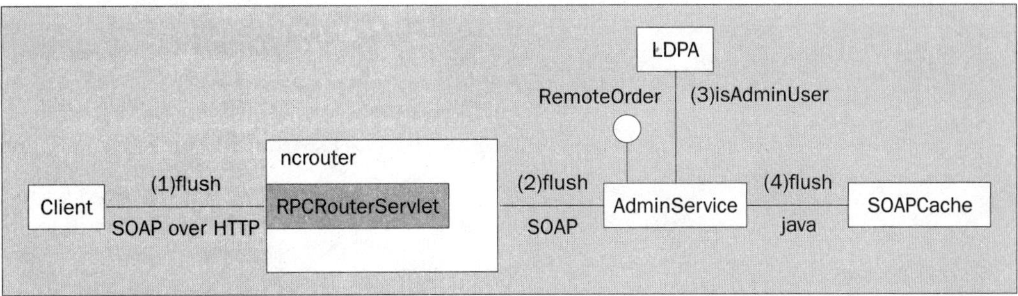

The `flush()` method has the following signature:

```
public void flush(String userName, String password) throws SavonException;
```

Note that the signature of the `flush()` method includes a user name and a password. This is because a higher level of security is required for methods that implement administrative features. Let's review the different steps involved in the processing of the `flush()` request:

1. `flush()`
   The client calls `flush()` using SOAP over HTTP. The target URL for the client in this diagram is the *ncrouter.*

2. `flush()`
   On receiving the request, *ncrouter* forwards the request to the `AdminService` class.

3. `isAdminUser(username, password)`
   The user name and password are validated against the enterprise security system implemented by the LDAP object. This step is the authorization step: we validate that the user has administration privileges.

4. `flush()`
   The actual flushing of the cache is done by the `SOAPCache`. `AdminService` calls its `flush()` method to empty the cache of stored responses.

Before getting into the details of the router implementation, let's have a look at the class structure of the objects that we have described so far.

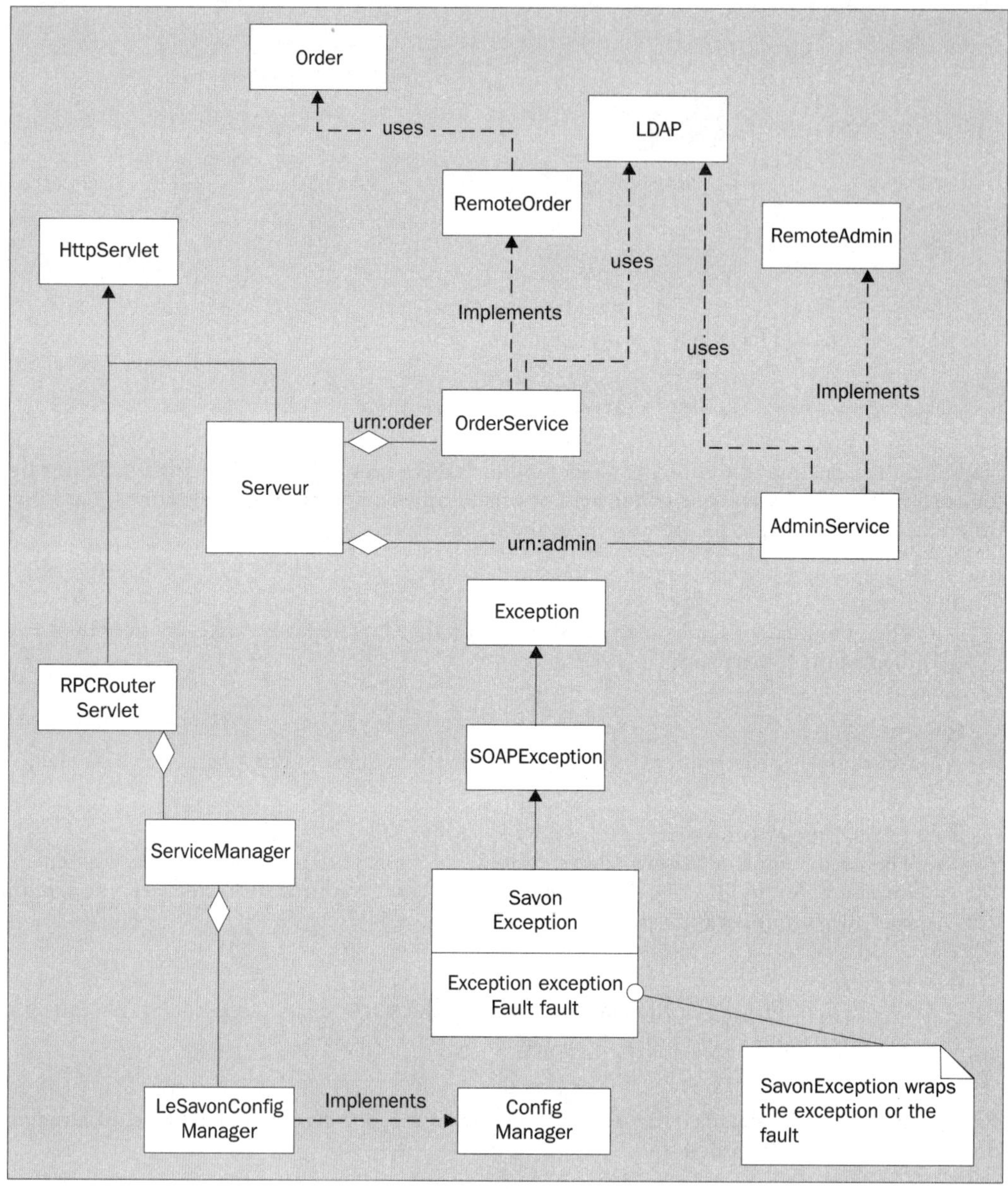
Order
uses
LDAP
RemoteOrder
uses
RemoteAdmin
HttpServlet
Implements
uses
Implements
urn:order
OrderService
Serveur
AdminService
urn:admin
Exception
RPCRouter Servlet
SOAPException
ServiceManager
Savon Exception
Exception exception
Fault fault
SavonException wraps the exception or the fault
LeSavonConfig Manager
Implements
Config Manager

The figure above shows the class diagram for the SOAP-server side of LeSavon.com. It should contain no surprises at this point. The `SavonException` must subclass `SOAPException`, otherwise the Apache SOAP framework will wrap it inside an instance of `SOAPException`. This makes it harder to manipulate, since we have to traverse an exception hierarchy to find out what went wrong. To make things simpler for us, all methods should throw a `SavonException` in case of error.

At this point, we have enough information to begin looking into the classes that make up the LeSavon.com application. We will start with a high level description of the Apache `RPCRouterServlet` that implements our *ncrouter*.

ncrouter

We will be using the Apache SOAP `RPCRouterServlet` without any modifications. A detailed discussion of its implementation is outside the scope of this book and is only relevant if you want to modify the implementation provided by Apache. You can find the code in the `org/apache/soap/server/http/RPCRouterServlet.java` file that comes with the source of Apache SOAP.

However, one point about exceptions needs to be made because it is relevant for the implementation of the `Serveur` class. The `doPost()` method of `RPCRouterServlet` does not throw a `ServletException` when things go wrong. The reason for this is that the `ServletException` is designed to handle HTML traffic over HTTP and as such generates an HTTP response with `text/html` content.

As we saw when we reviewed the SOAP specification, a SOAP server must always return a document with `text/xml` content. We will follow the same design in the `router`. If things go wrong (during the creation of the `SOAPException`, for instance) then the servlet falls back on the HTTP protocol.

Implementing the Service

Let's begin by looking at the *router* that will give us our caching capability. We will then look at the code for the administration and order services.

Router

The *router* is implemented by the `Serveur` servlet. The source code for this class is shown below:

```
// Serveur.java
package com.lesavon.service;


import java.io.IOException;
import java.io.StringWriter;
import java.io.OutputStream;
import java.io.ByteArrayInputStream;
import java.util.Enumeration;

import javax.servlet.ServletException;
```

```
import javax.servlet.ServletConfig;
import javax.servlet.http.HttpServlet;
import javax.servlet.http.HttpServletRequest;
import javax.servlet.http.HttpServletResponse;

import org.apache.soap.SOAPException;
import org.apache.soap.Fault;
import org.apache.soap.rpc.Call;
import org.apache.soap.rpc.SOAPContext;
import org.apache.soap.rpc.Parameter;
import org.apache.soap.rpc.Response;
import org.apache.soap.transport.TransportMessage;
import org.apache.soap.Constants;
import org.apache.soap.Envelope;
import org.apache.soap.encoding.SOAPMappingRegistry;

import com.lesavon.cache.SOAPCache;
import com.lesavon.SavonException;
```

As we saw in the collaboration diagram above, the router servlet makes use of the `SOAPCache` class. LeSavon throws `SavonException` when something goes wrong.

```
public final class Serveur extends HttpServlet {

    public void doPost(HttpServletRequest request,
                       HttpServletResponse response)
      throws IOException, ServletException {
        doGet(request, response);
    }
```

We mentioned in Chapter 3, when we were discussing the HelloWorld SOAP service, that the router servlet did not accept HTTP `GET` requests. As new requests come in, the `Serveur` class submits the request to the cache, which calculates a key. This key works like a hash key in that it uniquely represents the request. The `Serveur` class then submits the key to the cache, which checks the key for a cached response. If no cached response is found for that key the request is submitted to the *ncrouter*. The response is then cached against the cache key before being returned to the client.

A client may also submit a cache key with no SOAP document in the body that is equivalent to providing a SOAP request. This cuts out the need for parsing the SOAP request thus improving performance. For this purpose, a `GET` request with a cache key in the header is a valid request. We begin by checking that the request is in UTF-8 format, the application only accepts this encoding:

```
    public void doGet(HttpServletRequest request,
                      HttpServletResponse response)
      throws IOException, ServletException {
     try {
       // We only handle UTF-8
       final String UTF8 = "text/xml; charset=utf-8";
       if(!request.getContentType().equals(UTF8)) {
         throw new SavonException("This server only handles: " + UTF8);
       }
```

We look for a cache key in the request. If it cannot be found, the request must contain a valid SOAP request or an exception will be thrown. The cache key is computed at this point. Another possible exception is a malformed SOAP request:

```
String cacheKey    = request.getHeader("LeSavon-Cache-Key");
byte[] cacheData   = null;
byte[] inputBytes  = null;

// If we don't have a cache key, we must compute it
if(cacheKey == null) {
  try {
    inputBytes = readInputBytes(request);
    cacheKey = SOAPCache.getCache().computeCacheKey(request,
                                  new ByteArrayInputStream(inputBytes),
                                getServletConfig().getServletContext());
  } catch(Exception exception) {
    throw new SavonException("Internal error in computing cache key");
  }
}
```

Using the computed cache key, we check the cache to see if the response is already there.

```
cacheData = SOAPCache.getCache().getCacheData(cacheKey);
if(cacheData == null) {
```

A bug currently means that `request.getServerPort()` always returns port 80. We have therefore hardcoded port 8080 to the URL for *ncrouter*:

```
  String ncRouterURL = "http://localhost:"
                     + 8080 // prefer to use request.getServerPort()
                     + request.getContextPath()
                     + "/ncrouter";
```

Next, we read in any information submitted in the request, using the helper method `readInputBytes()` discussed in a moment.

```
if(inputBytes == null) {
  inputBytes = readInputBytes(request);
}
```

We attempt to get the response from the cache. If the response is not in the cache, then we will ask the cache to submit the request on our behalf and cache the response. The `SOAPCache` class provides a method, `submitAndCache()`, that does this:

```
try {
  byte [] soapResponse = SOAPCache.getCache().submitAndCache(inputBytes,
                                           ncRouterURL, cacheKey);

  response.setContentType(request.getContentType());
  response.getOutputStream().write(soapResponse);
} catch (Exception exception) {
  throw new SavonException("Error while submiting request.", exception);
}
```

We wrap the call around a `try..catch` block that will throw a `SavonException` in the case of error.

```
      } else {
        response.setContentType(request.getContentType());
        response.getOutputStream().write(cacheData);
      }
    } catch (Throwable throwable) {
      buildFault(request, response, throwable);
    }
  }
```

The `buildFault()` helper method attempts to build a SOAP fault based on the exception caught.

```
  private void buildFault(HttpServletRequest request,
    HttpServletResponse response,
    Throwable exception) throws ServletException {
    try {
      SOAPException soapException = (exception instanceof SOAPException)
           ? (SOAPException)exception
           : new SOAPException(Constants.FAULT_CODE_SERVER
                   + ".Exception:", "", exception);
```

We want to make sure that we are working with a `SOAPException` since the constructor for the `Fault` class requires a `SOAPException`. The additional test ensures that we avoid nesting a `SOAPException` into another one.

```
      Fault fault = new Fault(soapException);

      String faultString = soapException.getMessage();
      if(soapException.getTargetException() != null) {
        faultString += ": " + soapException.getTargetException().toString();
      }

      fault.setFaultString(faultString);

      if(request != null) {
        fault.setFaultActorURI(request.getRequestURI());
      }

        // CODE CLONED FROM APACHE REMOVED FROM LISTING ...

      } catch(Throwable throwable) {
        throw new ServletException(throwable);
      }
    }
  }
```

The remainder of `buildFault()` was copied verbatim from `RPCRouterServlet`. This attempts to extract as much information as possible from the current call to build a response with a `SOAP:FAULT` section.

Notice that we only handle UTF-8 in the application. If we were to handle other formats, we would need to check the content type and encoding to make sure that the cached version of the response is in the same text encoding as the request. For example, it is an error for the application to return a cached URF-8 response for a UTF-16 request. One solution is to pass the encoding as part of the cache key.

Perhaps, a better solution would be to store all cached responses encoded with UTF-8 and do the conversion before sending the response back. Note that for most applications UTF-8 is the better solution since it is more efficient in terms of memory.

The `init()` method starts the background thread that refreshes and flushes the contents of the cache based on rules that are in the system. The `destroy()` method stops this thread:

```
public void init(ServletConfig servletConfig) throws ServletException {
  super.init(servletConfig);
  try {
    SOAPCache.getCache().startCacheThread(
                                    servletConfig.getServletContext());
  } catch (Throwable throwable) {
    servletConfig.getServletContext().log(
                "Cannot start Cache thread: " + throwable);
  }
}

public void destroy() {
  try {
    SOAPCache.getCache().stopCacheThread();
  } catch (Throwable throwable) {
    // Destroy fails silently (may not throw ServletExcepion)
  }
}
```

The `readInputBytes()` method is the helper method that we call to read any input from `GET` calls.

```
private byte[] readInputBytes(HttpServletRequest request)
      throws IOException {
  byte[] inputBytes = new byte[request.getContentLength()];
  request.getInputStream().read(inputBytes);
  return inputBytes;
}
```

At this point, we have both the routers, the `RPCRouterServlet` class, and the `Serveur` class that handles cached responses. We need to design and write the application-specific work: the administration and the order service itself. Let's review the code for these two SOAP services.

RemoteOrder and the OrderService

Here, we will separate the interface definition from its implementation. It is not only good object-oriented development practice, but it is also a necessity for our use of the proxy pattern on the client side. The reason for this design will become clear in the next chapter when we work on a client-side framework.

```
// RemoteOrder.java

package com.lesavon;

import org.w3c.dom.Element;

public interface RemoteOrder {

  public Order[] getOrderList(String userName) throws SavonException;

  public Element getOrder(String userName, int orderId)
     throws SavonException;
}
```

The `OrderService` class implements the `RemoteOrder` interface. The implementation is brief and straightforward, thanks to the data access layer that we developed in Chapter 4.

```
/*
 * OrderService.java    1.0 02/06/2001
 */

package com.lesavon.service;

import java.io.StringReader;

import javax.xml.parsers.DocumentBuilderFactory;
import javax.xml.parsers.DocumentBuilder;
import javax.xml.parsers.ParserConfigurationException;

import org.w3c.dom.Document;
import org.w3c.dom.Element;
import org.xml.sax.InputSource;

import com.lesavon.Order;
import com.lesavon.SavonException;
```

We will use the XML parser to parse the XML that comes out of the `Order.toXML()` method.

```
public class OrderService implements com.lesavon.RemoteOrder {
  private DocumentBuilder docBuilder;     // Re-use the document builder
  private DataAccess      dataAccess;     // Re-use the data access object

  public OrderService() throws SavonException {
    try {
      docBuilder = DocumentBuilderFactory.
                                  newInstance().newDocumentBuilder();
    } catch(ParserConfigurationException parserConfigurationException) {
      throw new SavonException(
                    "Cannot create document builder for OrderService",
                    parserConfigurationException);
    }

    try {
      // Create a JDBCAccess for JDBC-ODBC bridge
      dataAccess = new JDBCAccess();
     //dataAccess = new TextAccess();
```

To use the text-based data access layer, simply create an instance of `TextAccess()` instead of an instance of `JDBCAccess()`. Both data access classes were described in Chapter 4. Any exception will arise because the application was unable to load the JDBC-ODBC bridge driver:

```
    } catch(Exception exception) {
      throw new SavonException(
                  "Cannot load jdbc/odbc bridge for OrderService", exception);
    }
  }

  public Order[] getOrderList(String userName) throws SavonException {
    return dataAccess.getOrderList(userName);
  }
```

As we mentioned at the beginning of this code review, the data access layer does most of the work for us. The implementation of the `getOrder()` method is straightforward: loop on the list of orders until you find the one identified by the order identifier passed as argument.

We call the `toXML()` method on the relevant order. The resultant string is wrapped in a `StringReader` that is then submitted to the constructor of the `InputSource` class, which the `parse()` method of the `DocumentBuilder` class requires as an argument:

```
  public Element getOrder(String userName, int orderId)
       throws SavonException {

    Order orders[]  = getOrderList(userName);
    for(int index = 0; index < orders.length; index++) {
      if(orders[index].getId() == orderId) {
        try {
          return docBuilder.parse(
                    new InputSource(
                    new StringReader(
                              orders[index].toXML()))).getDocumentElement();

        } catch (Exception exception) {
          System.out.println("Exception:  " + exception);
          throw new SavonException("Cannot create XML response", exception);
        }
      }
    }

    throw new SavonException("Order " + orderId + " not found!");
  }
```

We therefore call the `getDocumentElement()` method to returned the desired `Element`.

We can see this in the following response from the server (formatted for readability):

```
HTTP/1.0 200 OK
Content-Type: text/xml; charset=utf-8
Content-Length: 547
Servlet-Engine: Tomcat Web Server/3.2.1 (JSP 1.1; Servlet 2.2; Java 1.3.0;
Windows 2000 5.0 x86; java.vendor=Sun Microsystems Inc.)

<?xml version='1.0' encoding='UTF-8'?>
<SOAP-ENV:Envelope
```

```
            xmlns:SOAP-ENV="http://schemas.xmlsoap.org/soap/envelope/"
            xmlns:xsi="http://www.w3.org/1999/XMLSchema-instance"
            xmlns:xsd="http://www.w3.org/1999/XMLSchema">

  <SOAP-ENV:Body>
    <ns1:getOrderResponse
        xmlns:ns1="urn:order"
        SOAP-ENV:encodingStyle="http://xml.apache.org/xml-soap/literalxml">
      <return>
        <order article="atase"
               client="Eau de Mouille"
               id="123456005"
               quantity="2"
               totalPrice="100"
               unitPrice="50"/>
      </return>
    </ns1:getOrderResponse>
  </SOAP-ENV:Body>
</SOAP-ENV:Envelope>
```

The last method of the `Order` service is the `getOrderObject()` method that returns the same output as `getOrder()` but as a Java object. As you can see, its implementation contains little surprises since it follows the same pattern as `getOrder()` but without the XML document generation.

```
  public Order getOrderObject(String userName, int orderId)
       throws SavonException {
    Order orders[]  = getOrderList(userName);
    for(int index = 0; index < orders.length; index++) {
      if(orders[index].getId() == orderId) {
        return orders[index];
      }
    }
    throw new SavonException("Order " + orderId + " not found!");
  }
}
```

RemoteAdmin and the Admin Service

The `RemoteAdmin` interface is similar to the `RemoteOrder` interface. We must, however, use a password since authorization is necessary for controlling access to the service administration facility.

```
// RemoteAdmin.java
package com.lesavon;

public interface RemoteAdmin {
  public void flush(String userName, String password)
     throws SavonException;

  public void refresh(String userName, String password)
     throws SavonException;
}
```

Methods of the `RemoteAdmin` interface have a user name and password as part of their argument list, as they are only accessible to administrator users. The actual authorization is performed by an LDAP utility class.

In the argument list, the password is in clear text, which constitutes a possible security risk. A more secure implementation could use a public key certificate with an expiration time.

The `AdminService` class implements the `RemoteAdmin` interface:

```
/*
 * AdminService.java    1.0 02/07/2001

package com.lesavon.service;

import java.io.StringReader;

import com.lesavon.SavonException;
import com.lesavon.util.LDAP;
import com.lesavon.cache.SOAPCache;

public class AdminService implements com.lesavon.RemoteAdmin {

    public AdminService() throws SavonException {
    }
```

The `flush()` method checks for authorization with the LDAP proxy class. Until we are ready to explore LDAP, we will implement this class minimally such that it will check the passed values against hard coded values. The work of flushing the cache is performed by the cache itself:

```
public void flush(String userName, String password) throws SavonException {
  try {
    // Must be admin
    if(LDAP.getLDAP().isAdminUser(userName, password)) {
      SOAPCache.getCache().flush();
    } else {
      throw new SavonException(
                    "You must be an administrator to run this command");
    }
  } catch (Exception exception) {
    throw new SavonException("Flush was not successful.", exception);
  }
}
```

Refresh works in more or less exactly the same way:

```
    public void refresh(String userName, String password)
          throws SavonException {
        try {
            // Must be admin
            if(LDAP.getLDAP().isAdminUser(userName, password)) {
                SOAPCache.getCache().refresh();
            } else {
                throw new SavonException(
                    "You must be an administrator to run this command");
            }
        } catch (Exception exception) {
            throw new SavonException("Refresh was not successful.",
                                      exception);
        }
    }
}
```

The LDAP Proxy class

In order to make this code run, we will need to provide a simplified implementation of the LDAP module. The implementation of the interface to LDAP is isolated in one class: `com.lesavon.util.LDAP`. That class is accessed using the singleton design pattern. The singleton pattern ensures that only one copy of the class exists. This is usually done by making the constructor private and giving access to the class only through a static method.

In the class below, the `getLDAP()` method is called in order to retrieve the instance of this class.

```
package com.lesavon.util;

import javax.naming.NamingException;

public final class LDAP {
  static private LDAP ldap = new LDAP();    // The one and only

  // Constructor is hidden to enforce the singleton
  private LDAP() {
  }

  static public LDAP getLDAP() {
    return ldap;
  }

  public boolean isAdminUser(String user, String password)
      throws NamingException {
    return true;
  }
}
```

The `isAdminUser()` currently allows any user, password combination to be passed in.

We must also provide a minimum (non-working) implementation of `SOAPCache`, in order to make this code run so far:

SOAPCache

The `SOAPCache` class again runs on the singleton pattern. It can be retrieved using the `getCache()` method.

The `ServletContext`, `HttpServletRequest`, and `InputStream` objects are passed in to the `computeKey()` method if you recall. The SOAP related classes and the `URL` class will be used to call the *ncrouter* as we shall see in a moment:

```
package com.lesavon.cache;

import javax.servlet.ServletContext;
import javax.servlet.http.HttpServletRequest;
import java.io.InputStream;
```

```
import org.apache.soap.SOAPException;
import org.apache.soap.rpc.SOAPContext;
import org.apache.soap.transport.TransportMessage;
import org.apache.soap.util.net.HTTPUtils;

import java.net.URL;

import com.lesavon.SavonException;

public class SOAPCache {

  // The one and only cache for this VM
  private static SOAPCache theCache;

  private SOAPCache() throws SavonException {
  }

  public static SOAPCache getCache() throws SavonException{
    if(theCache == null) {
      theCache = new SOAPCache();
    }

    return theCache;
  }
```

Until we come to implement the cache, the cache key returned from the `computerCacheKey()` method will always be a meaningless value:

```
  public String computeCacheKey(HttpServletRequest request,
                                InputStream inputStream,
                                ServletContext servletContext)
     throws SavonException {
    return "test";
  }
```

This doesn't matter, because the `getCacheData()`, which should check the cache for data matching the passed in key, always returns `null`:

```
  public byte[] getCacheData(String key) {
    return null;
  }
```

The `submitAndCache()` method is the interesting one at this point. It forwards the request to the *ncrouter*. It is supposed to also cache the request, but it will not do so for now. The method uses the `org.apache.soap.transport.TransportMessage` class to make the call. This class represents a transport independent encapsulation of a SOAP call.

We begin by creating a new `SOAPContext` required by the `TransportMessage` class. We pass to the `TransportMessage` the SOAP request as a `String`, the SOAP context created earlier, and a hash table of SOAP headers; in this case a `null` represents no headers. We can now save the message.

We can post this message to our *ncrouter* using the `org.apache.soap.util.net.HTTPUtils` class's port method as shown below. The returned value is of also of type `TransportMessage`, its `getBytes()` method returns the response in the byte array format that the client expects.

```
    public byte[] submitAndCache(byte[] requestText, String url, String key)
        throws SOAPException {

      TransportMessage request = null;
      TransportMessage response = null;
      SOAPContext ctx = new SOAPContext();

      try {
        request = new TransportMessage(new String(requestText), ctx, null);
        request.save();

        response = HTTPUtils.post(new URL(url), request, 0, null, 0);

      } catch(Exception exception) {
          System.err.println("SOAPCache.submitAndCache: caught exception: "
                             + exception + ", ignored.");
      }
      return response.getBytes();
    }
```

In line with previous method, the methods for starting and stopping the cache cleanup thread are empty methods as are the methods for flushing and refreshing the cache:

```
    public synchronized void startCacheThread(ServletContext context) {
    }

    public synchronized void stopCacheThread() {
    }

    public synchronized void flush() {
    }

    public synchronized void refresh() {
    }
  }
```

Before we compile the application, we should provide a client to test the code we have written so far.

Simple Client

As part of this chapter, we will write a simple SOAP client for the `Order` service that gets a list of the orders for the user. The `GetOrders` client is similar to the `HelloWorldClient`:

```
  // GetOrders.java
```

```
package com.lesavon.test;

import java.net.URL;
import java.util.Vector;
import java.util.Arrays;

import org.apache.soap.*;
import org.apache.soap.rpc.*;

import org.apache.soap.encoding.SOAPMappingRegistry;
import org.apache.soap.encoding.soapenc.BeanSerializer;

import org.apache.soap.util.xml.QName;
```

We need to import quite a few SOAP classes in this code, which is in sharp contrast to our server-side development, where we did not import any.

```
import com.lesavon.Order;

public class GetOrders {
  public static void main(String args[]) {

  if(args.length != 1) {
    System.out.println("Usage is /"java GetOrders URLtoRouter/"");
    System.out.println("Where URLtoRouter is" +
                       "\"http://server:port/lesavon/ncrouter\"");
    System.exit(1);
  }

  String url = args[0];
```

We will pass in the URL for the service as a command line argument. This will be of the form:

http://localhost:8080/lesavon/ncrouter

for testing with Tomcat on port 8080. We can also use `tcpTrace` or `TcpTunnelGUI` for debugging by changing the port number to 8081 (by default), or port 80 for testing through a web server such as Apache.

The name of the service we want to test is *order*. Its URN is "urn:order". The method we wish to call is `getOrderList()`; we will pass in a user name of "atase":

```
String uri          = "urn:order";
String remoteMethod = "getOrderList";
String user         = "atase";

System.out.println("com.lesavon.test.GetOrders.main: Starting test...");
```

Here we create a `Call` object and add the user name parameter. Recall that the `getOrderList()` method takes a user name as a property. The `Parameter` class takes the name of the parameter, the java class of the parameter, the value, and the type of encoding style for the URI:

```
try {
  Call call  = new Call();
  Parameter param = new Parameter("userName",
                                  user.getClass(),
                                  user,
                                  Constants.NS_URI_SOAP_ENC);
```

The target of the call is the URI of the service that we pass in as a command line argument. The method name is defined above.

The parameter is assigned to the call. The `setParams()` method takes a vector of the required parameters for the remote method call. We create an array with the parameter as its content, convert this to a list with which to create a `Vector` and submit the vector to the `setParams()` method:

```
call.setTargetObjectURI(uri);
call.setMethodName(remoteMethod);
call.setParams(new Vector(Arrays.asList(new Parameter [] {param})));
```

We must tell the Apache SOAP framework how to serialize the `Order` class.

A `SOAPMappingRegistry` object maps between java and XML using pre-registered serializers and deserializers for SOAP. Its `mapTypes()` method (which inherits from its ancestor `org.apache.soap.util.xml.XMLJavaMappingRegistry`) takes as argument the encoding style URI, a fully qualified element type (our `Order` class), the class name of the java class to be serialized, the serializer, and finally the deserializer.

We register the mapping for the `Order` class with the registry with the `org.apache.soap.encoding.soapenc.BeanSerializer` class as the serializer/deserializer. The `Call` class uses this class to serialize and deserialize the `Order` class by calling its `marshall()` and `unmarshall()` methods. The `BeanSerializer` will deconstruct our `Order` bean and turn it into a SOAP call (XML) parameter using the accessors, and likewise reconstruct an order class calling the empty constructor to make an instance and loading the values into the properties using the class's mutators.

Once the registry mapping is created, we assign it to the call:

```
SOAPMappingRegistry smr = new SOAPMappingRegistry();
BeanSerializer      ser = new BeanSerializer();

smr.mapTypes("http://schemas.xmlsoap.org/soap/encoding/",
             new QName("urn:lesavon-order", "order"),
             Order.class, ser, ser);
call.setSOAPMappingRegistry(smr);
```

The actual SOAP call is done through the `invoke()` method of the `Call` class. Notice that to get the return value (an array of `Order` objects) we simply need to cast the `Object` returned by the `invoke()` method.

```
Response resp = call.invoke(new URL(url), "");
```

We check the response for a fault, and unpack the fault to report on it if this has happened:

```
// Check the response.
  if (resp.generatedFault()) {
    Fault fault = resp.getFault();

    System.out.println(methodName
                       + ": Call to " + remoteMethod
                       + " returned a fault!");

    System.out.println("  Fault code: " + fault.getFaultCode());
    System.out.println("  Fault string: " + fault.getFaultString());
```

If we have a valid response, we unpack it instead. The return value is an array of order objects. We retrieve the array, casting it to type `Order` as explained previously; the deserializer will convert the returned values to `Order` objects so that we can safely do this.

We then loop through each order in the response, outputting the value to the screen:

```
} else {
  if (resp.getReturnValue() != null) {
    Order[] orders = (Order[])resp.getReturnValue().getValue();

    System.out.println("Orders:");
    for(int index = 0; index < orders.length; index++) {
      System.out.println("    " + orders[index]);
    }
  }
}
```

And that completes the test client. Currently, it requires a deep understanding of SOAP. In future clients, we will need to abstract this understanding to make writing clients simpler:

```
        } catch (Exception exception) {
      System.err.println(methodName + ": Error, caught exception: "
      + exception);
    }

    System.out.println(methodName + ": All done!");
  }
}
```

Now that we have a server and a client, we can build the code and test it.

Compiling the Code

In order to compile and deploy the code, we have chosen a utility similar to *make* by Apache called ANT. Throughout the remainder of the book, scripts will be provided to enable automated compilation of the application. In order to understand what is happening, we will briefly explain how ANT works.

Before we do so, it is worth copying the contents of the `admin` folder in the `webapps\soap` for soap into our application. This will mean that we can check services have indeed been deployed. Copy this folder and its contents into the `Chapter05` directory, in a subdirectory called `web`. We will get ANT to automatically copy the contents to the relevant folder in our web application.

ANT

In the old days of C and C++ development, we used to create space and tab-sensitive *make* files, that would tell the *make* utility what shell commands to invoke in order to compile or link our C/C++ code.

The main drawback of the *make* file methodology, aside from the quirks of rigid *make* file syntax, is the fundamentally platform-centric nature of the technology: write once, run on one, and only one, OS.

An answer that the author has found to be more than satisfactory is ANT. ANT is a Java-based build tool that uses XML to define the syntax of build files. The Java-based architecture is a step toward the write once, run anywhere goal. The XML syntax of build files should not be an obstacle for SOAP developers.

The ANT utility can be downloaded from http://jakarta.apache.org/ant. Follow the relevant link to download version 1.4:

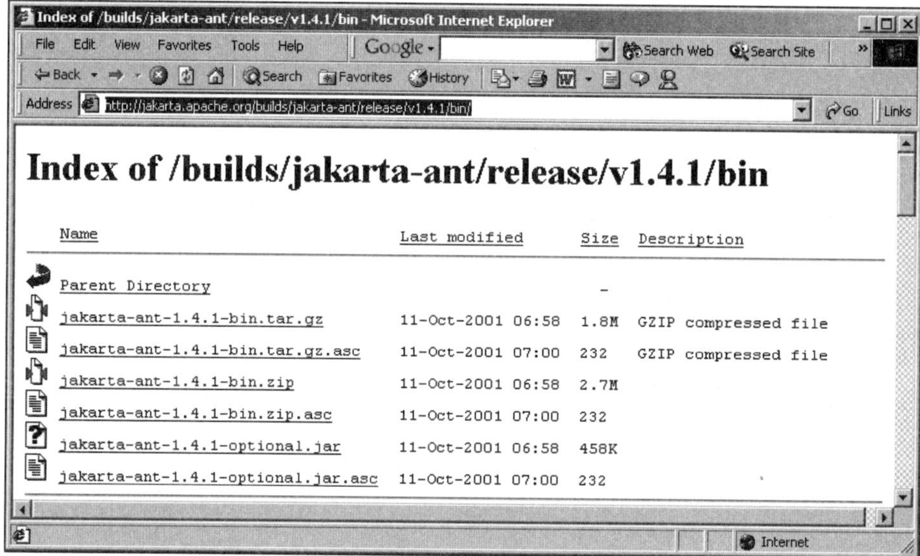

The samples in this book have been built using ANT 1.3 and ANT 1.4. The installation is straightforward, and does not require any special steps as far as SOAP development is concerned.

After downloading and exploding the compressed file, you should have a directory structure like the following:

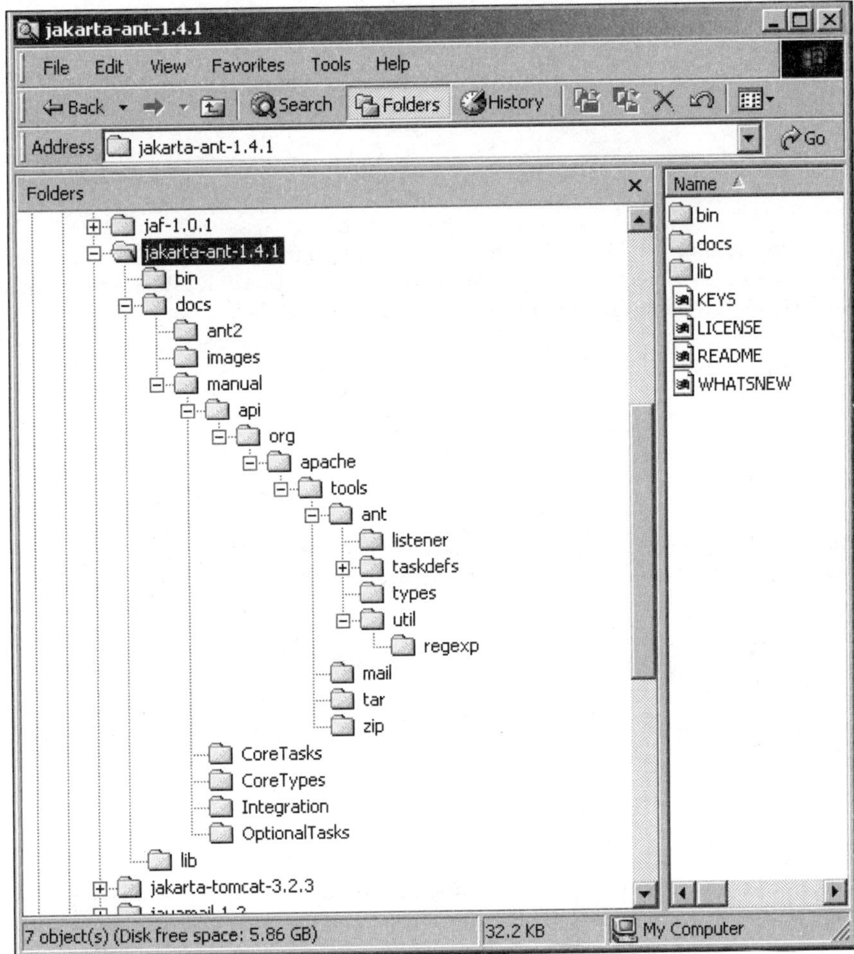

An in-depth description of all the capabilities of ANT is outside the scope of this book, so we will limit ourselves to a description of the features that we will use as part of the build files for LeSavon.com. If you want to learn more about ANT, check the `C:/jakarta-ant-1.4.1/docs/index.html` file that comes with the download. It contains a detailed list of all the available commands.

The principle of ANT is simple and similar to *make*: you write an XML document that contains definitions, targets, and commands. ANT will use the build file to build a dependency graph to "fire" the execution of the commands contained inside the target definitions.

Explaining the ANT file

To see how this works in practice, let's create a build file for our project. The top level element of an ANT file is the `<project>` element. The top-level element contains the name of the project (`lesavon`), the default target (`compile`) and the base directory (the current directory or C:\ProJavaSoap\Chapter05).

We then define several properties or variables to provide location-independence. Notice that the file paths includes a '/' as the file separator; this will work equally well on Windows and UNIX.

```
<project name="lesavon" default="compile" basedir=".">

<!-- This project is used to build the leSavon website -->

  <property name="app.name"         value="lesavon"/>
  <property name="deploy.home"      value="/webapps/${app.name}"/>
  <property name="dist.home"        value="${deploy.home}"/>
```

The LeSavon application will be created inside a directory named `webapps` within the current directory. The deployment and distribution directory are the `lesavon` folder within webapps. Java docs, will be created in a subdirectory of the web application called `javadoc`.

The `clean` target simply deletes files from previous compilations:

```
<target name="clean">
  <delete dir="${deploy.home}"/>
</target>
```

The next target, `prepare`, contains the steps necessary to create the output directory structure. The steps are self-explanatory and are identical to what we would do to manually build the application.

```
<target name="prepare">
  <mkdir  dir="${deploy.home}"/>
  <copy todir="${deploy.home}">
    <fileset dir="web"/>
  </copy>

  <mkdir  dir="${deploy.home}/WEB-INF"/>
</target>
```

The `compile` target requires the execution of the `prepare` target since we must have a directory structure in place prior to compiling. This is specified using the `depends` attribute of the target `<element>`.

The `javac` element is a built-in command to compile Java using `javac`. The `destdir` attributes defines the output directory, which in this case is the `WEB-INF/classes` directory of our Web application. This script assumes that the source files are all stored in the `src` directory directly underneath c:\ProJavaSoap\Chapter05. The other attributes are self-explanatory.

```
<target name="compile" depends="prepare">
  <javac srcdir="src"
         destdir="${deploy.home}/WEB-INF/classes"
         debug="off"
         optimize="on"
         deprecation="off"/>
</target>
```

The javadoc target simply runs javadoc on our classes. The all target is a convenient target to trigger a fresh build. Note that it is not normally a good idea to include the javadoc command as part of your compile target because it always rebuilds the entire documentation tree as opposed to simply rebuilding the documentation for the modified files.

```
  <target name="all" depends="clean,prepare,compile,javadoc"/>
</project>
```

As the project build file is at the moment, the last target will not be run. The default target called is compile and therefore it will be run by ANT. It depends on the prepare target, which ANT will run first, before running the compile target. The deletion of previous files is not referenced and will currently not be run. In order to run all of the targets, we would need to specify all as the target in the call to ANT. For example, we would call:

```
C:\ProJavaSoap\Chapter05>ant all -buildfile BuildLeSavon.xml
```

To run ANT, it is a good idea to include the ant executable in your path. The command line contains several options that can be found by calling ant –help.

Before we compile, we must make sure that the soap.jar, servlet.jar, archive is available on the classpath. This can be done by hand, added permanently, or through a batch or shell file. We can now build the project for LeSavon.com with the following command:

```
C:\ProJavaSoap\Chapter05>ant -buildfile BuildLeSavon.xml
```

As we hinted before, ANT is a more complex tool than we have shown in this section, but the simple build file that we just developed will give us enough functionality to easily build the leSavon project.

Assuming that all compiled well, we can go on to deploy the application and run it.

Deploying the Application

In order to compile and deploy the application, we will need to create a few more files. We will begin by creating a descriptor for the administration and order services.

Deployment Descriptors

LeSavon.com exposes two services so we will need two deployment descriptors. The deployment descriptor for the Admin service, RemoteAdmin.xml, is almost identical to the HelloWorld deployment descriptor:

```
<isd:service xmlns:isd="http://xml.apache.org/xml-soap/deployment"
             id="urn:admin">
  <isd:provider type="java"
                scope="Request"
                methods="flush refresh">
    <isd:java class="com.lesavon.service.AdminService" static="false"/>
```

```
    </isd:provider>

    <isd:faultListener>
      org.apache.soap.server.DOMFaultListener
    </isd:faultListener>
  </isd:service>
```

The deployment descriptor for the `Order` service is also quite simple. It should saved in the file, `RemoteOrder.xml`:

```
  <isd:service
   xmlns:isd="http://xml.apache.org/xml-soap/deployment"
   id="urn:order">
    <isd:provider type="java"
                  scope="Request"
                  methods="getOrderList getOrder">
      <isd:java class="com.lesavon.service.OrderService" static="false"/>
    </isd:provider>

    <isd:faultListener>
      org.apache.soap.server.DOMFaultListener
    </isd:faultListener>
```

We must, however, provide a mapping for the `Order` class. This corresponds to the encoding we previously defined programmatically using the `SOAPMappingRegistry` class.

```
    <isd:mappings>
      <isd:map encodingStyle="http://schemas.xmlsoap.org/soap/encoding/"
               xmlns:x="urn:lesavon-order" qname="x:order"
               javaType="com.lesavon.Order"
        java2XMLClassName="org.apache.soap.encoding.soapenc.BeanSerializer"
        xml2JavaClassName="org.apache.soap.encoding.soapenc.BeanSerializer"/>
    </isd:mappings>
  </isd:service>
```

We must specify mapping for our custom classes, otherwise the Apache SOAP framework will not know how to serialize the objects in and out of XML. If we submit a request for an object that has no known mappings, we will get a fault similar to the one below. This is the result of a call to `getOrderList()` without the mapping for `Order` begin provided on the server:

```
HTTP/1.0 500 Internal Server Error
Content-Type: text/xml; charset=utf-8
Content-Length: 1793
Set-Cookie2: JSESSIONID=9n6k9wo8v1;Version=1;Discard;Path="/lesavon"
Set-Cookie: JSESSIONID=9n6k9wo8v1;Path=/lesavon
Servlet-Engine: Tomcat Web Server/3.2.1 (JSP 1.1; Servlet 2.2; Java 1.3.0;
Windows 2000 5.0 x86; java.vendor=Sun Microsystems Inc.)

<?xml version='1.0' encoding='UTF-8'?>
<SOAP-ENV:Envelope
xmlns:SOAP-ENV="http://schemas.xmlsoap.org/soap/envelope/"
```

```
xmlns:xsi="http://www.w3.org/1999/XMLSchema-instance"
xmlns:xsd="http://www.w3.org/1999/XMLSchema">
<SOAP-ENV:Body>
<SOAP-ENV:Fault>
<faultcode>SOAP-ENV:Server</faultcode>
<faultstring>java.lang.IllegalArgumentException: No mapping found for
'com.lesavon.Order' using encoding style
'http://schemas.xmlsoap.org/soap/encoding/'.</faultstring>
<faultactor>/lesavon/ncrouter/</faultactor>
<detail>
<stackTrace>[SOAPException: faultCode=SOAP-ENV:Server;
msg=java.lang.IllegalArgumentException: No mapping found for
'com.lesavon.Order' using encoding style
'http://schemas.xmlsoap.org/soap/encoding/'.]
<!-- stack trace removed from listing -->
</stackTrace>
</detail>
</SOAP-ENV:Fault>

</SOAP-ENV:Body>
</SOAP-ENV:Envelope>
```

Many of `java.lang` classes (`String`, `Double`, etc.) and `java.util` classes (`Date`, `Vector`, etc.) have built-in serialization.

The last missing link in the SOAP server implementation of LeSavon.com is registration. We could register our services using the `ServiceManagerClient` class as what we did for the HelloWorld sample back in Chapter 3. However, as we will discuss in the next section, this client-based registration has several drawbacks.

Before reviewing more code, let's look at what we have achieved so far. We have defined two interfaces and their implementation to provide the `Admin` and the `Order` service. The implementation of those services had little to do with SOAP. We used JDBC code but very little actual SOAP code. If we had designed those services as an in-process API, it would have been very similar.

Well, this is almost true because of the `SavonException` that uses the `SOAPException` class as a base class. It is quite remarkable that the Apache SOAP framework isolates the developer so well from actual SOAP development.

Registration

In Chapter 3, we registered (or deployed) the HelloWorld Service using the `ServiceManagerClient` and the deployment descriptor `HelloWorld.xml`. This methodology, although adequate for development, is not suitable for a production system. If clients are allowed to register and un-register services at will, there is no way to predict the state of the system. Clearly, this is not acceptable in a mission critical system.

Another potential showstopper is security. The `ServiceManager()` methods do not follow our security scheme of having a user name and a password to protect administrator-level functionality. One could argue that since the web server handles authentication, if you were to deny all access to non-authenticated users, this would solve the problem. This is not the case, because you do not want your general user community to have access to administration capabilities. A more secure solution is required.

A potential solution to prevent your general user community from accessing administration functionalities is to restrict the access of administration URLs. However, this solution does not handle the issues related to the client-based registration. In addition, this kind of decentralized, ad-hoc solution tends to multiply the security points of failure. It is one more configuration step that the system administrator must perform when installing our application. Forgetting that step will not prevent the application from working, making it more likely that a breach of security will go undetected.

There are also other issues inherent in having client code handle the registration of our services. It makes it harder to write an installation program since we will have to write client code that will be invoked by the installation program. In addition, the set of registered services is saved to `DeployedServices.ds`, which is a serialized hash table. Using a binary file makes it slightly harder to debug the server since the services and their methods are not readily available.

An easy to manage and secure solution, that addresses the server problems as well as the client problems, is possible. The solution is to have the list of registered services on the server and move the responsibility of service registration to the `ServiceManager` when the server starts up. Actually, this is the way the `ServiceManager` handles its own registration, but it is with special code rather than populating the list of deployed services, as you can tell from the `ServiceManager.query()` implementation shown below:

```
public DeploymentDescriptor query(String id) throws SOAPException {
  if (id == null)
    return null;
  else if (id.equals (ServerConstants.SERVICE_MANAGER_SERVICE_NAME))
    return smsdd;
  else {
    DeploymentDescriptor dd = configMgr.query( id );
    if (dd != null)
      return dd;
```

Fortunately, the Apache SOAP framework comes with a customization mechanism that is designed to handle situations like this: the `ServiceManager` looks for a file called `soap.xml` at startup time. If it can find the `soap.xml` file, the `ServiceManager` will extract a class name for a configuration manager, instantiate the class for the manager and call its `setOptions()` method with the content of the `soap.xml` file.

The configuration manager created through this mechanism will be responsible for handling all registration-related requests: `deploy()`, `undeploy()`, `list()`, and `query()`. If you do not specify a custom configuration manager, the `ServiceManager` will instantiate a default configuration manager: `DefaultConfigManager`. The HelloWorld sample in Chapter 3 was using the default configuration manager.

Now that we are aware of the hooks that we can use in Apache SOAP to implement our own registration behavior, let's see how we can use them, starting with the configuration file `soap.xml`:

```
<!-- LeSavon SOAP Server Configuration File -->
<soapServer>
    <configManager value="com.lesavon.LeSavonConfigManager">
        <option name="defaultPackage" value="com.lesavon"/>
        <option name="services"
                value="RemoteAdmin,RemoteOrder"/>
    </configManager>
</soapServer>
```

This file should be stored in the C:\ProJavaSoap\Chapter5\etc folder. We will amend the ANT script file to copy it to the relevant folder in our web application.

LeSavonConfigManager handles the implementation of the registration for LeSavon.com. This is the class name specified as the value attribute on the <configManager> tag.

The options listed inside the <configManager> are specific to the relevant configuration manager. However, they must be name/value pairs since the ServiceManager reads them and puts them in a hashtable before passing them to the custom configuration manager.

The LeSavonConfigManager supports two options:

- defaultPackage
  This option specifies a default package name for the list of services. This frees us from having to specify the package name repeatedly in the services option.
- services
  The list of services that should be registered on this server. The list is comma-separated.

Let's see how this translates into code with LeSavonConfigManager:

```
// LeSavonConfigManager.java

package com.lesavon;

import java.util.Hashtable;
import java.util.Enumeration;
import java.util.StringTokenizer;
import java.io.File;
import java.io.FileReader;
import java.io.FileNotFoundException;
```

Since the deployment descriptors are read from disk and stored in a hashtable, we need classes from java.util and java.io. We do not need any DOM or SAX functionality since the parsing of the configuration file and the deployment descriptor file is handled outside of this class, by the Apache SOAP engine.

```
import javax.servlet.ServletContext;

import org.apache.soap.Constants;
import org.apache.soap.SOAPException;
import org.apache.soap.server.DeploymentDescriptor;
import org.apache.soap.util.ConfigManager;
```

We use the ServletContext object for logging.

```
public class LeSavonConfigManager implements ConfigManager {
  private String[] services;
  private ServletContext context;
  private Hashtable      descriptors = new Hashtable();
```

We keep the list of deployed services in the `descriptors` hashtable to support the `query()` and `list()` methods.

```
  public void setContext(ServletContext context) {
    this.context = context;
  }

  public void setOptions(Hashtable options) {
    if(options == null) return;

    String defaultPackage = (String)options.get("defaultPackage");
    if(null == defaultPackage) {
      defaultPackage = "";
    }

    String services   = (String) options.get("services");
    StringTokenizer tokenizer = new StringTokenizer(services, ",");
```

As we mentioned before, the default package and list of services is passed to `setOptions()` by the `ServiceManager` in the form of a hashtable. We look for the options we know and then use a `StringTokenizer` to parse the list of services.

```
    while(tokenizer.hasMoreTokens()) {
      String serviceName = tokenizer.nextToken();

      if(serviceName.indexOf('.') == -1) {
        serviceName = defaultPackage + "." + serviceName;
      }

      String fileName = context.getRealPath("\\WEB-INF\\classes\\")
                  + serviceName.replace('.', File.separatorChar) + ".xml";
```

The configuration manager assumes that it can find the descriptor files in the same directory as the interfaces for the services. In this case, this means the `C:\ProJavaSoap\Chapter05\webapps\lesavon\WEB-INF\classes\com\lesavon` directory.

```
      try {
        DeploymentDescriptor descriptor =
        DeploymentDescriptor.fromXML(new FileReader(fileName));
        descriptors.put(descriptor.getID(), descriptor);
        context.log("Service " + serviceName + " (" + fileName
                 + ") has been registered.");
      } catch(FileNotFoundException fileNotFoundException) {
       context.log("LeSavonConfigManager.setOptions: Cannot open "
                 + fileName + " for reading");
      }
    }
  }
```

For each service that we need to register, we build a path name to the descriptor file and parse the file using the `DeploymentDescriptorfromXML()` helper method. We save registered services in the `descriptors` hashtable. The `context.log()` method adds a message to the servlet engine log. This should be used rather than `System.out()` or `System.err()` to allow the servlet engine to control what is logged.

```
public void init() throws SOAPException {
}

public void deploy( DeploymentDescriptor dd ) throws SOAPException {
  throw new SOAPException(Constants.FAULT_CODE_SERVER,
                          "Operation not supported");
}

public DeploymentDescriptor undeploy( String id ) throws SOAPException {
  throw new SOAPException(Constants.FAULT_CODE_SERVER,
                          "Operation not supported");
}
```

The methods `deploy()` and `undeploy()` cannot be called, for the security reasons that we discussed earlier. Only the automatic registration of the services on startup is supported.

```
  public String[] list() throws SOAPException {
    if(services == null) {
      services = new String[descriptors.size()];
      Enumeration enum = descriptors.keys();
      for(int index = 0; index < descriptors.size(); index++) {
        services[index] = (String)enum.nextElement ();
      }
    }

    return services;
  }

  public DeploymentDescriptor query(String id) throws SOAPException {
    return (DeploymentDescriptor)descriptors.get(id);
  }
};
```

The implementation of `list()` and `query()` is straightforward with the `descriptors` hashtable. We cache the list of services for performance reasons.

By using a custom configuration manager, we have a registration solution that is easy to use and secure. To add or remove services, you simply need to modify the `soap.xml` file.

To illustrate the new security, unlike in the default manager, if you were to try to deploy a service for LeSavon.com with the following command:

```
C:\projavasoap\Chapter05>java org.apache.soap.server.ServiceManagerClient
http://localhost:8080/lesavon/ncrouter deploy RemoteAdmin.xml
```

You would get the following answer; (the "*Ouch*"is hard-coded in the `ServiceManagerClient`):

```
Ouch, the call failed:
  Fault Code   = SOAP-ENV:Server
  Fault String = Operation not supported
```

However, `query()` and `list()` methods are still accessible.

```
C:\projavasoap\Chapter05>java org.apache.soap.server.ServiceManagerClient
http://localhost:8080/lesavon/ncrouter list
```

This call to `list` will return the following response:

```
Deployed Services:
        urn:order
        urn:admin
```

In Chapter 12, we will add Universal Description, Discovery, and Integration (UDDI) support to LeSavon.com, which will provide the same functionality but using a *de facto* standard.

This concludes our description of the SOAP server. We have seen in the previous pages that the Apache SOAP frees the SOAP developer from low-level SOAP API coding: as an application developer, you can concentrate on the problem you are trying to solve.

Build and Test

Before we can continue, we must define the mappings in our lesavon web application for Tomcat.

```
<!DOCTYPE web-app
    PUBLIC "-//Sun Microsystems, Inc.//DTD Web Application 2.2//EN"
    "http://java.sun.com/j2ee/dtds/web-app_2_2.dtd">

<web-app>
    <display-name>Le Savon Application</display-name>
    <description>
        This is the Le Savon Application.
    </description>
```

We map `com.lesavon.service.Serveur` to the name "Le Serveur". We now route all calls to /serveur to this servlet. This will mean that any client that attempts to connect to `http://localhost:8080/lesavon/serveur` will have its request forwarded to the Serveur (cached) router.

```
<servlet>
  <servlet-name>Le Serveur</servlet-name>
  <servlet-class>com.lesavon.service.Serveur</servlet-class>
</servlet>
```

```
<servlet-mapping>
  <servlet-name>Le Serveur</servlet-name>
  <url-pattern>/serveur</url-pattern>
</servlet-mapping>

<servlet-mapping>
  <servlet-name>Le Serveur</servlet-name>
  <url-pattern>/serveur/</url-pattern>
</servlet-mapping>
```

The `RPCRouterServlet` is named "Non-Cached Router" and it is mapped to any calls for `/ncrouter` in the lesavon web application.

```
  <servlet>
    <servlet-name>Non-Cached Router</servlet-name>
    <display-name>Apache-SOAP RPC Router</display-name>
    <description>A router with no cache.</description>
    <servlet-class>
      org.apache.soap.server.http.RPCRouterServlet
    </servlet-class>
    <init-param>
      <param-name>faultListener</param-name>
      <param-value>org.apache.soap.server.DOMFaultListener</param-value>
    </init-param>
  </servlet>

  <servlet-mapping>
    <servlet-name>Non-Cached Router</servlet-name>
    <url-pattern>/ncrouter</url-pattern>
  </servlet-mapping>

  <servlet-mapping>
    <servlet-name>Non-Cached Router</servlet-name>
    <url-pattern>/ncrouter/</url-pattern>
  </servlet-mapping>
</web-app>
```

The `web.xml` file should be stored in a folder named `C:\ProJavaSoap\Chapter5\etc` together with the `soap.xml` file created earlier. We must now add a couple of lines to the ANT script to make sure that the new files are copied to the correct destinations.

The `web.xml` file must be placed inside the WEB-INF directory of the lesavon web application, ofcourse. We add the following lines to the BuildLeSavon.xml file:

```
<target name="prepare">
  <mkdir  dir="${deploy.home}"/>
  <mkdir dir="${deploy.home}/WEB-INF/";
  <copy  file="etc/web.xml" tofile="${deploy.home}/WEB-INF/web.xml"/>
```

Next, we must copy the `RemoteAdmin.xml` and `RemoteOrder.xml` descriptors to the C:\ProJavaSoap\Chapter05\webapps\lesavon\WEB-INF\classes\com\lesavon directory. Our configuration manager will look for these files here. We must also copy the `soap.xml` file to the lesavon web application directory:

```
<copy file="RemoteAdmin.xml"
      tofile="${deploy.home}/WEB-INF/classes/com/lesavon/RemoteAdmin.xml"/>
<copy file="RemoteOrder.xml"
      tofile="${deploy.home}/WEB-INF/classes/com/lesavon/RemoteOrder.xml"/>

<copy  file="etc/soap.xml" tofile="${deploy.home}/soap.xml"/>
```

The resultant ANT file is called `BuildLeSavon_2.xml` in the code download.

The sample code for this chapter can be found in the `ProJavaSoap\Chapter05\leSavon` directory in the code download. The following screenshot shows a build on a Windows 2000 machine:

```
C:\WINNT\SYSTEM32\CMD.EXE
C:\ProJavaSoap\Chapter05>ant -buildfile BuildLeSavon_2.xml
Buildfile: BuildLeSavon_2.xml

prepare:
    [mkdir] Created dir: C:\ProJavaSoap\Chapter05\webapps\lesavon
    [mkdir] Created dir: C:\ProJavaSoap\Chapter05\webapps\lesavon\WEB-INF
     [copy] Copying 1 file to C:\ProJavaSoap\Chapter05\webapps\lesavon\WEB-INF
     [copy] Copying 1 file to C:\ProJavaSoap\Chapter05\webapps\lesavon\WEB-INF\classes\com\lesavon
     [copy] Copying 1 file to C:\ProJavaSoap\Chapter05\webapps\lesavon\WEB-INF\classes\com\lesavon
     [copy] Copying 1 file to C:\ProJavaSoap\Chapter05\webapps\lesavon

compile:
    [javac] Compiling 14 source files to C:\ProJavaSoap\Chapter05\webapps\lesavon\WEB-INF\classes

BUILD SUCCESSFUL

Total time: 5 seconds
C:\ProJavaSoap\Chapter05>
```

You will have to adjust the classpath to your particular settings, but the list of JAR files should be the same. The `servlet.jar` file must be included in the classpath now since we are compiling servlets. As shown in the previous figure, ANT does most of the work for us.

We will also need to add the following context to Tomcat's `server.xml` as we did in Chapter 3.

```
<Context path="/lesavon"
  docBase="C:\ProJavaSoap\Chapter05\webapps\lesavon"
  reloadable="true" >
</Context>
```

Alternatively, the entire contents of Chapter 5's webapps directory may be moved to Tomcat's directory; this will have the same effect. We can test that the application is installed as we did in Chapter 3, by navigating to http://localhost:8080/lesavon/ncrouter. This should give the message: "Sorry, I don't speak via HTTP GET- you have to use HTTP POST to talk to me" as before. Remember that the ncrouter is being provided by the soap servlet that does not accept GET requests.

To test the `GetOrders` client, you first need to make sure that Tomcat is running. The instructions to set up Tomcat are described in Chapter 3. As usual, pay particular attention to classpath issues. You must make sure that Tomcat can load the new classes by making sure that the system classpath for Tomcat includes the `webapps/lesavon/WEB-INF/classes` as shown in the following screenshot:

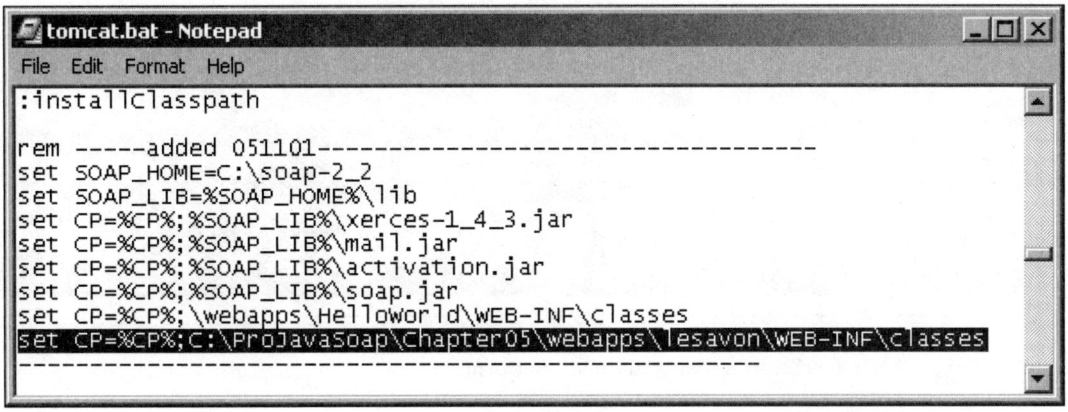

tomcat.bat - Notepad

File Edit Format Help

```
:installClasspath

rem -----added 051101--------------------------------------
set SOAP_HOME=C:\soap-2_2
set SOAP_LIB=%SOAP_HOME%\lib
set CP=%CP%;%SOAP_LIB%\xerces-1_4_3.jar
set CP=%CP%;%SOAP_LIB%\mail.jar
set CP=%CP%;%SOAP_LIB%\activation.jar
set CP=%CP%;%SOAP_LIB%\soap.jar
set CP=%CP%;\webapps\Helloworld\WEB-INF\classes
set CP=%CP%;C:\ProJavaSoap\Chapter05\webapps\lesavon\WEB-INF\classes
-----------------------------------------------------
```

Prior to running, you also need to make sure that the database is set up correctly. Detailed instructions are available in Chapter 4. If you have any problems, or if you are running the application on Linux, the easiest set up that works for all platforms is to run with the `TextAccess` class as shown in the following extract from `OrderService.java`:

```
...//rest of class as before
public OrderService() throws SavonException {
  try {
    docBuilder = DocumentBuilderFactory.
    newInstance().newDocumentBuilder();
  } catch(ParserConfigurationException parserConfigurationException) {
    throw new SavonException(
                    "Cannot create document builder for OrderService",
                    parserConfigurationException);
  }

  try {
    // Create a JDBCAccess for JDBC-ODBC bridge
    //dataAccess = new JDBCAccess();
    dataAccess = new TextAccess();
  } catch(Exception exception) {
    throw new SavonException(
             "Cannot load jdbc/odbc bridge for OrderService", exception);
  }
}
...// rest of class as before
```

For the `TextAccess` object to work, you need to make sure that the path to the text file is a valid one as we did in Chapter 4 as shown in the following few lines out of `TextAccess.java`:

```
...
public class TextAccess implements DataAccess {
  final String FILE_PATH =
                        "C:\\ProJavaSoap\\Chapter04\\Database\\orders.txt";
  final int    MIN_SIZE  = 13;    // Vector of result initial size
...
```

Note that we have added the `lesavon/WEB-INF/classes` directory to the classpath to include `GetOrders.java`.

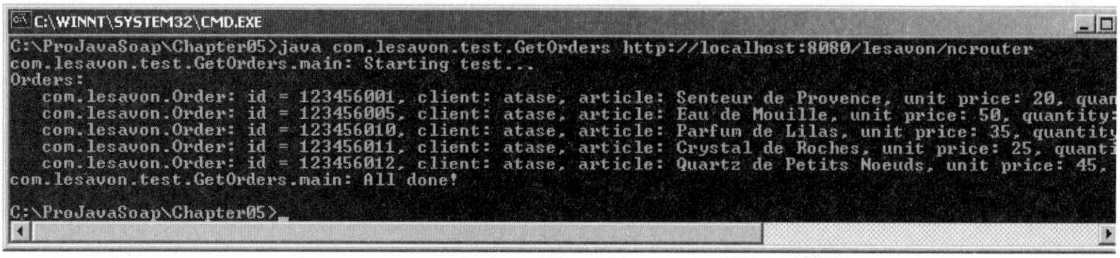

```
C:\WINNT\SYSTEM32\CMD.EXE
C:\ProJavaSoap\Chapter05>java com.lesavon.test.GetOrders http://localhost:8080/lesavon/ncrouter
com.lesavon.test.GetOrders.main: Starting test...
Orders:
   com.lesavon.Order: id = 123456001, client: atase, article: Senteur de Provence, unit price: 20, quan
   com.lesavon.Order: id = 123456005, client: atase, article: Eau de Mouille, unit price: 50, quantity:
   com.lesavon.Order: id = 123456010, client: atase, article: Parfum de Lilas, unit price: 35, quantit
   com.lesavon.Order: id = 123456011, client: atase, article: Crystal de Roches, unit price: 25, quanti
   com.lesavon.Order: id = 123456012, client: atase, article: Quartz de Petits Noeuds, unit price: 45,
com.lesavon.test.GetOrders.main: All done!

C:\ProJavaSoap\Chapter05>_
```

The output of the execution is identical on all platforms:

```
C:\ProJavaSoap\Chapter05>java com.lesavon.test.GetOrders http://localhost:8080/lesavon/ncrouter
com.lesavon.test.GetOrders.main: Starting test...
Orders:
  com.lesavon.Order: id = 123456001, client: atase, article: Senteur de Provence, unit price: 20,
quantity: 5
, total price: 100
  com.lesavon.Order: id = 123456005, client: atase, article: Eau de Mouille, unit price: 50, quantity:
2, tot
al price: 100
  com.lesavon.Order: id = 123456010, client: atase, article: Parfum de Lilas, unit price: 35, quantity:
1, to
tal price: 35
  com.lesavon.Order: id = 123456011, client: atase, article: Crystal de Roches, unit price: 25,
quantity: 1,
total price: 25
  com.lesavon.Order: id = 123456012, client: atase, article: Quartz de Petits Noeuds, unit price: 45,
quantit
y: 1, total price: 45
com.lesavon.test.GetOrders.main: All done!
```

The request that was sent to the server contains a simple SOAP call with one argument:

```
POST /lesavon/ncrouter HTTP/1.0
Host: localhost
Content-Type: text/xml; charset=utf-8
Content-Length: 456
SOAPAction: ""

<?xml version='1.0' encoding='UTF-8'?>
<SOAP-ENV:Envelope xmlns:SOAP-ENV="http://schemas.xmlsoap.org/soap/envelope/"
xmlns:xsi="http://www.w3.org/1999/XMLSchema-instance"
xmlns:xsd="http://www.w3.org/1999/XMLSchema">
  <SOAP-ENV:Body>
    <ns1:getOrderList xmlns:ns1="urn:order">
      <username
         xsi:type="xsd:string"
         SOAP-ENV:encodingStyle="http://schemas.xmlsoap.org/soap/encoding/">
         atase
```

```
      </userName>
    </ns1:getOrderList>
  </SOAP-ENV:Body>
</SOAP-ENV:Envelope>
```

The response from the server contains the serialization of an array of `Order` objects:

```
HTTP/1.0 200 OK
Content-Type: text/xml; charset=utf-8
Content-Length: 2184
Set-Cookie2: JSESSIONID=bqlf3p0ym1;Version=1;Discard;Path="/lesavon"
Set-Cookie: JSESSIONID=bqlf3p0ym1;Path=/lesavon
Servlet-Engine: Tomcat Web Server/3.2.1 (JSP 1.1; Servlet 2.2; Java 1.3.0; Windows
2000 5.0 x86; java.vendor=Sun Microsystems Inc.)

<?xml version='1.0' encoding='UTF-8'?>
<SOAP-ENV:Envelope xmlns:SOAP-ENV="http://schemas.xmlsoap.org/soap/envelope/"
xmlns:xsi="http://www.w3.org/1999/XMLSchema-instance"
xmlns:xsd="http://www.w3.org/1999/XMLSchema">
<SOAP-ENV:Body>
<ns1:getOrderListResponse xmlns:ns1="urn:order" SOAP-
ENV:encodingStyle="http://schemas.xmlsoap.org/soap/encoding/">
<return xmlns:ns2="http://schemas.xmlsoap.org/soap/encoding/" xsi:type="ns2:Array"
xmlns:ns3="urn:lesavon-order" ns2:arrayType="ns3:order[5]">
<item xsi:type="ns3:order">
<totalPrice xsi:type="xsd:int">100</totalPrice>
<client xsi:type="xsd:string">Senteur de Provence</client>
<unitPrice xsi:type="xsd:int">20</unitPrice>
<quantity xsi:type="xsd:int">5</quantity>
<article xsi:type="xsd:string">atase</article>
<id xsi:type="xsd:int">123456001</id>
</item>
```

The `<item xsi:type="ns3:order"> ... </item>` element is the serialization of an `Order` object.

```
<item xsi:type="ns3:order">
<totalPrice xsi:type="xsd:int">100</totalPrice>
<client xsi:type="xsd:string">Eau de Mouille</client>
<unitPrice xsi:type="xsd:int">50</unitPrice>
<quantity xsi:type="xsd:int">2</quantity>
<article xsi:type="xsd:string">atase</article>
<id xsi:type="xsd:int">123456005</id>
</item>
<item xsi:type="ns3:order">
<totalPrice xsi:type="xsd:int">35</totalPrice>
<client xsi:type="xsd:string">Parfum de Lilas</client>
<unitPrice xsi:type="xsd:int">35</unitPrice>
<quantity xsi:type="xsd:int">1</quantity>
<article xsi:type="xsd:string">atase</article>
<id xsi:type="xsd:int">123456010</id>
</item>
<item xsi:type="ns3:order">
```

```
<totalPrice xsi:type="xsd:int">25</totalPrice>
<client xsi:type="xsd:string">Crystal de Roches</client>
<unitPrice xsi:type="xsd:int">25</unitPrice>
<quantity xsi:type="xsd:int">1</quantity>
<article xsi:type="xsd:string">atase</article>
<id xsi:type="xsd:int">123456011</id>
</item>
<item xsi:type="ns3:order">
<totalPrice xsi:type="xsd:int">45</totalPrice>
<client xsi:type="xsd:string">Quartz de Petits Noeuds</client>
<unitPrice xsi:type="xsd:int">45</unitPrice>
<quantity xsi:type="xsd:int">1</quantity>
<article xsi:type="xsd:string">atase</article>
<id xsi:type="xsd:int">123456012</id>
</item>
</return>
</ns1:getOrderListResponse>

</SOAP-ENV:Body>
</SOAP-ENV:Envelope>
```

With the completion of our custom registration, we have achieved a significant milestone: we have designed, written, and deployed two functional SOAP services. These services are not complete enough to meet the requirements of LeSavon.com, but this might be enough for your application. The main missing link in this particular case is an interface to an enterprise directory system. Another significant missing link is the cache. We will work on these components as we continue through the book.

We will conclude this chapter by looking at another extension to the Apache SOAP server: custom serialization.

Custom Serialization

The objects that we have been dealing with so far are serialized using the `org.apache.soap.encoding.soapenc.BeanSerializer` class, or with Apache SOAP built-in serialization. Most of the objects that you will be using in your application can be handled in the same manner. However, there are a few cases where this methodology will not work or at least will not be very efficient. For instance, if you need to serialize a final class that is not a Java Bean, you can either wrap the class into a Bean or write a custom serializer.

As an example of custom serialization, we will look at the `java.sql.Timestamp` class. This class is not handled by the SOAP Apache framework out of the box. Before we start, let's agree on some definitions regarding the serialization process. Note that these definitions are tailored for the context of this book: SOAP development.

> *A time stamp is not a data type supported by the XML schema specification. See http://www.w3.org/TR/xmlschema-2/ for further details.*

- **Serialization** or **marshaling** is the process of writing Java objects to an XML document.
- **Deserialization** or **unmarshaling** is the process of reading an object definition from an XML document and creating a Java object based on that definition.

To implement custom serialization we will provide two methods: one method to marshal a time stamp and another to un-marshal it. For the purposes of this example, we will define a new SOAP service, `TimeStampService`.

The URN of the service is `urn:timestamp` and the service has one method:

```
public Timestamp getTimestamp() {
    return new Timestamp(System.currentTimeMillis());
}
```

So far, this is very similar to what we did for the HelloWorld service. Things start being different with the `<isd:mappings>` tag:

```
<isd:service
  xmlns:isd="http://xml.apache.org/xml-soap/deployment" id="urn:timestamp">
  <isd:provider type="java"
                scope="Request"
                methods="getTimestamp">
    <isd:java class="com.lesavon.service.TimestampService" static="false"/>
  </isd:provider>
  <isd:mappings>
    <isd:map encodingStyle="http://schemas.xmlsoap.org/soap/encoding/"
             xmlns:x="http://www.wrox.com/lesavon/XMLSchema"
             qname="x:timestamp"
             javaType="java.sql.Timestamp"
             java2XMLClassName="com.lesavon.TimestampSerializer"
             xml2JavaClassName="com.lesavon.TimestampDeserializer"/>
  </isd:mappings>
</isd:service>
```

We define a namespace that is specific to our application, along with the class that we need to serialize and we assign a `qname` (namespace-qualified name). We will see the use of the `qname` shortly. We also specify what class should be used to marshal our object: `java2XMLClassName`, and also another class to un-marshal our objects: `xml2JavaClassName`.

Let's have a look at the serializer class (`com.lesavon.TimestampSerializer`):

```
// TimestampSerializer.java

package com.lesavon;

import java.io.Writer;
import java.io.IOException;
import java.sql.Timestamp;

import org.apache.soap.util.xml.Serializer;
import org.apache.soap.util.xml.NSStack;
import org.apache.soap.util.xml.XMLJavaMappingRegistry;
import org.apache.soap.encoding.soapenc.SoapEncUtils;
import org.apache.soap.rpc.SOAPContext;
```

```
public class TimestampSerializer implements Serializer {

    */
    public void marshall(String inScopeEncStyle, Class javaType, Object src,
        Object context, Writer sink, NSStack nsStack,
        XMLJavaMappingRegistry xjmr,
        SOAPContext ctx) throws IllegalArgumentException, IOException {
        // src must be a time stamp
        if(src instanceof Timestamp) {
            Timestamp ts = (Timestamp)src;
```

We can ignore most of the arguments that are passed to us by the framework. However, it is valuable to understand what they are, should you need them in another situation:

- `String inScopeEncStyle`
  This string is the URI of the encoding being used for the current element. For instance, the value for the SOAP encoding is `http://schemas.xmlsoap.org/soap/encoding`.
- `Class javaType`
  The class of the type currently being marshaled. In our case it should be `java.sql.TimeStamp`.
- `Object src`
  The object being marshaled. For our sample, it should be an instance of `java.sql.TimeStamp`.
- `Object context`
  The name of the SOAP accessor for the element that will contained the result of the serialization. For instance, when serializing a time stamp as a return value for a method, the accessor will be `return` (`<return/>`).
- `Java.io.Writer sink`
  The `unmarshall()` method is expected to write the result of the serialization to this `Writer` which is typically an instance of `java.io.StringWriter`.
- `org.apache.soap.util.xml.NSStack nsStack`
  The namespace stack is used to keep track of namespace of the current element (see below).
- `org.apache.soap.util.xml.XMLJavaMappingRegistry xjmr`
  The SOAP mapping registry that we already encountered during registration. In practice it will be an instance of the `SOAPMappingRegistry`, which is an `XMLJavaMappingRegistry` with pre-registered serializers for SOAP (for example `String`, `Date`, etc.).
- `org.apache.soap.rpc.SOAPContext ctx`
  The SOAP context aggregates the SOAP body and the MIME part of the SOAP message, if any.

Since we do not support other encoding than SOAP encoding, and we do not need to look at other mappings or the SOAP call in progress, we can ignore most of the arguments.

The `src` object is the object to serialize, which will be a `Timestamp` if everything went well during the registration process.

The next statement in the `TimeStampSerializer` class requires a few comments:

```
nsStack.pushScope();    // We are entering a new name space scope
```

The `nsStack` object keeps track of name space declarations. A call to `pushScope()` creates a vector of prefix/URI pairs. A call to `popScope()` deletes the top vector. When methods need to add a namespace declaration to the current scope, they call the stack `addNSDeclaration()` method to add a namespace to the top-level vector.

The use of a vector allows the framework to keep track of all the namespaces that have been declared for an element. Without this vector, unrelated methods would potentially declare the same namespace multiple times. The use of a stack allows unrelated methods to keep track of nested namespace declarations.

The next instruction also requires further explanation:

```
SoapEncUtils.generateStructureHeader(inScopeEncStyle,
                javaType, context, sink, nsStack, xjmr);
```

The `SoapEncUtils.generateStructureHeader()` is a helper function that writes the tag for our time stamp. For instance, if the context of the call was `return`, the output of `generateStructureHeader()` would be the following XML element:

```
<return
 xmlns:ns2="http://www.wrox.com/lesavon/XMLSchema"
 xsi:type="ns2:timestamp">
```

Once we have the XML element generated, we can write it to the `sink` object as shown in the following statement:

```
            sink.write(ts + "</" + context + '>');

            nsStack.popScope();     // We are leaving a naming scope
        } else {
            throw new IllegalArgumentException(
               "Argument must be a Timestamp");
        }
    }
}
```

Once we have the tag, we still need to write the actual value, along with the closing tag. Again, if the context is `return`, then the closing tag would be `</return>`. We finally pop the namespace stack scope.

The de-serializer class (`com.lesavon.TimestampDeserializer`) follows a similar pattern:

```
// TimestampDeserializer.java

package com.lesavon;

import java.sql.Timestamp;
```

```
import org.apache.soap.util.xml.Deserializer;
import org.apache.soap.util.xml.QName;
import org.apache.soap.util.xml.XMLJavaMappingRegistry;
import org.apache.soap.rpc.SOAPContext;
import org.apache.soap.util.Bean;
import org.apache.soap.util.xml.DOMUtils;

import org.w3c.dom.Node;
import org.w3c.dom.Element;

public class TimestampDeserializer implements Deserializer {

  public Bean unmarshall(String inScopeEncStyle, QName elementType,
                         Node src, XMLJavaMappingRegistry xjmr,
                         SOAPContext ctx)
       throws IllegalArgumentException {
```

Most arguments are identical to those we saw in the `marshall()` method. The `elementType` argument is not a Java type; rather it is the `qname` that we defined in the deployment descriptor. The `src` object contains the DOM element that is the XML representation of our object, in this case a `Timestamp`.

```
    Element root = (Element)src;
    String value = DOMUtils.getChildCharacterData(root);
```

We extract the value (what is contained inside the beginning and end tags) as a string.

```
    return new Bean(Timestamp.class, Timestamp.valueOf(value));
  }
}
```

We finally create an instance of the `Timestamp` object and wrap it inside an `org.apache.soap.util.Bean` object. This works fine with objects that are not Java Beans, like the `Timestamp` object.

Now that all the pieces for custom serialization are in place, let's have a look at the client code (`com.lesavon.test.SerializerTestClient`):

```
// SerializerTestClient.java     1.0 08/162001

package com.lesavon.test;

import java.net.URL;
import java.util.Vector;
import java.util.Arrays;
import java.sql.Timestamp;

import org.apache.soap.Constants;
import org.apache.soap.SOAPException;
import org.apache.soap.Envelope;
import org.apache.soap.Fault;
```

```
import org.apache.soap.rpc.Call;
import org.apache.soap.rpc.Response;
import org.apache.soap.rpc.Parameter;
import org.apache.soap.encoding.SOAPMappingRegistry;
import org.apache.soap.util.xml.QName;

import com.lesavon.TimestampSerializer;
import com.lesavon.TimestampDeserializer;
```

We need to import the serializer and the de-serializer because they must be registered manually.

```
public class SerializerTestClient {
    public static void main(String args[]) {
        String  methodName   = "com.lesavon.test.SerializerTestClient.main";
        String  url          = "http://localhost:8081/helloworld/rpcrouter";
        String  uri          = "urn:timestamp"; // must match Timestamp.xml
        String  remoteMethod = "getTimestamp";

        if(args.length != 0) {
            System.err.println(
                "SerializerTestClient: invokes a SOAP service.");
            System.err.println("Usage: SerializerTestClient");
            System.exit(1);
        }

        System.out.println(methodName + ": Starting test...");

        try {
            Call call  = new Call();

            call.setTargetObjectURI(uri);
            call.setMethodName(remoteMethod);

            // We register a custom string serializer
            SOAPMappingRegistry smr = new SOAPMappingRegistry();

            smr.mapTypes(Constants.NS_URI_SOAP_ENC,
                new QName("http://www.wrox.com/lesavon/XMLSchema",
                          "timestamp"),
                     Class.forName("java.sql.Timestamp"),
                     new TimestampSerializer(),
                     new TimestampDeserializer());
            call.setSOAPMappingRegistry(smr);
```

To register custom serialization objects for a given class, we need to create a qualified name that associates a short name (`timestamp`) to a URL (`http://www.wrox.com/lesavon/XMLSchema`). We also need to specify the class that we want to serialize and the objects that are going to handle the marshaling and un-marshaling operations.

```
            Response resp = call.invoke(new URL(url), "");

            // Check the response.
```

```
            if (resp.generatedFault()) {
                Fault fault = resp.getFault();

                System.out.println(methodName + ": Call to " + remoteMethod
                    + " returned a fault!");
                System.out.println("  Fault code: " + fault.getFaultCode());
                System.out.println("  Fault string: "
                    + fault.getFaultString());
            } else {
                if (resp.getReturnValue() != null) {
                    Object result = resp.getReturnValue().getValue();

                   System.out.println("Timestamp on the server: " + result);
                }
            }
        } catch (Exception exception) {
            System.err.println(methodName + ": Error, caught exception: "
                + exception);
        }

        System.out.println(methodName + ": All done!");
    }
}
```

The rest of the code is very similar to the HelloWorld client. Before running the test, we must build and register the `TimeStampService`. The files we have created are added to the relevant folders as below:

C:\ProJavaSoap\Chapter05\TimeStampt.xml
C:\ProJavaSoap\Chapter05\src\com\lesavon\TimestampDeserializer.java
C:\ProJavaSoap\Chapter05\src\com\lesavon\TimestampSerializer.java
C:\ProJavaSoap\Chapter05\src\com\lesavon\service\TimestamptService.java
C:\ProJavaSoap\Chapter05\src\com\lesavon\test\SerializerTestClient.java

In order to make sure that ncrouter registers our service, we must also add it to the `soap.xml` file. This will ensure it is automatically deployed:

```
<!-- LeSavon SOAP Server Configuration File -->
<soapServer>
    <configManager value="com.lesavon.LeSavonConfigManager">
        <option name="defaultPackage" value="com.lesavon"/>
        <option name="services"
                value="RemoteAdmin,RemoteOrder,TimeStamp"/>
    </configManager>
</soapServer>
```

We will also need to add a line to the ANT script that copies `TimeStamp.xml` to the `com.lesavon` directory for the `configManager` to pick up for deployment:

```
<copy  file="RemoteOrder.xml"
   tofile="${deploy.home}/WEB-INF/classes/com/lesavon/RemoteOrder.xml"/>
<copy  file="TimeStampt.xml"
   tofile="${deploy.home}/WEB-INF/classes/com/lesavon/TimeStamp.xml"/>
    <copy  file="etc/soap.xml" tofile="${deploy.home}/soap.xml"/>
```

Compile the code using ANT:

>ant –buildfile BuildLeSavon.xml

We can check that the service is registered using the admin service as usual.

It is perfectly acceptable to register the timestamp service with the HelloWorld router that we created in Chapter 3. The router will handle any service that is deployed at its URL.

Running the test gives us the following output:

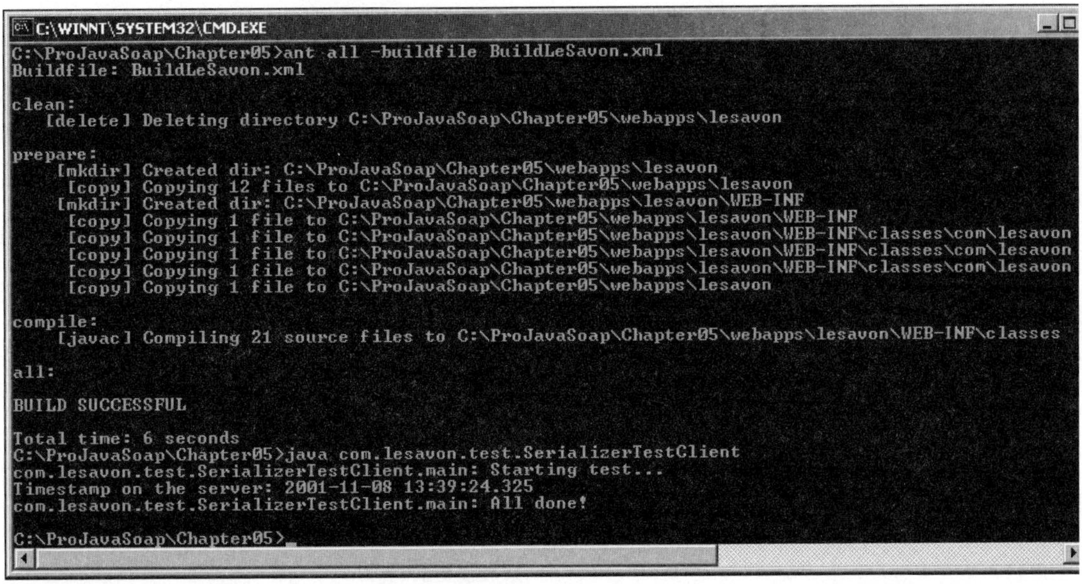

```
C:\WINNT\SYSTEM32\CMD.EXE
C:\ProJavaSoap\Chapter05>ant all -buildfile BuildLeSavon.xml
Buildfile: BuildLeSavon.xml

clean:
   [delete] Deleting directory C:\ProJavaSoap\Chapter05\webapps\lesavon

prepare:
    [mkdir] Created dir: C:\ProJavaSoap\Chapter05\webapps\lesavon
     [copy] Copying 12 files to C:\ProJavaSoap\Chapter05\webapps\lesavon
    [mkdir] Created dir: C:\ProJavaSoap\Chapter05\webapps\lesavon\WEB-INF
     [copy] Copying 1 file to C:\ProJavaSoap\Chapter05\webapps\lesavon\WEB-INF
     [copy] Copying 1 file to C:\ProJavaSoap\Chapter05\webapps\lesavon\WEB-INF\classes\com\lesavon
     [copy] Copying 1 file to C:\ProJavaSoap\Chapter05\webapps\lesavon\WEB-INF\classes\com\lesavon
     [copy] Copying 1 file to C:\ProJavaSoap\Chapter05\webapps\lesavon\WEB-INF\classes\com\lesavon
     [copy] Copying 1 file to C:\ProJavaSoap\Chapter05\webapps\lesavon

compile:
    [javac] Compiling 21 source files to C:\ProJavaSoap\Chapter05\webapps\lesavon\WEB-INF\classes

all:

BUILD SUCCESSFUL

Total time: 6 seconds
C:\ProJavaSoap\Chapter05>java com.lesavon.test.SerializerTestClient
com.lesavon.test.SerializerTestClient.main: Starting test...
Timestamp on the server: 2001-11-08 13:39:24.325
com.lesavon.test.SerializerTestClient.main: All done!

C:\ProJavaSoap\Chapter05>_
```

The request is an empty method call over SOAP:

```
POST /helloworld/rpcrouter HTTP/1.0
Host: localhost
Content-Type: text/xml; charset=utf-8
Content-Length: 343
SOAPAction: ""

<?xml version='1.0' encoding='UTF-8'?>
<SOAP-ENV:Envelope xmlns:SOAP-ENV="http://schemas.xmlsoap.org/soap/envelope/"
xmlns:xsi="http://www.w3.org/1999/XMLSchema-instance"
xmlns:xsd="http://www.w3.org/1999/XMLSchema">
<SOAP-ENV:Body>
```

```
<ns1:getTimestamp xmlns:ns1="urn:timestamp">
</ns1:getTimestamp>
</SOAP-ENV:Body>
</SOAP-ENV:Envelope>
```

The response contains the serialized time stamp object:

```
HTTP/1.0 200 OK
Content-Type: text/xml; charset=utf-8
Content-Length: 544
Set-Cookie2: JSESSIONID=4jqw51r5b1;Version=1;Discard;Path="/helloworld"
Set-Cookie: JSESSIONID=4jqw51r5b1;Path=/helloworld
Servlet-Engine: Tomcat Web Server/3.2.1 (JSP 1.1; Servlet 2.2; Java 1.3.0; Windows
2000 5.0 x86; java.vendor=Sun Microsystems Inc.)

<?xml version='1.0' encoding='UTF-8'?>
<SOAP-ENV:Envelope xmlns:SOAP-ENV="http://schemas.xmlsoap.org/soap/envelope/"
xmlns:xsi="http://www.w3.org/1999/XMLSchema-instance"
xmlns:xsd="http://www.w3.org/1999/XMLSchema">
<SOAP-ENV:Body>
<ns1:getTimestampResponse xmlns:ns1="urn:timestamp" SOAP-
ENV:encodingStyle="http://schemas.xmlsoap.org/soap/encoding/">
<return xmlns:ns2="http://www.wrox.com/lesavon/XMLSchema"
xsi:type="ns2:timestamp"> 2001-11-08 13:39:24.325</return>
</ns1:getTimestampResponse>

</SOAP-ENV:Body>
</SOAP-ENV:Envelope>
```

Now that we have seen how to serialize and de-serialize classes using custom code, we can reflect on the pros and cons of this approach. An advantage of custom serialization is that it gave us the functionality that we need: we just got a `Timestamp` in and out of a SOAP request. The major disadvantage is the loss of interoperability: a non-Java developer would not know what a `java.sql.Timestamp` is. A Java developer would need to get a copy of our custom serialization code or recreate the equivalent. Since openness is a key advantage of SOAP, it is a shame to weaken that advantage by losing interoperability on some methods.

For that reason, it is better to wrap classes that cannot be serialized into Java Beans that can be serialized in an open way. However, there are times when the success of your application depends on custom serialization. A typical reason is performance: without custom serialization, your application could be crippled and unusable.

For instance, if you return long XML documents as strings, any XML special characters will have to be escaped: a '<' must be escaped as '`<`'. This escaping mechanism can significantly increase the size of your documents and noticeably slow down your performance. As a remedy, you could encode the strings in a more straightforward way, such as using Base 64. Once again, this has to be measured against the loss of interoperability.

It is possible to get the best of both worlds by providing an open interface and a performance-oriented interface. In the case of the string, you can define a custom string type that will serialize more efficiently and overload some of your methods: one method returns a string and another method returns a custom string. The methods would have to have different names, as overloading in Java cannot depend on the return value alone.

SOAP Interface Design

Based on the two interfaces that we have designed for retrieving orders and administering the server, we can define some general guidelines on the design of SOAP services:

1. **Make sure that all methods of a SOAP service are stateless.**
   The SOAP specification uses HTTP, a stateless protocol, as transport. Although it is possible to define state by sending values back and forth between the clients and the server, it does not serve scalability and availability very well.

2. **Ensure that all methods of a SOAP service return the same exception.**
   Because the SOAP specification does not include serialized objects in a fault, no exception thrown on the server can make it to the client. By insisting that all methods throw the same exception, no matter what goes wrong, the client can handle all calls in a similar fashion.

3. **Separate the interface definition from the implementation.**
   This rule is a good object-oriented principle, but in designing SOAP services, it becomes a necessity. Without the definition of an interface, it is impossible to write a Proxy-based client. We will elaborate on this issue when we implement the `SavonProxy` in the next chapter.

4. **Use Java Beans in your arguments and return values.**
   By using Java Beans for the objects that you send to and get back from the server, you can rely on the automated serialization provided by Apache SOAP, and thus improve the interoperability of your application.

If you follow those simple rules in designing and writing your SOAP services, you should have no problem leveraging the power of SOAP in your application.

Summary

In this chapter, we have presented the architecture of the sample application in more detail. The architecture choices that we have made so far satisfy our openness requirements. Not only is the application written in Java, but also the web services architecture allows legacy applications to interface to the SOAP API, no matter what their native platform is.

In the design of our web services, we have been careful to separate the interface definition from the implèmentation. Although not required to have a running service, this decision will pay off when we expose our services to clients. The Apache SOAP framework does a good job of hiding the intricacies of distributed development, as our service implementations contain no protocol-level code.

We have developed a secure registration methodology. This alternate registration scheme contains the deployment information on the server in XML files, and prevents unauthorized clients from modifying server configurations, a true nightmare in a replicated server environment.

To test our `Order` service, we wrote a simple client that probably contains more protocol-level code that we would like, including such things as `Call` objects and mappings.

The serialization in and out of XML documents is handled automatically by the Apache SOAP framework. However, there are times when, for performance or design reasons, one needs to write a custom serializer. Apache SOAP provides an extensible mechanism that we easily leveraged to handle the serialization of the JDBC `timestamp` class.

Now that we have a working server running the two web services of the sample application (LeSavon.com), we can concentrate on writing client code. That is the topic of Chapter 6.

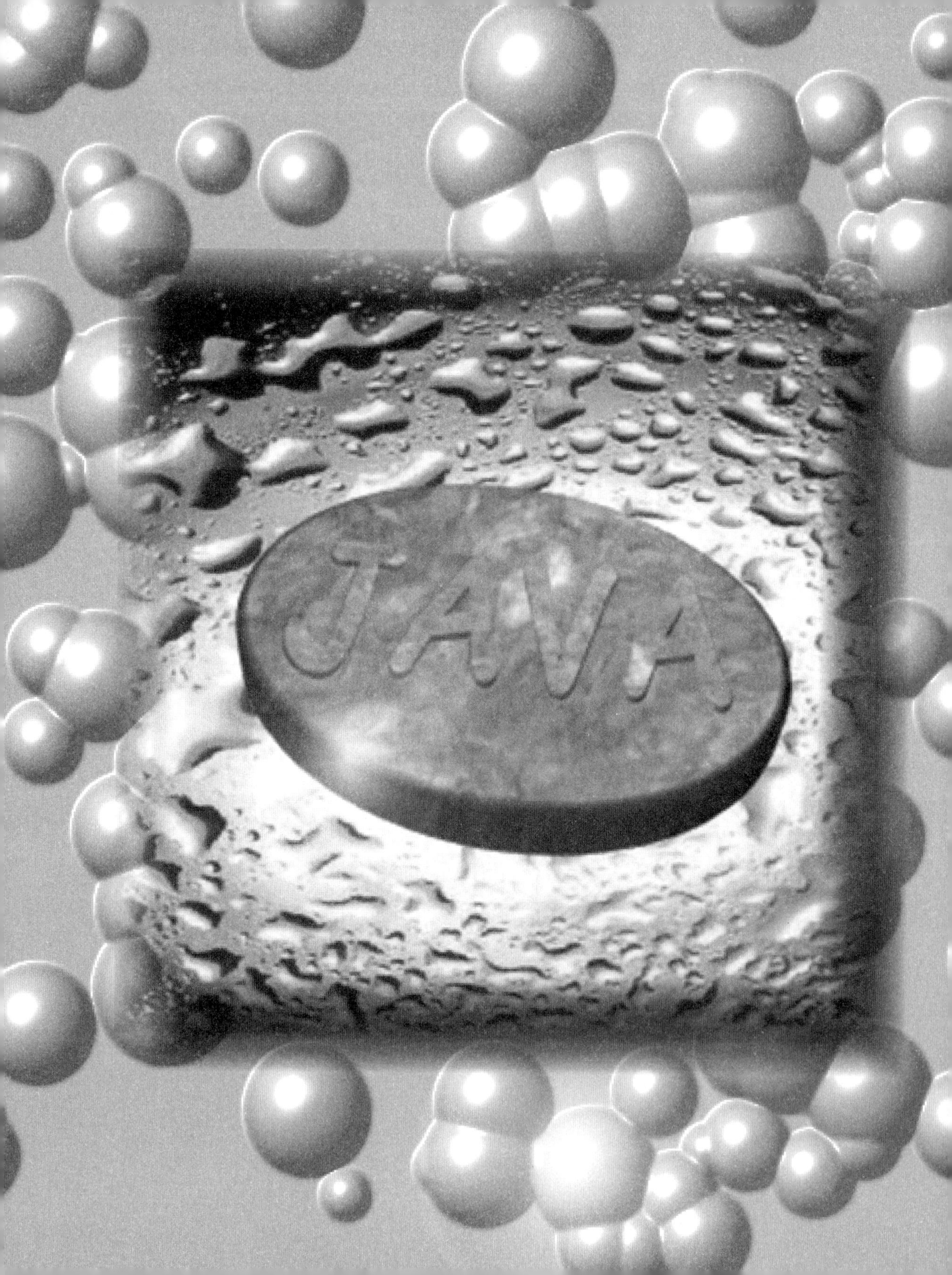
JAVA

6

SOAP Clients

In Chapter 5, we developed SOAP services without accessing a SOAP-level API, but we saw that the client code had to deal with low-level SOAP objects like a `Call` or a `DeploymentDescriptor`.

The main goal of this chapter is to design and implement a client-side framework that will allow us to write client code (almost) as if we were writing in-process Java code. We will never completely achieve total transparency when writing SOAP services and clients, because the protocols that we use have their limitations compared to a programming language like Java. For instance, SOAP is a stateless protocol that passes all objects by value; this is not the case in Java since we pass objects by reference to method calls.

All distributed protocols have similar limitations: RMI methods must throw `RemoteExceptions` and pass arguments in a special way, DCOM methods must not throw C++ exceptions, and so on. However, by design SOAP has more restrictions than most distributed frameworks. In addition, we have to reckon with the particular limitations of Apache SOAP, such as the lack of support for multi-references.

When designing the interfaces, we also need to be aware that ultimately the method calls are marshaled to an XML document that travels over (slow) network connections.

Nevertheless, we can free the client-code developer from the intricacies of SOAP development, and that's a step in the right direction. We will encapsulate this new level of abstraction in the `SavonProxy` class. We will now discuss the advantages and the limitations of this approach, so you will be able to make an informed decision for your own code.

The SavonProxy class uses the proxy pattern to hide calls to the Apache SOAP framework. In addition to taking care of the protocol details, the SavonProxy class uses a custom transport that improves our performance by putting hints for the server in HTTP headers. The SavonProxy also registers mappings for the classes that the framework needs to serialize in and out of XML documents. To achieve this goal, the SavonProxy uses a mechanism similar to the server-side registration that we saw earlier.

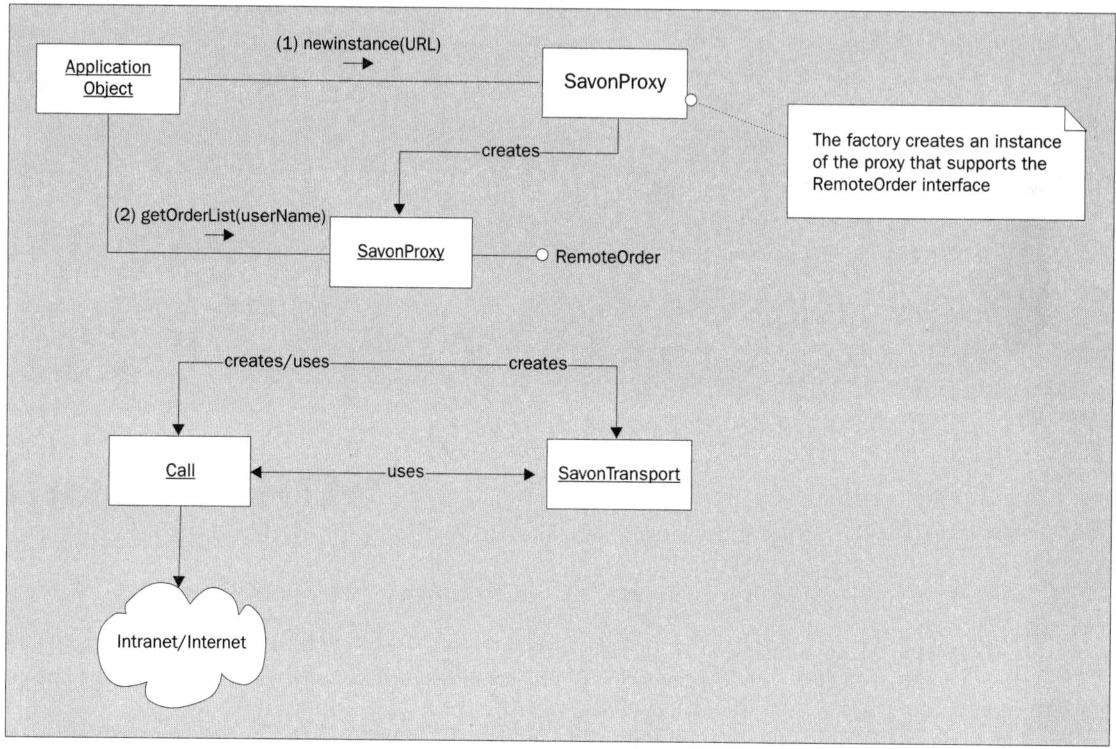

For the purpose of this implementation, the SavonProxyFactory will be coded as a static method of the SavonProxy class as opposed to a separate class.

As you can see in the above figure, instances of the SavonProxy class are created using the factory pattern. Before getting into the code, you should make a copy of the code developed for Chapter 5 into a folder named Chapter06 within the ProJavaSoap that contains the code for this book. We will be developing the SOAPCache class that we wrote earlier from it and adding a number of classes to our code. Let's briefly begin by describing the design patterns that we will use: the **proxy pattern** and the **factory pattern**. Let's start with the proxy.

The Proxy Pattern

The goal of the proxy design pattern is to control the access to another object without modifying its class. It is different from the façade or the adapter design pattern in that the proxy pattern deals with only one object and does not modify the interface of the existing class. Method calls to the object are forced to go through a surrogate object, or proxy, which usually implements additional functionality such as logging or authorization.

For a thorough description of the design patterns used in this book, consult Design Patterns *by Erich Gamma et al. (Addison-Wesley – ISBN 0-201-63361-2).*

Examples of the functionality that is typically implemented with the proxy pattern are security interceptors, logging, or remote calls. In our case, we are interested in making remote calls transparently – that is, remote calls should look like local calls to the client of the object. Specifically, we would like to make a SOAP remote call to an instance of the `OrderService` that we developed in Chapter 5 without having to worry about the specifics of SOAP development. In other words, we would like to replace the code that we had in `GetOrders`:

```
Call      call  = new Call();
Parameter param = new Parameter("userName", user.getClass(),
  user, Constants.NS_URI_SOAP_ENC);

call.setTargetObjectURI(uri);
call.setMethodName("getOrderList");
call.setParams(new Vector(Arrays.asList(new Parameter [] {param})));

// We register mapping for the Order class
SOAPMappingRegistry smr = new SOAPMappingRegistry();
BeanSerializer      ser = new BeanSerializer();

smr.mapTypes("http://schemas.xmlsoap.org/soap/encoding/",
             new QName("urn:lesavon-order", "order"),
             Order.class, ser, ser);
call.setSOAPMappingRegistry(smr);

Response resp = call.invoke(new URL(url), "");
```

with something more compact, such as:

```
RemoteOrder remoteOrder = (RemoteOrder)
SavonProxy.newInstance(url, urn, serviceClass);

Order orders[] = remoteOrder.getOrderList(user);
```

A classic implementation of the proxy design pattern is summarized in the following UML diagram:

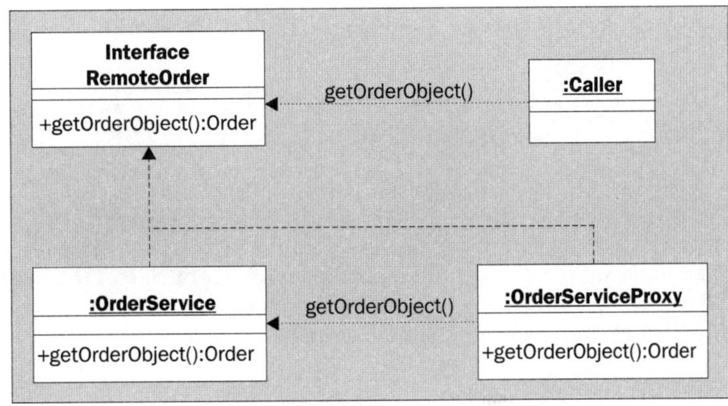

Both OrderService and OrderProxy implement RemoteOrder. This allows clients to bind to the RemoteOrder interface and treat local calls as remote calls. This implementation will do the work, but it has one major drawback: the OrderProxy class is specific to the RemoteOrder interface. Therefore, every time we define an interface to use over SOAP, we will define two classes instead of one: the service class and the proxy class.

There is an elegant solution to this problem: the dynamic proxy implemented by the java.lang.reflect.Proxy class introduced in the JDK 1.3. The proxy class implements a set of interfaces that are specified at runtime. Each method call on the class will be encoded as a java.lang.reflect.Method class, and an array of type Object containing the arguments. Both these are passed to an invocation handler that forwards the request to the relevant object.

There are some restrictions as to what interfaces can be implemented using the dynamic proxy, but for the most part, it will satisfy our requirements. For a detailed description of the Proxy class and its limitations, please consult the documentation for JDK 1.3 (or later JDK releases).

> *The JDK 1.3 documentation for the dynamic proxy is available on line at:*
> *http://java.sun.com/j2se/1.3/docs/guide/reflection/proxy.html*

When using the dynamic proxy, the UML diagram above is slightly modified:

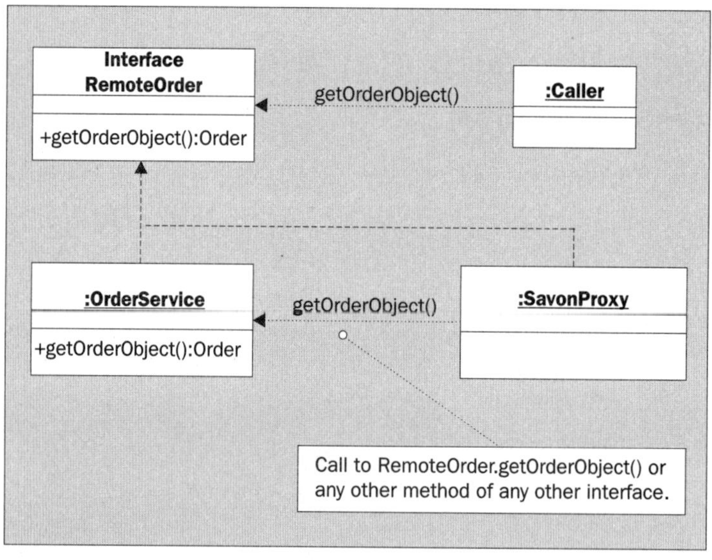

However, this apparently simple change will reduce the number of classes that we will need to implement by a factor of two. In addition, the implementation of a dynamic proxy is straightforward, as we will see shortly. Before that, let's discuss the factory design pattern.

The Factory Pattern

The creational factory pattern provides an interface for creating one or more related objects without specifying their implementation class.

The main use of the factory pattern is to give a third-party control over what objects should be created. Typically, the factory pattern uses a global state or a flag to decide what objects should be instantiated. A key advantage of the factory pattern is the reduction in complexity: the client does not need to worry about how the decision is made; it just needs to worry about the object or interface implementation that is returned by the factory. Another advantage is the centralization of the decision that makes it easier to modify the object creation algorithm. However, the same mechanism can easily be implemented through sub-classing.

We have seen in the previous section that the client needed to decide which implementation of the `RemoteOrder` interface should be created: a proxy to the `OrderService` class or the class itself. Abstracting that decision to another class besides the client is a good application of the factory pattern.

As we said earlier, the factory needs some information to decide what object to create. For SOAP development, we want the decision of which objects to create to be based on the target URL: local calls are made to inproc:// and remote calls are made to http://. We also need to pass enough information to the factory for the creation of a SOAP call: the service class and the URN of the service.

The following UML diagram summarizes the factory pattern:

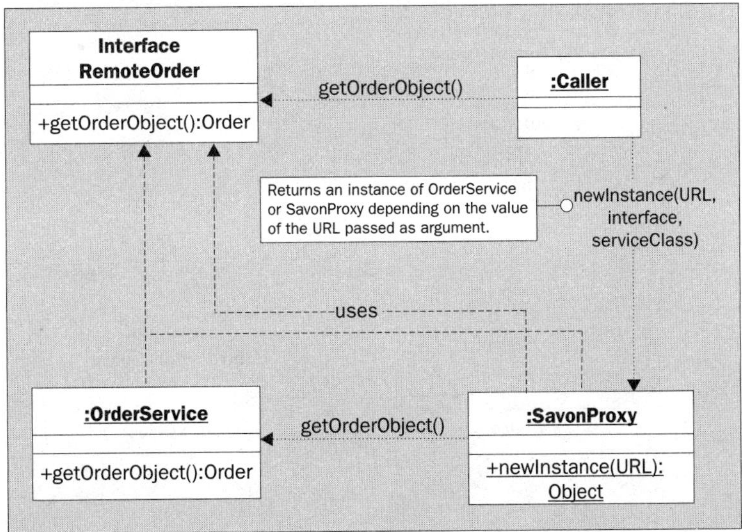

In the figure above, the factory is implemented as a static method on the `SavonProxy`, but that is not a requirement. It is a valid decision in our case since we have only one methodology to create objects and one factory method, but you could create a factory class to bundle several factory methods together.

The `newInstance()` method can be used to create implementations of `RemoteOrder` and `RemoteAdmin` since we pass both the service class and the URN as arguments to `newInstance()`. Note that we do not need to pass the class of the interface, since the signature of the `newInstance()` method calls for an `Object` to be returned: we can cast the result to the desired interface.

We are now ready to look at the code of the `SavonProxy` class.

The SavonProxy

There is no special class for the factory; we simply use a static method of the `SavonProxy` class. The sample code for this chapter (including the `SavonProxy.java` file) is available in the ProJavaSoap/Chapter06/ directory in the code download for this book.

```
// SavonProxy.java     1.0 02/06/2001

package com.lesavon.proxy;

import java.lang.reflect.*;
import java.io.*;
import java.net.*;
import java.util.*;
```

The reflection API (`java.lang.reflect.*`) allows Java programs to discover and invoke at runtime methods in a Java class. The dynamic proxy (`java.lang.reflect.Proxy`) uses reflection to implement the generic incarnation of the proxy pattern. The `java.lang.reflect.InvocationHandler` defines the `invoke()` method, which we will override to provide an implementation. In fact, the dynamic proxy creates a class that will use our implementation of the `InvocationHandler` interface to implement the proxy pattern, as shown in the following diagram:

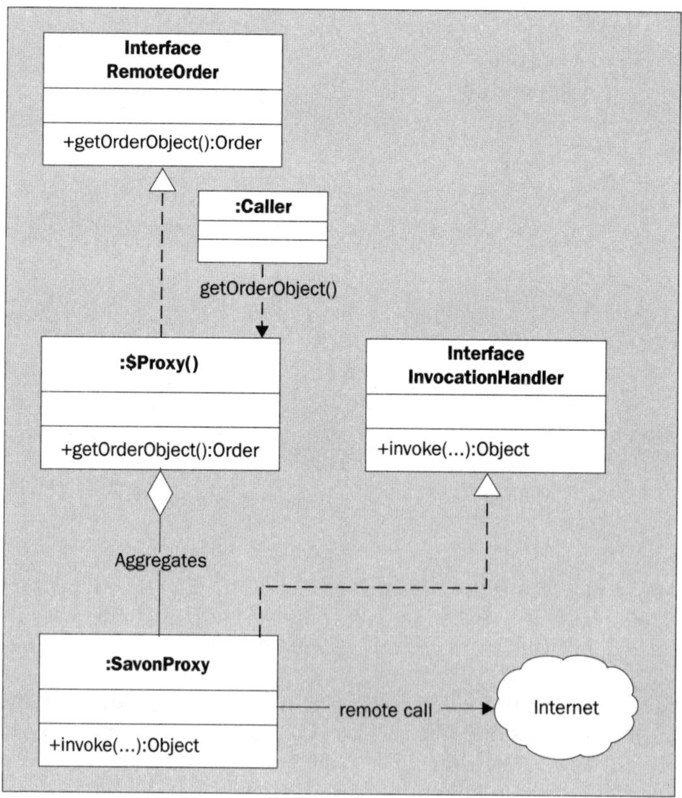

The IO classes are needed for the registration features of the proxy.

```
import javax.xml.parsers.DocumentBuilderFactory;
import javax.xml.parsers.DocumentBuilder;
import javax.xml.parsers.ParserConfigurationException;

import org.w3c.dom.*;

import org.xml.sax.InputSource;

import org.apache.soap.util.xml.QName;
import org.apache.soap.util.xml.XMLParserUtils;
import org.apache.soap.Fault;
import org.apache.soap.Constants;
import org.apache.soap.rpc.*;
import org.apache.soap.encoding.SOAPMappingRegistry;
import org.apache.soap.encoding.soapenc.BeanSerializer;
import org.apache.soap.server.DeploymentDescriptor;

import org.apache.xpath.XPathAPI;
```

As we saw earlier in Chapter 3, the registration of SOAP services relies on XML documents that we must parse. The XPath API will give us a convenient and robust way of searching for nodes in XML documents.

```
import com.lesavon.LeSavonConfigManager;
import com.lesavon.SavonException;
import com.lesavon.cache.SOAPCache;
```

We use the classes we have defined on the server-side. Note that we do not need the `Order`, the `RemoteOrder` or the `Admin` classes: the proxy is not specific to a particular interface or class.

```
public class SavonProxy implements InvocationHandler {
  public static Object newInstance(String url,
                                   String uri,
                                   String targetClass)
    throws ClassNotFoundException, IllegalAccessException,
           InstantiationException, MalformedURLException {

    Object result = null;

    if (url.startsWith("inproc:")) {
      result = Class.forName(targetClass).newInstance();
    } else {
      result = Proxy.newProxyInstance(
                         Class.forName(targetClass).getClassLoader(),
                         Class.forName(targetClass).getInterfaces(),
                         new SavonProxy(targetClass, new URL(url), uri));
    }
    return result;
  }
```

The implementation of the `SavonProxy.newInstance()` method can be used to create a local or a remote object. To create a local object, specify a URL that starts with `inproc:`, and to create a remote object, specify the URL of the SOAP service. In practice, this will be `http://<server-name>`, but it could specify any URL that does not start with `inproc:`. The second argument of the call is the name of the class that implements the service (`com.lesavon.service.OrderService` in this case).

Note that you must pass the fully qualified name of your class. When the URL of the SOAP service is specified, no actual object is created on the remote machine, but an instance of the `SavonProxy` class is created.

The `Proxy.newProxyInstance()` method requires further explanation. The signature of `newProxyInstance()` method is:

```
public static Object newProxyInstance(ClassLoader loader,
                                      Class[] interfaces,
                                      InvocationHandler handler)
       throws IllegalArgumentException
```

The three input arguments to this factory method are:

1. `ClassLoader loader`
   The proxy object is created with respect to one class loader. In practice, you will often specify the class loader of the target class.

2. `Class[] interfaces`
   The list of interfaces that we need to proxy.

3. `InvocationHandler handler`
   This is the class that implements the `InvocationHandler` interface. The dynamic proxy calls our implementation of `InvocationHandler.invoke()`. We will review how this works in a few moments.

As you can see by the granularity of the arguments, the `newProxyInstance()` method allows us to dynamically create a proxy object based on interfaces rather than objects. As far as LeSavon is concerned, we have one proxy object for all the interfaces of a class. This implementation meets our requirements since we have defined the behavior of a proxy (namely in-process versus remote) based on an instance of class, not on an implementation of an interface.

The `newProxyInstance()` method returns an instance of an `Object` which is the internal proxy that it created, and is not to be confused with our `SavonProxy` class (the implementation of the `InvocationHandler` interface).

Let's go back to the implementation of the `SavonProxy` class and have a look at its constructor:

```
// Instance data
private URL            savonURL;
private Call           call;
private SavonTransport transport;
private String         targetClass;
```

```
    public SavonProxy(String targetClass, URL url, String uri) {
        call = new Call();
        call.setTargetObjectURI(uri);
        call.setSOAPTransport(transport = new SavonTransport());
        this.targetClass = targetClass;
        this.savonURL    = url;

        // We read the service manager config file (soap.xml) to register
        // the same mappings as the server
        loadMappings();
    }
```

We will talk about the `SavonTransport` later, for now we will concentrate on the rest of the class. The constructor creates an `org.apache.soap.rpc.Call` object that we will reuse for all invocations of the interface. We must save the URL of the service to be able to make the remote calls. We also need the name of the target class (`OrderService` or `AdminService`) to compute the cache key. The `loadMappings()` method that performs our client-side registration will be reviewed later as well.

If you look at the figure below, we see how the collaboration diagram we saw earlier is modified for a local call: the proxy simply returns an instance of the `OrderService` class.

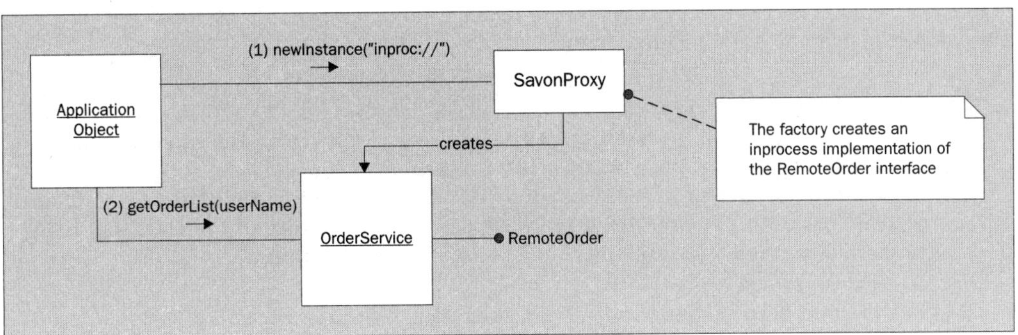

For a remote call, the following code can be used to create the proxy. Note that we use the `RemoteAdmin` interface rather than the `RemoteOrder` interface to emphasize that the `SavonProxy` is not specific to one service implementation.

```
RemoteAdmin remoteAdmin = (RemoteAdmin) SavonProxy.newInstance(
                             "http://myserver/lesavon/ncrouter", "urn:admin",
                             "com.lesavon.service.AdminService");
```

For a local call, the following code should be used:

```
RemoteAdmin remoteAdmin = (RemoteAdmin)SavonProxy.newInstance(
                "inproc:", "urn:admin", "com.lesavon.service.AdminService");
```

Once created, the implementation of the interface can be used in the same manner, whether it represents a remote or a local object:

```
RemoteAdmin.flush("atase", "lesavon");
```

Designing our SOAP services with an interface definition distinct from its implementation is essential to our use of the factory and the proxy patterns.

We have two tasks left for the implementation of the `SavonProxy` class: we need to implement the `invoke()` method as defined in Java's implementation of the proxy pattern and we need to automate registration. Let's start with the `invoke()` method.

The Invoke() Method

The Java 1.3 `InvocationHandler` interface provides the `invoke()` method as a way to trap all the calls going to the hidden object:

```
public Object invoke(Object proxy, Method method, Object[] args)
     throws Throwable {
```

The `invoke()` method has three arguments:

1. The proxy object: `Object proxy`
   The proxy object is of no use in this context. This proxy is *not* the same as `this` (no pun intended). A call to `this.getClass().getName()` returns "`com.lesavon.proxy.LeSavonProxy`" but a call to `proxy.getClass().getName()` returns "`$ProxyN`" where *N* is `0, 1, ...` `$ProxyN` is an instance of the class that is dynamically created to implement the proxy pattern at run time.

2. The method being called: `java.lang.reflect.Method method`
   The `method` object describes the method being invoked. We will use it to build the SOAP call.

3. The arguments of the method being called: `Object[] args`
   Each `arg` object describes one argument of the call. We will use them to build the SOAP call.

```
Object result = null;

try {
  // Encoding is NS_URI_SOAP_ENC, except if the method returns a DOM
  Class  elementClass   = Class.forName("org.w3c.dom.Element");
  String callEncoding   = elementClass.equals(method.getReturnType())
                          ? Constants.NS_URI_LITERAL_XML
                          : Constants.NS_URI_SOAP_ENC;
  String paramEncoding = elementClass.equals(method.getReturnType())
                          ? Constants.NS_URI_SOAP_ENC
                          : null;
```

We saw earlier in Chapter 2, when we talked about SOAP payloads, that the Apache SOAP framework supports three modes of encoding: SOAP encoding, literal XML encoding, and XMI. When the return type of the method is the `org.w3c.dom.Element` (in other words, the methods returns an XML document) we select literal XML encoding, otherwise we use SOAP encoding. For our purposes, we do not support XMI encoding, mainly because it is not widely used and it offers no advantages to us over the SOAP and literal XML encoding.

> *XMI is the XML Metadata Interchange standard supported by the OMG. More information can be found at* http://www.omg.org.

For the encoding of the argument, we force SOAP encoding if the call is encoded using literal XML, since we want to pass any type of argument, not just an `org.w3c.dom.Element`. This could be decided with a finer granularity by checking the actual type of the argument. However, this would not benefit the sample application since we do not have a method with an XML document as argument.

As we mentioned earlier, we use the reflection API to serialize the call to SOAP. Setting the method name for the SOAP call is done using `Call.setMethodName()` and the arguments are serialized with a loop on the argument list passed to the `invoke()` method by the dynamic proxy. Note that arguments are serialized with the generic names `arg0`, `arg1`, etc, instead of the real argument name.

This is not an issue for the Apache SOAP framework, but it is an issue for other environments, like Microsoft .NET that relies on argument names rather than method signatures to un-marshall SOAP calls.

```
// Build the call.
call.setMethodName(method.getName());
call.setEncodingStyleURI(callEncoding);

Vector params = new Vector ();
for (int index = 0; index < args.length; index++) {
  params.addElement (new Parameter("arg" + index,
                                  method.getParameterTypes()[index],
                                  args[index],
                                  paramEncoding));
}
call.setParams(params);
```

With the exception of the cache key and the mappings that we will discuss shortly, this code should be familiar since it uses the same methods and classes as the simple SOAP client (`GetOrders`) that we wrote in Chapter 5.

```
    // We set the cache key to free the server from computing it
    transport.setCacheKey(
                    SOAPCache.computeCacheKey(targetClass, method, args));

    // The mappings have been set at construction time (loadMappings)
    Response resp = call.invoke(savonURL, "");

    // Check the response.
    if (resp.generatedFault()) {
      Fault fault = resp.getFault();
      throw new SavonException(fault);
```

```
      } else {
        if (resp.getReturnValue() != null) {
          result = resp.getReturnValue().getValue();
        }
      }
    } catch (Exception exception) {
      throw exception;
    }

    return result;
  }
```

If the call was successful then the `invoke()` method returns the response to the caller (always an object). In case of trouble, a `SavonException` is built and thrown back to the caller. This simple construction forces us to have all methods throw the same exception class. This limitation is not a major issue for most applications but it can be a problem.

The root cause of this restriction lies in the content of a SOAP fault. We saw in Chapter 2 that there were four subelements to a fault element: `faultcode`, `faultstring`, `faultactor`, and `detail`. None of these elements carries the definition of an exception, nor should they since an exception is very language-specific.

However, the SOAP specification also says the following: *Other* `Fault` *subelements MAY be present, provided they are namespace-qualified.* In other words, nothing prevents us from adding our own `lesavon:exception` element to include a serialized exception. This solution is not implemented for LeSavon.com, but you might find it useful for your application.

Registration

In Chapter 5, we discussed a secure and flexible deployment methodology, which we referred to as registration or deployment. It is clear that there is no need to deploy services on the client side. However, there is a need to register mappings with the SOAP Apache engine, since we must serialize objects to and from XML documents on the client as well as on the server.

On the server, we relied on the configuration manager that was invoked by the service manager to register mappings. On the client, we will rely on the `SavonProxy` class to manage the process. We saw before that `SavonProxy` invokes `SavonProxy.loadMappings()` in its constructor to load the XML to Java and Java to XML mappings:

```
  private void loadMappings() {
    final String CONFIG_FILE     = "etc/soap.xml";
    final String OPTION          = "option";
    final String NAME            = "name";
    final String VALUE           = "value";
    final String MGR_PATH        = "/soapServer/configManager";
    final String DEFAULT_PACKAGE = "defaultPackage";
    final String SERVICES        = "services";

    DocumentBuilder xdb = XMLParserUtils.getXMLDocBuilder();
```

We will parse `soap.xml` ourselves looking for mappings. Note that the hard-coded file approach could be replaced by a resource looked up through `ClassLoader.getResourceAsStream()`.

```
try {
  FileReader reader = new FileReader(new File(CONFIG_FILE));
  Document document = xdb.parse(new InputSource(reader));
  Element configMgr = (Element)XPathAPI.selectSingleNode(
                                  document.getDocumentElement(), MGR_PATH);
```

We use XPath to get to the `<configmanager/>` node that contains the class name of the configuration manager.

> *To learn more about XPath, consult* XSLT Programmer's Reference *by Michael Kay (Wrox Press, ISBN - 1861005067).*

```
if(configMgr == null) {
  // The soap.xml file must exist and have a <configManager/>
  throw new SavonException("Can't find " + MGR_PATH + " in " + CONFIG_FILE);
}

// It is OK not to have any service with mappings to register
  NodeList optionsList = configMgr.getElementsByTagName(OPTION);
  if(optionsList != null) {
    for(int ndx=0; optionsList!=null && ndx<optionsList.getLength(); ndx++) {
Element optionElement = (Element)optionsList.item(ndx);
        String name = optionElement.getAttribute(NAME);
        String value = optionElement.getAttribute(VALUE);

        if(name != null && value != null) {
          if(name.equals(SERVICES)) {
            registerServices(value);
          }
        }
      }
    }
    reader.close();

  } catch(Throwable throwable) {
    System.err.println("Error processing configuration file ("
                       + CONFIG_FILE + ")" );
    System.err.println( "Error was: " + throwable);
  }
}
```

We loop on the comma-separated list of services and call `registerServices()` for each service.

```
private void registerServices(String services) {
  StringTokenizer tokenizer = new StringTokenizer(services, ",");

  while(tokenizer.hasMoreTokens()) {
    String serviceName = tokenizer.nextToken();
    String fileName    = serviceName + ".xml";

    try {
      DeploymentDescriptor descriptor =
      DeploymentDescriptor.fromXML(new FileReader(fileName));
      SOAPMappingRegistry smr =
           DeploymentDescriptor.buildSOAPMappingRegistry(descriptor,
                                                     call.getSOAPContext());
      call.setSOAPMappingRegistry(smr);
```

We read the same deployment descriptor on the client as the one we used earlier on the server. The Apache SOAP helper method `DeploymentDescriptor.buildSOAPMappingRegistry()` conveniently constructs a deployment descriptor based on the document we just parsed.

```
        } catch(FileNotFoundException fileNotFoundException) {
          System.err.println(
                        "SavonProxy.registerServices.setOptions: Cannot open "
                        + fileName + " for reading");
        }
      }
    }
  }
```

We looked at deployment descriptors in Chapter 3, but here is the deployment descriptor for the `OrderService`, `RemoteOrder.xml`:

```
<isd:service xmlns:isd="http://xml.apache.org/xml-soap/deployment"
             id="urn:order">
  <isd:provider type="java"
                scope="Request"
                methods="getOrderList getOrder">
    <isd:java class="com.lesavon.service.OrderService" static="false"/>
  </isd:provider>

  <isd:faultListener>
    org.apache.soap.server.DOMFaultListener
  </isd:faultListener>

  <isd:mappings>
    <isd:map encodingStyle="http://schemas.xmlsoap.org/soap/encoding/"
     xmlns:x="urn:lesavon-order" qname="x:order"
     javaType="com.lesavon.Order"
     java2XMLClassName="org.apache.soap.encoding.soapenc.BeanSerializer"
     xml2JavaClassName="org.apache.soap.encoding.soapenc.BeanSerializer"/>
  </isd:mappings>
</isd:service>
```

As you have probably guessed, the `SOAPMappingRegistry` object is built based on the `<isd:mappings/>` element. Once we have a `SOAPMappingRegistry` instance constructed, we can pass it to the call objects so that SOAP calls made with this proxy will have enough information to serialize Java objects.

The content of the `soap.xml` document on the client drives which deployment descriptors are going to be used by the client. They can be identical to the list of services registered on the server, but they can be a subset as well. Here is the listing of the `soap.xml` document that we use in this chapter (you can find it with the rest of the code in `ProJavaSoap/Chapter06/leSavon/etc/soap.xml`):

```
<!-- LeSavon SOAP Server Configuration File -->
<soapServer>
    <configManager value="com.lesavon.LeSavonConfigManager">
        <option name="defaultPackage" value="com.lesavon"/>
        <option name="services"
                value="RemoteAdmin,RemoteOrder"/>
    </configManager>
</soapServer>
```

You could easily refine this methodology, depending on your specific needs. For instance, clients and servers can be synchronized by ensuring that both pull the `soap.xml` document (with the deployment descriptors) from a directory service. We will see an example of this implementation in Chapter 7.

Another variation on this theme would be to have the clients get the list of services that are registered on the server. This can be done with one call to `ServiceManager.list()` followed by a set of calls to `ServiceManager.query()` for each deployed service. We can then register mappings identical to those of the server. We will see a refinement of this technology when we talk about the **Universal Dynamic Discovery Interface (UDDI)** in Chapter 12.

Caching

Web servers are often required to serve a large community of users with similar needs. For instance, a business intelligence application can provide identical key performance indicators to many users. Similarly, a traffic report system can return identical data for the same city. In the case of LeSavon, several employees from client companies may request the same information.

Business Intelligence (BI) is the field of computer science that provides business decision tools, including data marts and data warehouses.

Key Performance Indicators (KPIs) are variables that measure the success or failure of your business. For instance, in a call center, a KPI would be the average length of a call for the last 4 weeks. KPIs are cached, because their computation is usually CPU-intensive, and also because the same KPIs are common to many users. For instance, all workers in a call center would be interested in the average call length.

Typically, web servers improve performance by caching the data returned to users. The principle is simple enough: store the data (files or other) in a memory structure such as a vector or a hash table and use a key to quickly determine if the data is in memory or not. Caching is straightforward in the case of static data such as web pages, since we can use the URL of the web page as a key and save the file content in memory. However, in the case of dynamic data, things can be more challenging, since we do not necessarily have a URL that uniquely identifies the resource. For instance, if you want to cache the result of an HTML form submitted to the server using an HTTP `POST`, part of the key is the URL of the page processing the form, and the rest of the key is the content of the HTTP request.

The use of SOAP provides an easy way to define a key for a request: the serialization of the input arguments. That serialization is readily available since it is used by the Apache SOAP implementation to generate the SOAP request. In Chapter 8, we will talk at length about the cache, its server implementation, and its implications for the performance of your application. For now, let's simply state that with the key the server can quickly return a pre-computed SOAP response.

The `SavonProxy.invoke()` method computes the cache key and adds it to the header of the HTTP request, via the use of the `SavonTransport.setCacheKey()` method. The advantage of computing the cache key on the client is that the server can simply look at the HTTP header and, if the cache key is present, avoid parsing the request thus improving performance. If the cache key is not present in the HTTP header, the server must parse the request to compute the cache key.

The optional presence of the cache key in the HTTP header allows the server to support clients that provide the optimization and clients that do not. When the response cannot be found in the cache, the server can simply forward the request to the SOAP service for processing. It might seem to be only a small computational saving, but if thousands of users are hitting the site with similar requests this will save many CPU cycles.

The SavonTransport class extends the SOAPHTTPConnection class to override the send() method and add the cache key to the HTTP header. The cache is populated by saving the response from the service to a file, and the key, along with the file name, in a map.

Let's look at the code for the SavonTransport class. Once again, you will be pleased at how easy it is to customize the Apache SOAP framework to fit your needs.

```
/*
 * SavonTransport.java    1.0 03/05/2001

package com.lesavon.proxy;

import java.net.URL;
import java.util.Hashtable;

import org.apache.soap.Envelope;
import org.apache.soap.SOAPException;
import org.apache.soap.rpc.SOAPContext;
import org.apache.soap.encoding.SOAPMappingRegistry;
import org.apache.soap.transport.http.SOAPHTTPConnection;

public class SavonTransport extends SOAPHTTPConnection {
  private String cacheKey;

  final private String HEADER_CACHE_KEY = "LeSavon-Cache-Key";
```

The name of the header we will use is "LeSavon-Cache-Key". The java.net.URL class and the org.apache.soap packages are needed for the arguments of the send() method that we override from the base class: SOAPHTTPConnection. The HTTP header is called: LeSavon-Cache-Key. The HTTP header entries are stored in java.util.Hashtable.

If the cache key has been set by the SavonProxy.invoke() method, we add it to the header entries, making sure that the hashtable is indeed not null. We simply let the base class handle the rest of the send() method:

```
  public void send (URL sendTo,
                    String action,
                    Hashtable headers,
                    Envelope envelope,
                    SOAPMappingRegistry mappings,
                    SOAPContext context)
     throws SOAPException {
    if(cacheKey != null) {
      if(headers == null) {
        headers = new Hashtable();
      }
      headers.put(HEADER_CACHE_KEY, cacheKey);
    }

    super.send(sendTo, action, headers, envelope, mappings, context);
    cacheKey = null;    // one use
  }

  public void setCacheKey(String cacheKey) {
    this.cacheKey = cacheKey;
  }

  public String getCacheKey() {
    return cacheKey;
  }
}
```

There is one piece missing in this code review you have probably noticed. When we wrote the `SavonProxy.invoke()` method, we made use of the `SOAPCache` class to compute the cache key:

```
transport.setCacheKey(SOAPCache.computeCacheKey(targetClass, method, args));
```

The computation of the cache key is straightforward:

```
...// rest of SOAPCache class as before
    public static String computeCacheKey(String targetClass,
        Method method, Object[] args) {
        String cacheKey = targetClass + "." + method.getName();
        for(int index = 0; index < args.length; index++) {
            cacheKey += "." + args[index];
        }

        return cacheKey;
    }
...
```

We can see what the cache key looks like in the following SOAP message, which is transported over HTTP for a call to `RemoteOrder.getOrderList()`:

```
POST /lesavon/serveur/ HTTP/1.0
Host: localhost
Content-Type: text/xml; charset=utf-8
Content-Length: 448
SOAPAction: ""
LeSavon-Cache-Key: com.lesavon.service.OrderService.getOrderList.atase

<?xml version='1.0' encoding='UTF-8'?>
<SOAP-ENV:Envelope xmlns:SOAP-ENV="http://schemas.xmlsoap.org/soap/envelope/"
xmlns:xsi="http://www.w3.org/1999/XMLSchema-instance"
xmlns:xsd="http://www.w3.org/1999/XMLSchema">
<SOAP-ENV:Body>
<ns1:getOrderList xmlns:ns1="urn:order" SOAP-
ENV:encodingStyle="http://schemas.xmlsoap.org/soap/encoding/">
<arg0 xsi:type="xsd:string">atase</arg0>
</ns1:getOrderList>
</SOAP-ENV:Body>
</SOAP-ENV:Envelope>
```

You can see in the listing above that the call:

```
getOrderList(atase)
```

corresponds to the key:

```
com.lesavon.service.OrderService.getOrderList.atase
```

It is time to reap the fruits of our labor and see for ourselves that we have indeed simplified the development of SOAP clients. We cannot really see the previous code in action without a client, so let's look at a test client: `GetOrders2`. We will build the server code (from Chapter 5) and the client code in the *Building* section.

GetOrders2

GetOrders2 is a modified version of the GetOrders client program that we wrote in Chapter 5: it retrieves a list of the orders for a user and prints the order. Look at the code – if you ignore the URL, can you tell that this is a SOAP service test program?

```
// GetOrders2.java     1.0 08/21/2001

package com.lesavon.test;

import com.lesavon.Order;
import com.lesavon.RemoteOrder;
import com.lesavon.SavonException;
import com.lesavon.proxy.SavonProxy;
```

As you would expect, there are no imports for the Apache SOAP framework – only imports specific to our application: com.lesavon.*.

```
public class GetOrders2 {
  public static void main(String args[]) {
    String methodName   = "com.lesavon.test.GetOrders2.main";
    String url          = "";
    String remoteMethod = "getOrderList";
    String user         = "atase";
    String urn          = "urn:order";  // the service urn
    String serviceClass = "com.lesavon.service.OrderService";
                          // fully qualified service class name

    if(args.length != 1) {
      System.err.println("GetOrders2: invokes a SOAP service.");

      System.err.println("Usage: java GetOrders2 " +
                         "http://servert:port/lesavon/ncrouter ");
      System.exit(1);
    }

    url = args[0];

    System.out.println(methodName + ": Starting test for url "
                     + url + "...");
```

A call to the SavonProxy factory returns an instance of the serviceClass that we cast to an interface reference: RemoteOrder.

```
try {
  RemoteOrder remoteOrder = (RemoteOrder)
  SavonProxy.newInstance(url, urn, serviceClass);
```

We call the `getOrderList()` method and print the array of orders returned by the remote method. To run the same test as a local test, simply change the value of the variable `url` to `"inproc:"`.

```
        System.out.println("  remoteOrder.getOrderList...");
        Order orders[] = remoteOrder.getOrderList(user);

        System.out.println("Orders:");
        for(int index = 0; index < orders.length; index++) {
          System.out.println("    " + orders[index]);
        }
      } catch (Exception exception) {
        System.err.println(methodName + ": Error, caught exception: "
                           + exception);
      }

      System.out.println(methodName + ": All done!");
    }
  }
```

Before we can build this project, we need to introduce Xalan, the API we used during the parsing of the `soap.xml` file.

Xalan

Since we have been using the XPath API in the `SavonProxy`, we need an implementation of that API. One possible choice is Xalan. Xalan is an XSLT processor for transforming XML documents into HTML, text, or XML document types. It comes out of the Apache organization.

Xalan implements the W3C Recommendations for XSL Transformations (XSLT) and the XML Path Language (XPath). As we have seen earlier, we are only interested in the XPath API. You can get `xalan.jar` from the following URL: http://xml.apache.org/xalan-j/index.html.

Depending on the platform you want to use, you will need to select either the `xalan-j_2_2_D11.zip` for Windows or `xalan-j_2_2_D11.tar.gz` for UNIX. Following the same procedure as we did in Chapter 4, you should expand the compressed file and copy the `xalan.jar` file to the `soap/lib` directory.

Building

We are now ready to build the files used for this sample. This can be done either manually, creating the structure shown in the following screenshot and compiling the source files or simply relying on ANT to do the work for us. The ANT script from the previous chapter will work for this chapter too with a little modification:

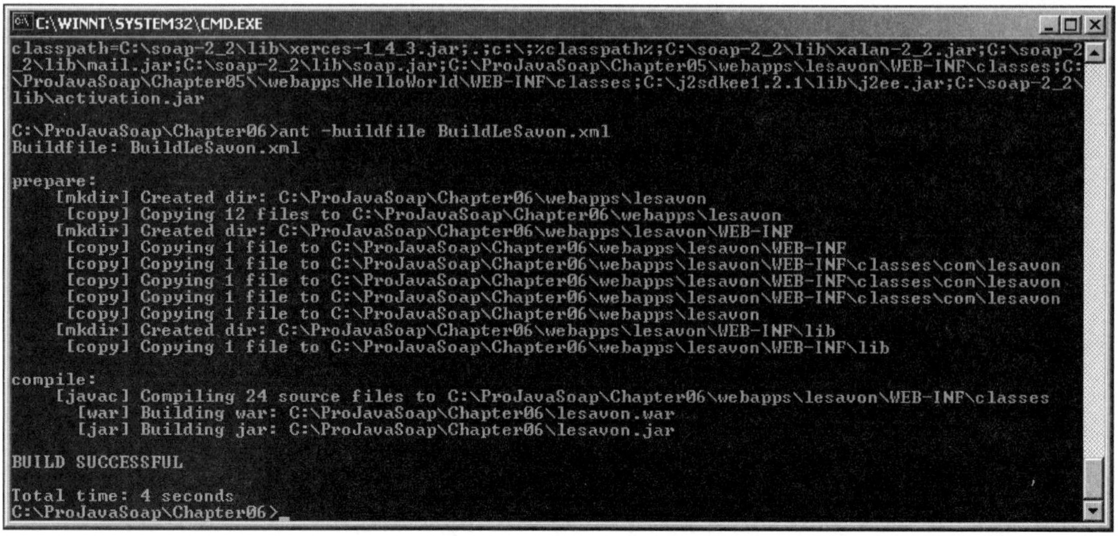

```
C:\WINNT\SYSTEM32\CMD.EXE
classpath=C:\soap-2_2\lib\xerces-1_4_3.jar;.;c:\;%classpath%;C:\soap-2_2\lib\xalan-2_2.jar;C:\soap-2_2\lib\mail.jar;C:\soap-2_2\lib\soap.jar;C:\ProJavaSoap\Chapter05\webapps\lesavon\WEB-INF\classes;C:\ProJavaSoap\Chapter05\\webapps\HelloWorld\WEB-INF\classes;C:\j2sdkee1.2.1\lib\j2ee.jar;C:\soap-2_2\lib\activation.jar

C:\ProJavaSoap\Chapter06>ant -buildfile BuildLeSavon.xml
Buildfile: BuildLeSavon.xml

prepare:
    [mkdir] Created dir: C:\ProJavaSoap\Chapter06\webapps\lesavon
     [copy] Copying 12 files to C:\ProJavaSoap\Chapter06\webapps\lesavon
    [mkdir] Created dir: C:\ProJavaSoap\Chapter06\webapps\lesavon\WEB-INF
     [copy] Copying 1 file to C:\ProJavaSoap\Chapter06\webapps\lesavon\WEB-INF
     [copy] Copying 1 file to C:\ProJavaSoap\Chapter06\webapps\lesavon\WEB-INF\classes\com\lesavon
     [copy] Copying 1 file to C:\ProJavaSoap\Chapter06\webapps\lesavon\WEB-INF\classes\com\lesavon
     [copy] Copying 1 file to C:\ProJavaSoap\Chapter06\webapps\lesavon\WEB-INF\classes\com\lesavon
     [copy] Copying 1 file to C:\ProJavaSoap\Chapter06\webapps\lesavon
    [mkdir] Created dir: C:\ProJavaSoap\Chapter06\webapps\lesavon\WEB-INF\lib
     [copy] Copying 1 file to C:\ProJavaSoap\Chapter06\webapps\lesavon\WEB-INF\lib

compile:
    [javac] Compiling 24 source files to C:\ProJavaSoap\Chapter06\webapps\lesavon\WEB-INF\classes
      [war] Building war: C:\ProJavaSoap\Chapter06\lesavon.war
      [jar] Building jar: C:\ProJavaSoap\Chapter06\lesavon.jar

BUILD SUCCESSFUL

Total time: 4 seconds
C:\ProJavaSoap\Chapter06>_
```

As you can see on the previous screenshot, the first step is to set the classpath. The classpath must include `xalan.jar`. Before compiling, you can check that the target directory is indeed empty. After that, you can let ANT do the hard work for you. You can find the build file in the `ProJavaSoap\Chapter06` directory. It takes care of creating the directory and copying the `web.xml` to the `WEB-INF` directory as specified in the J2EE specifications.

We also create a `lib` directory in `ProJavaSoap\Chapter06` and put `xalan.jar` in it since SOAP does not require it. The build script creates a `/lib` folder in `/WEB-INF` and copies `xalan.jar` into it:

```
<copy  file="etc/soap.xml" tofile="${deploy.home}/soap.xml"/>

<mkdir  dir="${deploy.home}/WEB-INF/lib"/>
<copy todir="${deploy.home}/WEB-INF/lib">
  <fileset dir="lib"/>
</copy>

<mkdir  dir="${deploy.home}/WEB-INF/classes"/>
```

Alternatively, you could modify the system classpath of Tomcat to include `xalan.jar`, as we did for other files such as `xerces.jar`.

The build file also creates a WAR file and a JAR file using the `<war>` and `<jar>` options in ANT. We can use the WAR file to deploy the application on another server, and the JAR file to write our own clients using the proxy. Let's briefly examine these options:

```
<war warfile="${app.name}.war" webxml="etc/web.xml">
  <fileset dir="web"/>
  <classes dir="${deploy.home}/WEB-INF/classes"/>
</war>

<jar jarfile="${app.name}.jar">
  <fileset dir="${dist.home}/WEB-INF/classes" excludes="*/test/*"/>
</jar>
```

The war command in ANT takes the name of the war file in the warfile attribute, the path to the web.xml file, and the path to the static files and class in the fileset and classes elements. From this a WAR file is built that can be deployed to any J2EE compliant server; Tomcat will deploy this application automatically if we were to drop the file into its /webapps directory.

The jar file simply jars up all of our lesavon classes in a lesavon.jar file. This can then be distributed to clients. If you wish to build the application by hand, check against the code download for the required structure.

The target directory is the C:\ProJavaSoap\Chapter06\webapps directory; as previously mentioned you will need to modify the target of the lesavon web application to match the context defined in your server.xml file, which resides in your Tomcat installation. For a refresher on Tomcat, go back to Chapters 3 and 5 where we set up the Apache SOAP server and the LeSavon.com application respectively. In addition, tomcat.bat will need to be amended to include the class file for Chapter06 as we have done previously:

```
set CP=%CP%;C:\ProJavaSoap\Chapter06\webapps\lesavon\WEB-INF\classes
```

Testing

To execute the test, you will need to modify your classpath to include the target file. Make sure that you execute from a current directory where etc/soap.xml can be found (this execution is from a Windows 2000 machine):

```
cd C:\ProJavaSoap\Chapter06
set classpath=C:\soap-2_2\lib\xerces-1_4_3.jar;%classpath%
set classpath=%classpath%;C:\soap-2_2\lib\xalan-2_2.jar
set classpath=%classpath%;C:\soap-2_2\lib\mail.jar
set classpath=%classpath%;C:\soap-2_2\lib\soap.jar
set classpath=%classpath%;C:\j2sdkee1.2.1\lib\j2ee.jar
set classpath=%classpath%;C:\soap-2_2\lib\activation.jar

java com.lesavon.test.GetOrders2 http://localhost:8081/lesavon/ncrouter
```

Note that the URL above assumes that we have the tcpTunnel on and redirecting calls from 8081 to 8080. Both the local and the remote test return the same output, except for the URL. The remote test output is:

```
C:\ProJavaSoap\Chapter06>java com.lesavon.test.GetOrders2
http://localhost:8081/lesavon/ncrouter
com.lesavon.test.GetOrders2.main: Starting test for url
http://localhost:8081/lesavon/ncrouter...
  remoteOrder.getOrderList...
Orders:
   com.lesavon.Order: id = 123456001, client: atase, article: Senteur de Provence, unit price:
20, quantity: 5, total price: 100
   com.lesavon.Order: id = 123456005, client: atase, article: Eau de Mouille, unit price: 50,
quantity: 2, total price: 100
   com.lesavon.Order: id = 123456010, client: atase, article: Parfum de Lilas, unit price: 35,
quantity: 1, total price: 35
```

```
com.lesavon.Order: id = 123456011, client: atase, article: Crystal de Roches, unit price: 25,
quantity: 1, total price: 25
  com.lesavon.Order: id = 123456012, client: atase, article: Quartz de Petits Noeuds, unit
price: 4
5, quantity: 1, total price: 45
com.lesavon.test.GetOrders2.main: All done!
```

The SOAP packet that we send to the server is the example that we saw earlier when we looked at the value of the cache key. The response from the server is:

```
HTTP/1.0 200 OK
Content-Type: text/xml; charset=utf-8
Content-Length: 2184
Set-Cookie2: JSESSIONID=ff4m3t2gj1;Version=1;Discard;Path="/lesavon"
Set-Cookie: JSESSIONID=ff4m3t2gj1;Path=/lesavon
Servlet-Engine: Tomcat Web Server/3.2.3 (JSP 1.1; Servlet 2.2; Java 1.3.0; Windows
2000 5.0 x86; java.vendor=Sun Microsystems Inc.)

<?xml version='1.0' encoding='UTF-8'?>
<SOAP-ENV:Envelope xmlns:SOAP-ENV="http://schemas.xmlsoap.org/soap/envelope/"
xmlns:xsi="http://www.w3.org/1999/XMLSchema-instance"
xmlns:xsd="http://www.w3.org/1999/XMLSchema">
<SOAP-ENV:Body>
```

The content of the HTTP response is an XML document; more specifically it is a SOAP envelope. The body of the envelope is the return value (or response) to a call to `getOrderList()`:

```
<ns1:getOrderListResponse xmlns:ns1="urn:order" SOAP-
ENV:encodingStyle="http://schemas.xmlsoap.org/soap/encoding/">
```

The return value is an array of orders (5 elements formatted for readability):

```
<return xmlns:ns2="http://schemas.xmlsoap.org/soap/encoding/"
        xsi:type="ns2:Array" xmlns:ns3="urn:lesavon-order"
        ns2:arrayType="ns3:order[5]">
  <item xsi:type="ns3:order">
    <totalPrice xsi:type="xsd:int">100</totalPrice>
     <client xsi:type="xsd:string">atase</client>
     <unitPrice xsi:type="xsd:int">20</unitPrice>
     <quantity xsi:type="xsd:int">5</quantity>
     <article xsi:type="xsd:string">Senteur de Provence</article>
     <id xsi:type="xsd:int">123456001</id>
   </item>
  <item xsi:type="ns3:order">
    <totalPrice xsi:type="xsd:int">100</totalPrice>
    <client xsi:type="xsd:string">atase</client>
    <unitPrice xsi:type="xsd:int">50</unitPrice>
    <quantity xsi:type="xsd:int">2</quantity>
    <article xsi:type="xsd:string">Eau de Mouille</article>
    <id xsi:type="xsd:int">123456005</id>
  </item>
```

```
    <item xsi:type="ns3:order">
      <totalPrice xsi:type="xsd:int">35</totalPrice>
      <client xsi:type="xsd:string">atase</client>
      <unitPrice xsi:type="xsd:int">35</unitPrice>
      <quantity xsi:type="xsd:int">1</quantity>
      <article xsi:type="xsd:string">Parfum de Lilas</article>
      <id xsi:type="xsd:int">123456010</id>
    </item>
    <item xsi:type="ns3:order">
      <totalPrice xsi:type="xsd:int">25</totalPrice>
      <client xsi:type="xsd:string">atase</client>
      <unitPrice xsi:type="xsd:int">25</unitPrice>
      <quantity xsi:type="xsd:int">1</quantity>
      <article xsi:type="xsd:string">Crystal de Roches</article>
      <id xsi:type="xsd:int">123456011</id>
    </item>
    <item xsi:type="ns3:order">
      <totalPrice xsi:type="xsd:int">45</totalPrice>
      <client xsi:type="xsd:string">atase</client>
      <unitPrice xsi:type="xsd:int">45</unitPrice>
      <quantity xsi:type="xsd:int">1</quantity>
      <article xsi:type="xsd:string">Quartz de Petits Noeuds</article>
      <id xsi:type="xsd:int">123456012</id>
    </item>
  </return>
```

We can run the same test as a local call simply by changing the URL to inproc://

Note that if you run the two tests one after the other and Tomcat is still running, the file that we use as our backend database will be locked by Tomcat. Before running the second test, you need to stop (or restart) Tomcat.

```
java com.lesavon.test.GetOrders2 inproc://
```

The local test output is identical to the previous run.

With the help of the factory and the proxy patterns, and in relatively few lines of code, we have designed and implemented a straightforward client-side framework that simplifies the development of SOAP clients. However, the `GetOrders2` implementation has one major flaw: the URL of the SOAP service is hard-coded. This is not acceptable for a production system, especially for a distributed application environment. A minor issue with `GetOrders2` is the fact that the class used to implement the service is known to the client, when the interface should be enough. You might want to avoid this level of coupling in an application that you will maintain for years.

A solution that is typically used in these kinds of situations is to isolate the dependency to a single file – typically an XML document since we are developing SOAP applications. However, files are hard to keep track of in a distributed environment, so a more desirable solution is to isolate the URL and the class name to a central location. Such a central location is readily available if your application has access to a directory system like LDAP. For now, we will assume that an LDAP-aware `SavonProxy` implementation is possible.

The decision to use the `SavonProxy` class is a design decision that has advantages and disadvantages, so let's take a few moments to review them.

Pros and Cons

The major cost of the simplicity provided by the `SavonProxy` is in the dynamic proxy and the `SavonProxy.invoke()` method. Arguably, the few instructions contained in that method constitute a negligible cost compared to the latency associated with a network, even in the case of an Intranet.

Since there is no proxy involved in the case of a local implementation, the only cost is the implementation of the factory pattern: a string comparison against `"inproc:"`.

The restriction on the exceptions that can be thrown is worthy of consideration, but we have mentioned earlier how that restriction can now be lifted with some additional development.

Another disadvantage of the `SavonProxy`, that can also be overcome with minor development, is the restriction on argument encoding that we mentioned during the code review: all arguments must be encoded using the same encoding (SOAP/XML Schema encoding or literal XML encoding).

Finally, it is worth reiterating that the `SavonProxy` relies on the dynamic proxy introduced in the JDK 1.3, with the caveats that not all classes can be supported by the dynamic proxy, and that it requires 1.3 functionality. This last issue would prevent you from using the `SavonProxy` if you had to deploy SOAP in a JDK 1.1 environment.

> **For a discussion on the limitations of the dynamic proxy, please visit**
> **http://java.sun.com/j2se/1.3/docs/guide/reflection/proxy.html**

The major advantage of the `SavonProxy` is in the simplicity that it provides to the client developer: one need not be concerned with low-level protocol-aware methods. To invoke a remote method you simply make a method call like `remoteAdmin.flush(usr, pwd)`. In addition, this transparency makes our job more simple for two important reasons: it makes debugging and deployment easier.

Debugging

Debugging remote services like JSP and Servlets can be a tedious task, especially if you do not have access to sophisticated IDEs. Even when using an IDE, the latency involved in debugging servlets as opposed to standalone applications can hurt productivity and shorten tempers.

The `SavonProxy` implementation offers an alternative since the service can be debugged as a local object simply by changing the URL passed to the factory.

Flexibility of Deployment

The actual load of a web application tends to be hard to predict. The problem becomes more complicated when the web application is sold to many customers as opposed to being deployed on a specific web site. By easily switching from a remote to a local deployment, the `SavonProxy` implementation offers flexibility in that area.

As we mentioned earlier, the actual URL of a SOAP service can come from a directory service similar to LDAP. In that environment, a site administrator can change the deployment machines easily. Since there is no penalty for local calls, this flexibility does not compromise the performance of the application. We could take this deployment strategy a step further by implementing a monitoring service that would automatically adjust the target servers according to the requirements of your application. Alternatively, if you simply want to distribute the load across several servers, a better solution is probably to rely on HTTP load balancing.

If high availability of the service is a requirement, a background thread can test the remote service and switch to local when things go wrong with the remote service. The same methodology could be used to maximize the use of hardware: work with local calls when the load is low and start distributing the requests when the load increases.

This level of sophistication is not required for most applications, but it is comforting to know that you have a design that can evolve with the requirements of your application.

Summary

In this chapter, we have enhanced the client-side development of SOAP applications in several ways:

In the first instance, we have freed the application developer from having to manually register mappings for the serialization of Java objects, both in and out of XML documents. We were able to easily implement this improvement by borrowing the server-side implementation.

Secondly, we have isolated the remote invocation of objects via SOAP in a dynamic proxy. Coupled with the use of the factory pattern, this feature allows the client-side programmer to easily create a local or a remote instance of SOAP services. In addition, the use of an interface allows local and remote instances to be used in the exact same way.

Finally, we have slightly modified the HTTP transport to pass a cache key as part of the HTTP header. This hint allows the server to skip parsing the SOAP request. Because the cache key is an optional entry in the HTTP header, we have preserved compatibility with clients and servers that are not aware of this optimization.

Our sample application now includes a functional, scalable, and robust SOAP server along with a client framework that offers a productive development environment. However, we still need to plug our web services in to an enterprise security system. In addition, we need to improve the performance of requests and responses that can be cached on the server.

The integration to an LDAP-based security system is presented in Chapter 7 and Chapter 8 is dedicated to the development of an intelligent cache.

JAVA

7

Security and Personalization

This chapter presents a possible architecture and implementation for a security and personalization system that can be used by your SOAP application. The main advantages of the proposed architecture are that it integrates well with the existing security system and does not require a custom user administration tool.

Briefly, it relies on the web server to authenticate requests and uses LDAP to store authorization and personalization information. The burden of owning an LDAP server is somewhat eased by the growing popularity of LDAP and by the availability of free LDAP systems like OpenLDAP. We will download and set up OpenLDAP in this chapter to run the samples. We do not pretend that the security and personalization architecture presented in this chapter is a panacea. It does, however, fulfill our modest requirements.

Security is a vast topic that we will not explore in detail. We will confine this discussion to how we connect a SOAP application to an existing security system and how we handle security and personalization using LDAP. We will integrate our sample application to an LDAP-based security system and to the Windows NT and 2000 security infrastructure. To demonstrate how LDAP-authentication can be set up, we will use Apache.

Before jumping into an overview of LDAP, it is important to point out that security is a chain as strong as its weakest link. In particular, correctly implementing an LDAP system is not a trivial task and the high level description of LDAP contained in this chapter will not prepare you to design and deploy your first LDAP-based security system.

However, this chapter will provide you with enough knowledge to design and deploy your SOAP application using an existing LDAP implementation to handle security and personalization.

> *For a more in-depth description of LDAP than one appropriate in a book on SOAP, please refer to* Implementing LDAP, *ISBN 1-861002-21-1, from Wrox Press.*

If you are already familiar with LDAP and JNDI, and you're impatient to see how you can use LDAP in your SOAP applications, feel free to jump to the *Roles and Privileges* section.

Naming Services

The primary feature of a **naming service** is to associate a human-readable name to an object. The word object should be taken in a broad sense here; it could be a Java object, an XML document, or a bitmap. There are a lot of naming services in use today. To name only a few:

- **Your computer file system**
  The computer file system associates file names with file data.
- **The Domain Name Service (DNS)**
  DNS associates computer names with IP addresses. For instance, the human-readable address such as www.wrox.com, is currently mapped to 204.148.170.161.
- **Your online corporate directory**
  The online corporate directory typically associates names of employees with their data: phone number, department, and so on.

Naming services impose constraints on the syntax of the names that they can store and retrieve. For instance, the DOS and Windows file systems use drive letters followed by a set of names separated by a backslash (\) – as in `C:\temp\MyFile.txt`.

Directory Services

A **directory service** or **system** is an extension of a naming system: it not only associates names with data, but also allows data to have attributes. Users of a directory service can then use those attributes to perform complicated queries on attribute values. The result of a directory service query is a set of objects (also known as **entities**) and their **attributes**.

One way to visualize the benefits of a directory service is to think of the yellow pages or your phone book. If you had a phone book with *only* the names and phone numbers of businesses, then that would be equivalent to a naming service: within such a book, you have a list of names and some data (a phone number) associated with each name. The addition of attributes (like type of business, brands sold, or even discount coupons), turns the yellow pages into a directory service, and makes it more valuable.

Lightweight Directory Access Protocol (LDAP)

Like phone books, directories are only useful if they are used to share information. Sharing information in the computing world means defining standards supported by vendors. An early standard aimed at standardizing the structure and the protocols used in distributed directory systems is the **X.500 Directory Access Protocol**. However, X.500 was complex and restrictive (it specified how a directory service should be implemented), so the **Internet Engineering Task Force** (**IETF**) started working on the **Lightweight Directory Access Protocol (LDAP)**.

LDAP focuses on what matters as far as a standard is concerned – how programs access the data. It does not matter if a phone book is printed on recycled gray paper or on white paper, but it is important that the phone book's entries are sorted alphabetically.

An exhaustive presentation of LDAP and X.500 directory services is outside the scope of this book, so we will limit ourselves to an introduction to directory services and LDAP, accompanied by a review of the concepts and features that are used by the sample application. RFC 2251, which defines LDAP version 3, can be found at http://www.ietf.org/rfc/rfc2251.txt. Version 3 of LDAP was published in 1997.

More and more LDAP systems are developed and deployed standalone. In such systems, an LDAP client is used to talk to a directory service that provides the X.500 subset required by LDAP. In this book, we work exclusively with LDAP systems. As we progress through this discussion, we will use the terms *LDAP* and *directory service* synonymously.

It's OK to do this, as long as we do not lose track of the fact that LDAP is only an *access protocol* to a directory service – and as such, it does not specify how the directory service should be implemented. We will now refine our understanding of directory services.

The screenshot below shows how objects are organized within a tree called the **Directory Information Tree** (**DIT**). Each 'entry' (or 'object', or 'entity' – the terms are synonymous in this context) contains a name, also called the **Distinguished Name** (**DN**), and attributes. The DN of our top-level entry is `o=LeSavonWrox`.

In LDAP, names are ordered from left to right. The components of a name are delimited using the comma (`,`) operator and each component is always composed of a name/value pair separated by the equal (=) operator.

We will use names like:

- o (an **organization** like a company or a research institute)
- ou (an **organizational unit** like the Human Resources or Accounting department)
- cn (a **common name** like Engineering or HR Manager)

These names are defined in LDAP schemas that we will introduce in the next section.

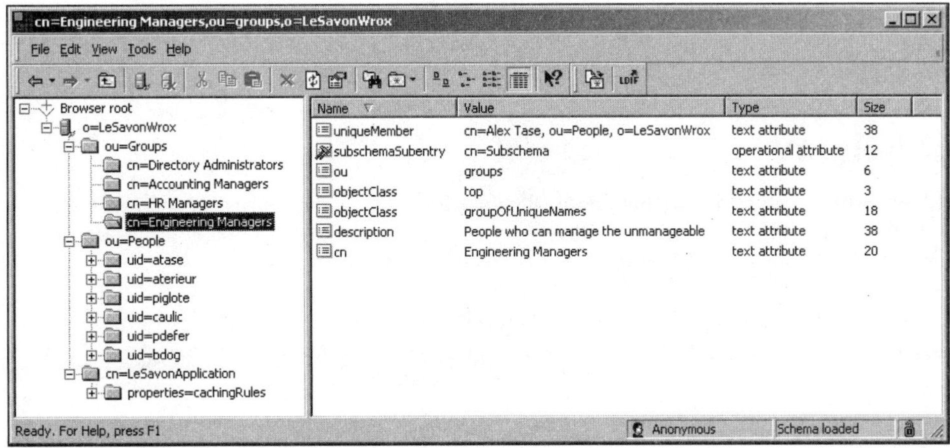

The screenshot above is taken from the example that we will meet during the course of this chapter, using Softerra LDAP Browser 2.0. More on this later.

Naming an object is sometimes referred to as **binding**, like a computer name is bound to an IP address in DNS.

At first glance, naming objects might not seem like a big deal. It becomes a big deal when most, if not all, of your applications use the same service. You have probably encountered this situation in your work or on the Internet: you use several applications in the course of your daily work and each application has its own set of users. For instance, the human resource web uses a different set of user accounts from the e-mail system. Soon, the proliferation of user accounts becomes hard and expensive to manage.

Very often, this multiplication of interdependent security systems weakens security, because it multiplies the number of potential points of failure. Another important point to consider is the fact that users tend to take the path of least resistance by using the same password in all systems, or worse, by not protecting their accounts at all.

A directory service is not for users alone. It can contain a representation of just about anything: a printer, a network, a server, and so on. In the screenshot above, you can see that there is an entry called `cn=LeSavonApplication` to represent our sample application. We will revisit this entry later.

In addition to providing naming and security for applications and users, LDAP also provides the designer of a distributed application with a central location in which to save and retrieve slowly-changing data. For instance, if you need to save the default background color for a given end user, you can save it using LDAP, and automatically give access to the saved data from any location. The same argument can be made to save application data, like cache settings.

We mentioned earlier that in addition to storing names for objects, a directory service can store attributes. For instance, in the screenshot, the `cn=Engineering Managers` object has an attribute called `description` (whose value gives more information about the object).

Note the `objectClass` attribute, which is a special attribute in LDAP. The object class gives a type to the object. From the screenshot, you can see that an object can have multiple types. For instance, the entry `cn=Engineering Managers` has two object classes: `top` and `groupOfUniqueNames`. Among its other attributes are its **Common Name** (`CN` or `cn`) and its `description`, which we've already met. To further explain types and attributes, we must discuss LDAP schemas.

LDAP Schema

An LDAP schema contains the **meta data** (data about data) for the entries stored in LDAP. The meta data defines what can be stored in the directory service. An LDAP schema contains definitions for objects, attributes, and matching rules.

The object type definition is similar to a structure (a class with no methods but only properties) definition; it defines the list of attributes that an entry of that class must have and a list of attributes an entry may have. Each entry must have at least one object class.

In practice, entries have more than one object class. In the screenshot, you will notice that the top-level element has two object classes, `top` and `organization`. Those two classes are defined in RFC 2256 (http://www.ietf.org/rfc/rfc2256.txt) and can be found in the `core.schema` file, along with other schema files, in the `Schema` directory of the OpenLDAP distribution:

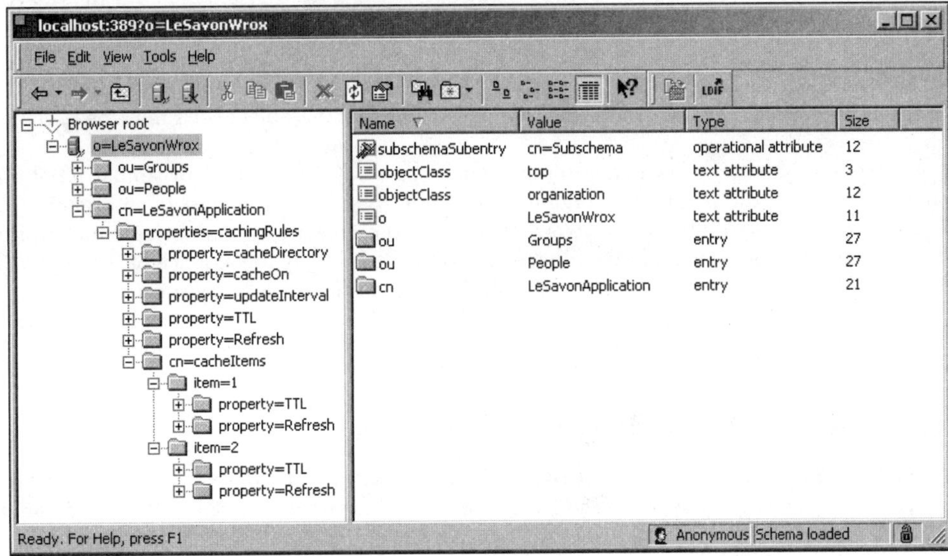

Let's have a look at the definitions of the `top` and `organization` classes from the `core.schema` file. First, here's the definition of the top-level class of a hierarchy:

```
objectclass ( 2.5.6.0 NAME 'top' ABSTRACT
   MUST objectClass )
```

And here's the definition of the organization (company, research institute, school, ...) class:

```
objectclass ( 2.5.6.4 NAME 'organization' SUP top STRUCTURAL
   MUST o
   MAY ( userPassword $ searchGuide $ seeAlso $ businessCategory $
      x121Address $ registeredAddress $ destinationIndicator $
      preferredDeliveryMethod $ telexNumber $ teletexTerminalIdentifier $
      telephoneNumber $ internationaliSDNNumber $
      facsimileTelephoneNumber $ street $ postOfficeBox $ postalCode $
      postalAddress $ physicalDeliveryOfficeName $ st $ l $ description ) )
```

The **Object Identifier** (**OID**) of the class `top` is `2.5.6.0`, as indicated by this statement:

```
objectclass ( 2.5.6.0 NAME 'top' ABSTRACT
   MUST objectClass )
```

OIDs uniquely identify classes and attributes. Each schema element is identified by an OID. When defining what you want to store in LDAP, you might find out that you need to add new attributes and new objects on top of what is defined in RFC 2256. It is possible to define your own object classes and attributes, but they must be assigned unique OIDs.

Rather than making up your own OID, you should apply for one with the **Internet Assigned Numbers Authority** (IANA at http://www.iana.org, follow the Application Forms->Private Enterprise Numbers (SNMP) links). Note that since OIDs are hierarchical, you can obtain one for your organization and then branch off your root. For instance, we will use the number assigned to Wrox Press (`4412`) to create a hierarchy of object classes: `4412.1.1.1.1` for the `roles` class, `4412.1.1.2` for the `properties` class, and so on.

The `ABSTRACT` keyword means that the top object class must either be accompanied by another object class or be sub-classed. The `MUST` keyword simply means that the object class must be specified.

The organization object class is meant to represent a company, or a school, or similar – but not a department, which is the realm of an organizational unit (ou). The superclass of an organization is the top object class. The `STRUCTURAL` keyword means that the object class cannot be removed from the entity. The intent is that removing the object class would take away the essence of the object. The `MAY` keyword is followed by a list of attributes that an instance of the object may specify.

We will have a second look at schema files when we review how our sample application uses LDAP.

LDAP Data Interchange Format

The **LDAP Data Interchange Format (LDIF)** is a file format suitable for exchanging additions or modifications to a directory system. The LDIF specification is defined in RFC 2849, and can be found at http://www.ietf.org/rfc/rfc2849.txt.

Most LDAP implementations, including OpenLDAP, provide capabilities to save and load directory data to and from LDIF files. We will have a closer look at an LDIF file when we review the use of LDAP in our sample application.

Another common use of LDIF files is to present data in a human-readable form. When reading articles and books about LDAP, you are likely to see the data presented using LDIF.

Replication

An important feature that is often implemented in standalone LDAP systems is **replication**. One can set up an LDAP directory service as part of a federation of directory services. This level of replication allows for high availability, which is a desirable feature for a distributed application.

Pitfalls

Before discussing what we will do with a directory system accessible through LDAP, we should discuss what should be avoided. A good rule of thumb is to keep in mind that LDAP is not SQL and LDAP databases are not meant to replace RDBMSs.

Three types of operations are not well suited for an LDAP system:

- First, we should not use LDAP for storage and retrieval of fast changing data. LDAP is best suited for "read-mostly" applications such as validating your user name, your password, or retrieving the IP address of a printer. I don't recommend that you use LDAP for, say, saving and retrieving the session variables of an e-commerce application. This is not the kind of data that you want to store in LDAP, and the performance of your application would suffer in this kind of operation.

  In addition, remember that LDAP databases can be replicated (or **federated**) across a wide network. In that case, it might take a while for the modifications to propagate throughout the network. Your application must be designed with that latency in mind. In the case of the sample application, we will use LDAP to store personalization settings such as users' preferred background color, which are not frequently changed.

- Second, we do not want to store large objects using LDAP. A directory system is not a database or a file system. If you need to have access to large amounts of data by name, for instance a directory of MP3 files, you should store pointers using LDAP and leave the music on your file system or in an object database.

  The performance of your application will deteriorate if you store large objects in your LDAP database. As we will see shortly, the sample application only stores very small amounts of data in LDAP.

- Finally, as we hinted earlier in our phone book analogy, directory systems are used for sharing data. If your data is only used by one application on a specific host, then the use of a directory system probably increases the complexity of your product without any tangible benefit.

LDAP Security and Personalization

Now that you have a better idea about the capabilities of LDAP, you might be wondering just what it has to do with security and personalization. Well, without going into too many details, we can divide the subject of security into two parts:

- **Authentication**
  This is the operation confirming that the user is who they say they are.

- **Authorization**
  Based on an authenticated user name, this operation confirms the user is allowed to do what they are trying to do.

Authenticating users with LDAP is usually done in two phases. First, the client connects to the server using an anonymous connection or using a pre-defined user account stored in a configuration file.

For instance, our sample application uses the `uid=atase,ou=People,o=LeSavonWrox` user as the root user. Once the client is connected to the server, it then performs a search by passing the user identifier and the user password as search criteria for the attributes.

This two-phase process is necessary because typically, the client does not know the DN; it only knows the RDN. That's because users like to log in with a portion of the RDN (such as `atase`) rather than the entire DN (in this case `uid=atase,ou=People,o=LeSavonWrox`).

> *We will see a practical example of this process when we use LDAP to authenticate users coming through the Apache web server. Note that if your application knows the exact DN to look for, then you can authenticate in a single phase.*

Another issue critical to the security of the overall system is how LDAP itself authenticates. Does it send the username and password in clear text over the wire? In a production environment, the answer is most definitely no. Very often, the biggest security risk comes not from the outside of the corporate network, but from the inside.

The way an LDAP client securely authenticates to the server is quite complex and outside the scope of this book. For the sake of illustration, we will store the passwords in clear text in the database and authenticate using basic authentication.

How does personalization get into this picture? Personalization is about the storage and retrieval of data that is associated with a user, with the intent of using that data to customize the user's experience. GUI applications have been storing user preferences on your local computer for years. This concept is being taken to the next step with web-based distributed applications that not only personalize the look and feel, but also the data that actually gets delivered to you. *MyYahoo!* is a well-known example – it's a feature of the *Yahoo!* portal that allows you to configure it according to your own preferences.

When your application is distributed, user preferences must be available globally to provide the same user experience regardless of the entry point. LDAP was designed with these requirements in mind.

If you're going to remember what each user wants, you need to uniquely identify your users. After a successful authentication phase, you have a unique user identifier that you can then use to build and populate an LDAP entry.

The sample application uses the background color and the default font to demonstrate how to implement personalization, but you can extend the concept to the data pertinent to your application. The important point is that once we have authenticated a user, we have a container in the LDAP database to store user data for a given application. We will define more specifically how we store user data in the *Roles and Privileges* section.

Java Naming and Directory Interface (JNDI)

There are many naming and directory systems in use today. To name only a few:

- OpenLDAP (http://www.openldap.org/)
- NT Domains (http://www.microsoft.com/ntserver/)
- Novell's NDS (http://www.novell.com/products/nds/)
- iPlanet (http://www.iplanet.com/)
- Windows 2000 Active Directory Service (http://www.microsoft.com/windows2000/server/)

The situation is similar to what database developers have faced for years, with RDBMS vendors supporting the SQL standard with slight variations such as data types and query syntax. As the next figure shows, client applications must code to several vendor-defined APIs in order to support more than one directory system.

This multiplication of vendor-specific code makes application development more complex and tends to decrease quality. In addition, whenever new directory services are released (as ADS was, fairly recently), application developers have to roll out a new version that supports the new service.

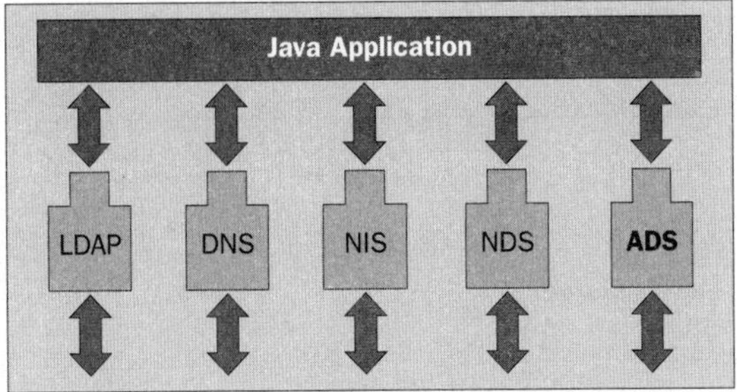

Following a strategy similar to JDBC, Sun designed and implemented the **Java Naming and Directory Interface** (**JNDI**). Like JDBC, which provides one interface to a variety of RDBMS systems, JNDI provides a common interface to a variety of naming and directory systems:

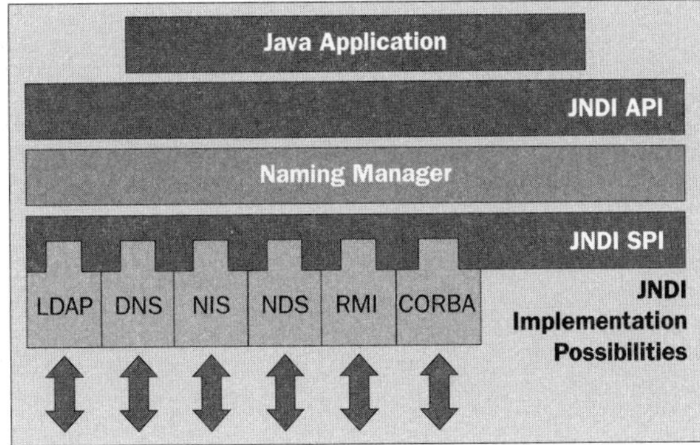

Even with a common API like JNDI, there are still differences in how a directory service names its entries. Those differences are removed if the directory service vendor provides an LDAP interface to its storage system because the LDAP interface handles the necessary conversion.

A detailed JNDI tutorial is outside the scope of this book, so we will restrict this discussion to the concepts and API calls that are used by the sample application.

Roles and Privileges

Before we can look at a meaningful example of how these concepts are translated into code using JNDI, we must explain how we assign privileges to the users of our sample application.

Since the number of operations is limited, the security scheme of the sample application can be made effective by defining just two simple roles: **user** and **administrator**. Users in the role of administrator can perform any operation on the system. For instance, only users in the administrator role will be allowed to flush or refresh the cache.

As the screenshot below shows, since `uid=atase` is our root user, she assumes the role of administrator. There can be as many administrators as necessary.

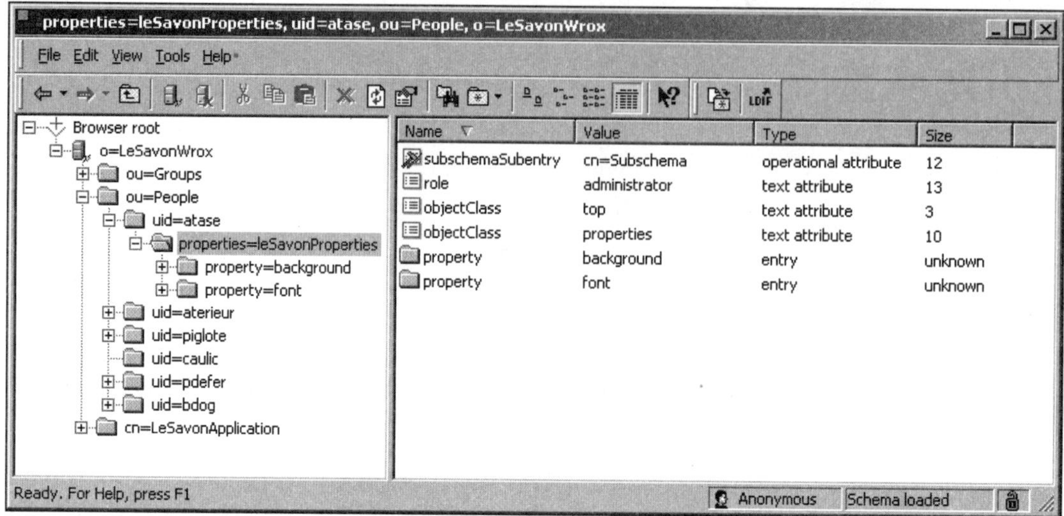

You might be wondering how, if we needed to, we could implement a more sophisticated scheme. At least two strategies could be used. We could refine the role-based security of the sample application with a privilege-based implementation. In such an implementation, we would define a more granular set of operations, like this:

- May edit an object
- May delete an object
- May create an object
- May read an object

The definition of these privileges depends on the application. The code would have to check for the list of privileges assigned to the user, before granting the right to perform the operation. This approach is very similar to the checks that you'll find for the administrator role in the sample application.

If you try this, you might want to facilitate the management of privileges by regrouping them – by defining each role as being a group of privileges. LDAP is a convenient place to put the definition of roles, since it allows system administrators to assign role names that are meaningful to their organization. In particular, it allows for easy localization of role names.

If you were to plug in to an enterprise LDAP-based security infrastructure, then you'd probably find that the users in its database already had some kind of privileges and roles assigned to them. In this case, you could use these existing roles and privileges for your own application. This strategy has the advantage of minimizing the required user administration, but has the drawback that you must marry your design to a specific existing security implementation.

Adding Users to LeSavon

We are now ready to have a look at a simple LDAP client, which you can use to grant users access to LeSavon: `AddLeSavonUser`. This client expects that the entry for the user (that you pass as an argument) already exists. Thus, it is similar to what would happen if you were to install your application at a customer site already using LDAP.

This example assumes some understanding of how we store entities and attributes for the sample *Non-Platform Specific/* application. We will discuss these topics in detail in the *Configuration Files* section, but for the purpose of understanding the next few paragraphs one only needs to know that application-wide settings are stored under `cn=LeSavonApplication` and that user-specific settings are stored under `properties=LeSavonProperties,uid=<user-name>`.

> *The sample code for this chapter can be found in `ProJavaSoap/Chapter07/`. The sample code for `AddLeSavonUser` can be found in `ProJavaSoap/Chapter07/AddLeSavonUser.java`.*

Let's begin to piece this client together:

```
// AddLeSavonUser.java
package com.lesavon.util;

import javax.naming.Context;
import javax.naming.directory.InitialDirContext;
import javax.naming.directory.DirContext;
import javax.naming.directory.Attributes;
import javax.naming.directory.ModificationItem;
import javax.naming.directory.BasicAttribute;
import javax.naming.directory.BasicAttributes;
import javax.naming.directory.AttributeInUseException;
import javax.naming.NamingException;
import javax.naming.NameNotFoundException;
import java.util.Hashtable;
```

JNDI provides two packages, one for naming (`javax.naming`) and one for directory access (`javax.naming.directory`).

```
public class AddLeSavonUser {
  private static final String APP_NAME = "com.lesavon.test.AddLeSavonUser";
  private static final String LDAP_URL =
                                      "ldap://localhost:389/o=LeSavonWrox";
  private static final String AUTH_TYPE = "simple";
  private static final String ROOT_USR =
                                      "uid=atase,ou=People,o=LeSavonWrox";
  private static final String ROOT_PWD = "lesavon";
  private static final String TRAILER = ",ou=People";
  private static final String UID = "uid=";
  private static final String PROPERTIES = "properties=LeSavonProperties,";
  private static final String ROLE = "user";
```

This example can connect to any LDAP server that supports LDAP version 3. As you can see from the static constants defined in the fragment above, the default connection URL is `localhost`, but feel free to change it to your server URL. Also, note that the port number is typically `389`, but any port can be used. The `AddLeSavonUser` will connect to the LDAP server using `uid=atase` – this is because an anonymous connection would not allow us to add and modify entities in the directory.

The use of the other static constants will become apparent in the `run()` method. We provide a private constructor that assigns the user name passed in at the command line:

```
private final String userName;

// Construct an instance of AddLeSavonUser for a given user name.
// @return the global cache ttl value
private AddLeSavonUser(String userName) {
  this.userName = userName;
}

// Public entry point.
// @arg args arg[0] contains a user identifier (e.g. pdefer)
public static void main(String args[]) {
  System.out.println(APP_NAME + ": Starting...");

  if (args.length != 1) {
    System.err.println("AddLeSavonUser: Grants access to LeSavon.");
    System.err.println("Usage :java AddLeSavonUser <user-name>");
    System.err.println("Sample:java AddLeSavonUser pdefer");
    System.exit(-1);   // something went wrong...
  }

  AddLeSavonUser addLeSavonUser = new AddLeSavonUser(args[0]);
  addLeSavonUser.run();

  System.out.println(APP_NAME + ": All done!");
}
```

The JNDI environment is used to store information like the LDAP server URL and authentication setting. Also, we're using our root user account to connect. We need to use this account, since we are going to modify the database:

```
private void run() {
  try {
    Hashtable jndiEnv = new Hashtable(1);
    jndiEnv.put(Context.INITIAL_CONTEXT_FACTORY,
                              "com.sun.jndi.ldap.LdapCtxFactory");
    jndiEnv.put(Context.PROVIDER_URL, LDAP_URL);
    jndiEnv.put(Context.SECURITY_AUTHENTICATION, AUTH_TYPE);

    jndiEnv.put(Context.SECURITY_PRINCIPAL, ROOT_USR);
    jndiEnv.put(Context.SECURITY_CREDENTIALS, ROOT_PWD);
```

In JNDI, the connection is specified using a hash table, which contains name/value pairs that define the behavior of the initial context. The `Context` class defines constants for the names that it understands: `Context.SECURITY_AUTHENTICATION` for the authentication type (which in this case is `simple`), `Context.SECURITY_PRINCIPAL` for the user name (`uid=atase,ou=People,o=LeSavonWrox`), and so on.

A context is essentially equivalent to an entity in the hierarchy. In a file system, a context would be akin to a directory. Since the LDAP URL that we set up in the JNDI environment specifies `o=LeSavonWrox` as a root DN, all names that we will use from now on will be relative to that root DN.

We are now ready to connect. The result of successful connection to a JNDI provider is a `DirContext` object:

```
DirContext rootContext = new InitialDirContext(jndiEnv);
```

An exception will be thrown if something goes wrong during the connection. For instance, a bad password would throw a `NamingException` with the following message:

```
[LDAP: error code 49 - Invalid Credentials]
```

The list of LDAP error codes can be found in RFC 2251 (http://www.ietf.org/rfc/rfc2251.txt). Typically, the server will send an explanation of the error code along with the error.

Once we are connected, we can verify that the user passed in actually exists in our LDAP database. To accomplish this, we query the root context that we got back from our connection for the entity associated to the user ID. If that operation is successful, we get back a collection of attributes. If, by contrast, that user could not be found in our LDAP database, we would get a `NameNotFoundException`, a subclass of `NamingException`, with the following error message:

```
[LDAP: error code 32 - No Such Object]
```

If we get a `NameNotFoundException` error, it's our cue to create an entry for the `LeSavon` properties of that user. We initially give it the object class `top`, but we must also make sure that it has the object class `properties`. The custom object class `properties` is used for a collection of property objects. We will review the `properties` object class further when we look at `lesavon.schema`. We must also add a role to the `properties` entry. Our default role is `user`:

```
Attributes uidAttributes
              = rootContext.getAttributes(UID + userName + TRAILER);
System.out.println("Found user " + uidAttributes.get("cn").get());
```

If the user does not already have a properties entry, we create one. The properties distinguished name for user pdefer would result in the following entry:

```
properties=LeSavonProperties,uid=pdefer,ou=People
```

The next line will search in the directory tree from right to left down from LeSavon through each category. If the entry is not found then we catch the `NameNotFoundException` that will be thrown and create the user's properties.

```
String propertiesDN = PROPERTIES + UID + userName + TRAILER;
try {
  Attributes propAttributes = rootContext.getAttributes(propertiesDN);
} catch (NameNotFoundException nameNotFoundException) {
  System.out.println("Creating LeSavonProperties for user "
                     + uidAttributes.get("cn").get() + "...");
```

We add the top object class, and add it to the DN:

```
  Attributes newAttributes = new BasicAttributes("objectClass", "top");
  rootContext.createSubcontext(propertiesDN, newAttributes);
}
```

We must now ensure that the properties collection is marked appropriately:

```
rootContext.modifyAttributes(propertiesDN,
             new ModificationItem[] {
               new ModificationItem(DirContext.REPLACE_ATTRIBUTE,
                                    new BasicAttribute("objectclass",
                                                       "properties"))
             }
);

// Make sure that the user has a role
rootContext.modifyAttributes(propertiesDN,
             new ModificationItem[] {
               new ModificationItem(DirContext.REPLACE_ATTRIBUTE,
                                    new BasicAttribute("role", ROLE))
             }
);
```

The remainder of our properties can now be added with the `addEntry()` helper method. In this case, we just add `background` and `font` properties for user personalization of the application:

```
      addEntry(rootContext, propertiesDN, "property",
               "property=background", "white");
      addEntry(rootContext, propertiesDN, "property", "property=font",
               "arial");

      rootContext.close();
    } catch (NamingException namingException) {
      System.err.println(APP_NAME + ": Error, caught exception: "
                         + namingException);
    }
  }
```

Finally, here's the definition of the `addEntry()` helper function that we used above:

```
  private void addEntry(DirContext rootContext, String dn,
                        String objectClass, String name, String value)
      throws NamingException {
    String newElementDN = name + "," + dn;
    try {
      Attributes propAttributes = rootContext.getAttributes(newElementDN);
    } catch (NameNotFoundException nameNotFoundException) {
      System.out.println("Creating " + newElementDN + "...");
```

```
      Attributes newAttributes = new BasicAttributes("objectClass", "top");
      rootContext.createSubcontext(newElementDN, newAttributes);
    }

    rootContext.modifyAttributes(newElementDN, new ModificationItem[] {
      new ModificationItem(DirContext.REPLACE_ATTRIBUTE,
                           new BasicAttribute("objectclass", objectClass))
    });

    if (objectClass.compareTo("properties") == 0) {
      // We need to add/replace the role
      rootContext.modifyAttributes(newElementDN, new ModificationItem[] {
        new ModificationItem(DirContext.REPLACE_ATTRIBUTE,
                             new BasicAttribute("role", ROLE))
      });
    }

    if (value != null) {
      rootContext.modifyAttributes(newElementDN, new ModificationItem[] {
        new ModificationItem(DirContext.REPLACE_ATTRIBUTE,
                             new BasicAttribute("value", value))
      });
      System.out.println("Property " + newElementDN
                         + " has been set to value " + value);
    }
  }
}
```

The `addEntry()` uses JNDI methods that we have previously discussed. Note that we could replace the JNDI code that creates the entry for the `LeSavon` properties of the user, with a call to `addEntry()`:

```
addEntry(rootContext, UID + userName + TRAILER, "properties",
         "properties=leSavonProperties", null);
```

By now, you are probably keen to run this sample and see how it modifies the database. Before we can do that, we need to have an LDAP server configured to handle our requests.

LDAP Browsers

When developing LDAP applications, it is useful to have an interactive tree view of the database and be able to modify entities and attributes. There are many tools available. Some, like the LDAP Browser/Editor from Softerra (currently freely available from http://www.ldapbrowser.com) are platform-specific.

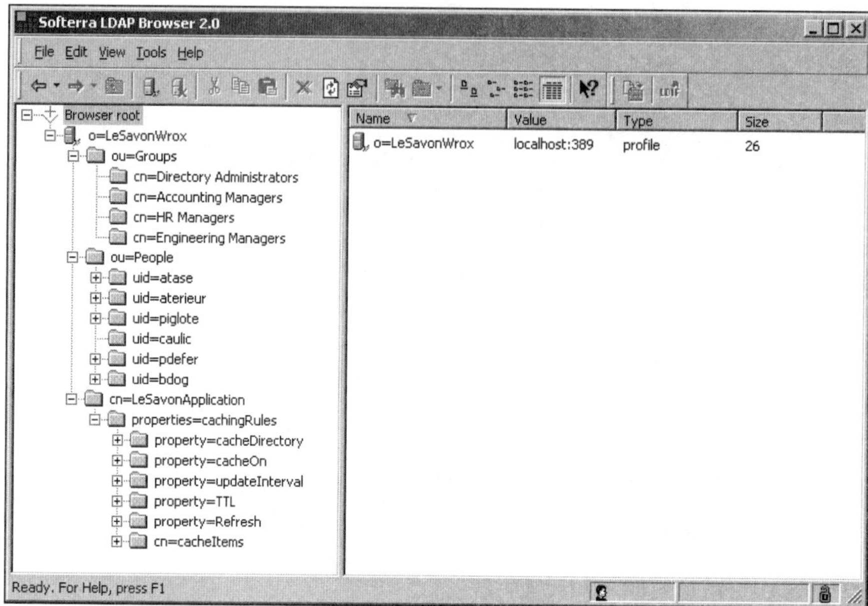

The illustration above shows the Softerra LDAP Browser/Editor, which we will be using in this book to show views of our LDAP database. When you've downloaded the file (`ldapbrowser20.msi`), run it and follow the install instructions.

Others browsers are java based like the LDAP Browser/Editor written and maintained by Jarek Gawor (see http://www.iit.edu/~gawojar/ldap).

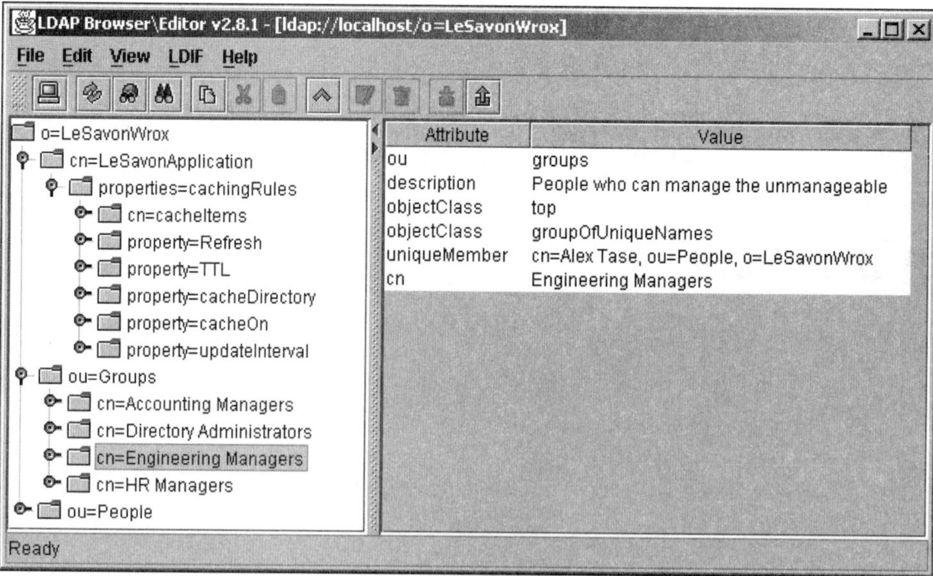

We will now set up LDAP on Windows 2000 as an example for the Windows family. The setup on Windows NT is similar.

LDAP Setup

Whether you're setting up your LDAP server on Windows or LINUX, the set up process is similar – although there are a few differences that are worth pointing out. We will go through the setup instructions for Windows 2000 and LINUX Red Hat 7.1. If you do not need to set up LDAP on a computer running Windows, you can go directly to the *LDAP Setup for LINUX* section. If you are already familiar with LDAP and how to set it up on your platform, then you can jump to the *Non-Platform Specific/ Configuration Files* section where we discuss settings specific to the sample application.

In the *LDAP Setup for Windows* and *LDAP Setup for LINUX* sections that follow, there is some duplicate information; the intention was to ensure that each section is self-contained.

LDAP Setup for Windows

The first step is naturally to get the software. You can download the source from http://www.openldap.org and build it for Windows. Alternatively, you can go to http://www.fivesight.com/downloads/openldap.asp and download a compiled version for Windows:

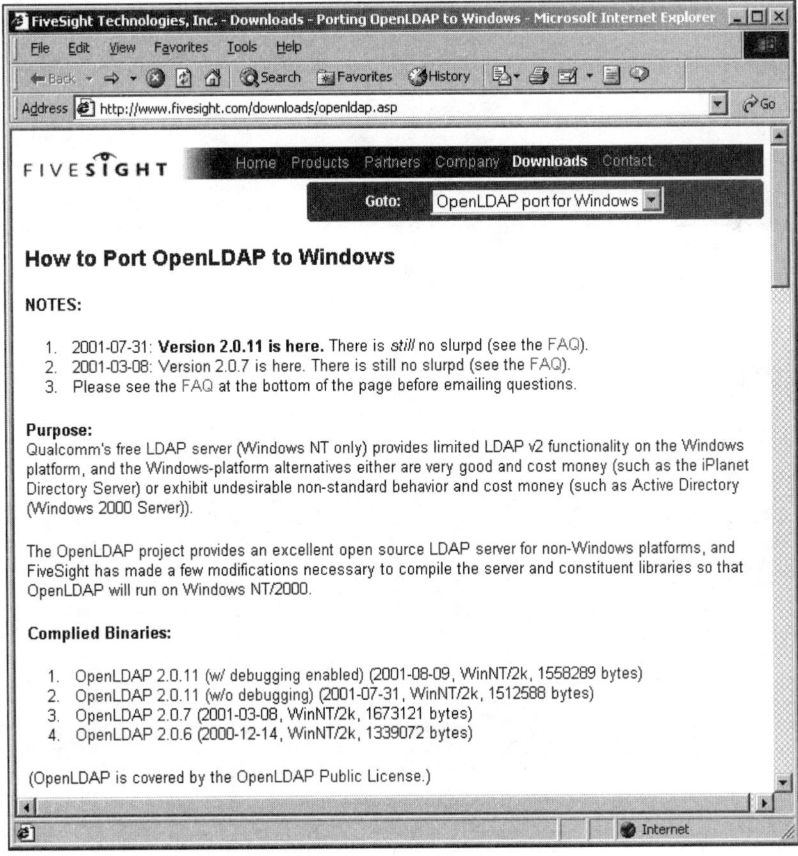

The examples in the book have been tested against version 2.0.7; you might want to select the same version from the list of available binaries. Click on the OpenLDAP 2.0.7 link, and download the tar file called `openldap-2_0_7-win32-20010308.tar.gz`. Once you've got the file, you can view its contents using a program like WinZip:

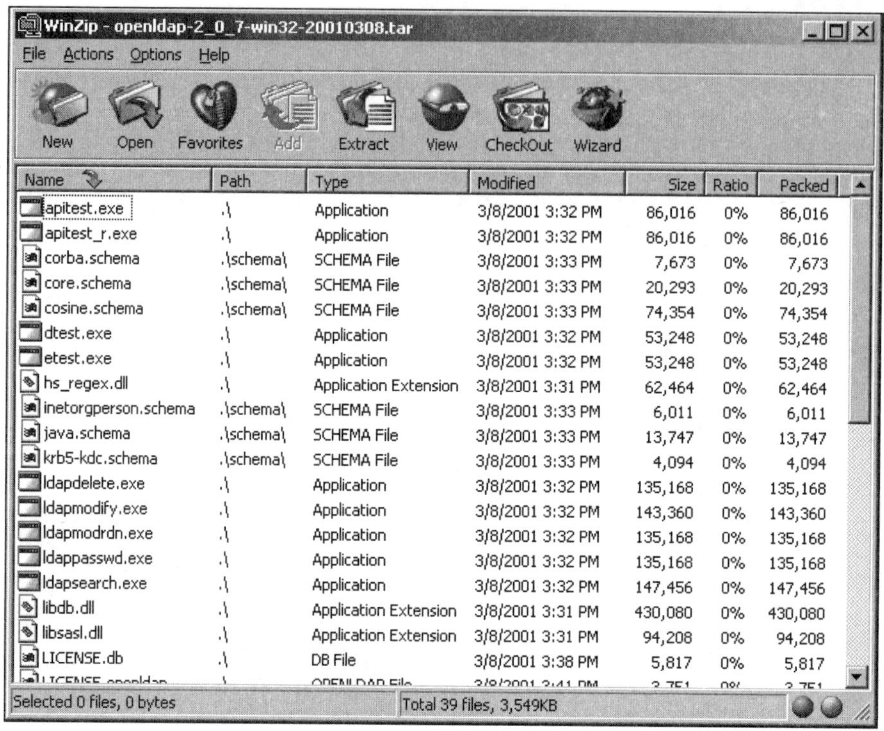

We need to extract the contents of the `.tar` file to a place on the machine's hard drive. In these screenshots, you'll see that I'm using a drive labeled c:. Extract the tar file into c:\ProJavaSoap\Chapter07\openLDAP as you can see in the following screenshot:

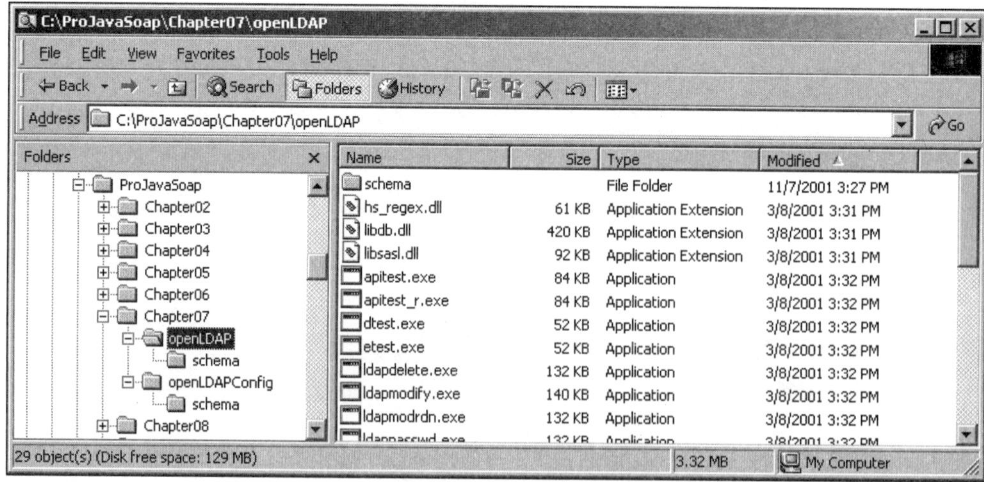

At this point, we're almost ready to run the LDAP server. However, we need to add the configuration files specific to the sample application.

Like most programs that find their roots in UNIX, OpenLDAP is configured using setup files. The main files we need to look into are:

- The `slapd.conf` file, which contains essential information such as the schema and the root account.
- The `lesavon.schema` file, which defines the objects and attributes that are specific to the sample application.
- The `lesavon.ldif` file, which is used to seed the database.

The last two of these files are not platform-specific, so we will review them in the *Non-Platform Specific/Configuration Files* section, a few pages on from here. However, we must present them now because LDAP will not work with an empty directory. We must seed the LDAP database with data to use it. We decided to work with real data from the sample application, rather than forcing the reader to go through two LDAP configurations.

For your convenience, the configuration files are available in c:\ProJavaSoap\Chapter07\OpenLDAPConfig as you can see in the next figure:

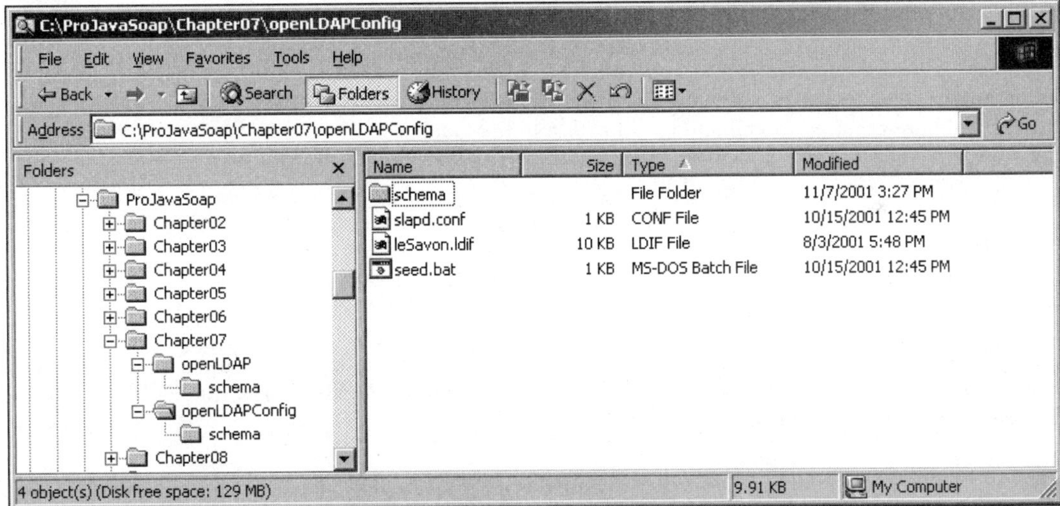

You need to copy the contents of the openLDAPConfig directory to the OpenLDAP directory. You may be asked if you want to overwrite the existing slapd.conf file – if so, say Yes. You can perform the copy either by drag-and-drop in your Windows Explorer, or at the command prompt, by navigating to the \openLDAP directory and then using the following commands:

```
c:\ProJavaSoap\Chapter07\openLDAP>copy ..\openLDAPConfig .
c:\ProJavaSoap\Chapter07\openLDAP>copy ..\openLDAPConfig\schema .\schema
```

In a few moments, we will look at the seed.bat file (which is used to create the LDAP directory). Before that, let's have a closer look at the `slapd.conf` file. The statements that we need to add or amend are in bold:

```
# slapd.conf
include     C:/ProJavaSoap/Chapter07/OpenLDAP/schema/core.schema
include     C:/ProJavaSoap/Chapter07/OpenLDAP/schema/cosine.schema
include     C:/ProJavaSoap/Chapter07/OpenLDAP/schema/inetorgperson.schema
include     C:/ProJavaSoap/Chapter07/OpenLDAP/schema/java.schema
include     C:/ProJavaSoap/Chapter07/OpenLDAP/schema/lesavon.schema

backend ldbm

database    ldbm
directory   C:/ProJavaSoap/Chapter07/OpenLDAP/ldbm

suffix ""

rootdn "uid=atase, ou=People, o=LeSavonWrox"
rootpw lesavon
```

In the `slapd.conf` file, any lines beginning with a # character are comments and are not executed. Otherwise, `slapd.conf` contains three types of statements or directives: global statements, backend statements and database statements.

The global statements can be `include` directives, timeouts for client connections, and logging statements. The `include` statements for the schema definitions are global statements. The schemas specified here are used to validate modification to the database.

```
include     C:/ProJavaSoap/Chapter07/OpenLDAP/schema/core.schema
include     C:/ProJavaSoap/Chapter07/OpenLDAP/schema/cosine.schema
include     C:/ProJavaSoap/Chapter07/OpenLDAP/schema/inetorgperson.schema
include     C:/ProJavaSoap/Chapter07/OpenLDAP/schema/java.schema
include     C:/ProJavaSoap/Chapter07/OpenLDAP/schema/lesavon.schema
```

Note that most servers will not enforce compliance with a schema when they open a database. Rather they will check the schema when a modification is attempted. We will review the schema for the sample application later in the chapter.

There is only one backend statement in this `slapd.conf` file:

```
backend ldbm
```

As we mentioned previously, LDAP is an access protocol – so it does not actually implement storage and retrieval for the data. The `backend` statement allows you to specify the database system used to store and retrieve the data. The sample application uses a shareware database, LDBM, which comes with your installation and is the default.

Database directives apply to one particular instance of a database. The `database` statement marks the beginning of a new database instance definition.

```
database     ldbm
directory    C:/ProJavaSoap/Chapter07/OpenLDAP/ldbm

suffix ""

rootdn "uid=atase, ou=People, o=LeSavonWrox"
rootpw lesavon
```

We will create the `/ldbm` directory that is listed for the database. The `suffix` statement states that all DNs that end with the specified suffix should be passed to this database. That statement is required. In the case of the sample application, all queries should go to the only database that is supported. Finally, the `rootdn` and `rootpwd` define the credentials that are used to define the **superuser**. The root DN is not subject to access and modification restrictions. Other directives in this section include read only status, replication, and log file directives.

The next file that we need to modify with the settings for your computer is seed.bat. The file that we've supplied looks like this:

seed.bat - Notepad

File Edit Format Help

```
@echo off
rem seed.bat
rem Henry Bequet 05/29/01
rem Regenerate the LDAP database based on lesavon.ldif. Slapd must not be running...

pushd C:\ProJavaSoap\Chapter07\OpenLDAP

rem Then we delete the database
if exist C:\ProJavaSoap\Chapter07\OpenLDAP\ldbm\*.dbb del C:\ProJavaSoap\Chapter07\OpenLDAP\ldbm\*.dbb

rem Finally we repopulate the database
slapadd -f slapd.conf -v -l lesavon.ldif

popd
```

If you've extracted OpenLDAP into a directory other than C:\ProJavaSoap\Chapter07\OpenLDAP, then you'll need to reflect that by changing the directory path in `slapd.conf` and `seed.bat`. Once you have made those simple changes, creating the database is straightforward. First, we create a new directory for our database and use `seed.bat` to populate the database. Once that's done, we can start the slapd server. That's all done using these three commands:

```
cd C:\ProJavaSoap\Chapter07\openLDAP
mkdir ldbm
seed
slapd
```

The screenshot shows the output you can expect to see:

```
E:\WINNT\System32\cmd.exe - slapd
C:\ProJavaSoap\Chapter07\openLDAP>mkdir ldbm

C:\ProJavaSoap\Chapter07\openLDAP>seed
added: "o=LeSavonWrox" (00000001)
added: "ou=Groups, o=LeSavonWrox" (00000002)
added: "cn=Directory Administrators, ou=Groups, o=LeSavonWrox" (00000003)
added: "cn=Accounting Managers,ou=groups,o=LeSavonWrox" (00000004)
added: "cn=HR Managers,ou=groups,o=LeSavonWrox" (00000005)
added: "cn=Engineering Managers,ou=groups,o=LeSavonWrox" (00000006)
added: "ou=People, o=LeSavonWrox" (00000007)
added: "uid=atase, ou=People, o=LeSavonWrox" (00000008)
added: "uid=aterieur, ou=People, o=LeSavonWrox" (00000009)
added: "uid=piglote, ou=People, o=LeSavonWrox" (0000000a)
added: "uid=caulic, ou=People, o=LeSavonWrox" (0000000b)
added: "uid=pdefer, ou=People, o=LeSavonWrox" (0000000c)
added: "uid=bdog, ou=People, o=LeSavonWrox" (0000000d)
added: "cn=LeSavonApplication, o=LeSavonWrox" (0000000e)
added: "properties=cachingRules, cn=LeSavonApplication, o=LeSavonWrox" (0000000f)
added: "property=cacheDirectory, properties=cachingRules, cn=LeSavonApplication, o=LeSavonWrox
added: "property=cacheOn, properties=cachingRules, cn=LeSavonApplication, o=LeSavonWrox" (0000
added: "property=updateInterval, properties=cachingRules, cn=LeSavonApplication, o=LeSavonWrox
added: "property=TTL, properties=cachingRules, cn=LeSavonApplication, o=LeSavonWrox" (00000013
added: "property=Refresh, properties=cachingRules, cn=LeSavonApplication, o=LeSavonWrox" (0000
added: "cn=cacheItems, properties=cachingRules, cn=LeSavonApplication, o=LeSavonWrox" (0000001
added: "item=1, cn=cacheItems, properties=cachingRules, cn=LeSavonApplication, o=LeSavonWrox"
added: "property=TTL, item=1, cn=cacheItems, properties=cachingRules, cn=LeSavonApplication, o
added: "property=Refresh, item=1, cn=cacheItems, properties=cachingRules, cn=LeSavonApplicatio
added: "item=2, cn=cacheItems, properties=cachingRules, cn=LeSavonApplication, o=LeSavonWrox"
added: "property=TTL, item=2, cn=cacheItems, properties=cachingRules, cn=LeSavonApplication, o
added: "property=Refresh, item=2, cn=cacheItems, properties=cachingRules, cn=LeSavonApplicatio
added: "properties=leSavonProperties, uid=atase, ou=People, o=LeSavonWrox" (0000001c)
added: "property=background, properties=leSavonProperties, uid=atase, ou=People, o=LeSavonWrox
added: "property=font, properties=leSavonProperties, uid=atase, ou=People, o=LeSavonWrox" (000
added: "properties=leSavonProperties, uid=aterieur, ou=People, o=LeSavonWrox" (0000001f)
added: "property=background, properties=leSavonProperties, uid=aterieur, ou=People, o=LeSavonW
added: "property=font, properties=leSavonProperties, uid=aterieur, ou=People, o=LeSavonWrox" (

C:\ProJavaSoap\Chapter07\openLDAP>slapd
starting slapd...
_
```

By default, the slapd server takes LDAP requests on port 389.

Fire up the browser (double-click on LB.exe or start it from the Start menu). You'll need to set up a new profile. Select File->New Profile; you'll be asked for a profile name (say, o=LeSavonWrox), host (localhost), port (389), base DN (o=LeSavonWrox); and select Anonymous Bind. The LDAP Browser user interface is similar to Windows Explorer.

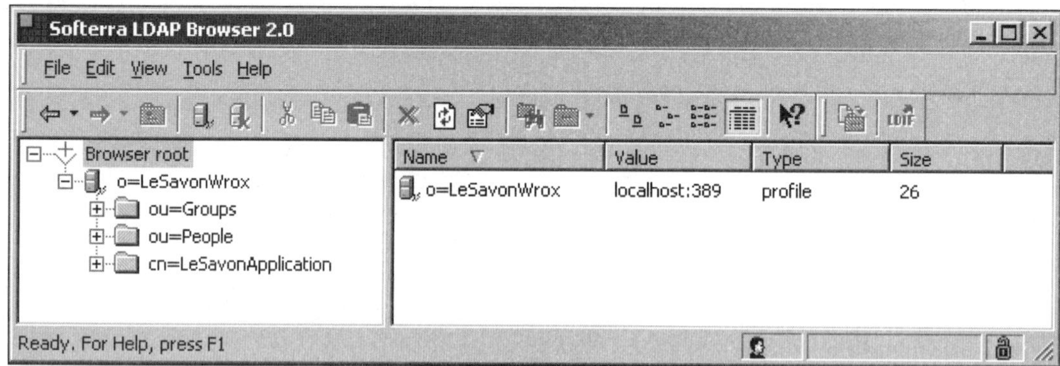

Your LDAP database is now fully configured for the sample application and ready to take requests. We will demonstrate our simple LDAP client shortly, but first, we will look at setting up an LDAP server on a LINUX machine.

LDAP Setup for LINUX

Red Hat LINUX 7.1 comes bundled with OpenLDAP, so it should already be installed on your server. If for some reason OpenLDAP has been removed from your system, you will need to re-install OpenLDAP RPM. You can download the LDAP RPM from http://www.redhat.com/swr/i386/openldap12-1.2.11-4.i386.html.

To configure your LDAP server on LINUX, you will need the files in the ProJavaSoap/Chapter07/OpenLDAPConfig directory: lesavon.ldif, sladp.conf, seed.sh, and lesavon.schema. We will only look at the two platform-specific files here – sladp.conf and seed.sh here. We will examine the non-platform-specific files lesavon.ldif and lesavon.schema in the *Non-Platform Specific-Configuration Files* section, which follows this section.

We moved the configuration files to a directory called OpenLDAP in the user home directory. The resultant directory structure for our user `soap` is as follows:

/home/soap/openLDAP/
/home/soap/openLDAP/lesavon.ldif
/home/soap/openLDAP/seed.sh
/home/soap/openLDAP/slapd.conf
/home/soap/openLDAP/schema/
/home/soap/openLDAP/schema/lesavon.schema
/home/soap/openLDAP/ldbm/

The last directory will hold our database. Before seeding the LDAP database, you will need to make sure that slapd.conf and seed.sh reflect your settings.

In a few moments, we will look at the seed.sh file that is used to create the LDAP directory. Before that, we'll look at the slapd.conf file (the statements that you are likely to need to change are in **bold**):

```
# slapd.conf
include     /usr/local/etc/openldap/schema/core.schema
include     /usr/local/etc/openldap/schema/cosine.schema
include     /usr/local/etc/openldap/schema/inetorgperson.schema
include     /usr/local/etc/openldap/schema/java.schema
include     /home/hbequet/openLDAP/schema/lesavon.schema
schemacheck off
pidfile  /home/hbequet/OpenLDAP/slapd.pid
argsfile /home/hbequet/OpenLDAP/slapd.args

backend ldbm

database   ldbm
threads
suffix "o=LeSavonWrox"

rootdn "uid=atase, ou=People, o=LeSavonWrox"
rootpw lesavon
directory  /home/hbequet/openLDAP/ldbm
```

In the `slapd.conf` file, any lines beginning with a # character are comments and are not executed (they're not shown here). Otherwise, `slapd.conf` contains three types of statements or directives: global statements, backend statements and database statements.

The `include` statements for the schema definitions are global statements. The schemas specified here are used to validate modification to the database. Note that most servers will not enforce compliance with a schema when they open a database. Rather, they will check the schema when a modification is attempted. We will review the schema specific for the sample application later.

There is only one backend statement in this `slapd.conf` file (the line beginning with the keyword `backend`, and followed by a backend type). As we mentioned previously, LDAP is an access protocol – so it does not actually implement storage and retrieval for the data. The `backend` statement allows you to specify the database system used to store and retrieve the data. The sample application uses a shareware database, LDBM, which comes with your installation and is the default.

Database directives apply to one particular instance of a database. The `database` statement marks the beginning of a new database instance definition.

The `suffix` statement states that all DNs that end with the specified suffix should be passed to this database. That statement is required. In the case of the sample application, all queries should go to the only database that is supported. The `rootdn` and `rootpwd` define the credentials that are used to define the **superuser**. The root DN is not subject to access and modification restrictions. Other directives in this section include read only status, replication, and log file directives.

The `schemacheck` statement allows you to turn schema checking on or off, and the `pidfile` and `argsfile` are the names of the files where the process identifier of slapd and its arguments are stored.

The next file that we need to modify with the settings for your computer is seed.sh. The changes are pretty trivial since you only need to replace the paths for the LDAP installation and the configuration files:

```
# seed.sh
# Henry Bequet 05/29/01
# Regenerate the LDAP database based on lesavon.ldif. Slapd must not be running...

# Then we delete the database
rm -f /home/soap/openLDAP/ldbm/*

# Finally we repopulate the database
/usr/local/sbin/slapadd -f slapd.conf -v -l lesavon.ldif
```

We must first run this command before starting slapd:

```
/usr/local/libexec/slapd –f /home/soap/openLDAP/ldap.conf –h ldap://172.17.1.89:8300
```

The path to `ldap.conf` and the server address will need to be changed to your system.

Note that if you want to start slapd on the default port (389) you will need super-user privileges. The command shown on the previous screenshot starts slapd on port 8300 on the server.

Non-Platform Specific Configuration Files

Now that our LDAP server is up and running, we can have a closer look at the configuration files that are not platform-dependent: the schema file `LeSavon.schema` and the LDIF file, `LeSavon.ldif`.

The Schema File

As we have previously mentioned, schema files define the rules that objects and attributes must follow to be valid entries in an LDAP database. There can be as many schema files as you need. A typical server installation like OpenLDAP comes with standard schemas for companies, people, groups, and even software components. The `core.schema` file contains the definition of objects like organizations, groups, people, and users, amongst other things. Schema files have a somewhat peculiar syntax that will look foreign to eyes accustomed to markup languages, As you will see as we step through parts of `LeSavon.schema`, the schema file used by the sample application. It begins as follows:

```
# leSavonSchema
#
# The object classes and attributes required for the sample application.
# The IANA Private Interprise number 4412 is assigned to Wrox Press.
# You must apply for a new number for your company (it is free).
#
attributetype ( 4412.1.1.1.1 NAME 'role'
    DESC 'security role'
    EQUALITY caseIgnoreMatch
    ORDERING caseIgnoreOrderingMatch
    SYNTAX 1.3.6.1.4.1.1466.115.121.1.26 )
```

As in the `slapd.conf` file, blank lines and lines beginning with a # character are ignored. Beware that most schema file parsers are more sensitive that you might like. In particular, make sure that you have spaces between keywords and parentheses.

The first entry in `LeSavon.schema` defines an attribute with the name `role`. As we mentioned earlier in this chapter, the IANA Private Enterprise Number `4412` belongs to Wrox Press. You may not use it in your own schemas. The long number (`1.3`....) in the syntax definition is an OID, similar to the one we discussed for objects earlier. You can find syntax definitions in RFC 2252 that can be downloaded from http://www.ietf.org/rfc/rfc2252.txt. In this particular case, a `role` is a string.

```
attributetype ( 4412.1.1.1.7 NAME ( 'app' 'applicationName' ) SUP name
    DESC 'application name'
    EQUALITY caseIgnoreMatch
    ORDERING caseIgnoreOrderingMatch
    SYNTAX 1.3.6.1.4.1.1466.115.121.1.26
    SINGLE-VALUE )

objectclass ( 4412.1.1.4 NAME 'application' SUP top STRUCTURAL
    DESC 'The LeSavon Application'
    MUST ( objectclass $ applicationName ) )
```

The application object is top-level entry for application-wide settings. The application name is a string.

```
objectclass ( 4412.1.1.2 NAME 'properties'
    DESC 'container for properties'
    MAY role
    MUST ( objectclass ) )

attributetype ( 4412.1.1.1.6 NAME 'value'
    DESC 'property value'
    EQUALITY caseIgnoreMatch
    ORDERING caseIgnoreOrderingMatch
    SYNTAX 1.3.6.1.4.1.1466.115.121.1.26
    SINGLE-VALUE )

objectclass ( 4412.1.1.5 NAME 'property'
    DESC 'Property (user or application) object'
    MUST objectclass
    MAY ( value ) )
```

Properties are name/value pairs that we use to set up application-wide and user-specific parameters, such as the cache directory and the default background color.

```
attributetype ( 4412.1.1.1.8 NAME ( 'regexp' 'regularexpression' ) SUP name
    DESC 'regular expression'
    EQUALITY caseIgnoreMatch
    ORDERING caseIgnoreOrderingMatch
    SYNTAX 1.3.6.1.4.1.1466.115.121.1.26
    SINGLE-VALUE )

objectclass ( 4412.1.1.6 NAME 'cacheItems'
    DESC 'container for cache items'
    MUST ( objectclass ) )

objectclass ( 4412.1.1.7 NAME 'cacheItem' SUP properties
    DESC 'container for cache item properties'
    MUST ( objectclass $ regexp ) )
```

A cache item defines a rule for the cache. Cache items are matched using regular expressions. We will explore the definition of cache items and cache rules in Chapter 8.

The LDIF File

Armed with the understanding of schema files, we are now ready to attack the `leSavon.ldif` file:

```
dn: o=LeSavonWrox
o: LeSavonWrox
objectclass: top
objectclass: organization

dn: ou=Groups, o=LeSavonWrox
ou: Groups
objectclass: top
```

```
objectclass: organizationalunit

dn: cn=Directory Administrators, ou=Groups, o=LeSavonWrox
cn: Directory Administrators
objectclass: top
objectclass: groupofuniquenames
ou: Groups
uniquemember: userid=atase, ou=People, o=LeSavonWrox
uniquemember: userid=aterieur, ou=People, o=LeSavonWrox
uniquemember: userid=pdefer, ou=People, o=LeSavonWrox

dn: cn=Accounting Managers,ou=groups,o=LeSavonWrox
objectclass: top
objectclass: groupOfUniqueNames
cn: Accounting Managers
ou: groups
uniquemember: cn=Paul Iglote, ou=People, o=LeSavonWrox
description: People who can manage accounting entries

dn: cn=HR Managers,ou=groups,o=LeSavonWrox
objectclass: top
objectclass: groupOfUniqueNames
cn: HR Managers
uniquemember: cn=Bert Dog, ou=People, o=LeSavonWrox
ou: groups
description: People who can manage HR entries

dn: cn=Engineering Managers,ou=groups,o=LeSavonWrox
objectclass: top
objectclass: groupOfUniqueNames
cn: Engineering Managers
ou: groups
uniquemember: cn=Alex Tase, ou=People, o=LeSavonWrox
description: People who can manage the unmanageable

dn: ou=People, o=LeSavonWrox
ou: People
objectclass: top
objectclass: organizationalunit

dn: uid=atase, ou=People, o=LeSavonWrox
cn: Alex Tase
uid: atase
sn: Tase
userPassword: lesavon
mail: atase@lesavonwrox.com
telephonenumber: +1 303 442 2838
facsimiletelephonenumber: +1 303 440 3523
jpegphoto:: 9j/4AAQSkZJRgABAQAAAQABAAD/xAAfAAABBQEBAQEBAQAAAAAAAAAAAQIDBAUGB
#rest of image cut out.
objectclass: top
objectclass: person
objectclass: organizationalPerson
objectclass: inetOrgPerson
```

As we have discussed before, an LDIF file is a list of human-readable representations of LDAP entries. The DN is always present since it is the unique name to get to the object. After the DN, you will find a list of object classes and a list of attributes with their values.

For instance, the entry for the accounting managers has the DN `cn=Accounting Managers,ou=groups,o=LeSavonWrox` and a value for the `uniquemember` attribute. The `uniquemember` attribute is actually used to get around the tree nature of LDAP: the hierarchy presented by LDAP is a tree, not a graph. By using attributes, one can define more than one "parent" for an entry.

The entry for the `uid=atase,ou=People,o=LeSavonWrox` user contains one binary attribute, a JPEG photo, encoded into Base 64 which allows it to be represented as a text string within the file.

> *Base 64 encoding is one of the techniques employed by the MIME standard that we discussed in Chapter 2. Base 64 encodes binary data into 6-bit ASCII characters (2^6=64, hence the name Base 64 encoding). The Base64 algorithm can be found at* http://www.ietf.org/rfc/rfc1521.txt.

The `leSavon.ldif` file contains several entries similar to the ones we discussed. The next entry of interest is the `cn=LeSavonApplication,o=LeSavonWrox` entry:

```
dn: cn=LeSavonApplication, o=LeSavonWrox
applicationName: LeSavon
objectclass: top
objectclass: application

dn: properties=cachingRules, cn=LeSavonApplication, o=LeSavonWrox
objectclass: top
objectclass: properties

dn: property=cacheDirectory, properties=cachingRules, cn=LeSavonApplication,
o=LeSavonWrox
value: leSavonCache
objectclass: top
objectclass: property

dn: property=cacheOn, properties=cachingRules, cn=LeSavonApplication,
o=LeSavonWrox
value: true
objectclass: top
objectclass: property

dn: property=updateInterval, properties=cachingRules, cn=LeSavonApplication,
o=LeSavonWrox
value: 300000
objectclass: top
objectclass: property
```

The fragment above is used to create a hierarchy under the `cn=LeSavonApplication` to store the configuration properties that define the default behavior of the sample application. The screenshot below shows how we can view that fragment in an LDAP browser, after it has been created, using the Softerra LDAP Browser:

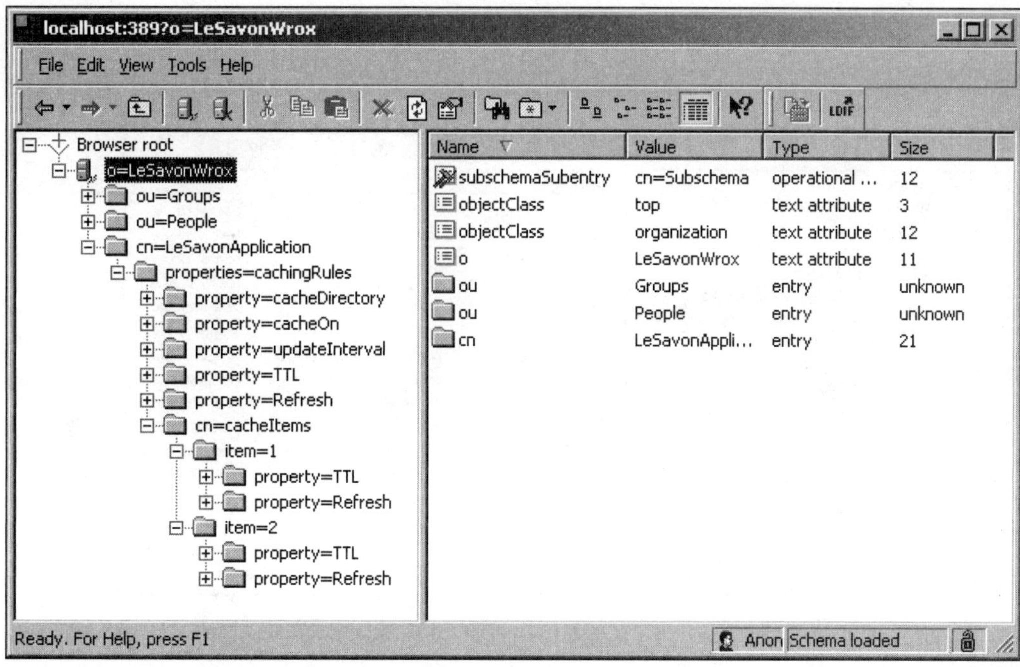

User-specific application properties are stored under the entry for that specific user. For instance, the application data for `uid=atase`, the sample application default user, is created using the following LDIF file:

```
dn: properties=leSavonProperties, uid=atase, ou=People, o=LeSavonWrox
role: administrator
objectclass: top
objectclass: properties

dn: property=background, properties=leSavonProperties, uid=atase, ou=People,
o=LeSavonWrox
value: white
objectclass: top
objectclass: property

dn: property=font, properties=leSavonProperties, uid=atase, ou=People,
o=LeSavonWrox
value: arial
objectclass: top
objectclass: property
```

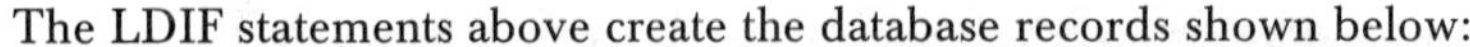

The LDIF statements above create the database records shown below:

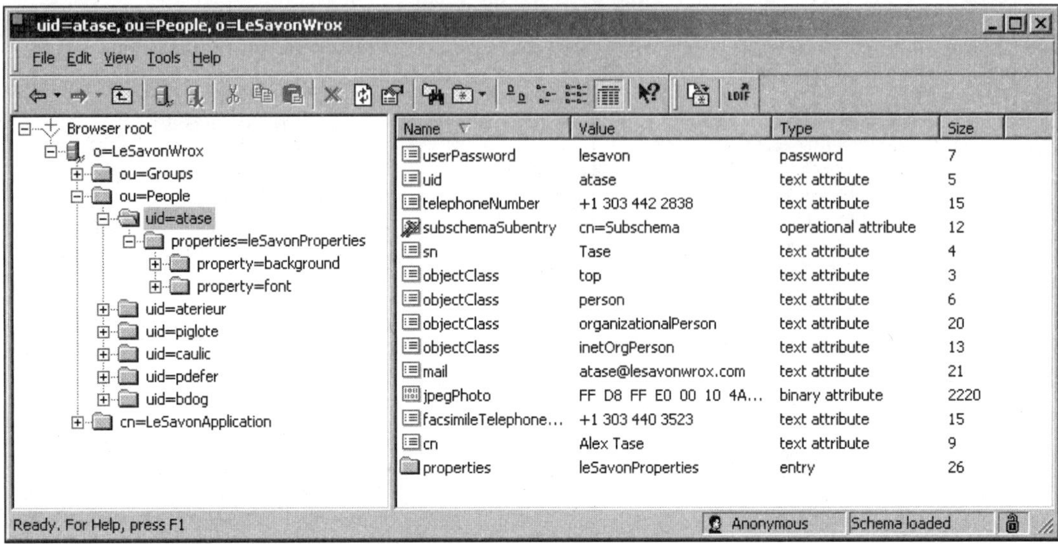

We are now ready to build and run the simple LDAP client that we wrote earlier.

Sample Execution

In this section, we will describe the instructions to build and run `AddLeSavonUser` on Windows 2000. The instructions for LINUX are similar. The easiest way to build the sample is to rely on ANT (which we met in Chapter 5) and the BuildAddLeSavonUser.xml build file:

```
<project name="AddLeSavonUser" default="compile" basedir=".">
  <property name="app.name"  value="AddLeSavonUser"/>
  <property name="deploy.home"
            value="/ProJavaSoap/Chapter07/${app.name}/classes"/>

  <target name="prepare">
    <mkdir  dir="${deploy.home}"/>
  </target>

  <target name="clean">
    <delete dir="${deploy.home}"/>
  </target>

  <target name="compile" depends="prepare">
    <javac srcdir="src" destdir="${deploy.home}"
           debug="off" optimize="on" deprecation="off"/>
  </target>

  <target name="all" depends="clean,prepare,compile"/>
</project>
```

The build file simply compiles the only source file of the sample and puts the resulting class file under the classes/ directory. No JAR file needs to be added to the classpath since all packages that are used in the sample are part of the standard JDK 1.3. So on Windows machine, there are just two build steps:

```
c:\ProJavaSoap\Chapter07\AddLeSavonUser>set CLASSPATH=
c:\ProJavaSoap\Chapter07\AddLeSavonUser>ant -buildfile BuildAddLeSavonUser.xml
```

The following figure shows the build steps on a Windows machine, and the output you can expect:

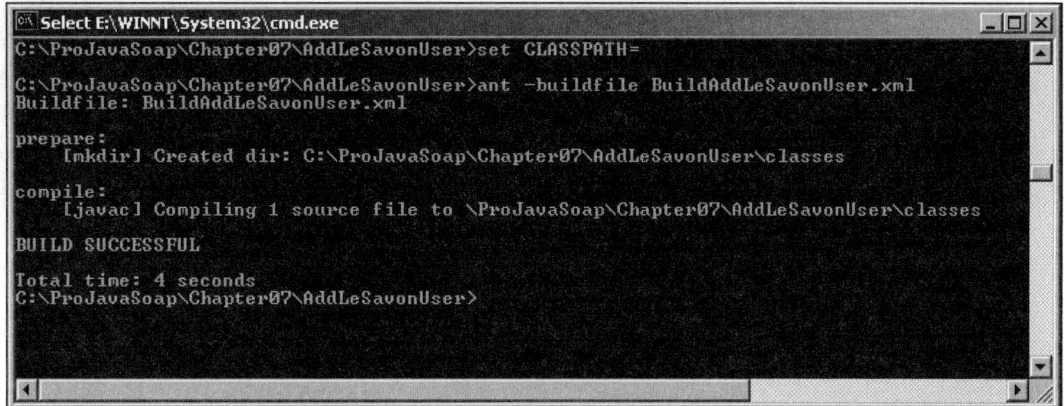

Let's see how running the `AddLeSavonUser` utility affects our LDAP database. Make sure that the LDAP server (`slapd.conf`) is running before launching `AddLeSavonUser`. In the screenshot below, the Softerra LDAP Browser shows the state of the database *before* running the utility. To bring up the LDAP browser, double-click on LB.exe (or run it from the Start menu) and connect to LDAP as described earlier in the chapter:

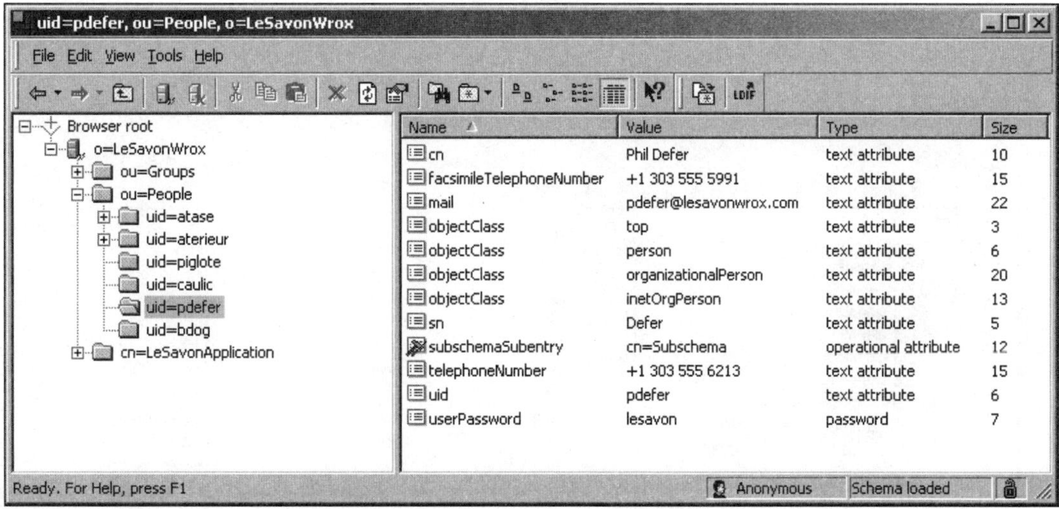

Running is equally straightforward, but you need to make sure that the classes/ directory is part of the classpath:

```
c:\ProJavaSoap\Chapter07\AddLeSavonUser>set CLASSPATH=./classes
c:\ProJavaSoap\Chapter07\AddLeSavonUser>java com.lesavon.util.AddLeSavonUser pdefer
```

The following screenshot shows you what to expect, the first time you run the program:

```
E:\WINNT\System32\cmd.exe
C:\ProJavaSoap\Chapter07\AddLeSavonUser>set CLASSPATH=./classes

C:\ProJavaSoap\Chapter07\AddLeSavonUser>java com.lesavon.util.AddLeSavonUser pdefer
com.lesavon.test.AddLeSavonUser: Starting...
Found user Phil Defer
Creating LeSavonProperties for user Phil Defer...
Creating property=background,properties=LeSavonProperties,uid=pdefer,ou=People...
Property property=background,properties=LeSavonProperties,uid=pdefer,ou=People has been set to value white
Creating property=font,properties=LeSavonProperties,uid=pdefer,ou=People...
Property property=font,properties=LeSavonProperties,uid=pdefer,ou=People has been set to value arial
com.lesavon.test.AddLeSavonUser: All done!

C:\ProJavaSoap\Chapter07\AddLeSavonUser>
```

Note that if you've forgotten to set `slapd` running, then you'll get the following error:

```
com.lesavon.test.AddLeSavonUser: Error, caught exception:
javax.naming.CommunicationException: localhost:389 [Root exception is
java.net.ConnectException: Connection refused: no further information]
```

In that case, simply start a command prompt and set `slapd` running as described earlier in the chapter, and then run `AddLeSavonUser` again.

As you can see from the output commentary in the image above, on this first execution the program finds the user represented by the RDN `uid=pdefer`, and *creates* a `properties` entry and two `property` entries for it. It also sets the values of the two `property` entries.

We can see the result of this by viewing the LDAP Browser again (press *F5* to refresh the Browser view if necessary). Note the new properties=LeSavonProperties entry:

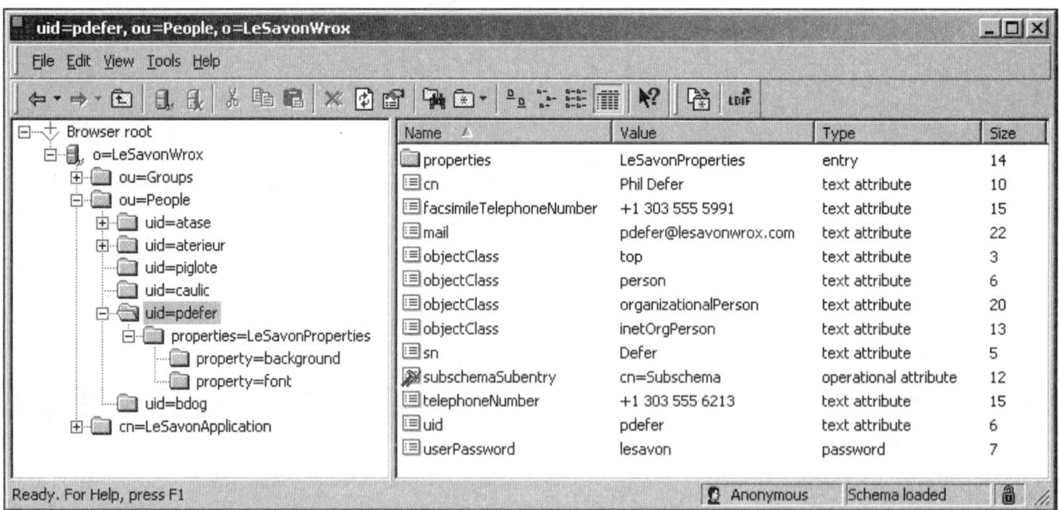

The screenshot below shows that the default role set for user `uid=pdefer` is indeed `user`:

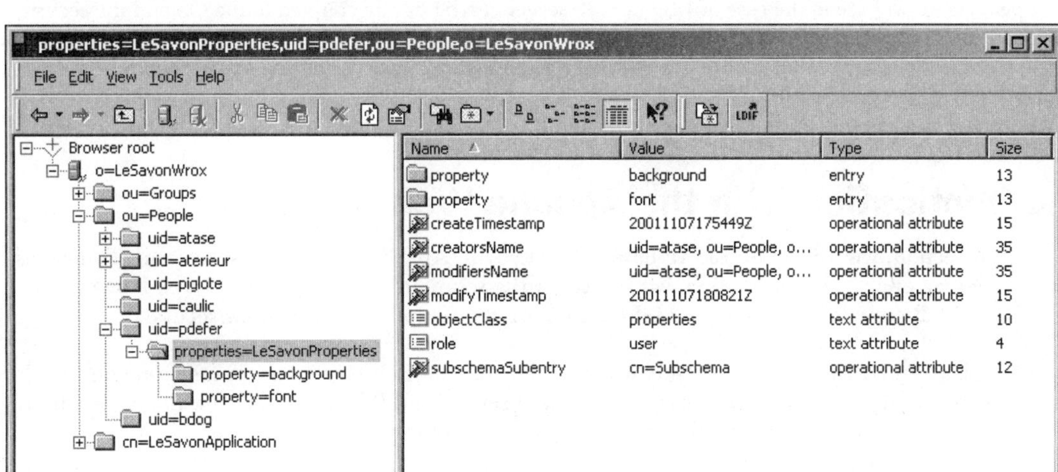

If you run the utility a second time, the program will simply *reset* the existing property values. The program output reflects this subtle difference:

```
E:\WINNT\System32\cmd.exe
C:\ProJavaSoap\Chapter07\AddLeSavonUser>java com.lesavon.util.AddLeSavonUser pdefer
com.lesavon.test.AddLeSavonUser: Starting...
Found user Phil Defer
Property property=background,properties=LeSavonProperties,uid=pdefer,ou=People has been set to value white
Property property=font,properties=LeSavonProperties,uid=pdefer,ou=People has been set to value arial
com.lesavon.test.AddLeSavonUser: All done!

C:\ProJavaSoap\Chapter07\AddLeSavonUser>
```

So far in this chapter, we have presented an overview of LDAP and discussed how our sample application was making use of it to handle personalization by storing user properties. We have also reviewed how users would be authorized based on the administrator and user roles. In addition, we looked at how one can authenticate with LDAP using a two-phase binding. However, because a SOAP application is running in the context of a web server, there are specific issues to consider. This is the subject of the next section.

Authentication

The authentication portion of security is best left to the web server when developing a SOAP application, and there are several reasons for this. One important reason is that web servers usually have a proven solution to the authentication problem. If we were to add an extra link to the security chain, we thereby increase the likelihood of creating a weak link.

Another good reason for relying on the web server for authentication is that it makes your application more open. As we will see in the case of IIS, the web server can be tightly coupled to the OS and the security protocol it relies on (NTLM and IIS for instance). By letting the web server handle authentication, our application takes advantage of the OS-Web server integration without limiting our portability.

Let's see how we can authenticate our users with the two most popular web servers: Apache and IIS.

Authentication with the Apache Web Server

In this section, we will set up LDAP-based security with Apache as the Web server and Tomcat as the JSP/Servlet engine. In this section, we will cover the setup only at a fairly high level. However, Appendix B contains more detailed information on the setup described in this section.

We will assume that you have already installed the Apache web server and Tomcat on your machine, and configured Apache so that it uses Tomcat as a servlet and JSP server for Apache. Appendix B contains notes on the Apache setup and configuration requirements.

There are a variety of solutions freely available for authenticating Apache users via an LDAP database. The list of modules registered with Apache can be found at `http://modules.apache.org/`. One freely available module, which we will use in our application, is `mod_ldap.c`. This module is based on the work of Lyonel Vincent and Norman Richards, and is currently maintained by Jeff Morrow.

The `mod_ldap.c` source must be compiled into an object file, `ldap_module.so`, or a DLL, `ldap_module.dll`, which is then used by Apache in its communications with the LDAP database. We'll return to this in a moment.

Before we compile or use the object file or DLL, you will also need to download the Netscape LDAP SDK, and install it to the correct location on your machine. You can get this from http://www.iplanet.com/downloads/developer/2091.html. Again, see Appendix B for more information on this.

Having installed the LDAP SDK, we can compile `mod_ldap.c` and its links into a DLL, `ldap_module.dll`. If you want to avoid doing the compilation, you can simply use the `ldap_module.dll` that we've provided with the sample code for this book – you'll find it in the folder \ProJavaSoap\Chapter07\mod_ldap.

If, by contrast, you want to compile the C source for yourself, then you can download the `mod_ldap.c` source code from http://www.kie.berkeley.edu/people/jmorrow/mod_ldap.

> *If you're working on Windows 2000 and have a Visual C++ compiler, you can use the Visual C++ project provided in the sample code for this book (again, look in the \ProJavaSoap\Chapter07\mod_ldap directory). C code compilation is beyond the scope of this chapter, but compilation of this project is described in Appendix B.*
>
> *If you need to use `mod_ldap.c` for use in your own applications, you can find more detailed configuration instructions at the same URL.*

The compiled `ldap_module.dll` or `ldap_module.so` should be placed in the `modules` directory of your Apache installation (in this chapter and in Appendix B, we've assumed that this is c:\Apache\Apache\modules). The next step is to add the necessary LDAP configuration information to the Apache web server's `httpd.conf` file. `httpd.conf` is the file that contains your Apache web server's configuration details. To do this, we append the following to the end of the `httpd.conf` file:

```
# LDAP Authentication Module
LoadModule ldap_module c:/Apache/Apache/modules/ldap_module.dll
AddModule mod_ldap.c

# We protect /examples
<Location "/examples">
    AuthType Basic
    AuthName LeSavonAuthentication
    LDAPAuth On
    LDAPServer "ldap://localhost:389/"
    LDAPBindName uid=atase,ou=People,o=LeSavonWrox
    LDAPBindPass lesavon
    LDAPuseridAttr uid
    LDAPBase o=LeSavonWrox
    LDAPSearchMode subtree
    require valid-user
</Location>
```

Let's take a look at the information that we're adding to the configuration here, attribute by attribute:

- `AuthType Basic`
  Basic authentication will use clear-text passwords. (To secure password transmission you should further secure the site with HTTPS).
- `AuthName LeSavonAuthentication`
  This is a label that will be shown to the user when she is prompted to authenticate.
- `LDAPAuth On`
  Dictates that LDAP authentication is turned on.
- `LDAPServer "ldap://localhost:389/"`
  This is the URL for the LDAP server.
- `LDAPBindName uid=atase,ou=People,o=LeSavonWrox`
  This is the user name for the initial binding. See the two-phase binding described in the *LDAP Security and Personalization* section for more details.
- `LDAPBindPass lesavon`
  This is the password for the initial user.
- `LDAPuseridAttr uid`
  This is the attribute for the user name. The authentication module performs a query with `uid=<user-name>` where `<user-name>` is the user name passed in for authentication.
- `LDAPBase o=LeSavonWrox`
  This is the base DN. Searches are started from this point.

- ❑ `LDAPSearchMode subtree`
  This describes how a search will be performed. By default, searches are limited to one level (`onelevel`).
- ❑ `require valid-user`
  This dictates that only valid users have access to the resource; in this case the virtual directory examples.

To demonstrate the authentication mechanism, we will use the `snoop.jsp` JSP that comes in the Tomcat `/examples` directory. Since `snoop.jsp` is in the `/examples` directory, we will protect it to see the effect of requiring LDAP authentication. For the sample application, we will need to protect the `/serveur` and `/ncrouter` URLs.

The `snoop.jsp` JSP displays server-side variables using the JSP request object. The code of `snoop.jsp` is straightforward (Formatted for readability):

```
<html>

  <body bgcolor="white">
    <h1> Request Information </h1>
    <font size="4">
      JSP Request Method:  <%= request.getMethod() %>         <br>
      Request URI:         <%= request.getRequestURI() %>     <br>
      Request Protocol:    <%= request.getProtocol() %>       <br>
      Servlet path:        <%= request.getServletPath() %>    <br>
      Path info:           <%= request.getPathInfo() %>       <br>
      Path translated:     <%= request.getPathTranslated() %><br>
      Query string:        <%= request.getQueryString() %>    <br>
      Content length:      <%= request.getContentLength() %> <br>
      Content type:        <%= request.getContentType() %>    <br>
      Server name:         <%= request.getServerName() %>     <br>
      Server port:         <%= request.getServerPort() %>     <br>
      Remote user:         <%= request.getRemoteUser() %>     <br>
```

The call to `request.getRemoteUser()` is what interests us in this discussion, since the effect of modifying security settings will be to expose a remote user to the servlet or JSP developer.

```
      Remote address:      <%= request.getRemoteAddr() %>     <br>
      Remote host:         <%= request.getRemoteHost() %>     <br>
      Authorization scheme:<%= request.getAuthType() %>       <br>
      Locale:              <%= request.getLocale() %>         <hr>
      The browser you are using is <%= request.getHeader("User-Agent") %>
      <hr>
    </font>
  </body>
</html>
```

The screenshot below shows the output that we can expect from `snoop.jsp` *without* the LDAP authentication configuration in place (that is, before making the changes to `httpd.conf`):

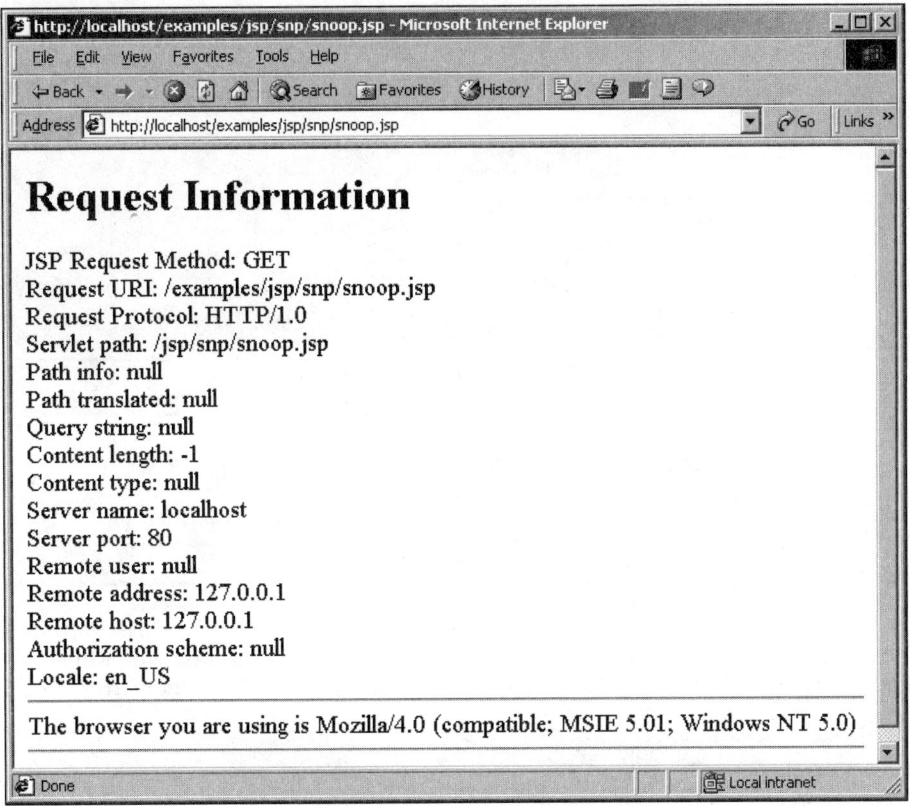

Once you have modified the `httpd.conf` file, by adding the `include` directive and the `<Location/>` statement, you will need to restart Apache for the modifications to take effect. If you attempt to refresh the output of your browser, you should get prompted for a user name and password, as we can see in the screenshot below. Note that the **Realm** is the label that we specified in the `<Location/>` statement with the `AuthName` attribute:

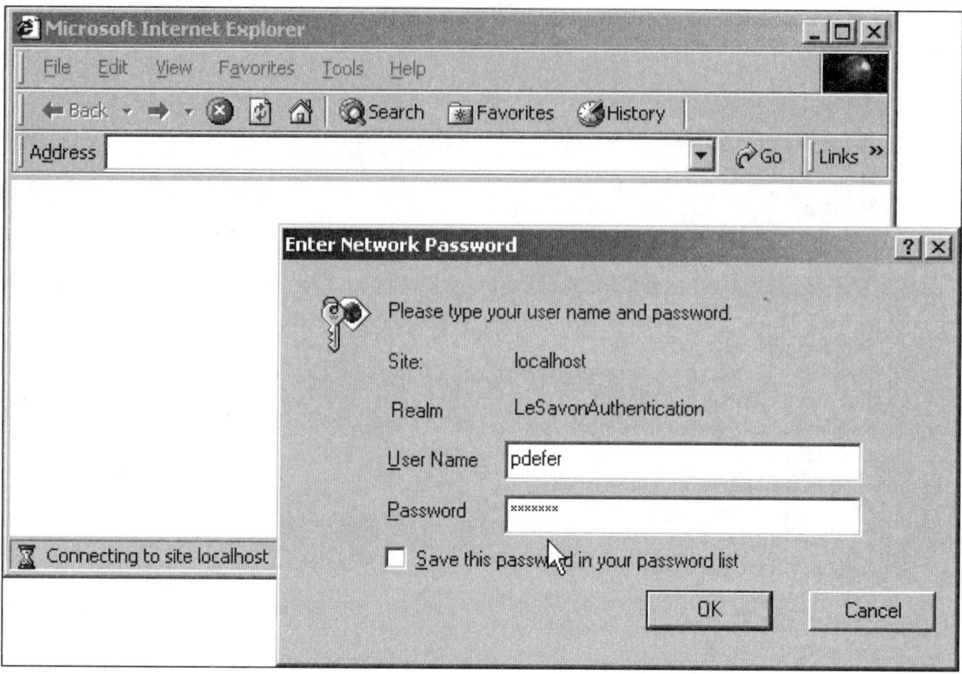

If we enter credentials which are are not accepted (because the user name or password password is invalid), then we get an error message similar to the one below. In this case, you will get the default Apache error message for a `401` HTTP error code, indicating an authorization error:

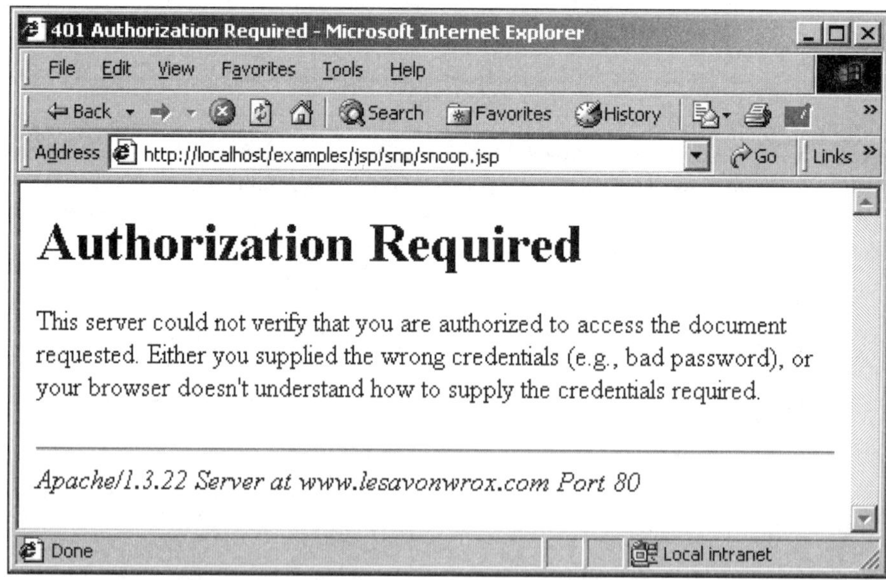

However, if we enter valid credentials, then we will get the output below. Note that the Remote User line contains the DN of the authenticated user:

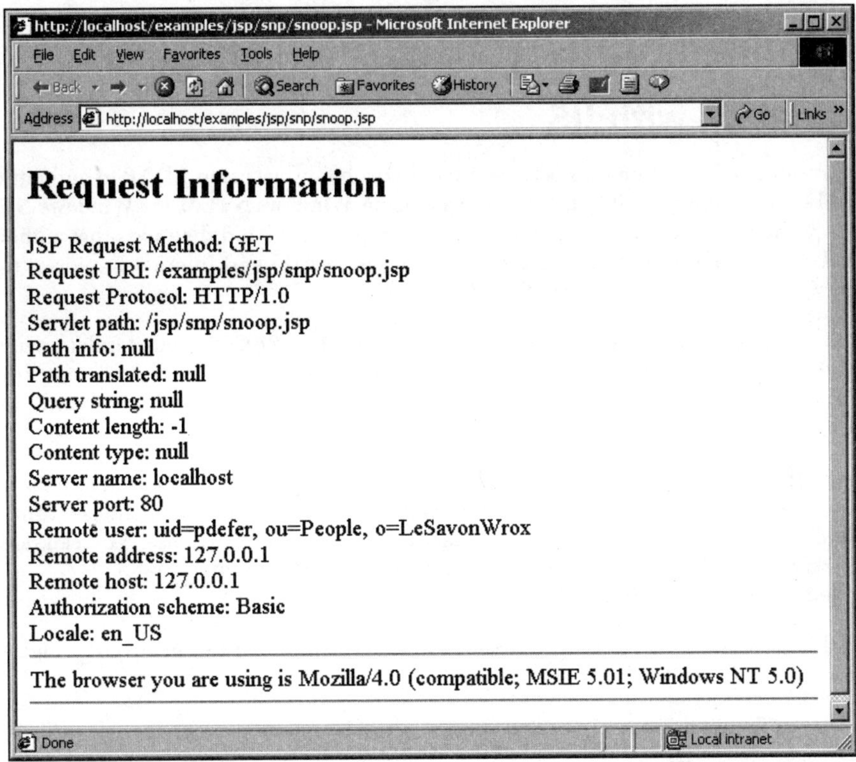

We can apply the same methodology to protect the sample application servlets and virtual directory. Note that `snoop.jsp` does not display the remote password, although it is included in the HTTP header:

```
GET /examples/jsp/snp/snoop.jsp HTTP/1.1
Accept: */*
Accept-Language: en-us
Accept-Encoding: gzip, deflate
User-Agent: Mozilla/4.0 (compatible; MSIE 5.5; Windows NT 5.0)
Host: localhost:8081
Connection: Keep-Alive
Cookie: JSESSIONID=2gjz409811
Authorization: Basic cGRlZmVyOmxlc2F2b24=
```

Note that we can ask a JSP to get this information for us, by including a `request.getHeader("Authorization")` method call. We would expect it to return the sam string, Authorization: Basic cGRlZmVyOmxlc2F2b24=. The series of characters at the end of this string is the base 64-encoded value of the following:

```
pdefer:lesavon
```

(Recall that base 64 is an encoding of binary data into 6-bit ASCII characters – see the Base64 algorithm at http://www.ietf.org/rfc/rfc1521.txt.) We will see in Chapter 10 how to extract the user name and password – in other words, to decode a base64-encoded string.

We will now review how to use the IIS authentication features.

Authentication with IIS

If you are running IIS on Windows NT, then you're probably *not* using LDAP to authenticate your users. The best option is probably to authenticate using **Windows NTLM** (or **Windows NT LAN Manager** – a challenge/response-based authentication protocol), and then pass that authentication to your SOAP application. In this short section we will see that IIS and Internet Explorer (from version 2.0) support a feature that allows secure single sign-on.

We will take a look at what needs to be done when Tomcat is acting as your servlet engine, and we will see that, other than the name of the filter used in IIS, everything is generic. To demonstrate that we are getting the remote user that we need, we will once again use `snoop.jsp` that is found in the Tomcat `examples` directory.

To connect IIS and Tomcat, you typically set up a **filter** in IIS. The filter is used to forward servlet and JSP requests from IIS to Tomcat. There are several freely available filters to choose from; Apache recommends `isapi_redirect.dll`, and so that is the one that we will use. You can download `isapi_redirect.dll` from http://jakarta.apache.org/builds/jakarta-tomcat/release/v3.2.3/bin/win32/i386/.

So in this demonstration, the first thing we need to do is set up the filter in IIS. At a high level, this involves:

- Placing the filter, `isapi_redirect.dll`, on the system
- Registering the filter, and a number of keys, in the Windows Registry
- Configuring IIS to be aware of the filter

Complete instructions for these tasks can be found at http://jakarta.apache.org/tomcat/tomcat-3.3-doc/tomcat-iis-howto.html, and also in the /doc/tomcat-iis-howto.html file in your Tomcat installation. As you'll see, the instructions are a little laborious but quite straightforward. Rather than repeating those instructions here, I refer you to the steps contained there for full details.

Once you've completed those steps, and restarted IIS, there is one further step to undertake before we can see the results of this demonstration. Namely, we must complete the web service authentication settings in IIS.

In this case, there is no authentication information like the `Authorization` HTTP header that we saw with Apache (when we set up the filter according to the instructions provided by Apache). Before we describe how we can get access to authentication information, we need to explain how IIS and IE handle authentication.

When an IE browser submits a resource request to IIS, IIS will attempt to obtain the resource using the (possibly internal) user account associated with to an *anonymous* request. IIS uses a *specific* user account to service anonymous requests: by default, the `IUSR_`*`<machine-name>`* user account is used, although it's possible to configure IIS to use a different account for such requests.

There are many security-related reasons that would cause such a request to fail. For example, it might be that anonymous access to the web server is disabled altogether. Another common reason is that the resource requested (typically a file) is protected – that is, that anonymous users are not entitled to access that resource. If the request fails for security reasons, then IIS responds with an HTTP `401` (access denied) error.

At this stage, if the user is already logged on to an NT domain, IE will then automatically send the user's NTLM credentials to IIS, in an attempt to access the resource using that account context. (This happens automatically: the user is not prompted to log on again.) However, if IIS is still not permitted access to the resource using these new credentials then the user is prompted for a domain, user name, and password. The prompting will happen if you are logged on a domain (for instance your local machine) with a user name and password that the server cannot authenticate.

To trigger this authentication dialog between IIS and IE, we simply need to prevent IIS from starting up the `isapi_redirect.dll` filter using anonymous access. We can do this by changing the security settings in the virtual directory in which the filter lives. Assuming you've placed the filter into a virtual directory called jakarta (as suggested in the instructions in /tomcat-iis-howto.html), then we can do this as follows:

- In the IIS management console, bring up the Properties of the jakarta virtual directory and select the Directory Security tab. In the Anonymous access and authentication control pane, click Edit.
- Uncheck the Anonymous access checkbox, and ensure that the Integrated Windows authentication checkbox is checked (as shown below). Submit these settings.

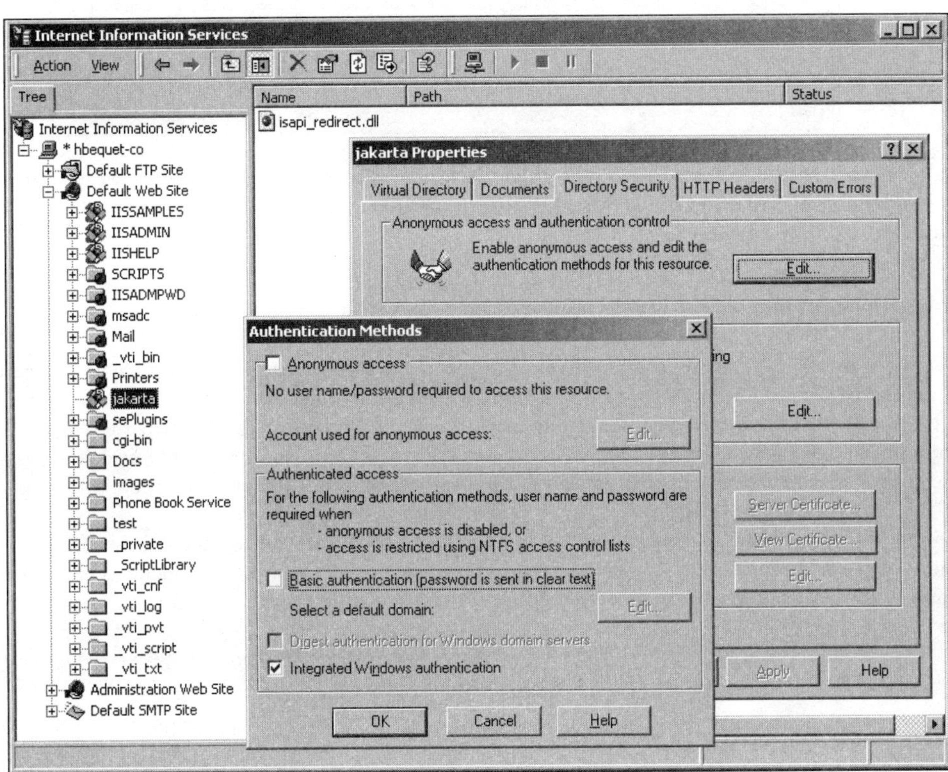

After restarting IIS and starting Tomcat, you can browse to `snoop.jsp`JSP. Your browser output should look like this:

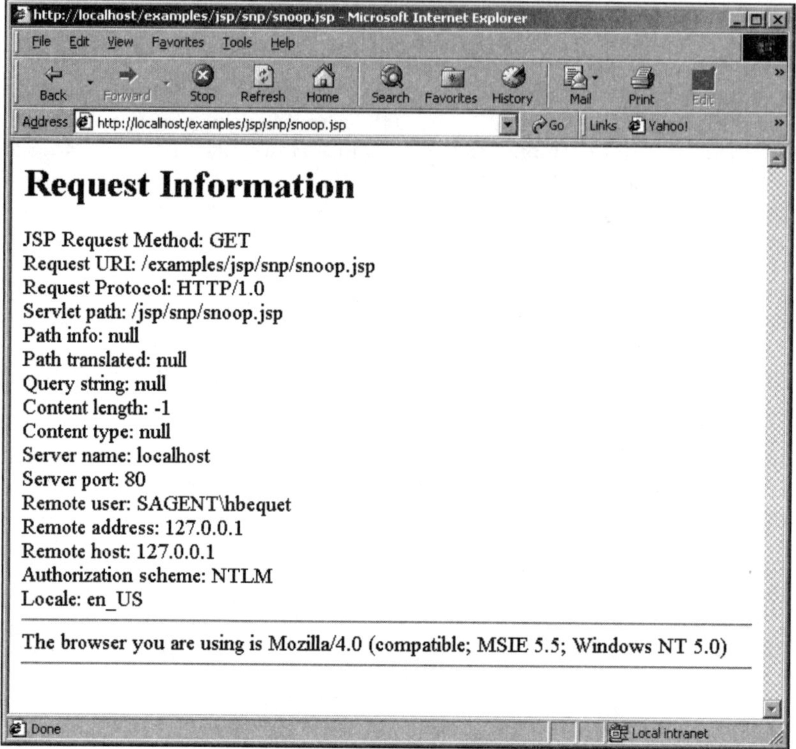

Finally, note that if you leave Basic authentication on and turn Integrated Windows authentication off, you will be able to log on to other domains or to non-Microsoft web servers using basic (plain-text) authentication.

Servlet Engine Security

Once the web server is satisfied with the credentials presented by the user, it forwards the request to the servlet engine (or web container). The web container will have access to the remote user name and (in the case of basic authentication) the remote user password. Since our design calls for the servlet engine to rely on the web server for authenticating users, it must accept that the remote user has passed in as a valid user, and hence proceed with handling the request without further authentication.

This presents a potential security issue: what if a client was to call the servlet engine directly with the remote user set? In order to address this issue, you must prevent remote connections to your servlet engine. With Tomcat, this is easily achieved by un-commenting the line in `tomcat.properties` that says:

```
#security.allowedAddresses=127.0.0.1
```

Finally, before we move to the code review of the LDAP utility class used by our sample application, I want to make one final important point about security of basic authentication.

As we said, *NTLM* authentication uses a challenge/response protocol that has the advantage of being secure since the user name and passwords do not travel in clear text over the Internet. However, when relying on *basic* authentication, the user name and password travel non-encrypted (although encoded) over the wire. That open line of communication presents a security risk that you would need to address if you're using basic authentication – perhaps by using HTTPS to carry your payload. The extra overhead of SSL is well worth a secure communication line.

LDAP Utility Class

In the sample application, all access to LDAP (with one exception – granting existing users permission to use the application – which we saw earlier in this chapter) is concentrated through the `com.lesavon.util.LDAP` class, which we first mentioned in Chapter 5. Based on our review of the `AddLeSavonUser` utility, most of the JNDI code should be straightforward. Let's step through that class now.

```
// LDAP.java
package com.lesavon.util;

import javax.naming.Context;
import javax.naming.directory.InitialDirContext;
import javax.naming.directory.DirContext;
import javax.naming.directory.Attributes;
import javax.naming.directory.ModificationItem;
import javax.naming.directory.BasicAttribute;
import javax.naming.directory.BasicAttributes;
import javax.naming.directory.SearchResult;
import javax.naming.NamingException;
import javax.naming.NamingEnumeration;

import java.util.Hashtable;
import java.util.Vector;
import java.util.Arrays;
import java.util.Comparator;

import org.apache.oro.text.perl.Perl5Util;
```

The `javax.naming` and `javax.naming.directory` packages are part of JNDI. The `Hashtable` is used to store the initial configuration of a JNDI configuration object, and the `org.apache.oro` package provides a Perl5-compatible regular expression parser.

> *The ORO package can be downloaded from* http://jakarta.apache.org/oro. *It is a zip file or a tar file that contains the jar file, source, and documentation. The jar file should be extracted and placed on the classpath.*

```
public final class LDAP {
  // Where to find the various properties we are interested in
  final static String TRAILER =
                    ", properties=cachingRules, cn=LeSavonApplication";
  final static String CACHE_DIRECTORY =
                    "property=cacheDirectory" + TRAILER;
  final static String CACHE_ON = "property=cacheOn" + TRAILER;
  final static String CACHE_UPDATE_INTERVAL =
                    "property=updateInterval" + TRAILER;
  final static String CACHE_TTL = "property=TTL" + TRAILER;
  final static String CACHE_REFRESH = "property=Refresh" + TRAILER;
  final static String CACHE_ITEMS = "cn=cacheItems" + TRAILER;
  final static String PASSWORD = "userPassword";
  final static String ROLE = "role";
  final static String ADMIN = "administrator";

  // The name of the user properties
  final static String BACKGROUND = "background";
  final static String FONT       = "font";

  final static String VALUE   = "value";    // The value of a property
  final static String REG_EXP = "regexp";   // The name of the regular
                                            // expression property

  static private LDAP      ldap     = new LDAP();     // The one and only
  static private Perl5Util perlUtil = new Perl5Util();// For Perl5 reg exp

  static private CacheRule[] cacheRules;           // As read from LDAP

  private Hashtable jndiEnv = new Hashtable(17);  // Our JNDI environment

  private String  cacheDirectory;
  private boolean cacheOn;
  private boolean cacheOnRead = false; // I would love a tri state type :)
  private boolean cacheRefresh;
  private boolean cacheRefreshRead = false;
  private long    cacheTTL;
  private long    cacheUpdateTime;
```

There is only one LDAP-utility class per JVM, and so we hide the constructor to enforce the singleton:

```
  private LDAP() {
    jndiEnv = new Hashtable(11);
    jndiEnv.put(Context.INITIAL_CONTEXT_FACTORY,
                              "com.sun.jndi.ldap.LdapCtxFactory");
    jndiEnv.put(Context.PROVIDER_URL, "ldap://localhost:389/o=LeSavonWrox");

    // We could limit authenticated connections to write operations
    jndiEnv.put(Context.SECURITY_AUTHENTICATION, "simple");
    jndiEnv.put(Context.SECURITY_PRINCIPAL,
                            "uid=atase, ou=People, o=LeSavonWrox");
    jndiEnv.put(Context.SECURITY_CREDENTIALS, "lesavon");
  }

  static public LDAP getLDAP() {
    return ldap;
  }
```

The security protocol used by the LDAP class is the simple authentication protocol. As we discussed earlier, in a production environment the simple authentication scheme of the sample application would need to be replaced by a more secure protocol.

We let the ORO package handle regular expression matching:

```
static public boolean matchCacheKey(String cacheKey, String regExp) {
  return perlUtil.match("/" + regExp + "/i", cacheKey);
}
```

The getCacheDirectory() method is the first of a number of methods that access LDAP:

```
public String getCacheDirectory() throws NamingException {
  if(cacheDirectory == null) {
    DirContext ctx   = new InitialDirContext(jndiEnv);
    Attributes attrs = ctx.getAttributes(CACHE_DIRECTORY);

    cacheDirectory = (String)attrs.get(VALUE).get();

    ctx.close();
  }

  return cacheDirectory;
}
```

All the methods that access attribute values from LDAP use the following pattern:

- They cache the attribute value locally, and return the cached value if it is available.
- They create an initial context object based on the default JNDI settings.
- They query for the specific attribute.
- They fetch the attribute value.
- They close the context object.
- They return the attribute value.

Creating a new context is not a performance issue since the attribute value is cached locally. All methods that access LDAP throw a NamingException in case of error. Note that if you are tempted to hold on to a context object for a long time, you will run the risk of nasty surprises – since most LDAP servers implement a connection timeout mechanism. You will need to age your contexts and refresh them after a few minutes. The exact latency will depend on your LDAP server and its settings.

```
public long getCacheTTL() throws NamingException {
  if(cacheTTL == 0) {
    DirContext ctx   = new InitialDirContext(jndiEnv);
    Attributes attrs = ctx.getAttributes(CACHE_TTL);
    cacheTTL = Long.parseLong((String)attrs.get(VALUE).get());
    ctx.close();
  }
```

```
    return cacheTTL;
  }

  public boolean getCacheRefresh() throws NamingException {
    if(!cacheRefreshRead) {
      DirContext ctx   = new InitialDirContext(jndiEnv);
      Attributes attrs = ctx.getAttributes(CACHE_REFRESH);
      cacheRefresh =
          Boolean.valueOf((String)attrs.get(VALUE).get()).booleanValue();
      cacheRefreshRead = true;
      ctx.close();
    }
    return cacheRefresh;
  }

  public long getCacheUpdateInterval() throws NamingException {
    if(cacheUpdateTime == 0) {
      DirContext ctx   = new InitialDirContext(jndiEnv);
      Attributes attrs = ctx.getAttributes(CACHE_UPDATE_INTERVAL);
      cacheUpdateTime = Long.parseLong((String)attrs.get(VALUE).get());
      ctx.close();
    }
    return cacheUpdateTime;
  }

  public boolean isCacheOn() throws NamingException {
    if(!cacheOnRead) {
      DirContext ctx   = new InitialDirContext(jndiEnv);
      Attributes attrs = ctx.getAttributes(CACHE_ON);
      cacheOn =
          Boolean.valueOf((String)attrs.get(VALUE).get()).booleanValue();
      cacheOnRead = true;
      ctx.close();
    }
    return cacheOn;
  }

  public boolean isValidUser(String user) throws NamingException {
    boolean isValidUser = false;
    try {
      // All users have these (value is irrelevant)
      getUserProperty(user, BACKGROUND);
      getUserProperty(user, FONT);
      isValidUser = true;
    } catch (NamingException namingException) {
      // Ignore, he is not a valid user for whatever reason
    }
    return isValidUser;
  }
```

To validate that a user has been granted the use of the sample application, we simply check that it has the attributes added by `AddLeSavonUser`. In this case, we check for the existence of background color and default font entries under the entry `cn=LeSavonProperties,uid=<user-name>,...`. In our application, existence of such entries is enough to prove that the user has been granted use.

> *Alternatively, we could have chosen to add a* `leSavonUser` *role attribute to the entry at the time the user is granted access to the application. In that case we would validate the user by checking for existence of the* `leSavonUser` *attribute at this time.*

To validate that a user is a valid *administrator*, we first check that the user is a valid user (with a call to `isValidUser()`); then we check that the user has the role of administrator. Since administrator-level operations require a password, we also check the password here:

```
public boolean isAdminUser(String user, String password)
      throws NamingException {
   boolean isAdminUser = false;

   try {
      if(isValidUser(user)) {
         // check password (only clear text password in this sample)
         DirContext ctx = new InitialDirContext(jndiEnv);
         Attributes usrattrs = ctx.getAttributes("uid=" + user +
                                                  ", ou=People");
         String passwordInLDAP =
                          new String((byte[])usrattrs.get(PASSWORD).get());
         if(passwordInLDAP.compareTo(password) == 0) {
            // check role
            Attributes attrs =
                  ctx.getAttributes("properties=leSavonProperties, uid=" +
                                    user + ", ou=People");
            String role = (String)attrs.get(ROLE).get();
            isAdminUser = role.compareToIgnoreCase(ADMIN) == 0;
         }
         ctx.close();
      }
   } catch (NamingException namingException) {
      // Ignore, not a valid user for whatever reason
   }

   return isAdminUser;
}
```

If your application needs to secure the general user community, you will want to perform this check for all operations.

To fetch the value of a user property from the LDAP database, we use the context.getAttributes method (passing RDN of the user property). To *modify* a user property, we use the `context.modifyAttributes()` method and pass an array with one `ModificationItem` object.

```
public String getUserProperty(String user, String property)
   throws NamingException {
   String propertyValue = null;
   // We could cache to optimize apps that read a lot
   DirContext ctx    = new InitialDirContext(jndiEnv);
   Attributes attrs = ctx.getAttributes("property=" + property +
                      ", properties=leSavonProperties, uid=" + user +
                      ", ou=People");
   propertyValue = (String)attrs.get(VALUE).get();
   ctx.close();
   return propertyValue;
}
```

```
public void setUserProperty (String user, String property,
   String value) throws NamingException {
   DirContext ctx = new InitialDirContext(jndiEnv);
   String name  = "property=" + property +
                            ", properties=leSavonProperties, uid=" + user +
                            ", ou=People";
    ctx.modifyAttributes(name,
           new ModificationItem[] {
               new ModificationItem(DirContext.REPLACE_ATTRIBUTE,
                   new BasicAttribute(VALUE, value))});
   ctx.close();
}
```

Finally, we have some cache capability. A `CacheAction` is made up of a time to live (TTL) and a refresh flag. These two properties govern what action should be performed on a cache item when the update interval is up: do nothing, delete the cache item, or refresh the cache item:

```
public static class CacheAction {
  public long ttl;
  public boolean refresh;

  public CacheAction(long ttl, boolean refresh) {
    this.ttl = ttl;
    this.refresh = refresh;
  }
}
```

A `CacheRule` is a cache item with a regular expression (to identify a cache item) and a rank (to prioritize the caching rules):

```
private static class CacheRule extends CacheAction {
  public String regExp;
  public int    rank;

  public CacheRule(int rank, long ttl, boolean refresh, String regExp) {
    super(ttl, refresh);
    this.rank   = rank;
    this.regExp = regExp;
  }

  public static class CacheRuleComparator implements Comparator {

    public int compare(Object o1, Object o2) {
      int rank1 = ((CacheRule)o1).rank;
      int rank2 = ((CacheRule)o2).rank;
      return rank1 < rank2 ? -1 : (rank1 > rank2 ? 1 : 0);
    }
  } // CacheRuleComparator
} // CacheRule
```

Since LDAP has no standard capability for server-side sorting, we use the `item=<integer>` mechanism in the database to order cache rules. Some servers (such as iPlanet) support extensions that will allow clients to request server-side sorting, as opposed to client-side sorting.

As we will see in Chapter 8, the order in which rules are triggered is important. The `CacheRuleComparator` class is used to compare two cache rules during the sort performed by `Arrays.sort`:

```
private void getCacheRules() throws NamingException {
  if(cacheRules == null) {
    Vector     rules   = new Vector();
    DirContext ctx     = new InitialDirContext(jndiEnv);
    Attributes select = new BasicAttributes(true);

    NamingEnumeration answer = ctx.search(CACHE_ITEMS, select);
    while(answer.hasMore()) {
      SearchResult result = (SearchResult)answer.next();
      Attributes   attrs  = ctx.getAttributes("property=TTL, " +
                                  result.getName() + ", " + CACHE_ITEMS);
      long ttl = Long.parseLong((String)attrs.get(VALUE).get());

      attrs = ctx.getAttributes("property=Refresh, " +
                                  result.getName() + ", " + CACHE_ITEMS);
      boolean refresh =
         Boolean.valueOf((String)attrs.get(VALUE).get()).booleanValue();
      rules.add(new CacheRule(Integer.parseInt(
                 result.getName().substring(5)), ttl, refresh,
                 (String)(result.getAttributes().get(REG_EXP).get())));
    }

    cacheRules = (CacheRule[])rules.toArray(new CacheRule[rules.size()]);
    Arrays.sort(cacheRules, new CacheRule.CacheRuleComparator());

    ctx.close();
  }
}
```

Cache rules are read in memory and saved in a sorted array. The array of rules is used to find the first matching rule based on a cache key in `computeCacheAction()`:

```
public CacheAction computeCacheAction(String cacheKey)
  throws NamingException {
  long    ttl     = 0;
  boolean refresh = false;

  // We get a list of all the caching rules
  getCacheRules();

  // We traverse the list of rules to see if one (or more) matches
  for(int index = 0; index < cacheRules.length; index++) {
    if(matchCacheKey(cacheKey, cacheRules[index].regExp)) {
      ttl     = cacheRules[index].ttl;
```

```
            refresh = cacheRules[index].refresh;
          }
        }

        // If not, we use the default one (ttl == 0 is not a valid ttl...)
        if(ttl == 0) {
          ttl     = getCacheTTL();
          refresh = getCacheRefresh();
        }

        return new CacheAction(ttl, refresh);
      }
    }
```

Serialization

Before concluding this chapter, let's say a word about serialization of Java objects in an LDAP database. In this chapter, we've saved properties (in the form of name/value pairs) within an LDAP database, in order to persist a "state" of the user interface. We can generalize this simple approach to serializing Java objects in LDAP – and there are several techniques for this. In this section we will review three techniques and discuss their pros and cons.

Whichever methodology you choose for your application, keep in mind that LDAP does not work well for all objects, and that there is no concurrency management or transaction concept in LDAP.

Name/Value Pairs Serialization

An incremental step from the personalization strategy used in the sample application is to package user preferences into one Java object, preferably a bean, and save the properties to an LDAP database. Any object can be stored using this strategy, either by saving a string representation of the data or by encoding binary data that cannot easily be converted to a string.

The key advantages of this approach are its simplicity and its openness. A variety of LDAP clients can be used to view and even modify properties. This open methodology allowed us to modify the default settings of the sample application using an LDAP browser. A drawback of this approach is that you need to write a custom serializer for each class that you want to serialize to and from your LDAP database. However, this burden can be alleviated with the bean serializer provided by Apache SOAP that we met in the previous chapter, which is able to produce a string representation of a class (in SOAP).

XML Serialization

A variation on the name/value pair serialization strategy is that of XML serialization. If an object is to transit in SOAP payloads then it must have an XML representation; the idea is to extend that requirement to your configuration classes.

This is an improvement over the name/value pairs serialization strategy, because you can use the serialization code provided by Apache SOAP – and hence avoid the need to write custom serializers.

However, viewing and modifying XML inside an LDAP browser can be tricky. Potentially more seriously, this strategy is also destined to make your object store that much bigger, because of the added weight of the XML format. If you're planning to serialize many large objects in XML, then size and performance of the LDAP database may become issues.

Java Serialization

RFC 2713 (http://www.ietf.org/rfc/rfc2713.txt) defines a schema for Java objects in LDAP. OpenLDAP ships with a schema file, `schema/java.schema`, that follows the recommendations of RFC 2713. If you're interested in serializing Java objects in LDAP using the RFC 2713 schema, then take a look at the *Storing Objects in the Directory* track, in SUN's JNDI tutorial at http://java.sun.com/products/jndi/tutorial.

If an object implements the `Serializable` interface, then we gain an element of simplicity from serializing it to an LDAP database. However, we lose on the interoperability front with that strategy, because objects serialized in that manner can only be understood by Java. In particular, we lose the ability to use *any* LDAP browser to modify users' settings.

Summary

In this chapter, we have presented a high-level overview of LDAP and discussed why LDAP is a viable solution for handling security and personalization. Specifically, the openness and the distributed nature of LDAP make it well suited to store infrequently changing data used by a distributed application. We have also pointed out why some operations should not rely on LDAP. For instance, fast changing objects are best handled by other systems like relational databases.

The sample application relies on JNDI to access an LDAP database. JNDI is an attractive choice for the Java developer because it shields Java code from vendor-specific APIs that increase the complexity and size of applications.

We looked at authentication. We concluded that web servers are best suited to handle the authentication portion of the security chain, because they are typically well integrated to the operating system and have a proven solution in place.

Finally, we discussed several options for personalization – storing data that is associated with a user, and using it to customize the user's experience. We demonstrated the simple solution used by the sample application, and hinted at other options for storing such data (by serializing Java objects in an LDAP database using XML or a Java-specific schema).

Before we can take a closer look at the clients of our SOAP server, we must make sure that the server can perform according to the requirements. This is the topic of Chapter 8.

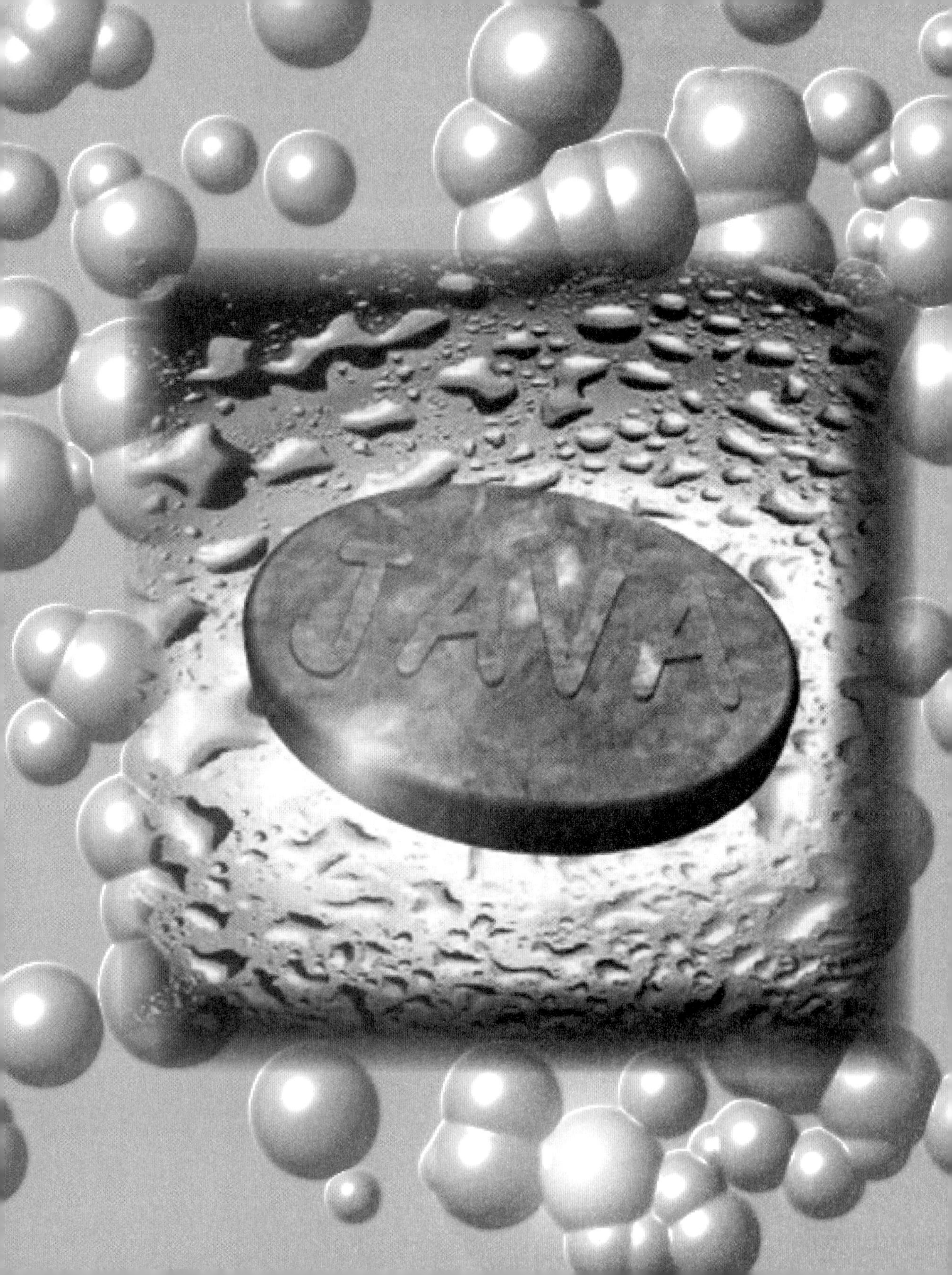
JAVA

8

Caching

In this chapter, we will discuss how to significantly improve the performance of a SOAP server by caching SOAP requests and responses. We will start by discussing the applicability of caching, and then we will dive into the requirements and implementation.

As you will discover in the following pages, there is more to managing caching than meets the eye, but armed with the guidelines and the code that we will present in this chapter, you will be able to quickly and easily raise the responsiveness of your application.

We will review the implementation of the `com.lesavon.cache.SOAPCache` class as part of this chapter. For the sake of simplicity, not all of the features discussed in this chapter are implemented in the SOAP cache class, but the infrastructure presented is functional and can easily be modified to accommodate the needs of your application.

The narrative of this chapter builds on many concepts that have been introduced previously in this book; in particular, we will assume that the reader is familiar with the high-level architecture of the sample application as well as with our use of LDAP. The high-level architecture of LeSavon.com is explained in Chapter 4 and our use of LDAP is discussed in Chapter 7.

Definition

We define **caching** as the addition of a storage and retrieval module to an existing application with the intent of improving its performance. The data structure that contains cached documents is simply referred to as the **cache** and the documents in the cache are called **cache items**.

Caching only applies to applications that follow a request/response model: a client sends a request to a server, which processes the request and then sends a response back. A web application that uses SOAP to implement Remote Procedure Calls (RPC) like the sample application can potentially use caching. The following diagram shows that process (a more detailed diagram was presented in Chapter 5):

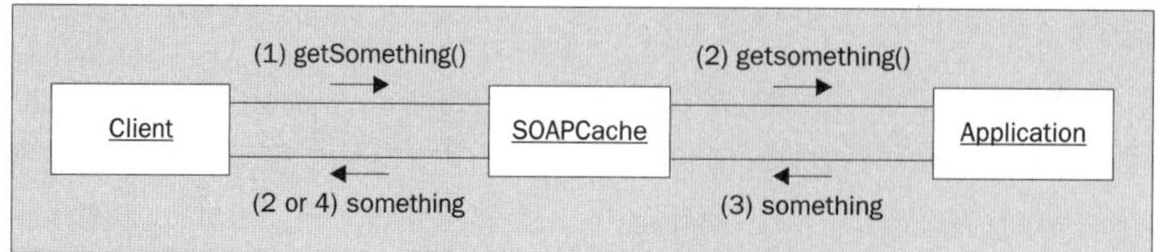

In the previous diagram, the client requests something using a SOAP request (`getSomething()`); if the requested data (`something`) is in the cache then it is returned immediately, if not then the requested data is forwarded to the backend server that hosts the original application. As you can see, when using a cache, the client application makes requests to the cache rather than to the original application.

In the case of a SOAP application, a convenient way to support this mechanism is to add a URL for the cache. Clients make requests to the cache that checks if the response is already cached and then forwards the request to the application URL if it needs to be generated. LeSavon.com uses this simple design: the URL that does not cache responses is ncrouter and the URL that caches responses is serveur:

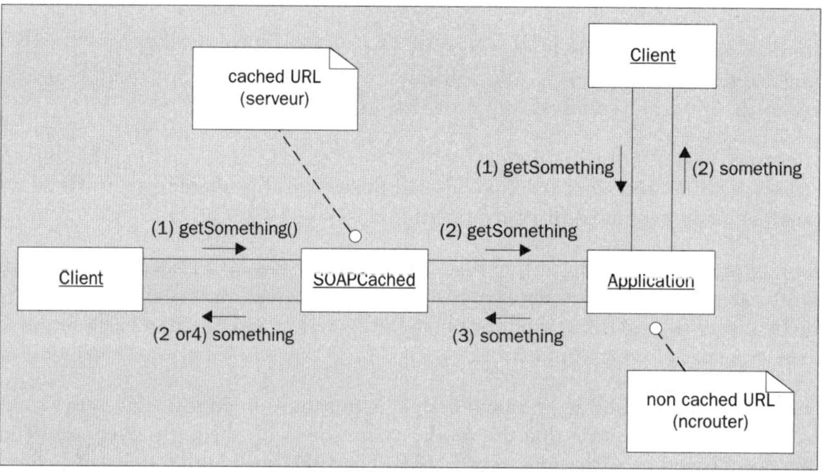

Another way to look at caching is that it simulates the real application to improve perceived response times. To perform its simulation, the cache stores responses to user requests so that it can return them faster than the application it serves. The data can be saved in memory or on disk: the important point is that retrieving the document from the cache is faster than the normal course of actions.

For instance, when a web server such as Apache caches a document, it saves the HTML in memory because accessing the disk is far slower than accessing Random Access Memory (RAM). This difference in performance comes from the mechanical movements of disk heads: data retrieval times for disk drives are measured in milliseconds while they are measured in nanoseconds for RAM. In SOAP-based applications, the issue is not disk versus RAM, it is generated responses versus saved responses since the majority of machine time is spent processing the request and creating the response.

As you have probably realized by now, speed is of the essence when designing and implementing a cache. To quickly identify the document that must be returned, a cache associates a key to a response document; however, it must be possible to compute the key from the request. In the case of the web server that we mentioned earlier, the key is the URL of the HTML page requested by the user.

For SOAP requests, the definition of the key is a little trickier since you do not have a static document to return, but it is possible, as we will see in a moment. Note that the cache as we have defined it so far is used to store responses, but we will see that there are some benefits in storing the requests as well.

For the remainder of this chapter, we will focus on a SOAP cache that contains SOAP requests and SOAP responses. Since we are using SOAP as a vehicle for RPC calls in the context of the sample application, a SOAP request is a method call and a SOAP response is the return value of the method. We will use that interpretation of SOAP documents in the following sections when reviewing the details of the cache.

Pros and Cons

A key advantage of caching is that it improves the response time of the application.

Another potential benefit of caching is the ability to work in an "off-line" mode in which the client or the web server can be disconnected from the backend server that supports the application.

There are at least three disadvantages to introducing a cache in the architecture of a SOAP server:

1. **Complexity**
   This is obvious, but sometimes overlooked: the addition of a cache increases the complexity of the overall application, which will cost more to develop and will be harder to test and debug. We will see in Chapter 9 when we measure performance that under the right circumstances the rewards can be well worth the trouble.

   Another issue related to complexity that we will discuss in the next section is the definition of what should and should not be cached.

2. **Latency**
   If caching is done right, the latency or time it takes for one user to get a response back, will be improved. However, because the response might be cached, it might have been sitting in the cache for a while and therefore the value of the data might have diminished. In other words, it might be quick to get an answer but the answer may be no longer correct. Situations can be widely different from one application to another, but it is important that the design of the cache includes functionality to address this issue.

3. **Performance**
   Because of the added complexity and of the requirement for managing the cache, the performance of the overall application might be negatively impacted. To measure that potential problem, it is important to keep a URL that can serve non-cached responses. During testing, and even during production, you will be able to use the non-cached URL to measure that the cache is actually improving performance. The sample application maintains a URL for cached requests and a URL for non-cached requests.

Now that we have defined what we expect from a cache and have a better understanding of the tradeoffs involved, we can discuss when it is appropriate to use a cache in a SOAP application.

To Cache or Not To Cache

The question is actually two fold:

- When is returning a cached document valid?
- When is returning a cached document faster?

It is not always correct to return a cached document. For instance, if the SOAP request updates a value in an enterprise database, then caching the request and the response is obviously not the correct answer since repeated SOAP calls would not modify the enterprise database. Caching SOAP responses is only valid when the request is read only.

In other words, if your application only deals with SOAP requests that trigger a modification of the state of the system, then caching is not for you. However, most applications are a mix of read-only and read-write operations.

Not all read-only operations should be cached. An obvious example is a time service: you want to return the most up-to-date information. Essentially, you want to be careful when caching time-sensitive data. However, the situation is not black or white since there are some time-sensitive data that you can cache for some time. The definition of "some time" depends on the context.

A good example of that situation is a stock quote server: depending on the service that you provide, you might want to cache the price of a stock for different lengths of time. For instance, responses to requests from regular customers could be cached for 20 minutes and responses to requests from premium customers could be in real-time, i.e. not cached at all.

As you can infer from the examples above, determining what operations can be cached and what operations cannot be cached must be done in the context of your application. In order to accommodate a variety of applications, our cache must have a straightforward way of turning caching on and off, not only for the application as a whole, but also for individual cached documents.

The issue of the speed of the cache is, once again, mostly a function of your application. As a general rule, the slower your backend server, the more benefits you will gain from caching. However, there are several issues that span most applications.

One issue to consider is the time it takes to parse a SOAP request and to build a Java call: the bigger the document, the longer it takes to parse it. As we will see in a few moments, when using the cache, the SOAP document must not always be parsed, which can lead to significant savings. When returning a cached SOAP response no time is spent generating the requests; this usually provides significant performance improvements, but not always as we discuss in the next paragraph.

Another issue to consider is the size of the cache: when the cache can no longer fit in RAM, it must be moved to disk and retrieval from disk will be significantly slower than from RAM. It might even be slower than parsing and generating the SOAP requests!

This is clearly the worst-case scenario for the cache since it actually slows down your application. Your best defense against this issue is carefully considering what you put in the cache and for how long it should stay in the cache. To validate your choices, you will need to test your application for performance. We will describe a tool to perform adequate performance testing in Chapter 9.

What's in a Key?

We mentioned previously that to speed up the access to the saved responses, the cache defines a key which can quickly be computed from the request. Using that key, the cache can query its internal structures to retrieve the desired response. We have seen earlier that for a web server, the URL of the requested document could serve as the key to the document. However, this approach will not work for a SOAP application since all clients make their requests to the same URL: the router.

An RPC SOAP request contains a method name, followed by its arguments. An easy way to create a key from a SOAP call is to concatenate the string representation of the fully qualified method name and its arguments into one long string. Each component of the key is separated by a period. For instance, let's consider the following SOAP request that retrieves the description of an item:

```
<?xml version="1.0" encoding="UTF-8" ?>
<SOAP-ENV:Envelope
 xmlns:SOAP-ENV="http://schemas.xmlsoap.org/soap/envelope/"
 xmlns:xsi="http://www.w3.org/1999/XMLSchema-instance"
 xmlns:xsd="http://www.w3.org/1999/XMLSchema">
 <SOAP-ENV:Body>
  <ns1:getItemDescription xmlns:ns1="urn:savon"
   SOAP-ENV:encodingStyle="http://xml.apache.org/xml-soap/literalxml">
   <arg0 xsi:type="xsd:string"
  SOAP-ENV:encodingStyle="http://schemas.xmlsoap.org/soap/encoding/">
  usr
   </arg0>
   <arg1 xsi:type="xsd:string"
  SOAP-ENV:encodingStyle="http://schemas.xmlsoap.org/soap/encoding/">
  Channel numéro cinq
   </arg1>
  </ns1:getItemDescription>
 </SOAP-ENV:Body>
</SOAP-ENV:Envelope>
```

Based on this SOAP document, the cache generates this simple key:

```
        com.lesavon.OrderService.getItemDescription.usr.Channel numéro cinq
```

This might seem obscure at first, but it becomes trivial when you look at the equivalent Java call:

```
com.lesavon.OrderService.getItemDescription("usr", "Channel numéro cinq");
```

Note that based on the discussion in Chapters 5 and 6, when we wrote the SOAP server and client, the call might be coming from `RemoteOrder` (an interface) instead of `OrderService` (a class name). To resolve that ambiguity, we adopt the convention of using the class name.

This algorithm to compute a key has two key advantages that are desirable in any storage system:

- It is fast to compute – The algorithm is simple and linear.
- It is short compared to the size of the document – The 676-characters request has shrunk into a 67-character key. You can expect to see a similar reduction when comparing the cache key to the SOAP response.

We have seen in previous chapters that the Apache SOAP engine takes care of parsing the XML request and creating the objects required to make the call (service class, arguments, etc.). The time spent doing this can constitute the majority of the processing, when the actual work that needs to be done is relatively trivial. For instance, in the previous example of returning a description for Channel No 5, looking up the text in a database or in memory would typically be faster than parsing the request and building the hierarchy of objects.

Based on this simple definition of a key, we can expect the cache to provide us with improved performance. To improve the performance of the cache further, we can ask the client to compute the cache key for the server and submit the cache key as part of the request in the HTTP header.

For instance, the `getItemDescription` request we looked at earlier could have the following HTTP header:

```
POST /lesavon/serveur HTTP/1.0
Host: localhost
Content-Type: text/xml; charset=utf-8
LeSavonCacheKey: com.lesavon.OrderService.getItemDescription.usr.Channel numéro
cinq
Content-Length: 676
```

If you are not sure how this header got computed, please refer to Chapter 2 where we discuss the use of the HTTP protocol as a transport for SOAP.

Using the HTTP header brings us extra savings because it frees the server from having to parse the SOAP request: the cache can extract the key from the HTTP header, check its data structure and then return the response to the client without looking at the document contained in the HTTP request. In all fairness, we must mention that there is a little extra processing required by the server to check for the presence of the cache key when a request is received without failing if the cache key is not present. We will see how this works in practice shortly.

The choice of the delimiter within the key is arbitrary. In this case, we have chosen the period because it makes the cache key identical to a fully qualified method name. However, it has the disadvantage of making regular expressions a little more complicated, as we will discuss shortly.

One critical concern in an Internet application is security. Since the client generates the cache key, it is possible that the wrong key will be generated. Worse, could a client impersonate another user by generating a key containing someone else's credentials? Not at all, because in order to generate a valid cache key one must be able to generate a valid SOAP request.

The cache key is a compact subset of the SOAP request, not a replacement for it. However, it is worth re-iterating the point that we made in Chapter 7: to protect your SOAP request against prying eyes, you should use HTTPS rather than HTTP. The use of HTTPS will also protect the cache key since it is part of the HTTP header.

However, as we will see when we talk about caching rules, careful setup is essential to maintain your site's security. A cache key submitted to the server that does not have a match in the cache will cause the server's behavior to be unpredictable depending on its current state. If you want to guarantee that the SOAP request matches the cache key, then you must parse the entire request and forgo the savings.

The cache key strategy is based on the premise that concurrent method calls with the same arguments will lend the same result. This is true of methods with no side effects made against stateless servers. However, a SOAP request contains more information than the method call itself. For instance, you can request a specific encoding (differing from the one registered on the server) as part of the SOAP payload. If you need this level of customization, you will have to refine the definition of the cache key.

Cache Data Structure

Based on the definition of the cache key, we can select the data structure that we want to use to store and retrieve cache keys, SOAP requests, and SOAP responses.

The data structure must be dynamic because the content of the cache depends on the runtime characteristics of the application and can vary widely from one day to the next. Another requirement that is implied by the definition of the cache (it must be faster than the original application) leads us to a data structure that can be quickly queried for a match on an arbitrary key. Finally, the cache data structure must be easy and quick to save to disk because you do not want a server restart to completely wipe out your cache.

A hash table is a data structure that meets all these requirements and that is supported by the JDK, so we will use it for the cache.

> *For a description of a hash table and its implementations by the JDK, please visit* *http://java.sun.com/j2se/1.3/docs/api/java/util/Hashtable.html.*

We said previously that we needed to serialize the cache to disk to allow the server to maintain a persistent state across restarts and reboots. To keep the serialized structure as small as possible, we will serialize SOAP documents in separate files. As we will see when we review the code, this organization allows us to optimize the use of memory.

Functionality of the Cache

In the beginning of this chapter, we have discussed the basics of caching, the definition of a key, and the pros and cons of caching. We will now refine our understanding of the cache by refining the model and laying out the functionality of the cache.

Storing and Retrieving

Now that we have our design for the cache and a unique key for cache items, we can start populating the cache with SOAP responses. Typically, the most cost efficient strategy is to save responses as the application generates them. However, there are cases where you want the cache to be pre-populated. For instance, if you were to run some lengthy report every morning, the cache could be seeded with the results of that report during the night.

Saving SOAP responses as they are generated seems simple on the surface; however, we must take care on the issue of concurrent accesses. It is entirely possible for two or more clients to submit the same request at the same time. When that happens, we want to avoid building the same response from two different threads of execution. We would rather have one thread to generate the SOAP response while the other is blocking.

We will look at the details when we review the code, but the basic idea is to add an item in the cache before submitting the response. Once we have an object, the cache item, we can synchronize multiple threads to avoid processing the same request multiple times.

One feature that is not part of the sample application, but that you might find useful for your own applications, is to time stamp the cached responses by using something similar to `inCacheSince="the-date-of-the-save"`. Using that information, the client can test whether or not the SOAP response was returned from the cache. The client could also test how old the response really is.

The cache item contains that information so the implementation on the server side boils down to reading the response in a DOM and adding the `inCacheSince` attribute to the SOAP envelope. We will see when we review the code that the cache saves the responses in a background thread. If you were to implement the same design in your application, then the overhead of modifying the responses would be incurred in the background thread, not in the thread handling client requests.

Off-Line Operation

Once the cache has been populated, it is possible to operate the application off-line. More precisely, the application is off-line, but the cache stays on line. This is similar to off-line browsing offered by most popular Internet browsers. However, the off-line mode applies to the SOAP server, rather than to the client.

The off-line mode can be used to temporarily update the back-end of your application without completely disabling the service. It can also be used by a client application to work in a disconnected mode, but this requires the SOAP server to be installed on the client machine.

It might seem like a bad idea to have a SOAP server on a client machine, but the client machine might be a powerful server. For instance, if you think of the sample application, LeSavon.com, the user interface is implemented as a web application that sends requests to a SOAP server to get data like the status of an order. The web server could cache the SOAP responses and keep providing service to its clients, even when the SOAP server is not available.

We will discuss below a system for client-side caching that does not require the SOAP application to be installed on the client. This capability is not implemented in the `SOAPCache` class because it is not very generic, but it can be useful in some applications.

Administering the Cache

The administration of the cache consists of getting items in and out of the cache and defining the rules governing the lifetime of the cache items. All cache configurations are properties stored in our LDAP database under the name:

properties=cachingrules, cn=LeSavonApplication, o=LeSavonWrox

Please refer to Chapter 7 for a description of the use of LDAP in the sample application.

In order to specify what needs to happen to a specific cache item, we need to identify cache items. We already know that a cache key uniquely identifies a cache item. A convenient way to extend this mechanism to identify a group of cache items is to use regular expressions. The `SOAPCache` classes use Perl5-compatible expressions because they are well known and parsing packages are readily available to support them. The sample application uses the ORO package available from http://jakarta.apache.org/oro/api/.

Instructions to download and install the ORO package can be found in Chapter 7.

Regular Expressions

A description of regular expression syntax can be found at the same URL. For the sake of this discussion, we will limit ourselves to explaining any regular expression we use. A period (.) is a special character that instructs the expression matching engine to match against any character. The star (*) is appended to a character to mean that the search should look for any number of instances of the character.

The following expression:

```
Hel.o
```

would match Hello, but it would also match Hel:o, Helpo, or Heldo, among others. The expression

```
Hel*o
```

looks for the letters 'H' and 'e' followed by any number of 'l' characters and ending in 'o'. That means that the words Heo, Helo, Hello, Helllo, etc would all match.

In addition, if we are searching for a period, it must be escaped by a backslash (\), otherwise it will be taken as meaning any character. For instance, all methods of the class:

```
com.lesavon.service.OrderService
```

can be specified as:

```
com\.lesavon\.service\.OrderService\..*
```

Similarly, all calls to `getOrderList()` can be specified as:

```
com\.lesavon\.service\.OrderService\.getOrderList\..*
```

In both cases, any keys that the expressions above followed by any value would be returned. For example, the first expression will match:

```
com.lesavon.OrderService.getOrderList.Channel numero cinq
```

but would also match:

```
com.lesavon.OrderService.someOtherMethod.argument list
```

The trailing '`\..*`' matches the arguments of the call to `getOrderList()`. If you recall, we mentioned earlier that using a period as a delimiter in cache key values would complicate the code; this is the reason. We must escape every instance of a period in our expression – that is all.

The screenshot of the LDAP browser below shows the entity for all the methods (for all classes) of the `com.lesavon.service` package.

The LDAP browser was described in Chapter 7.

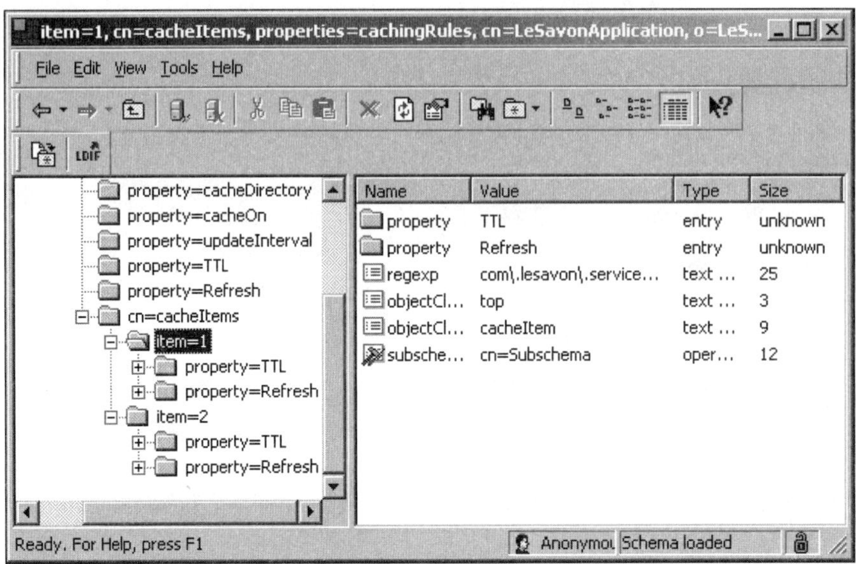

In addition to regular expressions, we need to define some properties for administering the cache. The sample application supports two properties:

- **TTL (Time To Live)**
  This property must be specified with an integer number that defines how long the items that match the pattern stay in the cache. This property is in milliseconds. The sample application does not define a maximum value for the TTL.

- **Refresh**
  If the value of the refresh flag is true then the cache items that match the pattern will be refreshed when the TTL expires (see below). Otherwise it will be deleted.

Properties are case-insensitive.

The screenshot below shows the entry for the `getOrderList()`. The `item={1, 2}` name can be used to order the rules from the more general to the more specific. You can see on the right-hand panel that the refresh flag for `getOrderList()` is `true` to force the cache to refresh the list of orders on a regular basis.

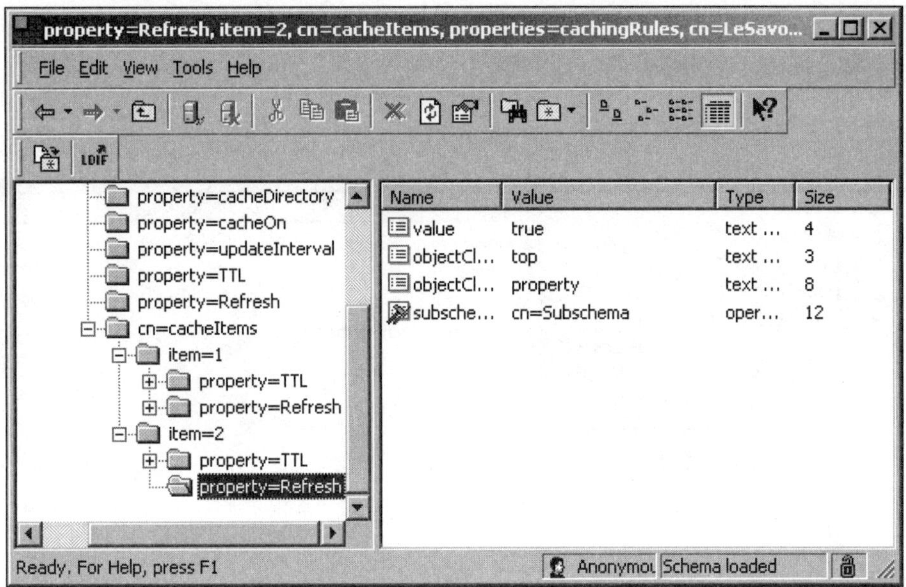

In addition to the properties that apply to individual cache items, a few properties apply to the cache as a whole, as shown in the diagram above. These are:

- `cacheDirectory`
  A valid directory path to store the cache in.
- `cacheOn`
  The cache is ON or OFF.
- `updateInterval`
  This property must be specified with an integer number that defines how often the cache is saved to disk in milliseconds.
- `TTL`
  Default time to live when no rule can be found for a key.
- `Refresh`
  Default value for the refresh flag. In the LDAP server provided with the code download, by default, cache items will not be refreshed unless specified otherwise.

The cache level properties are stored under the `properties=cachingRules` entity as you can see in the following figure:

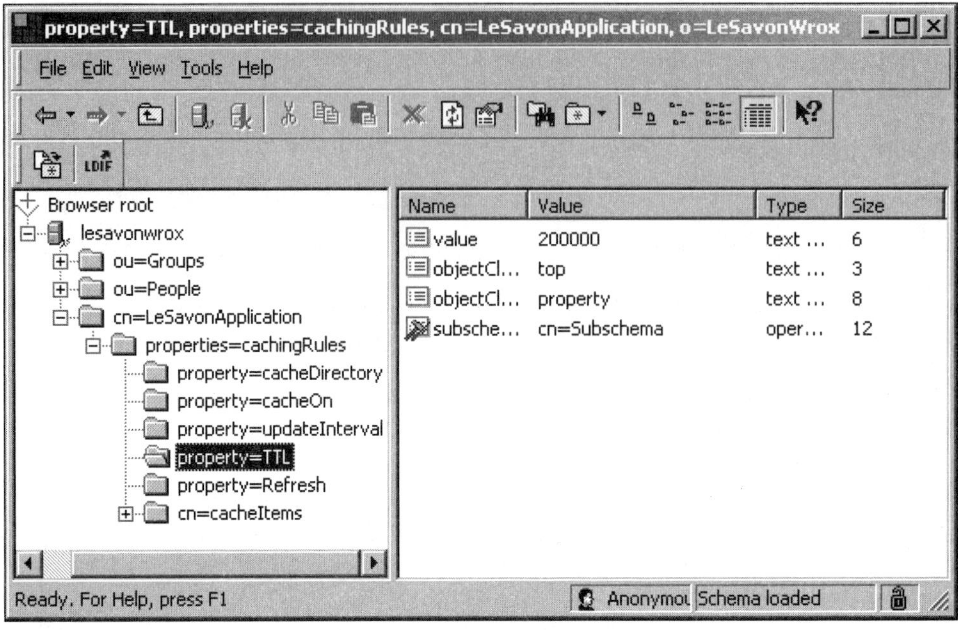

The screenshot above shows the value for the default TTL value: cache items that are not matched by a specific rule will be deleted after 200,000 milliseconds (3 minutes and 20 seconds) since the default value of the refresh flag is false (do not refresh).

The default values are defined in the `lesavon.ldif` file that we reviewed in Chapter 7. By modifying `lesavon.ldif`, you can alter the default values. You can also change the "live" values in LDAP using the LDAP browser or an LDAP client similar to `AddLeSavonUser` that we wrote in Chapter 7.

Cache Commands

We have discussed how it is possible for a system administrator to modify the settings in LDAP to configure how the cache behaves. Those settings are read when the cache starts and are in effect until the cache is restarted.

The administrator may also administer the cache itself through cache commands. Cache administration commands are not cached since they do more than returning documents and as such are not read-only.

Our implementation supports two commands:

- `flush`
  This command empties the cache.
- `refresh`
  This command refreshes all the items currently in the cache.

Both operations have subtleties that we will discuss in a few moments.

It is possible to augment this set of commands with other functionality, such as changing the `TTL` or the `refresh` flag. Supporting a pattern in the `refresh` and `flush` commands to selectively apply them is also possible. One has to be careful because of the nature of LDAP: there are no transactions and no locking in LDAP, so it is easy to leave the LDAP configuration in an inconsistent state. One simple strategy is to design your application so that the state stored in LDAP can be changed with one call to LDAP. You will notice that `flush` and `refresh` do not modify the LDAP database and therefore do not need to be synchronized across machines.

There is no command to turn off the cache. To submit a request with the cache turned off, simply send it to the `ncrouter` (non-cached router) URL. Please refer to Chapter 5 for a description of the `serveur` and `ncrouter` URLs.

One last note on cache commands: they are only accessible to users with the administrator privilege.

Refreshing the Cache

We have previously mentioned that you can indicate when cache items should become obsolete and what to do when this happens. In a nutshell, the cache item is either deleted or refreshed on the user's behalf when the TTL is reached. Obviously, refreshing the result can only happen if the cache saves the request along with the result.

The Cache Thread

A low-priority thread inspects the cache for expired items to refresh or delete. Another task that is well suited for that thread is to save the cache to disk from time to time. That way, if the server is interrupted or crashes for some reason, the entire content of the cache will not be lost. The same thread does some cleanup that will become clearer when we review the code.

Note that thanks to the cache thread, the implementation of the `refresh` command is straightforward: set a flag that will force the items to be refreshed when the low-priority thread fires. Using this implementation, the refresh might take a while to take effect, but the `refresh` command will come back right away.

The Danger of Flush

Flushing the cache is a potentially dangerous operation because it involves deleting files that may be being used to send a response back to a client. The first temptation is to synchronize access to the cache and delete the items along with their associated files as they become available. The problem with that simplistic approach is that a flush could take a very long time.

A more responsive way to handle the situation is to remove items from the cache and attempt to delete the file associated with the item. If the file is in use, the deletion will fail but that is not an issue since the cache thread that is responsible for cleaning up and refreshing expired cache items also removes dangling files periodically. With this methodology, the `flush` command can safely return in a reasonable amount of time. These details will be more obvious when we review the code later.

When Something Goes Wrong

Care must be taken to make sure that the cache does not remember "wrong" answers. For instance, let's imagine that you have set up the cache to ignore the user name and the password when caching requests and let's assume that the first request that comes through the server for the `getItemDescription()` request contains an invalid user name/password combination. The HTTP status is going to be perfectly `OK` (presumably `200`), but the SOAP response is going to contain a `FAULT` section with a description of the error.

If the cache were to simply save the response, then every request to `getItemDescription()` would fail with the same error message! This behavior is clearly not acceptable. Our implementation takes care of that requirement by using `org.apache.soap.util.net.HTTPUtils.POST` that throws a `SOAPException` when the reply contains a `FAULT` section.

Client-Side Caching

As we have discussed before, it is possible for a SOAP server to work off-line: all SOAP requests are returned from the cache rather than from the backend. This mode does not allow a user to take a laptop on the road and work with the application, unless the SOAP server has been installed on the laptop. This is not always practical and there is at least one alternative.

The SOAP requests and responses could be cached on the client rather than on the server. However, this requires that the server-side application reside on the client.If this fat client approach is not a problem for your application then this might be a viable solution for your users to work off-line. The major drawbacks of this approach are the same as for all fat client applications: size of the download, maintenance, etc. A more detailed discussion on the pluses and minuses of fat and thin clients is outside of the scope of this book, but you can find a good discussion of those issues at http://developer.java.sun.com/developer/technicalArticles/GUI/frontends/.

The sample application does not implement client-side caching.

Code Review

Now that we have defined the requirements and the design guidelines of the cache, it is time to look at the code and see how the cache is actually implemented. We will first look at the code for the `com.lesavon.cache.SOAPCache` class and then we will review the SOAP service that provides distributed access to the administration of the cache. Finally, we will look at two short test programs: `com.lesavon.test.GetAllOrders` and `com.lesavon.test.TestAdmin`.

The samples for this chapter can be found in \ProJavaSoap\Chapter08

Cache Implementation

In this section we will review the code of the cache itself and the SOAP service that makes the administration interface of the cache available as a web service. In the sample application not all the functionality of the cache is meant to be accessible through SOAP, but you might consider it for your application. For instance, through a SOAP interface, you could remotely administer cache wide values.

The SOAPCache Class

The cache fits in one class: `SOAPCache`. That class is in a package by itself to allow for potential growth without moving classes around.

The flow of a SOAP request was briefly described in the introduction and more thoroughly discussed in Chapter 4. You might want to quickly review it before continuing.

```
// SOAPCache.java

package com.lesavon.cache;

import java.io.*;
import java.net.*;
import java.util.*;
import java.lang.reflect.Method;
```

The first section of code shows the packages we will include:

- We will be working with the `java.io` package to save the cache to file.
- The `java.net` package is used to submit our requests.
- The memory cache is a `HashTable`, which comes with the `java.util` package.
- We need the `java.servlet` package to get access to the text of the request when the cache key needs to be computed. Recall that the cache key is a representation of the SOAP request. We will also use the servlet context to build the physical path to the cache directory.
- The use of the `java.lang.reflect` package might seem surprising, but we need to use reflection to compute a cache key.
- The `org.apache.soap` and `org.w3c` packages will allow us to have a closer look at SOAP requests and responses by inspecting the component XML of the documents – for instance, when we check for the presence of a `SOAP:FAULT` tag or compute a cache key.

The code download specified the exact classes imported. Such details were removed here for the sake of brevity.

We will use the LDAP utility class that we worked on in Chapter 7 to access the LDAP system.

```
import javax.servlet.ServletContext;
import javax.servlet.http.HttpServletRequest;

import javax.mail.MessagingException;
import javax.xml.parsers.*;
import javax.naming.NamingException;

import org.apache.soap.*;
import org.apache.soap.server.*;
import org.apache.soap.rpc.*;
import org.apache.soap.transport.TransportMessage;
import org.apache.soap.util.net.HTTPUtils;

import org.w3c.dom.Document;
```

```
import org.w3c.dom.NodeList;

import com.lesavon.SavonException;
import com.lesavon.util.LDAP;

public class SOAPCache {
  // milliseconds between iterations for the cache thread
  private static final long DELAY = 30000;

  // The (base) name for the cache file
  private static final String CACHE_FILE_NAME = "Cache.dat";

  // The (base) name for the cache item files (responses)
  private static final String RESPONSE_FILE_NAME = "Response";

  // The (base) name for the cache item files (requests)
  private static final String REQUEST_FILE_NAME = "Request";

  // The (base) name for the cache request files
  private static final String CACHE_ITEM_REQUEST_FILE_NAME = "Request";

  private String cacheDirectory;
  private long cacheUpdateInterval;
  private ServletContext  context = null;
  private Hashtable hashtable = new Hashtable();
  private Thread cacheThread;
  private boolean keepRunning = false; // stops cache thread
  private long counter = 0;
  private boolean forceRefresh = false;
  private DocumentBuilder docBuilder; // Re-use the document builder

  // The one and only cache for this VM
  private static SOAPCache theCache;
  // SOAP cache constructor is private to enforce singleton.
```

There is only one cache per server, so we make it a static variable and we enforce the singleton pattern with the `getCache()` method. Having more than one cache per server, in other words more than one `serveur` servlet that calls the cache, would be detrimental to performance since it would duplicate the memory taken by the cache and the work done by the background thread. As we will see later in Chapter 9, the stateless nature of our server allows you to replicate it over as many computers as you want.

In this environment, each cache works independently. For requests that can take a very long time, we could make the multiple instances of the cache aware of each other. This shared knowledge allows a cache that does not have a response already saved to ask its peers for the response.

```
private SOAPCache() throws SavonException {
  try {
  DocumentBuilderFactory factory = DocumentBuilderFactory.newInstance();
  factory.setNamespaceAware(true);
  docBuilder = factory.newDocumentBuilder();
  } catch(ParserConfigurationException parserConfigurationException) {
  throw new SavonException(
             "Cannot create document builder for OrderService",
             parserConfigurationException);
```

```
    }

    try {
    cacheDirectory     = LDAP.getLDAP().getCacheDirectory();
    cacheUpdateInterval = LDAP.getLDAP().getCacheUpdateInterval();
    } catch(NamingException namingException) {
    throw new SavonException("Cannot get cache directory from LDAP",
                 namingException);
    }
  }

  public static SOAPCache getCache() throws SavonException{
    if(theCache == null) {
    theCache = new SOAPCache();
    }

    return theCache;
  }
```

The cache is a hash table of `CacheItem` objects. The cache item contains all the information to save and refresh the response if necessary. The request and the response are not serialized as part of the cache item because saving them as standalone XML files makes it a lot easier to debug your application.

```
  // A cache item
  private static class CacheItem implements Serializable {
    String url;
    String key;
    String responseFileName;
    String requestFileName;
    long lastRefresh;
    boolean populated;
    transient byte[] request;
    transient byte[] response;
```

Most of the instance data of a cache item are self-explanatory. The `url` is the URL of the application. The `populated` flag will be set to true, once we have the response that goes along with the request. This flag is used by the cache thread to avoid saving incomplete requests.

```
  CacheItem(String url, String key) {
    counter++;
    this.key = key;
    this.url = url;

    String trailer = "_" + System.currentTimeMillis() + "_"
         + counter + ".xml";
```

The `javax.servlet.ServletContext.getRealPath()` method converts a relative pathname like the one we store in LDAP (see the description of the cacheDirectory in the *Administering the Cache* section) into a fully qualified pathname.

```
    this.responseFileName = SOAPCache.this.context.getRealPath(cacheDirectory
              + File.separator + RESPONSE_FILE_NAME + trailer);
    this.requestFileName = SOAPCache.this.context.getRealPath(cacheDirectory
```

```
                + File.separator + REQUEST_FILE_NAME + trailer);

    // We need to make sure that the cache directory exists
    File cacheDir = new File(
            SOAPCache.this.context.getRealPath(cacheDirectory));
    cacheDir.mkdir();
  }
```

The save method below writes the request and the response files to disk. It will be called by the cache thread, which we will review in a few moments.

```
    // Saves the file content to disk (including the request)
    void save() throws IOException {
    if(response != null) {
      FileOutputStream os = new FileOutputStream(responseFileName);
      os.write(response);
      os.close();
    }

    if(request != null) {
      FileOutputStream os = new FileOutputStream(requestFileName);
      os.write(request);
      os.close();
    }
    }
  }
```

The computeCacheKey() methods below need a little explanation. The first is straightforward: it first extracts the fully qualified name of the method and then concatenates the value of the toString() method of the arguments. As we have said before, if your application needs to use arguments in pattern patching, you might want to use another delimiter than the period.

```
  public static String computeCacheKey(String targetClass,
                         Method method,
                         Object[] args) {
    String cacheKey = targetClass + "." + method.getName();
    for(int index = 0; index < args.length; index++) {
    cacheKey += "." + args[index];
    }

    return cacheKey;
  }
```

The second overload of the computeCacheKey() method looks a little more complex at first because it needs to build a Call object from the input stream before computing the cache key. However, the fundamental idea is similar: build a cache key by concatenating the arguments of the method call.

As you will see shortly, the fully qualified name of the method comes from the DeploymentDescriptor. For an explanation of deployment descriptors and our registration strategy, please refer to Chapter 6.

```
public String computeCacheKey(HttpServletRequest request,
                InputStream inputStream,
                ServletContext servletContext)
   throws SavonException {
  ServiceManager serviceManager = null;
  Call call = null;
  SOAPContext soapContext = new SOAPContext();
  Envelope callEnv = null;
```

The `org.apache.soap.server.ServiceManager` was discussed in Chapter 6 when we introduced the `DeploymentDescriptor`; it is essentially a container for all the supported services. The `org.apache.soap.rpc.Call`, `org.apache.soap.rpc.SOAPContext`, and `org.apache.soap.Envelope` classes are also part of the Apache SOAP framework. The `Call` models a SOAP call, the `Envelope` represents a `<SOAP:Envelope/>` element, and the `SOAPContext` is used to encapsulates a MIME part of a SOAP document, if any (in the case of the sample application there is none).

```
try {
  serviceManager =
      ServerHTTPUtils.getServiceManagerFromContext(servletContext);
```

We get the current service manager from the servlet context with the intention of accessing the deployment information for the SOAP service being called.

```
callEnv = ServerUtils.readEnvelopeFromInputStream(docBuilder,
                        inputStream,
                        request.getContentLength(),
                        request.getContentType(),
                        null,
                        soapContext);
```

We read the content of the request (the SOAP envelope) into the `Envelope` object.

```
call = RPCRouter.extractCallFromEnvelope(serviceManager,
                      callEnv,
                      soapContext);
```

Once we have an envelope, we can build an instance of the `Call` class, which we can use to loop on the arguments of the call. The remainder of the implementation of this version of `computeCacheKey()` is similar to the simple overload that we reviewed earlier.

```
  DeploymentDescriptor descriptor =
             serviceManager.query(call.getTargetObjectURI());
  Vector params = call.getParams();
  String cacheKey = descriptor.getProviderClass()
           + "."
           + call.getMethodName();

  for(int index = 0; index < params.size(); index++) {
    cacheKey += "." + ((Parameter)params.elementAt(index)).getValue();
  }

  return cacheKey;
```

```
    } catch (Exception exception) {
    throw new SavonException("Cannot compute cache key", exception);
    }
}
```

The next method, `submitAndCache()`, is responsible for submitting requests and saving them to the cache. We have already seen its use back in Chapter 5 when we wrote the `Serveur` servlet that is accessed using the lesavon/serveur URL.

```
public byte[] submitAndCache(CacheItem item)
    throws MalformedURLException, IOException, MessagingException,
        SOAPException {
  if(item.request == null) { // request in memory?
  item.request = readFile(it.requestFileName);
  }

  byte[] data = null;

  if(item.request != null) { // Could we read the file if null?
  data = submitAndCache(item.request, item.url, item.key);
  }
  return data;
}
```

There are two overloads of `submitAndCache()`. The first version takes a cache item as argument. It is used during a refresh, as we will see later when we talk about the background thread of the cache. The second overload is where things happen. So let's have a closer look at that method.

```
public byte[] submitAndCache(byte[] requestText, String url, String key)
    throws MalformedURLException, IOException,
        MessagingException, SOAPException {
  TransportMessage request = null;
  TransportMessage response = null;
  SOAPContext ctx = new SOAPContext();
  CacheItem cacheItem = null;
  boolean success = false;
```

The caller of that method is expected to only call `submitAndCache()` if the response is not already in the cache. The method starts by adding an entry to the cache for the new response:

```
  try {
  synchronized(hashtable) {
    cacheItem = (CacheItem)hashtable.get(key);
    if(cacheItem == null) {
    cacheItem = new CacheItem(url, key);
    hashtable.put(key, cacheItem);
    }
  }
```

The previous block of code must be synchronized on the cache (the hash table) to prevent duplicate entries from being added. The code above will work when multiple clients submit the same request that is not cached yet: all clients will call `submitAndCache()` but only one of them will make it in the critical section.

The other clients will get the cache item rather than `null` and will therefore not create a new cache item. Once we have created a cache item, we can synchronize multiple clients as shown in the next few lines of code.

```
synchronized(cacheItem) {
  if(!cacheItem.populated) {
  request = new TransportMessage(new String(requestText), ctx, null);
  request.save();

  response = HTTPUtils.post(new URL(url), request, 0, null, 0);
```

It is possible for the client that creates the cache item and the client that submits the request to be different, which is not a problem. What is important is that we do not submit the same request twice, which is guaranteed by the test on `cacheItem.populated` above. The request is forwarded to the application URL (lesavon/ncrouter for the sample application).

As we mentioned before, we must check that the SOAP response does not contain any faults. We perform a quick check using `String.indexOf()`. This is quick but can lead to false positives. This situation could arise if a valid SOAP response contained the word "Fault" in its return value. Hence, the more thorough check that parses the SOAP response, as you can see below:

```
// We must make sure that nothing went wrong, otherwise,
// we would cache failures!
if(response.getEnvelope().indexOf("Fault") != -1) {
  Document respDoc = DocumentBuilderFactory.newInstance().
  newDocumentBuilder().parse(response.getEnvelope());

  String prefix = respDoc.getDocumentElement().getPrefix();
  String uri = respDoc.getDocumentElement().getNamespaceURI();

  if(uri.compareToIgnoreCase(
            "http://schemas.xmlsoap.org/soap/envelope/") == 0) {
  NodeList nl = respDoc.getElementsByTagName(prefix + ":Fault");

  success = (nl.getLength() == 0);
}
```

The point of the code above is to assign a value to `success` based on the content of the response from the application: if the response contains a SOAP fault then the operation is not a success so the value of `success` must be false.

We have to be careful when looking for the fault: first we must parse the request, second we must find the prefix assigned to the SOAP namespace, third we must look for a node with the `<SOAP:Fault/>` element in the response. This might seem like a lot of work, but is required to be accurate and is only done is rare cases because of the quick test that surrounds this block of code.

```
  } else {
  success = true;
  }

  if(success) {
  cacheItem.request = requestText;
```

```
    cacheItem.response = response.getBytes();
    cacheItem.populated = true;
    cacheItem.lastRefresh = System.currentTimeMillis();
    }
```

The statements above populate the cache item with the data from the response.

```
        }
    }
    } catch(Exception exception) {
    System.err.println("SOAPCache.submitAndCache: caught exception: "
              + exception + ", ignored.");
    } finally {
    if(!success) {
      hashtable.remove(key);
    }
    }

    return cacheItem.response;
  }
```

If the operation is a success then we leave the synchronized block to allow other clients to proceed and retrieve the response from the cache items they have obtained earlier.

If something went wrong, e.g. a SOAP fault is returned, we delete the cache entry. Note that by default `success` is false, so if an exception is thrown, the cache item is removed from the cache. This is the correct behavior since the response in this case is questionable at best.

One last word needs to be said on `submitAndCache()`. As described earlier, the synchronization happens on a cache item (`synchronized(cacheItem)`), so if the request does not need to be cached, what do we do? The easiest solution is to force all non-cached calls to go through the `ncrouter` URL. Calls aimed at that URL do not execute any of the code described in this chapter; they go directly to the Apache SOAP router. Another possibility would be to modify the `Serveur` code that we reviewed in Chapter 5 so that a cache entry with a TTL equal to zero would not go through `submitAndCache()`.

The following portion of the code has to do with returning a cached response. Let's start by looking at `getCacheData()`:

```
  public byte[] getCacheData(String key) {
    CacheItem cacheItem = null;
    byte[] data = null;
```

That `getCacheData()` method takes a cache key as argument and returns the response found in the cache item. Keep in mind that the cache is restored lazily. That is, when the hashtable, that stores a list of keys against their responses, is deserialized from file the cache items that it stores are not. They must be deserialized separately.

`getCacheData()` does this by checking if the cache item that the hash table returns when given a key has a null object in the `response` property, and if so reloads the cache item's value from file. This means that objects that are in the cache and do not get requested before their expiration are not wastefully deserialized. We will define a method, `cleanupCacheDirectory()` that will delete any files that are no longer referenced by the hash table.

```
    cacheItem = (CacheItem)hashtable.get(key);
```

```
if(cacheItem != null) {
  synchronized (cacheItem) {
  // File content is brought in memory lazily
  if(cacheItem.response == null) {
  try {
    data = readFile(cacheItem.responseFileName);
  } catch (Exception exception) {
    // handle as data == null
  }
  } else {
  data = cacheItem.response;
  }
}
```

You will notice the test `if(cacheItem.response == null)`: the response contained in the cache item is `null` by default; in particular, when the cache is serialized from disk (see below), all responses are `null`. This allows us to lazily bring the content of the cache in memory: only when a specific request is sent do we bring up the corresponding response. The main advantage of this approach is that you will conserve your precious RAM space and will not see a delay when the hash table that implements the cache is serialized from disk. There are no significant drawbacks to this methodology. As you can see in the following code, we return null (and log a message) when the data of the response cannot be found. The caller is expected to resubmit the request, which would populate the cache in case of success.

```
    if(data == null) {
      hashtable.remove(key);
      System.err.println("SOAPCache.getCacheData: Cannot read "
                + cacheItem.responseFileName
                + ", removing entry from the cache.");
    }
    }

    return data;
  }

  private String getCacheFileName() {
    return context.getRealPath(cacheDirectory + File.separator
                + CACHE_FILE_NAME);
  }
```

The method `getCacheFileName()` simply returns the physical path of the file used to serialize the hash table. The `readFile()` method reads a file as bytes, it is used to read SOAP responses and requests.

```
  private static byte[] readFile(String filePath) throws IOException {
    File file   = new File(filePath);
    int length = (int)file.length();
    byte[] data = null;

    if(length > 0) {
```

```
    InputStream is = new FileInputStream(file);
    data = new byte[length];
    int offset = 0;
    while(length > 0) {
      int read = is.read(data, offset, length);
      if (read < 0) {
      break;
      }
      offset += read;
      length -= read;
    }
    is.close();
    }
    return data;
  }
```

Before we can look into the cache thread, we must look at a couple of helper methods. `cleanupCacheDirectory()` below, scans the cache directory and removes files that do not have a corresponding entry in the cache. Initially, this code was written to protect the server against a forceful stop or a crash, which can happen from time to time in debug.

The implementation of `cleanupCacheDirectory()` is straightforward: get a list of the files managed by the cache (SOAP responses and requests) and make sure that each of them can be found in the hash table of the cache. The files that are not referenced in the hash table can safely be deleted since the cache will never use them.

```
  private void cleanupCacheDirectory() {
    try {
    File cacheDir = new File(context.getRealPath(cacheDirectory));
    File files[] = cacheDir.listFiles(
              new FilenameFilter() {
                 public boolean accept(File dir, String name) {
                 // The cache only handles XML files that are
                 // either a request or a response.
                 return (name.startsWith(REQUEST_FILE_NAME) ||
                     name.startsWith(RESPONSE_FILE_NAME)) &&
                     name.endsWith(".xml");
                 } // end accept
              }); // end file name filter. end listFile()

    if (files!= null) {
      for(int index = 0; index < files.length; index++) {
      Iterator iter   = hashtable.values().iterator();
      boolean remove = true;

      while(iter.hasNext()) {
        CacheItem item = (CacheItem)iter.next();
        String fileName = context.getRealPath(cacheDirectory +
                File.separator + files[index].getName());
        if(fileName.equalsIgnoreCase(item.responseFileName) ||
         fileName.equalsIgnoreCase(item.requestFileName)) {
        remove = false;
        break;
```

```
        }
      }

      if(remove) {
        files[index].delete();
      }
      }
    }
    } catch (Exception exception) {
    System.err.println("SOAPCache.cleanupCacheDirectory: Caught "
              + exception + ", ignored.");
    }
  }
```

Next, we look at cleanupAndRefresh():

```
  private void cleanUpAndRefresh(CacheItem item, boolean forceRefresh) {
    try {
    LDAP.CacheAction cacheAction =
                  LDAP.getLDAP().computeCacheAction(item.key);
```

The cleanupAndRefresh() method implements the caching rules that we mentioned earlier. The cache thread calls it on a regular basis to check if a cache item needs either to be refreshed or deleted. A call to computeCacheAction() gives us the caching rule that applies to the cache item that was passed in. The LDAP.CacheAction class is a nested class inside LDAP since it is LDAP's view of a cache action, not the cache's.

```
  // Is the item stale yet or do we have to refresh?
  if(forceRefresh ||
      item.lastRefresh + cacheAction.ttl <= System.currentTimeMillis()) {

    // The item is stale, it should either be deleted or refreshed
    if(forceRefresh || cacheAction.refresh) {
    submitAndCache(item);
```

We test if the cache item needs to be looked at: if the TTL has not expired yet, then the item does not need to deleted or the cached response recalculated and we do not need to take any further action; if the TTL has expired, the entry must either be refreshed or deleted. To refresh the entry, we call submitAndCache() that we reviewed earlier. The forceRefresh flag is set by the cache thread after a call to the refresh command. We will review the cache thread or background thread in a moment.

A call to hashtable.remove() deletes the entry from the cache (the clean up work in the cache directory is left to cleanupCacheDirectory():

```
      } else {
      hashtable.remove(item.key); // It is history
      }
    }
    } catch (Exception exception) {
    System.err.println("SOAPCache.cleanUpAndRefresh: Caught "
              + exception + ", ignored.");
    }
  }
```

One last comment can be said on expired items in the cache. Since the `getCacheData()` method that we reviewed earlier is not synchronized, there is a slight chance that it will get an entry from the cache and by the time it reads the file content, the file has been deleted by the cache thread. This circumstance is taken care of by the silent failure of the `hashtable.remove()` method in the code above.

More precisely, because the file IO fails in `getCacheData()`, the code attempts to delete the entry in the cache but the entry is gone at this point so the call to `remove` fails as well, but no exception is thrown. The caller to `getCacheData()` receives `null` for its cached response, meaning that the response is not in the cache.

We are now ready to look into the cache thread that we mentioned earlier. The background cache thread is created by a call to `startCacheThread()`, which is synchronized since we do not want more than one cache thread to be running:

```
public synchronized void startCacheThread(ServletContext context) {
  // If there is already a cache thread, then there is nothing to do...
  if(cacheThread != null) {
  return;
  }

  this.context = context;

  // Make sure we have a cache directory
  new File(context.getRealPath(cacheDirectory)).mkdir();

  // If there is a saved cache, we read it
  try {
  File cacheFile = new File(getCacheFileName());

  ObjectInputStream is =
         new ObjectInputStream(new FileInputStream(cacheFile));

  hashtable = (Hashtable)is.readObject();
  is.close();
```

The method starts by reading the hash table from disk if one was previously saved, otherwise it creates an empty one. Note that any file IO exception (file not found, read only file, etc.) will result in the creation of an empty cache.

Once we have a hash table, we are ready to start the cache thread since the cache items will be populated lazily with the requests and responses saved on disk, if any.

```
} catch (Exception exception) {
  hashtable = new Hashtable();

  System.err.println("SOAPCache.startCacheThread: Caught "
           + exception + ", ignored.");
}

counter = hashtable.size();

keepRunning = true;

cacheThread = new Thread(new Runnable() {
```

```
public void run() {
long lastSave = -1;

while(keepRunning) {
```

The cache thread runs for as long as the keepRunning flag is true. The run method performs the work that we have been discussing so far. After getting a list of the items in the cache, it calls the cleanupAndRefresh method that we reviewed earlier.

This first block scans the hash table to find cache items that need to be refreshed or have expired and need to be deleted. Note that we must synchronize on the hashtable since it is not thread safe and we might be adding items from other threads.

```
try {
  CacheItem items[] = null;

  synchronized(hashtable) {
  Iterator iter1 = hashtable.values().iterator();
  Vector itemVector = new Vector();

  while(iter1.hasNext()) {
    CacheItem item = ((CacheItem)iter1.next());

    if(item.populated) { // skip partial entries
    itemVector.add(item);
    }
```

The test on the populated flag of the CacheItem might seem a bit obscure. If you go back to submitAndCache(), you will see that when we were processing a SOAP request, we created a cache item, but we did not set the request in the CacheItem until we had a response back. By testing the populated flag, we make sure that we do not refresh, or worse delete, a request already being processed.

We convert the vector to an array of type CacheItem since this is what cleanUpAndRefresh() expects:

```
  }
  items = (CacheItem[])itemVector.toArray(new CacheItem[vector.size()]);
}
```

Now that we have an array of the cache items that are populated, we call the cleanUpAndRefresh() helper method that we reviewed earlier:

```
for(int index = 0; index < items.length; index++) {
  cleanUpAndRefresh(items[index], forceRefresh);
}
```

Next, we check if we need to save the cache: the hash table and the cache items. The value for cacheUpdateInterval instance variable comes from LDAP.

```
// Time to save?
if((System.currentTimeMillis() - lastSave) > cacheUpdateInterval) {
  // Save the cache item files
  for(int ndx = 0; ndx < items.length; ndx++) {
```

```
    items[ndx].save();
    }

    // Save the hash table
    ObjectOutputStream os = new ObjectOutputStream(
                new FileOutputStream(getCacheFileName()));

    synchronized(hashtable) {
    os.writeObject(hashtable);
    os.close();
    }

    lastSave = System.currentTimeMillis();

    // Clean up directory
    cleanupCacheDirectory();
}
```

Saving cache items is handled by the `CacheItem.save()` method that we previously discussed. A possible alternate implementation of the `CacheItem.save()` method would be to remember when the last save occurred and avoid saving the same file content twice. If your application generates many cached SOAP documents, you might want to consider this.

Saving the hash table is straightforward using an `ObjectOutputStream`. We also make sure to store the current time so that the last time the cache has been saved is known and we clean up the cache directory.

Finally, in the last statements of the `run` method, we set the `forceRefresh` flag to false since it has been handled by now and then we sleep for a while (`DELAY`).

If an exception is thrown, we report it and output the value of the cache to the output stream:

```
      } catch (Exception exception) {
        System.err.println("SOAPCache Thread (run): Caught "
                  + exception + ", ignored.");

    Object objects[] =  hashtable.values().toArray();
    System.out.println("Hashtable contains " + objects.length + " elements:");
    for(int index = 0; index < objects.length; index++) {
    System.out.println("  objects[" + index + "]: " + objects[index]);
  }
```

Then we cause the thread to sleep for DELAY milliseconds before repeating all this again:

```
      } finally {
        try {
        // Wait for the next iteration
        forceRefresh = false;
        Thread.sleep(DELAY);
        } catch (Exception exception) {
        }
      }
      }
```

```
    }
    });

    cacheThread.setPriority(Thread.MIN_PRIORITY);
    cacheThread.start();
  }
```

As we mentioned earlier, the cache thread is a low priority thread, so we set its priority to `Thread.MIN_PRIORITY` before starting it.

The `stopCacheThread()` method sets the `keepRunning` flag to false and waits for the cache thread to cleanly finish:

```
  public synchronized void stopCacheThread() {
    keepRunning = false;

    try {
    cacheThread.join(DELAY * 2); // Do not wait forever...
    } catch (Exception exception) {
    System.err.println(
        "SOAPCache.stopCacheThread: Caught "+ exception + ", ignored.");
    }
  }
```

The last two methods we should look at are `flush` and `refresh`.

```
    public synchronized void flush() {
    // We attempt to delete all files. Failure typically indicates
    // that the file is in use.
    Iterator iter = hashtable.values().iterator();

    while(iter.hasNext()) {
      CacheItem item = ((CacheItem)iter.next());

      try {
      File fileRequest  = new File(item.requestFileName);
      File fileResponse = new File(item.responseFileName);

      fileRequest.delete();
      fileResponse.delete();
      } catch (Exception exception) {
    }
    }

    hashtable.clear();
  }
```

The `flush()` and `cache()` methods must be synchronized on the cache since they have some significant consequences on the cache itself. The implementation of `flush()` does not contain any surprises, with the exception of error handling. If another thread has a handle on a file then the `delete` operation will fail. This is another case where the method `cleanupCacheDirectory()` comes to our rescue by deleting files that have no corresponding cache entry.

The implementation of refresh is quite trivial:

```
    public synchronized void refresh() {
      forceRefresh = true;
    }
  } // public class SOAPCache
```

This concludes our review of the `com.lesavon.cache.SOAPCache` class. We are now ready to look at the SOAP service that exposes `flush` and `refresh`.

The Administration Service

We will conclude the code review for the cache with a look at the administration SOAP service. This section will build on the knowledge that we acquired in Chapter 5, when we created the `RemoteOrder` service. As we did in Chapter 5, we will define an interface, an implementation of that interface, and a deployment descriptor. You could bundle the `RemoteAdmin` interface with the `RemoteOrder` interface, but that would be confusing to users since the methods of the administration service are restricted to administrators.

The interface definition for the administration service contains the `flush()` and `refresh()` methods:

```
// RemoteAdmin.java  1.0 02/07/2001
package com.lesavon;

public interface RemoteAdmin {

  public void flush(String userName, String password) throws SavonException;

  public void refresh(String userName, String password)
      throws SavonException;
}
```

If we wanted our application to handle more administration operations over SOAP, then we would need to add additional methods here.

Aside from the security issues that we discussed in Chapter 7, the implementation of this service is simple:

```
// AdminService.java
package com.lesavon.service;

import java.io.StringReader;

import com.lesavon.SavonException;
import com.lesavon.util.LDAP;
import com.lesavon.cache.SOAPCache;

public class AdminService implements com.lesavon.RemoteAdmin {
  /**
   * Construct the AdminService
   */
  public AdminService() throws SavonException {
  }
```

Let's have a look at `flush()`; `refresh()` is almost a carbon copy of it. We check with LDAP if the user is an administrator and if the answer is positive, we forward the request to the cache.

```
public void flush(String userName, String password)
    throws SavonException {
     try {
       // Must be admin
       if(LDAP.getLDAP().isAdminUser(userName, password)) {
         SOAPCache.getCache().flush();
       } else {
         throw new SavonException(
           "You must be an administrator to run this command");
       }
     } catch (Exception exception) {
       throw new SavonException("Flush was not successful.", exception);
     }
   }

   public void refresh(String userName, String password)
    throws SavonException {
     try {
       // Must be admin
       if(LDAP.getLDAP().isAdminUser(userName, password)) {
         SOAPCache.getCache().refresh();
       } else {
         throw new SavonException(
           "You must be an administrator to run this command");
       }
     } catch (Exception exception) {
       throw new SavonException("Refresh was not successful.",
                   exception);
     }
   }
}
```

The deployment descriptor contains only the service and method definitions since `flush()` and `refresh()` have no argument and do not return any value:

```
<isd:service xmlns:isd="http://xml.apache.org/xml-soap/deployment
       id="urn:admin">
  <isd:provider type="java"
        scope="Request"
        methods="flush refresh">
  <isd:java class="com.lesavon.service.AdminService" static="false"/>
  </isd:provider>

  <isd:faultListener>
  org.apache.soap.server.DOMFaultListener
  </isd:faultListener>
</isd:service>
```

Our remote administration interface is complete and ready for testing.

Test Admin

The code for `com.lesavon.test.TestAdmin` *can be found in ProJavaSoap\Chapter08 \src\com\lesavon\test\TestAdmin.java.*

We will test the administration service with the `com.lesavon.test.TestAdmin` class. The `TestAdmin` code is straightforward and very similar to the client code that we reviewed in previous chapters:

```
// TestAdmin.java
package com.lesavon.test;

import com.lesavon.RemoteAdmin;
import com.lesavon.SavonException;
import com.lesavon.proxy.SavonProxy;
```

We import the `SavonProxy` to handle SOAP calls; (the use of `SavonProxy` implies an understanding of sections of Chapter 6; please review it in case of doubt). The proxy throws a `SavonException` when events take an unexpected turn. The `RemoteAdmin` is the interface that we just reviewed.

```
public class TestAdmin {
  final static String FLUSH  = "flush";
  final static String REFRESH  = "refresh";
  final static String USER   = "atase";
  final static String PASSWORD = "lesavon";
```

We support flush and refresh; `atase` is our super user, i.e. the user with administration privileges.

```
public static void main(String args[]) {
  String methodName = "com.lesavon.test.TestAdmin.main";
  String userName   = "user";
  String url    = "http://localhost:8080/lesavon/ncrouter/";
```

Since flush and refresh modify the state of the system, they must go through the uncashing router (`ncrouter`).

```
        String command    = null;

        if(args.length > 2 || args.length < 1) {
            System.err.println("TestAdmin: test the admin commands");
            System.err.println("Usage    : TestAdmin <command> {<url>}");
            System.err.println(
"Example  : TestAdmin flush http://localhost:8081/lesavon/ncrouter/");
            System.exit(1);
        }

        command = args[0];
        if(args.length > 1) {
            url = args[1];
        }
```

```
        System.out.println(methodName + ": Starting test for command '"
+ command              + "' at url '"              + url + "'...");

        try {
            RemoteAdmin remoteAdmin =
     (RemoteAdmin)SavonProxy.newInstance(url, "urn:admin",
"com.lesavon.service.AdminService");
```

We create an instance of the SavonProxy to serialize the SOAP calls to and from the wire.

```
            if(command.compareToIgnoreCase(FLUSH) == 0) {
                System.out.println("  Testing flush...");
                remoteAdmin.flush(USER, PASSWORD);
```

We invoke the `flush` command over SOAP with a simple Java call on the `RemoteAdmin` interface. The invocation of the `refresh` command is similar.

```
        System.out.println("  -----------");
      } else {
        if(command.compareToIgnoreCase(REFRESH) == 0) {
            System.out.println("  Testing refresh...");
            remoteAdmin.refresh(USER, PASSWORD);
            System.out.println("  -----------");
        } else {
          throw new SavonException("Unknown command: " + command);
        }
      }
    } catch (SavonException exception) {
      System.err.println(methodName + ": Caught savon exception : "
                         + exception);
    } catch (Exception exception) {
      System.err.println(methodName + ": Caught exception : " + exception);
      exception.printStackTrace();
    }

    System.out.println(methodName + ": All done!");
  }
}
```

GetAllOrders

The code of this test program is similar to what we have done in previous chapters; however, it retrieves all the orders of a user to give us more variety in the data traveling between the server and the client.

> *The code for `com.lesavon.test.GetAllOrders` can be found in ProJavaSoap\Chapter08\src\com\lesavon\test\GetAllOrders.java.*

```
package com.lesavon.test;

import org.w3c.dom.Element;
import org.apache.soap.util.xml.DOM2Writer;
```

We need the `org.w3c.dom.Element` to handle the XML DOM element, which is the return value of `com.lesavon.RemoteOrder.getOrder()`, and we will use `org.apache.soap.util.xml.DOM2Writer` to print the XML.

```
import com.lesavon.Order;
import com.lesavon.RemoteOrder;
import com.lesavon.SavonException;
import com.lesavon.proxy.SavonProxy;

public class GetAllOrders {
    public static void main(String args[]) {
        String methodName = "com.lesavon.test.GetAllOrders.main";
        String userName   = "atase";
        String url        = "http://localhost:8080/lesavon/serveur";
```

The requests will go to the URL of the cache: `serveur`. We will discuss that URL further when we review the code of the cache.

```
if(args.length > 0) {
  url = args[0];
}

System.out.println(methodName + ": Starting test for url '"
                   + url + "'...");

try {
  System.out.println("  Getting list of orders...");
  RemoteOrder remoteOrder = (RemoteOrder)SavonProxy.newInstance(
                   url, "urn:order", "com.lesavon.service.OrderService");
```

We create an instance of the `com.lesavon.proxy.SavonProxy` to handle the SOAP calls. The `SavonProxy` was discussed in Chapter 6.

```
            System.out.println("  remoteOrder.getOrderList...");
            Order orderList[] = remoteOrder.getOrderList(userName);
```

A call to `com.lesavon.RemoteOrder.getOrderList()` gives us a list of the orders for the customer `atase`.

```
// We get the XML of all the orders
System.out.println("  Getting order descriptions...");
for (int index = 0; index < orderList.length; index++) {
  System.out.println("    Getting description for order " +
                   orderList[index] + ") ...");
  Element OrderResult = remoteOrder.getOrder(userName,
                                      orderList[index].getId());
```

We get the XML description of each order by calling `com.lesavon.RemoteOrder.getOrder()` and we print it in the next statement.

```
            System.out.println("        " + DOM2Writer.nodeToString(OrderResult));
            System.out.println("    Done!");
          }

            System.out.println("-----------");
          } catch (SavonException exception) {
            System.err.println(methodName + ": Caught savon exception :(: " +
                               exception);
          } catch (Exception exception) {
            System.err.println(methodName + ": Caught exception : " +
                               exception);
            exception.printStackTrace();
          }

          System.out.println(methodName + ": All done!");
        }
      }
```

We are now ready to build and test the code that we have reviewed.

Build

We will rely on ANT to handle our build like we did in the previous chapters. The build file from previous chapters will suffice:

```
<project name="AddLeSavonUser" default="compile" basedir=".">
  <property name="app.name"        value="AddLeSavonUser"/>
  <property name="deploy.home"
            value="/ProJavaSoap/Chapter07/${app.name}/classes"/>

  <target name="prepare">
    <mkdir  dir="${deploy.home}"/>
  </target>

  <target name="clean">
    <delete dir="${deploy.home}"/>
  </target>

  <target name="compile" depends="prepare">
    <javac srcdir="src" destdir="${deploy.home}"
           debug="off" optimize="on" deprecation="off"/>
  </target>

  <target name="all" depends="clean,prepare,compile"/>
</project>
```

We copy the deployment descriptors for the benefit of the server-side registration that we described in Chapter 5.

Using ANT and the build file above, we can easily build the sample application and its test routines. The classpath must include the following JAR files (in that order):

- xerces.jar
- xalan.jar
- soap.jar
- activation.jar
- mail.jar
- servlet.jar
- oro.jar

In previous chapters we put all of these in the SOAP /lib/ directory, which was added to the system classpath. If you compare this classpath to earlier versions, you will notice that we added the oro.jar library that we use in the cache to handle regular expressions.

For a discussion on the required JAR files to build and run a SOAP application, please refer to Chapter 3. In addition, the code from Chapter 6 and Chapter 7 should be moved to Chapter 8. To build, simply enter the command as before (on all platforms):

```
ant –buildfile BuildLeSavon.xml
```

Remember to set the classpath as in previous examples.

The resulting class files will be in the target directory specified in the build file, which in this example is C:\ProJavaSoap\Chapter08\webapps\lesavon. Note that the build file puts the server and the test routines in the same directorystructure. Tomcat's server.xml will need amending once more to point to the code in Chapter 8.The code download for chapter 8 includes all the required files, in the correct folder structure.

We are now ready to run the tests.

Sample Executions

Although we introduced the TestAdmin class first, we will start with the GetAllOrders class because it is simpler to execute since it does not directly use LDAP. The execution of TestAdmin also builds on the results of GetAllOrders.

GetAllOrders

On top of the classpath that we used during the build, you need to include the target directory of the build to pick up GetAllOrders.class. You should also check tomcat.bat to ensure that the /classes/ directory in the /lesavon/ web application is in the classpath. Since we have moved the code to/ProJavaSoap/Chapter08/, the old reference will be out of date.

Before running, make sure that etc\soap.xml and the deployment descriptors can be accessed from the current directory. In addition Tomcat and LDAP (slapd from the openLDAP directory) must be running.

The remainder of the text assumes that you have followed the book from the beginning up to this point.

You may wish to check http://localhost:8080/lesavon/admin/index.html to see that the two services, `admin` and `order` are running.

The first time you start this application with the new file developed in this chapter, the directory will not exist. If you have already sent transactions to the server, the cache directory will exist and might already have data in it. You can safely delete all the files in the cache directory that is created by the constructor of the `CacheItem` class as we saw earlier but you must make sure that you first stop Tomcat, which may have a lock on the files. Since our deployment directory is C:\ProJavaSoap\Chapter08\webapps\lesavon, the cache directory is C:\ProJavaSoap\Chapter08\webapps\lesavon\leSavonCache.

As the screenshot below shows, the cache directory is empty before we send any request to the server:

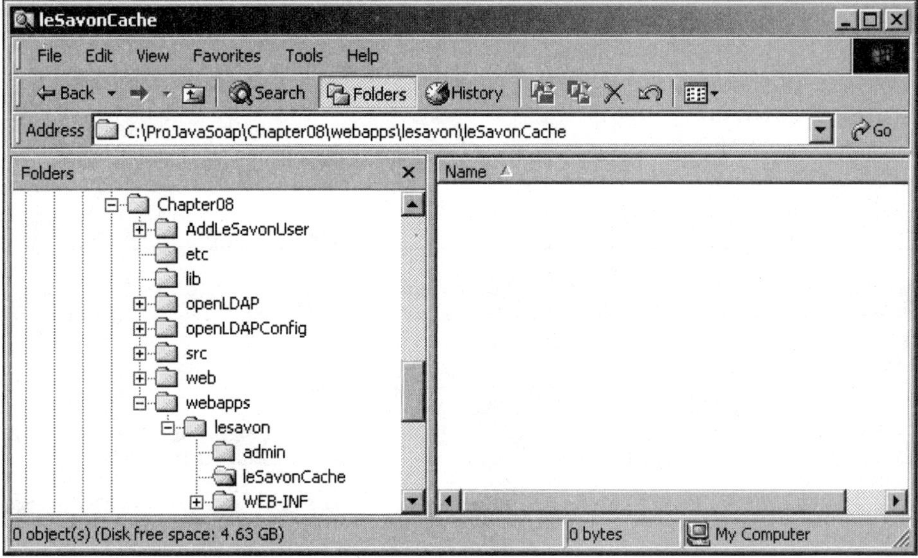

To speed things up a little during this walkthrough we have changed the following values in LDAP:

- The cache-level `updateInterval` property has been set to 90 seconds.
- The cache-level `TTL` property has been set to 120 seconds.
- The `getOrderList() TTL` property has been set to 240 seconds.

To modify LDAP values, you can either modify the `lesavon.ldif` file and regenerate the database (calling `seed` from the `/openLDAP/` directory – the directory references in `leSavon.dif`, `seed.bat`, `slapd.conf` will need updating to point to Chapter 08). Alternatively, use an LDAP browser that allows amends. The following screenshots shows the LDAP browser view of those changes:

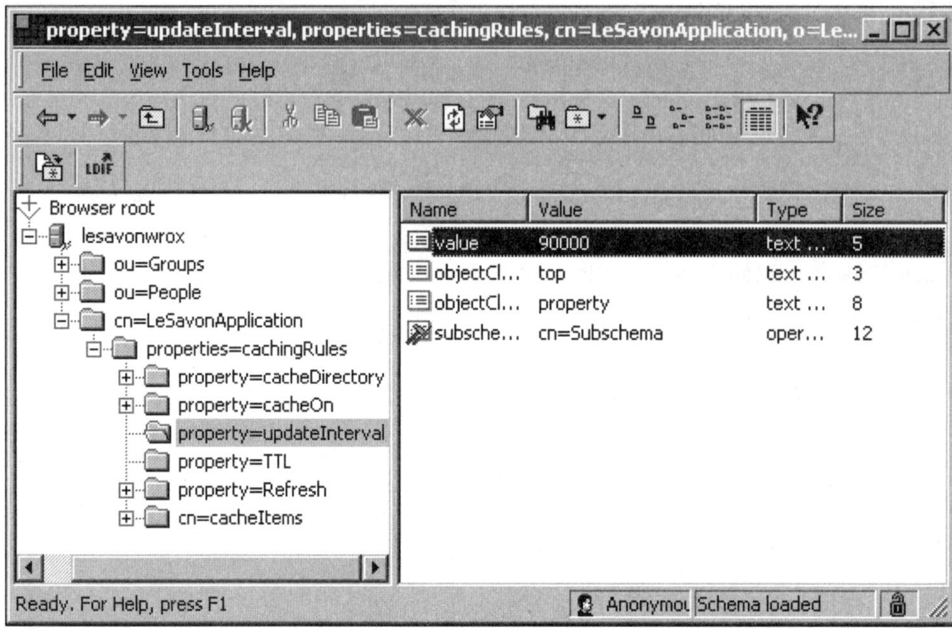
property=updateInterval, properties=cachingRules, cn=LeSavonApplication, o=Le...
File Edit View Tools Help
Browser root
lesavonwrox
ou=Groups
ou=People
cn=LeSavonApplication
properties=cachingRules
property=cacheDirectory
property=cacheOn
property=updateInterval
property=TTL
property=Refresh
cn=cacheItems
Name Value Type Size
value 90000 text ... 5
objectCl... top text ... 3
objectCl... property text ... 8
subsche... cn=Subschema oper... 12
Ready. For Help, press F1
Anonymou Schema loaded

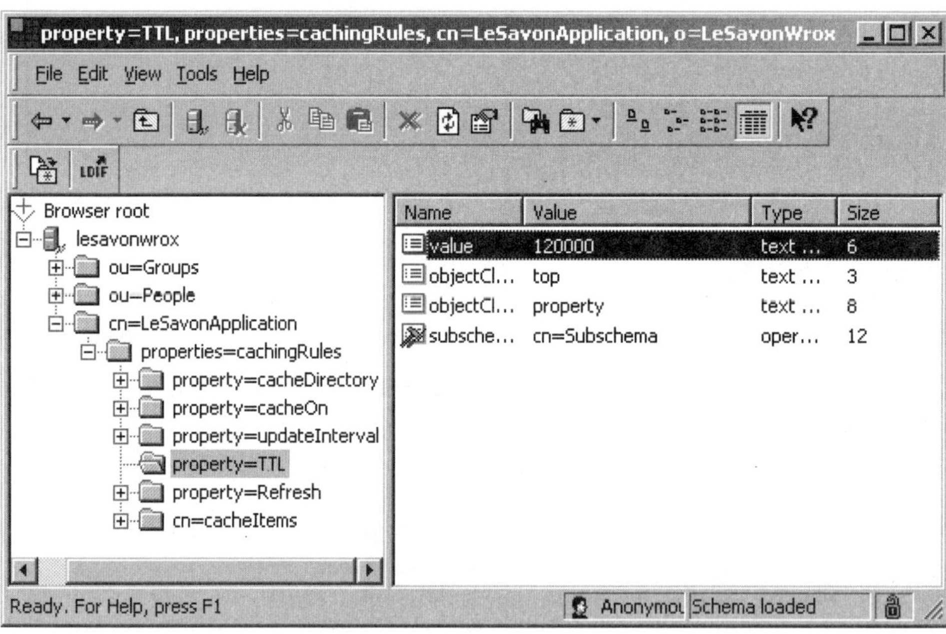
property=TTL, properties=cachingRules, cn=LeSavonApplication, o=LeSavonWrox
File Edit View Tools Help
Browser root
lesavonwrox
ou=Groups
ou=People
cn=LeSavonApplication
properties=cachingRules
property=cacheDirectory
property=cacheOn
property=updateInterval
property=TTL
property=Refresh
cn=cacheItems
Name Value Type Size
value 120000 text ... 6
objectCl... top text ... 3
objectCl... property text ... 8
subsche... cn=Subschema oper... 12
Ready. For Help, press F1
Anonymou Schema loaded

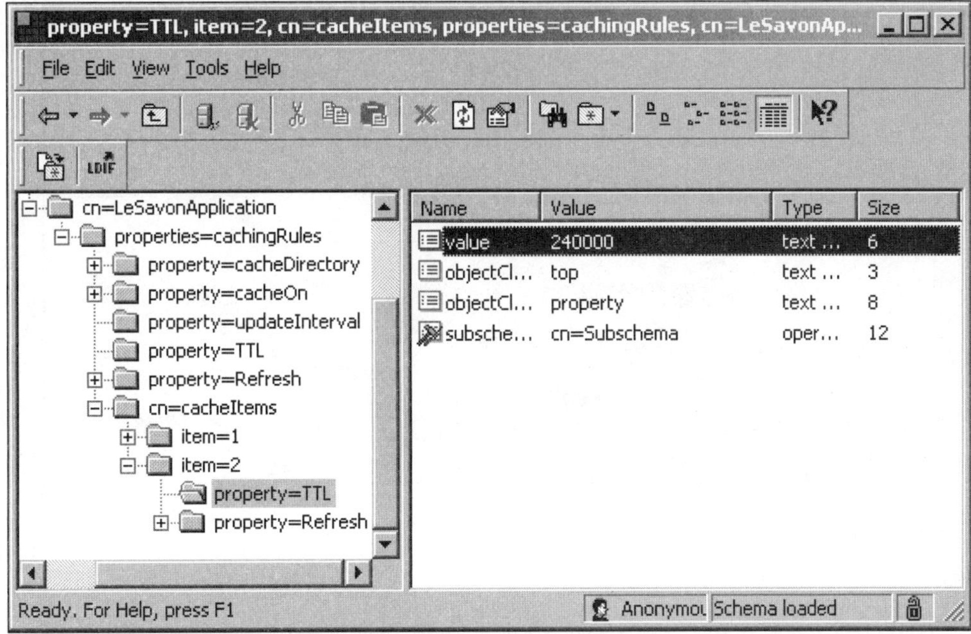

Let's run the `GetAllOrders` program and see what happens. The following figure shows the results of the execution of `GetAllOrders`.

```
C:\ProJavaSoap\Chapter08>java com.lesavon.test.GetAllOrders
com.lesavon.test.GetAllOrders.main: Starting test for url 'http://localhost:8080/les
  Getting list of orders...
  remoteOrder.getOrderList...
  Getting order descriptions...
    Getting description for order com.lesavon.Order: id = 123456001, client: atase,
        <order article="Senteur de Provence" client="atase" id="123456001" quantity=
    Done!
    Getting description for order com.lesavon.Order: id = 123456005, client: atase,
        <order article="Eau de Mouille" client="atase" id="123456005" quantity="2" t
    Done!
    Getting description for order com.lesavon.Order: id = 123456010, client: atase,
        <order article="Parfum de Lilas" client="atase" id="123456010" quantity="1"
    Done!
    Getting description for order com.lesavon.Order: id = 123456011, client: atase,
        <order article="Crystal de Roches" client="atase" id="123456011" quantity="1
    Done!
    Getting description for order com.lesavon.Order: id = 123456012, client: atase,
        <order article="Quartz de Petits Noeuds" client="atase" id="123456012" quant
    Done!
    ---------
com.lesavon.test.GetAllOrders.main: All done!

C:\ProJavaSoap\Chapter08>_
```

If this is the first set of transactions that you have sent to the server, you should get the result shown in the screenshot below because the cache thread is started during the initialization of the servlet, and the first save will happen right away. The next save will be after the value saved in the `updateInterval` property.

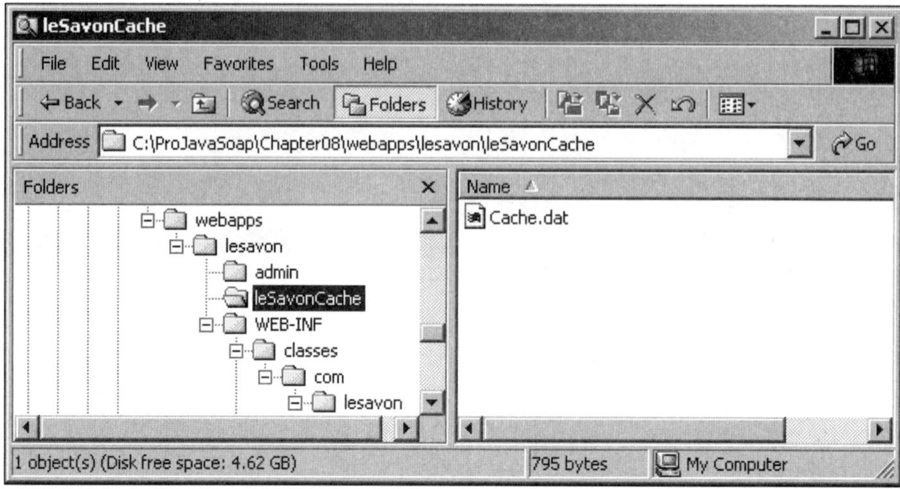

By now `GetAllOrders` should be done and after a few seconds, your computer should show a picture similar to the screenshot below. The file names will be different on your machine but they should start with either `Request_` or `Response_`.

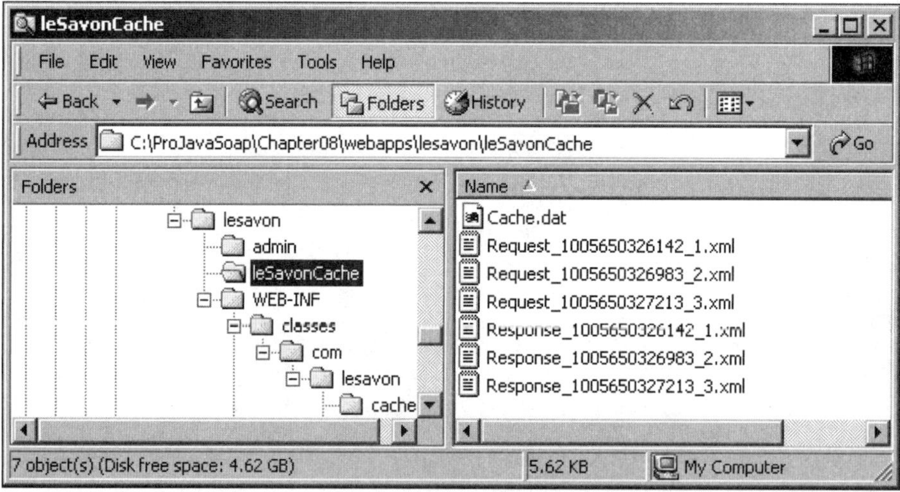

There are three request-response pairs (the trailing part of the filenames are identical) because the `GetAllOrders` program generates three transactions with the default data. Let's have a look at the first request (easily identified by its file name since the number after the '_' is the result of a call to `System.currentTimeMillis` followed by _ and an index value to handle the cases when a response is generated in less than a millisecond.

The request stored in the `Request_1005650326142_1.xml` file looks like this:

```
<?xml version='1.0' encoding='UTF-8'?>
  <SOAP-ENV:Envelope
   xmlns:SOAP-ENV="http://schemas.xmlsoap.org/soap/envelope/"
   xmlns:xsi=http://www.w3.org/1999/XMLSchema-instance
```

```
    xmlns:xsd="http://www.w3.org/1999/XMLSchema">
     <SOAP-ENV:Body>
       <ns1:getOrderList
        xmlns:ns1="urn:orders"
        SOAP-ENV:encodingStyle="http://schemas.xmlsoap.org/soap/encoding/">
       <arg0 xsi:type="xsd:string">user</arg0>
     </ns1:getOrderList>
   </SOAP-ENV:Body>
</SOAP-ENV:Envelope>
```

The response stored in the `Response_1005650326142_1.xml` file looks like this:

```
<?xml version='1.0' encoding='UTF-8'?>
<SOAP-ENV:Envelope
 xmlns:SOAP-ENV="http://schemas.xmlsoap.org/soap/envelope/"
 xmlns:xsi="http://www.w3.org/1999/XMLSchema-instance"
 xmlns:xsd="http://www.w3.org/1999/XMLSchema">
  <SOAP-ENV:Body>
    <ns1:getOrderListResponse
     xmlns:ns1="urn:orders"
     SOAP-ENV:encodingStyle="http://schemas.xmlsoap.org/soap/encoding/">
      <return
       xmlns:ns2="http://schemas.xmlsoap.org/soap/encoding/"
       xsi:type="ns2:Array"
       xmlns:ns3="urn:lesavon-order"
       ns2:arrayType="ns3:order[2]">
        <item xsi:type="ns3:order">
          <description xsi:type="xsd:string">Savon de lilas</description>
          <id xsi:type="xsd:string">First Order</id>
        </item>
        <item xsi:type="ns3:order">
          <description xsi:type="xsd:string">
            Savon de lavande
          </description>
          <id xsi:type="xsd:string">Second Order</id>
        </item>
      </return>
    </ns1:getOrderListResponse>
  </SOAP-ENV:Body>
</SOAP-ENV:Envelope>
```

The other requests and responses are for the calls to `getOrder()`. Because of the rules governing the behavior of our cache, in a little time, the only request that should remain in the cache directory is the call to `getOrderList()`. Consequently, if you let your computer sit for another save cycle (90 seconds), your cache directory will only contain the request and response from `getOrderList()` and look like the screenshot below.

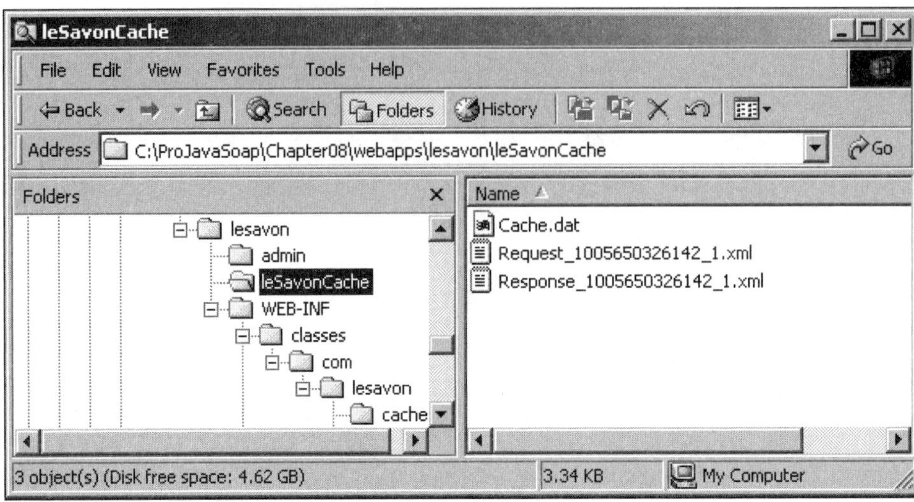

Now that we have seen the effects of our cache in action, it is time to look at the code that makes it possible.

TestAdmin

To run this test, let's change the default update interval to 30 seconds in LDAP:

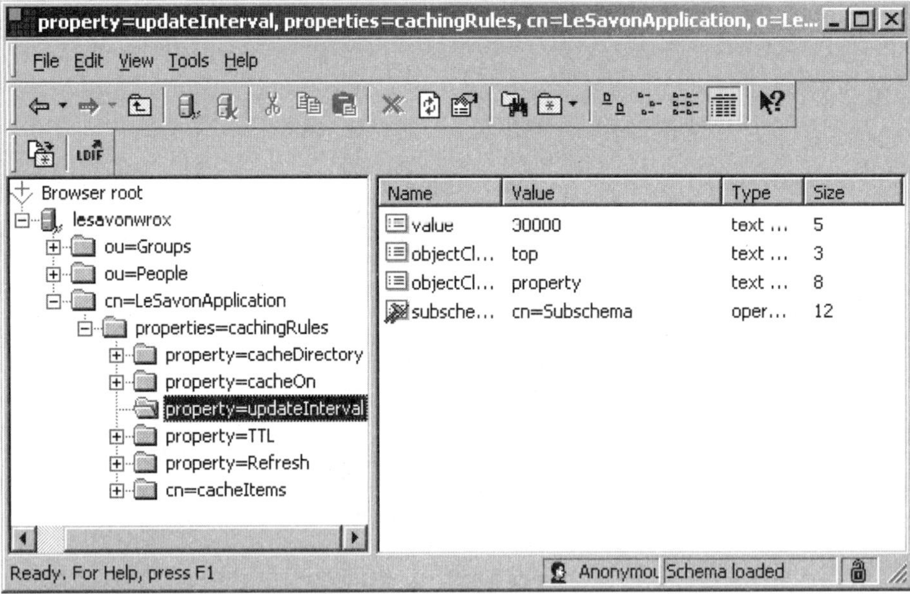

To seed the cache, we run the `GetAllOrders` test program. After 30 seconds or less, the cache on disk will look as it did before. Now let's invoke the test from the same command window typing the command:

```
java com.lesavon.test.TestAdmin flush
```

The classpath and the current directory must be identical to those we used for GetAllOrders.

We get the following output:

```
com.lesavon.test.TestAdmin.main: Starting test for command 'flush' at url
'http://localhost:8080/lesavon/ncrouter/'...
  Testing flush...
  -----------
com.lesavon.test.TestAdmin.main: All done!
```

After 30 seconds or less, the cache will be empty, because the permanent list of orders request will have been flushed out.

Summary

We started this chapter by introducing the concept of a SOAP cache that stores results from SOAP calls in order to improve the performance of your SOAP server. We then discussed the circumstances in which the use of a cache is desirable. After a presentation of the overall design of the cache and a description of the algorithm to compute a cache key, we described the functionality of the cache. We augmented the concept of a SOAP cache by saving SOAP requests along with the SOAP responses. The availability of the SOAP requests allows the cache to automatically refresh itself. We also developed rules that identify SOAP requests using regular expressions to control the automatic operations of the cache.

As an example of administration capabilities, we implemented a flush and a refresh. Flush removes SOAP documents from the cache. Refresh resubmits SOAP requests to get an up-to-date version of the SOAP responses.

We reviewed the code of the `SOAPCache` class and explored several variations on the proposed design. We concluded the code reviews with the description of two test programs, `GetAllOrders` and `TestAdmin` that we used to demonstrate the behavior of the cache.

This chapter gave us the opportunity to see a practical proof of the points we made in Chapter 7 regarding the choice of LDAP to store slowly changing data in a distributed application. By using an off-the-shelf LDAP browser, we could modify the behavior of the cache. The same modifications can be applied to a set of servers since they would all go back to LDAP to get the configuration parameters.

In the next chapter, we will review other techniques that can improve scalability and responsiveness in your application.

JAVA

9

Performance

Now that we have a functional SOAP server with a client framework, it is time to look at our performance requirements. Will the sample application meet its performance specifications? How do we measure its performance?

We must define what we mean by performance before proceeding further. The definition of performance is in the eye of the beholder. For some applications, the faster you can get an answer back, the better. For successful web sites, the more users you can handle, the better. For mission-critical operations, uptime is the ultimate measure of the performance. For your application, performance might be a combination of two or more of these requirements.

Based on the requirements that we outlined in Chapter 3, the sample application needs to maintain a balance between the following indicators:

- Latency
- Scalability
- Robustness

Latency is defined as the time it takes for a client to get an answer back. In other words, the latency measures the responsiveness of your application. The client can be a program if it is calling the SOAP API or it may be a human being who is operating the **User Interface (UI)** that we will develop in Chapter 10. If the user is a person, then latency is important up to the point where it becomes irrelevant because it appears instantaneous to humans.

Scalability measures how latency is affected when the user community increases in size. Alternatively, scalability can be measured by the number of transactions per second that the system can handle, as the size of user community increases. The term "throughput" is also used in this context, but scalability is more descriptive since it implies that the application scales, or, in other words, it can handle increasing numbers of users.

Robustness measures how often the server returns a valid answer back to the client. As we will see later in this chapter, when the load increases, the SOAP server is put under stress and HTTP connections can fail.

This chapter presents the major compromises that a SOAP application needs to make in order to improve scalability at the expense of latency, but without compromising robustness. We will review the design choices that you can make early on in order to provide a scalable solution to your end users. In particular, the separation walls between local and remote calls must be kept flexible. The transport presented in Chapter 6 makes this separation practical, since it does not require us to re-evaluate architectural decisions or to rewrite code.

While we are on the topic of scalability, we will review how SOAP programs can take advantage of HTTP **load balancing**. We will also discuss designing our application to work seamlessly with popular software and hardware load balancers.

Robustness is not a performance issue as such, although when the application no longer delivers its services, one could argue that this is the ultimate loss of performance. More importantly, robustness comes into the picture because, with a minor modification, the solution that we discussed earlier to improve scalability improves robustness as well. We will see that careful management of the state of your application can significantly help scalability and robustness.

You might have heard of **server capacity planning**, which is the art of determining what hardware you will need to ensure a given capacity; in other words, it is used to ascertain a pre-defined scalability level. Since we will concentrate on the relative improvements that can be made to a SOAP application, we will not be giving specific recommendations for hardware requirements. One motivation for staying clear of the subject is that a significant factor in server capacity planning is going to be your backend application, and in the case of our sample application we have already reduced this to its simplest form.

Before, we jump to measurements and solutions, let's have a cursory look at some potential problems.

Bottlenecks

As we will see in this section, the performance issues faced by SOAP applications are linked to the nature of the protocol and to the problems solved using SOAP.

XML Parsing

As we saw in Chapter 2, openness is a major goal in the design of SOAP, if not the essence of the protocol. By using a UNICODE-based protocol to encode its payload, SOAP forces its applications to get data, typically objects, in and out of XML documents. This process of parsing (XML to objects) and serialization (objects to XML) is usually slower than a binary serialization that would simply move data structures from memory to the wire.

Network Bandwidth

Another fundamental characteristic of SOAP is that it is a network protocol: it defines how to exchange application data in XML over HTTP. As we saw in Chapter 2, other protocols like SMTP can be used to carry SOAP payloads, but HTTP is the only protocol that has bindings defined in the SOAP 1.1 specification.

Network performance is not only limited by the physical bandwidth and routing hardware, but more importantly by the fact that it is shared among many users. Most of the time, it is not possible or practical to predict the amount of network usage that will be going on when your application is running. One fact is almost certain for most applications: network resources are going to be in short supply and their use should be minimized to improve responsiveness.

State Management

Because SOAP is by nature a stateless protocol, when a request comes to the server, some minimal state must be reconstructed. The HTTP connection must be re-established, and a SOAP context must be rebuilt. However, keep-alive connections may help. The Apache SOAP framework does a good job of minimizing the effort needed to recreate a minimal state. Your application can also help by using session or application scope objects, and by caching objects rather than creating them when it makes sense to do so. It is also possible to share the burden between the client and the server, as we will see shortly.

Your application can also optimise the overhead of SOAP by maintaining some minimal state. For instance, the cache that we built in Chapter 8 maintains a state on the server. However, as we will discuss in depth shortly, it is important not to depend on that state being on the server. In the example of the cache, the sample application will work equally well whether or not the SOAP response is in the cache; the response will simply come back faster if the item is found in the cache.

Backend

SOAP is designed to open applications outside of their normal realm. SOAP is a middleware protocol whose primary mission is to relay requests from users to backend applications and send the response back to the user when it is available. We have seen in Chapter 8 that it was possible to minimize the load put on the backend via the use of a SOAP cache.

We have also discovered that it was not always possible to shield applications from having to serve requests. If a request must go all the way to the backend application, SOAP applications lose some control over the performance. The amount of the loss of control clearly depends on the backend application: in the case of the sample application, it is almost negligible, but in the case of a lengthy database query, it might be more significant.

Benchmark

In this section, we will develop a test client to measure the performance of the sample application. We will use the test client, `PerfTest`, before and after making changes to our SOAP server to measure their effectiveness. We will establish a reference point for our tests based on an HTTP transaction returning an empty HTML document.

PerfTest

The sample code for this chapter can be found in `/ProJavaSoap/Chapter09/PerfTest`. Note that the `Chapter09` directory contains a directory for LeSavon.com that simply adds an empty HTML page to the web site. Please refer to Chapter 8 for instructions on how to build and run this version of the sample application.

If you cannot measure a variable, you will not be able to optimize it. In this case, we need to measure three variables: latency, scalability, and robustness. As we said earlier, scalability can be measured in terms of average latency and transactions per second. This means that if we measure latency and the number of transactions per second as a function of the number of users, we will have the measurements we need.

We will use a small test program, `PerfTest`, to make our measurements against our SOAP server. `PerfTest` gives us the ability to submit raw XML or use the client framework that we developed in Chapter 6:

We will use `org.apache.soap.util.net.HTTPUtils` to submit raw XML documents and the `SavonProxy` to submit requests to the `RemoteOrder` service. For a sample of the use of `HTTPUtils` to submit XML documents, please refer to Chapter 8 where we described the implementation of the `SOAPCache.SubmitAndCache()` method.

```
// PerfTest.java
package com.lesavon.test;

import java.net.URL;

import org.apache.soap.util.net.HTTPUtils;
import org.apache.soap.transport.TransportMessage;
import org.apache.soap.Constants;

import com.lesavon.proxy.SavonProxy;
import com.lesavon.RemoteOrder;
import com.lesavon.Order;
```

The `DELIM` constant allows us to support multiple text-based file formats such as **Comma-Separated Values (CSV)** or tab-delimited. The others are self-explanatory.

```
public class PerfTest {
  private static final  String APP_NAME   = "com.lesavon.test.PerfTest";
  private static final  int  MAX_CLIENTS = 1024;
  private static String    url         = "http://hbequet-co:8080";
  private static final  String DELIM      = "\t"; // csv, tab, ...
  private Thread[] threads          = new Thread[MAX_CLIENTS];
  private int     nbrOfThreads      = 0;
  private int     nbrOfErrors       = 0;
  private int     nbrOfTransactions = 0;
  private double   latency          = 0;
  private boolean  inProgress       = false;
  private boolean  pause          = false;

  // Interface to do some work (empty, call one method, ...)
  interface Worker {
    public boolean doWork(); // true if everything was ok
  }
```

We now define a number of inner classes, one class per test. Each of these classes implements the `Worker` interface. The `doWork()` method should return true for successful operations and false for failures. This boolean value is used to count errors during a test.

The `DoNothing` class is provided for a baseline test:

```
static class DoNothing implements Worker {
  public boolean doWork() {
    boolean returnValue = true;

    try {
    } catch (Exception exception) { // unlikely ☺
      System.err.println("DoNothing.doWork caught: " + exception);
      returnValue = false;
    }

    return returnValue;
  }
}
```

Both the `DoNothing` and `DoEmptyHTTP` clients define the baseline metrics for latency, scalability, and robustness when doing nothing and returning empty HTTP responses respectively.

```
static class DoEmptyHttp implements Worker {
  public boolean doWork() {
    boolean returnValue = true;

    try {
      final String xmlRequest = "";

      TransportMessage request   = new TransportMessage (null, null, null);
      URL targetURL = new URL(url + "/lesavon/empty.html");
```

```
            request.setContentType(Constants.HEADERVAL_CHARSET_UTF8);
            //Constants.HEADERVAL_CHARSET_UTF8 == "text/xml;charset=utf-8"
            request.setBytes(xmlRequest.getBytes());
            HTTPUtils.post(targetURL, request, 0, null, 0, 10);
        } catch (Exception exception) {
            returnValue = false;
        }

        return returnValue;
    }
}
```

The DoHTTP class submits a pre-defined SOAP request to the server: a call to the RemoteOrder.getOrderList("atase").

```
static class DoHttp implements Worker {
    public boolean doWork() {
        boolean returnValue = true;
        try {
            final String xmlRequest =
"<?xml version='1.0' encoding='UTF-8'?>\n" +
"<SOAP-ENV:Envelope\n" +
"  xmlns:SOAP-ENV=\"http://schemas.xmlsoap.org/soap/envelope/\"\n" +
"  xmlns:xsi=\"http://www.w3.org/1999/XMLSchema-instance\"\n" +
"  xmlns:xsd=\"http://www.w3.org/1999/XMLSchema\">\n" +
"<SOAP-ENV:Body>\n" +
"  <ns1:getOrderList xmlns:ns1=\"urn:order\" \n" +
"    SOAP-ENV:encodingStyle=" +
"      \"http://schemas.xmlsoap.org/soap/encoding/\">\n" +
"    <arg0 xsi:type=\"xsd:string\">atase</arg0>\n" +
"  </ns1:getOrderList>\n" +
"</SOAP-ENV:Body>\n" +
"</SOAP-ENV:Envelope>\n";

            TransportMessage request   = new TransportMessage(null, null, null);
            URL targetURL = new URL(url + "/lesavon/router");

            request.setContentType(Constants.HEADERVAL_CHARSET_UTF8);

            request.setBytes(xmlRequest.getBytes());
            HTTPUtils.post(targetURL, request, 0, null, 0, 10000);
        } catch (Exception exception) {
            returnValue = false;
        }

        return returnValue;
    }
}
```

The statement where we actually submit the request (HTTPUtils.post(targetURL...), requires further elaboration. We have seen in Chapter 8 that checking the validity of a SOAP response is not trivial: we need to parse the XML document and search for a SOAP fault.

During testing, the point is to submit as many transactions as possible, so parsing the responses is a burden we do not want to put on a performance test client. Nevertheless, it is important to make sure that the responses that we are getting denote a successful transaction. We can use two methodologies to that end.

In the first methodology, we run a first execution of the test through the tcpTrace utility that we introduced back in Chapter 2. While the test is running, we can watch the transactions and verify that they contain the data that we expect.

In the second, which is perhaps a better strategy, we print the length of the SOAP response during a first run and execute some code similar to that in Chapter 8, using the `SubmitAndCache()` method to validate that everything goes according to our expectations. Using that length, which must be the same for all transactions, we can perform a quick and dirty test that will not disturb our performance measurements in any significant way for subsequent executions of the test.

```
static class GetOrderList implements Worker {
  private RemoteOrder remoteOrder = null;

  public GetOrderList() {
    try {
      remoteOrder = (RemoteOrder)SavonProxy.newInstance(
                              url +  "/lesavon/ncrouter",
                              "urn:order", "com.lesavon.service.OrderService");
    } catch (Exception exception) {
      System.err.println("GetOrderList.GetOrderList caught: " + exception);
    }
  }

  public boolean doWork() {
    boolean returnValue = true;

    try {
      remoteOrder.getOrderList("atase");
    } catch (Exception exception) {
      System.err.println("GetOrderList.doWork caught: " + exception);
      returnValue = false;
    }

    return returnValue;
  }
}
```

The `GetOrderList` class performs the same SOAP call as `DoHTTP` but using the `SavonProxy`.

Each client is a thread that runs for as long as `inProgress` is true. The test might be paused to simulate the load on a server going up and down. We measure the number of successful transactions, the latency, and the number of errors.

```
// A PerfTest client runs in its own thread
class Client extends Thread {
  private int  clientId = -1;
  private Worker worker   = null;

   Client(int clientId, Worker worker) {
    this.clientId = clientId;
    this.worker   = worker;
  }
```

```
    public void run() {
      synchronized(PerfTest.this) { nbrOfThreads++; }

      try {
        while(inProgress) {

          long before = System.currentTimeMillis();
          boolean returnValue = worker.doWork();
          long after = System.currentTimeMillis();

          // Do not count failed transactions!
          if(returnValue) {
            synchronized(PerfTest.this) {
              nbrOfTransactions++;
              latency += (after - before) * 0.001;
            }
          } else {
            synchronized(PerfTest.this) { nbrOfErrors++; }
          }

          while(pause) {
            Thread.sleep(1000);
          }
        }
      } catch (Exception exception) {
        System.err.println("Client::run: Error (Exception) for client "
                           + clientId + ": " + exception);
        exception.printStackTrace(System.out);
        synchronized(PerfTest.this) { nbrOfErrors++; }
      } finally {
        synchronized(PerfTest.this) { nbrOfThreads--; }
      }
    }
  }
```

Finally, the `main()` method:

```
  public static void main(String args[]) {
    new PerfTest().runTest(args);
  }
```

The test is executed by `PerfTest.runTest()`, which begins by validating the arguments.

```
  public void runTest(String args[]) {
    final String innerPrefix = "com.lesavon.test.PerfTest$";
```

The `innerPrefix` is the prefix used by `javac` for `PerfTest`'s inner classes. For instance, the fully qualified name of `DoHttp` nested inside `com.lesavon.PerfTest` is `com.lesavon.PerfTest$DoHttp`.

The format for a test is PerfTest <number-of-clients> <length-of-test> <worker>. The arguments to this class in order are:

- The number of concurrent clients.
- The length of the test in seconds.
- The name of the inner class worker.

```
if(args.length != 3) {
  System.err.println("PerfTest: Multi-client performance test for " +
                     "LeSavon.com.");
  System.err.println("Usage : PerfTest <number-of-clients>" +
                     " <length-of-test> <worker>");
  System.err.println("Sample: PerfTest 5 30 DoNothing");
  System.exit(-1);
}

try {
  int maxNbrOfClients = Integer.parseInt(args[0]);
  int duration = Integer.parseInt(args[1]);
  String workerClass = args[2];

  if(maxNbrOfClients <= 0 || maxNbrOfClients > MAX_CLIENTS) {
    System.out.println(APP_NAME
                       + ": number of clients must be between 1 and "
                       + MAX_CLIENTS + ", not " + maxNbrOfClients);
    System.exit(-1);
  }

  if(duration <= 0) {
    System.out.println(APP_NAME +
      ": duration must be > 0, it is " + duration);
    System.exit(-1);
  }

  System.out.println(APP_NAME + ": Starting test with up to "
    + maxNbrOfClients + " client(s) for " + duration
    + " second(s), using worker " + workerClass + "...");
```

We begin by creating all the threads before the test, in order to avoid counting the thread creation time as part of the test:

```
for(int clientIndex = 0; clientIndex < maxNbrOfClients; clientIndex++) {
  Thread thread = new Client(clientIndex,
          (Worker)Class.forName(innerPrefix + workerClass).newInstance());
  threads[clientIndex] = thread;
}
```

`runTest()` also goes through one iteration to avoid counting the time it takes to load classes and to verify that the worker class returns a valid response.

```
Worker firstWorker = (Worker)(Class.forName(innerPrefix
                                               + workerClass).newInstance());
if(!firstWorker.doWork()) {
  // If the first transaction fails then this is hopeless
  System.out.println(APP_NAME + ": first invocation of "
                  + workerClass + " failed! Aborting test.");
  System.exit(-1);
}
```

We can now begin the test:

```
// Run the test
int    clientCounts[] = new int[maxNbrOfClients];
double latencies[]   = new double[maxNbrOfClients];
double transactions[] = new double[maxNbrOfClients];
int    errors[]      = new int[maxNbrOfClients];
int    currentIndex    = 0;
int    threadIndex   = 0;
```

The previous arrays store the intermediate results of each iteration.

```
inProgress = true;
for (int nbrOfClients = 1;
     nbrOfClients <= maxNbrOfClients;
     nbrOfClients += nbrOfClients >= 8? nbrOfClients : 1) {
```

The previous `for()` statement loops on the number of clients (threads). The loop on the number of clients is unconventional since it increments by one for fewer clients than 8 and then doubles after that. The number of clients will therefore be: 1, 2, 3, 4, 5, 6, 7, 8, 16, etc.

This allows us to see the trend for a few clients and then test the scalability for more than eight clients.

```
  for (; threadIndex < nbrOfClients; threadIndex++) {
    threads[threadIndex].start();
  }
```

The call to `java.lang.Thread.start()` is only required for new clients. Existing clients have already been started and paused at the end of the last iteration.

```
System.out.print("Iteration for " +  nbrOfClients + " clients: ");
for(int tick = 0; tick < duration; tick++) {
  System.out.print(".");

  Thread.sleep(1000);
}
```

The main thread prints "." to show the operator that everything is moving, while the threads that simulate clients do the work.

```
// We store the results (if we got at least one transaction)
if(nbrOfTransactions > 0) {
  clientCounts[currentIndex] = nbrOfClients;
  latencies[currentIndex] = latency / nbrOfTransactions;
  transactions[currentIndex] =
                        (double)nbrOfTransactions / (latency/nbrOfClients);
  errors[currentIndex] = nbrOfErrors;
  currentIndex++;
}
```

We store the intermediate results in the arrays that we defined earlier. We pause for duration / 2 in between runs (we assume that no transactions take longer than duration / 2; however we do not pause for the last one.

```
  // This would mean that all threads have exited
  if(0 == nbrOfThreads) {
    break;
  }

  if(nbrOfClients * 2 <= maxNbrOfClients) {
    pause = true;
    Thread.sleep(duration * 500);

    nbrOfTransactions = 0;
    nbrOfErrors = 0;
    latency = 0;

    pause = false;
  }
  System.out.println();
}
```

Pausing for a while simulates activity in bursts; it also allows the JVM to perform some optimizations.

```
// Stop everyone, but don't wait forever
inProgress = false;
for(int clientIndex = 0; clientIndex < maxNbrOfClients; clientIndex++) {
  try {
    if(threads[clientIndex].isAlive()) {
      System.out.print(":");
    }

    threads[clientIndex].join(5000);
  } catch (InterruptedException exception) {
    break;
  }
}
```

We wait for all the threads to stop and then we print the results:

```
        System.out.println();

        // Print the results in a csv or tab-separated format
        System.out.println("numberOfClients" + DELIM + "latency" + DELIM
                         + "numberOfTransactions" + DELIM + "numberOfErrors");

        for(int clientIndex = 0; clientIndex < currentIndex; clientIndex++) {
          System.out.println(clientCounts[clientIndex] + DELIM
                           + latencies[clientIndex] + DELIM
                           + transactions[clientIndex] + DELIM
                           + errors[clientIndex]);
        }

        System.out.println(APP_NAME + ": All done!");
      } catch (Exception exception) {
        System.out.println(APP_NAME + ": Caught exception: " + exception);
      }

      System.exit(0);
    }
  }
```

The rest of the code is straightforward. Note that we output the result in a CSV format, for easy inclusion to Microsoft Excel that we used to generate the diagrams. Other possibilities include a tab-delimited file (implemented in `PerfTest`) or an XML document (not implemented in `PerfTest`).

Build

As we did in previous chapters, we will build the sample code with ANT. The easiest way to do this is to use the last chapter's code file. Copy `PerfTest` to the `/src/` directory and run `BuildLeSavon.xml` again.

Test

To run the tests, we will use the following hardware:

- **Server**
  Pentium processor at 400 MHz with 256 MB of memory running Windows 2000 Professional
- **Client**
  Dual Pentium processor at 550 MHz with 360 MB of memory running Windows 2000 Server

The client machine is actually more powerful than the server machine since we intend to optimize the server-side and not the client-side. Also, we are interested in how various optimizations will improve the performance in relative terms, so raw performance numbers are unimportant. But, in case you are curious, on a quad 550 MHz Pentium with 1GB of memory, LeSavon.com can serve over 1,200 SOAP transactions per second for more than 50 simultaneous users.

However, because of the stateless nature of LeSavon.com, the sample application can virtually scale to as many clients as needed. These numbers are somewhat impressive, but keep in mind that they only reflect the time spent in cached SOAP calls; they do not consider the backend application.

Note that if you run the tests that we present in this chapter on different hardware than what we have presented here, you will see different results, but the relative numbers should be similar.

To run, you need to make sure that the classpath gives you access to `PerfTest.class`. In the following figure, we change the current directory to `\ProJavaSoap\Chapter08` and depend on the `setclasspath` batch file, to enable it to read the directory we are running the code from. We run the following test:

```
cd C:\ProJavaSoap\Chapter08\
setclasspath
java com.lesavon.test.PerfTest 4 5 DoEmptyHttp
```

The result is as follows:

```
com.lesavon.test.PerfTest: Starting test with up to 4 client(s) for 5 second(s), using worker
DoEmptyHttp...
Iteration for 1 clients ..... – 4.9569999999999625, 459, 0
Iteration for 2 clients ..... – 9.464999999999966, 390, 0
Iteration for 1 clients ..... – 13.938999999999963, 388, 0
Iteration for 1 clients ..... – 34.12099999999994, 748, 0
::
numberOfClients,latency,numberOfTransactions,numberOfErrors
1,0.010799564270152424,91.8,0
2,0.022426923076923068 2,78.0,0
3,0.03592525773195867,77.6,0
4,0.04564133333333325,150.0,0
com.lesavon.test.PerfTest: All Done.
```

The primary goal of the `PerfTest` program is to measure latency and the total number of transactions per second when the CPU usage is close to 100%. As a base line for our test, let's run `PerfTest` with the `DoEmptyHTTP` class:

```
C:\ProJavaSoap\Chapter08\PerfTest\classes>java com.lesavon.test.PerfTest
4 60 DoEmptyHttp
```

We will use the same classpath for all executions of `PerfTest` presented in this chapter. We will not show a screenshot of the actual results of individual executions, but simply the charts plotted from the results of each execution. The charts are easier to understand than the raw numbers. However, the numbers of each run are available as both a CSV file and a Microsoft Excel spreadsheet with the source code under the `results/` directory. The Microsoft Excel spreadsheets include the charts presented in this chapter.

Note that an empty request or response is not really empty because of the HTTP headers. The request is:

```
POST /lesavon/empty.html HTTP/1.0
Host: localhost
Content-Type: text/xml;charset=utf-8
Content-Length: 0
```

And the response is:

```
HTTP/1.0 200 OK
Content-Type: text/html
Content-Length: 0
Last-Modified: Wed, 29 Aug 2001 17:57:58 GMT
Servlet-Engine: Tomcat Web Server/3.2.3 (JSP 1.1; Servlet 2.2; Java 1.3.0; Windows
2000 5.0 x86; java.vendor=Sun Microsystems Inc.)
```

However, in both cases the content length is 0 bytes.

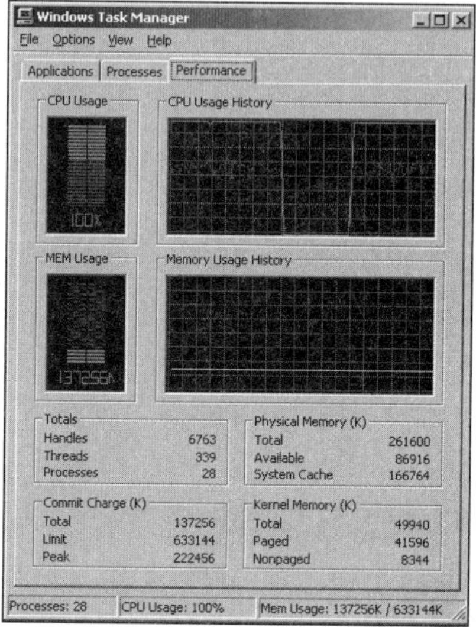

Even with one client, the server is saturated. The client is barely busy with four client threads as shown below. The valleys happen when the client pauses for `duration / 2`.

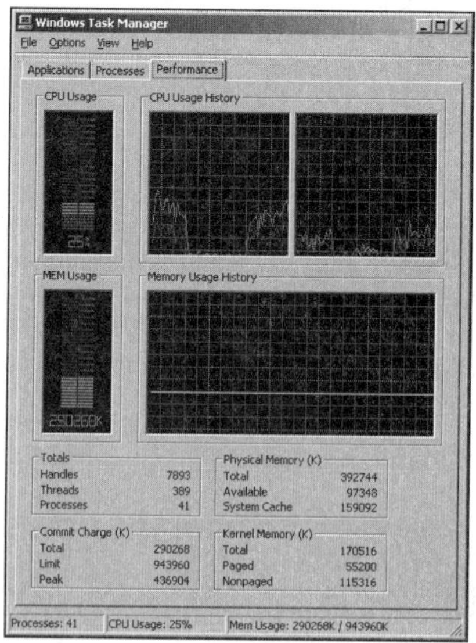

These numbers should constitute our upper limit, since in this case the server is not doing anything. Actually, this is not exactly true as we will see shortly, mostly because some IO operations are required, even to discover that the file that you need to return is empty.

The latency per number of clients is given in the next figure. The latency is in seconds.

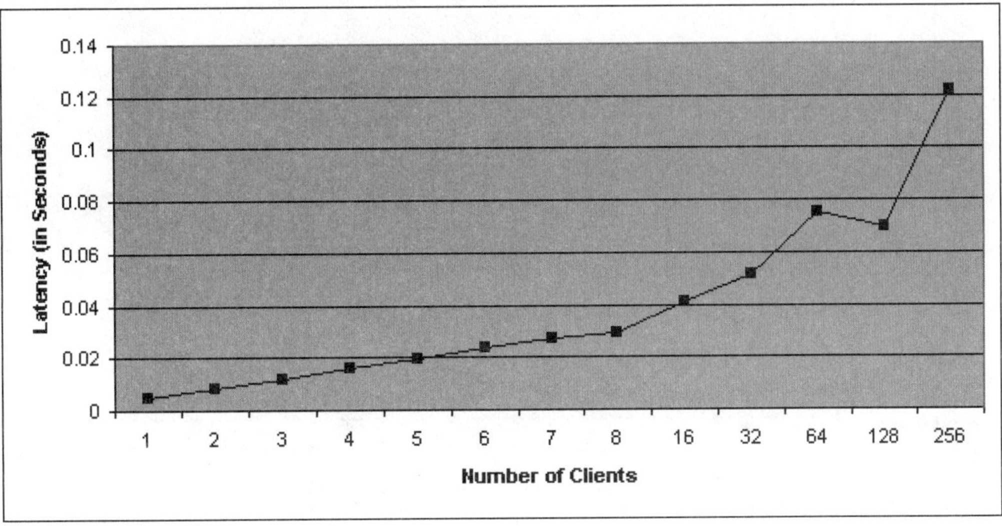

Obviously, the lower numbers represent greater latency. The next figure shows the number of transactions per second for `DoEmptyHTTP` client. Higher numbers represent a good speed for the transactions per second.

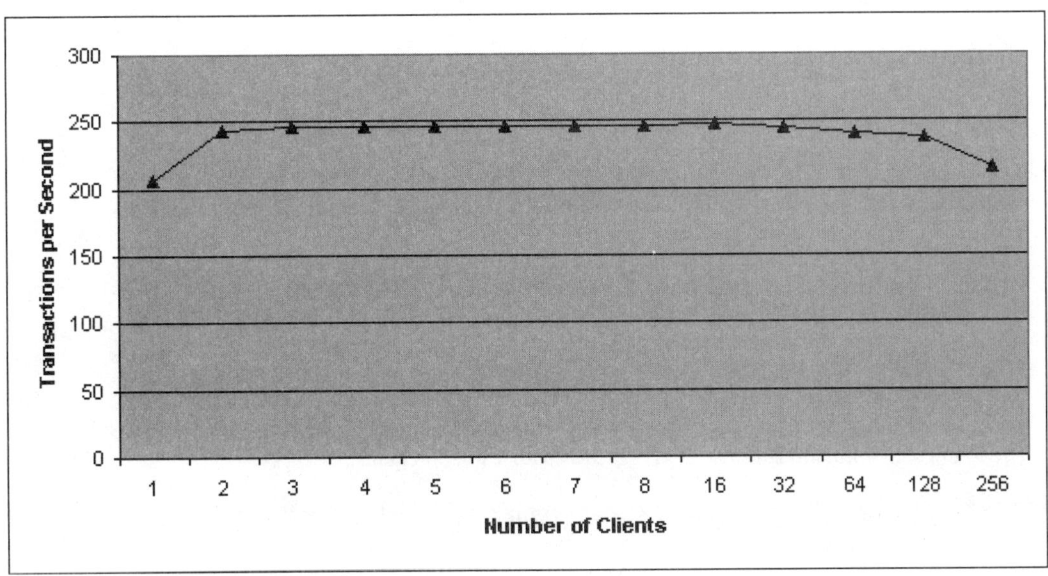

This last diagram shows the number of errors plotted against number of clients. Note that with more than eight clients, you will start getting a sizeable number of exceptions with connections refused. We will revisit this issue.

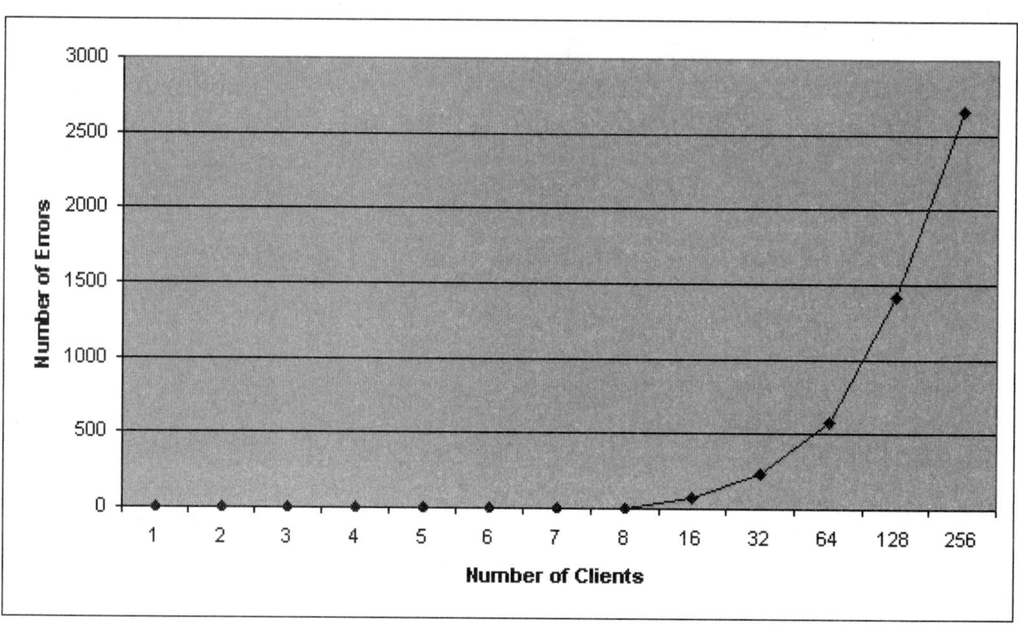

We have seen in the code review of the `PerfTest` client that the `DoHTTP` class submits a simple SOAP request, which is a call to `RemoteOrder.getOrderList("atase")`:

```
<?xml version='1.0' encoding='UTF-8'?>
<SOAP-ENV:Envelope
xmlns:SOAP-ENV="http://schemas.xmlsoap.org/soap/envelope/"
  xmlns:xsi="http://www.w3.org/1999/XMLSchema-instance"
  xmlns:xsd="http://www.w3.org/1999/XMLSchema">
<SOAP-ENV:Body>
  <ns1:getOrderList xmlns:ns1="urn:order"
   SOAP-ENV:encodingStyle="http://schemas.xmlsoap.org/soap/encoding/">
   <arg0 xsi:type="xsd:string">atase</arg0>
  </ns1:getOrderList>
</SOAP-ENV:Body>
</SOAP-ENV:Envelope>
```

–We can use the `DoHTTP` class to compare the retrieval of an empty HTML document to a SOAP request. The following command runs the `DoHTTP` class with 1 to 256 clients:

```
java com.lesavon.test.PerfTest 256 60 DoHttp
```

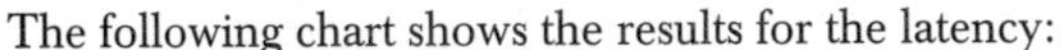

The following chart shows the results for the latency:

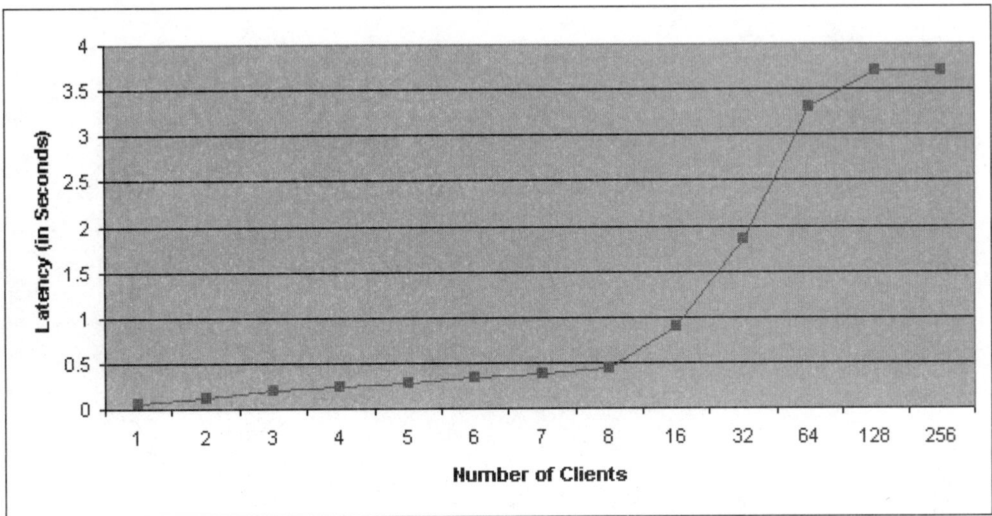

Since the `DoHTTP` client actually performs some work and returns more data then the `DoEmptyHTTP` client, the latency increases and the number of transactions per second goes to around 15, down from over 200.

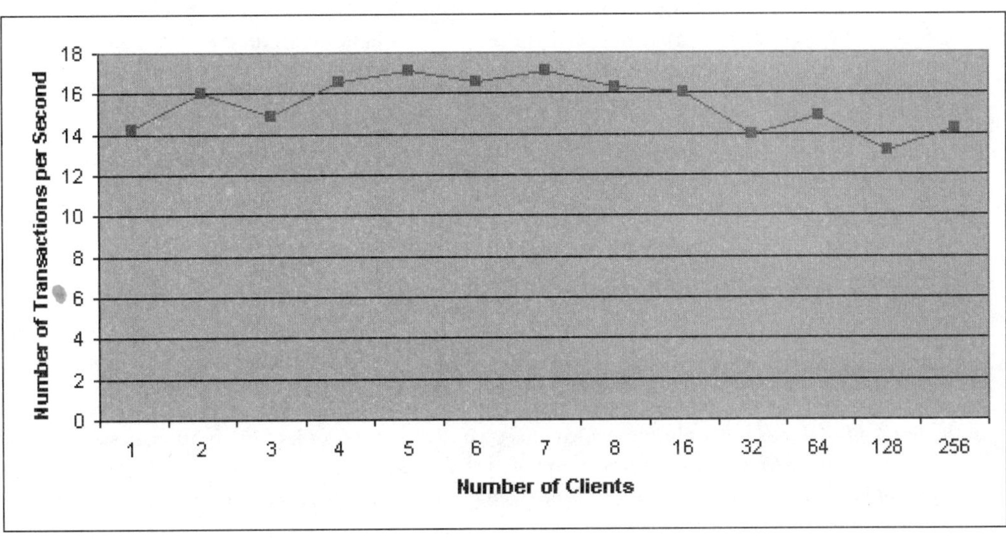

The number of errors is roughly similar:

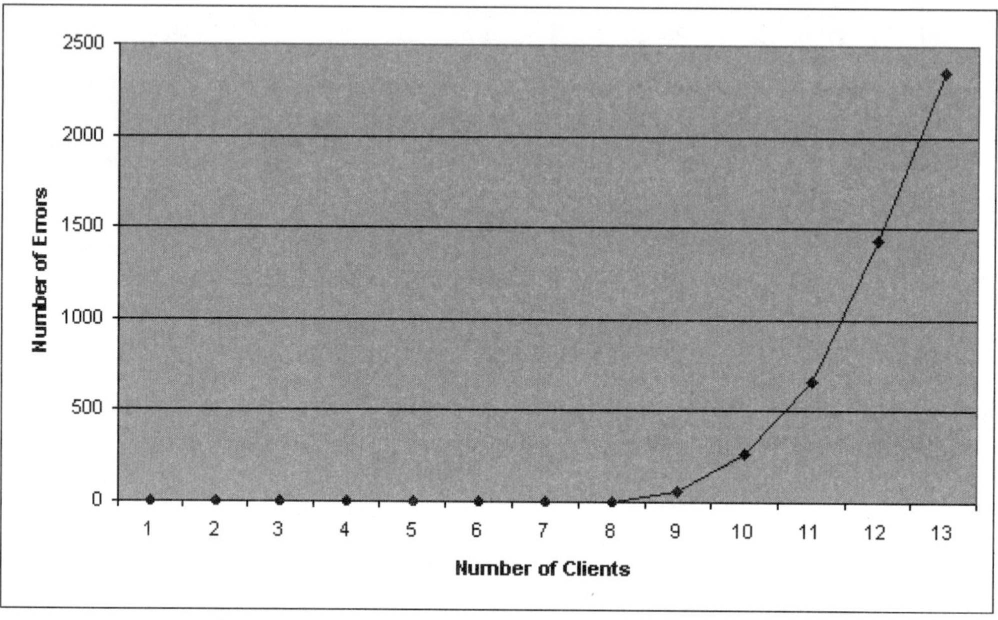

Note that caching was off (the target URL was `ncrouter`, not `serveur`). Please refer to Chapter 4 where we discussed the architecture of the sample application for collaboration diagrams describing the high-level interactions between the non-cached and the cache router. Chapter 8 contains a detailed description of the cached URL.

As you can see, there is room for improvement: about one order of magnitude, both in terms of the latency of the number of transactions per second.

Now that we have the tools to measure our performance indicators, we can work on improving their values.

Optimization Techniques

In the first half of this chapter about performance, we took a close look at the bottlenecks of a SOAP application and we wrote a client application tailored to measuring the performance issues that we identified. We also confirmed that there is room for improvement in the performance of our application.

In the second half of this chapter, we will be looking at ways to improve the bottlenecks that we discussed. In this section, we begin our discussion with the optimization of the sample application as a standalone server. In the next section, we will be looking at the benefits we can get from replicating our application, with a close eye on the applicability of server redundancy.

Hardware Optimization

From a hardware standpoint, we can improve scalability and latency using the following methodologies:

- **Scaling in**
  This form of scaling could also be labeled "internal scaling". When scaling in, we improve the performance of our software by getting more or better hardware for our server: more CPUs, more memory, and faster network bandwidth. Typically, this is the easiest route from a software point of view, with the exception of thread safety. Once our application is thread-safe, we let the hardware do its job.

- **Scaling out**
  This form of scaling could also be labeled "external scaling" or "distributed scaling". When scaling out, we improve the performance of our application by distributing the load over multiple servers. Scaling out is usually harder to achieve because it requires the distributed application to either be stateless or share its state across multiple machines.

Scaling in is an easy solution: you only need to buy more processing power and let the hardware do the rest. However, you can only put so much memory or CPUs in your server: scaling in has physical constraints that you cannot overcome. If it were not for the fact that we can only scale in to a point, scaling in would be the ideal solution for scalability and latency.

Scaling in can also improve the availability of our application through internal hardware redundancy: redundant power supply, dual network cards, amongst other things. However, once again, you can only take those solutions to their physical limits.

It is important to maintain flexibility as far of your deployment is concerned. You might run a battery of tests before going live with your application, only to discover after a few weeks of utilization that the load patterns of your servers are completely different from what was anticipated. This is where the `SavonTransport` comes to the rescue. It allows you change the target machine of your services from an `in-proc` call to a SOAP call that can be distributed over multiple servers (see below) without changing your design, or even your code.

Since this book is about software development, we will assume that we have the best machines that money can buy and work on maximizing their use. First, we will investigate what we can do to optimize the use of one machine and then we will work on distributing the load across multiple machines.

Object Life Time

We have seen in Chapter 5 that there were three settings for the scope of remote objects created by the Apache SOAP framework. In reality, there is also the page scope: the object will remain available until the target servlet sends a response back to the client or forwards the request to another servlet. This will not happen unless you use a custom deployment mechanism:

- **Request**
  The remote object is available for the duration of the request.

- **Session**
  The remote object is available for the duration of the session.

- **Application**
  The remote object is available until the router servlet is destroyed. In addition, all requests will share the same object.

For instance, the `RemoteAdmin` service is set up with the scope set for the request:

```
<isd:service xmlns:isd="http://xml.apache.org/xml-soap/deployment"
             id="urn:admin">
  <isd:provider type="java"
                scope="Request"
                methods="flush refresh">
    <isd:java class="com.lesavon.service.AdminService" static="false"/>
  </isd:provider>

  <isd:faultListener>
     org.apache.soap.server.DOMFaultListener
  </isd:faultListener>
</isd:service>
```

The `RemoteOrder` service is set up the same way. Since object creation is usually an expensive operation in Java, it seems natural to optimize our services using the application scope. However, before we jump to that solution, we need to consider two significant issues: **security** and **threading**.

By giving an application scope to the remote object, we are telling Apache SOAP to create one, and only one, remote object for all clients. In other words, all client requests will be served by the same object, regardless of the security credentials of the client. When writing our SOAP service, we must keep in mind that all clients share the instance data of our objects.

The threading issue is obvious: when multiple clients are hitting the server for the same SOAP service, multiple threads are going to be executing code on the same object.

Neither issue is a problem for the order service, so we can safely change the scope from request to application.

The following figure shows the latency for the `DoHttp` test with the scope set to application. The command to execute the `PerfTest` client is identical to what we did earlier for the `DoHttp` class.

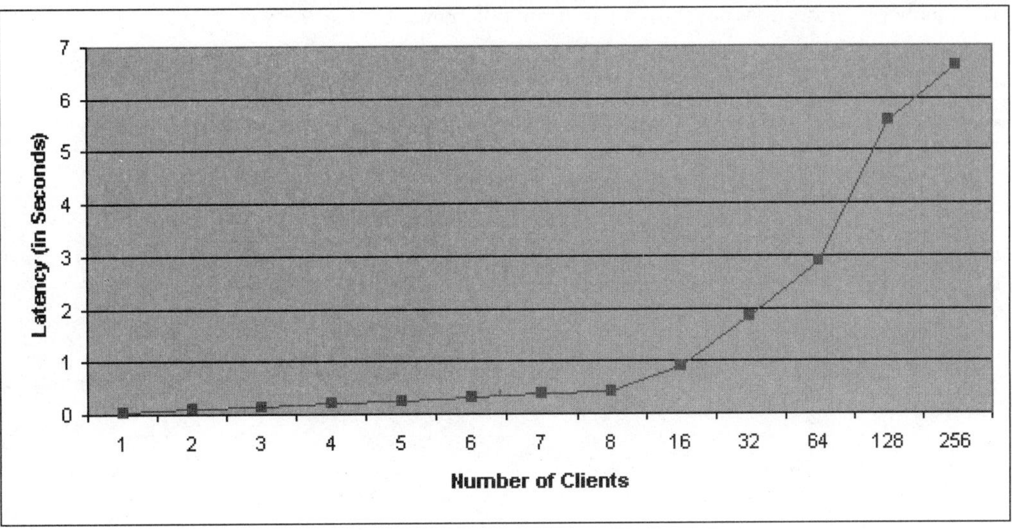

The latency has improved for a small number of clients by almost a factor of 2. A similar improvement can be seen for the number of transactions per second, which improves when the number of clients is small, but starts to degrade as the number of clients increases.

If you use the application scope, you will see a decrease in performance when the load increases on the server since all clients must synchronize on one SOAP service object. The session scope does not have that problem; however, if sessions are short, then SOAP services will be created often. Alternatively, you could implement a more sophisticated object-caching scheme, like a pool of objects with the session scope.

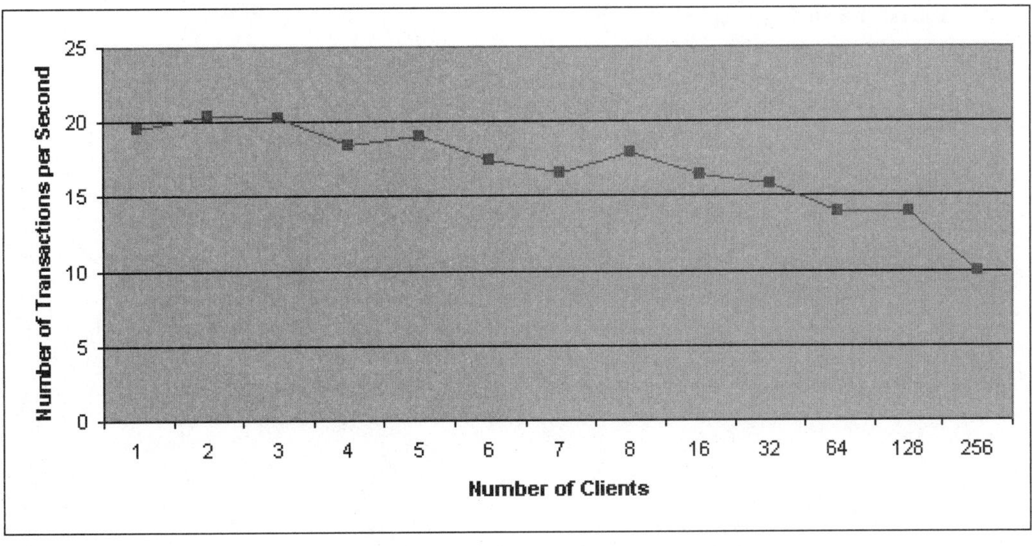

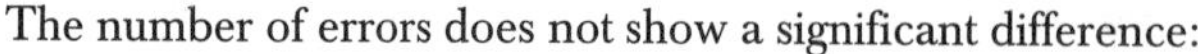

The number of errors does not show a significant difference:

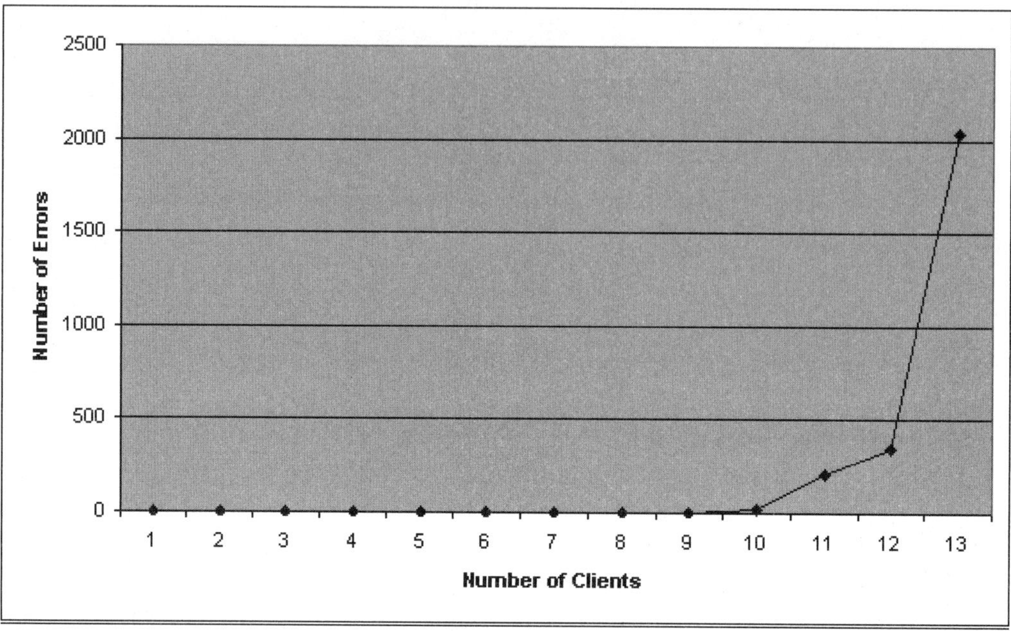

The previous diagrams show that the use of the application scope is not always desirable, since the performance actually decreases for the sample application when it is under stress. As we hinted before, we will see better savings with objects that are expensive to create. We will also see shortly that this undesirable effect can be curtailed by caching.

Caching

To enable caching, we simply modify the code of `DoHttp.doWork()` to hit the `serveur` URL rather than the `ncrouter` URL. For this test, the cache key is not included in the HTTP header:

```
...
        URL         targetURL = new URL(url + "/lesavon/serveur");
//        URL         targetURL = new URL(url + "/lesavon/ncrouter");

        request.setContentType(Constants.HEADERVAL_CHARSET_UTF8);

...
```

The improvements are shown in the figure below. You will notice that cached documents are returned faster than web pages. This is a testimony to the fact that Tomcat is optimized to run servlets, not to return static web pages.

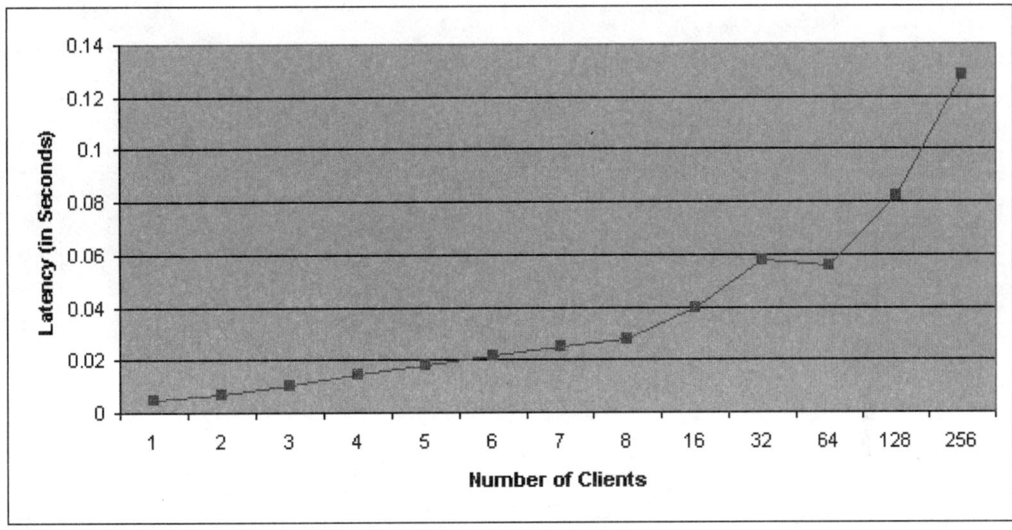

Using the cache improves on three of the potential bottlenecks that we identified at the beginning of this chapter. The cache helps prevent the bottlenecks in the backend systems, since it reduces the number of hits on the backend. The cache also improves upon any bottlenecks in the SOAP services, for the same reason. Finally, the cache reduces the time spent serializing objects to XML documents since cached responses are returned either from memory or from disk on the first access.

The cache itself puts some burden on the SOAP server, so it should only be used when a significant percentage of the requests can be cached.

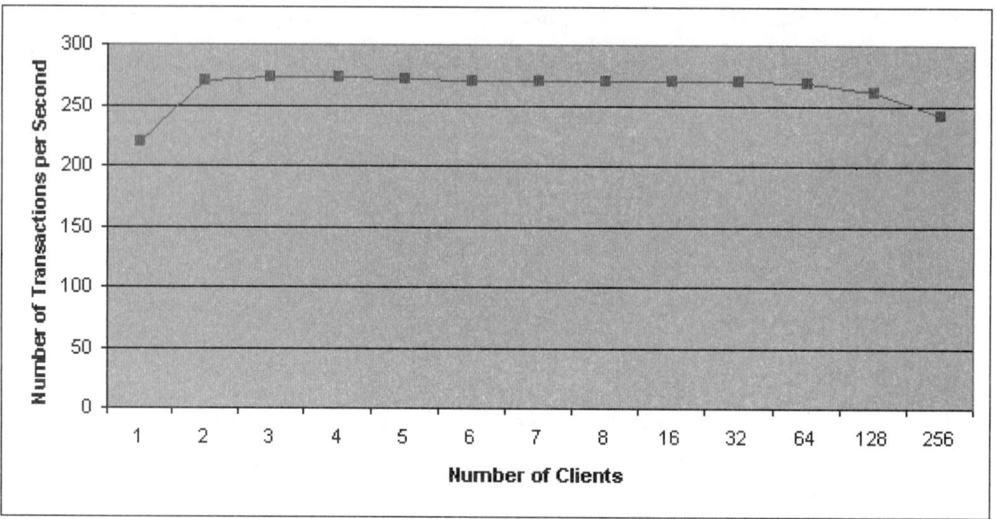

The number of errors has actually increased. This is attributable to the fact that the server is busier handling a lot more connections (over 200) than previously.

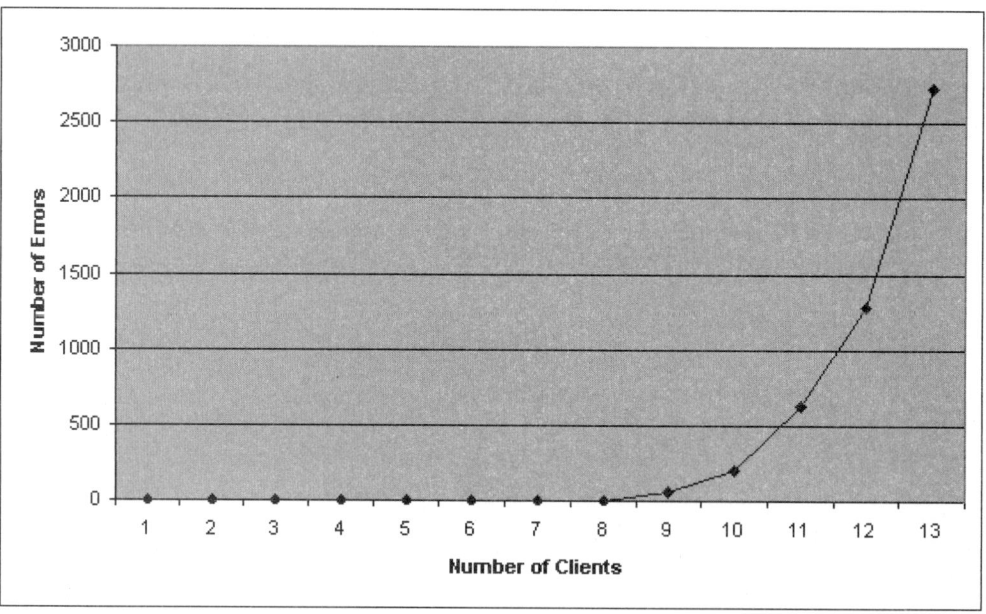

The cache does not improve on problems inherent in network bandwidth, nor does it reduces the overhead incurred during un-marshalling. Both these issues can be addressed with a little help from the client.

Client-Side Cache Key

We have seen in Chapter 8 that the server did not need to parse the incoming request if a cache key is already present in the HTTP header and if the response is already cached. We can easily add the cache key by adding the following statement to the `DoHTTP.doWork()` method:

```
...
request.setContentType("text/xml; charset=utf-8");
request.setHeader("LeSavon-Cache-Key",
                   "com.lesavon.service.OrderService.getOrderList.atase");
request.setBytes(xmlRequest.getBytes());
...
```

Run the test exactly as we did before:

```
C:\ProJavaSoap\Chapter09>java com.lesavon.test.PerfTest 256 60 DoHttp
```

If we include the cache key in the HTTP header and rerun the previous `DoHTTP` test against the cache (`serveur`), we get the results shown below.

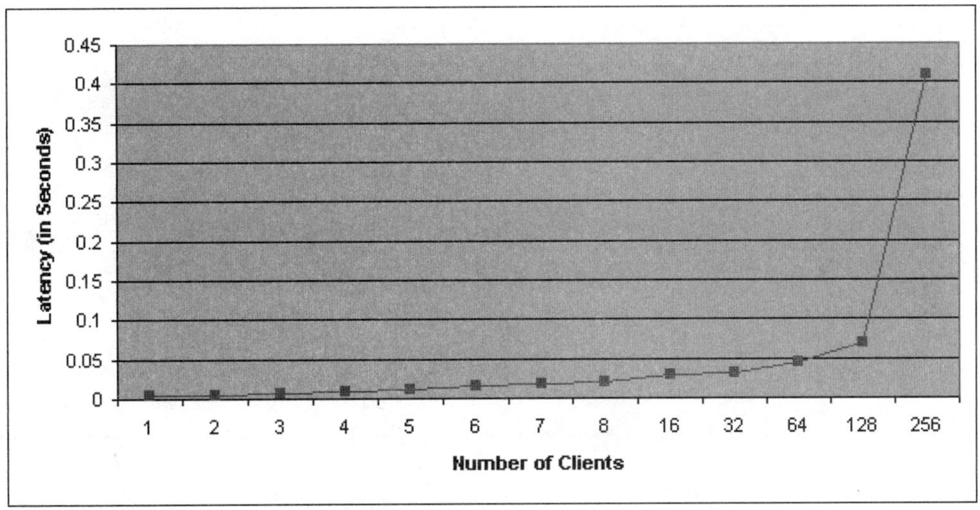

As you can see, the results are significantly better than the previous ones for up to 64 clients. The latency for 16 clients goes down to 0.029 from 0.039. This improvement (of about 30%) can be seen for up to 64 clients.

The number of transactions per second has almost doubled. The savings are proportional to the size of the input. Therefore, if our application has method calls that take more complicated inputs than the `getOrderList()` method, we will see better results. However, keep in mind that for most applications, we will not be able to hit the cache for every single request.

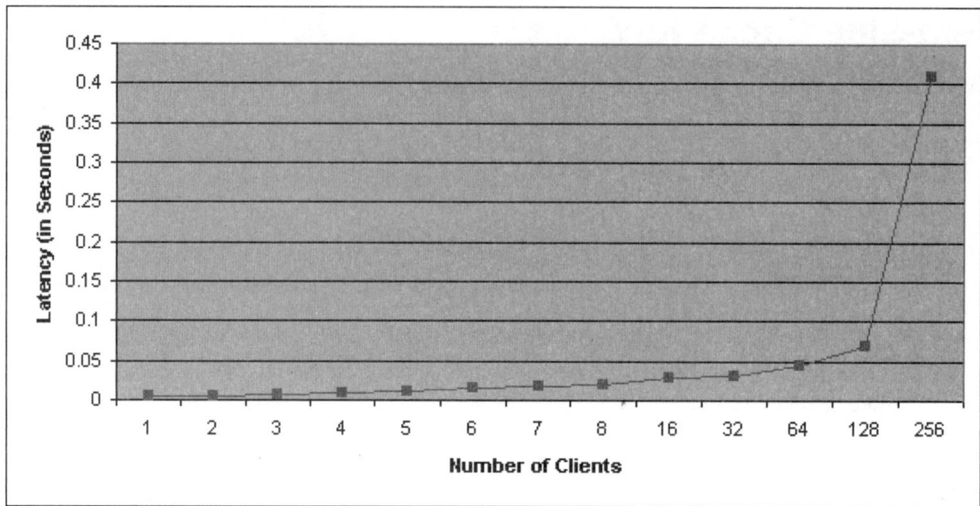

The number of errors is still higher than one would hope, as you can see in the following diagram:

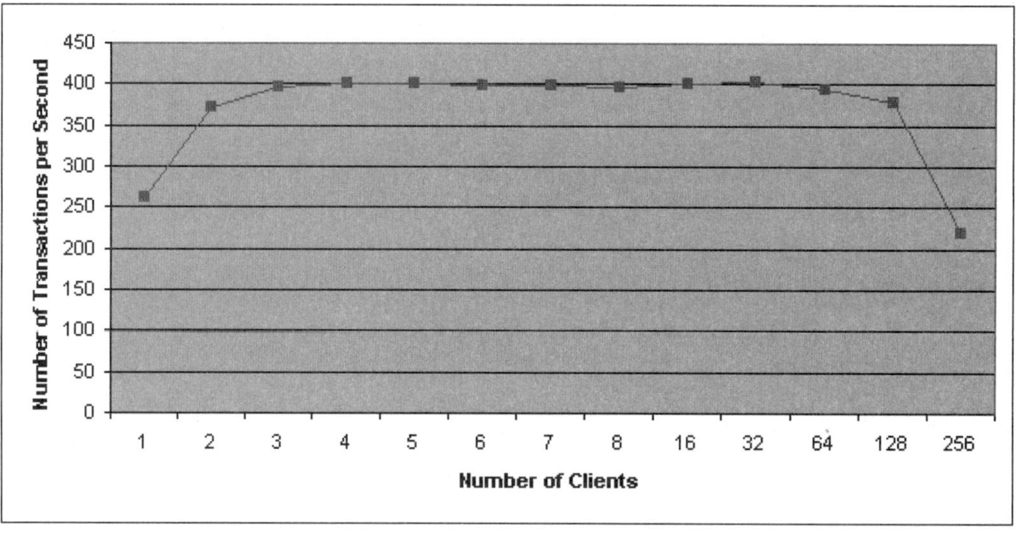

The scope is of little importance here since the Apache SOAP router will not be hit after the first request.

In addition to reducing the CPU overhead associated with the serialization of objects in and out of XML, the cache key can also help with network bandwidth. If there is a good chance that a response to a request will be in the cache, you can `POST` a request with no SOAP payload. If the response cannot be found in the cache, then the server will fail with a SOAP fault.

However, if your client re-submits the request with the SOAP payload, then the server will be able to process the request normally. As we mentioned earlier, this methodology only makes sense if there is a good chance that the response will be cached, because more traffic will be generated when the server needs the request. We will work on a variation of this theme when we talk about robustness.

Client State

To minimize the number of round trips to the server and optimize network bandwidth, we might want to consider caching some state on the client. For instance, let's assume that our application needs to update customer records in a database via calls to the `RemoteCustomer` interface. You could implement `RemoteCustomer` with `set*()` methods that post the information on the server. To support a client-side state, you can define a `Customer` object that implements the `set*()` methods along with a `save()` method that posts the data to the server.

The same reasoning can be applied to `get*()` methods, especially for objects with a deep tree of objects. There is a balance between how much information you want to exchange in a call and how many roundtrips you want to make to the server. Typically, this kind of optimization depends on your particular application: how deep should your local copies be? How much granularity do you implement?

These questions must be addressed on a case-by-case basis. The design pattern that we have just described is known as the **Data Transfer Object** or **Value Object**. You can find a more in-depth discussion of the Value Object on the Java site at http://java.sun.com/j2ee/blueprints/design_patterns/value_object/index.html.

Server Virtual Machine

The HotSpot™ VM offers significant improvement over the classic JVM in three major areas:

- **Garbage Collection**
  The new generational copying garbage collector takes advantage of the fact that most objects in a computer program have a short lifespan to improve the speed of garbage collection. It also reduces the pauses seen when the garbage collector kicks in.

- **Just In Time Compiling (JIT)**
  The adaptive JIT finds the "hot spot" of your program: pieces of your code that are executed often. The hot spots are then compiled into native code for maximum speed.

- **Native Thread Synchronization**
  HotSpot relies on the operating system to implement the Java synchronization primitives.

The HotSpot VM comes in two flavors: client and server. The server VM is optimized for server-like operations, mostly at the expense of the speed of JIT compilation. For more information on the Java HotSpot™ Server VM, you can visit http://java.sun.com/products/hotspot/2.0/README.html.

The HotSpot Server VM is platform-specific, so it might not be available for your platform. At the time of this writing, it is only available as a separate install for the Windows operating system. The installation process is similar to the JRE, which is a prerequisite. The first step is to get the installation program from http://java.sun.com/products/hotspot/:

Click on Download Java HotSpot Server VM 2.0 for Win32. You will go through a few prompts until you get to the actual download (there is an HTTP link and several FTP sites, pick the one closest to your location). Choose to "Run this program from its current location" and once the file is downloaded, it will automatically execute the setup (you might get prompted by your browser, depending on your security settings).

After the unavoidable licensing agreement, you will be prompted for the JDK or simply the runtime. We will select the runtime. The setup will then locate your JRE and prompt you to install the HotSpot Server VM at that location:

The setup will also give you the option to select which VM should be the default: server or client. Click on Next to start the installation process.

You can easily compare the client and server version by specifying, or omitting, the `-server` switch when starting the VM. Another switch that you might find useful is the `-Xms` (minimum heap size) and `-Xmx` (maximum heap size) since the default (64MB) is usually too small for most server applications. The heap size must be a multiple of 1024 and at least 2MB. You can use `k` or `K` to specify kilobytes and `m` or `M` to specify megabytes.

For instance, the following command line would start the HotSpot Server VM with the `DoHttp` client:

```
java -server -Xms80m -Xmx80m com.lesavon.test.PerfTest 256 60 DoHttp
```

Setting the minimum and maximum to the same value will give you the fastest speed. After running a few tests, chances are that you will be convinced that the server VM is the best solution for your servers. All benchmarks presented in this chapter are executed with the server version of HotSpot.

If you run our performance test (`PerfTest`) for a long period of time, you will see the performance improve gradually. Note that `PerfTest` contains a pause between successive tests. Those pauses are designed to give the JIT compiler a chance to optimize the code.

Load Balancing

In the previous pages, we have been concentrating on maximizing the performance of one server. Once you have taken optimizations in your code to their maximum potential, you can start thinking of dividing the work between multiple servers.

As we mentioned earlier, this division of labor, also called scaling out, will improve your application in two areas: performance and reliability. We will start by looking at an easy and inexpensive solution that can be implemented on the client side.

Client-Side Load Sharing

The client can maintain a list of servers that process its requests and hit the target servers in a round-robin fashion. This solution is very easy to implement in most cases. The following simple modification to the `GetOrders` test case adds client-side load sharing to the sample application.

The code for the GetOrders3 class can be found in
`C:\ProJavaSoap\Chapter09\leSavon\src\com\lesavon\test`.

```
public class GetOrders3 {
  static final String urls[] = new String [] {
      "http://localhost:8081/lesavon/ncrouter",
      "inproc://",
      "http://localhost:8080/lesavon/ncrouter"
  };
  private static String getUrl() {
    int index = (int)(System.currentTimeMillis() % urls.length);
    return urls[index];
  }
  public static void main(String args[]) {
    String methodName   = "com.lesavon.test.GetOrders3.main";
    String uri          = "urn:order";
    String remoteMethod = "getOrderList";
    String user         = "atase";
    String url          = getUrl();
    String urn          = "urn:order";  // the service urn
    String serviceClass = "com.lesavon.service.OrderService";
                  // fully qualified service class name
```

A first execution might give you the following output. Some calls to `System.out.println()` have been removed from the `GetOrders2` version. For a description of how to build and test the `GetOrders` client, please see Chapter 5.

```
com.lesavon.test.GetOrders3.main: Starting test for url
http://localhost:8081/lesavon/ncrouter...
    (123456001)(123456005)(123456010)(123456011)(123456012)
com.lesavon.test.GetOrders3.main: All done!
```

Another execution might give you this output:

```
com.lesavon.test.GetOrders3.main: Starting test for url inproc://...
    (123456001)(123456005)(123456010)(123456011)(123456012)
com.lesavon.test.GetOrders3.main: All done!
```

This simple solution achieves load sharing because the load is shared amongst the servers that are in your list.

The first disadvantage of client-side load sharing is that the client is aware of the possible servers. This makes it harder for the servers to be re-deployed. A second disadvantage of this methodology is that it only shares the load between servers; it does not balance the load at all. Therefore, if one server is busy to the point that it cannot service any requests, while another server is almost idle, the client might still try to send it to the busy server. The same thing will occur if one of the servers is down.

These problems can be addressed with server-side solutions, that can range from the simple – an inexpensive DNS load sharing – to the more expensive HTTP load balancing. Let's first have a look at DNS load sharing.

DNS Load Sharing

The **Domain Name System (DNS)** translates commonly used machine names into **Internet Protocol (IP)** addresses usable by TCP/IP. For instance, `wrox.com` is the common name for `204.148.170.161`. Current implementations of the DNS protocol allow `A` (Address) records to be duplicated: the host name is the same, but the IP address is different. If you look at the output below, you will see the result of a name lookup using the Windows `nslookup` for a couple of addresses.

```
nslookup
>wrox.com

Non-authoritative answer:
Name:    wrox.com
Address:  204.148.170.161

ibm.com

Non-authoritative answer:
Name:    ibm.com
Addresses:  129.42.19.99, 129.42.16.99, 129.42.17.99, 129.42.18.99
```

The name `wrox.com` is associated to one address, but the name `ibm.com` is associated with four addresses. The records in the authoritative name server contain a Time To Live (`TTL`). The authoritative name server file contains the master copy of the `A` records. The DNS server caches the non-authoritative answers: once the `TTL` has expired for one record, the next record will be used to answer DNS queries.

So the first time a client application requests the IP of `ibm.com`, it might get `129.42.19.99` and the next time, it might get `129.42.16.99`.

On some OS, like Windows 2000, we would need to take DNS caching off to take full advantage of this feature.

As you can you can easily see in the illustration below, this methodology can be used to move the knowledge of server deployment away from the client. As the figure above demonstrates, the methodology can be used with various clients.

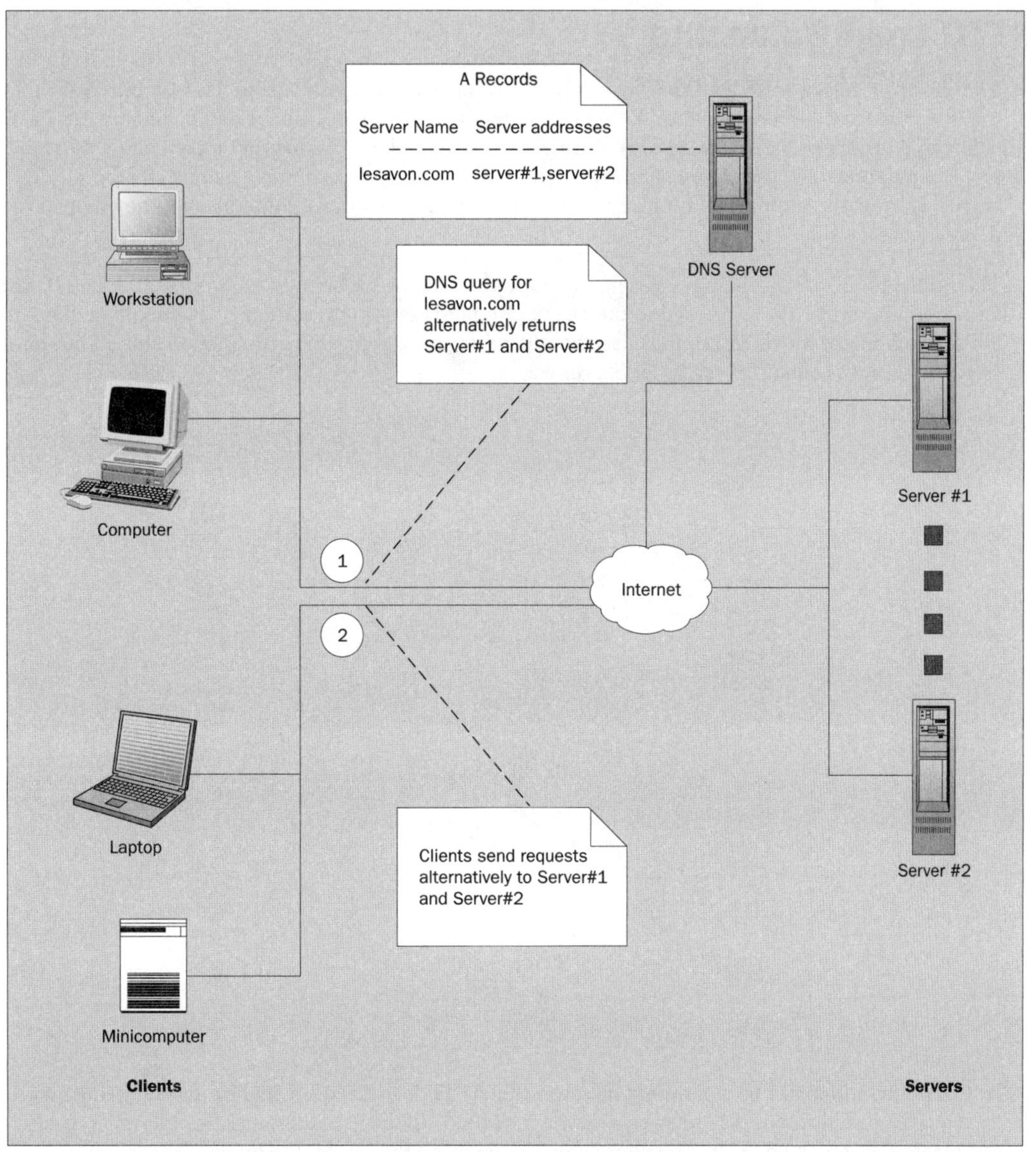

The main disadvantage of a DNS round robin is that it does not address the load balancing issue. Another significant drawback of the DNS round robin is that if a server is unavailable, its entry will still be returned from DNS queries. We will see shortly how that limitation can be overcome with a more intelligent client.

Despite those limitations, the DNS round robin has its merits because of its low cost and simplicity.

HTTP Load Balancing

The shortcomings of DNS load sharing can be overcome with load balancing. Here, a third machine that monitors the load and the health of the servers makes the routing decision. Load balancing can be achieved either by software or by hardware. It is more expensive than load sharing, but it provides a dynamic solution that can maximize the use of your hardware while maintaining maximum availability of the service to the clients. Hardware solutions are typically more expensive than software solutions, but they deliver better performance.

The principle of load balancing is simple. If you look at the figure below, you will see that one IP address, known as the virtual IP, is exposed to the clients. Requests sent to the virtual IP eventually make it to the HTTP load balancer, which can make an intelligent decision as to where the request should be routed. In this case, the choice is either Server #1 or Server #2.

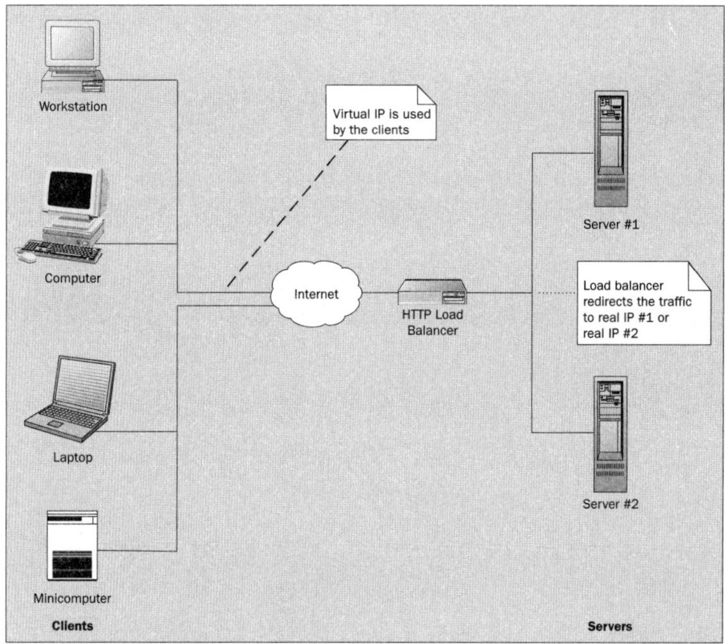

At this point, you might be wondering how can the HTTP load balancer make a more intelligent decision than a DNS round robin? The answer is simple: the load balancer continuously monitors the health of its servers. Based on how quickly a response comes back from the server, the load balancer can upgrade or downgrade its status. This process can happen several times per second with little impact on network traffic. We will discuss health monitoring further in a few minutes, but for now let's concentrate on setting up the servers and the load balancer.

The screenshots below show you how to set up virtual IP and real IP addresses for a popular hardware HTTP load balancer. Note that describing all the steps involved in setting up a load balancer are outside the scope of this book, but it is useful to understand the principles so that you can decide if it is worth taking it further for your application. Those tests were conducted inside an intranet. Most load balancers have either an HTTP interface or a telnet interface to set up their configuration. Sometimes both interfaces are available.

As we can see in the next screenshot, the first step is to define a virtual server. The virtual server does not really exist, since it is an IP address used re-distribute TCP/IP traffic to the real servers. In this case, we have two virtual servers: 172.17.1.39 and 172.17.1.52:

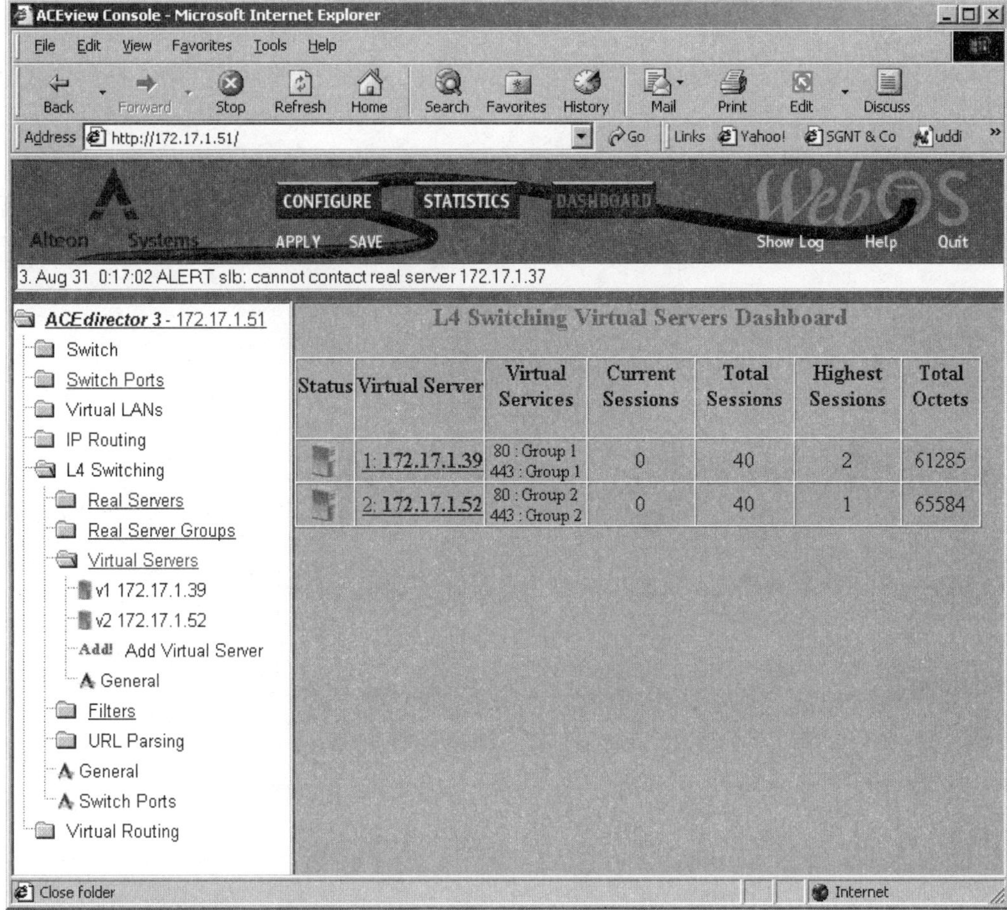

If you click on 172.17.1.39, as we do below, you can see that it is made of two real IP addresses: 172.17.1.43 and 172.17.1.45. These IP addresses are assigned to real servers.

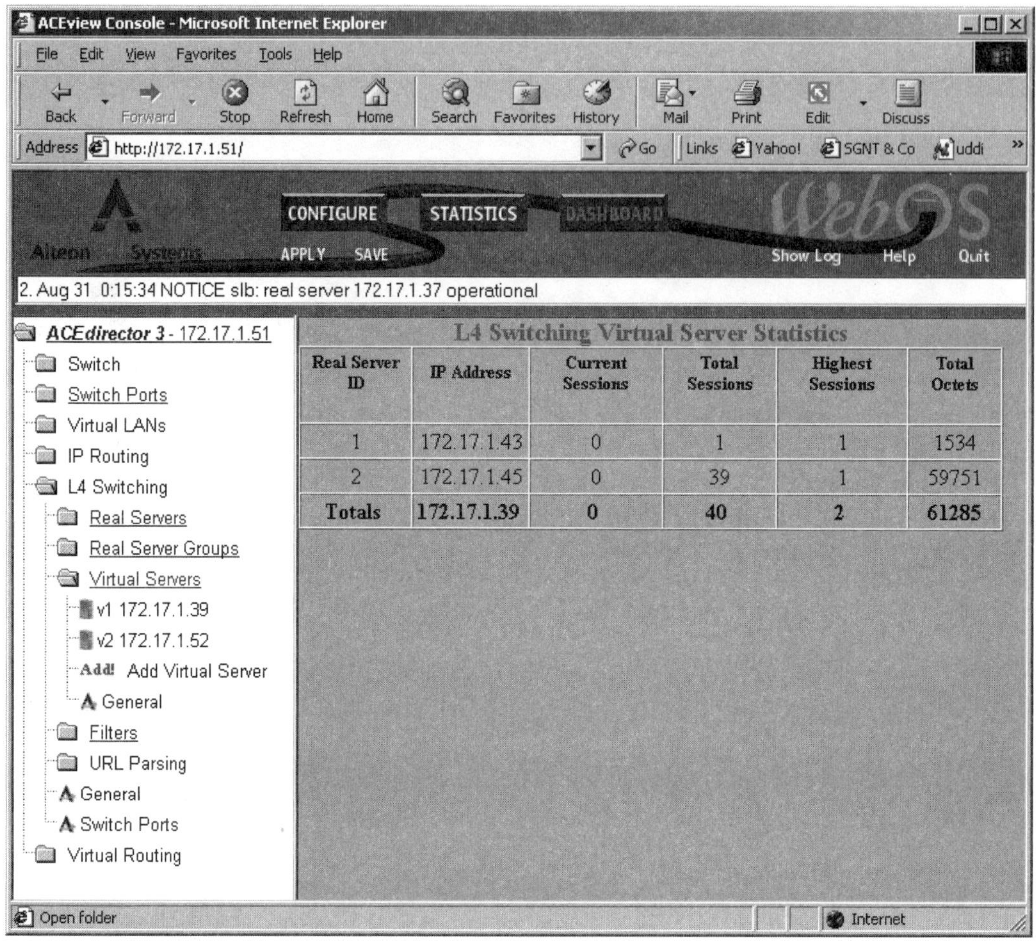

Real Server ID	IP Address	Current Sessions	Total Sessions	Highest Sessions	Total Octets
1	172.17.1.43	0	1	1	1534
2	172.17.1.45	0	39	1	59751
Totals	172.17.1.39	0	40	2	61285

To test the configuration described in the previous two figures, we create two almost identical web pages (`WhoAmI.jsp`) on our servers:

```
<!DOCTYPE HTML PUBLIC "-//IETF//DTD HTML//EN">
<html>
<head>
<title>Welcome To LeSavon1 (172.17.1.43)</title>
</head>
<body>
<h1>Welcome To LeSavon1 (172.17.1.43)!</h1>
</body>
</html>
```

Most HTTP load balancers have their own caching, so if you use an HTML page to do the same, you are likely to get the cached page, even when the machine that generated the cache page is down. Dynamically-generated pages like JSP or servlets are not cached by the load balancer.

Only the server name and the IP address are different for the version on LeSavon2:

```
...
<title>Welcome To LeSavon2 (172.17.1.45)</title>
</head>
<body>
<h1>Welcome To LeSavon2 (172.17.1.45)!</h1>
...
```

The first time we try to view the `WhoAmI.jsp` page, the load balancer directs the request to 172.17.1.43 and we get the result shown in the next figure.

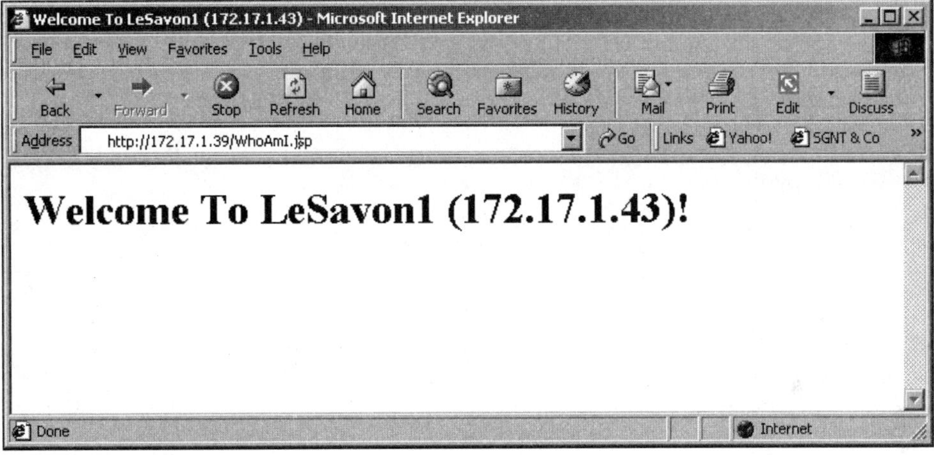

If we interrupt service on LeSavon1 by stopping the web server, we get the result shown in the next screenshot. Note that server switching happens almost instantly.

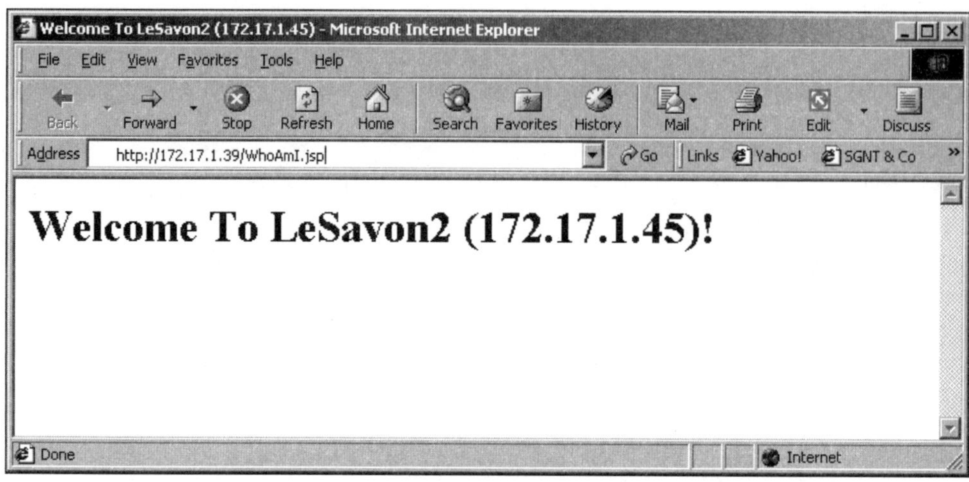

The obvious weak link in this configuration is the load balancer. The load balancer is a single point of failure: if it goes down then the entire network or service goes down. In any 24/7 deployment design, we must reduce the number of single points of failure, ideally down to zero.

An active-active configuration is shown below. The load balancers receive all the traffic, but they negotiate who should forward the packets at any given time.

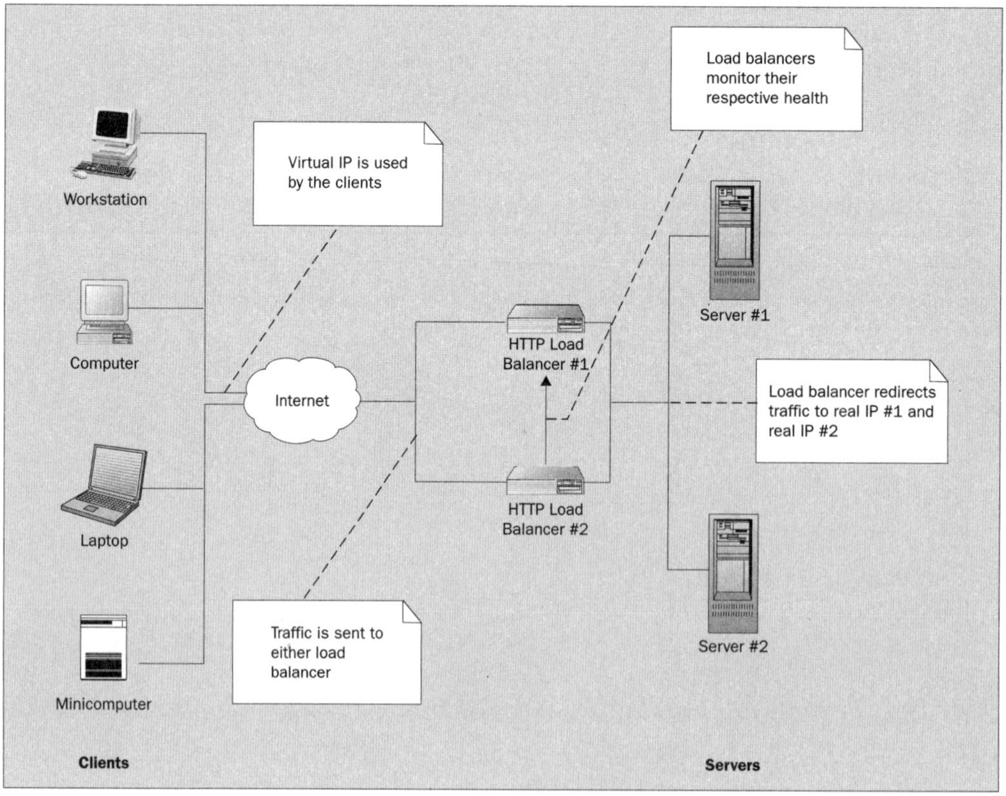

The probability that the load balancer will go down is far less than the probability that your application will go down. This is true for mainly two reasons: it is a simpler piece of hardware or firmware and it contains built-in redundancy. Nevertheless, it *might* go down. The solution above is to set up two, or more, load balancers in a configuration called active-active: the load balancers monitor each other's status and either one can take over when the other one goes down.

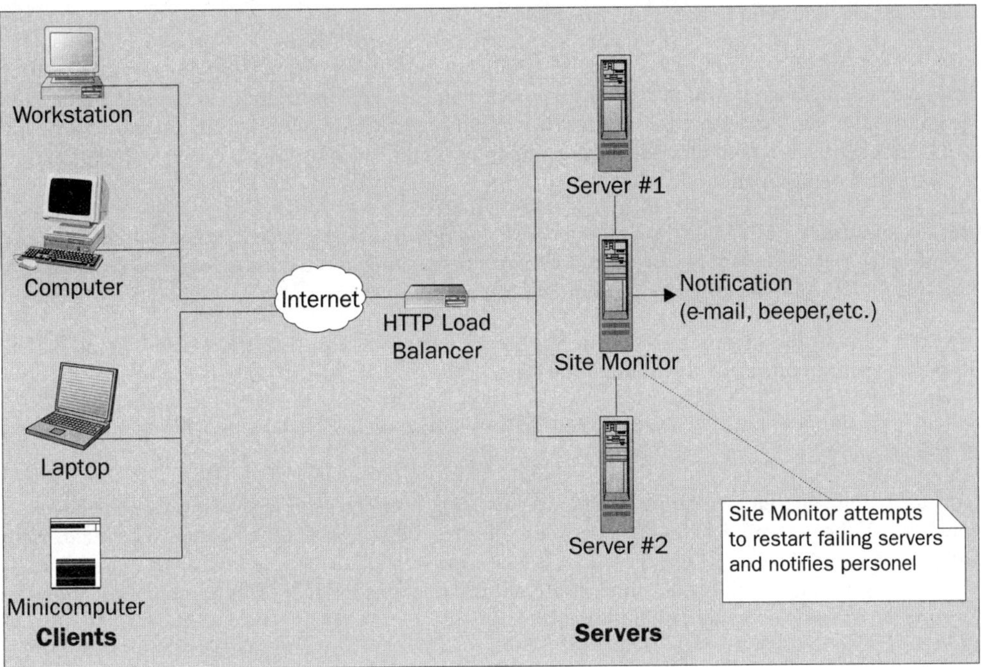

The health monitoring can take on several levels of sophistication. In its simplest form, health monitoring involves sending HTTP packets and monitoring how quickly they come back. A more sophisticated version involves application-specific HTTP requests that must reply with a known response. The load balancer can then compare the response against its master copy and take the server offline if they do not match. When a server starts failing, some remedies can be taken to improve the availability of the site: the servlet engine can be restarted, the web server can be restarted, or the server can be rebooted.

In addition, the JVM is a good old executable that throws an occasional unrecoverable exception. At the time of this writing, a search with the words "crash" and "VM" in Sun's bug database (http://developer.java.sun.com/developer/bugParade/) returns 178 open bugs (1,864 closed bugs). In other words, monitoring your JSP or servlet application with a recovery mechanism is necessary for a 24 hour, seven day, deployment.

You may be wondering how web sites relying purely on HTTP take advantage of load balancing, especially when they rely on sessions. The answer is simple. Most load balancers implement "stickiness" to a server: they monitor the client IP and HTTP cookies to keep sending requests coming from one specific client to the same server.

The same stickiness is used to optimize SSL. Setting up an SSL session can take several seconds. Without any preferred server, the client would have to wait for a new session to be re-established whenever the server is switched. Most load balancers have built-in awareness of SSL and HTTPS in their load balancing algorithms.

A notification of the problem, and a description, can be sent to the site administrator as well. The figure above shows how a site-monitoring machine can be added to our initial configuration. Some load balancers monitor the site and send notifications as well.

Before closing this discussion on hardware redundancy, it is worth noting that your servers are not the only components that can go down: you can lose power, you can lose connectivity to the Internet, and you can lose your router, amongst other things. In order to have a true 24/7 solution, you must provide redundancy from beginning to end. Note that there are companies that provide hosting services with the redundant hardware that we just mentioned.

After this discussion about hardware and network configurations, it is time to go back to SOAP. How do we take advantage of redundant hardware and network connections? We do nothing: the client application binds to the virtual IP address and the load balancing solution does the rest.

However, it is worth re-iterating that if our application is not stateless then the whole scheme falls apart without an application server distributing the state.

In the case of the sample application, we can take advantage of load balancing without any further changes to our code.

It is usually not a good idea to implement load balancing between remote sites because the latency and availability of the communication lines between the sites might lead the load balancer to make incorrect assumptions about the state of the servers. A better approach is to combine load sharing and load balancing by publishing virtual IP addresses, rather than real IP addresses in DNS. This combination allows us to keep our costs down while providing high availability.

Proximity of Servers

The sample application relies heavily on LDAP to store configuration and personalization information. If the accesses to the LDAP server are slow because the latency of the network is high, then the overall performance of the application will suffer accordingly. A similar point can be made concerning the backend databases of your application.

To limit the impact of network latency, design your network infrastructure so servers that need to communicate often are close to one another. You can also use techniques such as replication and caching to improve the speed of networks that have a rigid topology. Finally, an optimization to keep in mind is to dedicate a network (local or global) to a specific application and therefore avoid the problems inherent to sharing the bandwidth. This option will significantly increase the cost of deployment.

With the techniques that we have presented so far in this chapter, you should be able to get the most performance out of your application in terms of latency and scalability. However, we need to improve the robustness as well.

Caching (Reprise)

We have seen in the *Caching* section above that caching can dramatically improve the throughput of an application. The introduction of multiple servers complicates the issue, however, because one server might have cached a response while another server would still have to compute it.

For some applications, retrieving the cached response from another server might be faster. However, as you might imagine, this replication of servers raises the bar for development and deployment. A possible compromise that minimizes the increase of complexity for the application is to define the cache as a SOAP service and move it to a separate server, the cache server. The loss of redundancy for the cache is usually an acceptable compromise since the application will continue to function properly in case of a failure of the cache server, albeit in a somewhat degraded fashion.

Robustness

We have seen earlier in this chapter that the number of errors increases dramatically with the load applied on the server. After we have used up all the techniques that we have described earlier, the high server load and the increased error rate might be a permanent constraint on our application.

We can improve the perceived robustness of our application at the client level by making a small change to the transport that we will discuss in more detail shortly. To measure the impact of the change, let's run the `PerfTest` program with the `GetOrderLists` class (the classpath should be identical to what we had in the *Test* section above):

```
java com.lesavon.test.PerfTest 256 15 GetOrderLists
```

The next chart shows the latency for this test:

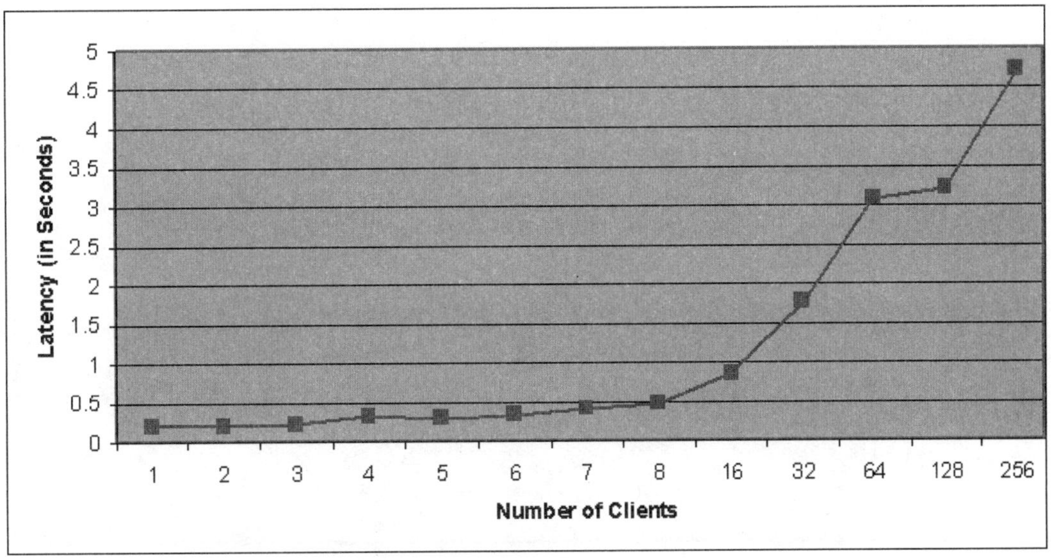

As you would expect, the latency and the number of transactions per second are similar to what we had for the DoHttp client that performed essentially the same work. The only significant difference is the work done by the SavonProxy, which is marginal compared to the other operations.

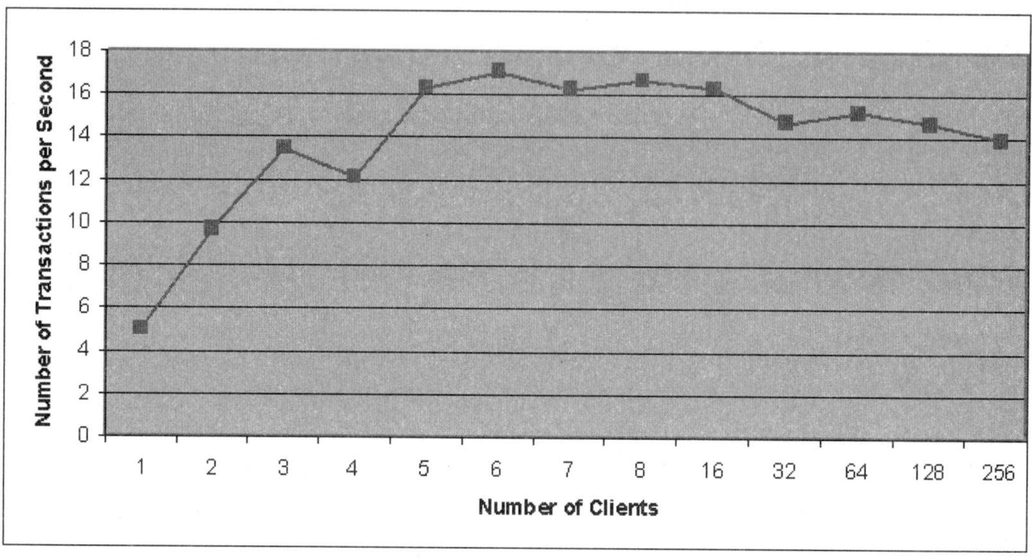

The next chart shows the number of errors, and is also similar to the results that we observed with the first DoHttp test:

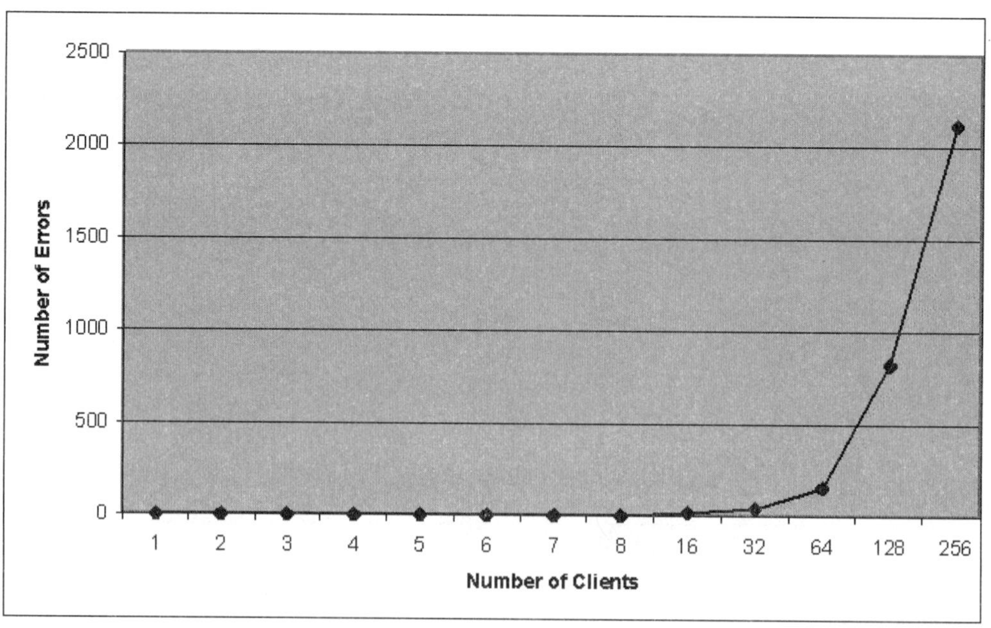

The improvement that we can make to the `SavonTransport` is based on a simple idea: we can increase the likelihood of getting a valid response to a SOAP request by submitting the request multiple times.

The changes are in the `send()` method of `SavonTransport`:

> *The sample code for `RobustSavonTransport.java` can be found in the `\ProJavaSoap\Chapter09\leSavon\src\com\lesavon\proxy` directory.*

```
// RobustSavonTransport.java
package com.lesavon.proxy;

import java.net.URL;
import java.util.Hashtable;

import org.apache.soap.Envelope;
import org.apache.soap.SOAPException;
import org.apache.soap.rpc.SOAPContext;
import org.apache.soap.encoding.SOAPMappingRegistry;
import org.apache.soap.transport.http.SOAPHTTPConnection;
import com.lesavon.SavonException;
```

We throw a `SavonException` as a last resort.

```
public class RobustSavonTransport extends SOAPHTTPConnection {
  private String cacheKey;

  final private String HEADER_CACHE_KEY = "LeSavon-Cache-Key";
  final private int  MAX_ATTEMPTS   = 5;
  final private long   DELAY      = 1000;  // Delay between attempts
```

We attempt to resubmit the request up to `MAX_ATTEMPTS` with a delay of `DELAY` milliseconds between attempts.

```
  public void send (URL sendTo, String action, Hashtable headers,
           Envelope envelope, SOAPMappingRegistry mappings,
           SOAPContext context)
    throws SOAPException {
    if(cacheKey != null) {
      if(headers == null) {
        headers = new Hashtable();
      }
      headers.put(HEADER_CACHE_KEY, cacheKey);
    }

    for(int index = 0; index < MAX_ATTEMPTS; index++) {
      try {
        super.send(sendTo, action, headers, envelope, mappings, context);
        break;
      } catch (Exception exception) {
        if(index == MAX_ATTEMPTS - 1) {
          String msg = "RobustSavonTransport: Aborting after "
```

```
                    + index + " attempts.";

          System.err.println(msg);
          if(exception instanceof SOAPException) {
            throw (SOAPException)exception;
          } else {
            throw new SavonException(msg, exception);
          }
```

We abort the `send()` after `MAX_ATTEMPTS` and throw a `SavonException` if the exception thrown is not a `SOAPException`. We could choose to only resubmit the request when some communication-related exceptions are thrown.

The way the `send()` method is coded here, other errors like installation problems will trigger useless multiple sends. However, it is more robust to always attempt to submit the request multiple times, because some problems that are not communication-related will be corrected by the site monitoring and/or the load balancing infrastructures.

```
        } else {
          try {
            Thread.sleep(DELAY * (index + 1));
          } catch (InterruptedException interruptedException) {
            // Abandon
            break;
          }
        }
      }
    }

    cacheKey = null;  // one use
  }
// REST OF THE CODE IS UNTOUCHED
```

As you can see, we have simply added a loop with an increased delay around the `send()` operation. This straightforward modification has some major impacts on the robustness of the client:

- **Overloaded Server**
  If the server is so busy that it cannot serve any more requests, resubmitting the request increases the likelihood that the server will be able to serve the request. Note that re-submitting a request to an overloaded server right after a failure would likely fail as well, hence the use of the delay.

- **Load Sharing**
  If you are using load sharing, resubmitting the request will direct the request to another server that might have a lighter load. This somewhat alleviates the limitation of load sharing when compared to load balancing, but at the expense of latency.

- **Load Balancing**
  There is always a small window of opportunity for a request to be directed to a server that cannot handle a request. If the client happens to send a request into that window, resubmitting the request after a small delay will allow the load balancer to redirect the request to an available server.

The figure below shows the improvements to the `GetOrderLists` test. The latency has increased slightly (up to 20%):

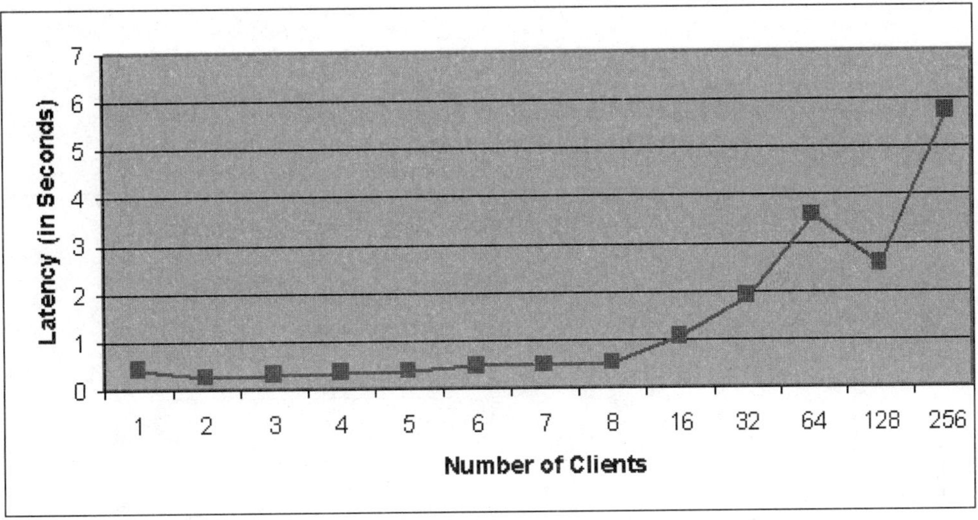

Notice that the throughput goes down dramatically. As we mentioned earlier, there is a compromise between raw performance and robustness.

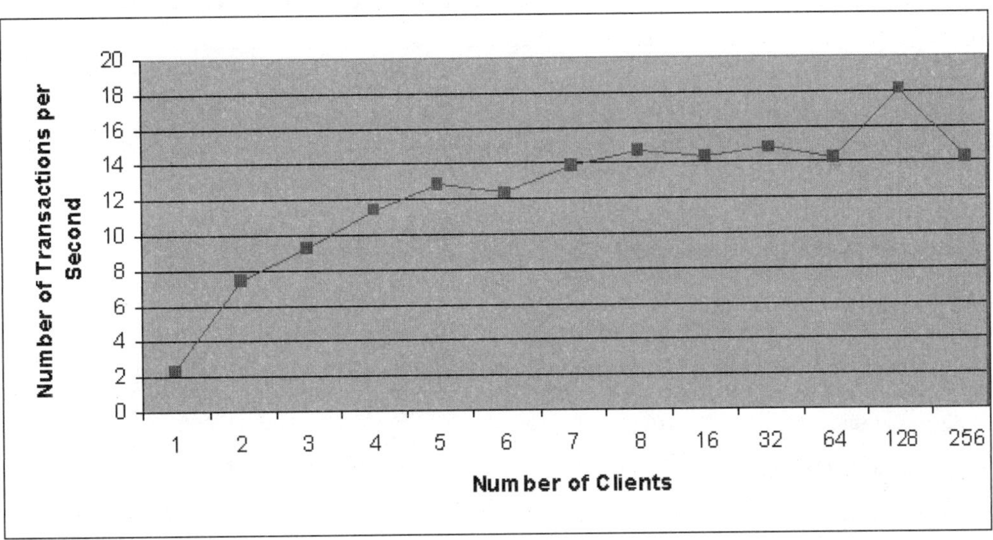

The number of errors has been reduced to zero for up to 128 clients. Once the server is completely saturated, at 256 clients, the number of errors is still reduced from over 2,000 to about 30.

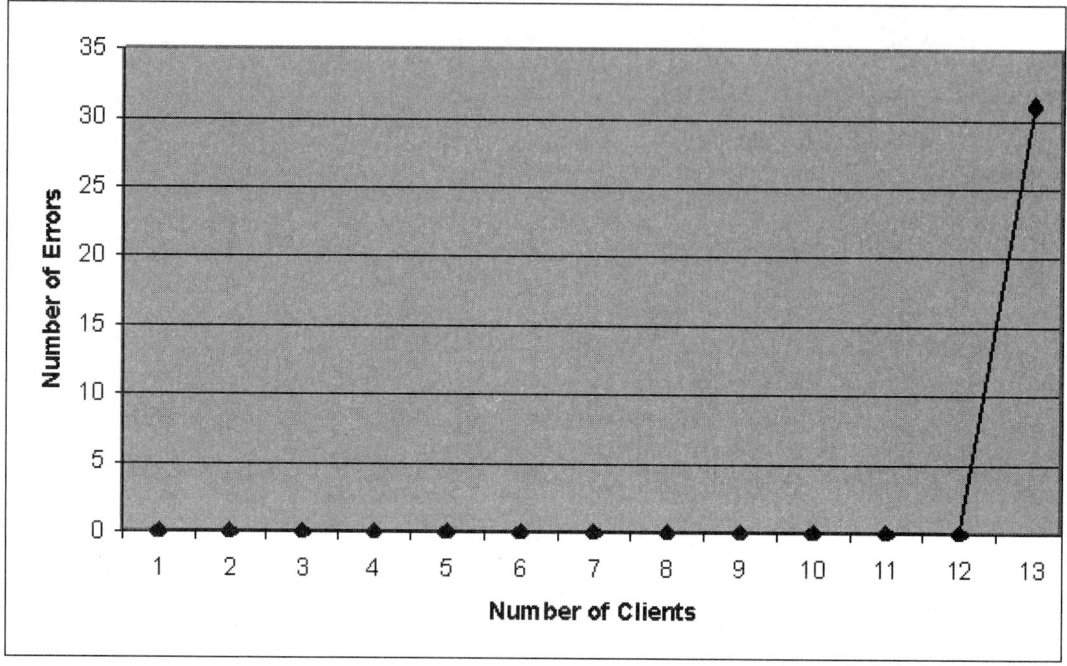

If you look at the chart on the previous page, you will notice that the number of transactions shows a spike at 128 clients. This is attributable to the fact that the `RobustLeSavonTransport` sleeps for one second in case of an error. The practical effect of the sleep is to effectively reduce the number of clients, hence the number of transactions going up. At 256 clients, the number of transactions goes back down again because the test program spends more cycles dealing with errors.

Summary

In this chapter, we have analyzed and improved the performance of the sample application on three fronts:

- Latency
- Scalability
- Robustness

We began by writing a test program to measure these three characteristics. We set up our test environment to isolate network issues from CPU issues. After improving the performance on one machine using various techniques from the HotSpot server VM to caching, we focused our attention on dividing the load across multiple servers.

The easiest and most affordable form of load distribution is load sharing, and this can be implemented on the client- or on the server-side through DNS round robin. However, load-sharing techniques have their shortcomings.

We addressed these limitations by introducing load balancing, which can be implemented by software or by hardware, depending on the robustness and performance level required.
Finally, we modified our transport to improve the perceived robustness at the client level. We saw that a simple change dramatically improved the error rate.

This chapter concludes the development of the SOAP server for the sample application. We now have in place a fast, robust, and scalable SOAP infrastructure that can be used by client applications to easily take advantage of the openness of web services without compromising performance.

We will use our infrastructure in the development of the user interface for the user communities that we defined in Chapter 3: users and administrators.

The development of the web application that implements the UI of LeSavon.com is the subject of Chapter 10.

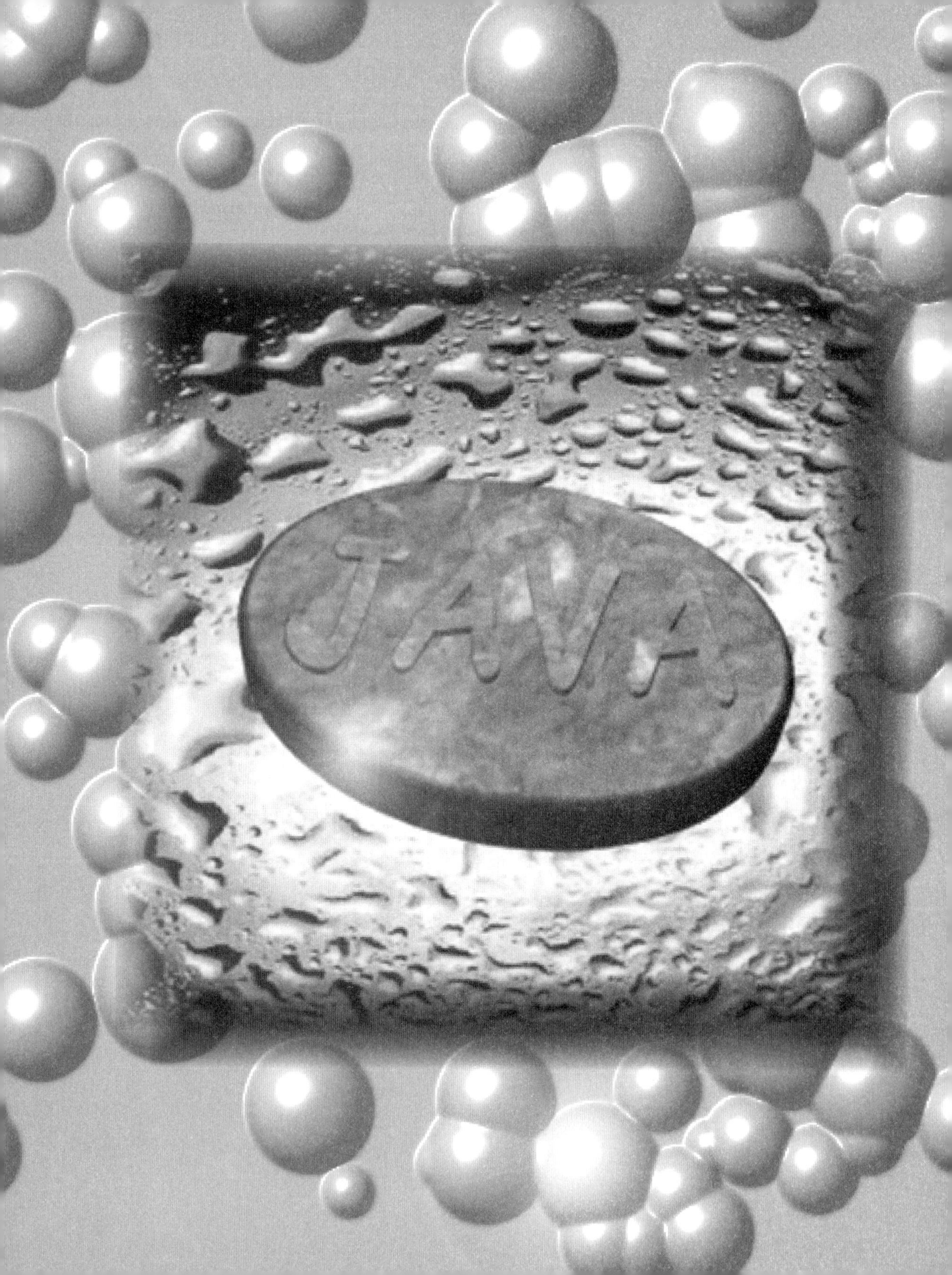
JAVA

10

Web Application

In the previous chapters, we have developed a set of SOAP services that acted as a front end to backend applications and databases. We have also developed a client infrastructure that simplifies the development of applications for RPC.

The next step in the development of a complete application is usually to write a UI to give end users access to the functionality. However, in the case of SOAP, this step is optional since SOAP is a technology for integrating applications in distributed computing, and not primarily about web front-end technology. To satisfy the specifications of the sample application we will develop a web application, but virtually any kind of application can talk to our SOAP server: a standalone GUI application such as an applet, or a portable device application such as a Wireless Application Protocol (WAP) client. Moreover, client applications can be written in a variety of languages and can be deployed on a variety of platforms.

Since this book is about SOAP development and not about web site design, we will keep the functionality of the web application as simple as possible and put the emphasis on the SOAP aspects of our development.

For the development of this user interface, we will use **JavaServer Pages** and **Java Beans**. In a production application, we could use other J2EE components to ease the maintenance and the localization of our application. For instance, you could use custom tag libraries to hide the JSP code or XSLT to transform your XML rather than parsing it. These technologies are useful for your production applications; however, they have little relevance in a book focused on SOAP development.

> *To learn more about the Java 2 Platform Enterprise Edition (J2EE), you can visit* *http://java.sun.com/j2ee/.*

We will begin our discussion with a high-level view of the architecture of the web application.

High-Level Architecture

The user interface of LeSavon.com is a web GUI that satisfies two main requirements:

- Allow end-users to review their orders
- Allow administrators to manage the site

The architecture of the web application is modeled after the **Model View Controller (MVC)** design pattern shown in the figure below:

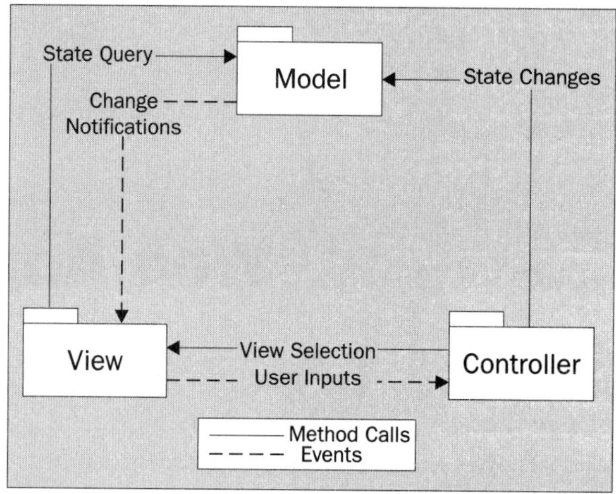

For a more detailed discussion of the Model View Controller design pattern and other design patterns used in the J2EE architecture, please go to http://java.sun.com/j2ee/blueprints/design_patterns.

The use of the MVC was popularized some twenty years ago when it made its appearance in SmallTalk 80. As you can see in the previous figure, the MVC design pattern contains three objects:

1. **The Model.**
   The model manages the state of the application. The name "model" comes from the fact that the application models the real life situation. The model responds to two types of operations: state changes and state queries. State changes are read write operations. State queries are read only operations.

2. **The View.**
   The view renders (generates a display for) the model. In addition, the view receives user interactions, but does not interpret them since that task is left to the controller.

3. **The Controller.**
   The controller interprets the user inputs into state changes to the model and display changes to the view.

The MVC also dictates the interactions between the members of the triad:

- The model does not modify itself. Only the controller is allowed to make calls to the model to alter its state.
- The model notifies the view of model changes.
- The view is allowed to access the model in a read-only fashion (state queries).
- The view notifies the controller of user actions.
- The view currently displayed is decided by the controller. For instance, if you had a set of tabular data, you could have two views to represent the same: textual data and a pie chart. The controller would decide which view should be displayed at anytime.

Aside from clearly defining the protagonists of the design pattern, the main advantages of MVC lie in its flexibility to handle multiple views or clients. For instance, if you design your web application using MVC, adding a WAP client does not require a modification of the model or the controller, it simply requires the development of an additional view.

The illustrations below show how we apply the MVC pattern to the sample application. Some obvious interactions like the calls from the Java beans to the proxy have been omitted.

Since LeSavon.com carries a state in two distinct places, the database and LDAP, the more straightforward way of showing how the MVC pattern is applied is to view the sample application as carrying two models: the application model and the LDAP model. In reality, there is only one model: the state of the application.

The first figure shows the interactions with the database:

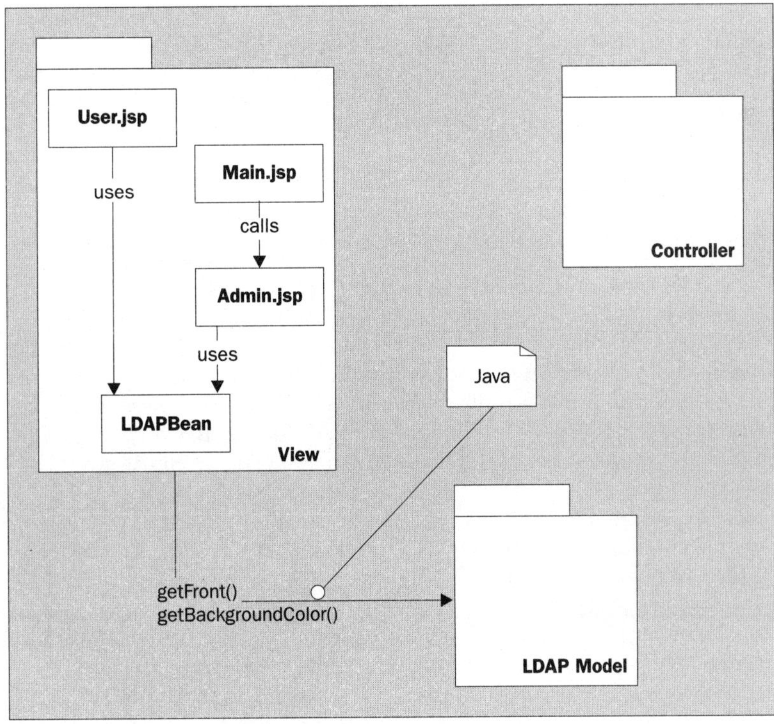

The application model is accessed via SOAP. The interactions between the view and the controller are handled with local (no SOAP) Java.

The second figure shows the interactions with LDAP. You will notice that the controller is empty, and idle, since we do not modify the LDAP database with the sample application.

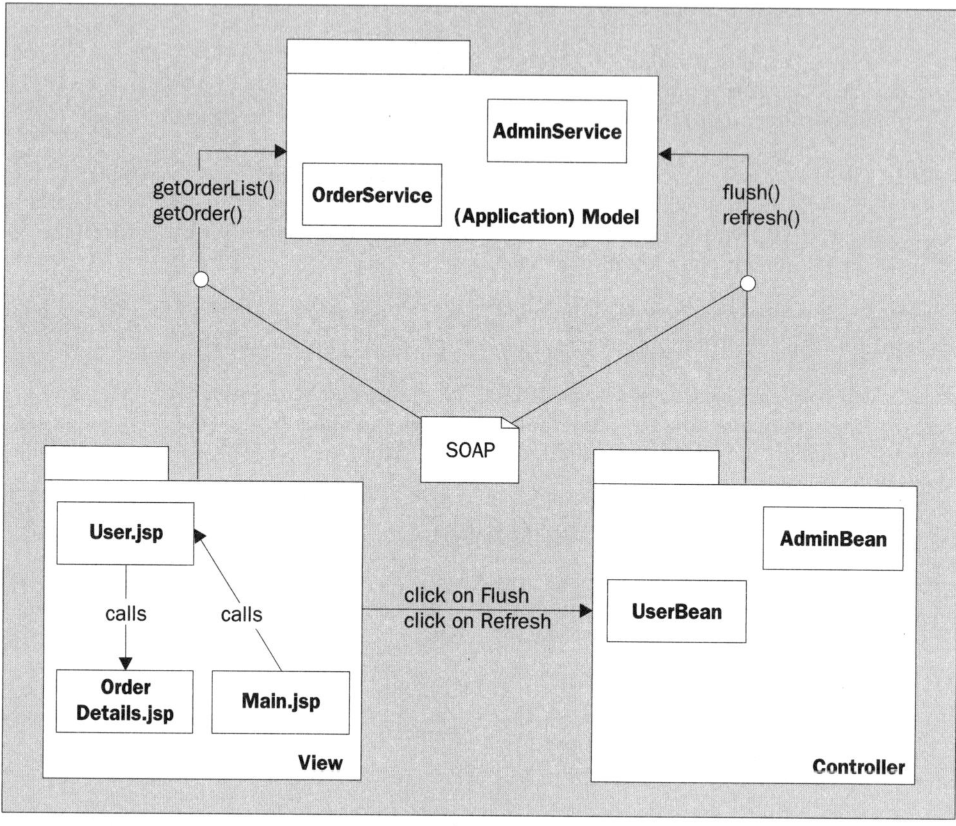

Despite the fact that we have presented the application model as two separate entities, we have only one controller and one view.

The controller is made up of two beans that we instantiate on a session basis: the `AdminBean` and the `UserBean`. The `AdminBean` is responsible for calling the `urn:admin` service (`flush` and `refresh`). The `UserBean` gets the list of orders and the order details for the user logged in. The `LDAPBean` is used to easily store and retrieve user preferences and to authorize administrators.

The view contains the `Main.jsp`, `Admin.jsp`, `User.jsp`, and the `OrderDetail.jsp` pages. `Main.jsp` is simply a link to the other pages. All pages get the user preferences from the LDAP database using the `LDAPBean` Java bean.

Now that we have a better idea of the high-level architecture of our sample application, we can have a look at the specifics. We will start with a description of the security architecture.

Security Architecture

In Chapter 7, we saw how you can set up the web server to authenticate users before the request reaches the servlet engine. The `Login.jsp` page checks that security credentials are present and saves them for the other pages.

```
<%@ page errorPage="LeSavonErrorPage.jsp" %>
<%@ page import="org.apache.soap.encoding.soapenc.Base64" %>
<html>
<comment>
  Login.jsp: gets the user name and password and puts it in the admin bean.
  In case of success, we redirect to Main.jsp, in case of failure we go to
  LeSavonErrorPage.

  @author       Henry Bequet
  @version      1.0 09/01/2001
  @since        1.0
</comment>
```

We will use the `org.apache.soap.encoding.soapenc.Base64` class to decode the user name and password. The Base64 encoding and its use in the context of web security is introduced in Chapter 7. All pages in the sample application web site use the same error page.

```
<head>
  <title>LeSavon.com - Login Page</title>
</head>
<body>
  <jsp:useBean id="adminBean" scope="session"
               class="com.lesavon.web.AdminBean" />
  <jsp:setProperty name="adminBean" property="*" />
```

We will describe the `AdminBean` in detail in the next section. For the purpose of this discussion, it is used to store the user name and the password. You will notice that we use the session scope to keep the `AdminBean` instance alive for as long as the JSP session is active.

```
<%
  // If the user name and password are already set then go to
  // the Main page
  String user     = adminBean.getUser();
  String password = adminBean.getPassword();

  if(user == null || user.length() == 0 ||
     password == null || password.length() == 0) {
```

If the user name and password are not set, we try to get them from the header:

```
    // only works for BASIC authentication. For other challenge-response
    // security schemes, use a X.509 cerificate in lieu of a password
    user = request.getRemoteUser();

    String authorization = request.getHeader("Authorization");
    int base64Index    = authorization.indexOf(' ') + 1;
```

```
        if(base64Index == 0) {
          throw new SecurityException("No valid password for user "  + user);
        }

        // We decode the BASE64 password
        String base64Password = authorization.substring(base64Index);

        // user:password
        password = new String(Base64.decode(base64Password)).
                                         substring(user.length() + 1);

        adminBean.setUser(user);
        adminBean.setPassword(password);
      } // if(user == null ...

      getServletContext()
                  .getRequestDispatcher("/Main.jsp").forward(request, response);
    %>
```

At this point, we have a user name and password and can forward the request to the main page. The code for the `Login.jsp` page only works for BASIC authentication. We saw in Chapter 7 that other authentication schemes like NTLM do not provide the password to the JSP. Another solution is required to handle those situations.

One possible solution is to overload the SOAP methods to take an X.509 certificate in lieu of a password. The certificate can either come from the client or be specific to the web application. As we saw in Chapter 7, we assume the web server has authenticated the user name and password passed by the web server to the servlet.

However, the administration methods still check that the user has administration permissions: the user has been authenticated but not authorized. We will see how the authentication is performed with the help of the `AdminBean` in the next section.

```
<h1>Login Page.</h1>
If you see this page, please contact your site administrator.
</body>
</html>
```

The conclusion of the login page might seem surprising at first, so let's review the flow of the pages:

1. The user navigates to Login.jsp.

2. The web server gets the request and authenticates the user. If the user is authenticated, the request for Login.jsp is sent to the servlet engine (Tomcat in our case). Chapter 7 contains an in-depth discussion of the negotiation protocol between the web server and the web browser that makes authentication possible.

3. The code in Login.jsp verifies that a user name and a password are part of the request and saves them in the `AdminBean`.

4. The request is forwarded to Main.jsp.

In other words, after step 4 has been performed, processing should be handled by Main.jsp and the remainder of Login.jsp should never be seen by the user.

The screenshot below shows the user name and password requested by the browser. This dialog box is the visible part of step 2 in the four-step process that we just described. Once again, the dialog box is displayed by your browser, not by the sample application.

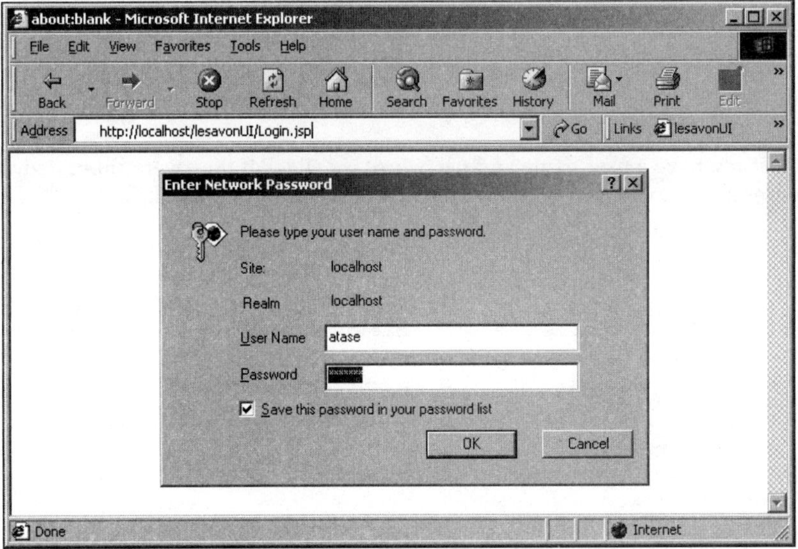

When debugging your application, you usually want to minimize the number of non-essential software systems to keep things as simple as possible. In particular, it is easy to simulate the authentication provided by the web server with a form in a JSP page. As an example of this simplification, the sample code also includes `DebugLogin.jsp` that prompts for a user name and password.

The code of `DebugLogin.jsp` is a slight variation of `Login.jsp`:

```
<%@ page errorPage="LeSavonErrorPage.jsp" %>
<html>
<comment>
  DebugLogin.jsp: debug page to let you enter a user name and password. In
  production, this is provided by the web server.

  @author       Henry Bequet
  @version      1.0 09/01/2001
  @since        1.0
</comment>
<head>
  <title>LeSavon.com - Debug Login Page</title>
</head>
  <jsp:useBean id="adminBean" scope="session"
               class="com.lesavon.web.AdminBean" />
  <jsp:setProperty name="adminBean" property="*" />
```

We use the same beans as `Login.jsp` since we want the remainder of the application to behave as if `Login.jsp` had been called.

```
<%
  // If the user name and password are already set then go to
  // the Main page
  String user     = adminBean.getUser();
  String password = adminBean.getPassword();

  if(user != null && user.length() > 0 &&
   password != null && password.length() > 0) {
   getServletContext()
     .getRequestDispatcher("/leSavonUI/Main.jsp")
       .forward(request, response);
  }
%>
```

If we do not already have a user name and password, we check if they were submitted with the request. If we have a user name and a password, we forward the request to Main.jsp.

```
<body>
  <h1>Debug Login Page.</h1>
    This debug login page allows you to set the user name and password.
    The login page extracts the user name and password from the HTTP header.
    <form method="post" action="Main.jsp">
      <br><br>
      <table width="30%">
        <tr>
          <td>User Name: </td>
          <td><input type="text" name="user" size=10></td>
        </tr>
        <tr>
          <td>Password : </td>
          <td><input type="password" name="password" size=10></td>
        </tr>
      </table>
      <input type="submit" name="Submit" value="Submit">
    </form>
  </body>
</html>
```

The remainder of the page contains an HTML form to prompt the user for their credentials. The following screenshot shows the `DebugLogin.jsp` as it appears to the user:

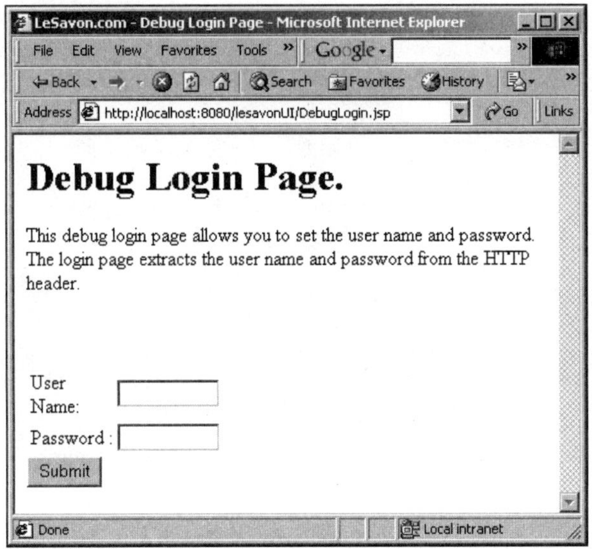

Notice that we directly go to port 8080, Tomcat's default port, to use the debug login JSP. In the next section, we will discuss the Java beans that will help us in the implementation of the web pages.

JavaBeans

As we have described in the section on the high-level architecture of the application, we will implement three Java beans as part of the web-based user interface of the sample application. The Java beans that we define here can be called from any Java program, in particular by JSPs, which is our main focus in this chapter.

AdminBean

The `AdminBean` is part of the controller and serves two purposes: it keeps track of the user name/password pair and it performs administration functions over SOAP:

```
// AdminBean.java
package com.lesavon.web;

import javax.naming.NamingException;

import com.lesavon.proxy.SavonProxy;
import com.lesavon.RemoteAdmin;

public class AdminBean {
  final private String url = "http://localhost:8080/lesavon/ncrouter";
```

The hard-coded URL above implies that the web application is executed on the same server as the SOAP server. This is simplistic and in a real system could be replaced by a URL stored in an LDAP server. Another possible solution is to store the SOAP server URL as part of the web application parameters and have the page creating the AdminBean (Login.jsp) pass the URL to the AdminBean.

```
final private String urn      = "urn:admin";
final private String svcClass = "com.lesavon.service.AdminService";

private String      operation    = "NOOP";
private String      user         = null;
private String      password     = null;
```

You could avoid storing the password in clear in a bean that will persist for more than one request by re-applying the Base64 decoding that we used in Login.jsp for each request.

```
private RemoteAdmin remoteAdmin = null;

public AdminBean() throws Exception {
  remoteAdmin = (RemoteAdmin)SavonProxy.newInstance(url, urn, svcClass);
}
```

The `SavonProxy` implementation and its usage are described in Chapter 6. The operation to be performed, `flush` or `refresh`, is set by the page.

```
public String getOperation() {
  return operation;
}

public void setOperation(String newValue) throws Exception {
  if (newValue != null) {
    if(newValue.equals("flush") || newValue.equals("refresh")) {
      operation = newValue;
    } else {
      throw new Exception("Invalid operation. Must be flush or refresh.");
    }
  }
}
```

The JSP page we saw earlier sets the user name and password for the bean. We provide accessor/mutator pairs for both for this purpose.

```
public String getPassword() {
  return password;
}

public void setPassword(String newValue) {
  if (newValue != null) {
    password = newValue;
  }
}

public String getUser() {
  return user;
}

public void setUser(String newValue) {
  if(newValue != null) {
    user = newValue;
  }
}
```

The RemoteAdmin interface reference is used to perform the SOAP calls. Because of the design of the application, this part of is very straightforward. doIt() is called to invoke the SOAP command. The method begins by checking:

```
public String doIt() throws Exception {
  String message = null;

  if(operation.compareTo("NOOP") == 0) {
    message = "Nothing to do!";
  } else if(operation.equals("flush")) {
    remoteAdmin.flush(user, password);
    message = "We performed a flush for " + user + " (" + password + ")";
  } else if(operation.equals("refresh")) {
    remoteAdmin.refresh(user, password);
    message = "We performed a refresh for " + user + " (" + password + ")";
  } else {
    throw new Exception("Invalid operation: " + operation);
  }
  return message;
}
```

The hasUser method is called on every page to check that a user name and password have been set.

```
  public boolean hasUser() throws SecurityException {
    if(user == null || user.length() == 0 ||
       password == null || password.length() == 0) {
      throw new SecurityException("The user/password is not set ("
                                  + user + ", " + password + ")");
    }
    return true;
  }
}
```

UserBean

The UserBean provides a page interface to make SOAP calls to the urn:order service. The code is similar to its administration counterpart:

```
// UserBean.java
package com.lesavon.web;

import org.w3c.dom.Element;

import com.lesavon.proxy.SavonProxy;
import com.lesavon.RemoteOrder;
import com.lesavon.Order;

public class UserBean {
  final private String url = "http://localhost:8080/lesavon/ncrouter";
  final private String urn = "urn:order";
  final private String svcClass = "com.lesavon.service.OrderService";

  private RemoteOrder remoteOrder;

  public UserBean() throws Exception {
    remoteOrder = (RemoteOrder)SavonProxy.newInstance(url, urn, svcClass);
```

```
    }

    public Order[] getOrderList(String user) {
      Order orders[] = null;

      try {
        orders = remoteOrder.getOrderList(user);
      } catch (Exception exception) {
        System.err.println("com.lesavon.web.UserBean.getOrderList: " +
                           "Error, caught: " + exception);
      }

      return orders;
    }

    public Order getOrder(String userName, int orderID) {
      Order order = null;

      try {
        Element orderDOM = remoteOrder.getOrder(userName, orderID);

        order = new Order(
                  orderID,
                  userName,
                  orderDOM.getAttribute("article"),
                  Integer.parseInt(orderDOM.getAttribute("unitPrice")),
                  Integer.parseInt(orderDOM.getAttribute("quantity")),
                  Integer.parseInt(orderDOM.getAttribute("totalPrice")));
      } catch (Exception exception) {
        System.err.println("com.lesavon.web.UserBean.getOrder:" +
                           " Error, caught: " + exception);
      }

      return order;
    }
  }
```

At this point, all the code in `UserBean` should look familiar to you. The `getOrder()` method returns an order object that will be displayed by the `OrderDetails.jsp` page.

Before we move on to the LDAP bean, let's consider the strategy that we use to deal with an order as it comes out of the `RemoteOrder.getOrder()` method. As you can see, we use the parsed result of the proxy and retrieve attribute values using calls to `Element.getAttribute()`. With an XML document as simple as the serialization of an order, this is probably the best solution. However, if your application produces more complex and larger XML documents, you might want to consider a more generic solution.

For instance, you could transform the SOAP body into HTML using the **Extensible Stylesheet Language Transformations** (**XSLT**) and **Cascading Style Sheets** (**CSS**) on a per user basis. The same technology can be applied to define different renderings for different types of peripherals: PC, WAP devices, reports, etc. The MVC-based architecture that we are using for the sample application provides a nice framework for implementing these requirements.

We can now look at the LDAP bean.

LDAPBean

The LDAPBean class is simply a Java bean wrapper around the LDAP class (much like the previous two). It allows us to retrieve the user name, and preferred background color, and font.

```
// LDAPBean.java
package com.lesavon.web;

import javax.naming.NamingException;
import com.lesavon.util.LDAP;

public class LDAPBean {
  private LDAP ldap   = null;
  private String user = null;

  public LDAPBean() throws Exception {
    ldap = LDAP.getLDAP();
  }

  public String getUser() {
    return user;
  }

  public String getBackgroundColor() throws NamingException {
    return ldap.getUserProperty(user, "background");
  }

  public String getFont() throws NamingException {
    return ldap.getUserProperty(user, "font");
  }

  public void setUser(String newValue) {
    if(newValue != null) {
      user = newValue;
    }
  }
}
```

Once again, this code should contain no surprises.

Now that we have coded the Java beans used by the web pages, we can have a look at the pages themselves.

Build and Test

Before looking at the Web pages, we will build the classes that we just wrote so that we can use them to test the UI.

The build is handled by ANT using the BuildLeSavonUI.xml file:

```
<project name="lesavonUI" default="compile" basedir=".">

<!-- This project is used to test the lesavonUI website -->
```

```
    <property name="app.name"     value="lesavonUI"/>
    <property name="app.dir"      value="C:/ProJavaSoap/Chapter10"/>
    <property name="deploy.home"  value="${app.dir}/webapps/${app.name}"/>
    <property name="dist.home"    value="${deploy.home}"/>
    <property name="dist.war"     value="${app.name}.war"/>

    <target name="prepare">
      <mkdir  dir="${deploy.home}"/>
      <copy todir="${deploy.home}">
        <fileset dir="." includes="*.jsp"/>
      </copy>
      <mkdir  dir="${deploy.home}/WEB-INF"/>
      <mkdir  dir="${deploy.home}/etc"/>
      <copy  file="etc/web.xml" tofile="${deploy.home}/WEB-INF/web.xml"/>
      <copy  file="RemoteAdmin.xml"
       tofile="${deploy.home}/WEB-INF/classes/com/lesavonUI/RemoteAdmin.xml"/>
      <copy  file="RemoteOrder.xml"
       tofile="${deploy.home}/WEB-INF/classes/com/lesavonUI/RemoteOrder.xml"/>
      <copy  file="etc/soap.xml" tofile="${deploy.home}/etc/soap.xml"/>
      <mkdir  dir="${deploy.home}/WEB-INF/classes"/>
    </target>

    <target name="clean">
      <delete dir="${deploy.home}"/>
    </target>

    <target name="compile" depends="prepare">
      <javac srcdir="src" classpath="${app.dir}/lesavon.jar"
             destdir="${deploy.home}/WEB-INF/classes"
             debug="on" optimize="off" deprecation="off"/>
      <war warfile="lesavonUI.war" webxml="etc/web.xml">
        <fileset dir="." includes="*.jsp"/>
        <classes dir="${deploy.home}/WEB-INF/classes"/>
      </war>
    </target>

    <target name="all" depends="clean,prepare,compile"/>
  </project>
```

The build file above is similar to what we have done in the past. The build steps for the web pages simply consist of copying the pages to the target directory: webapps\leSavonUI. We use the lesavon.jar file built in previous chapters to reference the classes from LeSavon.

The build steps contain no surprises other than the fact that the classpath can be limited to simply soap.jar since we do not need any of the internal Apache SOAP classes. We do need soap.jar because our remote interfaces throw `SavonException` which is a subclass of `SOAPException`.

To run, you simply need to start Tomcat as we did in Chapter 3 and LDAP as we did in Chapter 7. Now that we have the compiled our bean classes, we are ready to move to the web pages that implement the UI of the sample application.

Web Pages

The entry point of the web site is the `Login.jsp` page that redirects the user to the `Main.jsp` page that contains two links: `User.jsp` and `Admin.jsp`.

User Pages

As you might expect, the code for `Main.jsp` page is brief, but a few observations need to be made.

```
<%@ page errorPage="LeSavonErrorPage.jsp" %>
<html>
<comment>
  Main.jsp: gives you a link to either the admin or the login page.

  @author      Henry Bequet
  @version     1.0 09/01/2001
  @since       1.0
</comment>
<head>
<title>
LeSavon.com - Main Page
</title>
</head>
<jsp:useBean id="adminBean" scope="session" class="com.lesavon.web.AdminBean" />
<jsp:setProperty name="adminBean" property="*" />
<% adminBean.hasUser(); // Check if we have a user name and password %>
```

The user name and password must be in the `AdminBean` at this point or `hasUser()` will throw an exception that will redirect the user to the error page. The `hasUser_()` method throws an exception rather than simply returning false since not having a user at this point violates our design and should never happen. We also instantiate the LDAP bean as you can see in the following code snippet:

```
<jsp:useBean id="LDAPBean" scope="session"
 class="com.lesavon.web.LDAPBean" />
<% LDAPBean.setUser(adminBean.getUser()); %>
<body bgcolor="<%=LDAPBean.getBackgroundColor()%>">
<basefont face="<%=LDAPBean.getFont()%>">
```

The default background color and font are extracted from LDAP based on the user. For instance, the background color is set to `cyan` for user `atase`. The main page will have its background color set to cyan.

The sample application does not contain an interface to change the background color or the default font, but you can easily see how a page could use a bean like the `LDAPBean` to set values in LDAP to handle personalization.

The remainder of Main.jsp contains a little code embedded in HTML:

```
<h1>
  LeSavon.com Main Page
</h1>
  Welcome <%=adminBean.getUser()%>! From this page you can either go to the
  <a href="Admin.jsp">admin page</a> or to the
  <a href="User.jsp">user page</a>.
</body>
</html>
```

The resultant output from `Main.jsp` is as follows. In order to get this output we entered atase as the user name and lesavon as the password:

Let's now review the pages that are accessible from Main.jsp, starting with the `User.jsp` page that displays a list of the orders for the user logged in:

```
<%@ page errorPage="LeSavonErrorPage.jsp" %>
<%@ page import="com.lesavon.Order" %>
<html>
  <comment>
    User.jsp: user page: shows the list of orders for a given user.
  </comment>
<head>
  <title>LeSavon.com - User Page (List of Orders)
  </title>
</head>
  <jsp:useBean id="adminBean" scope="session"
               class="com.lesavon.web.AdminBean" />
  <jsp:setProperty name="adminBean" property="*" />
  <%
     adminBean.hasUser(); // Check if we have a user name and password
  %>
```

The use of the `AdminBean` is identical to what we have seen earlier in the Main.jsp page.

```
  <jsp:useBean id="userBean" scope="session"
               class="com.lesavon.web.UserBean" />
  <jsp:useBean id="LDAPBean" scope="session"
               class="com.lesavon.web.LDAPBean" />
  <%
    LDAPBean.setUser(AdminBean.getUser());
  %>

  <body bgcolor="<%=LDAPBean.getBackgroundColor()%>">
    <basefont face="<%=LDAPBean.getFont()%>">
```

We get the default background color and font from LDAP like we did in the Main.jsp page. After the personalization, we can deal with the orders for the current user:

```
    <%
      String user = adminBean.getUser();
    %>
    <h1>List of Current Orders for <%=user%></h1>#
```

```
        <br/>
        <%
          Order orders[] = userBean.getOrderList(user);
          if(orders == null || orders.length == 0) {
        %>
        <p>Sorry, there are no orders for <%=user%>.</p>

        <%
          } else {
        %>

          <table border=1 align="center" width="60%" cellpadding=3>
            <tr><th>Order ID</th><th>TotalPrice</th></tr>
            <%
              for(int index = 0; index < orders.length; index++) {
            %>
            <tr>
              <td>
                <a href=OrderDetails.jsp?orderid=<%=orders[index].getId()%>>
                  <%=orders[index].getId()%>
                </a>
              </td>
              <td align="right">$ <%=orders[index].getTotalPrice()%></td>
            </tr>
            <%
              }
            %>
          </table>

         <br/><br/>
         You can click on an order ID to get details about a specific order.
         <%
          }
        %>
      </body>
    </html>
```

The array of orders for the users are returned by a call to `userBean.getOrderList()` that calls the `SavonProxy` to make the SOAP call to the `OrderService`. You could make the call to the proxy directly from the page; however, it is nice to have Java bean on a JSP because of the integration that it provides. This is probably a case where you could hide the code in a custom tag library.
The output of the `User.jsp` page for `atase` is shown below.

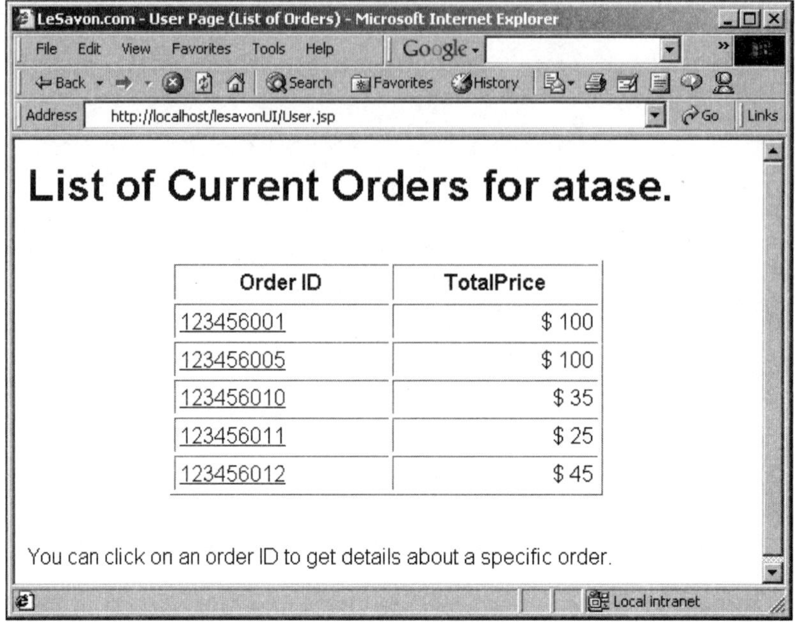

Each order is formatted into a hyperlink to the `OrderDetails.jsp` page. The `OrderDetails.jsp` page is built on the same model as `User.jsp`. An example of its output is shown in the screenshot below:

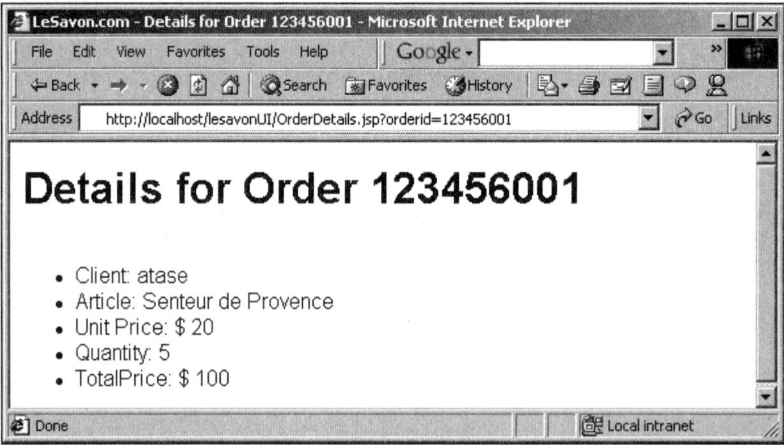

Admin Page

The design of the `Admin.jsp` page is very similar to what we have seen so far: the Java bean is created by the page and subsequently used to perform SOAP calls. In the case of the admin pages, the user name/password combination is verified to check that the user is in the administrator role. The output of the page, before an operation is shown below:

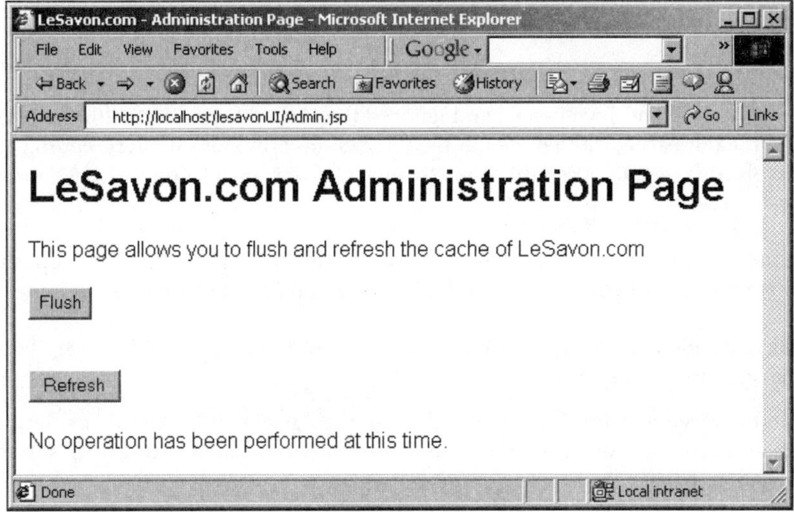

This is the output of the page after an operation:

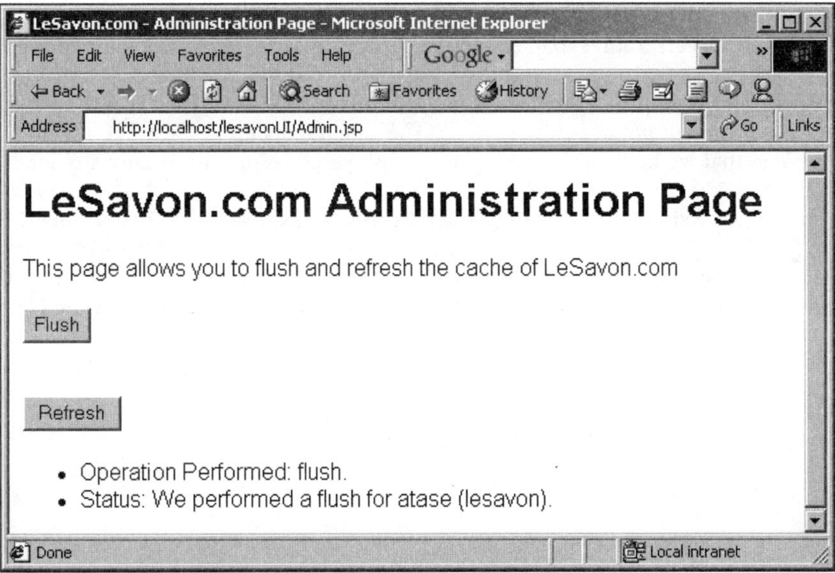

Administration operations are protected at the SOAP service level, so if you were to login as a user that does not have administrator privileges, the SOAP service (`AdminService`) would throw an exception that would make its way to the `LeSavonErrorPage.jsp`.

Summary

During the development of our simplified user interface, we concentrated mostly on web page technologies such as JSP and Java beans, and ignored the fact that we were calling SOAP in the back-end. Thanks to the infrastructure that we put together in the previous chapters, coding against a SOAP server only involved Java calls. We also took advantage of our integration to LDAP to provide a simple personalization solution.

Since this chapter concludes the development of the sample application using the Apache SOAP framework, it is time to take a step back and look at what we have achieved so far.

- We have developed two Java-based, portable SOAP services: the order service and the administration service.
- In addition, we have developed extensions to the Apache SOAP implementation. These extensions provide a distributed and secure registration scheme for SOAP services and serialization mappings.
- We have also developed a proxy class that increases the robustness of our application as well as shielding clients from the details of SOAP development.

In Chapter 7, we secured our application by integrating our services into existing security infrastructures like LDAP and web servers, rather than relying on a proprietary security implementation.

In Chapter 8, in order to improve the performance of our SOAP server, we added a flexible and versatile cache that can automatically keeps its SOAP documents up-to-date. We saw in Chapter 9 that the SOAP services that we have developed can be deployed to support virtually any load.

Finally, we developed a simple JSP-based web application to expose our SOAP services.

In the remainder of the book we will discuss WSDL and UDDI that allow us to publish SOAP services to the World-Wide Web. We will start with WSDL, which is the topic of the Chapter 11.

JAVA

11

WSDL

All of the features developed for LeSavon.com in the previous chapters could have been developed with a communication protocol other than SOAP. So why did we use SOAP? Beyond benefits that are largely attributable to the statelessness of SOAP, such as scalability and robustness, a major advantage of SOAP is that it opens up your applications to clients written in any language and running on any platform. As we stated in Chapter 1, interoperability was a main design goal for SOAP.

Interoperability, however, is not an endgoal. The end goal is to enable **electronic commerce** (**e-commerce**) or **electronic business** (**e-business**): the electronic exchange of goods, services, and their payments over the Internet. Interoperability is the key ingredient of the recipe that will allow companies to provide e-commerce services or **web services** that will talk to each other.

There will be little practical interoperability without the necessary plumbing: companies must be able to publish and subscribe to services in a dynamic fashion. The promises of e-commerce will not become true unless companies can quickly evaluate their suppliers against a variety of other suppliers. The evaluation should not be limited to whether or not the service can be provided, but it should also include other relevant information, such as the financial stability of the potential provider, the level of customer satisfaction, and so on.

The infrastructure that is required for companies to automatically do business over the Internet is the main topic of the last two chapters of this book. As you will see shortly, SOAP is a major player in this space, but it is not the only one. In this chapter, we will introduce a markup language that standardizes the definition of web services: the **Web Services Description Language** (**WSDL**). In Chapter 12, our focus will be the **Universal Description, Discovery, and Integration** (**UDDI**) specification that can be used to discover, and bind to, web services at runtime.

We will begin by defining what we mean by web services. We will then review the WSDL specification and discuss how it can be applied to our sample application, LeSavon.com.

To keep the focus on practical issues, we will generate the WSDL description of the `Order` service and use the same WSDL document to generate a Java proxy that simplifies client-side development, in the same way that we did in Chapter 6 (SOAP Clients) with the `SavonProxy`. We will also compare the pros and cons of both approaches.

As you will see in the coming pages, there is more to doing business over the Internet than exchanging XML files between backend servers: a process involving providers and suppliers needs to be set in place.

A word of caution is necessary before we go any further. UDDI and web services are still in their infancy and you will not find the same ease of use, robustness, and overall quality in UDDI and web services tools, as you have been accustomed to so far in the book. UDDI and web services are at the limit of what you might ideally wish to use in a mission-critical application. In testimony to this lack of maturity, you will see that tools provided by reputable companies like IBM still have some major shortcomings – these are characteristic of alpha releases.

The strategy that we are using in LeSavon.com is to provide access to the technology since it does not endanger the reliability of our application, but we have been careful not to depend on the technology for the critical operation of our software.

The Big Picture

In the late nineties, when the dot.com revolution was in full swing, companies were scrambling to provide browser-based interfaces to their products and services. This rush to provide browser-aware **business to business** (**B2B**) applications has come to fruition since, today, several major companies such as Dell, Amazon.com, and eBay conduct a sizeable portion of their business over the Internet using browser-based interfaces. This is only the tip of the iceberg: e-business will not reach its full potential until B2B transactions are completelyautomated.

For instance, if you are running a construction company and getting most of your supplies from supplier A, you might be interested in finding out that supplier B has overstocked some of the items that you need and is running a sale today. Companies do not typically do this kind of comparison-shopping in part because the overhead of finding the best price outweighs the savings. One way to reduce the cost of comparison-shopping is to automate the process and let computers do the hard work. However, this is hardly possible today since there is no widely available standard that supports such functionality. The promise of web services is to provide such a standard, a plug-and-play framework for Internet-aware software components.

It would be narrow-minded to think that the only reason why people and companies do not constantly switch providers is technical. There are many other factors that come into the picture, like established relationships, trust, and name-recognition to name only a few. However, technical limitations reduce the available choices and therefore play a role as a free trade inhibitor.

Before we get deeper in web service technology, we might wonder how likely it is to succeed as a free trade electronic standard. If the goal is 100% percent automation, then web services will most likely fail. The core reason goes back to human factor that we mentioned earlier. Business is conducted by human beings for human beings with the help of machines, not by machines for machines.

In other words, to be successful, web services must account for the human-side of the equation and enable flexible human-friendly interfaces to the technology. We will see in this chapter that WSDL was designed with that requirement in mind. We will also see in Chapter 12 that UDDI keeps the humans in the center of the picture. Nevertheless, by automating a significant portion of the work, web services have a chance to contribute to a smoother exchange of goods and services over the Internet.

Without any more delay, let's define web services.

Web Service Definition

The definition of web services has evolved significantly recently, and there is little agreement on what a web service is exactly, since definitions usually come out of software or service vendors that have an agenda: to sell their products and services. However, there is some consensus on the key points that we will use in our definition.

For the remainder of this chapter, we will adopt a developer-centric definition of a web service – relying on the use of specific technologies. You will see that a web service tends to define technologies as add-ons. This is not surprising since companies are trying to leverage their existing infrastructure while jumping on the web service train.

A web service is a software component or application that exhibits the following characteristics:

- **TCP/IP**
  A web service must provide its capabilities over TCP/IP or one of the transport protocols, such as HTTP layered on top of TCP/IP. The main idea behind TCP/IP-based protocols is to use the existing infrastructure of the Internet to enable B2B transactions. A web service may provide an additional interface that is not based on TCP/IP. For instance, a Java-based web service could provide both a SOAP and an RMI interface.

- **SOAP**
  A web service must provide its functionality over SOAP using the RPC or the document model. SOAP brings key ingredients to the table. Firstly, it defines a protocol that you can use to leverage your existing applications. You do not need to rewrite your backend applications to make them available via SOAP. Secondly, the use of SOAP leverages the interoperability of XML.

- **WSDL**
  A web service must provide a description of its functionality using WSDL. WSDL is a new technology that can easily be added to our existing applications. We will see soon that we do not need to modify our existing infrastructure to use WSDL as the descriptor for our web services.

- **UDDI**
  A web service must support the advertisement of its specifications in a UDDI registry. Like WSDL, UDDI is a new technology that can be added to an existing application.

You will notice that our definition does not include references to operating systems or languages. One can develop a web service in any language and deploy a web service on any platform.

The sample application, LeSavon.com, is not a web service at this point since it lacks WSDL and UDDI support. We will remedy these shortcomings in the remainder of this book. We will also revisit the integration of UDDI and WSDL in Chapter 12.

This definition of web services would be incomplete if it did not mention the availability of the tools and technologies that web services use: they must be readily available and inexpensive. As you have seen throughout this book, SOAP development and deployment can be done with freely downloadable utilities from the Internet. WSDL and UDDI follow the same pattern: we will use freely available tools for WSDL and the use of UDDI registries is free.

In summary, we can say that web services allow the interoperability of existing or new software programs over the Internet by re-using the existing infrastructure, and adding new inexpensive technologies, aimed at facilitating the exchange of information.

WSDL Specification

The specification for WSDL can be found at http://www.w3.org/TR/wsdl.

WSDL is an XML variant for describing web services. WSDL allows the web service to define what a service does, what protocol the service uses, and at what URL the service can be found. That is to say that WSDL describes the **What**, **Where**, and **How** of a particular web service.

As we will see in a few moments, the what question can be subdivided into two sub-questions: What language does the service speak? What does the service do? To answer those questions, WSDL describes web services as a set of **endpoints** operating on messages containing RPC-based or document-based data.

Web services are not limited to using SOAP: they can support simpler protocols such HTTP. WSDL supports the definition of more complicated protocols like DCOM, which technically agrees with our definition of web services, but which in practice locks us to one platform.

As we have seen earlier in this chapter, one of the main motivations of web services is to provide a plug-and-play environment for software components over the Internet. WSDL is a key ingredient in that recipe because it allows for a standard definition of web services. Without that standard definition, it would be impossible for companies to choose and switch between different ones.

Let's now have a look at WSDL, starting with the structure of a WSDL document. Conceptually, a WSDL document is a set of definitions, and contains two parts:

- The **interface definition**
- The **interface implementation**

We will examine both parts as being in the same document for the purposes of clarity; there is a WSDL file for each of these parts, but we will split the definition and the implementation when we actually work with WSDL files.

A WSDL document contains one `<definitions/>` element that is the container for one or more web service descriptions. As shown in the figure below, each service description contains an answer to the four fundamental questions that we can ask a web service:

- **What** language do you speak?
  This question is answered using the `<types/>` elements.
- **What** do you do?
  This question is answered using the `<message/>` and the `<portType/>` elements.

- **How** do I talk to you?
  This question is answered using the **<binding/>** elements.
- **Where** are you?
  This question is answered using the **<service/>** elements.

The following diagram shows you the structure of a WSDL document:

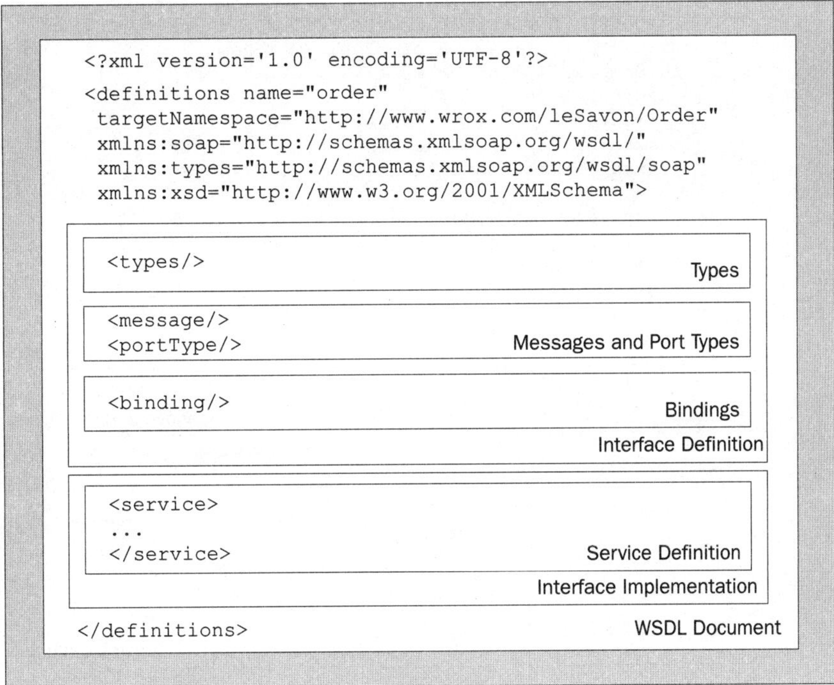

We will now have a closer look at each WSDL element.

Web Service Schema

WSDL relies on XML Schemas to define the data types that are used in the public interface of a web service. All the data types defined by XML Schemas are fair game and if your service only needs the basics then there is no need for a `<types/>` element. If the `<types/>` element is present, it must follow the `<definitions/>` element and precede the `<message/>` element.

WSDL is extensible in its definition of schemas. XML Schemas are the preferred way, but other technologies like the XML Metadata Interchange (XMI) format, as used by the business intelligence industry, are also possible. Please refer to Chapter 2 for a brief introduction to XML schemas.

If your service needs to use complex data types, such as the `Order` class, you must define what those are in terms of the data types defined by XML Schemas. If you look at the following figure, you will see that we define an order as a sequence of integers and strings.

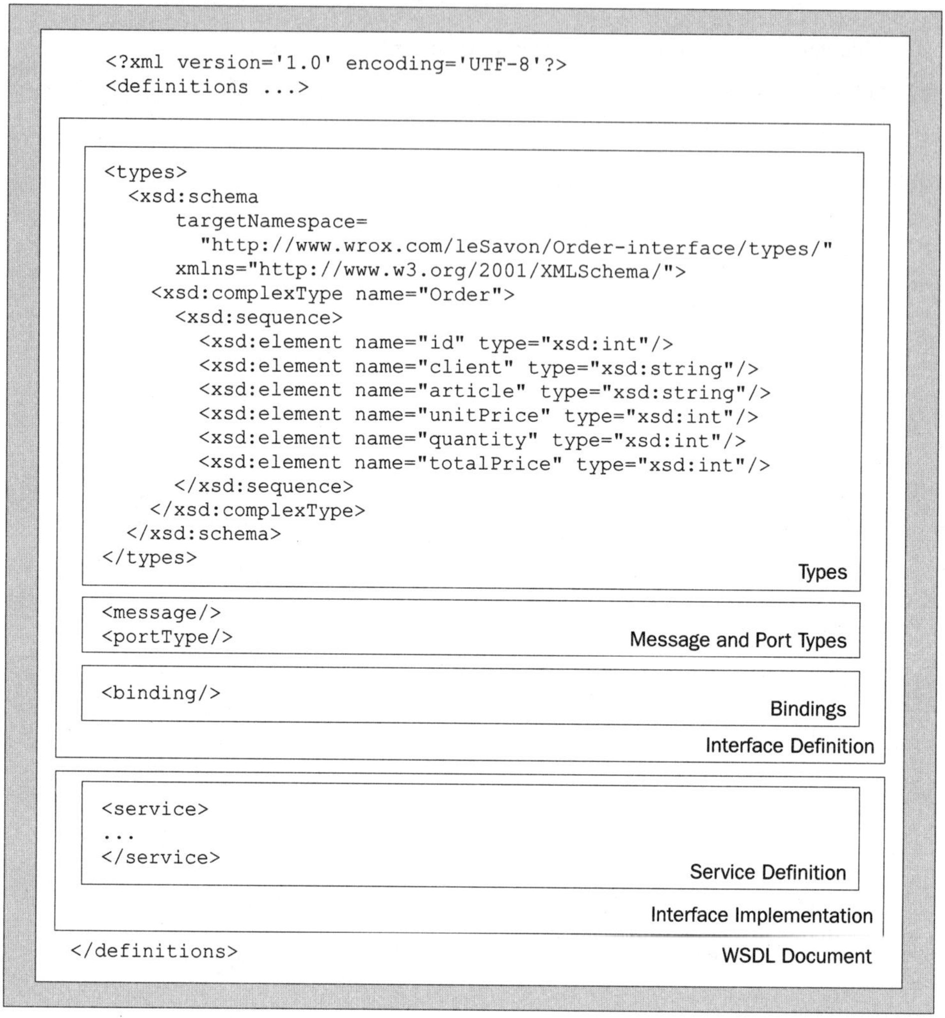

```
<?xml version='1.0' encoding='UTF-8'?>
<definitions ...>

<types>
  <xsd:schema
      targetNamespace=
        "http://www.wrox.com/leSavon/Order-interface/types/"
      xmlns="http://www.w3.org/2001/XMLSchema/">
    <xsd:complexType name="Order">
      <xsd:sequence>
        <xsd:element name="id" type="xsd:int"/>
        <xsd:element name="client" type="xsd:string"/>
        <xsd:element name="article" type="xsd:string"/>
        <xsd:element name="unitPrice" type="xsd:int"/>
        <xsd:element name="quantity" type="xsd:int"/>
        <xsd:element name="totalPrice" type="xsd:int"/>
      </xsd:sequence>
    </xsd:complexType>
  </xsd:schema>
</types>
```



```
<message/>
<portType/>
```



```
<binding/>
```



```
<service>
...
</service>
```



```
</definitions>
```


An integer is defined as `xsd:int`*. A string is defined as* `xsd:string`*. XML Schema Definition (XSD) is the recommended type system for WSDL for maximum interoperability and platform neutrality. WSDL treats XSD as the intrinsic type system. For a more in-depth discussion of the data types supported by XML schemas, please refer to Chapter 2.*

As we have seen in previous chapters, SOAP uses XML to encode its payloads. WSDL can be used to define web services that use XML as for encoding, but other standards like RMI can also be specified. In addition, it is legal to define multiple bindings for the same message. This flexibility allows WSDL to describe web services that use multiple protocols to communicate. For instance, a web service could use SOAP in an Internet situation and RMI in an intranet configuration.

After establishing what language is going to be spoken by the web service and its clients, we need to express what operations the web service can perform.

Web Service Operations

The operations supported by the web service are defined in two steps. The first step is to define the actual message that is going to transit from one endpoint to the other. A normal request-response exchange is made of two messages: one for the request and one for the response. For instance in the following figure, the `getOrderObject()` method contains a request made of a string (the user name) and an integer (the order identifier) and the response is one complex type (the `Order` object).

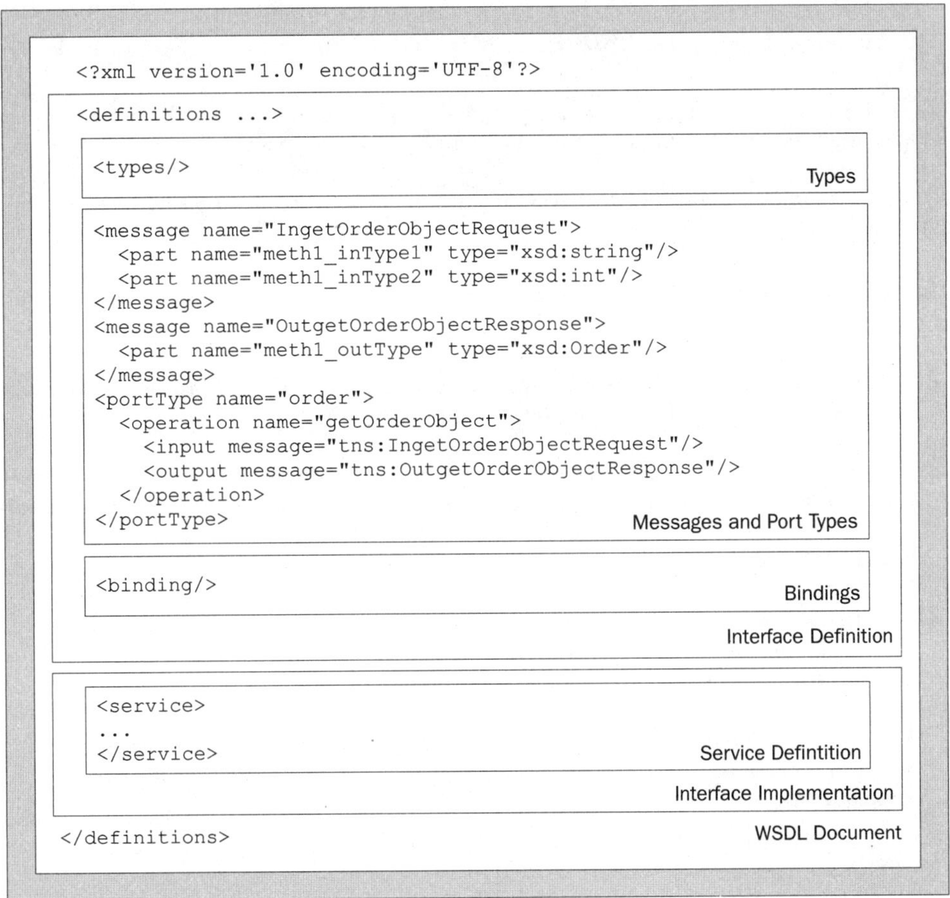

The components of a message are expressed as `<part/>` elements. Each message must have one or more parts. Each part usually has two attributes if XSD is used:

- `name="name of the component"`
- `type="xsd:type"`

XML namespaces are introduced in Chapter 2.

We may add our own attributes, if they are namespace-qualified to avoid conflicts with WSDL-defined attributes. An empty message used as a response denotes a method returning `void`. The `name` attribute exists for documentation purposes.

Speaking of documentation, there is one optional tag defined by WSDL that you might find useful to document your model: the `<documentation/>` tag is used to provide human-readable documentation. The `<documentation/>` tag is allowed inside any WSDL element.

> *The `xsd:mixed` XML schema data type denotes arbitrary text. The data type of the content of the `<documentation/>` tag in WSDL is `xsd:mixed` data.*

In the model used by WSDL, messages are grouped into operations that are themselves grouped into port types or endpoints. An operation must be named via the `name` attribute.

WSDL defines four **transmission primitives**, or ways of exchanging messages between an endpoint and its clients:

1. **One-way:** a message is sent to the endpoint. For instance, a client sends a message to a web service via SMTP.

2. **Request-Response**: this is what we are used to seeing in RPC protocols: we make a SOAP call and wait for the response from the server.

3. **Solicit-Response**: in this transmission mode, the endpoint is the client of another endpoint: it sends a message and receives a correlated response. RPC calls can also be initiated this way, however; in the solicit-response mode of operations, the web service makes the call.

4. **Notification**: this mode is another version of the one-way transmission primitive, where the endpoint sends the message rather than receiving it. This is similar to event notification in GUI development.

> *The Simple Mail Transfer Protocol (SMTP) is typically used to transfer human-readable e-mail over the Internet. SMTP can also be used as an asynchronous communication protocol for applications.*

The four transmission primitives we just described represent permutations of the presence or absence of the <input/> and <output/> tags. For instance, a one-way operation is:

```
...
<wsdl:operation: name="sayHelloToEndpoint">
  <wsdl:input: name="hello" message="helloMessage">
</wsdl:operation: ...>
...
```

The message referenced in the <input/> element must be a message defined in the WSDL document. The example below shows the `getOrderObject` operation as a Request-Response operation, since it defines an input message and an output message:

```
...
  <wsdl:operation name="getOrderObject">
    <wsdl:input message="IngetOrderObjectRequest"/>
    <wsdl:output message="OutgetOrderObjectResponse"/>
  </wsdl:operation>
...
```

The naming of the message is slightly different in this example: the input message starts with `In` and the output messages starts with `Out`. There is no particular significance to this notation; it only makes the intended use of the message more obvious. Also, nothing prevents you from using the output of one operation as the input to another operation.

Typically a web service supports more than one operation, so operations are placed in a container called a **port type** and marked up by the <portType/> tag.

This hierarchy of operations and port types is roughly analogous to what you find in an object-oriented language with classes (endpoints) and methods (operations). In fact, when WSDL describes an object, operations are the methods and port types are the classes or interfaces. In the previous example, you will probably have recognized the `RemoteOrder` interface, and one of its methods `getOrderObject()`.

We have been making the point that web services are about interoperability, but we have not seen anything in WSDL so far that facilitates the communication between software components written in different languages and running on different platforms. The <binding/> element is where the rubber hits the road when it comes to interoperability, as it defines how a web service operates.

Web Service Protocols

The <binding/> element, or simply **binding**, defines a concrete message format and a protocol for a given port type. For instance, in the figure below, we define a SOAP binding for the `tns:order` endpoint. As you can see, the binding references the port type using the `type` attribute. As we mentioned previously, other protocols like CORBA, DCOM, and RMI can be specified in addition to SOAP. The standard allows the definition of extensible bindings to support other protocols. To specify that the web service supports more than one protocol, we simply declare more than one binding for a given port type.

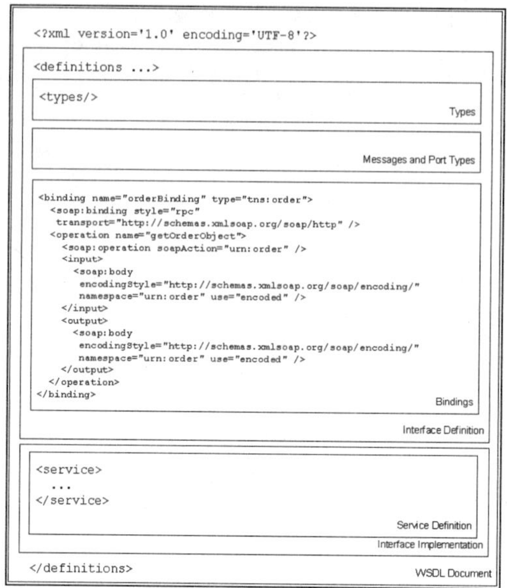

<?xml version='1.0' encoding='UTF-8'?>
<definitions ...>
<types/>
Types
Messages and Port Types
<binding name="orderBinding" type="tns:order">
<soap:binding style="rpc"
transport="http://schemas.xmlsoap.org/soap/http" />
<operation name="getOrderObject">
<soap:operation soapAction="urn:order" />
<input>
<soap:body
encodingStyle="http://schemas.xmlsoap.org/soap/encoding/"
namespace="urn:order" use="encoded" />
</input>
<output>
<soap:body
encodingStyle="http://schemas.xmlsoap.org/soap/encoding/"
namespace="urn:order" use="encoded" />
</output>
</operation>
</binding>
Bindings
Interface Definition
<service>
...
</service>
Service Definition
Interface Implementation
</definitions>
WSDL Document

You can see in the figure above that the type of the `<binding/>` matches the `<portType name="order"/>` defined earlier in the document. The `name` attribute is simply a unique name among all bindings defined in a particular WSDL document.

> *The word "binding" is overloaded by three meanings in this discussion, and it is important to keep a clear distinction among the three definitions:*
>
> 1. *The WSDL `<binding/>` element defines the protocol details for the operations of a port type.*
>
> 2. *The SOAP binding for WSDL as defined in Section 3 of the WSDL 1.1 specification, defines how WSDL `<binding/>` elements should define SOAP protocol details for port type operations.*
>
> 3. *The HTTP bindings for SOAP are defined in Section 6 of the SOAP 1.1 specification. They define how to use SOAP within HTTP. The HTTP bindings for SOAP have nothing to do with the WSDL `<binding/>` element.*

The binding in the previous example is a binding for the SOAP protocol. WSDL includes a binding for the SOAP protocol (version 1.1) along with bindings for HTTP `GET/POST` and `MIME`. We are mostly interested in the WSDL binding for SOAP; however, it is worth spending a few lines describing other possible bindings.

The bindings for HTTP `GET/POST` specify the grammar for defining web services that use simple HTTP methods like `GET` and `POST` as a programming interface. Essentially, the WSDL HTTP binding allows for the definition of the interactions between a web browser and a web server. However, the "web browser" can be any application. When using HTTP `GET`, the request is on the URL and the response is in the HTTP document. When using HTTP `POST`, the messages are in the HTTP document.

The main advantage of the HTTP binding is its simplicity: any web server can be transformed into a web service provider. However, that simplicity is also its major drawback: any interaction that does not fit the HTTP form model will stretch the model beyond its intended use.

The binding for MIME might seem surprising at first, but it is very convenient for providing additional data as part of a response. For instance, let's imagine that we want to implement a weather service. As part of that service, we provide a `getForecast()` method that we expose using SOAP. The response could be a structure (object) containing the usual elements of weather forecasting: minimum and maximum temperatures, humidity, cloud coverage and so on. In addition, we could also return a bitmap, JPEG or GIF, with the current satellite picture. We could specify the picture as an additional argument and encode it as part of a CDATA element; however, that encoding loses the type of the picture (a CDATA has no type other than "character data"). Alternatively, you could define an encoding for a JPEG and a GIF picture as an XML document.

Both solutions, although possible, are neither efficient nor elegant, as they merely re-invent what is solved by well-established standards. A better possibility that builds on existing technologies, and that does not lose the information about the data type of the picture, is to use the WSDL binding for MIME, which allows you to specify that in addition to the SOAP response, the `getForecast()` method also returns a picture.

The SOAP bindings for WSDL define complex rules to map message definitions to the content of a SOAP message, but here is a digest. Section 3 of the WSDL specification contains the SOAP binding rules.

The SOAP bindings are specified using four elements: `<soap:binding/>`, `<soap:operation/>`, `<soap:body/>`, and `<soap:fault/>`:

- `<soap:binding style="rpc|document" transport="uri"/>`
  A binding marked with this element must follow the SOAP protocol format: `Envelope`, `Header`, and `Body`. If the binding is for SOAP then the `<soap:binding/>` element must be present.

  The `style` attribute must be either `document` or `rpc`. The type `document` corresponds to a SOAP call that does not encode a method call, and is the default. Note that in the case of the example above, we use an RPC-style message since it is for a method call.

  The value of the `transport` attribute indicates which transport is being used to carry the SOAP payload. The URI `http://schemas.xmlsoap.org/soap/http/` corresponds to the HTTP bindings defined in the SOAP specification.

- `<soap:operation soapAction="uri" style="rpc|document"/>`
  The `<soap:operation/>` element provides information for the operation as a whole. The `soapAction` attribute defines the value of the `SOAPAction` header field. The `style` attribute has the same meaning as we saw earlier with `<soap:binding/>`.

- `<soap:body parts="nmtokens" use="literal|encoded" encodingStyle="uri-list" namespace="uri"/>`
  The <soap:body/> element defines how the message parts that we defined earlier in the document should appear inside the SOAP body. The parts attribute is optional, and its absence means that all the parts defined by the message are assumed to be included in the SOAP body. Its presence explicitly specifies what parts are included in the SOAP message. The data type of the parts attribute is nmtoken, which stands for the XML schema name token data type. In short, a name token is "any mixture of name characters". The list of the data types defined by XML schemas can be found at http://www.w3.org/TR/xmlschema-2/.

  The use attribute defines the type of encoding. This is similar to what we have been doing with the Apache SOAP framework: either your encoding maps to a schema, possibly self-described using xsd:types, or it is literal XML. The encodingStyle is a list of URIs that defines the encoding used. Most of the time it will be the encoding defined by SOAP in Section 5 of the SOAP 1.1 specification and referenced by the URI http://schemas.xmlsoap.org/soap/encoding/.

  The namespace attribute specifies the namespace of your application.

- `<soap:fault name="nmtokens" use="literal|encoded" encodingStyle="uri-list" namespace="uri"/>`
  The <soap:fault/> element defines the content of the SOAP fault element. The possible values for the attributes: name, use, encodingStyle, and namespace, are the same as for <soap:body/>.

With the rules taken into consideration, the meaning of the example above becomes clear:

- We define a binding for the endpoint order and we call it orderBinding.
- We define the binding for the getOrderObject() operation (method).
- The binding is for the SOAP protocol over the HTTP transport.
- The SOAP messages have an input and an output that will both be encoded using XML schemas and the rules defined in the SOAP 1.1 specification.

You will see shortly that tools are going to come to your rescue when it comes to putting together a WSDL document and the bindings for the SOAP protocol.

At this point, we know the what, the how, but we do not have the where. Where to find a web service is specified in the <service/> element that we describe in the next section.

Web Service Location

Once you have defined the protocols that are supported by your web service, you still need to give a specific URL where the clients can go. That definition is the main usage of the <service/> element.

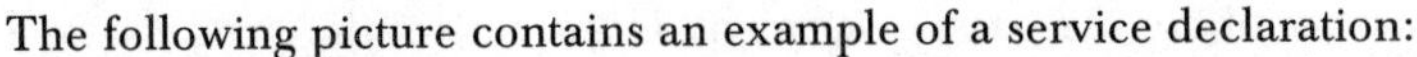

The following picture contains an example of a service declaration:

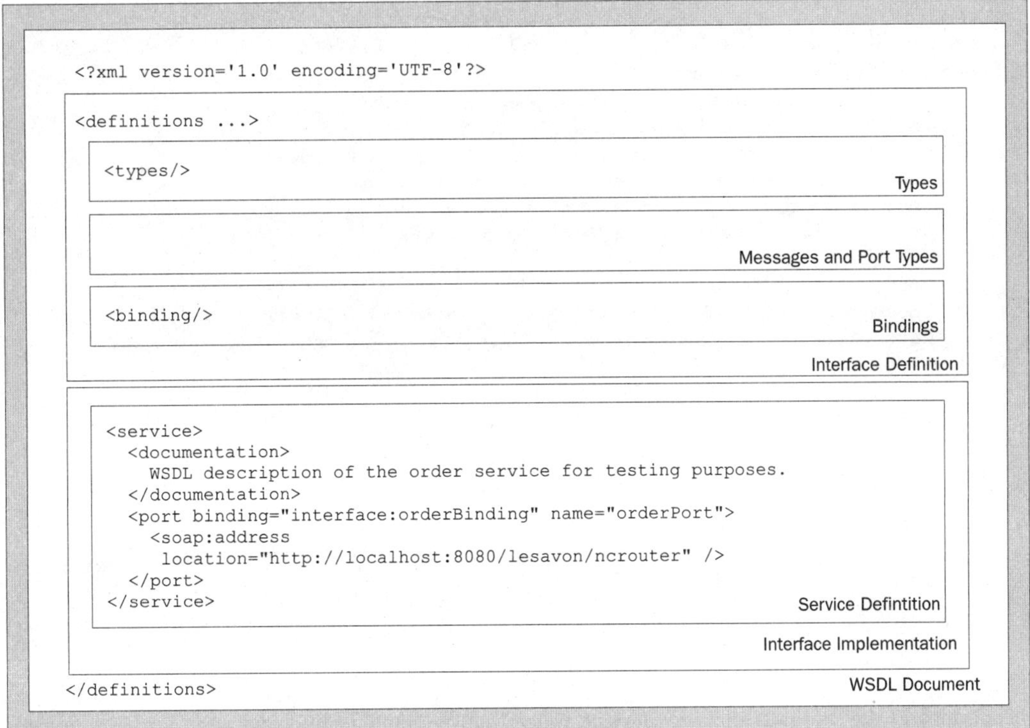

<?xml version='1.0' encoding='UTF-8'?>
<definitions ...>
<types/>
Types
Messages and Port Types
<binding/>
Bindings
Interface Definition
<service>
<documentation>
WSDL description of the order service for testing purposes.
</documentation>
<port binding="interface:orderBinding" name="orderPort">
<soap:address
location="http://localhost:8080/lesavon/ncrouter" />
</port>
</service>
Service Defintition
Interface Implementation
</definitions>
WSDL Document

The `binding` attribute must match one of the bindings defined earlier in the document, in this case `orderBinding`. As usual, the `name` attribute is a unique name for a service.

The `<documentation/>` element is the usual human-readable description that can be added to any WSDL element.

As we said previously, a service is a set of ports or endpoints, so when it comes to defining where to find a web service, you need to define exactly what ports are available. The `<port/>` element must reference a binding defined earlier in the WSDL document. In the example above, we reference the `orderBinding` binding.

Finally, we use the `<soap:address/>` element that is part of the SOAP binding for WSDL to assign a physical address (a URL) to the service port. The address of the service is http://localhost:8080/lesavon/ncrouter/, which is probably not a good address for outside clients, but does the job for debugging.

Before we conclude our introduction to WSDL, we need to go back to a point that we made at the beginning of this section about the separation of an interface definition from its implementation.

WSDL supports an `<import/>` element that allows you to include one WSDL document in another. The `<import/>` element can be used to keep the interface definition separated from the interface implementation. It can also be used to keep document sizes manageable.

Let's see a practical example of the use of the <import/> element. In the case of the Order service (order.wsdl), the interface implementation is quite short (most of the code is namespace definitions):

```
<?xml version="1.0" encoding="UTF-8"?>
<definitions name="order"
  targetNamespace="http://www.wrox.com/leSavon/Order"
  xmlns="http://schemas.xmlsoap.org/wsdl/"
  xmlns:interface="http://www.wrox.com/leSavon/Order-interface"
  xmlns:soap="http://schemas.xmlsoap.org/wsdl/soap/"
  xmlns:types="http://www.wrox.com/leSavon/Order"
  xmlns:xsd="http://www.w3.org/2001/XMLSchema">

<import
    location="http://localhost:8080/wsdl/order-interface.wsdl"
    namespace="http://www.wrox.com/leSavon/Order-interface">
</import>

<service name="order">
  <documentation>
     IBM WSTK V2.4 generated service definition file
  </documentation>
  <port binding="interface:OrderBinding" name="OrderPort">
   <soap:address location="http://localhost:8080/soap/servlet/rpcrouter"/>
  </port>
</service>

</definitions>
```

If you look at the <service> tag, you will notice that the name of the binding is from the interface definition, hence the qualified name interface:orderBinding.

This concludes our review of WSDL. We have seen that WSDL is used to answer three fundamental questions about a web service:

- **What?**
  The answer is defined in the <message/> and <portType/> elements.
- **How?**
  The answer is defined in the <binding/> elements.
- **Where?**
  The answer is defined in the <service/> elements.

We also saw that WSDL allows for the definition of the data types used by the web service inside a <types/> element, preferably using XML schemas.

Let's move from theory to practice and create a WSDL document for the sample application. To help us create a WSDL document for LeSavon.com, we will use a (free) utility provided by IBM: the web service ToolKit (WSTK).

The Web Services ToolKit (WSTK)

The Web Service Toolkit (WSTK) available at http://www.alphaworks.ibm.com/tech/webservicestoolkit/ is a set of tools that are built on top of the Apache SOAP and UDDI SOAP APIs. Among other things, it will help us in the generation of WSDL files. The download is free, but it requires registration. The download is rather large – about 38MB.

Most of the installation is straightforward. The following screenshots are from a Windows 2000 machine, but the installation is platform-independent.

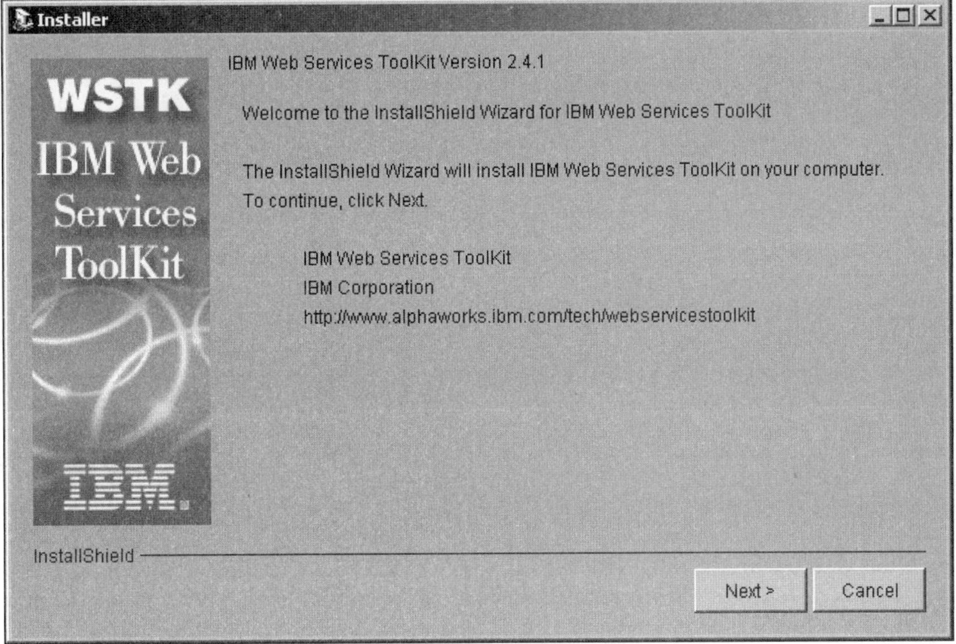

The install has the nasty habit of hanging after the first screen if you have a JDK prior to 1.3. So make sure that you have JDK 1.3 or later before running it. After clicking Next to take you through some installation tips, the licensing agreement, and confirming where your JAVA_HOME variable is and where you want the WSTK to be installed to (accept the default), you will come to the following:

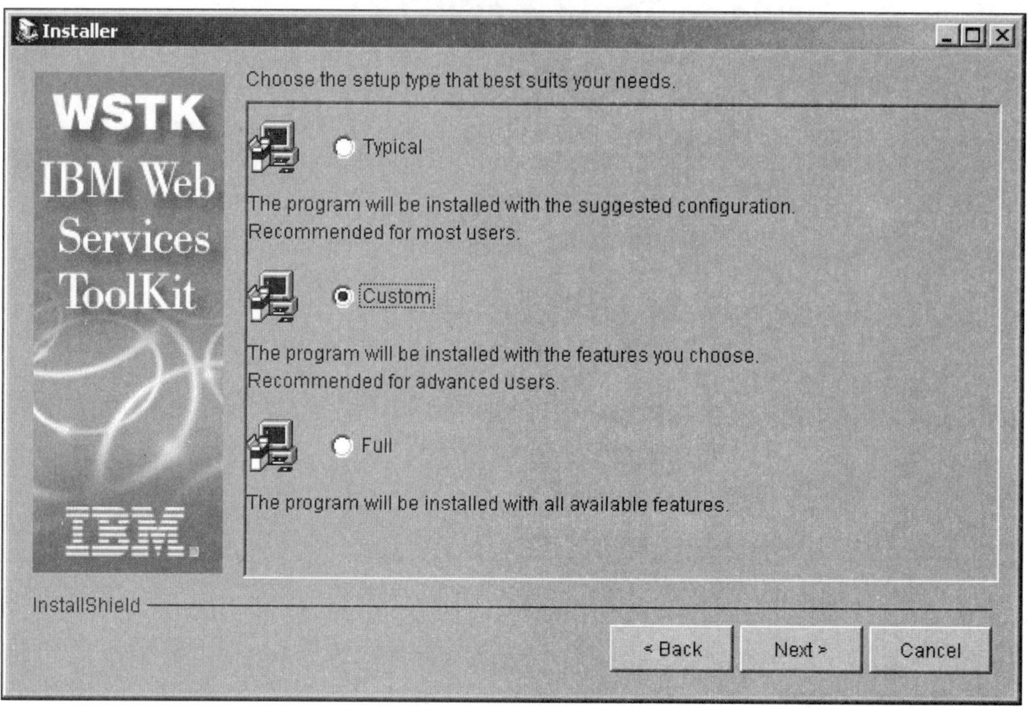

Be sure to select Custom to be able to select the servlet engine and the UDDI registry that you want to use. You can use the default for the other options in this wizard after this screen. The WSTK will now be installed.

Below is the Web Services Configuration Tool, which can be run after the installation to configure the web server and UDDI. We will work with the IBM test registry, but any other, including a local one, should work just fine. In the sample below, the directory of the Tomcat installation is C:\Jakarta-tomcat-3.2.3. You should replace this with the directory of your installation, if this is different.

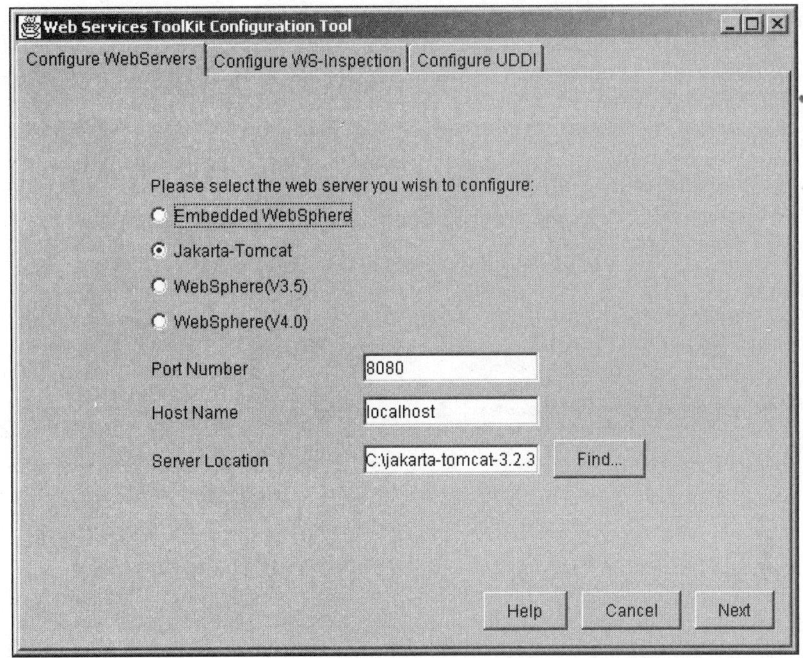

When you install WSTK, you might run into problems because the installation program tries to find the VM by itself and will not necessarily prompt you. So, if you have JDK 1.3 and the install still hangs, check that you do not have an older JVM hanging around.

Before going to the next step, which is used to configure your UDDI connection, you will need to apply for an account with one of the UDDI providers supported by the toolkit. For instance, to apply for an account with the IBM UDDI registry, go to the https://www-3.ibm.com/services/uddi/protect/registry.html URL as shown in the following figure:

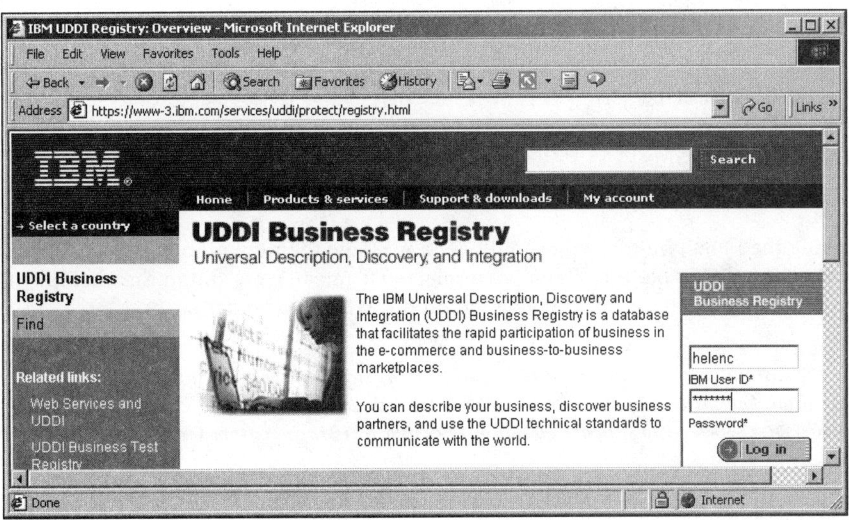

You can apply for an account by following the First Time? link. Applying for an account is free. Your account for the IBM UDDI registry can also be used for the test registry and vice-versa. However, you will have to enter an activation key the first time you login to each account. We will not use our UDDI account until Chapter 12 when we register LeSavon.com in a UDDI registry.

Once you have your account and password in hand, you have enough information to complete the last step. You can always leave the information blank and get back to it later by bringing up the WSTK configuration wizard: `wstkconfig.sh` or `wstkconfig.bat` in the `/bin/` directory of your WSTK installation.

You must provide a valid e-mail address during the registration process because IBM will mail you an activation key to enter the first time you logon to your account.

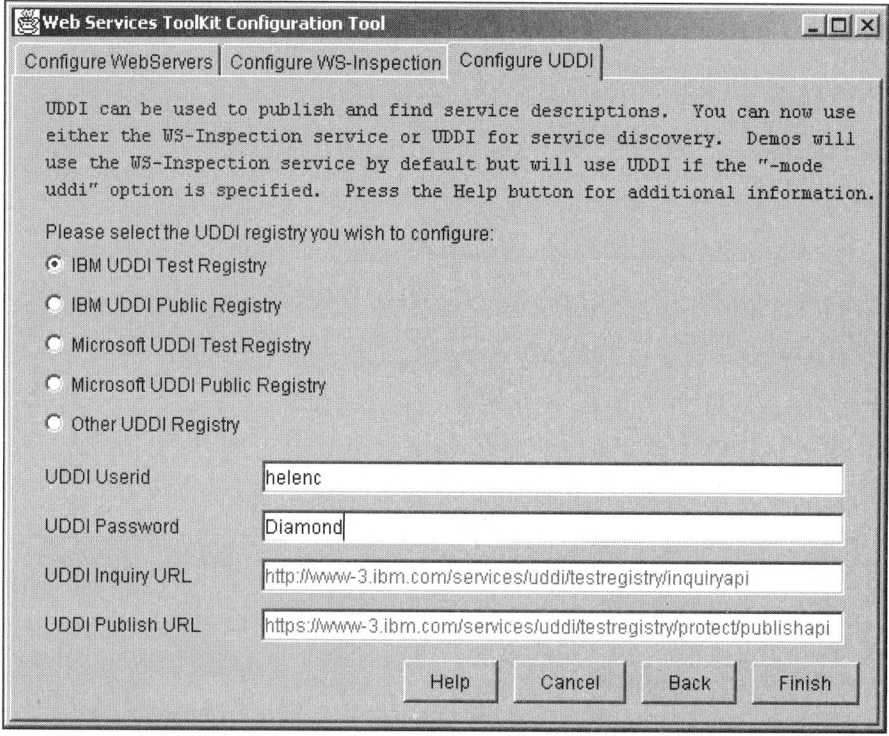

After clicking the Finish button, you should get a message telling you that The UDDI Registration Configuration [has] Completed. If you have selected Tomcat as we did in the example, the setup will modify your `tomcat.bat` or `tomcat.sh` to add the WSTK to your `CLASSPATH`.

After the installation, you will need to restart Tomcat if it is already running. The restart is required for Tomcat to take the new `CLASSPATH` into account. The WSTK installation modifies Tomcat's `CLASSPATH` to support UDDI queries and registrations from servlets and JSP pages.

We are now ready to generate the WSDL file for the `Order` service.

LeSavon.com WSDL

As you can see on the following figure, the WSDL Generation Tool supports the creation of WSDL files from a Java class, an Enterprise JavaBean JAR file, or a COM Dispatch interface (`IDispatch`). To open this utility, run the `wsdlgen.bat` program in `C:\wstk-2.4/bin`. We will only be using the Java class support of the utility.

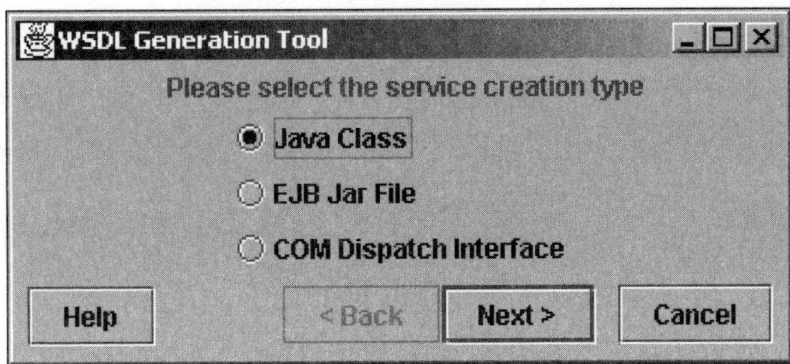

In fact, the WSDL Generation produces four outputs:

- **WSDL definition file:** contains the `<message/>`, `<portType/>`, and `<bindings/>`.
- **WSDL implementation file:** the `<service/>` tag along with an import of the WSDL definition file. This separation of a WSDL into two files has the advantage of decoupling the interface specification from the interface implementation. In theory, you could have multiple implementation files for one WSDL definition file.
- **Apache SOAP Deployment Descriptor:** these files should hold no secrets for us. We will not use the WSTK-generated deployment descriptor for the order service since we already have one from the previous chapters.
- **One or more serializers for complex types:** the serializers produced by the WSDL Generation Tool are equivalent in functionality to the `BeanSerializer` provided by the Apache SOAP implementation.

We will generate the WSDL files for the `RemoteOrder.getOrderObject()` method to give you an idea of the steps involved. The WSDL Generation Tool performs a valuable service by generating a skeleton WSDL we can use.

In order to utilize our WSDL files, we need to create a `/wsdl/` context to work inside. If you have configured the WSTK to work with Tomcat, run `wstkEnv.bat` or `wstkEnv.sh` (depending on your platform) in the `C:\wstk-2.4\bin` directory, and it will create the additional contexts it needs to run – except for `/wsdl/`, which we have to create manually.

The following snippet shows the new `tomcat.bat`, which is created by the environment utility. We have to alter the following line of code:

```
...
:chkClasspath
if "%CLASSPATH%" == "" goto noClasspath
set CP=%WSTK_CP%;%CP%;%CLASSPATH%
:noClasspath
...
```

We also need to create the `/wsdl/` context in `server.xml` in `C:\jakarta-tomcat-3.2.3\conf`. Add the following line of code:

```
<Context reloadable="true" path="/wsdl"
         docBase="c:\ProJavaSoap\Chapter11\webapps/wsdl/WEB-INF/classes"
         debug="0"/>
<Context reloadable="true" path="/ecounter_services"
         docBase="c:\wstk-2.4/demos/entity" debug="0"/>
```

Let's now specify the Java class to work with, as shown in this screenshot. First start the WSDL Generation Tool by running `wsdlgen.bat` in the `bin` directory of the Web Services Toolkit installation:

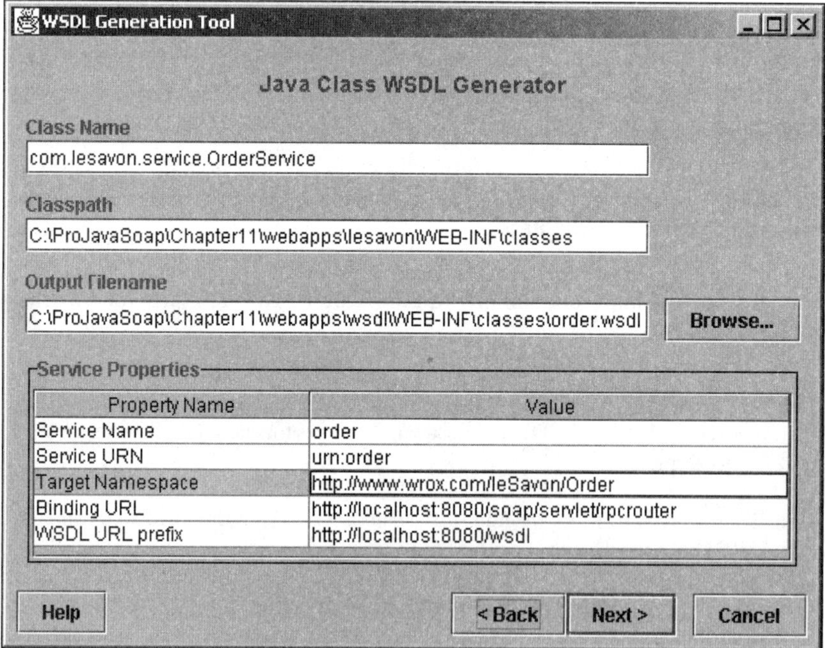

Make sure you enter the correct classpath and that you specify the service class, not the interface, since the tool does not work with an interface.

For the target namespace, it is reasonable to give the URL to your service. However, the target namespace will be used later to register the serializer for the `Order` class, and must match the namespace used by Apache SOAP. In our case, it is `urn:lesavon-order`, but the tool forces us to enter a path starting with http:// so we will enter http://www.wrox.com/leSavon/Order and manually modify the generated proxy to match our server-side definition.

The next step is where the "bugginess" of the tool comes to the surface. If you look at the next screenshot, you will notice that we selected the `getOrderObject()` method only. For some reason, the WSDL Generation could not generate the correct schema for an array of objects. If you encounter this issue in your application, you will have to hand-edit the schema contained in the generated WSDL file.

The red dots indicate the methods that do not return primitive types (`int`, `float`, `double`, `string`, and so on). It comes under the title **status**, presumably to indicate that its status of complex type might require manual intervention.

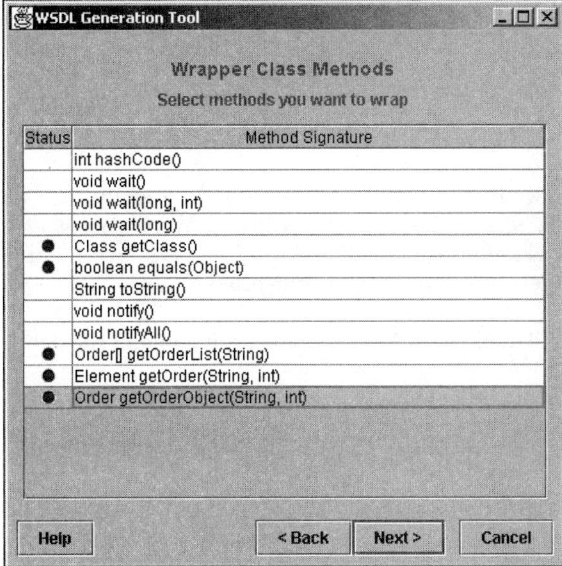

After selecting the `getOrderObject()` method, you will be asked to select the complex types for which the tool should generate a schema, as you can see on the next figure:

> *Another sign that the tool has not been given IBM's best efforts: complex is misspelled in the* Wrapper Comlex Types.

After selecting the complex types, you will be asked to confirm your choices and then the tool will do its magic and generate the aforementioned files. The two files that we are interested in are `order-interface.wsdl` and `order.wsdl`. These should now be in the `C:\ProJavaSoap\Chapter11\webapps\wsdl\WEB-INF\classes` folder.

Let's first look at the `order-interface.wsdl` file since it defines the interface of our web service:

```
<?xml version="1.0" encoding="UTF-8"?>
<definitions name="order"
  targetNamespace=
                  "http://www.orderserviceservice.com/OrderService-interface"
  xmlns="http://schemas.xmlsoap.org/wsdl/"
  xmlns:soap="http://schemas.xmlsoap.org/wsdl/soap/"
  xmlns:tns="http://www.orderserviceservice.com/OrderService-interface"
  xmlns:types=
        "http://www.orderserviceservice.com/OrderService-interface/types/"
  xmlns:xsd="http://www.w3.org/2001/XMLSchema">
```

When we generate our own files, it pays off to check them carefully – for some buggy reason, these files will sometimes be generated with the wrong namespaces. We are using `http://www.wrox.com/leSavon/Order` and `http://www.wrox.com/leSavon/Order-interface` for now, at least until we generate our proxy.

We saw earlier that a WSDL file is an XML document; it contains the definition of one service in this case: `order`.

```
<types>
  <xsd:schema
      targetNamespace=
         "http://www.orderserviceservice.com/OrderService-interface/types/"
      xmlns="http://www.w3.org/2001/XMLSchema/">
    <xsd:complexType
            name="Order"><xsd:sequence><xsd:element name="id"
            type="xsd:int"/><xsd:element name="client"
            type="xsd:string"/><xsd:element name="article"
            type="xsd:string"/><xsd:element name="unitPrice"
            type="xsd:int"/><xsd:element name="quantity"
            type="xsd:int"/><xsd:element name="totalPrice"
    type="xsd:int"/></xsd:sequence>
    </xsd:complexType>
  </xsd:schema>
</types>
```

Since we have a complex type (the `Order` class), the WSDL document contains the definition of an order using XML schema. The XML schema definition of an order is identical to the Java definition, as it should be.

```
<message name="IngetOrderObjectRequest">
 <part name="meth1_inType1" type="xsd:string"/>
 <part name="meth1_inType2" type="xsd:int"/>
</message>

<message name="OutgetOrderObjectResponse">
 <part name="meth1_outType"  type="types:Order"/>
</message>

<portType name="order">
  <operation name="getOrderObject">
   <input    message="tns:IngetOrderObjectRequest"/>
   <output message="tns:OutgetOrderObjectResponse"/>
  </operation>
</portType>
```

The `<message>` tag, along with the `<portType>` tag, defines what operations the service provides: there is one input or request message and one output or response message. The input message is made of a string (the user name) and one integer (the order identifier). The output message is made of one order object. There is one `portType` or method call in this case: `getOrderObject()`. However, we will not know that the message is for SOAP and that it represents an RPC call until we get to the `<binding>` tag.

```
<binding name="orderBinding" type="tns:order">
  <soap:binding style="rpc"
                transport="http://schemas.xmlsoap.org/soap/http"/>
 <operation name="getOrderObject">
   <soap:operation soapAction="urn:order"/>
    <input>
     <soap:body encodingStyle="http://schemas.xmlsoap.org/soap/encoding/"
                namespace="urn:order"
                use="encoded"/>
    </input>
    <output>
     <soap:body encodingStyle="http://schemas.xmlsoap.org/soap/encoding/"
                namespace="urn:order"
                use="encoded"/>
    </output>
  </operation>
</binding>
</definitions>
```

Now that we have a WSDL file that describes the `Order` service, the question is: what can you do with a WSDL file? Essentially, the WSDL file is useful for two things:

- **Publish your interface for others to use.**
  We will postpone this step until Chapter 12 where we introduce UDDI.
- **Generate a proxy to use the web service.**
  This is similar to what we did in Chapter 6, but with a different implementation. We will generate a proxy using WSDL in the next section.

WSTK Proxy

The proxy that is generated by the WSTK is based on a different philosophy than the `SavonProxy` that we developed in Chapter 6. The main difference is that it relies on a utility to generate the Java implementation of a proxy rather than using the dynamic proxy pattern. As we will see in the coming paragraphs, the end result is similar, except for the fact that the WSTK-generated proxy does not support the `inproc://` protocol that we used in Chapter 6.

> *The proxy sample is in the `ProJavaSOAP/Chapter11/Proxy` directory, as `src/com/lesavon/test/ProxyTest.java`.*

The `WSTK_HOME` shell variable, that points to the installation directory of WSTK, is defined by the WSTK installation and included in the user's list, as you can see in the following picture (on Windows 2000, right-click on My Computer, select the Advanced tab and then the Environment Variables... button):

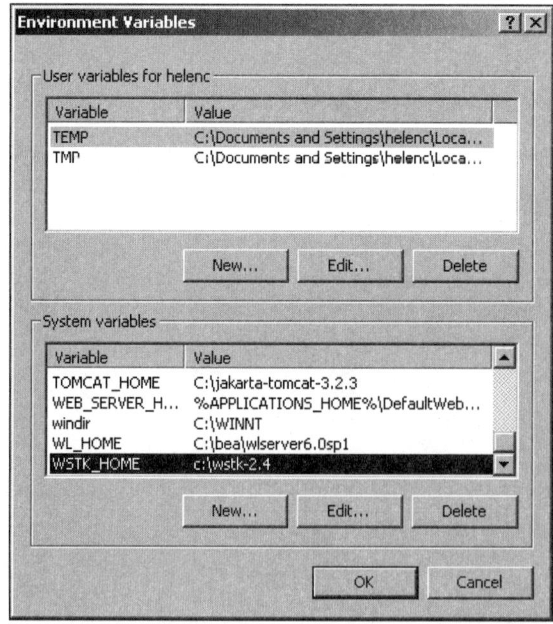

The following screenshot shows the steps required to perform this on a Windows 2000 machine.

Generating a proxy using the WSTK is easy, providing it throws no unexpected surprises. Key in the following commands, and make sure that your directory tree resembles the one below:

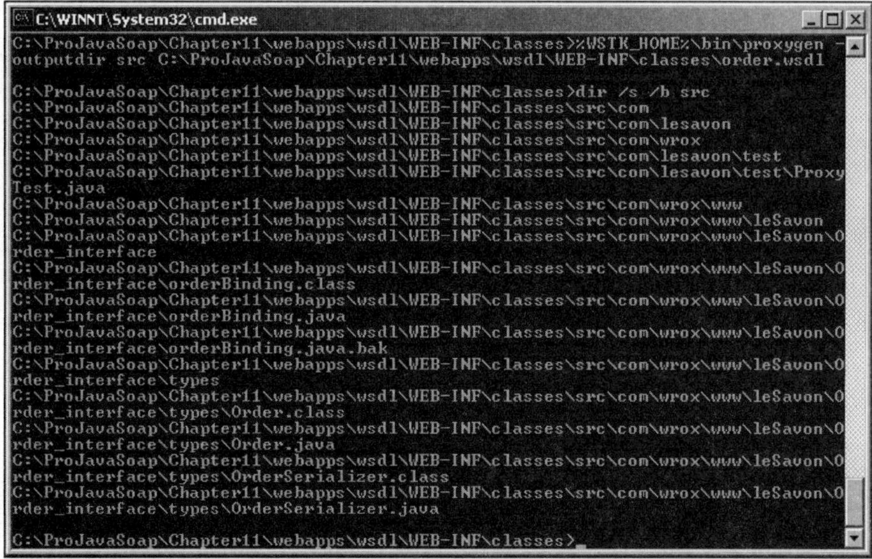

We can see in the output above the tool has generated three classes (the collaboration diagram below shows the interactions of the instances of the classes):

- `orderBinding.java`
  The proxy to the `Order` object
- `Order.java`
  The client-side version of the local object
- `OrderSerializer.java`
  A serializer for the `Order` object

Note that the class names are generated by the tool and do not always follow well established Java coding conventions. For instance, class names are not always capitalized and package names are not always in lower case. When we look at the code of the proxy, we will also see some irregularities and funny-looking variable names.

The mode of operations is as follows:

1. The client creates an instance of the proxy, `orderBinding`, and calls `orderBinding.getOrderObject()`.

2. The proxy, serializes the call into a SOAP call by calling `OrderSerializer.marshall()`.

3. The proxy makes the SOAP call using the Apache SOAP engine.

4. The proxy de-serializes the SOAP response with a call to `OrderSerializer.unmarshall()`.

5. The serializer/de-serializer creates an instance of the local `Order` object. Note that the local `Order` object has little resemblance to the `Order` object that we used in Chapter 5, since it does not follow the JavaBean design pattern and contains only one method: its constructor. We can see this in the following code snippet (formatted for readability):

```
/* Class for "com.wrox.www.leSavon.Order_interface.types.Order",  Schema source:
"http://www.wrox.com/leSavon/Order-interface/types/:Order" .*/
package com.wrox.www.leSavon.Order_interface.types;

public class Order
{
      public int        id;
      public java.lang.String   client;
      public java.lang.String   article;
      public int        unitPrice;
      public int        quantity;
      public int        totalPrice;

      public Order(){} //Default constructor required by de-serializer.

      public Order(int id, java.lang.String client,
                   java.lang.String article, int unitPrice,
                   int quantity, int totalPrice)
      {
            this.id= id;
            this.client= client;
            this.article= article;
            this.unitPrice= unitPrice;
            this.quantity= quantity;
            this.totalPrice= totalPrice;
      }
}
```

Let's now have a look at the proxy code. We will see that the implementation uses the Apache SOAP framework, in a similar fashion to the simple client that we developed in Chapter 5.

```
package com.wrox.www.leSavon.Order_interface;
/** Proxy object  "com.wrox.www.leSavon.Order_interface.orderBinding"  */

public class orderBinding{
  public static java.net.URL[] _KnownServiceLocations= null;
  private org.apache.soap.rpc.Call
        ________call=new  org.apache.soap.rpc.Call();
  private java.net.URL ________url= null;
  private java.lang.String SOAPActionURI = "";
  private org.apache.soap.encoding.SOAPMappingRegistry smr =
       ________call.getSOAPMappingRegistry();
```

The proxy object maintains an instance of a `Call` object and an instance of the `SOAPMappingRegistry` that we will initialize at the end of this file.

```
{static{
  try{
    _KnownServiceLocations=
        new java.net.URL[]{
           new java.net.URL("http://localhost:8080/soap/servlet/rpcrouter")
        };
  } catch(java.net.MalformedURLException e ){
  _KnownServiceLocations= new java.net.URL[0];
  };
}}

public orderBinding(java.net.URL endPointURL){
  ________call.setTargetObjectURI("urn:order");
  ________call.setEncodingStyleURI(
      "http://schemas.xmlsoap.org/soap/encoding/");
  this.________url = endPointURL;
  this.SOAPActionURI = "urn:order";
}
```

There is no empty constructor, so you must always specify a URL when constructing the proxy. However, you may use `_KnownServiceLocations` since it is public instance data.

```
public synchronized com.wrox.www.leSavon.Order_interface.types.Order
    getOrderObject (java.lang.String meth1_inType1, int   meth1_inType2)
    throws  org.apache.soap.SOAPException{
```

The signature of the `orderBinding.getOrderObject()` method is exactly the signature of the `RemoteOrder.getOrderObject()` method.

```
if(________url == null)
 throw new org.apache.soap.SOAPException(org.apache.soap.Constants.
         FAULT_CODE_CLIENT, "A URL must be specified \"orderBinding\"." );

this.________call.setMethodName("getOrderObject");
java.util.Vector ________parms  = new java.util.Vector(2);
________parms.addElement( new org.apache.soap.rpc.Parameter(
          "meth1_inType1", java.lang.String.class, meth1_inType1, null));
________parms.addElement( new org.apache.soap.rpc.Parameter(
              "meth1_inType2", java.lang.Integer.class,
              new java.lang.Integer(meth1_inType2), null));
this.________call.setParams(________parms);
org.apache.soap.rpc.Response ________resp =
              this.________call.invoke(________url, SOAPActionURI);
```

The instance of the Call object is initialized with the arguments of the call. If you forget about the unorthodox naming, this code should contain no surprises since we already used the same methodology in Chapter 5.

```
    if(________resp.generatedFault()){
      org.apache.soap.Fault ________fault = ________resp.getFault();
      throw new org.apache.soap.SOAPException(________fault.getFaultCode(),
                                              ________fault.getFaultString());
    }
    return(com.wrox.www.leSavon.Order_interface.types.Order)
  }

  ________resp.getReturnValue().getValue();
  }

    {
      com.wrox.www.leSavon.Order_interface.types.OrderSerializer ser_0 =
             new com.wrox.www.leSavon.Order_interface.types.OrderSerializer();
      smr.mapTypes("http://schemas.xmlsoap.org/soap/encoding/",
       new org.apache.soap.util.xml.QName("http://www.wrox.com/leSavon/
       Order-interface/types/", "Order"),
       com.wrox.www.leSavon.Order_interface.types.Order.class, ser_0,
       ser_0);

      new org.apache.soap.util.xml.QName("urn:lesavon-order",
      "order"),com.wrox.www.leSavon.Order_interface.types.Order.class,
      ser_0, ser_0);
    }
  }
```

This static initializer block is where we need to replace the namespace that we entered during the generation of the WSDL file with the namespace expected by our server: urn:lesavon-order. We also need to change the name of the complex type from Order to order since WSTK used the class name and we use the name order for the Order service. The generated code has been commented out above.

The introduction of the generated proxy will allow us to write a client as simple as the one we wrote in Chapter 6. We will review a simple client based on the WSTK-generated proxy in the next section and then we will compare the two methodologies. Let's begin with the client code.

ProxyTest

The ProxyTest class is a standalone console application that retrieves an order object using SOAP:

```
// ProxyTest.java
package com.lesavon.test;

import java.net.URL;
import com.wrox.www.leSavon.Order_interface.orderBinding;
import com.wrox.www.leSavon.Order_interface.types.Order;
```

We need to import the URL definition since it is used as an argument in the constructor of the proxy. We also need to import the proxy and the local definition of the `Order` class.

```
// A class to test the WSDL-generated proxy
public class ProxyTest {
  public static void main(String args[]) {
    System.out.println("com.lesavon.test.main: Entering...");

    try {
      orderBinding orderService = new orderBinding(
      new URL("http://localhost:8080/lesavon/ncrouter"));
```

We simply pass the URL for the service to the constructor of the proxy.

```
      Order order = orderService.getOrderObject("atase", 123456001);
```

The call to the `Order` service is a call to the proxy, and looks like a local Java method call: we get the `Order` object for order number `123456001` for user `"atase"`. Please refer to Chapter 5 for a description of the `RemoteOrder` interface and its methods.

```
      System.out.println("  The order #123456001 for atase is: ");
      System.out.println("    article     : " + order.article);
      System.out.println("    unit price  : " + order.unitPrice);
      System.out.println("    quantity    : " + order.quantity);
      System.out.println("    total price: " + order.totalPrice);

    } catch(Exception exception) {
      System.err.println("com.lesavon.test.main: Caught an exception: "
                         + exception);
    }
    System.out.println("com.lesavon.test.main: All done!");
  }
}
```

We print the fields of the `Order` object, which was returned by the server to show that everything went as expected. You will notice that our error handling strategy is simplistic, but adequate for a test application.

The `ProxyTest` class and the `GetOrders2` client that we wrote back in Chapter 6 are similar; however; there are differences on top of the obvious change in methodology. For instance, we saw in Chapter 6 that a limitation of the `SavonProxy` class, derived from its use of the dynamic proxy: it cannot handle interfaces that are not supported by the dynamic proxy.

Presumably, the WSTK-generated proxy would not suffer from the same restriction, although at the time of writing, the tool still contains some bugs and cannot handle all the data types used in our sample application. With time, the WSTK proxy should provide more coverage than a solution based on the dynamic proxy.

From a performance standpoint, the SOAP call from either proxy should be equivalent since they use the same technology, namely Apache SOAP. This statement is true with the exception of serialization: the WSTK-generated proxy uses a hard-coded serializer class that is potentially faster than the `BeanSerializer` used by Apache SOAP. However, that difference will be negligible unless you have very large objects to serialize.

Finally, the `SavonProxy` offers the advantage that it supports local and remote calls making it an ideal tool for debugging and deploying our application as we discussed in Chapter 6. It is possible to implement the same functionality for a WSTK-generated proxy, but at the time of this writing, it is not available.

As with many design decisions we have discussed in this book, it comes down to our application: do we need the flexibility of the `SavonProxy` class and are we willing to trade some performance for that flexibility? If not, we should consider using WSTK-generated proxies.

Build and Test

The ANT build file for the Proxy project is short and straightforward:

```
<project name="proxy" default="compile" basedir=".">
  <property name="app.name" value="proxy"/>
  <property name="deploy.home"
            value="C:/ProJavaSoap/Chapter11/webapps/wsdl/WEB-INF/classes"/>
  <property name="dist.home" value="${deploy.home}"/>

  <target name="prepare">
    <mkdir  dir="${deploy.home}"/>
  </target>
```

The output directory is the `/ProJavaSOAP/Chapter11/webapps/wsdl/WEB-INF/classes` directory and the `prepare` target simply consists of making sure the output directory exists.

```
  <target name="clean">
    <delete dir="${deploy.home}"/>
  </target>

  <target name="compile" depends="prepare">
    <javac srcdir="src" destdir="${deploy.home}"
           debug="off" optimize="on" deprecation="off"/>
  </target>

  <target name="all" depends="clean,prepare,compile"/>
</project>
```

The build of the application and the execution of `ProxyTest` is equally easy. Make sure that the classpath includes `soap.jar`, `mail.jar`, `activation.jar`, and `xerces.jar`.

The following screenshot shows the build steps and their results on Windows 2000:

```
C:\WINNT\System32\cmd.exe
C:\ProJavaSoap\Chapter11\webapps\wsdl\WEB-INF\classes>ant -buildfile BuildProxy.
xml
Buildfile: BuildProxy.xml

prepare:

compile:
    [javac] Compiling 4 source files to C:\ProJavaSoap\Chapter11\webapps\wsdl\WE
B-INF\classes

BUILD SUCCESSFUL

Total time: 2 seconds
C:\ProJavaSoap\Chapter11\webapps\wsdl\WEB-INF\classes>java com.lesavon.test.Prox
yTest
com.lesavon.test.main: Entering...
  The order #123456001 for atase is:
    article     : Senteur de Provence
    unit price  : 20
    quantity    : 5
    total price: 100
com.lesavon.test.main: All done!
```

Summary

With the introduction of the Web Services Description Language (WSDL), we have moved from the realm of SOAP development to the realm of web service development. We have defined a web service as a software component or application that facilitates interoperability across programming languages and operating systems by leveraging existing infrastructures rather than inventing new ones where possible. Specifically a web service exhibits four characteristics:

- A web service provides a TCP/IP-based interface.
- A web service provides a SOAP interface.
- A web service provides a definition of its capabilities using WSDL.
- A web service provides a publicly available description using a Universal Description, Integration and (UDDI) registry.

WSDL provides standardized answers to the questions that a client of a software component must ask:

- What language does the service speak? What functionality does the service provide?
- How do clients talk to the service?
- Where is the service?

In addition to providing a standardized answer to those questions, WSDL can also be used to generate `Proxy` classes and serializers that make the development of web service clients easier. In this chapter we introduced the Web Service Toolkit (WSTK) to demonstrate where the future of web service development lies.

We concluded the chapter by comparing the WSTK-generated proxy and the `SavonProxy` class that we developed back in Chapter 6. The type of proxy you choose will depend on the goals of your application.

To complete the transition of LeSavon.com from a SOAP service to a web service, we need to travel one last lap: we need to make the definition of our service publicly available. As we said in the introduction of this chapter, the potential of e-business will not be reached until companies can easily and dynamically select providers via their web services. In the last chapter of this book, we will bring LeSavon.com one step closer to that goal, by publishing its existence and definition in a UDDI registry.

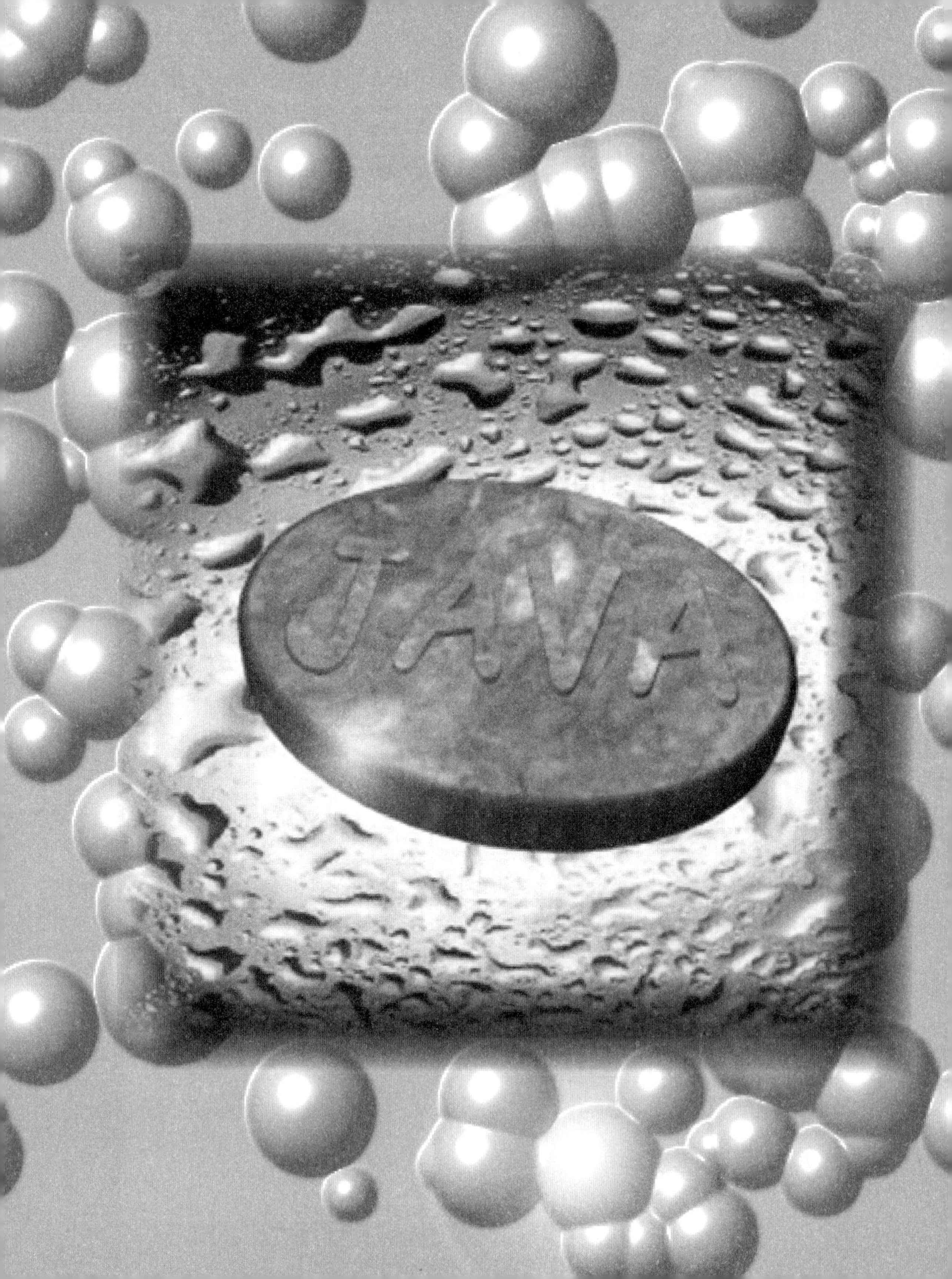
JAVA

12

UDDI

In the previous chapter, we defined the WSDL markup language and used it to define the capabilities of our web services. That definition is of little use if it is not published to potential users and customers. This is similar to the issues faced by a brick-and-mortar business: you need to get your name recognized, or at least available to get patrons to visit your establishment. A common way for people to find a business that provides a service that they need is to look in a phone book. A similar solution is needed for electronic business (e-business).

In addition to making the business and its description available, an electronic infrastructure and a standardized process are required for companies to automatically do business over the Internet. The main topic of this chapter is to refine the high-level definition of this problem and present a solution that is currently gaining momentum: the **Universal Description, Discovery, and Integration (UDDI)** industry standard.

UDDI is a vast topic and we will only scratch the surface of the technology and its applications in one chapter. In other words, do not expect this chapter to tell you everything that there is to know about UDDI. Rather, you should use this chapter as an introduction to UDDI and the APIs that are used to facilitate the access to the technology. We will provide several pointers to reference materials, should you want to learn more about the subject.

The same word of caution that we stated in the previous chapter about WSDL and the tools supporting it apply to UDDI: the technology is still in its infancy, and the tools are not always of the best quality. However, they are functional.

Before jumping into a technical description of what UDDI does, let's get some historical perspective.

History

UDDI grew out of the collaboration of three major industry players: IBM, Microsoft, and Ariba. IBM and Ariba have been active for a few years in the backend services that make Business-to-Business (B2B) possible. As we mentioned in Chapter 1 of this book, IBM and Microsoft were among the companies that collaborated on the SOAP specification. Ariba and Microsoft have collaborated in the XML space for BizTalk and commerce XML (cXML). A notable absentee from the list is Sun Microsystems, however, they have since embraced UDDI, only a couple of weeks after its announcement.

The UDDI organization runs a web site at http://www.uddi.org that serves both as a documentation web site and as a registry of services available over the Web. The community of companies that support UDDI is growing steadily and, at the time of this writing, counts over 300 members.

During the summer of 2001, Ariba dropped out of the triumvirate and the uddi.org web site is now only being run by IBM and Microsoft. However, the support of UDDI is not fading since other companies, such as Hewlett-Packard, are planning to launch their own registry. Additionally, in October 2001, SAP announced their plans to become a UDDI operator.

The UDDI registry on http://www.uddi.org went live on May 2, 2001.

Problem Statement

The three companies that we just mentioned decided to work together inside the UDDI partnership to solve three problems:

1. The discovery of services
2. The description of services
3. The integration of services

Each of these problems are solved independently, some with new technologies, some with a refinement of existing technologies.

Discovery of Services

The first problem is simply making people aware of the services that you offer. There is no Internet "backend server" phone book that gives a list of companies and their services. UDDI promises a solution to that problem by offering free registration and publication of company services. Note that this is not a revolutionary concept since CORBA supports a similar technology with Trading Services. Where UDDI differs, however, is in its simplicity.

Description of Services

Once the providers and consumers of web services have been put in contact, they are faced with the issue of describing their services in a manner that they can both understand. UDDI promises a solution to that problem by using an implementation-independent, XML-based description of services.

WSDL is fast becoming the standard for the description of web services, but it is not the only one. In fact, you can describe your service any way you want in a UDDI registry. For instance, you could use a modified version of the Apache SOAP deployment descriptors.

Integration of Services

The last problem UDDI wants to solve is the common language for web services: how do these backend services talk to each other? You are going to like the answer: they speak SOAP!

It is worth noting that UDDI is not just for web services – it can be used to store information about any of the software services of an enterprise.

Now that we have a better understanding of the problems, let's have a look at how UDDI intends to solve them.

UDDI Solutions

UDDI decided early on to rely on existing standards rather than inventing new ones. In other words, UDDI is not a revolution. This approach is similar to what the SOAP architects adopted. The technologies that UDDI decided to start from were:

- TCP/IP, HTTP, and HTTPS
- XML, XML Schemas, and WSDL
- SOAP

You might argue that packaging open protocols under one umbrella is no technology, but in the mind of the UDDI partners, allowing providers and consumers of web services to keep their existing solutions was a key requirement because the partners have radically different solutions to common problems.

Based on these existing technologies, UDDI defines a process for solving the three problems that we mentioned earlier. The UDDI process is described in the following figures. The first figure describes the process from a provider and consumer of web services point of view. Information on these web services are cached on portals and search engines, and then is accessed by potential business partners.

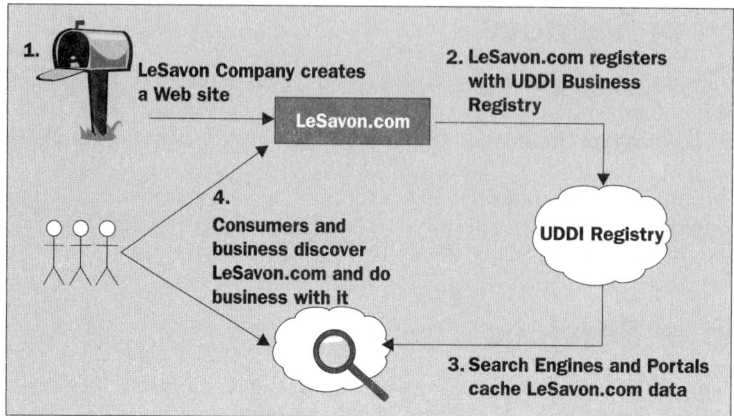

A portal is a web site that presents an integrated view of several sources of information or technologies. There are private portals built by companies for their employees and partners, and there are public portals built for a wide audience. A well-known example of a public portal is Yahoo!. A portal typically contains some customization capability, and, because they potentially integrate a lot of information, portals use search engines to speed up queries.

Search engines rely on a concept called spidering. Since they have to deal with a lot of information, querying web sites in real-time like you would do with a query to an RDBMS is not practical. Spiders are programs typically executed in a batch. They navigate the Web (hence the name spider) with the intention of caching descriptions and summaries of the web sites that they visit to a local storage. The access to the cached information is orders of magnitude faster than the access to the web sites.

The second figure describes the process from a registry of services standpoint.

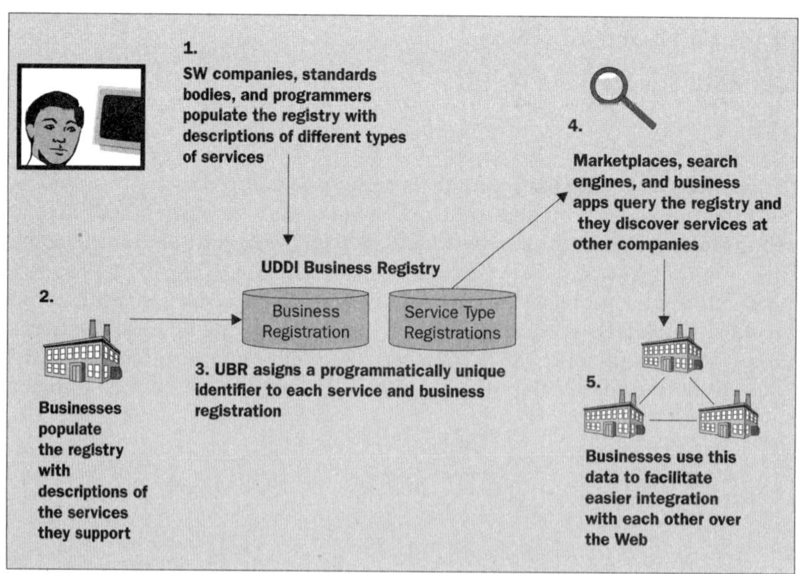

As you can see, the model is simple: LeSavon creates a web site, LeSavon.com, advertises the existence of the web site in the UDDI Business Registry, potential customers find out that the service is available by querying the registry, and finally clients use the service. As it is often the case, the problem is in the fine detail. So let's have closer look at the process.

The first step in the process is for software developers and standards organizations to decide what kind of services can be registered. Once the code is written and the registry initialized, the business can move in and register the services they want to offer. The registry is organized similarly to a phone book, and contains three kinds of pages:

- **White Pages**
  As you might expect, the white pages are indexed by the names of the businesses and contain information such as business name, contact information, phone number, fax number, and so on.

  In addition, White Pages contain data such as the DUNS identifier, a multi-language description of the business and its services, and so on. The Dun & Bradstreet Corporation provides data (including a credit rating) about businesses worldwide.

- **Yellow Pages**
  Yellow pages sort businesses by categories. This has a restricting effect on the number of taxonomies that you can use to register your business. The current version contains three taxonomies: NAICS, UN/SPSC, and location. The **North American Industry Classification System (NAICS)** provides common industry definitions for Canada, Mexico, and the United States. You can find out more about this at http://www.census.gov/epcd/www/naics.html. The **United Nations Standard Products and Services Code System (UN/SPSC)** provides a taxonomy for businesses and services based on a hierarchical system.

- **Green Pages**
  The green pages contain the business and technical descriptions of the web services offered. We will look more closely at the Green Pages shortly.

To implement this model, UDDI defines five primary data types. We will use those data types later when we write UDDI clients. A more detailed definition of these data types can be found at http://www.uddi.org/pubs/DataStructure-V2.00-Open-20010608.pdf.

- `businessEntity`
  The business entity is a placeholder for information about the business that we discussed earlier. The business entity is a service provider for one or more business services. The `businessEntity` stores the White and Yellow Pages data.

- `businessService`
  The business service record is the essence of the Green Pages since it contains the business and technical descriptions of a particular service. The business service is a container for a set of related web services. Examples of related web services are all the services for shipping or all the services for customer relationships management. The technical description of a web service is stored in a binding template.

- `bindingTemplate`
  A binding template is a container for a set of `tModels` (type of service), the actual technical description of the service. More precisely, a binding template is a container for `tModelInstanceInfo` records, which refer to the `tModel`.

- `tModel`
  The `tModel` is metadata about the service; `tModel` records contain three kinds of fields: the name of the service, the description of the service, and a set of URL pointers to the actual specifications of the web service.

- `publisherAssertion`
  The `publisherAssertion` describes the relationship between two parties, which is asserted by either one or both.

As web service developers, we are mostly interested in what goes inside a `tModel`. The specification for a `tModel` defines three attributes and five elements as you can see in the following XML schema snippet (the full UDDI schema can be found at http://www.uddi.org/schema/uddi_1.xsd):

```
<element name="tModel">
  <type content="elementOnly">
    <group order="seq">
      <element ref="name" />
      <element ref="description" minOccurs="0" maxOccurs="*" />
      <element ref="overviewDoc" minOccurs="0" maxOccurs="1" />
      <element ref="identifierBag" minOccurs="0" maxOccurs="1" />
      <element ref="categoryBag" minOccurs="0" maxOccurs="1" />
    </group>
    <attribute name="tModelKey" minOccurs="1" type="string" />
    <attribute name="operator" type="string" />
    <attribute name="authorizedName" type="string" />
  </type>
</element>
```

The attributes of a `tModel` are:

- `tModelKey`
  The `tModelKey` is the unique key assigned to the `tModel`. It is the only required attribute.

- `operator`
  The name of the UDDI registry site operator, (for instance, IBM UDDI Test Registry).

- `authorizedName`
  The name of the person who registered the `tModel`, (for instance, John Doe).

The elements of a `tModel` are:

- `name`
  A unique, human-readable identifier for the `tModel` record. The `name` is a required element.

- `description`
  A locale-aware description of the `tModel` record. The description is locale-aware because it carries a locale identifier, such as `en` (for England).

- `overviewDoc`
  This is a container element for remote descriptions and information. For instance, the overview URL contains a URL to a document that describes the web service. A recommended language to specify the description of a web service in a `tModel` is WSDL. Note that the WSDL document is referenced as a URL to keep the size of the registry manageable. This is similar to what we saw for LDAP in Chapter 7.

- `identifierBag`
  This is an optional list of name-value pairs that can be used during a search.

- `categoryBag`
  The category bag is a container for one or more name-value pairs called **keyed references**. The keyed references allow for a flexible taxonomy of `tModels`. If WSDL is used to describe the service, then the `tModel` should be classified using the `uddi-org:types` taxonomy, with the type `wsdlSpec`.

Here is an example of a `tModel` for LeSavon.com:

```
<tModel authorizedName="Alex Tase" operator="IBM UDDI Test Registry"
tModelKey="c1acf26d-9672-4404-9d70-39b756e62a5a">
  <name>LeSavon.com</name>
  <description xml:lang="en">
    WSDL description of the order service of LeSavon.com.
  </description>
  <overviewDoc>
    <description xml:lang="en">
      WSDL source document.
    </description>
    <overviewURL>
      http://www.wrox.com/leSavon/order.wsdl
    </overviewURL>
  </overviewDoc>
  <categoryBag>
    <keyedReference
     tModelKey="uuid=c1acf26d-9672-4404-9d70-39b756e62ab4"
     keyName="uddi-org:types"
     keyValue="wsdlSpec"/>
  </categoryBag>
</tModel>
```

LDAP and UDDI are directory services. LDAP is a general-purpose directory service. UDDI is a specialized directory service designed to store and retrieve web service descriptions. The slow-changing nature of the information stored in UDDI is compatible with the recommended usage of directory systems.

The UDDI organization has published a list of best practices for the use of WSDL in a UDDI registry. The recommended mappings between UDDI and WSDL can be found in the document Using WSDL in a UDDI Registry (the version number at the end of this link is irrelevant, only the latest version should be accessible) at http://www.uddi.org/.

UDDI APIs

UDDI supports two SOAP-based APIs: the inquiry API and the publication API.

> *The URL of the inquiry API for the IBM test registry is: http://www-3.ibm.com/services/uddi/testregistry/inquiryapi.*

> *The URL of the publication API for the IBM test registry is: https://www-3.ibm.com/services/uddi/testregistry/protect/publishapi. The publication API URL uses HTTPS.*

> *To manually login to the IBM test registry, you need to go to: https://www-3.ibm.com/services/uddi/testregistry/protect/registry.html.*

The inquiry API contains two classes of calls: `find_xx()` and `get_xx()`, where *xx* stands for `business`, `service`, `tModel` and so on. The `find_xx()` calls (for example, `find_business()`) are used to query the registry with search criteria, such as a regular expression, to match the business name. The `get_xx()` calls are direct calls to retrieve detailed information about a specific record in the UDDI registry. Records in the UDDI registry are identified by a unique key.

The publication API supports a set of calls to save business and service definitions in a UDDI registry: `save_xx()` (for example, `save_business()`).

We will use the inquiry API in the *FindLeSavon* section, when we look at an UDDI client that queries the registry to find `LeSavon.com`. We will go on to use the publication API in the *PublishLeSavon* section, when we look at an UDDI client that saves the definition of LeSavon.com along with the description of the `Order` service.

UDDI Support in LeSavon.com

As we mentioned earlier, LeSavon.com does not rely on UDDI to perform its operations, but it provides the necessary hooks for UDDI. Those hooks are:

- An entry in the IBM Test Registry describing the business and the web service (the Yellow and White Pages)
- A WSDL file at the company's URL describing the `OrderService` from a technical standpoint (Green Pages)

We will start by registering LeSavon.com and the `OrderService` with the UDDI registry, using the GUI provided by the IBM test registry. In the *FindLeSavon* section, we will write a UDDI client to query the registry and find the data we registered manually. Finally, in the *PublishLeSavon* section, we will write a more complicated UDDI client that programmatically registers LeSavon.com and the `OrderService`.

Registering LeSavon.com

We will register the `OrderService` class as a web service. Registering the `AdminService` class can be done by following the same process. In this case, we already have a class implemented (including a SOAP interface), so we simply need to register the information for the White, Yellow, and Green Pages. The White and Yellow Pages information is entered using the web pages provided by the IBM registry.

We will first register our business (LeSavon.com), we will then register a new service type (Order Service), and finally we will register a new service (`Order`). Note that if there was already an Order Service in the UDDI registry, we would use that existing type rather than inventing our own.

The following screenshot shows you an account that has no business and no service. The URL uses HTTPS as mandated by UDDI for registering or modifying businesses and services. Note that to get this page, you must first establish an account with the IBM test registry. This process is explained in Chapter 11, in the Web Services Toolkit set up section. The URL is http://www-3.ibm.com/services/uddi/testregistry/protect/publish.

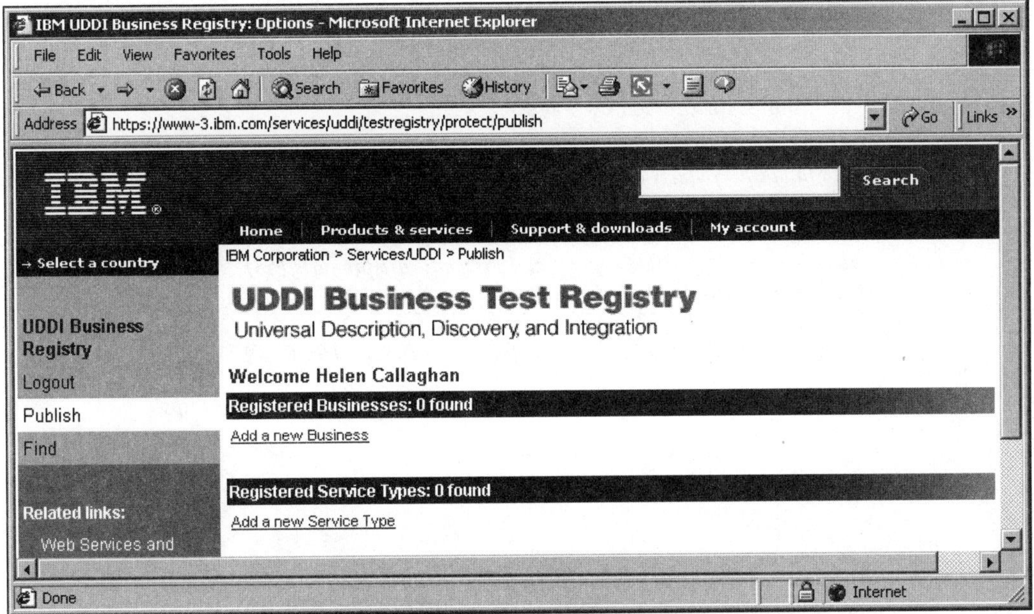

We will use IBM's test registry for the purpose of this demonstration, but you can use any other UDDI registry publicly available. The user interface will be different since UDDI does not standardize the user interface.

The first step is to create a business entry, so click on the Add a new Business link, and enter the name of the business as LeSavon.com.

Click on Continue to get to the next screen that allows you to enter a description of your business, business contacts, and a business locator. Click each of these the links and enter the required information:

- Business Description:
  Enter `Perfumes by catalog`.
- Business Contact:
  Enter under Name: `Henry Bequet` and under Role: `Java Developer`.
- Click on Continue, and more options will come up.
- EMAIL Address:
  Enter `hbequet@wrox.lesavon.com`.
- Business Locator:
  For Type: select the button specifying UNSPSC v7.3. Then select the Code button: 53.00.00.00.00. To get the correct value, you will need to drill down to the specific category by clicking on the arrow at the far right. Click on the subcategories until you get down to 53.13.16.20.00.
- The Description should now specify Perfumes or colognes or fragrances. Now click Add.

Entering the description of your business and its contacts is optional and straightforward. The locator is simply a list of taxonomies for the Yellow Pages.

The Universal Standard Products and Services Classification (UNSPSC) is a hierarchical classification of products and services For instance, the UNSPSC number for LeSavon is made of the following hierarchy:
- Top-level classification: Apparel, Luggage, and Personal care products (53)
- Family: Personal Care Products (53:13)
- Class: Bath and Body (53:13:16)
- Commodity: Perfumes, cologne, or fragrances (53:13:16:20:00)

For more information, you can go to the UNSPSC home page: http://eccma.org/unspsc/.

Click on **Continue** and then **Save** to apply your changes. Once you have entered all the information for your business, you should see a screen that looks like this:

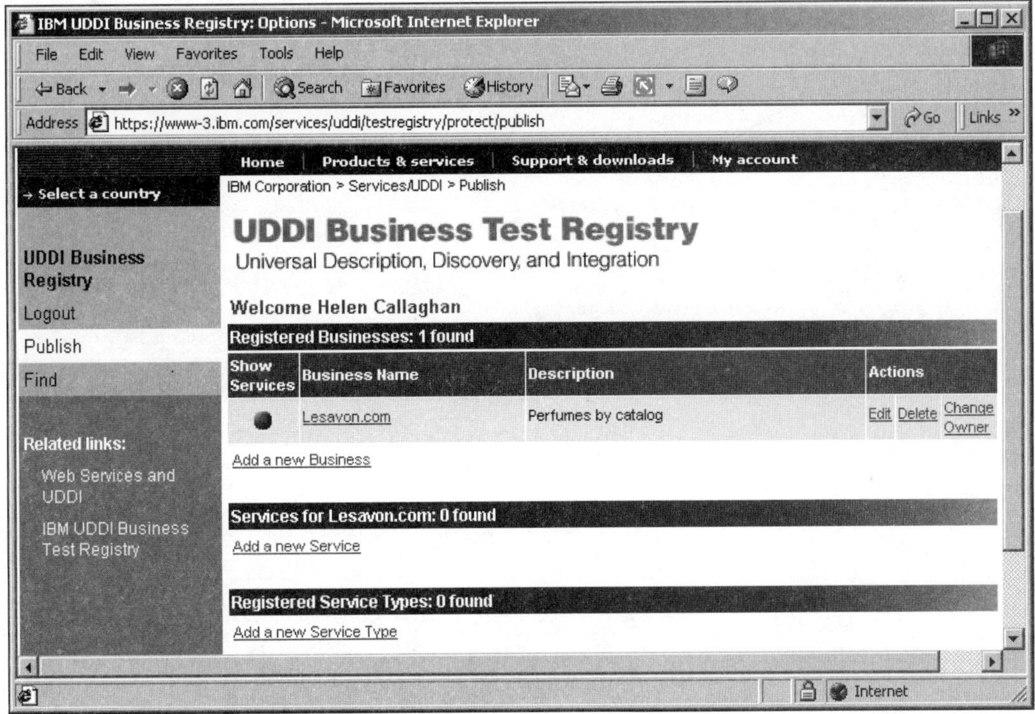

Before creating the order service, we will add a new service type with its description, the `order.wsdl` file. The service type that you register is public, because the more people that use the same service type definition, the more interoperable the service is. However, this is also a weakness of UDDI, and some would argue that this is a weakness of XML and its dialects. The problem is that nothing forces you to use the same service definition as another company and there is a risk of WSDL explosion. People's behavior, not the technology, will be the determining factor in the success of the promised interoperability of web services and UDDI.

To register a new service type, follow the **Add new Service Type** link on the bottom of the screen and enter the following information:

Name: `Order Service`

Click on **Continue** and follow the **Add an overview URL** link on the next page. This should bring up this page where you can enter the overview URL:

Overview URL: `http://www.wrox.com/lesavon/order.wsdl`

The overview URL is the URL to the description of our service, which is in WSDL. We will generate the WSDL description of our service in the next section. We can then accept our changes by clicking on Continue and Save on the following pages. Eventually, we will get back to the list of businesses and services, which should now include the new service type:

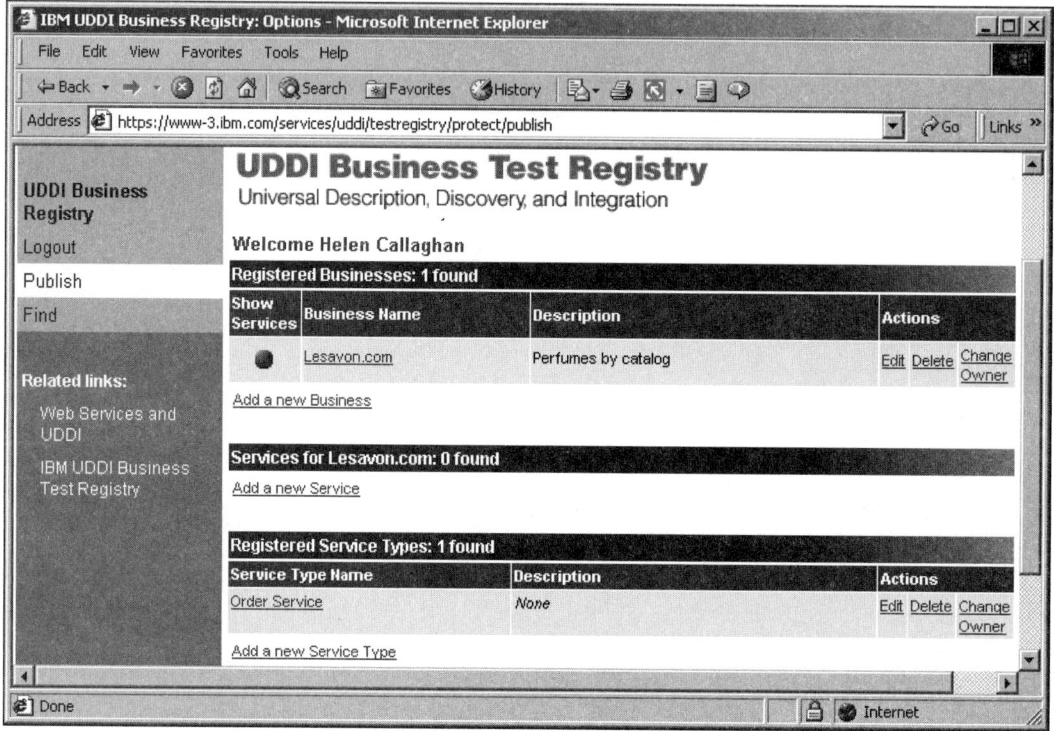

We can now proceed with the creation of a new service. Click on the Add a New Service link on the previous screen to bring you the next page where you enter the name of your service:

Under the Name link, enter `Orders`.

Click on Continue and then follow the link Add a new access point to bring up the next screen where you can enter the data for a new access point. An access point is a public URL for your service. Enter the following information:

- Service Type:
  Select http:
- Address:
  Enter `http://www.wrox.com/lesavon`

Make sure you select the service type as being HTTP. The possibilities at the time of this writing are `http`, `https`, `ftp`, `mailto`, `fax`, `phone`, and `other`. Click on Continue.

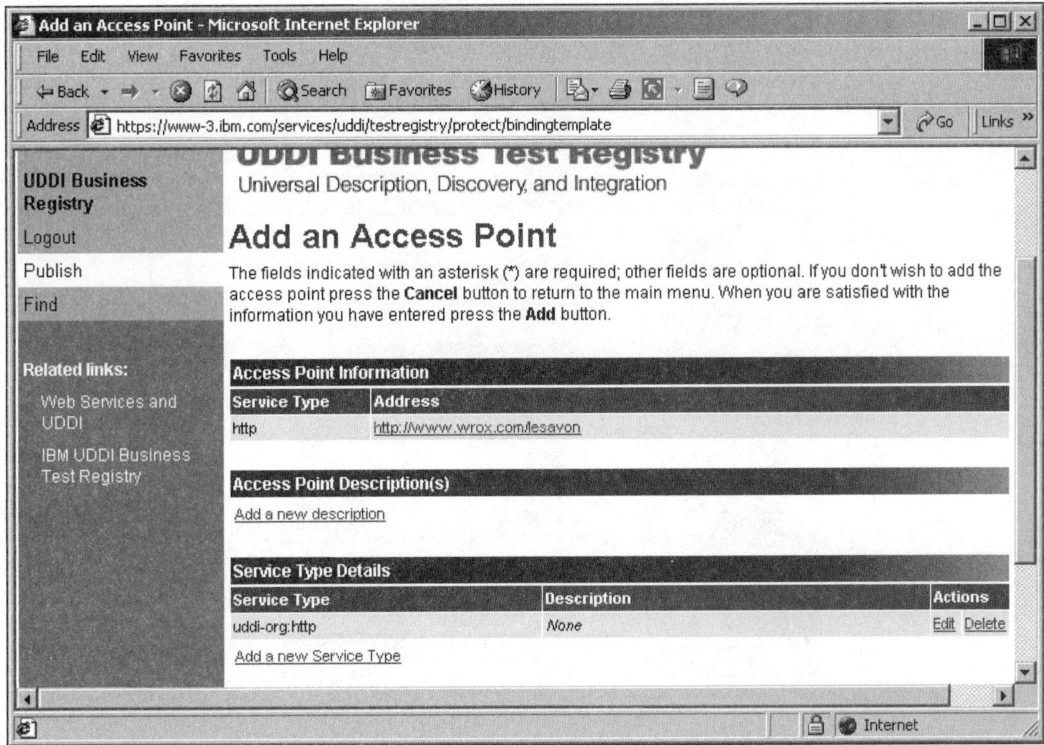

The access point description is optional – we can use it to enter descriptions in multiple languages.

We need to add another service type to point to the WSDL description of our service. To add a new service type to this access point, click on Add a new Service Type that should bring you the Find a Service Type page. This might be surprising at first: shouldn't we see a page displaying your service types? It all makes sense if you start thinking in terms of interoperability: web service developers should attempt to reuse existing service types as much as possible. Enter the name of the service type you are looking for as shown in the following picture:

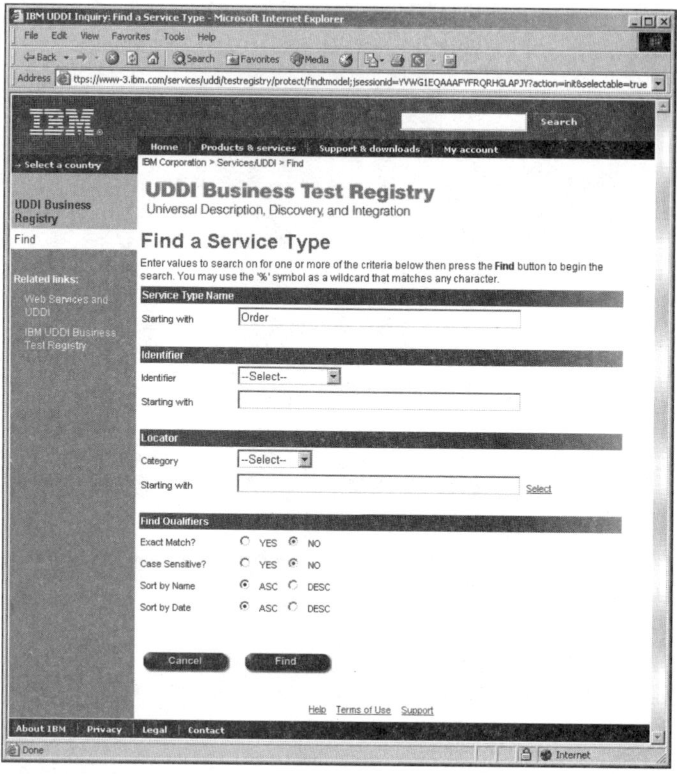

There are other ways to find a service type. For instance, you can use the locators that we encountered earlier. Click on Find, which will bring up the results:

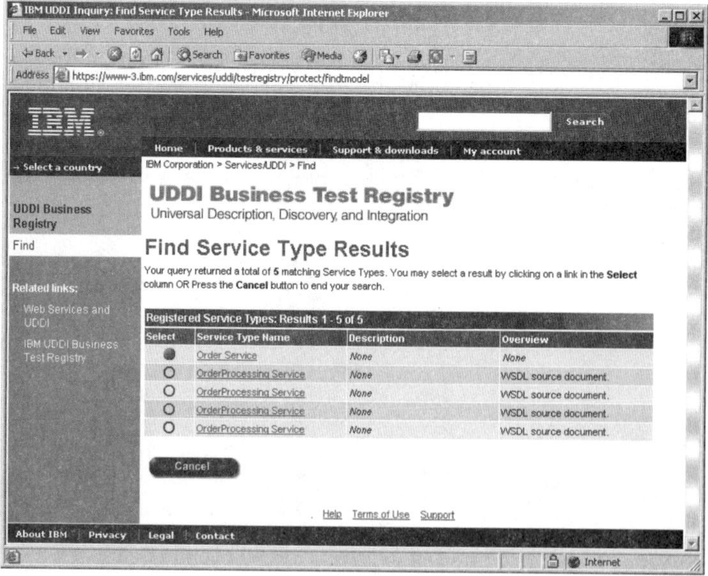

In this screen, we have already selected the service type that we want. The actual display might look different, depending upon the other service types with a name similar to ours that have been registered on the site. Click Return to go back and accept your changes:

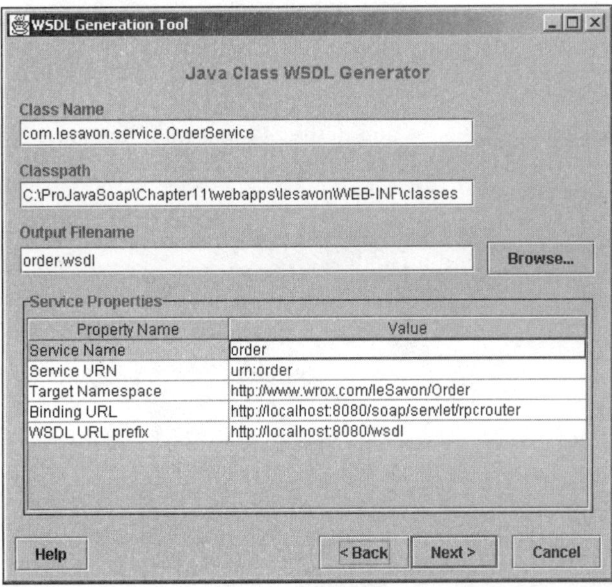

As you might have expected, the order service has two service types or `tModels`. Make sure to accept your changes and get back to the list of businesses and services, which should look similar to the illustration. Note that you will have to click on Continue and Save a few times before getting back to the final screen.

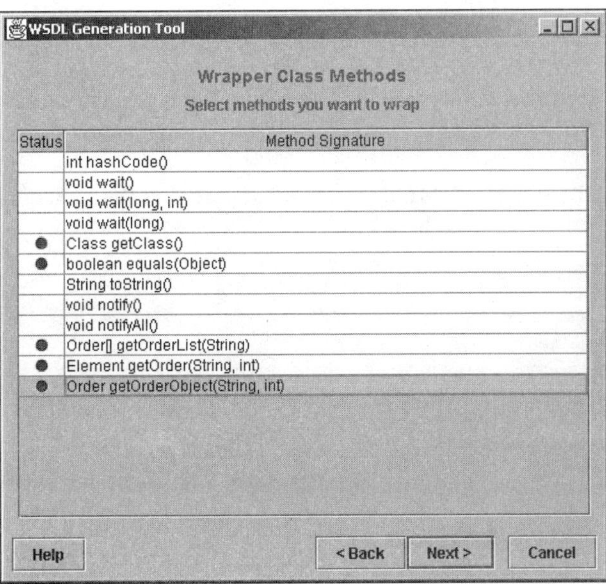

So what have we accomplished with this lengthy and tedious process? We have registered our service for others to use. We have not added any functionality to our service; we have simply made it available for people to search. This is the discovery portion of UDDI.

For instance, let's say that someone has heard that LeSavon.com offers an online service. They would go to the Find page (http://www-3.ibm.com/services/uddi/testregistry/find) of the UDDI registry and enter their search criteria:

In the Search for a: link, enter Business and in the Starting with: link enter `LeSavon`.

It should return the business that we entered previously:

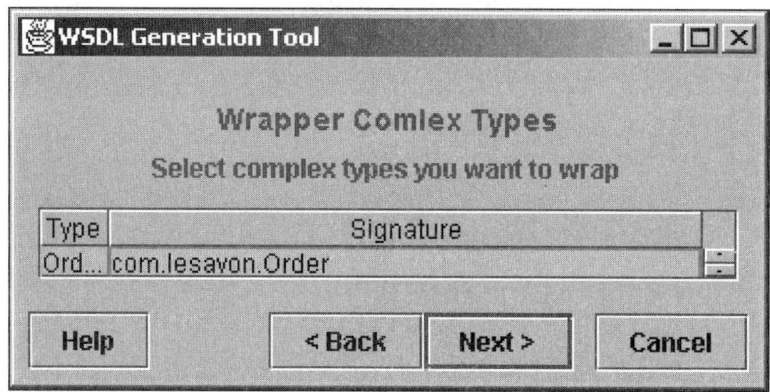

Alternatively, someone could be looking for any service in the perfumes, cologne, or fragrances industry and enter the UNSPC number 53:13:16:20:00 as a search criteria.

The discovery URL for a business contains the XML representation of the UDDI entry. The discovery URL of the service that we registered is http://www-3.ibm.com/services/uddi/testregistry/uddiget?businessKey=AC8AF3E0-B418-11D5-98D0-0004AC49CC1E. Note that by the time you read these pages, this business key will no longer be valid in the test registry. To test this feature, you will need to register your own business and enter your own key.

The UDDI registry GUI creates an XML document that describes the LeSavon.com business as well as the service that it supports:

```
<?xml version="1.0" encoding="utf-8" ?>
<businessDetail generic="1.0"
    xmlns="urn:uddi-org:api"
    operator="www.ibm.com/services/uddi" truncated="false">
  <businessEntity authorizedName="1000001JCG"
      operator="www.ibm.com/services/uddi"
      businessKey="AC8AF3E0-B418-11D5-98D0-0004AC49CC1E">
```

The business description is at the site operated by IBM. The business key is unique to LeSavon.com and assigned by the UDDI registry.

```
      <discoveryURLs>
        <discoveryURL useType="businessEntity">
            http://www-3.ibm.com/services/uddi/testregistry/uddiget?
            businessKey=AC8AF3E0-B418-11D5-98D0-0004AC49CC1E
        </discoveryURL>
      </discoveryURLs>
    <name>LeSavon.com</name>
    <description xml:lang="en">Perfumes by catalog</description>
    <contacts>
      <contact useType="Java Developer">
        <personName>Henry Bequet</personName>
        <email useType="Ask questions about the
            book.">hbequet@wrox.lesavon.com</email>
      </contact>
    </contacts>
  <businessServices>
    <businessService
        serviceKey="C7C44B10-B419-11D5-98D0-0004AC49CC1E"
        businessKey="AC8AF3E0-B418-11D5-98D0-0004AC49CC1E">
      <name>Orders</name>
      <bindingTemplates>
        <bindingTemplate
            bindingKey="C7C5F8C0-B419-11D5-98D0-0004AC49CC1E"
            serviceKey="C7C44B10-B419-11D5-98D0-0004AC49CC1E">
```

The `serviceKey` and `businessKey` will be different for your examples.

```
          <description xml:lang="en">
              Review your orders from LeSavon over the Web
          </description>
          <accessPoint
              URLType="http">http://www.wrox.com/lesavon
          </accessPoint>
        <tModelInstanceDetails>
          <tModelInstanceInfo
              tModelKey="UUID:68DE9E80-AD09-469D-8A37-088422BFBC36"/>
          <tModelInstanceInfo
              tModelKey="UUID:00FDA570-B41A-11D5-98D0-0004AC49CC1E"/>
        </tModelInstanceDetails>
```

The service key is assigned by the UDDI registry. Notice that you find the information that we entered earlier using the GUI. As you might expect, the order service contains two references to `tModels`: one for the HTTP access and one for the WSDL description.

```
        </bindingTemplate>
      </bindingTemplates>
    </businessService>
  </businessServices>
  <categoryBag>
```

```
        <keyedReference
            tModelKey="UUID:CD153257-086A-4237-B336-6BDCBDCC6634"
            keyName="Perfumes or colognes or fragrances"
            keyValue="53.13.16.20.00" />
      </categoryBag>
    </businessEntity>
    </businessDetail>
```

The category bag contains the key value for "`Perfumes or colognes or fragrances`": `53.13.16.20.00`. The `tModelKey` points to the UUID (unique universal identifier) assigned to UNSPSC by the UDDI operator.

To complete the registration, we must make the WSDL file that we generated in Chapter 11 (`order.wsdl`) available on our public web site. Since UDDI is a directory service, the WSDL file does not reside in the UDDI registry, it resides on the web server of LeSavon.com.

This addition of the discovery part of the UDDI specification is a milestone: the `OrderService` is now a web service since, according to the definition that we stated in Chapter 11, it meets all the criteria of a web service:

- **TCP/IP**
  The order service uses the HTTP transport.
- **SOAP**
  The order service uses the SOAP protocol.
- **Web Service Description Language (WSDL)**
  A public description of the order service is available from http://www.wrox.com/lesavon/order.wsdl.
- UDDI
  We have registered our service in a publicly available UDDI registry for all to use.

The registration of the `OrderService` in a UDDI registry allowed us to find the definition of the `Order` service through various queries, but what if the client wanted to fulfill the vision that we laid out at the beginning of this chapter? Namely, how does one query a UDDI registry programmatically? Writing a Java UDDI query program is the topic of the next section.

FindLeSavon

We mentioned earlier that a UDDI registry could be queried using SOAP. To ease the burden of SOAP development IBM has released the UDDI4J API (`uddi4j.jar`), which is included with the WSTK in the `uddi4j` directory. Note that the IBM Web Services Toolkit API (`com.ibm.wstk` package in `wstk.jar`) allows us to make higher-level calls that hide the UDDI data structures. For the purposes of this example, however, we have decided to use a lower-level API to demonstrate the practical use of the UDDI data structures, which we described earlier. If you decide to use the Web Services Toolkit API for your application, you will need to keep in mind that it uses the UDDI settings that we entered during the setup of the WSTK.

A detailed description of the UDDI4J API would take an entire book, so we will limit ourselves to two simple examples that will give you an idea of the possibilities. In this first example, we will query the UDDI registry for the information that we entered earlier using the web-based GUI.

Code Review

The sample is called `FindLeSavon.java` and the code can be found in the `ProJavaSOAP/Chapter12/FindLeSavon` directory.

```
// FindLeSavon.java
package com.lesavon.uddi.test;

import java.util.Vector;

import com.ibm.uddi.UDDIException;
import com.ibm.uddi.response.DispositionReport;
import com.ibm.uddi.response.BusinessList;
import com.ibm.uddi.response.BusinessInfo;
import com.ibm.uddi.response.ServiceInfos;
import com.ibm.uddi.response.ServiceInfo;
import com.ibm.uddi.client.UDDIProxy;
```

The UDDI4J API uses the `com.ibm.uddi` package. The `UDDIProxy` class is the main entry point of the API, and it contains the `find_xx()` and `get_xx()` methods of the inquiry API, as well as the `save_xx()` methods of the publication API.

```
public class FindLeSavon {
  public static void main(String args[]) {
    final String methodName = "com.lesavon.uddi.test.FindLeSavon.main";
    final String uddiSite =
        "http://www-3.ibm.com/services/uddi/testregistry/inquiryapi";
```

We will query the IBM UDDI test site, but you can change the value of the `uddiSite` variable to query other registries.

```
    if (args.length != 0) {
      System.err
        .println("FindLeSavon: finds LeSavon.com in IBM UDDI registry.");

      System.err.println("Usage: FindLeSavon");
      System.exit(1);
    }

    System.out.println(methodName + ": Starting test...");

    UDDIProxy proxy = new UDDIProxy();    // Create the UDDI proxy
```

We will use the proxy to query the registry. The `UDDIProxy` class contains methods to retrieve businesses, services, `tModels`, and so on. It also contains methods to register new entries in the UDDI registry: new businesses, new services, new entry points, and so on.

```
        try {

          // Set the UDDI registry to IBM UDDI site
          System.out.println("    Setting UDDI site to " + uddiSite);
          proxy.setInquiryURL(uddiSite);
        } catch (Exception exception) {
          System.err.println(methodName + ": Cannot set UDDI site to "
                             + uddiSite);
          System.exit(1);
        }

        try {

          // Find LeSavon
          System.out.println("    Searching for LeSavon...");
          BusinessList bizList = proxy.find_business("LeSavon", null, 0);
          Vector bizInfoVector =
              bizList.getBusinessInfos().getBusinessInfoVector();
```

We search for all names starting with `LeSavon`. You can query using other taxonomies like DUNS or UNSPSC.

Depending on the speed of your connection, you might see a noticeable delay since the `proxy.find_business()` method call actually makes a SOAP call to the UDDI registry.

```
          System.out.println("    Found " + bizInfoVector.size()
                             + " entry(ies):");

          // List the businesses
          for (int ndx = 0; ndx < bizInfoVector.size(); ndx++) {
            BusinessInfo businessInfo =
                (BusinessInfo) bizInfoVector.elementAt(ndx);
            System.out.println("      entry[" + ndx + "]: "
                + businessInfo.getNameString() + " ("
                + businessInfo.getDefaultDescriptionString()
                + "), business key is: " + businessInfo.getBusinessKey());
```

We display the name and the key for the businesses that we find. For each business, we then display the name and the key of the services that it owns.

```
            // For each business, we list the services
            ServiceInfos serviceInfos = businessInfo.getServiceInfos();
            Vector siv = serviceInfos.getServiceInfoVector();

            System.out.println("      There is(are) " + siv.size()
                + " service(s) registered for " + businessInfo.getNameString());
            for (int svcNdx = 0; svcNdx < siv.size(); svcNdx++) {
              ServiceInfo serviceInfo = (ServiceInfo) siv.elementAt(svcNdx);
```

```
              System.out.println("        " + serviceInfo.getNameString()
                  + ", service key is: " + serviceInfo.getServiceKey());
            }
          }
        } catch (UDDIException uddiException) {
          System.err.println(methodName + ": Cannot find LeSavon.com "
              + uddiException);

          DispositionReport dispReport = uddiException.getDispositionReport();
          if (dispReport != null) {
            System.out.println("  UDDIException faultCode:"
                + uddiException.getFaultCode() + "("
                + dispReport.getErrInfoText() + ")");
          }
```

In case things go badly, the DispositionReport gives us information on the cause of the problem.

```
          System.exit(1);
        } catch (Exception exception) {
          System.err.println(methodName + ": Cannot find LeSavon.com "
              + exception);
          exception.printStackTrace();
          System.exit(1);
        }

        System.out.println(methodName + ": All done!");
      }
    }
```

The remainder of the code is self-explanatory. Next, we will build and test this straightforward sample.

Build and Test

As we did for previous projects, we will build the FindLeSavon project using ANT and a build file: BuildFindLeSavon.xml, which can be found in the ProJavaSoap\Chapter12\FindLeSavon directory. The only difference between this project and the projects that we have built in the previous chapters is the addition of the uddi4j.jar file in the classpath. The following screenshot shows the now familiar build steps on a Windows 2000 computer:

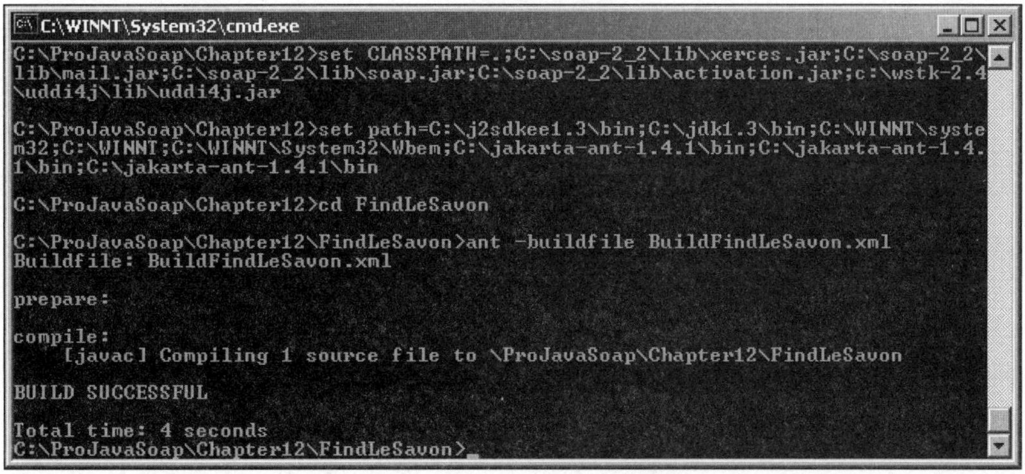

```
C:\WINNT\System32\cmd.exe
C:\ProJavaSoap\Chapter12>set CLASSPATH=.;C:\soap-2_2\lib\xerces.jar;C:\soap-2_2\
lib\mail.jar;C:\soap-2_2\lib\soap.jar;C:\soap-2_2\lib\activation.jar;c:\wstk-2.4
\uddi4j\lib\uddi4j.jar

C:\ProJavaSoap\Chapter12>set path=C:\j2sdkee1.3\bin;C:\jdk1.3\bin;C:\WINNT\syste
m32;C:\WINNT;C:\WINNT\System32\Wbem;C:\jakarta-ant-1.4.1\bin;C:\jakarta-ant-1.4.
1\bin;C:\jakarta-ant-1.4.1\bin

C:\ProJavaSoap\Chapter12>cd FindLeSavon

C:\ProJavaSoap\Chapter12\FindLeSavon>ant -buildfile BuildFindLeSavon.xml
Buildfile: BuildFindLeSavon.xml

prepare:

compile:
    [javac] Compiling 1 source file to \ProJavaSoap\Chapter12\FindLeSavon

BUILD SUCCESSFUL

Total time: 4 seconds
C:\ProJavaSoap\Chapter12\FindLeSavon>_
```

As you can see in the previous figure, the only output file is the `FindLeSavon.class` file.

If we run `FindLeSavon` against IBM's test registry, we will get the following results. Note that the key values will be different if you register your own business. As you would expect, the business and service keys are identical to those found in the XML document that we retrieved from the overview URL earlier:

```
C:\ProJavaSOAP\Chapter12\FindLeSavon\output>java com.lesavon.uddi.test.FindLeSavon
com.lesavon.uddi.test.FindLeSavon.main: Starting test...
   Setting UDDI site to http://www-3.ibm.com/services/uddi/testregistry/inquiryapi
   Searching for LeSavon...
   Found 1 entry(ies):
     entry[0]: LeSavon.com (Perfumes by catalog),
               business key is: AC8AF3E0-B418-11D5-98D0-0004AC49CC1E
     There is(are) 1 service(s) registered for LeSavon.com
       Orders, service key is: C7C44B10-B419-11D5-98D0-0004AC49CC1E
com.lesavon.uddi.test.FindLeSavon.main: All done!
```

Since the API ultimately understood by the UDDI registry is SOAP, we might be wondering what the SOAP messages look like. We can easily change the `uddiSite` variable to point to port 8081 of our local machine and use `tcpTrace` (which we discussed in Chapter 3) to look at the SOAP messages:

```
      final String uddiSite =
                    "http://localhost:8081/services/uddi/testregistry/inquiryapi";
```

If we run `FindLeSavon` a second time using `tcpTrace`, you will see that the request that goes to the UDDI registry is one of the `find_xx()` methods that we mentioned earlier – more specifically, a call to the `find_business()` method:

```
POST /services/uddi/testregistry/inquiryapi HTTP/1.0
Host: localhost
Content-Type: text/xml; charset=utf-8
Content-Length: 368
SOAPAction: ""

<?xml version='1.0' encoding='UTF-8'?>
<SOAP-ENV:Envelope xmlns:SOAP-ENV="http://schemas.xmlsoap.org/soap/envelope/"
xmlns:xsi="http://www.w3.org/1999/XMLSchema-instance"
xmlns:xsd="http://www.w3.org/1999/XMLSchema">
<SOAP-ENV:Body>
<find_business generic="1.0" xmlns="urn:uddi-
org:api"><name>LeSavon</name></find_business>
</SOAP-ENV:Body>
</SOAP-ENV:Envelope>
```

The response from the server is the UDDI data structure that describes LeSavon.com:

```
HTTP/1.1 200 ok
Connection: close
Proxy-Connection: close
Via: HTTP/1.1 www-3.ibm.com (IBM-PROXY-WTE-US)
Date: Sat, 29 Sep 2001 20:52:18 GMT
Server: IBM_HTTP_Server/1.3.12.2 Apache/1.3.12 (Unix)
Content-Length: 617
Content-Type: text/xml
Content-Language: en

<?xml version="1.0" encoding="UTF-8" ?>
<Envelope xmlns="http://schemas.xmlsoap.org/soap/envelope/">
  <Body><businessList generic="1.0" xmlns="urn:uddi-org:api"
operator="www.ibm.com/services/uddi" truncated="false">
    <businessInfos>
      <businessInfo businessKey="AC8AF3E0-B418-11D5-98D0-0004AC49CC1E">
        <name>LeSavon.com</name>
        <description xml:lang="en">Perfumes by catalog</description>
        <serviceInfos>
          <serviceInfo
            serviceKey="C7C44B10-B419-11D5-98D0-0004AC49CC1E"
            businessKey="AC8AF3E0-B418-11D5-98D0-0004AC49CC1E">
            <name>Orders</name>
          </serviceInfo>
        </serviceInfos>
      </businessInfo>
      </businessInfos>
    </businessList>
  </Body>
</Envelope>
```

In this case, the businessList contains only one entry.

PublishLeSavon

We will conclude this chapter by redoing programmatically what we did manually earlier: we will register the LeSavon.com business and OrderService with the IBM UDDI test registry. You will see in the following code that we use the data structures previously introduced as part of UDDI. One major difference between the inquiry API and the publish API is the level of security: UDDI mandates the use of HTTPS for any modification to the registry.

Code Review

Let's have a look at the code:

```
// PublishLeSavon.java

package com.lesavon.uddi.test;

import java.util.Vector;
```

```
import com.ibm.uddi.UDDIException;
import com.ibm.uddi.response.*;
import com.ibm.uddi.client.UDDIProxy;
import com.ibm.uddi.datatype.business.*;
import com.ibm.uddi.datatype.service.BusinessService;
import com.ibm.uddi.datatype.binding.*;
```

We can see that we need to import a lot more classes than we did in the `FindLeSavon` sample. The main reason for this is that we will build the data structures that make up the UDDI registry ourselves, as opposed to simply querying for business and services.

```
public class PublishLeSavon {
  public static void main(String args[]) {
    final String methodName = "com.lesavon.uddi.test.PublishLeSavon.main";
    final String uddiURL = "www-3.ibm.com/services/uddi/testregistry/";
    final String inquiryURL = "http://" + uddiURL + "inquiryapi";
    final String publishURL = "https://" + uddiURL + "protect/publishapi";
    final String tModelKey = "UUID:33752420-D778-11D5-8055-0004AC49CC1E";
```

We will use the inquiry API URL to query that our business and its service have been added to the registry. The publish API uses a different URL (`/protect/publishapi`) and, as we stated earlier, requires the use of the HTTPS protocol. Note that you will need to replace the value of the `tModelKey` if you want to run this sample against a service that you have registered yourself.

```
    if (args.length != 0) {
      System.err
        .println("PublishLeSavon: publish and finds LeSavon.com in UDDI.");

      System.err.println("Usage: PublishLeSavon");
      System.exit(1);
    }

    System.out.println(methodName + ": Starting test...");

    System.setProperty("java.protocol.handler.pkgs",
                       "com.ibm.net.ssl.internal.www.protocol");
    java.security.Security.addProvider(new com.ibm.jsse.JSSEProvider());
```

We specify IBM's SSL implementation for handling HTTPS. Note that since we are using HTTPS, you will not be able to use `tcpTrace` to look at the HTTPS packets as they travel between the client and the server, since they are encrypted.

```
  try {

    // Set the UDDI registry to IBM UDDI site
    System.out.println("    Setting UDDI site to " + publishURL
                       + ",\n      and " + inquiryURL);
    proxy.setPublishURL(publishURL);
    proxy.setInquiryURL(inquiryURL);
  } catch (Exception exception) {
    System.err.println(methodName + ": Cannot set UDDI site to "
                       + uddiURL);
```

```
    System.exit(1);
  }

  try {

    // We first publish the business and the service
    // Pass in userid and password registered at the UDDI site
    AuthToken token = proxy.get_authToken("user", "password");
```

We must provide a valid user name and password for the UDDI site in order to be allowed to publish business and service information in the registry. In order for this demonstration to work, you will have to substitute a valid user/password combination in the code above. The authorization token that is returned by the UDDI site using the `get_authToken()` method must be specified in all subsequent publishing calls. We assign the security token to the `token` variable.

```
    System.out.println("   Adding LeSavon business...");

    // We create a business entity for LeSavon with one contact
    BusinessEntity business = new BusinessEntity("", "LeSavon");
```

We will register LeSavon as opposed to LeSavon.com to avoid conflicting with the business that we registered manually.

```
    Contacts contacts = new Contacts();
    Contact contact = new Contact("Henry Bequet");
    Vector bVector = new Vector();     // businnesses
    Vector cVector = new Vector();     // contacts
    String bKey = null;                // business key

    business.setDefaultDescriptionString("Sells perfumes over the Web");
    cVector.addElement(contact);
    contacts.setContactVector(cVector);
    business.setContacts(contacts);

    // Save the business and its description in the UDDI registry
    bVector.addElement(business);
    BusinessDetail businessDetail =
        proxy.save_business(token.getAuthInfoString(), bVector);
```

We create a business entity data structure with one contact, and then we call the `proxy.save_business()` method to publish the definition of LeSavon in the UDDI registry. Note that there are more fields in a business entity object than just a contact: for example, there is a business key, a description, taxonomies, and so on.

If the call to `save_business()` is successful, then the method returns a `BusinessDetail` object, which is a container for a vector of `BusinessEntity` objects, each of which is a copy of the ones we passed as input, augmented with the business key returned by the UDDI registry. In this particular case, we have saved only one business, so the vector contains only one element. We will use the business key to register the service since a service must be associated with a business.

If you are using the IBM test registry for an execution of this sample, keep in mind that there is a maximum of one business definition per user account. In other words, you will have to delete any existing business prior to running this sample program. This can easily be achieved using the GUI that we reviewed earlier.

```
// We print the business entity returned to us by UDDI
bVector = businessDetail.getBusinessEntityVector();
bKey = ((BusinessEntity) bVector.elementAt(0)).getBusinessKey();
System.out.println("     Business key: " + bKey);

// We create the order service
BindingTemplates bindingTemplates = new BindingTemplates();
BindingTemplate bindingTemplate = new BindingTemplate();
Vector bndVector = new Vector();
Vector tVector = new Vector();

// We need a tModel retference to the OrderService type
TModelInstanceDetails tModelInstanceDetails =
    new TModelInstanceDetails();
TModelInstanceInfo tModelInstanceInfo = new TModelInstanceInfo();
tModelInstanceInfo.setTModelKey(tModelKey);
tVector.addElement(tModelInstanceInfo);
tModelInstanceDetails.setTModelInstanceInfoVector(tVector);

bindingTemplate.setTModelInstanceDetails(tModelInstanceDetails);
bndVector.addElement(bindingTemplate);
bindingTemplates.setBindingTemplateVector(bndVector);

// We create a business service object based on the binding template
// that we just created
BusinessService service = new BusinessService("", "order",
    bindingTemplates);
Vector sVector = new Vector();    // services
Vector sdVector = new Vector();   // service details

// Save the service and its description in the UDDI registry
service.setBusinessKey(bKey);
sVector.addElement(service);
ServiceDetail serviceDetail =
    proxy.save_service(token.getAuthInfoString(), sVector);
```

The creation of the business service is a little more complex than the creation of the business since it involves the definition of a `tModel`. The `tModel` key that we use points to the service type that we registered earlier. To use your own service type definition, you will have to replace the value of the `tModel` key with the value specific to our service type.

Saving the business service is similar to saving the business entity: we call the `proxy.save_service()` method and get a business service detail object back if everything went well.

```
// We print the service key of the service we just added
sdVector = serviceDetail.getBusinessServiceVector();
System.out.println("     Name        : "
    + ((BusinessService) sdVector.elementAt(0))
    .getNameString());
System.out.println("     Service key : "
    + ((BusinessService) sdVector.elementAt(0)).getServiceKey());

System.out.println("   ----- Done Adding -----");
```

The remainder of this test client is copied from the `FindLeSavon` example.

```
    // Find LeSavon
    System.out.println("   Searching for LeSavon and its services...");
    BusinessList bizList = proxy.find_business("LeSavon", null, 0);
    Vector bizInfoVector =
        bizList.getBusinessInfos().getBusinessInfoVector();


    System.out.println("   Found " + bizInfoVector.size()
        + " entry(ies):");

    // List the businesses
    for (int ndx = 0; ndx < bizInfoVector.size(); ndx++) {
      BusinessInfo businessInfo =
          (BusinessInfo) bizInfoVector.elementAt(ndx);
      System.out.println("     entry[" + ndx + "]: "
          + businessInfo.getNameString() + " ("
          + businessInfo.getDefaultDescriptionString()
          + "), \n       business key is: "
          + businessInfo.getBusinessKey());

      // For each business, we list the services
      ServiceInfos serviceInfos = businessInfo.getServiceInfos();
      Vector siv = serviceInfos.getServiceInfoVector();

      System.out.println("     There is(are) " + siv.size()
          + " service(s) registered for "
          + businessInfo.getNameString());
      for (int svcNdx = 0; svcNdx < siv.size(); svcNdx++) {
        ServiceInfo serviceInfo = (ServiceInfo) siv.elementAt(svcNdx);
        System.out.println("       " + serviceInfo.getNameString()
            + ", service key is: " + serviceInfo.getServiceKey());
      }
    }
  } catch (UDDIException uddiException) {
    System.err.println(methodName + ": " + uddiException);

    DispositionReport dispReport = uddiException.getDispositionReport();
    if (dispReport != null) {
```

```
            System.out.println("  UDDIException faultCode:"
                + uddiException.getFaultCode() + "("
                + dispReport.getErrInfoText() + ")");
          }

          System.exit(1);
        } catch (Exception exception) {
          System.err.println(methodName + ": caught an exception: "
              + exception);
          exception.printStackTrace();
          System.exit(1);
        }

        System.out.println(methodName + ": All done!");
      }
    }
```

Build and Test

If it were not for IBM SSL's implementation (included in the `ibmjsse.jar` library, found in the `%WSTK_HOME%\lib` directory), building the `PublishLeSavon` sample would be identical to building `FindLeSavon`.

Once again, we use an ANT build file (`BuildPublishLeSavon.xml`) as you can see in the following screenshot (which includes the new classpath):

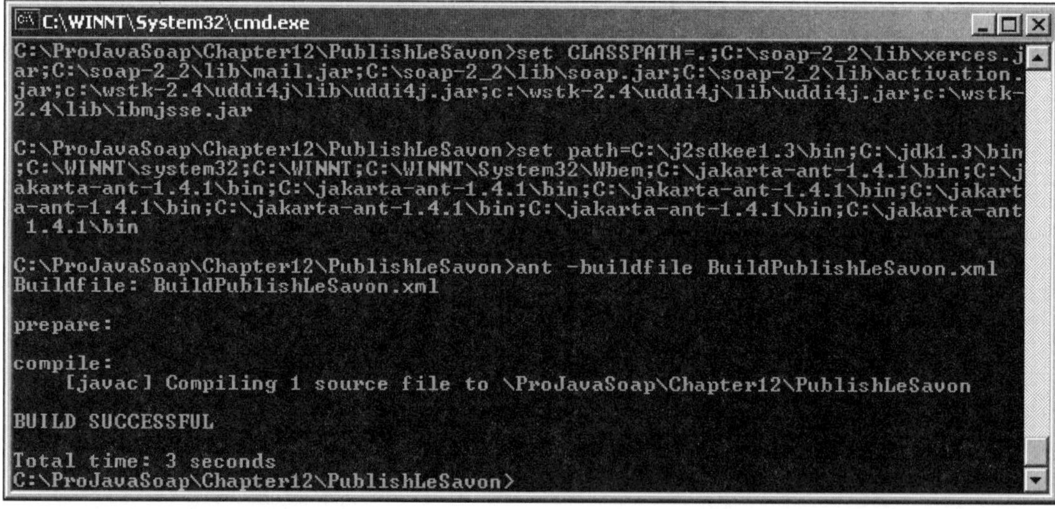

We said previously that the account used as the target for this test should not contain any business registration information if it is an IBM UDDI Test Registry account. Also, make sure that you have a valid `tModel` key. The key may point to a `tModel` defined by another account. If you are unsure of the key, visit the site below and click on the link, and the key will be displayed. The following screenshot shows the ideal state of the UDDI account, prior to running the sample:

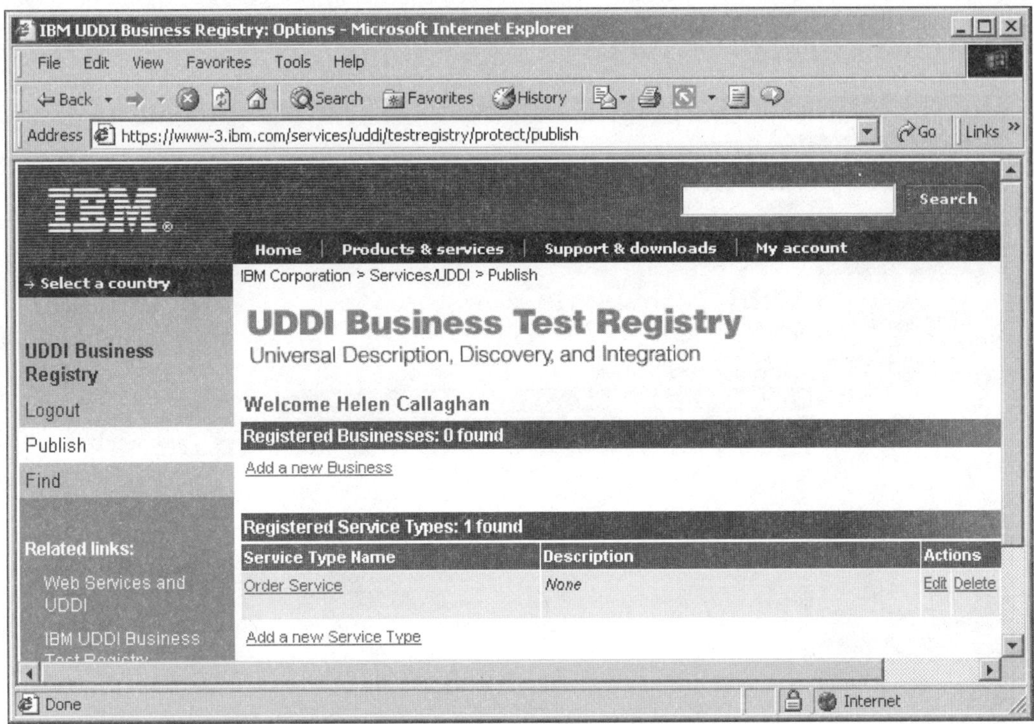

The command to run the sample is similar to the previous one:

```
C:\WINNT\System32\cmd.exe
C:\ProJavaSoap\Chapter12\PublishLeSavon>java com.lesavon.uddi.test.PublishLeSavo
n
com.lesavon.uddi.test.PublishLeSavon.main: Starting test...
   Setting UDDI site to https://www-3.ibm.com/services/uddi/testregistry/protect
/publishapi,
     and http://www-3.ibm.com/services/uddi/testregistry/inquiryapi
   Adding LeSavon business...
     Business key: E12AB240-DD33-11D5-9094-0004AC49CC1E
     Name        : order
     Service key : E1E7C0B0-DD33-11D5-9094-0004AC49CC1E
   ----- Done Adding -----
   Searching for LeSavon and its services...
   Found 3 entry(ies):
     entry[0]: LeSavon (Sells perfumes over the Web),
       business key is: F98D4CE0-CA27-11D5-A432-0004AC49CC1E
     There is(are) 1 service(s) registered for LeSavon
       order, service key is: FAAC7880-CA27-11D5-A432-0004AC49CC1E
     entry[1]: LeSavon (Sells perfumes over the Web),
       business key is: A198F1B0-BD0C-11D5-A432-0004AC49CC1E
     There is(are) 1 service(s) registered for LeSavon
       order, service key is: A2399E80-BD0C-11D5-A432-0004AC49CC1E
     entry[2]: LeSavon (Sells perfumes over the Web),
       business key is: E12AB240-DD33-11D5-9094-0004AC49CC1E
     There is(are) 1 service(s) registered for LeSavon
       order, service key is: E1E7C0B0-DD33-11D5-9094-0004AC49CC1E
com.lesavon.uddi.test.PublishLeSavon.main: All done!

C:\ProJavaSoap\Chapter12\PublishLeSavon>
```

The business and service keys will be different after each execution. The next screenshot shows that after running `PublishLeSavon` once, a new business and a new business service have been added to the IBM UDDI Test Registry:

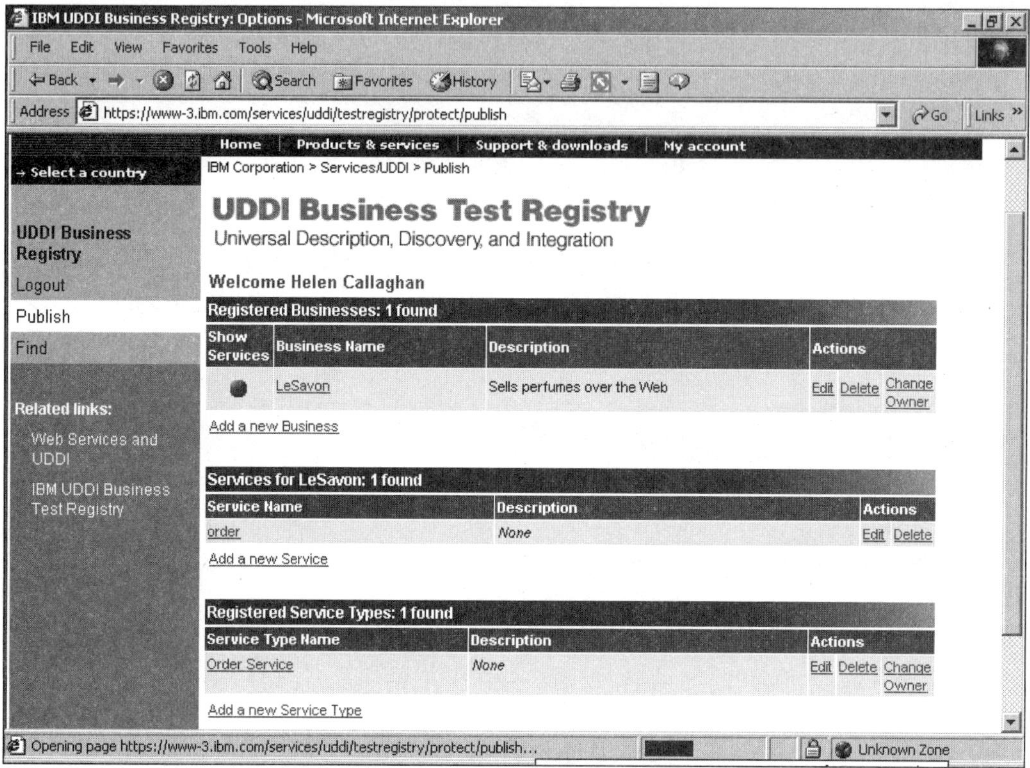

Summary

Web services and UDDI are still in their infancy. Working with UDDI in general requires a lot of manual data entry work, and is probably too much work at this point. However, UDDI is a step in the right direction since it facilitates e-commerce.

UDDI provides a global business registry that organizes businesses and their services in three categories:

- **White Pages**: provides the name and contacts for the business.
- **Yellow Pages**: provides taxonomies for easy discovery.
- **Green Pages**: provides the technical descriptions of the published services using `tModels`.

Since UDDI relies heavily on open standards, and technologies like WSDL and SOAP, it is likely to provide a framework for companies to leverage the potential of B2B integration. Supporting these technologies in LeSavon.com was a straightforward addition to the service.

We concluded the chapter by querying and publishing one business and one service to the UDDI registry, using the UDDI4J API, and we reviewed the SOAP messages exchanged between a query application and a UDDI registry.

The ultimate goal of technologies such as UDDI is to get to the point where companies can easily find a web service that meets their needs, and automatically switch from one provider of a web service to another. UDDI is not there yet. True interchangeability will only be possible when different web service providers not only use the same language to specify their services, but will also use the same XML schema and interface definitions. However, with XML, XML Schema, WSDL, and UDDI we have a common framework to define what the services do, how they do it, and where to find them.

The success of web services will depend on our use of the technologies: if web service types proliferate, then the realm of web services will become a Tower of Babel where software components do not collaborate. On the other hand, if people communicate and define a compact set of web service types, companies will be able to pick and choose from a reasonable list of possibilities.

However, a more important issue prevents the free flow of goods and services over the Internet. Simply stated, that problem is the way companies define their business processes. It does not matter if two companies use web services to expose and consume services, if those web services are designed to support incompatible processes. We hinted at that issue when we talked about ebXML back in Chapter 1.

Since ebXML is aimed at standardizing the definition of business processes, it offers a framework for companies to not only speak the same language, but to have meaningful e-commerce implementations. The road will be rocky, because despite the synergy between web services and ebXML, there are obstacles. For instance, ebXML defines its own UDDI-like service. Can we rise above those differences and make e-commerce an engine for economic opportunities? The challenge is ours.

JAVA

SOAP 1.1 Specifications

The SOAP 1.1 Specification can be downloaded from **http://www.w3.org/TR/SOAP/**

Simple Object Access Protocol (SOAP) 1.1

W3C Note 08 May 2000

This version:
http://www.w3.org/TR/2000/NOTE-SOAP-20000508
Latest version:
http://www.w3.org/TR/SOAP

Authors (alphabetically):
Don Box, DevelopMentor
David Ehnebuske, IBM
Gopal Kakivaya, Microsoft
Andrew Layman, Microsoft
Noah Mendelsohn, Lotus Development Corp.

Henrik Frystyk Nielsen, Microsoft
Satish Thatte, Microsoft
Dave Winer, UserLand Software, Inc.

Abstract

SOAP is a lightweight protocol for exchange of information in a decentralized, distributed environment. It is an XML based protocol that consists of three parts: an envelope that defines a framework for describing what is in a message and how to process it, a set of encoding rules for expressing instances of application-defined datatypes, and a convention for representing remote procedure calls and responses. SOAP can potentially be used in combination with a variety of other protocols; however, the only bindings defined in this document describe how to use SOAP in combination with HTTP and HTTP Extension Framework.

Status

This document is a submission to the World Wide Web Consortium (see Submission Request, W3C Staff Comment) to propose the formation of a working group in the area of XML-based protocols. Comments are welcome to the authors but you are encouraged to share your views on the W3C's public mailing list <xml-dist-app@w3.org> (see archives).

This document is a NOTE made available by the W3C for discussion only. Publication of this Note by W3C indicates no endorsement by W3C or the W3C Team, or any W3C Members. W3C has had no editorial control over the preparation of this Note. This document is a work in progress and may be updated, replaced, or rendered obsolete by other documents at any time.

A list of current W3C technical documents can be found at the Technical Reports page.

Table of Contents

1. Introduction

SOAP provides a simple and lightweight mechanism for exchanging structured and typed information between peers in a decentralized, distributed environment using XML. SOAP does not itself define any application semantics such as a programming model or implementation specific semantics; rather it defines a simple mechanism for expressing application semantics by providing a modular packaging model and encoding mechanisms for encoding data within modules. This allows SOAP to be used in a large variety of systems ranging from messaging systems to RPC.

SOAP consists of three parts:

- The SOAP envelope (see section 4) construct defines an overall framework for expressing **what** is in a message; **who** should deal with it, and **whether** it is optional or mandatory.

- The SOAP encoding rules (see section 5) defines a serialization mechanism that can be used to exchange instances of application-defined datatypes.

- The SOAP RPC representation (see section 7) defines a convention that can be used to represent remote procedure calls and responses.

Although these parts are described together as part of SOAP, they are functionally orthogonal. In particular, the envelope and the encoding rules are defined in different namespaces in order to promote simplicity through modularity.

In addition to the SOAP envelope, the SOAP encoding rules and the SOAP RPC conventions, this specification defines two protocol bindings that describe how a SOAP message can be carried in HTTP [5] messages either with or without the HTTP Extension Framework [6].

1.1 Design Goals

A major design goal for SOAP is simplicity and extensibility. This means that there are several features from traditional messaging systems and distributed object systems that are not part of the core SOAP specification. Such features include

- Distributed garbage collection

- Boxcarring or batching of messages

- Objects-by-reference (which requires distributed garbage collection)

- Activation (which requires objects-by-reference)

1.2 Notational Conventions

The keywords "MUST", "MUST NOT", "REQUIRED", "SHALL", "SHALL NOT", "SHOULD", "SHOULD NOT", "RECOMMENDED", "MAY", and "OPTIONAL" in this document are to be interpreted as described in RFC-2119 [2].

The namespace prefixes "SOAP-ENV" and "SOAP-ENC" used in this document are associated with the SOAP namespaces "http://schemas.xmlsoap.org/soap/envelope/" and "http://schemas.xmlsoap.org/soap/encoding/" respectively.

Throughout this document, the namespace prefix "xsi" is assumed to be associated with the URI "http://www.w3.org/1999/XMLSchema-instance" which is defined in the XML Schemas specification [11]. Similarly, the namespace prefix "xsd" is assumed to be associated with the URI "http://www.w3.org/1999/XMLSchema" which is defined in [10]. The namespace prefix "tns" is used to indicate whatever is the target namespace of the current document. All other namespace prefixes are samples only.

Namespace URIs of the general form "some-URI" represent some application-dependent or context-dependent URI [4].

This specification uses the augmented Backus-Naur Form (BNF) as described in RFC-2616 [5] for certain constructs.

1.3 Examples of SOAP Messages

In this example, a GetLastTradePrice SOAP request is sent to a StockQuote service. The request takes a string parameter, ticker symbol, and returns a float in the SOAP response. The SOAP Envelope element is the top element of the XML document representing the SOAP message. XML namespaces are used to disambiguate SOAP identifiers from application specific identifiers. The example illustrates the HTTP bindings defined in section 6. It is worth noting that the rules governing XML payload format in SOAP are entirely independent of the fact that the payload is carried in HTTP.

More examples are available in Appendix A.

Example 1 SOAP Message Embedded in HTTP Request

```
POST /StockQuote HTTP/1.1
Host: www.stockquoteserver.com
Content-Type: text/xml; charset="utf-8"
Content-Length: nnnn
SOAPAction: "Some-URI"

<SOAP-ENV:Envelope
  xmlns:SOAP-
ENV="http://schemas.xmlsoap.org/soap/envelope/"
  SOAP-
ENV:encodingStyle="http://schemas.xmlsoap.org/soap/encod
ing/">
   <SOAP-ENV:Body>
       <m:GetLastTradePrice xmlns:m="Some-URI">
           <symbol>DIS</symbol>
       </m:GetLastTradePrice>
   </SOAP-ENV:Body>
</SOAP-ENV:Envelope>
```

Following is the response message containing the HTTP message with the SOAP message as the payload:

Example 2 SOAP Message Embedded in HTTP Response

```
HTTP/1.1 200 OK
Content-Type: text/xml; charset="utf-8"
Content-Length: nnnn

<SOAP-ENV:Envelope
  xmlns:SOAP-
ENV="http://schemas.xmlsoap.org/soap/envelope/"
  SOAP-
ENV:encodingStyle="http://schemas.xmlsoap.org/soap/encod
ing/"/>
   <SOAP-ENV:Body>
       <m:GetLastTradePriceResponse xmlns:m="Some-URI">
           <Price>34.5</Price>
       </m:GetLastTradePriceResponse>
   </SOAP-ENV:Body>
</SOAP-ENV:Envelope>
```

2. The SOAP Message Exchange Model

SOAP messages are fundamentally one-way transmissions from a sender to a receiver, but as illustrated above, SOAP messages are often combined to implement patterns such as request/response.

SOAP implementations can be optimized to exploit the unique characteristics of particular network systems. For example, the HTTP binding described in section 6 provides for SOAP response messages to be delivered as HTTP responses, using the same connection as the inbound request.

Regardless of the protocol to which SOAP is bound, messages are routed along a so-called "message path", which allows for processing at one or more intermediate nodes in addition to the ultimate destination.

A SOAP application receiving a SOAP message MUST process that message by performing the following actions in the order listed below:

1. Identify all parts of the SOAP message intended for that application (see section 4.2.2)

2. Verify that all mandatory parts identified in step 1 are supported by the application for this message (see section 4.2.3) and process them accordingly. If this is not the case then discard the message (see section 4.4). The processor MAY ignore optional parts identified in step 1 without affecting the outcome of the processing.

3. If the SOAP application is not the ultimate destination of the message then remove all parts identified in step 1 before forwarding the message.

Processing a message or a part of a message requires that the SOAP processor understands, among other things, the exchange pattern being used (one way, request/response, multicast, etc.), the role of the recipient in that pattern, the employment (if any) of RPC mechanisms such as the one documented in section 7, the representation or encoding of data, as well as other semantics necessary for correct processing.

While attributes such as the SOAP encodingStyle attribute (see section 4.1.1) can be used to describe certain aspects of a message, this specification does not mandate a particular means by which the recipient makes such determinations in general. For example, certain applications will understand that a particular <getStockPrice> element signals an RPC request using the conventions of section 7, while another application may infer that all traffic directed to it is encoded as one way messages.

3. Relation to XML

All SOAP messages are encoded using XML (see [7] for more information on XML).

A SOAP application SHOULD include the proper SOAP namespace on all elements and attributes defined by SOAP in messages that it generates. A SOAP application MUST be able to process SOAP namespaces in messages that it receives. It MUST discard messages that have incorrect namespaces (see section 4.4) and it MAY process SOAP messages without SOAP namespaces as though they had the correct SOAP namespaces.

SOAP defines two namespaces (see [8] for more information on XML namespaces):

- The SOAP envelope has the namespace identifier "http://schemas.xmlsoap.org/soap/envelope/"

- The SOAP serialization has the namespace identifier "http://schemas.xmlsoap.org/soap/encoding/"

A SOAP message MUST NOT contain a Document Type Declaration. A SOAP message MUST NOT contain Processing Instructions. [7]

SOAP uses the local, unqualified "id" attribute of type "ID" to specify the unique identifier of an encoded element. SOAP uses the local, unqualified attribute "href" of type "uri-reference" to specify a reference to that value, in a manner conforming to the XML Specification [7], XML Schema Specification [11], and XML Linking Language Specification [9].

With the exception of the SOAP mustUnderstand attribute (see section 4.2.3) and the SOAP actor attribute (see section 4.2.2), it is generally permissible to have attributes and their values appear in XML instances or alternatively in schemas, with equal effect. That is, declaration in a DTD or schema with a default or fixed value is semantically equivalent to appearance in an instance.

4. SOAP Envelope

A SOAP message is an XML document that consists of a mandatory SOAP envelope, an optional SOAP header, and a mandatory SOAP body. This XML document is referred to as a SOAP message for the rest of this specification. The namespace identifier for the elements and attributes defined in this section is "http://schemas.xmlsoap.org/soap/envelope/". A SOAP message contains the following:

- The Envelope is the top element of the XML document representing the message.
- The Header is a generic mechanism for adding features to a SOAP message in a decentralized manner without prior agreement between the communicating parties. SOAP defines a few attributes that can be used to indicate who should deal with a feature and whether it is optional or mandatory (see section 4.2)
- The Body is a container for mandatory information intended for the ultimate recipient of the message (see section 4.3). SOAP defines one element for the body, which is the Fault element used for reporting errors.

The grammar rules are as follows:

1. Envelope
   - The element name is "Envelope".
   - The element MUST be present in a SOAP message
   - The element MAY contain namespace declarations as well as additional attributes. If present, such additional attributes MUST be namespace-qualified. Similarly, the element MAY contain additional sub elements. If present these elements MUST be namespace-qualified and MUST follow the SOAP Body element.
2. Header (see section 4.2)
   - The element name is "Header".
   - The element MAY be present in a SOAP message. If present, the element MUST be the first immediate child element of a SOAP Envelope element.
   - The element MAY contain a set of header entries each being an immediate child element of the SOAP Header element. All immediate child elements of the SOAP Header element MUST be namespace-qualified.
3. Body (see section 4.3)
   - The element name is "Body".
   - The element MUST be present in a SOAP message and MUST be an immediate child element of a SOAP Envelope element. It MUST directly follow the SOAP Header element if present. Otherwise it MUST be the first immediate child element of the SOAP Envelope element.

- The element MAY contain a set of body entries each being an immediate child element of the SOAP Body element. Immediate child elements of the SOAP Body element MAY be namespace-qualified. SOAP defines the SOAP Fault element, which is used to indicate error messages (see section 4.4).

4.1.1 SOAP encodingStyle Attribute

The SOAP encodingStyle global attribute can be used to indicate the serialization rules used in a SOAP message. This attribute MAY appear on any element, and is scoped to that element's contents and all child elements not themselves containing such an attribute, much as an XML namespace declaration is scoped. There is no default encoding defined for a SOAP message.

The attribute value is an ordered list of one or more URIs identifying the serialization rule or rules that can be used to deserialize the SOAP message indicated in the order of most specific to least specific. Examples of values are

```
"http://schemas.xmlsoap.org/soap/encoding/"
"http://my.host/encoding/restricted http://my.host/encod
ing/"
""
```

The serialization rules defined by SOAP in section 5 are identified by the URI "http://schemas.xmlsoap.org/soap/encoding/". Messages using this particular serialization SHOULD indicate this using the SOAP encodingStyle attribute. In addition, all URIs syntactically beginning with "http://schemas.xmlsoap.org/soap/encoding/" indicate conformance with the SOAP encoding rules defined in section 5 (though with potentially tighter rules added).

A value of the zero-length URI ("") explicitly indicates that no claims are made for the encoding style of contained elements. This can be used to turn off any claims from containing elements.

4.1.2 Envelope Versioning Model

SOAP does not define a traditional versioning model based on major and minor version numbers. A SOAP message MUST have an Envelope element associated with the "http://schemas.xmlsoap.org/soap/envelope/" namespace. If a message is received by a SOAP application in which the SOAP Envelope element is associated with a different namespace, the application MUST treat this as a version error and discard the message. If the message is received through a request/response protocol such as HTTP, the application MUST respond with a SOAP VersionMismatch faultcode message (see section 4.4) using the SOAP "http://schemas.xmlsoap.org/soap/envelope/" namespace.

4.2 SOAP Header

SOAP provides a flexible mechanism for extending a message in a decentralized and modular way without prior knowledge between the communicating parties. Typical examples of extensions that can be implemented as header entries are authentication, transaction management, payment etc.

The Header element is encoded as the first immediate child element of the SOAP Envelope XML element. All immediate child elements of the Header element are called header entries.

The encoding rules for header entries are as follows:

1. A header entry is identified by its fully qualified element name, which consists of the namespace URI and the local name. All immediate child elements of the SOAP Header element MUST be namespace-qualified.

2. The SOAP encodingStyle attribute MAY be used to indicate the encoding style used for the header entries (see section 4.1.1).

3. The SOAP mustUnderstand attribute (see section 4.2.3) and SOAP actor attribute (see section 4.2.2) MAY be used to indicate how to process the entry and by whom (see section 4.2.1).

4.2.1 Use of Header Attributes

The SOAP Header attributes defined in this section determine how a recipient of a SOAP message should process the message as described in section 2. A SOAP application generating a SOAP message SHOULD only use the SOAP Header attributes on immediate child elements of the SOAP Header element. The recipient of a SOAP message MUST ignore all SOAP Header attributes that are not applied to an immediate child element of the SOAP Header element.

An example is a header with an element identifier of "Transaction", a "mustUnderstand" value of "1", and a value of 5. This would be encoded as follows:

```
<SOAP-ENV:Header>
   <t:Transaction
      xmlns:t="some-URI" SOAP-ENV:mustUnderstand="1">
         5
   </t:Transaction>
</SOAP-ENV:Header>
```

4.2.2 SOAP actor Attribute

A SOAP message travels from the originator to the ultimate destination, potentially by passing through a set of SOAP intermediaries along the message path. A SOAP intermediary is an application that is capable of both receiving and forwarding SOAP messages. Both intermediaries as well as the ultimate destination are identified by a URI.

Not all parts of a SOAP message may be intended for the ultimate destination of the SOAP message but, instead, may be intended for one or more of the intermediaries on the message path. The role of a recipient of a header element is similar to that of accepting a contract in that it cannot be extended beyond the recipient. That is, a recipient receiving a header element MUST NOT forward that header element to the next application in the SOAP message path. The recipient MAY insert a similar header element but in that case, the contract is between that application and the recipient of that header element.

The SOAP actor global attribute can be used to indicate the recipient of a header element. The value of the SOAP actor attribute is a URI. The special URI "http://schemas.xmlsoap.org/soap/actor/next" indicates that the header element is intended for the very first SOAP application that processes the message. This is similar to the hop-by-hop scope model represented by the Connection header field in HTTP.

Omitting the SOAP actor attribute indicates that the recipient is the ultimate destination of the SOAP message.

This attribute MUST appear in the SOAP message instance in order to be effective (see section 3 and 4.2.1).

4.2.3 SOAP mustUnderstand Attribute

The SOAP mustUnderstand global attribute can be used to indicate whether a header entry is mandatory or optional for the recipient to process. The recipient of a header entry is defined by the SOAP actor attribute (see section 4.2.2). The value of the mustUnderstand attribute is either "1" or "0". The absence of the SOAP mustUnderstand attribute is semantically equivalent to its presence with the value "0".

If a header element is tagged with a SOAP mustUnderstand attribute with a value of "1", the recipient of that header entry either MUST obey the semantics (as conveyed by the fully qualified name of the element) and process correctly to those semantics, or MUST fail processing the message (see section 4.4).

The SOAP mustUnderstand attribute allows for robust evolution. Elements tagged with the SOAP mustUnderstand attribute with a value of "1" MUST be presumed to somehow modify the semantics of their parent or peer elements. Tagging elements in this manner assures that this change in semantics will not be silently (and, presumably, erroneously) ignored by those who may not fully understand it.

This attribute MUST appear in the instance in order to be effective (see section 3 and 4.2.1).

4.3 SOAP Body

The SOAP Body element provides a simple mechanism for exchanging mandatory information intended for the ultimate recipient of the message. Typical uses of the Body element include marshalling RPC calls and error reporting.

The Body element is encoded as an immediate child element of the SOAP Envelope XML element. If a Header element is present then the Body element MUST immediately follow the Header element, otherwise it MUST be the first immediate child element of the Envelope element.

All immediate child elements of the Body element are called body entries and each body entry is encoded as an independent element within the SOAP Body element.

The encoding rules for body entries are as follows:

1. A body entry is identified by its fully qualified element name, which consists of the namespace URI and the local name. Immediate child elements of the SOAP Body element MAY be namespace-qualified.

2. The SOAP encodingStyle attribute MAY be used to indicate the encoding style used for the body entries (see section 4.1.1).

SOAP defines one body entry, which is the Fault entry used for reporting errors (see section 4.4).

4.3.1 Relationship between SOAP Header and Body

While the Header and Body are defined as independent elements, they are in fact related. The relationship between a body entry and a header entry is as follows: A body entry is semantically equivalent to a header entry intended for the default actor and with a SOAP mustUnderstand attribute with a value of "1". The default actor is indicated by not using the actor attribute (see section 4.2.2).

4.4 SOAP Fault

The SOAP Fault element is used to carry error and/or status information within a SOAP message. If present, the SOAP Fault element MUST appear as a body entry and MUST NOT appear more than once within a Body element.

The SOAP Fault element defines the following four subelements:

faultcode
: The faultcode element is intended for use by software to provide an algorithmic mechanism for identifying the fault. The faultcode MUST be present in a SOAP Fault element and the faultcode value MUST be a qualified name as defined in [8], section 3. SOAP defines a small set of SOAP fault codes covering basic SOAP faults (see section 4.4.1)

faultstring
: The faultstring element is intended to provide a human readable explanation of the fault and is not intended for algorithmic processing. The faultstring element is similar to the 'Reason-Phrase' defined by HTTP (see [5], section 6.1). It MUST be present in a SOAP Fault element and SHOULD provide at least some information explaining the nature of the fault.

faultactor
: The faultactor element is intended to provide information about who caused the fault to happen within the message path (see section 2). It is similar to the SOAP actor attribute (see section 4.2.2) but instead of indicating the destination of the header entry, it indicates the source of the fault. The value of the faultactor attribute is a URI identifying the source. Applications that do not act as the ultimate destination of the SOAP message MUST include the faultactor element in a SOAP Fault element. The ultimate destination of a message MAY use the faultactor element to indicate explicitly that it generated the fault (see also the detail element below).

detail
: The detail element is intended for carrying application specific error information related to the Body element. It MUST be present if the contents of the Body element could not be successfully processed. It MUST NOT be used to carry information about error information belonging to header entries. Detailed error information belonging to header entries MUST be carried within header entries.

The absence of the detail element in the Fault element indicates that the fault is not related to processing of the Body element. This can be used to distinguish whether the Body element was processed or not in case of a fault situation.

All immediate child elements of the detail element are called detail entries and each detail entry is encoded as an independent element within the detail element.

The encoding rules for detail entries are as follows (see also example 10):

1. A detail entry is identified by its fully qualified element name, which consists of the namespace URI and the local name. Immediate child elements of the detail element MAY be namespace-qualified.

2. The SOAP encodingStyle attribute MAY be used to indicate the encoding style used for the detail entries (see section 4.1.1).

Other Fault subelements MAY be present, provided they are namespace-qualified.

4.4.1 SOAP Fault Codes

The faultcode values defined in this section MUST be used in the faultcode element when describing faults defined by this specification. The namespace identifier for these faultcode values is "http://schemas.xmlsoap.org/soap/envelope/". Use of this space is recommended (but not required) in the specification of methods defined outside of the present specification.

The default SOAP faultcode values are defined in an extensible manner that allows for new SOAP faultcode values to be defined while maintaining backwards compatibility with existing faultcode values. The mechanism used is very similar to the 1xx, 2xx, 3xx etc basic status classes classes defined in HTTP (see [5] section 10). However, instead of integers, they are defined as XML qualified names (see [8] section 3). The character "." (dot) is used as a separator of faultcode values indicating that what is to the left of the dot is a more generic fault code value than the value to the right. Example

```
Client.Authentication
```

The set of faultcode values defined in this document is:

Name	Meaning
VersionMismatch	The processing party found an invalid namespace for the SOAP Envelope element (see section 4.1.2)
MustUnderstand	An immediate child element of the SOAP Header element that was either not understood or not obeyed by the processing party contained a SOAP mustUnderstand attribute with a value of "1" (see section 4.2.3)

Table continued on following page

Client	The Client class of errors indicate that the message was incorrectly formed or did not contain the appropriate information in order to succeed. For example, the message could lack the proper authentication or payment information. It is generally an indication that the message should not be resent without change. See also section 4.4 for a description of the SOAP Fault detail sub-element.
Server	The Server class of errors indicate that the message could not be processed for reasons not directly attributable to the contents of the message itself but rather to the processing of the message. For example, processing could include communicating with an upstream processor, which didn't respond. The message may succeed at a later point in time. See also section 4.4 for a description of the SOAP Fault detail sub-element.

5. SOAP Encoding

The SOAP encoding style is based on a simple type system that is a generalization of the common features found in type systems in programming languages, databases and semi-structured data. A type either is a simple (scalar) type or is a compound type constructed as a composite of several parts, each with a type. This is described in more detail below. This section defines rules for serialization of a graph of typed objects. It operates on two levels. First, given a schema in any notation consistent with the type system described, a schema for an XML grammar may be constructed. Second, given a type-system schema and a particular graph of values conforming to that schema, an XML instance may be constructed. In reverse, given an XML instance produced in accordance with these rules, and given also the original schema, a copy of the original value graph may be constructed.

The namespace identifier for the elements and attributes defined in this section is "http://schemas.xmlsoap.org/soap/encoding/". The encoding samples shown assume all namespace declarations are at a higher element level.

Use of the data model and encoding style described in this section is encouraged but not required; other data models and encodings can be used in conjunction with SOAP (see section 4.1.1).

5.1 Rules for Encoding Types in XML

XML allows very flexible encoding of data. SOAP defines a narrower set of rules for encoding. This section defines the encoding rules at a high level, and the next section describes the encoding rules for specific types when they require more detail. The encodings described in this section can be used in conjunction with the mapping of RPC calls and responses specified in Section 7.

To describe encoding, the following terminology is used:

1. A "value" is a string, the name of a measurement (number, date, enumeration, etc.) or a composite of several such primitive values. All values are of specific types.

2. A "simple value" is one without named parts. Examples of simple values are particular strings, integers, enumerated values etc.

3. A "compound value" is an aggregate of relations to other values. Examples of Compound Values are particular purchase orders, stock reports, street addresses, etc.

4. Within a compound value, each related value is potentially distinguished by a role name, ordinal or both. This is called its "accessor." Examples of compound values include particular Purchase Orders, Stock Reports etc. Arrays are also compound values. It is possible to have compound values with several accessors each named the same, as for example, RDF does.

5. An "array" is a compound value in which ordinal position serves as the only distinction among member values.

6. A "struct" is a compound value in which accessor name is the only distinction among member values, and no accessor has the same name as any other.

7. A "simple type" is a class of simple values. Examples of simple types are the classes called "string," "integer," enumeration classes, etc.

8. A "compound type" is a class of compound values. An example of a compound type is the class of purchase order values sharing the same accessors (shipTo, totalCost, etc.) though with potentially different values (and perhaps further constrained by limits on certain values).

9. Within a compound type, if an accessor has a name that is distinct within that type but is not distinct with respect to other types, that is, the name plus the type together are needed to make a unique identification, the name is called "locally scoped." If however the name is based in part on a Uniform Resource Identifier, directly or indirectly, such that the name alone is sufficient to uniquely identify the accessor irrespective of the type within which it appears, the name is called "universally scoped."

10. Given the information in the schema relative to which a graph of values is serialized, it is possible to determine that some values can only be related by a single instance of an accessor. For others, it is not possible to make this determination. If only one accessor can reference it, a value is considered "single-reference". If referenced by more than one, actually or potentially, it is "multi-reference." Note that it is possible for a certain value to be considered "single-reference" relative to one schema and "multi-reference" relative to another.

11. Syntactically, an element may be "independent" or "embedded." An independent element is any element appearing at the top level of a serialization. All others are embedded elements.

Although it is possible to use the xsi:type attribute such that a graph of values is self-describing both in its structure and the types of its values, the serialization rules permit that the types of values MAY be determinate only by reference to a schema. Such schemas MAY be in the notation described by "XML Schema Part 1: Structures" [10] and "XML Schema Part 2: Datatypes" [11] or MAY be in any other notation. Note also that, while the serialization rules apply to compound types other than arrays and structs, many schemas will contain only struct and array types.

The rules for serialization are as follows:

1. All values are represented as element content. A multi-reference value MUST be represented as the content of an independent element. A single-reference value SHOULD not be (but MAY be).

2. For each element containing a value, the type of the value MUST be represented by at least one of the following conditions: (a) the containing element instance contains an xsi:type attribute, (b) the containing element instance is itself contained within an element containing a (possibly defaulted) SOAP-ENC:arrayType attribute or (c) or the name of the element bears a definite relation to the type, that type then determinable from a schema.

3. A simple value is represented as character data, that is, without any subelements. Every simple value must have a type that is either listed in the XML Schemas Specification, part 2 [11] or whose source type is listed therein (see also section 5.2).

4. A Compound Value is encoded as a sequence of elements, each accessor represented by an embedded element whose name corresponds to the name of the accessor. Accessors whose names are local to their containing types have unqualified element names; all others have qualified names (see also section 5.4).

5. A multi-reference simple or compound value is encoded as an independent element containing a local, unqualified attribute named "id" and of type "ID" per the XML Specification [7]. Each accessor to this value is an empty element having a local, unqualified attribute named "href" and of type "uri-reference" per the XML Schema Specification [11], with a "href" attribute value of a URI fragment identifier referencing the corresponding independent element.

6. Strings and byte arrays are represented as multi-reference simple types, but special rules allow them to be represented efficiently for common cases (see also section 5.2.1 and 5.2.3). An accessor to a string or byte-array value MAY have an attribute named "id" and of type "ID" per the XML Specification [7]. If so, all other accessors to the same value are encoded as empty elements having a local, unqualified attribute named "href" and of type "uri-reference" per the XML Schema Specification [11], with a "href" attribute value of a URI fragment identifier referencing the single element containing the value.

7. It is permissible to encode several references to a value as though these were references to several distinct values, but only when from context it is known that the meaning of the XML instance is unaltered.

8. Arrays are compound values (see also section 5.4.2). SOAP arrays are defined as having a type of "SOAP-ENC:Array" or a type derived there from.

   SOAP arrays have one or more dimensions (rank) whose members are distinguished by ordinal position. An array value is represented as a series of elements reflecting the array, with members appearing in ascending ordinal sequence. For multi-dimensional arrays the dimension on the right side varies most rapidly. Each member element is named as an independent element (see rule 2).

   SOAP arrays can be single-reference or multi-reference values, and consequently may be represented as the content of either an embedded or independent element.

   SOAP arrays MUST contain a "SOAP-ENC:arrayType" attribute whose value specifies the type of the contained elements as well as the dimension(s) of the array. The value of the "SOAP-ENC:arrayType" attribute is defined as follows:

```
arrayTypeValue = atype asize
atype          = QName *( rank )
rank           = "[" *( "," ) "]"
asize          = "[" #length "]"
length         = 1*DIGIT
```

   The "atype" construct is the type name of the contained elements expressed as a QName as would appear in the "type" attribute of an XML Schema element declaration and acts as a type constraint (meaning that all values of contained elements are asserted to conform to the indicated type; that is, the type cited in SOAP-ENC:arrayType must be the type or a supertype of every array member). In the case of arrays of arrays or "jagged arrays", the type component is encoded as the "innermost" type name followed by a rank construct for each level of nested arrays starting from 1. Multi-dimensional arrays are encoded using a comma for each dimension starting from 1.

   The "asize" construct contains a comma separated list of zero, one, or more integers indicating the lengths of each dimension of the array. A value of zero integers indicates that no particular quantity is asserted but that the size may be determined by inspection of the actual members.

   For example, an array with 5 members of type array of integers would have an arrayTypeValue value of "int[][5]" of which the atype value is "int[]" and the asize value is "[5]". Likewise, an array with 3 members of type two-dimensional arrays of integers would have an arrayTypeValue value of "int[,][3]" of which the atype value is "int[,]" and the asize value is "[3]".

   A SOAP array member MAY contain a "SOAP-ENC:offset" attribute indicating the offset position of that item in the enclosing array. This can be used to indicate the offset position of a partially represented array (see section 5.4.2.1). Likewise, an array member MAY contain a "SOAP-ENC:position" attribute indicating the position of that item in the enclosing array. This can be used to describe members of sparse arrays (see section 5.4.2.2). The value of the "SOAP-ENC:offset" and the "SOAP-ENC:position" attribute is defined as follows:

```
arrayPoint = "[" #length "]"
```

   with offsets and positions based at 0.

9. A NULL value or a default value MAY be represented by omission of the accessor element. A NULL value MAY also be indicated by an accessor element containing the attribute xsi:null with value '1' or possibly other application-dependent attributes and values.

Note that rule 2 allows independent elements and also elements representing the members of arrays to have names which are not identical to the type of the contained value.

5.2 Simple Types

For simple types, SOAP adopts all the types found in the section "Built-in datatypes" of the "XML Schema Part 2: Datatypes" Specification [11], both the value and lexical spaces. Examples include:

Type	Example
int	58502
float	314159265358979E+1
negativeInteger	-32768
string	Louis "Satchmo" Armstrong

The datatypes declared in the XML Schema specification may be used directly in element schemas. Types derived from these may also be used. An example of a schema fragment and corresponding instance data with elements of these types is:

```
<element name="age" type="int"/>
<element name="height" type="float"/>
<element name="displacement" type="negativeInteger"/>
<element name="color">
  <simpleType base="xsd:string">
    <enumeration value="Green"/>
    <enumeration value="Blue"/>
  </simpleType>
</element>

<age>45</age>
<height>5.9</height>
<displacement>-450</displacement>
<color>Blue</color>
```

All simple values MUST be encoded as the content of elements whose type is either defined in "XML Schema Part 2: Datatypes" Specification [11], or is based on a type found there by using the mechanisms provided in the XML Schema specification.

If a simple value is encoded as an independent element or member of a heterogenous array it is convenient to have an element declaration corresponding to the datatype. Because the "XML Schema Part 2: Datatypes" Specification [11] includes type definitions but does not include corresponding element declarations, the SOAP-ENC schema and namespace declares an element for every simple datatype. These MAY be used.

```
<SOAP-ENC:int id="int1">45</SOAP-ENC:int>
```

5.2.1 Strings

The datatype "string" is defined in "XML Schema Part 2: Datatypes" Specification [11]. Note that this is not identical to the type called "string" in many database or programming languages, and in particular may forbid some characters those languages would permit. (Those values must be represented by using some datatype other than xsd:string.)

A string MAY be encoded as a single-reference or a multi-reference value.

The containing element of the string value MAY have an "id" attribute. Additional accessor elements MAY then have matching "href" attributes.

For example, two accessors to the same string could appear, as follows:

```
<greeting id="String-0">Hello</greeting>
<salutation href="#String-0"/>
```

However, if the fact that both accessors reference the same instance of the string (or subtype of string) is immaterial, they may be encoded as two single-reference values as follows:

```
<greeting>Hello</greeting>
<salutation>Hello</salutation>
```

Schema fragments for these examples could appear similar to the following:

```
<element name="greeting" type="SOAP-ENC:string"/>
<element name="salutation" type="SOAP-ENC:string"/>
```

(In this example, the type SOAP-ENC:string is used as the element's type as a convenient way to declare an element whose datatype is "xsd:string" and which also allows an "id" and "href" attribute. See the SOAP Encoding schema for the exact definition. Schemas MAY use these declarations from the SOAP Encoding schema but are not required to.)

5.2.2 Enumerations

The "XML Schema Part 2: Datatypes" Specification [11] defines a mechanism called "enumeration." The SOAP data model adopts this mechanism directly. However, because programming and other languages often define enumeration somewhat differently, we spell-out the concept in more detail here and describe how a value that is a member of an enumerated list of possible values is to be encoded. Specifically, it is encoded as the name of the value.

"Enumeration" as a concept indicates a set of distinct names. A specific enumeration is a specific list of distinct values appropriate to the base type. For example the set of color names ("Green", "Blue", "Brown") could be defined as an enumeration based on the string built-in type. The values ("1", "3", "5") are a possible enumeration based on integer, and so on. "XML Schema Part 2: Datatypes" [11] supports enumerations for all of the simple types except for boolean. The language of "XML Schema Part 1: Structures" Specification [10] can be used to define enumeration types. If a schema is generated from another notation in which no specific base type is applicable, use "string". In the following schema example "EyeColor" is defined as a string with the possible values of "Green", "Blue", or "Brown" enumerated, and instance data is shown accordingly.

```
<element name="EyeColor" type="tns:EyeColor"/>
<simpleType name="EyeColor" base="xsd:string">
   <enumeration value="Green"/>
   <enumeration value="Blue"/>
   <enumeration value="Brown"/>
</simpleType>
<Person>
   <Name>Henry Ford</Name>
   <Age>32</Age>
   <EyeColor>Brown</EyeColor>
</Person>
```

5.2.3 Array of Bytes

An array of bytes MAY be encoded as a single-reference or a multi-reference value. The rules for an array of bytes are similar to those for a string.

In particular, the containing element of the array of bytes value MAY have an "id" attribute. Additional accessor elements MAY then have matching "href" attributes.

The recommended representation of an opaque array of bytes is the 'base64' encoding defined in XML Schemas [10][11], which uses the base64 encoding algorithm defined in 2045 [13]. However, the line length restrictions that normally apply to base64 data in MIME do not apply in SOAP. A "SOAP-ENC:base64" subtype is supplied for use with SOAP.

```
<picture xsi:type="SOAP-ENC:base64">
   aG93IG5vDyBicm73biBjb3cNCg==
</picture>
```

5.3 Polymorphic Accessor

Many languages allow accessors that can polymorphically access values of several types, each type being available at run time. A polymorphic accessor instance MUST contain an "xsi:type" attribute that describes the type of the actual value.

For example, a polymorphic accessor named "cost" with a value of type "xsd:float" would be encoded as follows:

```
<cost xsi:type="xsd:float">29.95</cost>
```

as contrasted with a cost accessor whose value's type is invariant, as follows:

```
<cost>29.95</cost>
```

5.4 Compound types

SOAP defines types corresponding to the following structural patterns often found in programming languages:

Struct
: A "struct" is a compound value in which accessor name is the only distinction among member values, and no accessor has the same name as any other.

Array
: An "array" is a compound value in which ordinal position serves as the only distinction among member values.

SOAP also permits serialization of data that is neither a Struct nor an Array, for example data such as is found in a Directed-Labeled-Graph Data Model in which a single node has many distinct accessors, some of which occur more than once. SOAP serialization does not require that the underlying data model make an ordering distinction among accessors, but if such an order exists, the accessors MUST be encoded in that sequence.

5.4.1 Compound Values, Structs and References to Values

The members of a Compound Value are encoded as accessor elements. When accessors are distinguished by their name (as for example in a struct), the accessor name is used as the element name. Accessors whose names are local to their containing types have unqualified element names; all others have qualified names.

The following is an example of a struct of type "Book":

```
<e:Book>
   <author>Henry Ford</author>
   <preface>Prefatory text</preface>
   <intro>This is a book.</intro>
</e:Book>
```

And this is a schema fragment describing the above structure:

```
<element name="Book">
<complexType>
  <element name="author" type="xsd:string"/>
  <element name="preface" type="xsd:string"/>
```

```
   <element name="intro" type="xsd:string"/>
</complexType>
</e:Book>
```

Below is an example of a type with both simple and complex members. It shows two levels of referencing. Note that the "href" attribute of the "Author" accessor element is a reference to the value whose "id" attribute matches. A similar construction appears for the "Address".

```
<e:Book>
   <title>My Life and Work</title>
   <author href="#Person-1"/>
</e:Book>
<e:Person id="Person-1">
   <name>Henry Ford</name>
   <address href="#Address-2"/>
</e:Person>
<e:Address id="Address-2">
   <email>mailto:henryford@hotmail.com</email>
   <web>http://www.henryford.com</web>
</e:Address>
```

The form above is appropriate when the "Person" value and the "Address" value are multi-reference. If these were instead both single-reference, they SHOULD be embedded, as follows:

```
<e:Book>
   <title>My Life and Work</title>
   <author>
       <name>Henry Ford</name>
       <address>
          <email>mailto:henryford@hotmail.com</email>
          <web>http://www.henryford.com</web>
       </address>
   </author>
</e:Book>
```

If instead there existed a restriction that no two persons can have the same address in a given instance and that an address can be either a Street-address or an Electronic-address, a Book with two authors would be encoded as follows:

```
<e:Book>
   <title>My Life and Work</title>
   <firstauthor href="#Person-1"/>
   <secondauthor href="#Person-2"/>
</e:Book>
<e:Person id="Person-1">
```

```
   <name>Henry Ford</name>
   <address xsi:type="m:Electronic-address">
       <email>mailto:henryford@hotmail.com</email>
       <web>http://www.henryford.com</web>
   </address>
</e:Person>
<e:Person id="Person-2">
   <name>Samuel Crowther</name>
   <address xsi:type="n:Street-address">
       <street>Martin Luther King Rd</street>
       <city>Raleigh</city>
       <state>North Carolina</state>
   </address>
</e:Person>
```

Serializations can contain references to values not in the same resource:

```
<e:Book>
   <title>Paradise Lost</title>
   <firstauthor href="http://www.dartmouth.edu/~milton/"
/>
</e:Book>
```

And this is a schema fragment describing the above structures:

```
<element name="Book" type="tns:Book"/>
<complexType name="Book">
   <!-- Either the following group must occur or else
the
        href attribute must appear, but not both. -->
   <sequence minOccurs="0" maxOccurs="1">
       <element name="title" type="xsd:string"/>
       <element name="firstauthor" type="tns:Person"/>
       <element name="secondauthor" type="tns:Person"/>
   </sequence>
   <attribute name="href" type="uriReference"/>
   <attribute name="id" type="ID"/>
   <anyAttribute namespace="##other"/>
</complexType>

<element name="Person" base="tns:Person"/>
<complexType name="Person">
   <!-- Either the following group must occur or else
```

```
the
        href attribute must appear, but not both. -->
    <sequence minOccurs="0" maxOccurs="1">
        <element name="name" type="xsd:string"/>
        <element name="address" type="tns:Address"/>
    </sequence>
    <attribute name="href" type="uriReference"/>
    <attribute name="id" type="ID"/>
    <anyAttribute namespace="##other"/>
</complexType>

<element name="Address" base="tns:Address"/>
<complexType name="Address">
    <!-- Either the following group must occur or else
the
        href attribute must appear, but not both. -->
    <sequence minOccurs="0" maxOccurs="1">
        <element name="street" type="xsd:string"/>
        <element name="city" type="xsd:string"/>
        <element name="state" type="xsd:string"/>
    </sequence>
    <attribute name="href" type="uriReference"/>
    <attribute name="id" type="ID"/>
    <anyAttribute namespace="##other"/>
</complexType>
```

5.4.2 Arrays

SOAP arrays are defined as having a type of "SOAP-ENC:Array" or a type derived there from (see also rule 8). Arrays are represented as element values, with no specific constraint on the name of the containing element (just as values generally do not constrain the name of their containing element).

Arrays can contain elements which themselves can be of any type, including nested arrays. New types formed by restrictions of SOAP-ENC:Array can also be created to represent, for example, arrays limited to integers or arrays of some user-defined enumeration.

The representation of the value of an array is an ordered sequence of elements constituting the items of the array. Within an array value, element names are not significant for distinguishing accessors. Elements may have any name. In practice, elements will frequently be named so that their declaration in a schema suggests or determines their type. As with compound types generally, if the value of an item in the array is a single-reference value, the item contains its value. Otherwise, the item references its value via an "href" attribute.

The following example is a schema fragment and an array containing integer array members.

```
<element name="myFavoriteNumbers"
        type="SOAP-ENC:Array"/>

<myFavoriteNumbers
  SOAP-ENC:arrayType="xsd:int[2]">
   <number>3</number>
   <number>4</number>
</myFavoriteNumbers>
```

In that example, the array "myFavoriteNumbers" contains several members each of which is a value of type SOAP-ENC:int. This can be determined by inspection of the SOAP-ENC:arrayType attribute. Note that the SOAP-ENC:Array type allows unqualified element names without restriction. These convey no type information, so when used they must either have an xsi:type attribute or the containing element must have a SOAP-ENC:arrayType attribute. Naturally, types derived from SOAP-ENC:Array may declare local elements, with type information.

As previously noted, the SOAP-ENC schema contains declarations of elements with names corresponding to each simple type in the "XML Schema Part 2: Datatypes" Specification [11]. It also contains a declaration for "Array". Using these, we might write

```
<SOAP-ENC:Array SOAP-ENC:arrayType="xsd:int[2]">
   <SOAP-ENC:int>3</SOAP-ENC:int>
   <SOAP-ENC:int>4</SOAP-ENC:int>
</SOAP-ENC:Array>
```

Arrays can contain instances of any subtype of the specified arrayType. That is, the members may be of any type that is substitutable for the type specified in the arrayType attribute, according to whatever substitutability rules are expressed in the schema. So, for example, an array of integers can contain any type derived from integer (for example "int" or any user-defined derivation of integer). Similarly, an array of "address" might contain a restricted or extended type such as "internationalAddress". Because the supplied SOAP-ENC:Array type admits members of any type, arbitrary mixtures of types can be contained unless specifically limited by use of the arrayType attribute.

Types of member elements can be specified using the xsi:type attribute in the instance, or by declarations in the schema of the member elements, as the following two arrays demonstrate respectively.

```
<SOAP-ENC:Array SOAP-ENC:arrayType="xsd:ur-type[4]">
   <thing xsi:type="xsd:int">12345</thing>
   <thing xsi:type="xsd:decimal">6.789</thing>
   <thing xsi:type="xsd:string">
      Of Mans First Disobedience, and the Fruit
      Of that Forbidden Tree, whose mortal tast
      Brought Death into the World, and all our woe,
   </thing>
   <thing xsi:type="xsd:uriReference">
```

```
      http://www.dartmouth.edu/~milton/reading_room/
   </thing>
</SOAP-ENC:Array>
<SOAP-ENC:Array SOAP-ENC:arrayType="xsd:ur-type[4]">
   <SOAP-ENC:int>12345</SOAP-ENC:int>
   <SOAP-ENC:decimal>6.789</SOAP-ENC:decimal>
   <xsd:string>
      Of Mans First Disobedience, and the Fruit
      Of that Forbidden Tree, whose mortal tast
      Brought Death into the World, and all our woe,
   </xsd:string>
   <SOAP-ENC:uriReference>
      http://www.dartmouth.edu/~milton/reading_room/
   </SOAP-ENC:uriReference >
</SOAP-ENC:Array>
```

Array values may be structs or other compound values. For example an array of "xyz:Order" structs :

```
<SOAP-ENC:Array SOAP-ENC:arrayType="xyz:Order[2]">
   <Order>
       <Product>Apple</Product>
       <Price>1.56</Price>
   </Order>
   <Order>
       <Product>Peach</Product>
       <Price>1.48</Price>
   </Order>
</SOAP-ENC:Array>
```

Arrays may have other arrays as member values. The following is an example of an array of two arrays, each of which is an array of strings.

```
<SOAP-ENC:Array SOAP-ENC:arrayType="xsd:string[][2]">
   <item href="#array-1"/>
   <item href="#array-2"/>
</SOAP-ENC:Array>
<SOAP-ENC:Array id="array-1" SOAP-
ENC:arrayType="xsd:string[2]">
   <item>r1c1</item>
   <item>r1c2</item>
   <item>r1c3</item>
</SOAP-ENC:Array>
<SOAP-ENC:Array id="array-2" SOAP-
```

```
ENC:arrayType="xsd:string[2]">
   <item>r2c1</item>
   <item>r2c2</item>
</SOAP-ENC:Array>
```

The element containing an array value does not need to be named "SOAP-ENC:Array". It may have any name, provided that the type of the element is either SOAP-ENC:Array or is derived from SOAP-ENC:Array by restriction. For example, the following is a fragment of a schema and a conforming instance array.

```
<simpleType name="phoneNumber" base="string"/>

<element name="ArrayOfPhoneNumbers">
  <complexType base="SOAP-ENC:Array">
    <element name="phoneNumber" type="tns:phoneNumber"
maxOccurs="unbounded"/>
  </complexType>
  <anyAttribute/>
</element>
<xyz:ArrayOfPhoneNumbers SOAP-
ENC:arrayType="xyz:phoneNumber[2]">
   <phoneNumber>206-555-1212</phoneNumber>
   <phoneNumber>1-888-123-4567</phoneNumber>
</xyz:ArrayOfPhoneNumbers>
```

Arrays may be multi-dimensional. In this case, more than one size will appear within the asize part of the arrayType attribute:

```
<SOAP-ENC:Array SOAP-ENC:arrayType="xsd:string[2,3]">
   <item>r1c1</item>
   <item>r1c2</item>
   <item>r1c3</item>
   <item>r2c1</item>
   <item>r2c2</item>
   <item>r2c3</item>
</SOAP-ENC:Array>
```

While the examples above have shown arrays encoded as independent elements, array values MAY also appear embedded and SHOULD do so when they are known to be single reference.

The following is an example of a schema fragment and an array of phone numbers embedded in a struct of type "Person" and accessed through the accessor "phone-numbers":

```
<simpleType name="phoneNumber" base="string"/>

<element name="ArrayOfPhoneNumbers">
```

```
  <complexType base="SOAP-ENC:Array">
    <element name="phoneNumber" type="tns:phoneNumber"
maxOccurs="unbounded"/>
  </complexType>
  <anyAttribute/>
</element>

<element name="Person">
  <complexType>
    <element name="name" type="string"/>
    <element name="phoneNumbers"
type="tns:ArrayOfPhoneNumbers"/>
  </complexType>
</element>
<xyz:Person>
   <name>John Hancock</name>
   <phoneNumbers SOAP-
ENC:arrayType="xyz:phoneNumber[2]">
       <phoneNumber>206-555-1212</phoneNumber>
       <phoneNumber>1-888-123-4567</phoneNumber>
   </phoneNumbers>
</xyz:Person>
```

Here is another example of a single-reference array value encoded as an embedded element whose containing element name is the accessor name:

```
<xyz:PurchaseOrder>
   <CustomerName>Henry Ford</CustomerName>
   <ShipTo>
       <Street>5th Ave</Street>
       <City>New York</City>
       <State>NY</State>
       <Zip>10010</Zip>
   </ShipTo>
   <PurchaseLineItems SOAP-ENC:arrayType="Order[2]">
       <Order>
           <Product>Apple</Product>
           <Price>1.56</Price>
       </Order>
       <Order>
           <Product>Peach</Product>
           <Price>1.48</Price>
```

```
        </Order>
    </PurchaseLineItems>
</xyz:PurchaseOrder>
```

5.4.2.1 Partially Transmitted Arrays

SOAP provides support for partially transmitted arrays, known as "varying" arrays in some contexts [12]. A partially transmitted array indicates in an "SOAP-ENC:offset" attribute the zero-origin offset of the first element transmitted. If omitted, the offset is taken as zero.

The following is an example of an array of size five that transmits only the third and fourth element counting from zero:

```
<SOAP-ENC:Array SOAP-ENC:arrayType="xsd:string[5]" SOAP-
ENC:offset="[2]">
   <item>The third element</item>
   <item>The fourth element</item>
</SOAP-ENC:Array>
```

5.4.2.2 Sparse Arrays

SOAP provides support for sparse arrays. Each element representing a member value contains a "SOAP-ENC:position" attribute that indicates its position within the array. The following is an example of a sparse array of two-dimensional arrays of strings. The size is 4 but only position 2 is used:

```
<SOAP-ENC:Array SOAP-ENC:arrayType="xsd:string[,][4]">
   <SOAP-ENC:Array href="#array-1" SOAP-
ENC:position="[2]"/>
</SOAP-ENC:Array>
<SOAP-ENC:Array id="array-1" SOAP-
ENC:arrayType="xsd:string[10,10]">
   <item SOAP-ENC:position="[2,2]">Third row, third
col</item>
   <item SOAP-ENC:position="[7,2]">Eighth row, third
col</item>
</SOAP-ENC:Array>
```

If the only reference to array-1 occurs in the enclosing array, this example could also have been encoded as follows:

```
<SOAP-ENC:Array SOAP-ENC:arrayType="xsd:string[,][4]">
  <SOAP-ENC:Array SOAP-ENC:position="[2]" SOAP-
ENC:arrayType="xsd:string[10,10]>
    <item SOAP-ENC:position="[2,2]">Third row, third
col</item>
    <item SOAP-ENC:position="[7,2]">Eighth row, third
```

```
col</item>
   </SOAP-ENC:Array>
</SOAP-ENC:Array>
```

5.4.3 Generic Compound Types

The encoding rules just cited are not limited to those cases where the accessor names are known in advance. If accessor names are known only by inspection of the immediate values to be encoded, the same rules apply, namely that the accessor is encoded as an element whose name matches the name of the accessor, and the accessor either contains or references its value. Accessors containing values whose types cannot be determined in advance MUST always contain an appropriate xsi:type attribute giving the type of the value.

Similarly, the rules cited are sufficient to allow serialization of compound types having a mixture of accessors distinguished by name and accessors distinguished by both name and ordinal position. (That is, having some accessors repeated.) This does not require that any schema actually contain such types, but rather says that if a type-model schema does have such types, a corresponding XML syntactic schema and instance may be generated.

```
<xyz:PurchaseOrder>
   <CustomerName>Henry Ford</CustomerName>
   <ShipTo>
       <Street>5th Ave</Street>
       <City>New York</City>
       <State>NY</State>
       <Zip>10010</Zip>
   </ShipTo>
   <PurchaseLineItems>
       <Order>
           <Product>Apple</Product>
           <Price>1.56</Price>
       </Order>
       <Order>
           <Product>Peach</Product>
           <Price>1.48</Price>
       </Order>
   </PurchaseLineItems>
</xyz:PurchaseOrder>
```

Similarly, it is valid to serialize a compound value that structurally resembles an arrray but is not of type (or subtype) SOAP-ENC:Array. For example:

```
<PurchaseLineItems>
    <Order>
        <Product>Apple</Product>
```

```
        <Price>1.56</Price>
    </Order>
    <Order>
        <Product>Peach</Product>
        <Price>1.48</Price>
    </Order>
</PurchaseLineItems>
```

5.5 Default Values

An omitted accessor element implies either a default value or that no value is known. The specifics depend on the accessor, method, and its context. For example, an omitted accessor typically implies a Null value for polymorphic accessors (with the exact meaning of Null accessor-dependent). Likewise, an omitted Boolean accessor typically implies either a False value or that no value is known, and an omitted numeric accessor typically implies either that the value is zero or that no value is known.

5.6 SOAP root Attribute

The SOAP root attribute can be used to label serialization roots that are not true roots of an object graph so that the object graph can be deserialized. The attribute can have one of two values, either "1" or "0". True roots of an object graph have the implied attribute value of "1". Serialization roots that are not true roots can be labeled as serialization roots with an attribute value of "1" An element can explicitly be labeled as not being a serialization root with a value of "0".

The SOAP root attribute MAY appear on any subelement within the SOAP Header and SOAP Body elements. The attribute does not have a default value.

6. Using SOAP in HTTP

This section describes how to use SOAP within HTTP with or without using the HTTP Extension Framework. Binding SOAP to HTTP provides the advantage of being able to use the formalism and decentralized flexibility of SOAP with the rich feature set of HTTP. Carrying SOAP in HTTP does not mean that SOAP overrides existing semantics of HTTP but rather that the semantics of SOAP over HTTP maps naturally to HTTP semantics.

SOAP naturally follows the HTTP request/response message model providing SOAP request parameters in a HTTP request and SOAP response parameters in a HTTP response. Note, however, that SOAP intermediaries are NOT the same as HTTP intermediaries. That is, an HTTP intermediary addressed with the HTTP Connection header field cannot be expected to inspect or process the SOAP entity body carried in the HTTP request.

HTTP applications MUST use the media type "text/xml" according to RFC 2376 [3] when including SOAP entity bodies in HTTP messages.

6.1 SOAP HTTP Request

Although SOAP might be used in combination with a variety of HTTP request methods, this binding only defines SOAP within HTTP POST requests (see section 7 for how to use SOAP for RPC and section 6.3 for how to use the HTTP Extension Framework).

6.1.1 The SOAPAction HTTP Header Field

The SOAPAction HTTP request header field can be used to indicate the intent of the SOAP HTTP request. The value is a URI identifying the intent. SOAP places no restrictions on the format or specificity of the URI or that it is resolvable. An HTTP client MUST use this header field when issuing a SOAP HTTP Request.

```
soapaction    = "SOAPAction" ":" [ <"> URI-reference <">
]
URI-reference = <as defined in RFC 2396 [4]>
```

The presence and content of the SOAPAction header field can be used by servers such as firewalls to appropriately filter SOAP request messages in HTTP. The header field value of empty string ("") means that the intent of the SOAP message is provided by the HTTP Request-URI. No value means that there is no indication of the intent of the message.

Examples:

```
SOAPAction: "http://electrocommerce.org/abc#MyMessage"
SOAPAction: "myapp.sdl"
SOAPAction: ""
SOAPAction:
```

6.2 SOAP HTTP Response

SOAP HTTP follows the semantics of the HTTP Status codes for communicating status information in HTTP. For example, a 2xx status code indicates that the client's request including the SOAP component was successfully received, understood, and accepted etc.

In case of a SOAP error while processing the request, the SOAP HTTP server MUST issue an HTTP 500 "Internal Server Error" response and include a SOAP message in the response containing a SOAP Fault element (see section 4.4) indicating the SOAP processing error.

6.3 The HTTP Extension Framework

A SOAP message MAY be used together with the HTTP Extension Framework [6] in order to identify the presence and intent of a SOAP HTTP request.

Whether to use the Extension Framework or plain HTTP is a question of policy and capability of the communicating parties. Clients can force the use of the HTTP Extension Framework by using a mandatory extension declaration and the "M-" HTTP method name prefix. Servers can force the use of the HTTP Extension Framework by using the 510 "Not Extended" HTTP status code. That is, using one extra round trip, either party can detect the policy of the other party and act accordingly.

The extension identifier used to identify SOAP using the Extension Framework is

```
http://schemas.xmlsoap.org/soap/envelope/
```

6.4 SOAP HTTP Examples

Example 3 SOAP HTTP Using POST

```
POST /StockQuote HTTP/1.1
Content-Type: text/xml; charset="utf-8"
Content-Length: nnnn
SOAPAction: "http://electrocommerce.org/abc#MyMessage"

<SOAP-ENV:Envelope...

HTTP/1.1 200 OK
Content-Type: text/xml; charset="utf-8"
Content-Length: nnnn

<SOAP-ENV:Envelope...
```

Example 4 SOAP Using HTTP Extension Framework

```
M-POST /StockQuote HTTP/1.1
Man: "http://schemas.xmlsoap.org/soap/envelope/";
ns=NNNN
Content-Type: text/xml; charset="utf-8"
Content-Length: nnnn
NNNN-SOAPAction:
"http://electrocommerce.org/abc#MyMessage"

<SOAP-ENV:Envelope...

HTTP/1.1 200 OK
Ext:
```

```
Content-Type: text/xml; charset="utf-8"
Content-Length: nnnn

<SOAP-ENV:Envelope...
```

7. Using SOAP for RPC

One of the design goals of SOAP is to encapsulate and exchange RPC calls using the extensibility and flexibility of XML. This section defines a uniform representation of remote procedure calls and responses.

Although it is anticipated that this representation is likely to be used in combination with the encoding style defined in section 5 other representations are possible. The SOAP encodingStyle attribute (see section 4.3.2) can be used to indicate the encoding style of the method call and or the response using the representation described in this section.

Using SOAP for RPC is orthogonal to the SOAP protocol binding (see section 6). In the case of using HTTP as the protocol binding, an RPC call maps naturally to an HTTP request and an RPC response maps to an HTTP response. However, using SOAP for RPC is not limited to the HTTP protocol binding.

To make a method call, the following information is needed:

- The URI of the target object
- A method name
- An optional method signature
- The parameters to the method
- Optional header data

SOAP relies on the protocol binding to provide a mechanism for carrying the URI. For example, for HTTP the request URI indicates the resource that the invocation is being made against. Other than it be a valid URI, SOAP places no restriction on the form of an address (see [4] for more information on URIs).

7.1 RPC and SOAP Body

RPC method calls and responses are both carried in the SOAP Body element (see section 4.3) using the following representation:

- A method invocation is modelled as a struct.
- The method invocation is viewed as a single struct containing an accessor for each [in] or [in/out] parameter. The struct is both named and typed identically to the method name.

- Each [in] or [in/out] parameter is viewed as an accessor, with a name corresponding to the name of the parameter and type corresponding to the type of the parameter. These appear in the same order as in the method signature.

- A method response is modelled as a struct.

- The method response is viewed as a single struct containing an accessor for the return value and each [out] or [in/out] parameter. The first accessor is the return value followed by the parameters in the same order as in the method signature.

- Each parameter accessor has a name corresponding to the name of the parameter and type corresponding to the type of the parameter. The name of the return value accessor is not significant. Likewise, the name of the struct is not significant. However, a convention is to name it after the method name with the string "Response" appended.

- A method fault is encoded using the SOAP Fault element (see section 4.4). If a protocol binding adds additional rules for fault expression, those also MUST be followed.

As noted above, method and response structs can be encoded according to the rules in section 5, or other encodings can be specified using the encodingStyle attribute (see section 4.1.1).

Applications MAY process requests with missing parameters but also MAY return a fault.

Because a result indicates success and a fault indicates failure, it is an error for the method response to contain both a result and a fault.

7.2 RPC and SOAP Header

Additional information relevant to the encoding of a method request but not part of the formal method signature MAY be expressed in the RPC encoding. If so, it MUST be expressed as a subelement of the SOAP Header element.

An example of the use of the header element is the passing of a transaction ID along with a message. Since the transaction ID is not part of the signature and is typically held in an infrastructure component rather than application code, there is no direct way to pass the necessary information with the call. By adding an entry to the headers and giving it a fixed name, the transaction manager on the receiving side can extract the transaction ID and use it without affecting the coding of remote procedure calls.

8. Security Considerations

Not described in this document are methods for integrity and privacy protection. Such issues will be addressed more fully in a future version(s) of this document.

9. References

[1] S. Bradner, "The Internet Standards Process -- Revision 3", RFC2026, Harvard University, October 1996

[2] S. Bradner, "Key words for use in RFCs to Indicate Requirement Levels", RFC 2119, Harvard University, March 1997

[3] E. Whitehead, M. Murata, "XML Media Types", RFC2376, UC Irvine, Fuji Xerox Info. Systems, July 1998

[4] T. Berners-Lee, R. Fielding, L. Masinter, "Uniform Resource Identifiers (URI): Generic Syntax", RFC 2396, MIT/LCS, U.C. Irvine, Xerox Corporation, August 1998.

[5] R. Fielding, J. Gettys, J. C. Mogul, H. Frystyk, T. Berners-Lee, "Hypertext Transfer Protocol -- HTTP/1.1", RFC 2616, U.C. Irvine, DEC W3C/MIT, DEC, W3C/MIT, W3C/MIT, January 1997

[6] H. Nielsen, P. Leach, S. Lawrence, "An HTTP Extension Framework", RFC 2774, Microsoft, Microsoft, Agranat Systems

[7] W3C Recommendation "The XML Specification"

[8] W3C Recommendation "Namespaces in XML".

[9] W3C Working Draft "XML Linking Language". This is work in progress.

[10] W3C Working Draft "XML Schema Part 1: Structures". This is work in progress.

[11] W3C Working Draft "XML Schema Part 2: Datatypes". This is work in progress.

[12] Transfer Syntax NDR, in "DCE 1.1: Remote Procedure Call"

[13] N. Freed, N. Borenstein, "Multipurpose Internet Mail Extensions (MIME) Part One: Format of Internet Message Bodies", RFC2045, Innosoft, First Virtual, November 1996

A. SOAP Envelope Examples

A.1 Sample Encoding of Call Requests

Example 5 Similar to Example 1 but with a Mandatory Header

```
POST /StockQuote HTTP/1.1
Host: www.stockquoteserver.com
Content-Type: text/xml; charset="utf-8"
Content-Length: nnnn
SOAPAction: "Some-URI"
<SOAP-ENV:Envelope
```

```
  xmlns:SOAP-
ENV="http://schemas.xmlsoap.org/soap/envelope/"
  SOAP-
ENV:encodingStyle="http://schemas.xmlsoap.org/soap/encod
ing/"/>
   <SOAP-ENV:Header>
       <t:Transaction
           xmlns:t="some-URI"
           SOAP-ENV:mustUnderstand="1">
               5
       </t:Transaction>
   </SOAP-ENV:Header>
   <SOAP-ENV:Body>
       <m:GetLastTradePrice xmlns:m="Some-URI">
           <symbol>DEF</symbol>
       </m:GetLastTradePrice>
   </SOAP-ENV:Body>
</SOAP-ENV:Envelope>
```

Example 6 Similar to Example 1 but with multiple request parameters

```
POST /StockQuote HTTP/1.1
Host: www.stockquoteserver.com
Content-Type: text/xml; charset="utf-8"
Content-Length: nnnn
SOAPAction: "Some-URI"

<SOAP-ENV:Envelope
  xmlns:SOAP-
ENV="http://schemas.xmlsoap.org/soap/envelope/"
  SOAP-
ENV:encodingStyle="http://schemas.xmlsoap.org/soap/encod
ing/"/>
   <SOAP-ENV:Body>
       <m:GetLastTradePriceDetailed
         xmlns:m="Some-URI">
           <Symbol>DEF</Symbol>
           <Company>DEF Corp</Company>
           <Price>34.1</Price>
       </m:GetLastTradePriceDetailed>
   </SOAP-ENV:Body>
</SOAP-ENV:Envelope>
```

A.2 Sample Encoding of Response

Example 7 Similar to Example 2 but with a Mandatory Header

```
HTTP/1.1 200 OK
Content-Type: text/xml; charset="utf-8"
Content-Length: nnnn

<SOAP-ENV:Envelope
  xmlns:SOAP-
ENV="http://schemas.xmlsoap.org/soap/envelope/"
  SOAP-
ENV:encodingStyle="http://schemas.xmlsoap.org/soap/encod
ing/"/>
   <SOAP-ENV:Header>
       <t:Transaction
         xmlns:t="some-URI"
         xsi:type="xsd:int" mustUnderstand="1">
           5
       </t:Transaction>
   </SOAP-ENV:Header>
   <SOAP-ENV:Body>
       <m:GetLastTradePriceResponse
         xmlns:m="Some-URI">
           <Price>34.5</Price>
       </m:GetLastTradePriceResponse>
   </SOAP-ENV:Body>
</SOAP-ENV:Envelope>
```

Example 8 Similar to Example 2 but with a Struct

```
HTTP/1.1 200 OK
Content-Type: text/xml; charset="utf-8"
Content-Length: nnnn

<SOAP-ENV:Envelope
  xmlns:SOAP-
ENV="http://schemas.xmlsoap.org/soap/envelope/"
  SOAP-
ENV:encodingStyle="http://schemas.xmlsoap.org/soap/encod
ing/"/>
   <SOAP-ENV:Body>
       <m:GetLastTradePriceResponse
```

```
          xmlns:m="Some-URI">
            <PriceAndVolume>
                <LastTradePrice>
                    34.5
                </LastTradePrice>
                <DayVolume>
                    10000
                </DayVolume>
            </PriceAndVolume>
        </m:GetLastTradePriceResponse>
    </SOAP-ENV:Body>
</SOAP-ENV:Envelope>
```

Example 9 Similar to Example 2 but Failing to honor Mandatory Header

```
HTTP/1.1 500 Internal Server Error
Content-Type: text/xml; charset="utf-8"
Content-Length: nnnn

<SOAP-ENV:Envelope
  xmlns:SOAP-
ENV="http://schemas.xmlsoap.org/soap/envelope/">
   <SOAP-ENV:Body>
       <SOAP-ENV:Fault>
           <faultcode>SOAP-
ENV:MustUnderstand</faultcode>
           <faultstring>SOAP Must Understand
Error</faultstring>
       </SOAP-ENV:Fault>
   </SOAP-ENV:Body>
</SOAP-ENV:Envelope>
```

Example 10 Similar to Example 2 but Failing to handle Body

```
HTTP/1.1 500 Internal Server Error
Content-Type: text/xml; charset="utf-8"
Content-Length: nnnn

<SOAP-ENV:Envelope
  xmlns:SOAP-
ENV="http://schemas.xmlsoap.org/soap/envelope/">
   <SOAP-ENV:Body>
       <SOAP-ENV:Fault>
           <faultcode>SOAP-ENV:Server</faultcode>
```

```
            <faultstring>Server Error</faultstring>
            <detail>
                <e:myfaultdetails xmlns:e="Some-URI">
                  <message>
                    My application didn't work
                  </message>
                  <errorcode>
                    1001
                  </errorcode>
                </e:myfaultdetails>
            </detail>
        </SOAP-ENV:Fault>
    </SOAP-ENV:Body>
</SOAP-ENV:Envelope>
```

W3C® DOCUMENT NOTICE AND LICENSE

THAT THE CONTENTS OF THE DOCUMENT ARE SUITABLE FOR ANY PURPOSE; NOR THAT THE IMPLEMENTATION OF SUCH CONTENTS WILL NOT INFRINGE ANY THIRD PARTY PATENTS, COPYRIGHTS, TRADEMARKS OR OTHER RIGHTS.
COPYRIGHT HOLDERS WILL NOT BE LIABLE FOR ANY DIRECT, INDIRECT, SPECIAL OR CONSEQUENTIAL DAMAGES ARISING OUT OF ANY USE OF THE DOCUMENT OR THE PERFORMANCE OR IMPLEMENTATION OF THE CONTENTS THEREOF.
The name and trademarks of copyright holders may NOT be used in advertising or publicity pertaining to this document or its contents without specific, written prior permission. Title to copyright in this document will at all times remain with copyright holders.

This formulation of W3C's notice and license became active on April 05 1999 so as to account for the treatment of DTDs, schema's and bindings. See the older formulation for the policy prior to this date. Please see our Copyright FAQ for common questions about using materials from our site, including specific terms and conditions for packages like libwww, Amaya, and Jigsaw. Other questions about this notice can be directed to site-policy@w3.org.
webmaster
(last updated by reagle on 1999/04/99.)

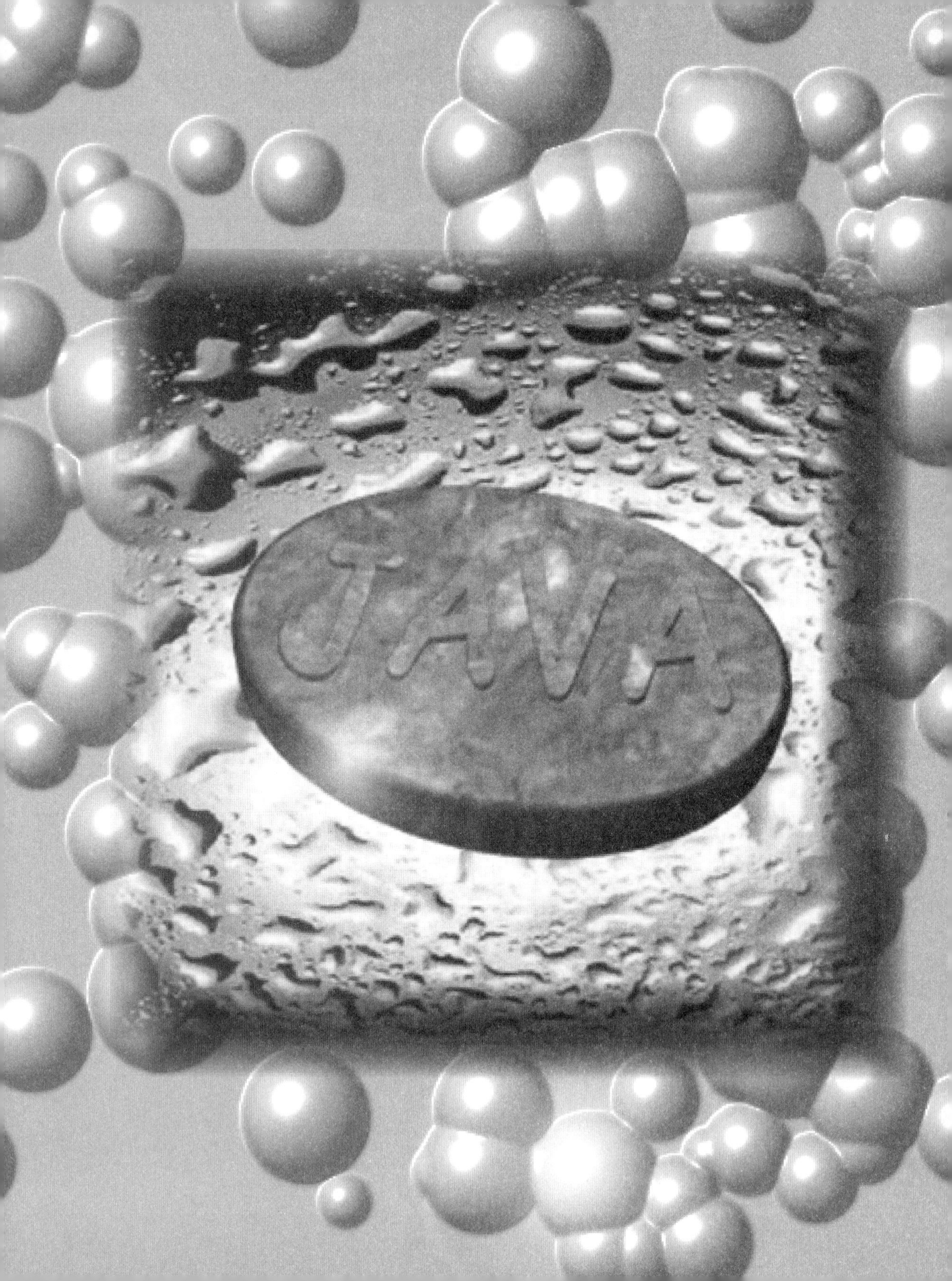
JAVA

B

Catalina (Tomcat 4.0)

This book is going to publication after the release of Catalina, the version 4.0 of Tomcat, and you are likely to find installations of that new release in production by the time you read these pages. Despite the fact that it is the 3.2 release of Tomcat which is recommended for use with SOAP, this may not always be practical or even desirable in some situations. This appendix aims to show the reader how to deploy their SOAP applications on Catalina. To give you an idea of what needs to be changed between Tomcat 3 and Tomcat 4, we will compile and deploy the `HelloWorld` sample that we wrote back in Chapter 3 under Catalina.

Things are actually simpler in Catalina because a few annoying problems that we had to deal with under Tomcat 3 no longer exist in Tomcat 4. The two main ones are the `xerces.jar` issue and the `/lib/` issue. Because Tomcat 3 shipped with an XML parser that was not compatible with SOAP, we had to explicitly include the `xerces.jar` library at the beginning of the system classpath. The `/lib/` issue had to do with the fact that Tomcat 3 would not always include JAR files included in the `WEB-INF/lib` as part of your classpath. As we said earlier, these problems are no more and the setup of Tomcat for SOAP development is more straightforward than ever.

The instructions are similar for Windows and Linux.

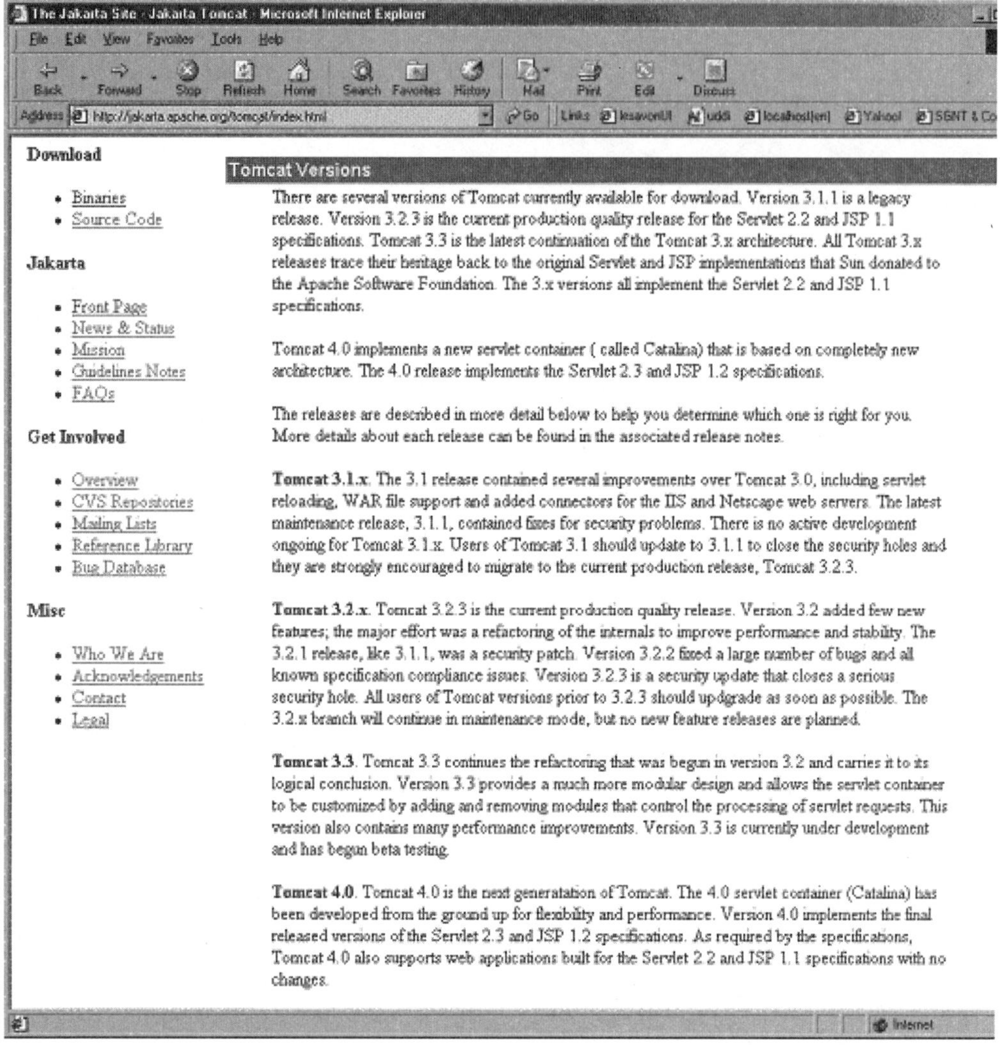

To get to the downloadable file, you can navigate through the binaries by following the Binaries link and a couple of other pages or directly go to http://jakarta.apache.org/builds/jakarta-tomcat-4.0/release/v4.0.1/bin/:

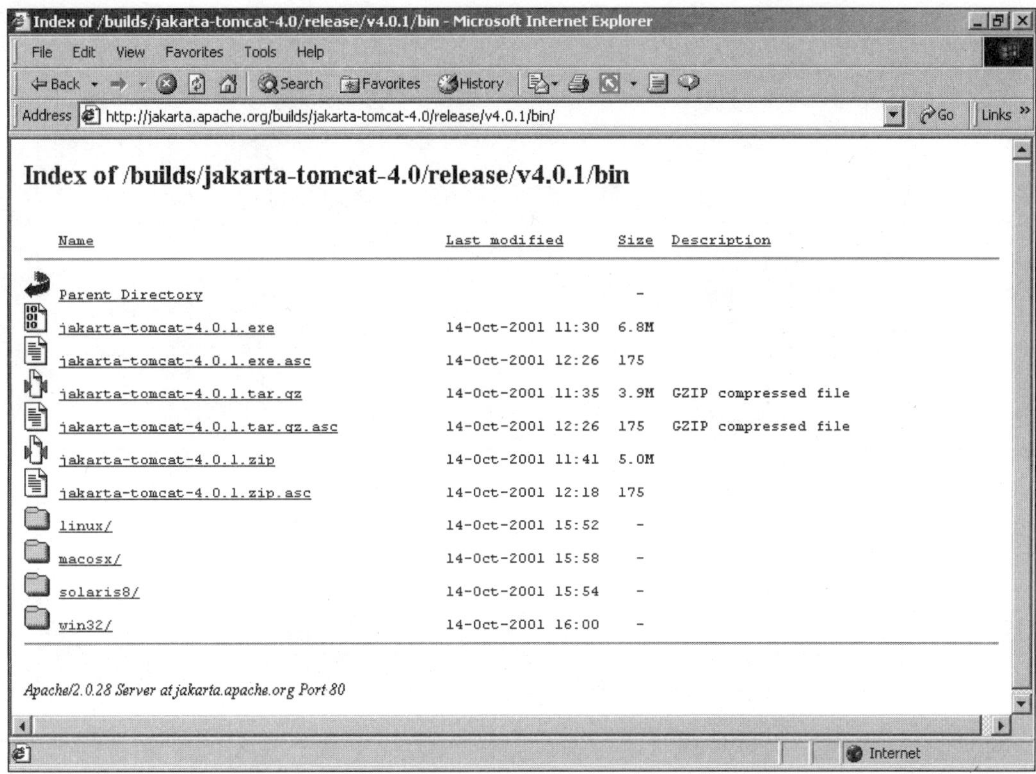

Select the file you need (for Windows you need jakarta-tomcat-4.0.1.zip, and for Linux you need jakarta-tomcat-4.0.1.tar.gz), and download it now. We will put the file in the `C:\` directory for now, but any other location will work.

The ZIP file can be exploded using the WinZip utility. We have chosen to extract Catalina directly to the `C:\` directory for ease of use:

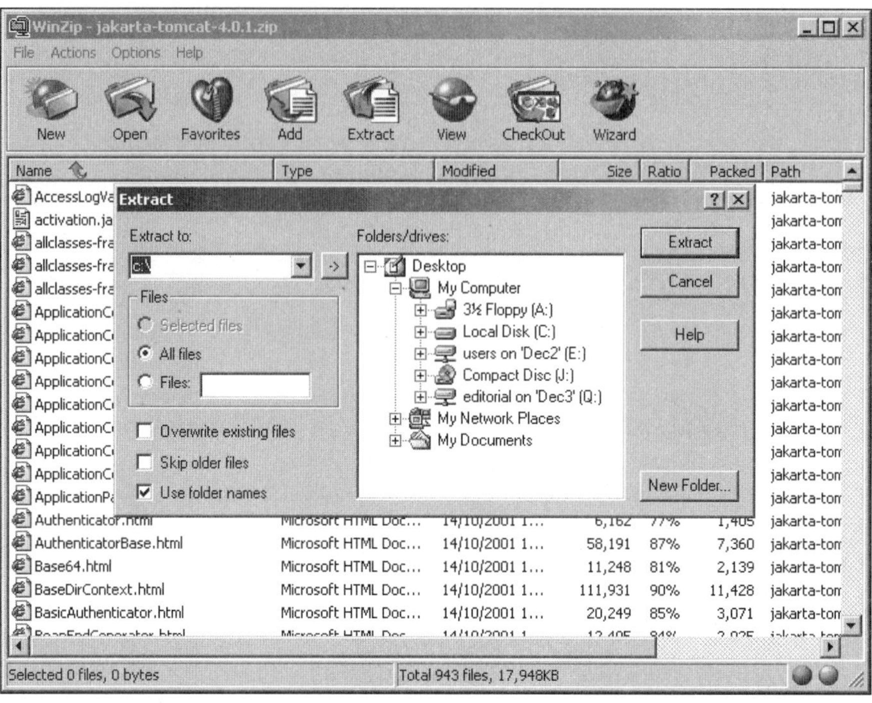

At the end of this process, your Tomcat 4 directory (`C:\jakarta-tomcat-4.0.1`) should look like the following screenshot.

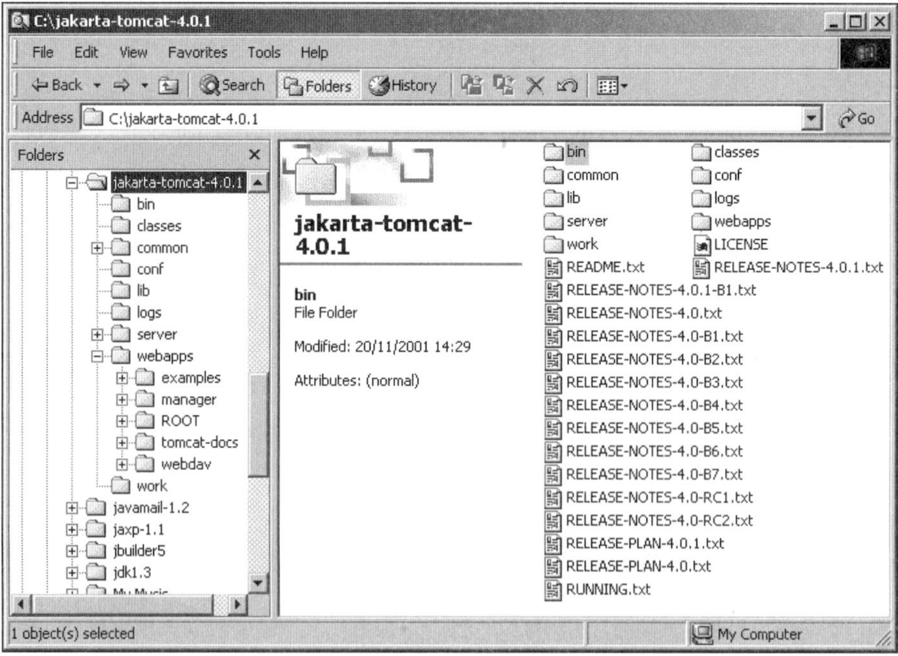

Catalina is now ready to run. You can use `startup.sh` on Linux and `startup.bat` on Windows as shown on the next picture:

```
C:\WINNT\System32\cmd.exe
Microsoft Windows 2000 [Version 5.00.2195]
(C) Copyright 1985-2000 Microsoft Corp.

C:\jakarta-tomcat-4.0.1\bin>startup
Using CATALINA_BASE:   ..
Using CATALINA_HOME:   ..
Using CLASSPATH:       ..\bin\bootstrap.jar;C:\jdk1.3\lib\tools.jar
Using JAVA_HOME:       C:\jdk1.3
C:\jakarta-tomcat-4.0.1\bin>
```

The Catalina process runs in its own window by default:

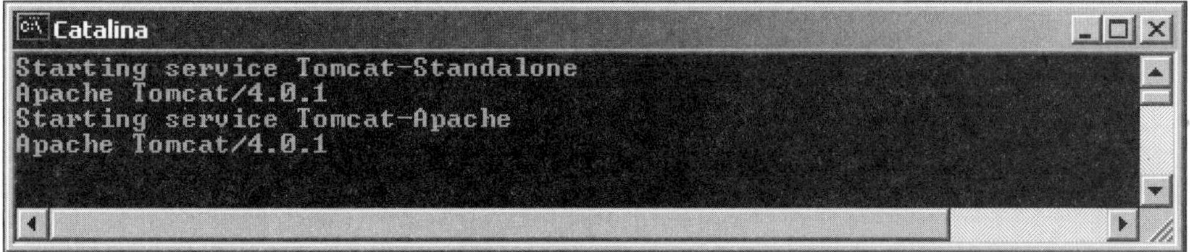

To test that Tomcat 4 is actually taking requests, we can go to the Tomcat homepage (http://localhost:8080/index.html). Port 8080 is the default):

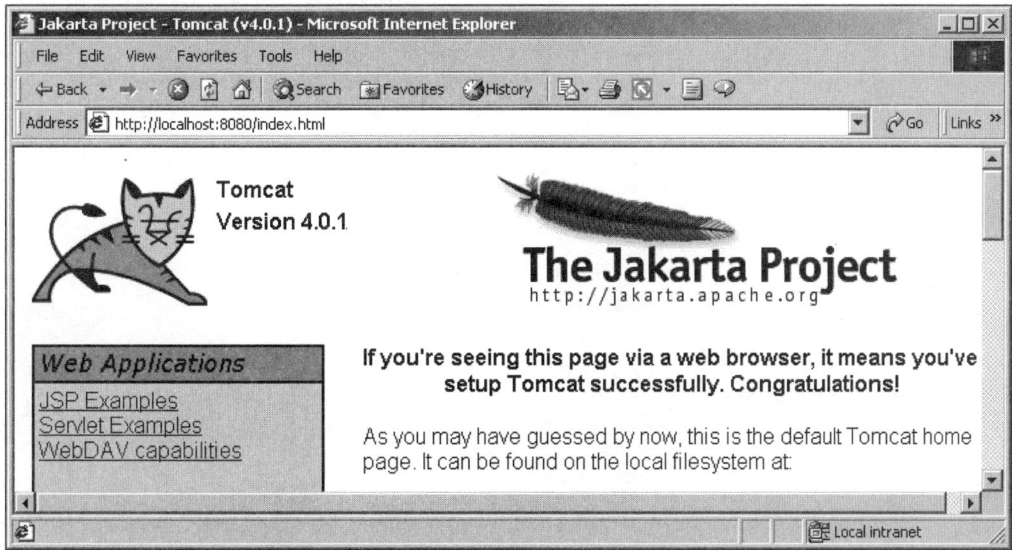

You can find the Appendix B version of HelloWorld in \ProJavaSoap\AppendixB\HelloWorld in the code download. The only difference between the version we wrote in Chapter 3 and this version is the copy of the jar files: soap.jar, activation.jar, and mail.jar to the WEB-INF/lib directory.

Here is the BuildHelloWorld.xml file:

```
<project name="HelloWorld" default="compile" basedir=".">
  <property name="app.name"         value="HelloWorld"/>
  <property name="deploy.home"      value="/ProJavaSoap/AppendixB/${app.name}"/>
  <property name="deploy.lib"       value="${deploy.home}/WEB-INF/lib"/>
  <property name="dist.home"        value="/ProJavaSoap/AppendixB/${app.name}"/>
  <property name="warfile"         value="${dist.home}/${app.name}.war"/>
  <property name="soap.home"       value="/soap-2_2"/>

  <target name="prepare">
    <mkdir  dir="${deploy.home}"/>
    <mkdir  dir="${deploy.home}/WEB-INF"/>
    <mkdir  dir="${deploy.home}/WEB-INF/classes"/>
    <mkdir  dir="${deploy.home}/WEB-INF/classes/lib"/>
  </target>

  <target name="clean">
    <delete dir="${deploy.home}"/>
    <delete file="${warfile}"/>
  </target>

  <target name="compile" depends="prepare">
   <copy  file="${soap.home}/lib/soap.jar" todir="${deploy.lib}"/>
   <copy  file="${soap.home}/lib/mail.jar" todir="${deploy.lib}"/>
   <copy  file="${soap.home}/lib/activation.jar" todir="${deploy.lib}"/>
   <copy  file="etc/web.xml" tofile="${deploy.home}/WEB-INF/web.xml"/>
   <javac srcdir="src" destdir="${deploy.home}/WEB-INF/classes"
            debug="on" optimize="off" deprecation="off"/>
   <war warfile="${warfile}" webxml="etc/web.xml">
     <classes dir="${deploy.home}/WEB-INF/classes"/>
     <lib dir="${deploy.lib}"/>
   </war>
  </target>

  <target name="all" depends="clean,prepare,compile"/>
</project>
```

With ANT the build steps are straightforward. Note that the classpath to build must include soap.jar, activation.jar, and mail.jar.

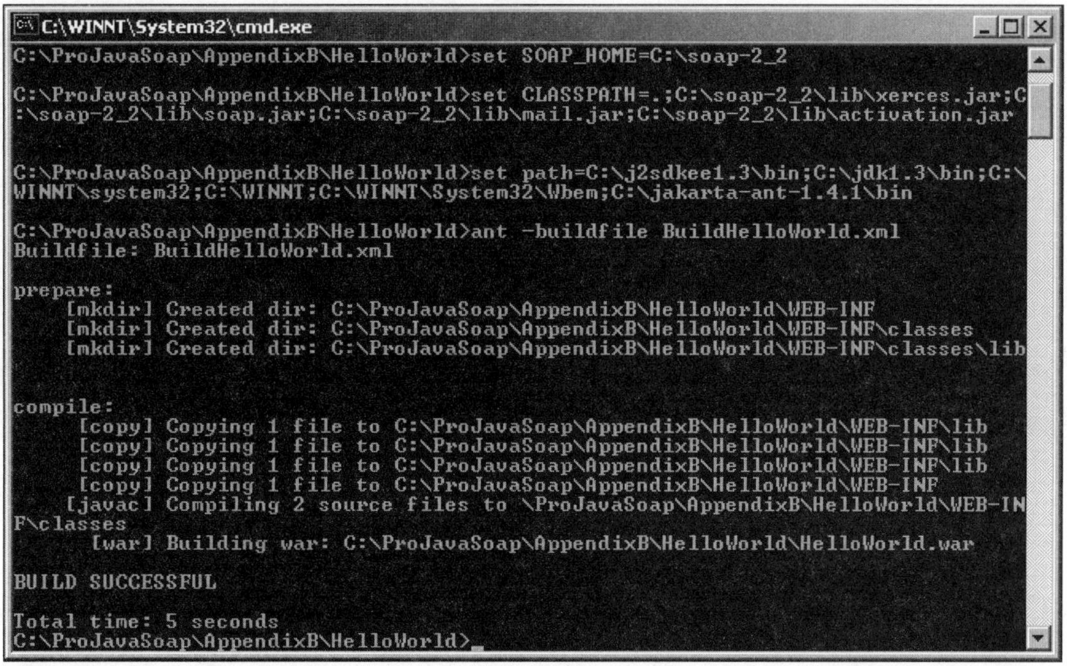

```
C:\WINNT\System32\cmd.exe
C:\ProJavaSoap\AppendixB\HelloWorld>set SOAP_HOME=C:\soap-2_2

C:\ProJavaSoap\AppendixB\HelloWorld>set CLASSPATH=.;C:\soap-2_2\lib\xerces.jar;C
:\soap-2_2\lib\soap.jar;C:\soap-2_2\lib\mail.jar;C:\soap-2_2\lib\activation.jar

C:\ProJavaSoap\AppendixB\HelloWorld>set path=C:\j2sdkee1.3\bin;C:\jdk1.3\bin;C:\
WINNT\system32;C:\WINNT;C:\WINNT\System32\Wbem;C:\jakarta-ant-1.4.1\bin

C:\ProJavaSoap\AppendixB\HelloWorld>ant -buildfile BuildHelloWorld.xml
Buildfile: BuildHelloWorld.xml

prepare:
    [mkdir] Created dir: C:\ProJavaSoap\AppendixB\HelloWorld\WEB-INF
    [mkdir] Created dir: C:\ProJavaSoap\AppendixB\HelloWorld\WEB-INF\classes
    [mkdir] Created dir: C:\ProJavaSoap\AppendixB\HelloWorld\WEB-INF\classes\lib

compile:
     [copy] Copying 1 file to C:\ProJavaSoap\AppendixB\HelloWorld\WEB-INF\lib
     [copy] Copying 1 file to C:\ProJavaSoap\AppendixB\HelloWorld\WEB-INF\lib
     [copy] Copying 1 file to C:\ProJavaSoap\AppendixB\HelloWorld\WEB-INF\lib
     [copy] Copying 1 file to C:\ProJavaSoap\AppendixB\HelloWorld\WEB-INF
    [javac] Compiling 2 source files to \ProJavaSoap\AppendixB\HelloWorld\WEB-IN
F\classes
      [war] Building war: C:\ProJavaSoap\AppendixB\HelloWorld\HelloWorld.war

BUILD SUCCESSFUL

Total time: 5 seconds
C:\ProJavaSoap\AppendixB\HelloWorld>_
```

We also need to tell Catalina that `C:\ProJavaSoap\AppendixB\HelloWorld` is a web application. This is easily achieved by modifying the `conf\server.xml` (below the Tomcat installation directory):

```
<!-- Tomcat Manager Context -->
<Context path="/manager" docBase="manager"
 debug="0" privileged="true"/>

<Context path="/helloworld" docBase="C:\ProJavaSoap\AppendixB\HelloWorld"
 debug="0" privileged="true"/>

<!-- Tomcat Examples Context -->
```

Since `HelloWorld` does not use the automatic registration that we designed in Chapter 5, we need to manually register it prior running. The classpath for the execution must include a path to the `HelloWorldClient` class:

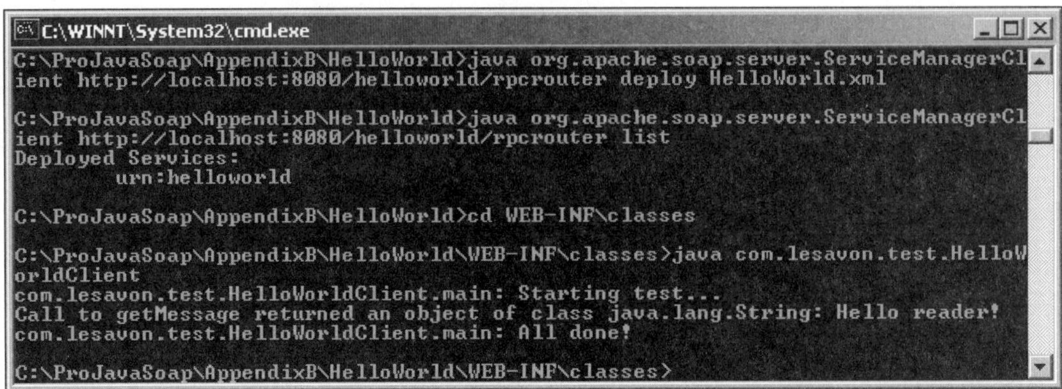

C:\WINNT\System32\cmd.exe
C:\ProJavaSoap\AppendixB\HelloWorld>java org.apache.soap.server.ServiceManagerCl
ient http://localhost:8080/helloworld/rpcrouter deploy HelloWorld.xml
C:\ProJavaSoap\AppendixB\HelloWorld>java org.apache.soap.server.ServiceManagerCl
ient http://localhost:8080/helloworld/rpcrouter list
Deployed Services:
urn:helloworld
C:\ProJavaSoap\AppendixB\HelloWorld>cd WEB-INF\classes
C:\ProJavaSoap\AppendixB\HelloWorld\WEB-INF\classes>java com.lesavon.test.HelloW
orldClient
com.lesavon.test.HelloWorldClient.main: Starting test...
Call to getMessage returned an object of class java.lang.String: Hello reader!
com.lesavon.test.HelloWorldClient.main: All done!
C:\ProJavaSoap\AppendixB\HelloWorld\WEB-INF\classes>

Here we have set the classpath, manually deployed our service, and then run our application. We can also use the `HelloWorld.war` file by copying it to the `jakarta-tomcat-4.0.1\webapps` directory and Tomcat will expand the directory structure to give the same hierarchy as we created in the `C:\ProJavaSoap\AppendixB\HelloWorld` directory.

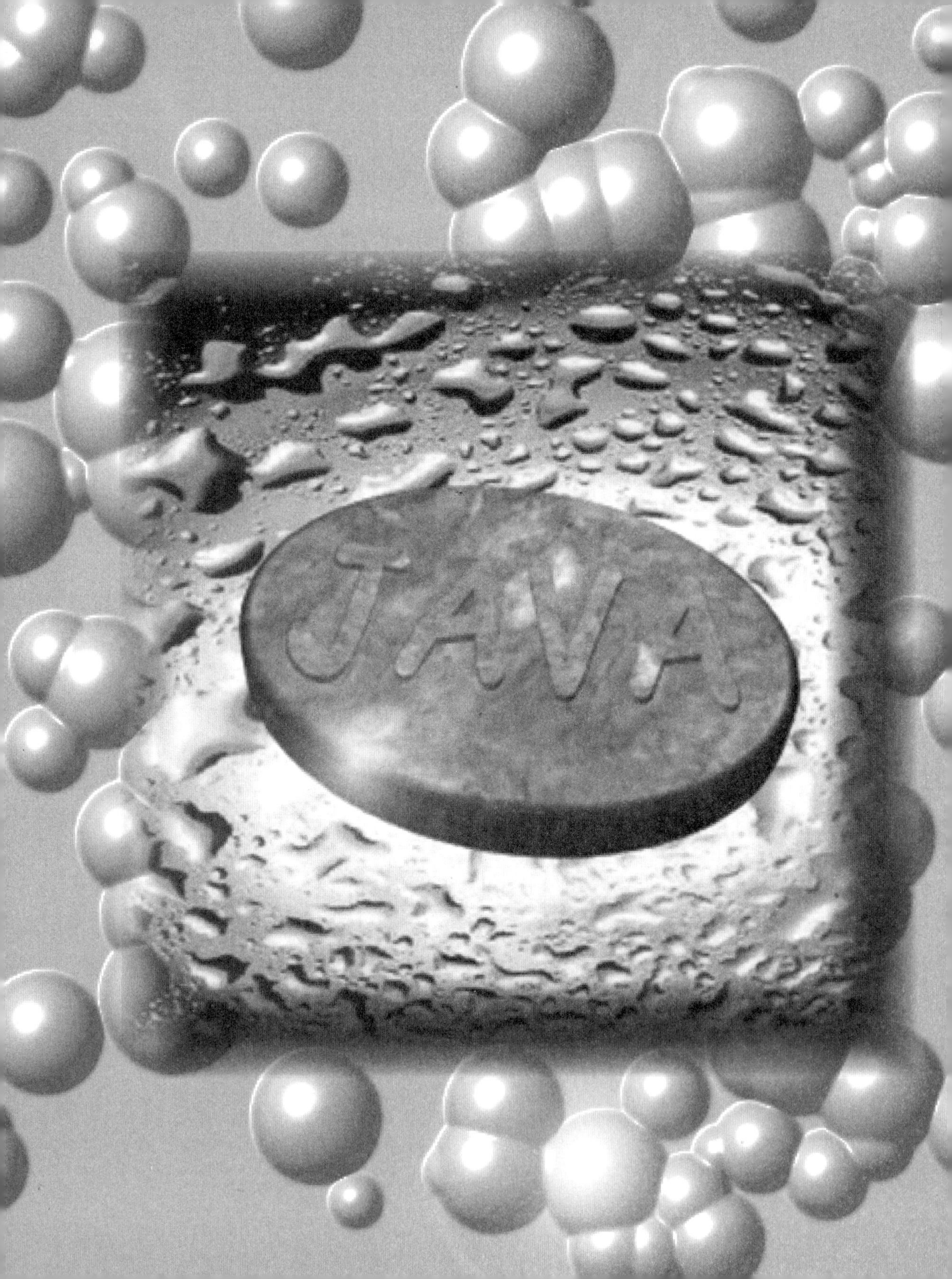
JAVA

C

Authentication with LDAP

In this appendix, we describe how to setup Apache and Tomcat with LDAP authentication on a Windows 2000 machine. We will assume that you have already downloaded and installed Tomcat as described in Chapter 3. We will use Apache 1.3.22 and Tomcat 3.2.3. We will also install Apache and Tomcat in C:\Apache. Feel free to replace that root path with your own settings.

> *The sample code covered in this appendix can be found in the \ProJavaSoap\Chapter07\mod_ldap directory.*

The Apache Web Server

The first step is to download `apache_1.3.22-win32-x86.exe` or `apache_1.3.22-win32-x86.msi` from http://httpd.apache.org/dist/httpd/binaries/win32/. In this appendix, we'll assume you've downloaded the executable version, though it doesn't really matter. The EXE is a self-extracting ZIP file that will start an installation program, as shown in the next screenshot:

Click Next to continue, accept the license agreement and fill out the required information as shown in the next figure:

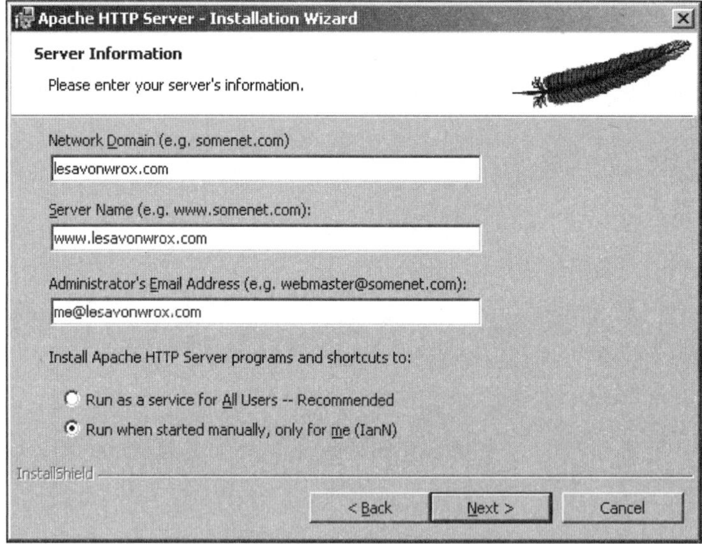

Click Next. You'll be asked what type of setup you require – select Complete, and Next to move onto the last screen before the installation. This last screen prompts you for the destination directory. The default directory path contains space characters, which can become problematic later on, so we're going to click the Change... button and change it to C:\Apache:

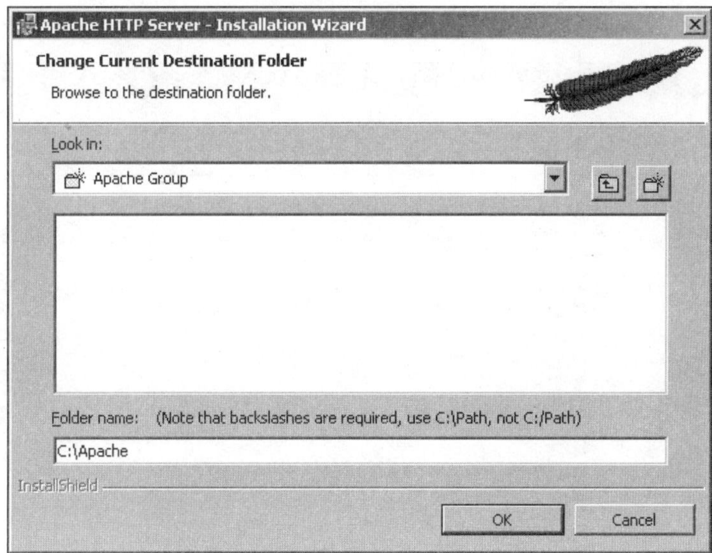

On the next screen, click on Install to start the installation process. Once the installation is complete, you will get the following dialog box:

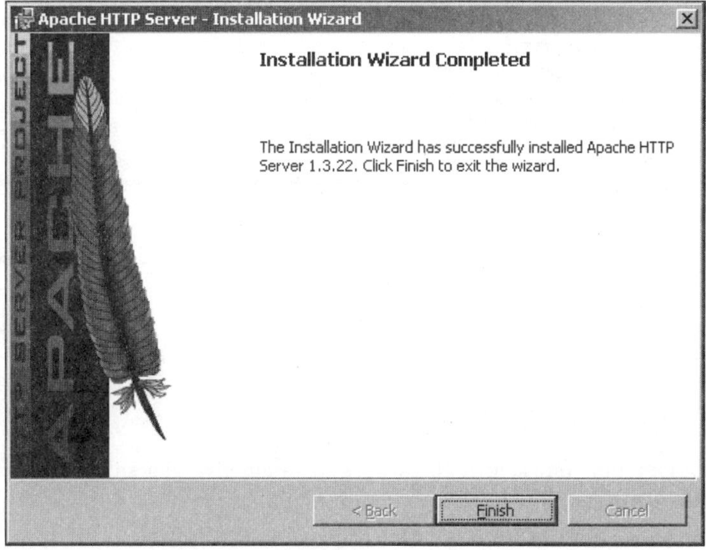

The installation created the c:\Apache\Apache directory as shown in the following figure:

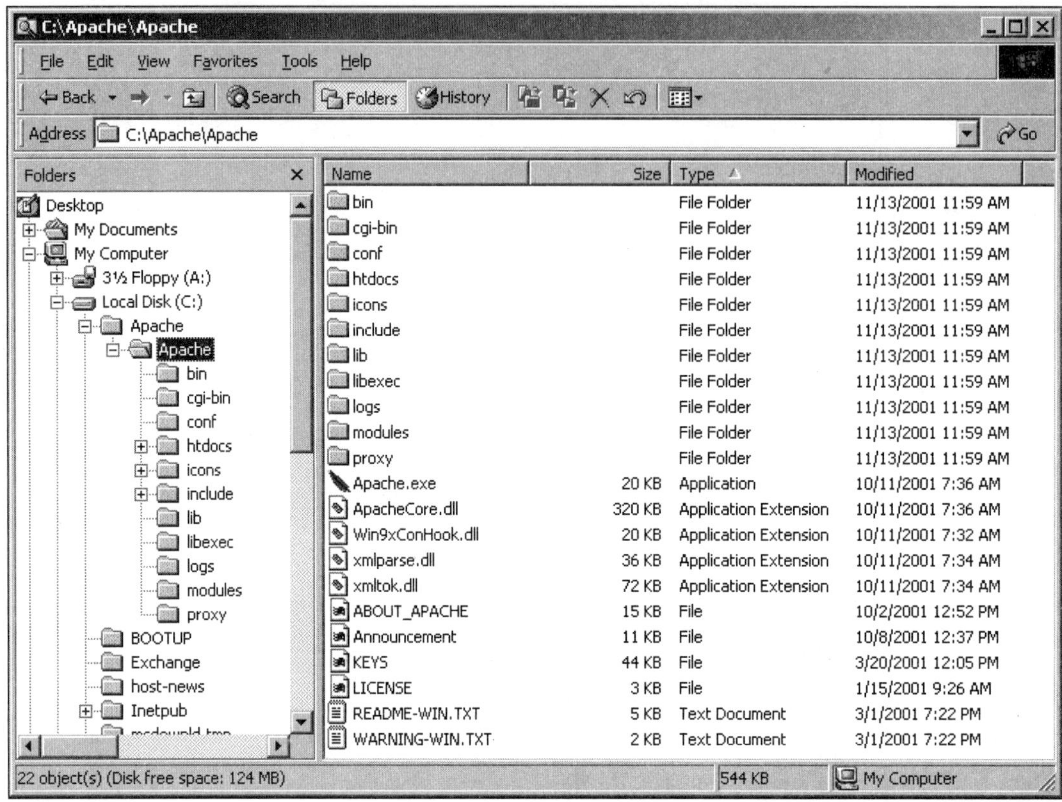

To test that your Apache installation works, you simply need to start the Apache server from the Command window, using the following commands (make sure that you do not have another web server, like IIS, already running) on port 80:

```
C:\>cd Apache\Apache
C:\Apache\Apache>Apache
Apache/1.3.22 (Win32) running...
```

Now type http://localhost into your favorite browser – it should give you a display similar to the following:

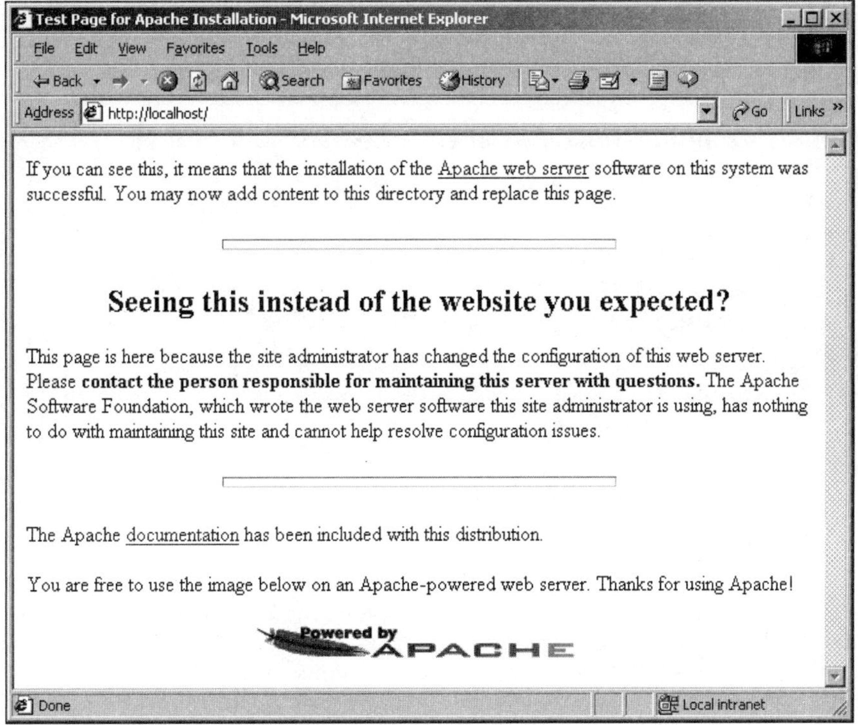

Integrating Apache and Tomcat

At this point, the Apache web server is successfully taking HTTP requests. We will now enable the Apache/Tomcat integration to allow Apache to handle servlet and JSP requests with Tomcat's help.

> *The following instructions are a digest of the Apache/Jakarta document that you can find in the file \doc\tomcat-apache-howto.html, under the root of your Tomcat installation.*

The integration between Apache and Tomcat is implemented with the `mod_jk.dll` module. You can download this module from http://jakarta.apache.org/builds/jakarta-tomcat/release/v3.2.3/bin/win32/i386/:

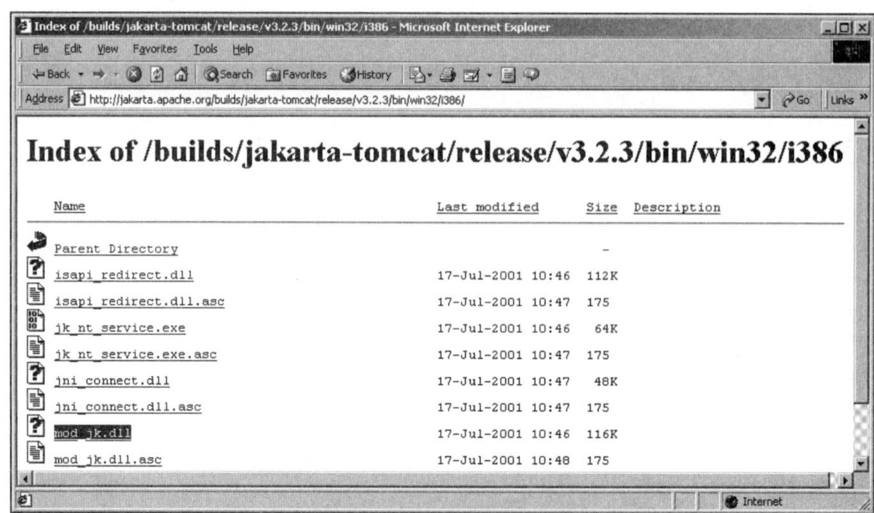

Click on the link, and download it to the C:\Apache\Apache\modules directory or its equivalent.

In order to let Apache know that servlet and JSP requests should be forwarded to Tomcat, we simply need to modify the conf\httpd.conf file to include the `mod_jk.conf-auto` file as shown in the following figure. To do so, add the following line to the very end of this file (It has over 1000 lines.) Here, C:/Apache/tomcat is the Tomcat installation directory; you may need to amend this value:

```
include C:/Apache/tomcat/conf/mod_jk.conf-auto
```

Note that the `mod_jk.conf-auto` file, specified here, is generated automatically by Tomcat upon startup.

To test that everything is working fine, restart Apache, start Tomcat, and enter the path to the snoop JSP (http://localhost/examples/jsp/snp/snoop.jsp) in your favorite browser:

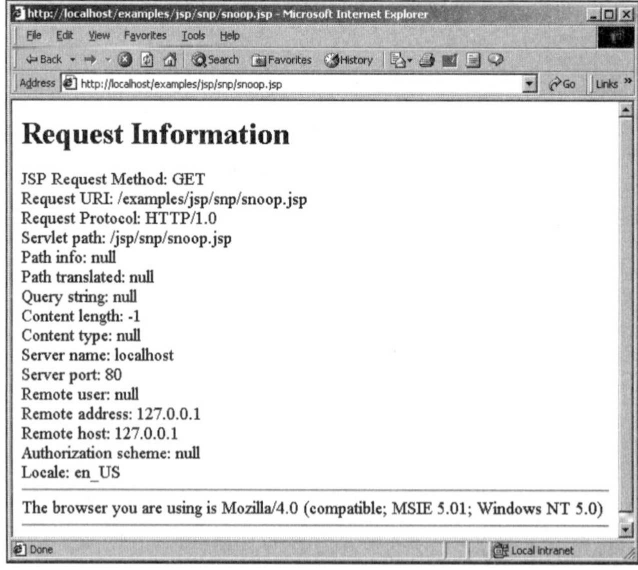

Securing the /samples Directory using LDAP

We now have configured Apache to forward HTTP requests to Tomcat for processing. Next, we will secure the access to the samples directory using LDAP. As discussed in Chapter 7, we are using `mod_ldap.c` to handle the integration between Apache and LDAP. Before we come to that, we need to obtain the LDAP SDK.

Obtaining the Netscape LDAP SDK

The **Netscape LDAP SDK** can be downloaded from http://www.iplanet.com/downloads/developer/2091.html:

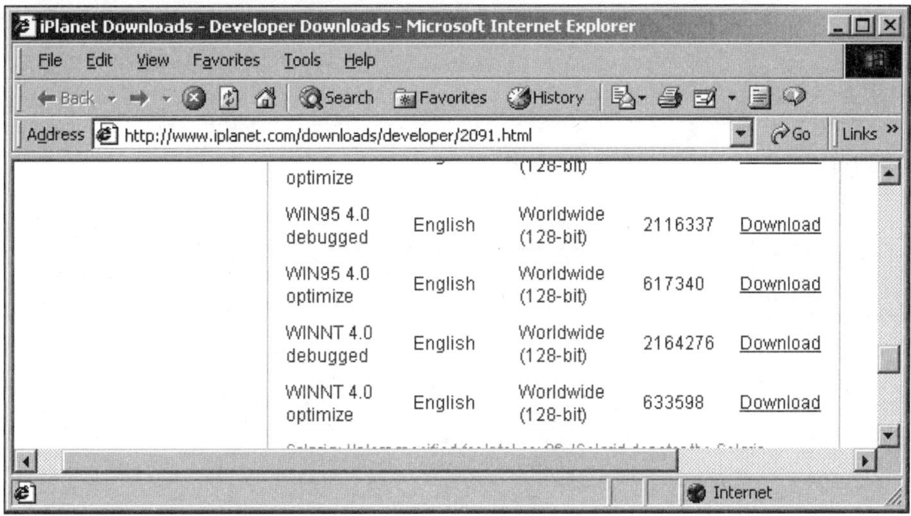

For Windows 2000, select the WINNT 4.0 optimize option, and follow the steps to download the SDK file, `ldapcsdk50-WINNT4[1].0_OPT.zip`. Now we can unpack the contents of the ZIP file, to the folder C:\Apache\Apache.

For brevity, we'll change the name of the download directory from C:\Apache\Apache\WINNT4.0_OPT.OBJ to C:\Apache\Apache\LDAPsdk:

Obtaining ldap_module.dll

Now we can think about the `ldap_module.dll` module. If you want to avoid the compilation process (for example, because you don't have Visual C++) then you can simply use the `ldap_module.dll` provided with the source code for this book (see the \ProJavaSoap\Chapter07\mod_ldap directory).

If you want to compile the DLL for yourself, you can download the source, `mod_ldap.c`, from http://www.kie.berkeley.edu/people/jmorrow/mod_ldap/. Alternatively, you can use the Visual C++ project files, which are available with the sample code, in the \ProJavaSoap\Chapter07\mod_ldap directory – in addition to the original C source code, these files contain the necessary configuration information for the project.

We are now ready to compile and link the `mod_ldap.c` file. We will use the Visual C++ project found in the \ProJavaSoap\Chapter07\mod_ldap directory.

Create a new directory called mod_ldap, somewhere on your system, and paste those three files (mod_ldap.c, mod_ldap.dsp, and mod_ldap.dsw) into it. Then start Visual C++ and open the workspace by using File->Open Workspace and navigating to the project file, `mod_ldap.dsw`. The project file assumes that your directory structure is set up as described in this Appendix.

You will need to update the include file path and the link file path if you have installed the software in different directories. (Specifically, select mod_ldap in the FileView pane; then select Project|Settings. On the C/C++ tab, check the file paths in the Project Options section. On the Link tab, do the same in the Output file name section under the General category, and in the Additional library path section under the Input category.)

Now you can build the DLL: select Build->Build ldap_module.dll. The following screenshot shows a successful build of the `mod_ldap.c` file inside Visual C++:

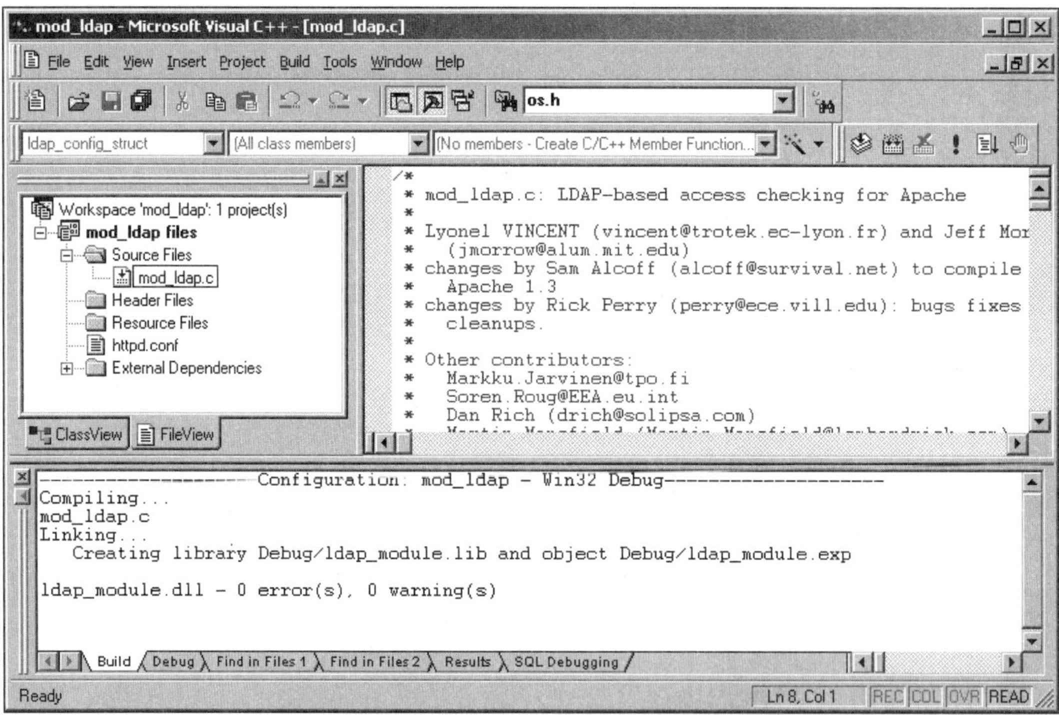

You will notice that the target DLL is created in the C:/Apache/Apache/modules directory (as specified in the Visual C++ project, in the General category under the Link tab on the project's Settings dialog):

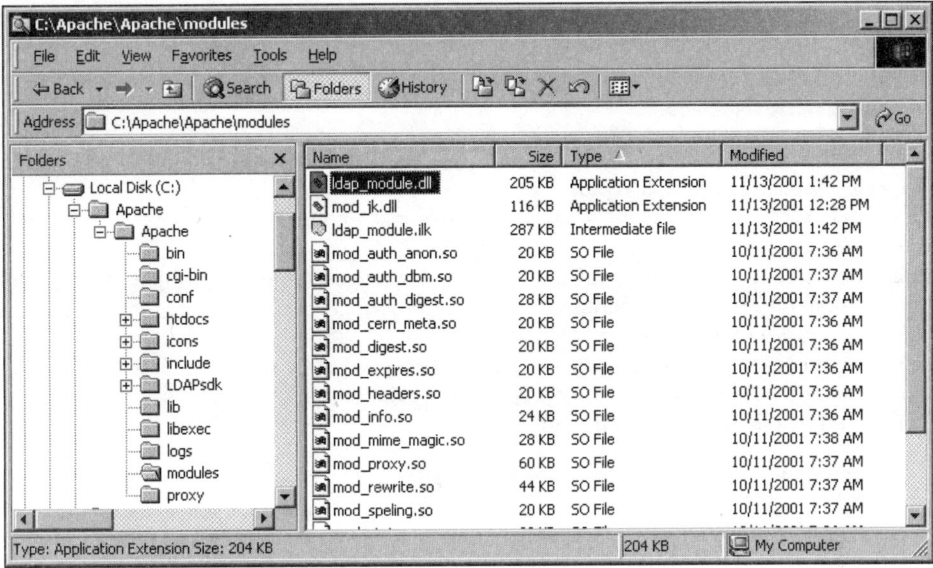

Configuring Apache and Running the Example

We are now ready to let Apache know that the access to the examples directory will be handled through LDAP. We can do this by adding the following instructions at the end of the C:\Apache\Apache\conf\httpd.conf file:

```
#LDAP Authentication Module
LoadModule ldap_module C:/Apache/Apache/modules/ldap_module.dll
AddModule mod_ldap.c

#We protect /examples
<Location "/examples">
     AuthType Basic
     AuthName LeSavonAuthentication
     LDAPAuth On
     LDAPServer "ldap://localhost:389/"
     LDAPBindName uid=atase,ou=People,o=LeSavonWrox
     LDAPBindPass lesavon
     LDAPUseridAttr uid
     LDAPBase o=LeSavonWrox
     LDAPSearchMode subtree
     require valid-user
</Location>
```

For a description of these instructions, please refer to Chapter 7. Once you have saved the `httpd.conf` file, you will need to stop and restart Apache using the following commands:

C:Apache\Apache>set path= C:Apache\Apache\LDAPsdk\lib
C:Apache\Apache>apache

The first of these commands modifies the path to include the LDAPsdk\lib directory, and hence allows Apache to find the LDAP SDK DLL. If you forget to do this, you will get an error like this:

```
C:\Apache\Apache>Apache
Syntax error on line 1036 of c:/apache/apache/conf/httpd.conf:
Cannot load c:/apache/apache/modules/ldap_module.dll into server: (126)
The specified module could not be found:
Note the errors or messages above, and press the <ESC> key to exit.  5....
```

The error message here is a little misleading at first, since it suggests that the problem is with the location of the ldap_module.dll file. Setting the path in the manner described above should eliminate this error.

Before requesting the `snoop.jsp` JSP, you must also start your LDAP server, as described in the *LDAP Setup* section of Chapter 7. When that's done, request http://localhost/examples/jsp/snp/snoop.jsp in your browser, and you'll be challenged for authentication:

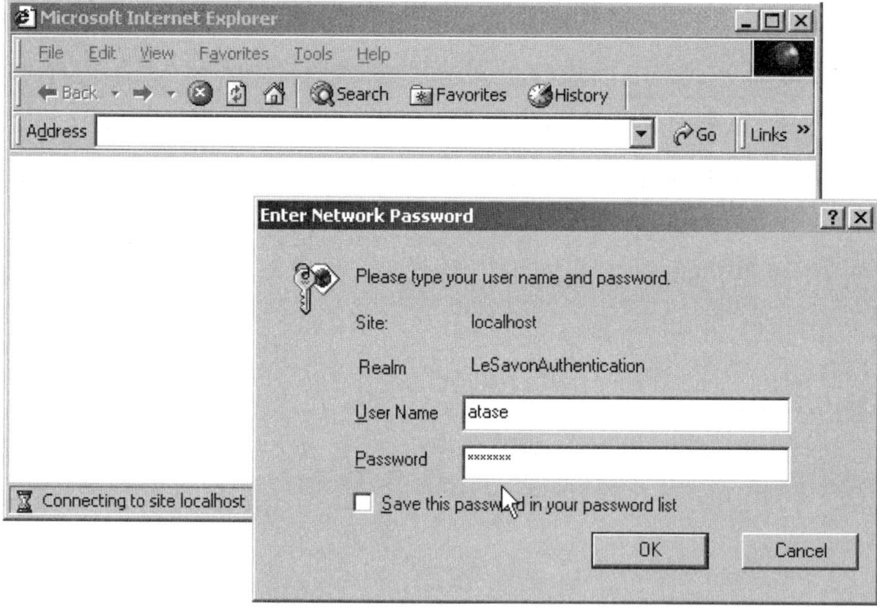

Type the username atase, and password lesavon. (Alternatively, use another username and password from the LDAP database. You can use a directory browser to get these details; see Chapter 7.) When the correct username and password are authenticated against the LDAP database, the `snoop.jsp` response should look like this:

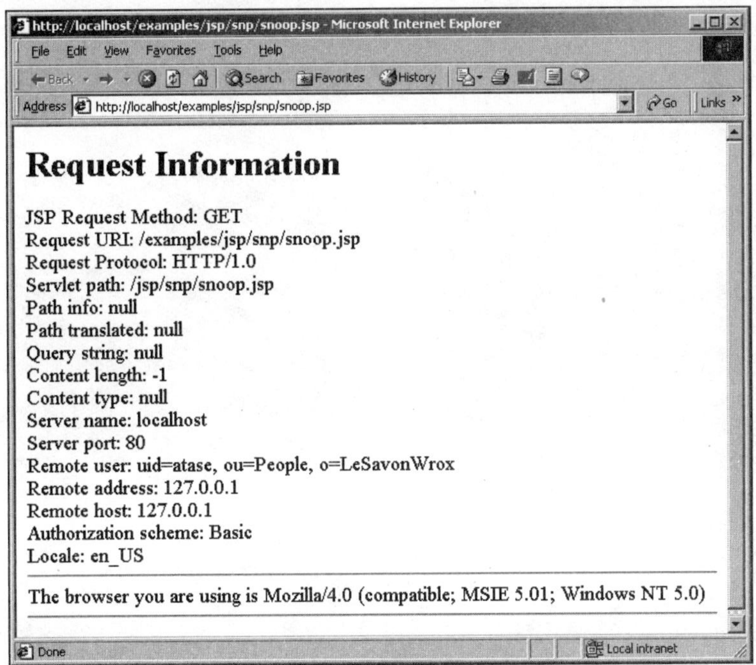
http://localhost/examples/jsp/snp/snoop.jsp - Microsoft Internet Explorer
File Edit View Favorites Tools Help
Back Search Favorites History
Address http://localhost/examples/jsp/snp/snoop.jsp
Go Links
Request Information
JSP Request Method: GET
Request URI: /examples/jsp/snp/snoop.jsp
Request Protocol: HTTP/1.0
Servlet path: /jsp/snp/snoop.jsp
Path info: null
Path translated: null
Query string: null
Content length: -1
Content type: null
Server name: localhost
Server port: 80
Remote user: uid=atase, ou=People, o=LeSavonWrox
Remote address: 127.0.0.1
Remote host: 127.0.0.1
Authorization scheme: Basic
Locale: en_US
The browser you are using is Mozilla/4.0 (compatible; MSIE 5.01; Windows NT 5.0)
Done
Local intranet

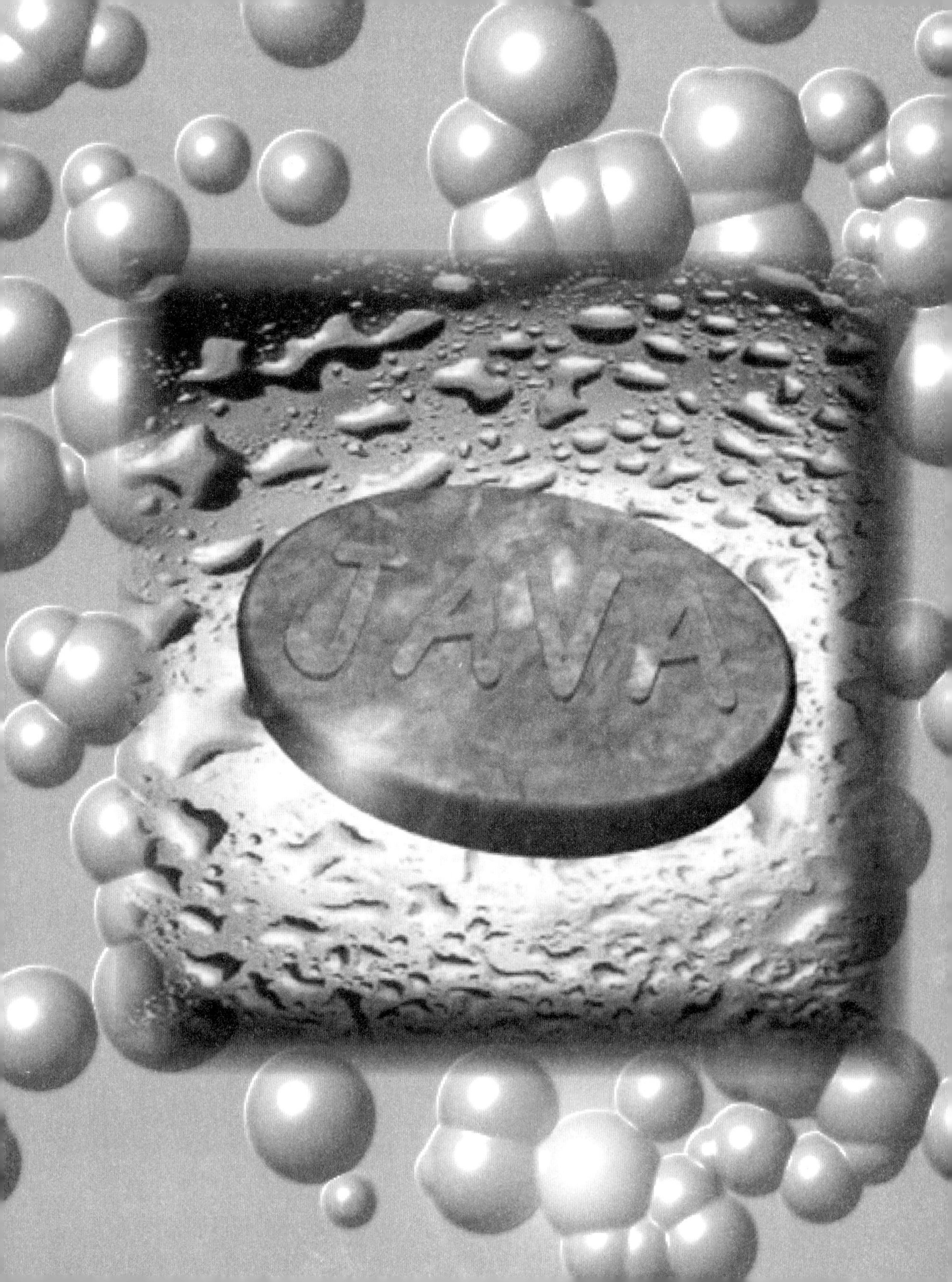
JAVA

D

The Apache Software License, Version 1.1

The Apache Software License, Version 1.1

The following is the license agreement for Apache software. Please read this carefully before using the software.

Redistribution and use in source and binary forms, with or without modification, are permitted provided that the following conditions are met:

1. Redistributions of source code must retain the above copyright notice, this list of conditions and the following disclaimer.

2. Redistributions in binary form must reproduce the above copyright notice, this list of conditions and the following disclaimer in the documentation and/or other materials provided with the distribution.

3. The end-user documentation included with the redistribution, if any, must include the following acknowledgment: "This product includes software developed by the Apache Software Foundation (http://www.apache.org/)." Alternately, this acknowledgment may appear in the software itself, if and wherever such third-party acknowledgments normally appear.

4. The names "Ant" and "Apache Software Foundation" must not be used to endorse or promote products derived from this software without prior written permission. For written permission, please contact `apache@apache.org`.

5. Products derived from this software may not be called "Apache", nor may "Apache" appear in their name, without prior written permission of the Apache Software Foundation.

THIS SOFTWARE IS PROVIDED ``AS IS'' AND ANY EXPRESSED OR IMPLIED WARRANTIES, INCLUDING, BUT NOT LIMITED TO, THE IMPLIED WARRANTIES OF MERCHANTABILITY AND FITNESS FOR A PARTICULAR PURPOSE ARE DISCLAIMED. IN NO EVENT SHALL THE APACHE SOFTWARE FOUNDATION OR ITS CONTRIBUTORS BE LIABLE FOR ANY DIRECT, INDIRECT, INCIDENTAL, SPECIAL, EXEMPLARY, OR CONSEQUENTIAL DAMAGES (INCLUDING, BUT NOT LIMITED TO, PROCUREMENT OF SUBSTITUTE GOODS OR SERVICES; LOSS OF USE, DATA, OR PROFITS; OR BUSINESS INTERRUPTION) HOWEVER CAUSED AND ON ANY THEORY OF LIABILITY, WHETHER IN CONTRACT, STRICT LIABILITY, OR TORT (INCLUDING NEGLIGENCE OR OTHERWISE) ARISING IN ANY WAY OUT OF THE USE OF THIS SOFTWARE, EVEN IF ADVISED OF THE POSSIBILITY OF SUCH DAMAGE.

This software consists of voluntary contributions made by many individuals on behalf of the Apache Software Foundation. For more information on the Apache Software Foundation, please see http://www.apache.org/.

JAVA

Index

A Guide to the Index

The index is arranged hierarchically, in alphabetical order, with symbols preceding the letter A. Most second-level entries and many third-level entries also occur as first-level entries. This is to ensure that users will find the information they require however they choose to search for it.

C

D

E

F

G

H

I

M

N

O

P

T

U

V

W

X

Y

JAVA

Wrox writes books for you. Any suggestions, or ideas about how you want information given in your ideal book will be studied by our team. Your comments are always valued at Wrox.

Free phone in USA 800-USE-WROX
Fax (312) 893 8001

UK Tel.: (0121) 687 4100 Fax: (0121) 687 4101

Professional Java SOAP Programming – Registration Card

Name ______________________

Address ______________________

____

____

____

City ____________ State/Region ____________

Country ____________ Postcode/Zip ____________

E-Mail ______________________

Occupation ______________________

How did you hear about this book?

- ❐ Book review (name) ____________
- ❐ Advertisement (name) ____________
- ❐ Recommendation ____________
- ❐ Catalog ____________
- ❐ Other ____________

Where did you buy this book?

- ❐ Bookstore (name) ____________ City ____________
- ❐ Computer store (name) ____________
- ❐ Mail order ____________
- ❐ Other ____________

What influenced you in the purchase of this book?

❐ Cover Design ❐ Contents ❐ Other (please specify):

____

How did you rate the overall content of this book?

❐ Excellent ❐ Good ❐ Average ❐ Poor

What did you find most useful about this book? ____________

____

____

What did you find least useful about this book? ____________

____

____

Please add any additional comments. ____________

____

____

What other subjects will you buy a computer book on soon?

____

What is the best computer book you have used this year?

____

Note: This information will only be used to keep you updated about new Wrox Press titles and will not be used for any other purpose or passed to any other third party.

 Check here if you DO NOT want to receive support for this book ❐ 6101

Note: If you post the bounce back card below in the UK, please send it to:

Wrox Press Limited, Arden House, 1102 Warwick Road,
Acocks Green, Birmingham B27 6HB. UK.

Computer Book Publishers

NO POSTAGE
NECESSARY
IF MAILED
IN THE
UNITED STATES

BUSINESS REPLY MAIL

FIRST CLASS MAIL PERMIT#64 CHICAGO, IL

POSTAGE WILL BE PAID BY ADDRESSEE

WROX PRESS INC.
29 S. LA SALLE ST.
SUITE 520
CHICAGO IL 60603-USA